STATISTICS USING R

An Integrative Approach

Using numerous examples with real data, this textbook closely integrates the learning of statistics with the learning of R. It is suitable for introductory-level learners, allows for curriculum flexibility, and includes, as an online resource, R-code script files for all examples and figures included in each chapter, for students to learn from and adapt and use in their future data analytic work. Other unique features created specifically for this textbook include an online R tutorial that introduces readers to data frames and other basic elements of the R architecture, and a CRAN library of datasets and functions that is used throughout the book. Essential topics often overlooked in other introductory texts, such as data management, are covered. The textbook includes online solutions to all end-of-chapter exercises and PowerPoint slides for all chapters as additional resources, and is suitable for those who do not have a strong background in mathematics.

Sharon Lawner Weinberg is Professor of Applied Statistics and Psychology, and the former Vice Provost for Faculty Affairs, at New York University (NYU). She is the recipient of the NYU Steinhardt Outstanding Teaching Award, and has taught statistics at both undergraduate and graduate levels. Her research has been supported by federal agencies and private foundations.

Daphna Harel is Associate Professor of Applied Statistics at New York University. She is known for her innovative approach to teaching both introductory and advanced statistics. Her research has been supported by federal agencies and foundations, such as the National Institutes for Health and the Canadian Institutes for Health Research.

Sarah Knapp Abramowitz is Professor of Mathematics and Computer Science, Department Chair, and Co-ordinator of Statistics Instruction at Drew University. She is Associate Editor of the *Journal of Statistics Education* and has presented at national conferences on topics related to the teaching of statistics.

Statistics Using R

AN INTEGRATIVE APPROACH

SHARON LAWNER WEINBERG

New York University

DAPHNA HAREL

New York University

SARAH KNAPP ABRAMOWITZ

Drew University, New Jersey

CAMBRIDGE
UNIVERSITY PRESS

CAMBRIDGE
UNIVERSITY PRESS

University Printing House, Cambridge CB2 8BS, United Kingdom

One Liberty Plaza, 20th Floor, New York, NY 10006, USA

477 Williamstown Road, Port Melbourne, VIC 3207, Australia

314–321, 3rd Floor, Plot 3, Splendor Forum, Jasola District Centre,
New Delhi – 110025, India

79 Anson Road, #06–04/06, Singapore 079906

Cambridge University Press is part of the University of Cambridge.

It furthers the University's mission by disseminating knowledge in the pursuit of
education, learning, and research at the highest international levels of excellence.

www.cambridge.org
Information on this title: www.cambridge.org/9781108719148
DOI: 10.1017/9781108755351

First published 2021

A catalogue record for this publication is available from the British Library.

Library of Congress Cataloging-in-Publication Data
Names: Weinberg, Sharon L., author. | Harel, Daphna, 1988– author. |
Abramowitz, Sarah Knapp, 1967– author.
Title: Statistics using R : an integrative approach / Sharon Lawner
Weinberg, Daphna Harel, Sarah Knapp Abramowitz.
Description: Cambridge ; New York, NY : Cambridge University Press, 2021. |
Includes bibliographical references and index.
Identifiers: LCCN 2019059928 (print) | LCCN 2019059929 (ebook) |
ISBN 9781108719148 (paperback) | ISBN 9781108755351 (ebook)
Subjects: LCSH: R (Computer program language) |
Mathematical statistics – Data processing. | Statistics – Data processing.
Classification: LCC QA276.45.R3 W45 2021 (print) | LCC QA276.45.R3 (ebook) |
DDC 519.50285/5133–dc23
LC record available at https://lccn.loc.gov/2019059928
LC ebook record available at https://lccn.loc.gov/2019059929

ISBN 978-1-108-71914-8 Paperback

Additional resources for this publication at www.cambridge.org/stats-r

To our families

Contents

Preface

This first edition of *Statistics Using R: An Integrative Approach* capitalizes on the versatility and power of the R software package to create a course of study that links good statistical and data science practice to the analysis of real data. It also benefits from the many years of the authors' experience teaching statistics to undergraduate students at a liberal arts university and to undergraduate and graduate students at a large research university from a variety of disciplines including education, psychology, health, and policy analysis. R is a free, open-source software, which provides a command line approach to the analysis of data. This textbook teaches readers the skills necessary to program statistical analyses using this command line approach.

Guiding Principles Underlying Our Approach

First, and perhaps most importantly, we believe that a good data analytic plan must serve to uncover the story behind the numbers; what the data tell us about the phenomenon under study. To begin, a good data analyst must know their data well and have confidence that it satisfies the underlying assumptions of the statistical methods used. Accordingly, we emphasize the usefulness of diagnostics in both graphical and statistical form to expose anomalous cases, which might unduly influence results, and to help in the selection of appropriate assumption-satisfying transformations so that ultimately we may have confidence in our findings. We also emphasize the importance of using more than one method of analysis to answer fully the question posed and understanding potential bias in the estimation of population parameters.

Second, because we believe that data are central to the study of good statistical practice, we have made available the datasets used in this textbook. The textbook's website contains the datasets used throughout the text. Also, we have published a software package, hosted on R's server, that can be downloaded as another means to access the datasets. This package, named *sur*, also contains several R functions that we have written to facilitate the application of several statistical methods.

The datasets used in this textbook provide examples of real-world data. Two are large sets of real data that we make repeated use of in both worked-out examples and end-of-chapter exercises. One dataset contains 48 variables and 500 cases from the education discipline that includes psychosocial measures such as self-concept; the other contains 49 variables and nearly 4,500 cases from the health discipline. By posing interesting questions about variables in these large, real datasets (e.g., Is there a gender difference in eighth graders' expected income at age 30? Is self-concept in eighth grade related to eighth graders' expected income at age 30?), we are able to employ a more meaningful and contextual approach to the introduction of statistical methods and to engage students more actively in the learning process. The repeated use of these datasets also contributes to creating a more cohesive presentation of statistics; one that links different methods of analysis to each other and avoids the perception that statistics is an often confusing array of so many separate and distinct methods of analysis, with no bearing or relationship to one another.

Third, to facilitate the analysis of these data, and to provide students with a platform for actively engaging in the learning process associated with what it means to be a good researcher and data analyst, we incorporate the functionality of R version 3.5.3 into the presentation of statistical material using a highly integrative approach that reflects practice. Students learn R along with each new statistical method covered, thereby allowing them to apply their newly learned knowledge to the real world of applications. In addition to demonstrating the use of R within each chapter, all chapters have an associated .R file, that may be accessed from the textbook's website (www.cambridge.org/stats-r) along with other ancillary materials and resources. The .R files are designed to allow students not only to replicate all worked-out examples within a chapter, but also to reproduce the figures embedded in a chapter, and to create their own .R files by extracting and modifying commands from them. Emphasizing data workflow management throughout the text using the .R file allows students to begin to appreciate one of the key ingredients in being a good researcher. Of course, another key ingredient to being a good researcher is content knowledge, and toward that end, we have included in the text a more comprehensive coverage of essential topics in statistics not covered by other textbooks at the introductory level, including regression to the mean, the weighted mean, and potential sources of bias in the estimation of population parameters based on the analysis of data from quasi-experimental designs. We also include a discussion of Simpson's paradox, counterfactuals, and other issues related to research design in an entire chapter (Chapter 12) devoted to this topic.

Fourth, in accordance with our belief that the result of a null hypothesis test (to determine whether an effect is real or merely apparent) is only a means to an end (to determine whether the effect is important or useful) rather than an end in itself, we stress the need to evaluate the magnitude of an effect if it is deemed to be real, and of drawing clear distinctions between statistically significant and substantively significant results. Toward this end, we introduce the computation of standardized measures of effect size as common practice following a statistically significant result. While we provide guidelines for evaluating, in general, the magnitude of an effect, we encourage readers to think more subjectively about the magnitude of an effect, bringing into the evaluation their own knowledge and expertise in a particular area.

Finally, we believe that a key ingredient of an introductory statistics text is a lively, clear, conceptual, yet rigorous approach. We emphasize conceptual understanding through an exploration of both the mathematical principles underlying statistical methods and real-world applications. We use an easy-going, informal style of writing that we have found gives readers the impression that they are involved in a personal conversation with the authors. And, we sequence concepts with concern for student readiness, reintroducing topics in a spiraling manner to provide reinforcement and promote the transfer of learning.

Overview of Content Coverage and Intended Audience

Along with the earlier topics mentioned, the inclusion of linear and nonlinear transformations, diagnostic tools for the analysis of model fit, tests of inference, an in-depth discussion of interaction and its interpretation in both two-way analysis of variance and multiple regression, and nonparametric statistics, the text provides a highly comprehensive coverage of essential topics in introductory statistics, and in so doing gives instructors flexibility in curriculum planning and provides students with more advanced material for future work in statistics. In addition, the text includes a large bibliography of references to relevant books and journal articles, and many end-of-chapter exercises with detailed answers on the textbook's website.

The book, consisting of 18 chapters, is intended for use in a one- or two-semester introductory applied statistics course for the behavioral, social, or health sciences at either the graduate or undergraduate level, or as a reference text as well. It is not intended for readers who wish to acquire a more theoretical understanding of mathematical statistics. To offer another perspective, the book may be described as one that begins with modern approaches to exploratory data analysis (EDA) and descriptive statistics, and then covers material similar to what is found in an introductory mathematical statistics text, designed, for example, for undergraduates in math and the physical sciences, but stripped of calculus and linear algebra, and grounded instead in data examples. Thus, theoretical probability distributions, Bayes' theorem, the law of large numbers, sampling distributions and the central limit theorem are all covered, but in the context of solving practical and interesting problems.

Finally, to facilitate learning R, an online tutorial has been written to accompany the textbook. The tutorial covers the basic use and manipulation of datasets, also referred to as data frames in R. The activities covered in the tutorial are designed to help students understand the examples in each chapter and to complete end-of-chapter exercises in the textbook. It also is designed to teach some basic coding skills that will be helpful when working with data frames in R, complete more complex analyses, and, ultimately, to learn the larger statistical concepts covered throughout the textbook.

Acknowledgments

This book has benefited from the many helpful comments of our New York University and Drew University students, too numerous to mention by name, and from the insights and suggestions of several colleagues. For their help, we would like to thank (in alphabetical order) Chris Apelian, Ellie Buteau, Chris Casement, Miao Chi, Sarah Friedman, Andrea Hassler, Jennifer Hill, Michael Karchmer, Steve Kass, Jon Kettenring, Linda Lesniak, Yi Lu, Kathleen Madden, Isaac Maddow-Zimet, Meghan McCormick, Joel Middleton, and Marc Scott. Of course, any errors or shortcomings in the text remain the responsibility of the authors.

# CHAPTER ONE

INTRODUCTION

Welcome to the study of statistics! It has been our experience that many students face the prospect of taking a course in statistics with a great deal of anxiety, apprehension, and even dread. They fear not having the extensive mathematical background that they assume is required, and they fear that the contents of such a course will be irrelevant to their work in their fields of concentration.

Although it is true that an extensive mathematical background is required at more advanced levels of statistical study, it is not required for the introductory level of statistics presented in this book. Greater reliance is placed on the use of the computer for calculation and graphical display so that we may focus on issues of conceptual understanding and interpretation. While hand computation is de-emphasized, we believe, nonetheless, that a basic mathematical background – including the understanding of fractions, decimals, percentages, signed (positive and negative) numbers, exponents, linear equations and graphs – is essential for an enhanced conceptual understanding of the material.

As for the issue of relevance, we have found that students better comprehend the power and purpose of statistics when it is presented in the context of a substantive problem with real data. In this information age, data are available on a myriad of topics. Whether our interests are in health, education, psychology, business, the environment, and so on, numerical data may be accessed readily to address our questions of interest. The purpose of statistics is to allow us to analyze these data to extract the information that they contain in a meaningful way and to write a story about the numbers that is both compelling and accurate.

Throughout this course of study, we make use of a series of real datasets that may be found either on the website for this book (www.cambridge.org/stats-r), or as a part of the R package we have created for this book, called **sur** (for Statistics Using R). Instructions on how to download and load this R package onto your computer are presented later in this chapter as are instructions for downloading the R software itself. We will pose relevant questions and learn the appropriate methods of analysis for answering such questions. Students will learn that more than one statistic or method of analysis typically is needed to address a question fully. Students also will learn that a detailed description of the data, including possible anomalies, and an ample characterization of results, are critical components of any data analytic plan. Through this process we hope that this book will help students come to view statistics as an integrated set of data analytic tools that, when used together in a meaningful way, will serve to uncover the story contained in the numbers.

THE ROLE OF STATISTICAL SOFTWARE IN DATA ANALYSIS

From our own experience, we have found that the use of a statistics software package to carry out computations and create graphs not only enables a greater emphasis on conceptual understanding and interpretation, but also allows students to study statistics in a way that reflects statistical practice. We have selected the latest version of R available to us at the time of writing (R version 3.5.3) for use with this text. It is available for free download from https://cran.r-project.org/. We have selected R because it is a well-established, comprehensive, open-source, and free software that is widely used by behavioral and social scientists. Like MINITAB, JMP, SPSS, and Stata, R is powerful enough to handle the analysis of large datasets quickly. By the end of this book, students will have obtained a conceptual understanding of statistics as well as an applied, practical skill in how to carry out statistical operations.

STATISTICS: DESCRIPTIVE AND INFERENTIAL

The subject of statistics may be divided into two general branches: descriptive and inferential. *Descriptive statistics* are used when the purpose of an investigation is to *describe* the data that have been (or will be) collected. Suppose, for example, that a third-grade elementary school teacher is interested in determining the proportion of children who are firstborn in her class of 30 children. In this case, the focus of the teacher's question is her own class of 30 children and she will be able to collect data on all of the students about whom she would like to draw a conclusion. The data collection operation will involve noting whether each child in the classroom is firstborn or not; the statistical operations will involve counting the number who are, and dividing that number by 30, the total number of students in the class, to obtain the proportion sought. Because the teacher is using statistical methods merely to describe the data she collected, this is an example of descriptive statistics.

Suppose, on the other hand, that the teacher is interested in determining the proportion of children who are firstborn in *all* third-grade classes in the city where she teaches. It is highly unlikely that she will be able to (or even want to) collect the relevant data on all individuals about whom she would like to draw a conclusion. She will probably have to limit the data collection to some randomly selected smaller group and use *inferential statistics* to generalize to the larger group the conclusions obtained from the smaller group. *Inferential statistics* are used when the purpose of the research is not to describe the data that have been collected, but to generalize or make inferences based on it. The smaller group on which she collects data is called the *sample*, whereas the larger group to whom conclusions are generalized (or inferred), is called the *population*. In general, two major factors influence the teacher's confidence that what holds true for the sample also holds true for the population at large. These two factors are the method of sample selection and the size of the sample. Only when data are collected on *all* individuals about whom a conclusion is to be drawn (when the sample *is* the population and we are therefore in the realm of descriptive statistics), can the conclusion be drawn with 100 percent certainty. Thus, one of the major goals of inferential statistics is to assess the degree of certainty of inferences when such inferences are drawn from sample data. Although this text is divided roughly into two parts, the first on descriptive statistics and the second on inferential statistics, the second part draws heavily on the first.

VARIABLES AND CONSTANTS

In the previous section, we discussed a teacher's interest in determining the proportion of students who are firstborn in the third grade of the city where she teaches. What made this question worth asking was the fact that she did not expect everyone in the third grade to be firstborn. Rather, she quite naturally expected that in the population under study, birth order would vary, or differ, from individual to individual and that only in certain individuals would it be first.

Characteristics of persons or objects that vary from person to person or object to object are called *variables*, whereas characteristics that remain constant from person to person or object to object are called *constants*. Whether a characteristic is designated as a variable or as a constant depends, of course, on the study in question. In the study of birth order, birth order is a variable; it can be expected to vary from person to person in the given population. In that same study, grade level is a constant; all persons in the population under study are in the third grade.

EXAMPLE 1.1 Identify some of the variables and constants in a study comparing the math achievement of tenth grade boys and girls in the southern United States.

Solution
Constants: Grade level; Region of the United States
Variables: Math achievement; Sex

EXAMPLE 1.2 Identify some of the variables and constants in a study of math achievement of secondary-school boys in the southern United States.

Solution
Constants: Sex; Region of the United States
Variables: Math achievement; Grade level

Note that grade level is a constant in Example 1.1 and a variable in Example 1.2. Because constants are characteristics that do not vary in a given population, the study of constants is neither interesting nor informative. The major focus of any statistical study is therefore on the variables rather than the constants. Before variables can be the subject of statistical study, however, they need to be numerically valued. The next section describes the process of measuring variables so as to achieve that goal.

THE MEASUREMENT OF VARIABLES

Measurement involves the observation of characteristics on persons or objects, and the assignment of numbers to those persons or objects so that the numbers represent the amounts of the characteristics possessed. As introduced by S. S. (Stanley Smith) Stevens (1946) in a paper, "On the theory of scales of measurement," and later described by him in a chapter, "Mathematics, measurement, and psychophysics," in the *Handbook of Experimental Psychology*, edited by Stevens (1951), we describe four levels of measurement in this text. Each of the four levels is defined by the nature of the observation and the way in which the numbers assigned correspond to the amount of the underlying characteristic that has been observed. The level of measurement of a variable determines which numerical operations (e.g., addition, subtraction, multiplication, or division) are permissible on that variable. If other than the permissible numerical operations are used on a variable given its level of measurement, one can expect the statistical conclusions drawn with respect to that variable to be questionable.

NOMINAL LEVEL

The nominal level of measurement is based on the simplest form of observation – whether two objects are similar or dissimilar: for example, whether they are short versus non-short, male versus female, or college student versus non-college student. Objects observed to be similar on some characteristic (e.g., college student) are assigned to the same class or category, while objects observed to be dissimilar on that characteristic are assigned to different classes or categories. In the nominal level of measurement, classes or categories are *not* compared as say, taller or shorter, better or worse, or more educated or less educated. Emphasis is strictly on observing whether the objects are similar or dissimilar. As befitting its label, classes or categories are merely named, but not compared, in the *nominal* level of measurement.

Given the nature of observation for this level of measurement, numbers are assigned to objects using the following simple rule: if objects are dissimilar, they are assigned different numbers; if objects are similar, they are assigned the same number. For example, all persons who are college students would be assigned the same number (say, 1); all persons who are non-college students also would be assigned the same number different from 1 (say, 2) to distinguish them from college students. Because the focus is on distinction and not comparison, in this level of measurement, the fact that the number 2 is larger than the number 1 is irrelevant in terms of the underlying characteristic being measured (whether or not the person is a college student). Accordingly, the number 1 could have been assigned, instead, to all persons who are non-college students and the number 2 to all persons who are college students. Any numbers other than 1 and 2 also could have been used as well.

While the examples in this section (e.g., college student versus non-college student) may be called *dichotomous* in that they have only two categories, nominal variables also may have more than two categories (e.g., car manufacturers – Toyota, Honda, General Motors, Ford, Chrysler, etc.).

ORDINAL LEVEL

The ordinal level of measurement is not only based on observing objects as similar or dissimilar, but also on ordering those observations in terms of an underlying characteristic. Suppose, for example, we were not interested simply in whether a person was a college student or not, but rather in ordering college students in terms of the degree of their success in college (e.g., whether the college student was below average, average, or above average). We would, therefore, need to observe such ordered differences among these college students in terms of their success in college, and we would choose numbers to assign to the categories that corresponded to that ordering. For this example, we might assign the number 1 to the below average category, the number 2 to the average category, and the number 3 to the above average category. Unlike in the nominal level of measurement, in the ordinal level of measurement, it is relevant that 3 is greater than 2, which, in turn, is greater than 1, as this ordering conveys in a meaningful way the ordered nature of the categories relative to the underlying characteristic of interest. That is, comparisons among the numbers correspond to comparisons among the categories in terms of the underlying characteristic of success in college. In summary, the ordinal level of measurement applies two rules for assigning numbers to categories: (1) different numbers are assigned to persons or objects that possess different amounts of the underlying characteristic, and (2) the higher the number assigned to a person or object, the less (or more) of the underlying characteristic that person or object is observed to possess. From these two rules it does *not* follow, however, that equal numerical differences along the number scale correspond to equal increments in the underlying characteristic being measured in the ordinal level of measurement. While the differences between 3 and 2 and between 2 and 1 in our college student success example are both equal to 1, we cannot infer from this that the difference in success between above average college students and average college students equals the difference in success between average college students and below average college students.

We consider another example that may convey more clearly this idea. Suppose we line 10 people up according to their height and assign a number from 1 to 10, respectively to each person so that each number corresponds to the person's place in line. We could assign the number 1 to the shortest person, the number 2 to the next shortest person, and so forth, ending by assigning the number 10 to the tallest person. While according to this method, the numbers assigned to each pair of adjacent people in line will differ from each other by the same value (i.e., 1), clearly, the heights of each pair of adjacent people will not necessarily also differ by the same value. Some adjacent pairs will differ in height by only a fraction of an inch, while other adjacent pairs will differ in height by several inches. Accordingly, only some of the features of this size place ranking are reflected or modeled by the numerical scale. In particular, while, in this case, the numerical scale can be used to judge the relative order of one person's height compared to another's, differences between numbers on the numerical scale cannot be used to judge how much taller one person is than another. As a result, statistical conclusions about variables measured on the ordinal level that are based on anything other than an ordering or ranking of the numbers (including taking sums or differences) cannot be expected to be meaningful.

INTERVAL LEVEL

An ordinal level of measurement can be developed into a higher level of measurement if it is possible to assess how near to each other the persons or objects are in the underlying characteristic being observed. If numbers can be assigned in such a way that equal numerical differences along the scale correspond to equal increments in the underlying characteristic, we have what is called an *interval level of measurement.* As an example of an interval level of measurement, consider the assignment of yearly dates, the chronological scale. Because one year is defined as the amount of time necessary for the Earth to revolve once around the Sun, we may think of the yearly date as a measure of the number of revolutions of the Earth around the Sun up to and including that year. Hence, this assignment of numbers to the property *number of revolutions of the Earth around the Sun* is on an interval level of measurement. Specifically, this means that equal numerical differences for intervals (such as 1800 CE to 1850 CE and 1925 CE to 1975 CE) represent equal differences in the number of revolutions of the Earth around the Sun (in this case,

50). In the interval level of measurement, therefore, we may make meaningful statements about the amount of *difference* between any two points along the scale. As such, the numerical operations of addition and subtraction (but not multiplication and division) lead to meaningful conclusions at the interval level and are therefore permissible at that level. For conclusions based on the numerical operations of multiplication and division to be meaningful, we require the ratio level of measurement.

RATIO LEVEL

An interval level of measurement can be developed into a higher level of measurement if the number zero on the numeric scale corresponds to zero or "not any" of the underlying characteristic being observed. With the addition of this property (called an *absolute zero*), ratio comparisons are meaningful, and we have, what is called the *ratio level of measurement*. Consider once again the chronological scale and, in particular, the years labeled 2000 CE and 1000 CE. Even though 2000 is numerically twice as large as 1000, it does not follow that the number of revolutions represented by the year 2000 is twice the number of revolutions represented by the year 1000. This is because on the chronological scale, the number 0 (0 CE) does not correspond to zero revolutions of the Earth around the Sun (i.e., the Earth had made revolutions around the Sun many times prior to the year 0 CE). In order for us to make meaningful multiplicative or ratio comparisons of this type between points on our number scale, the number 0 on the numeric scale must correspond to 0 (none) of the underlying characteristic being observed.

In measuring height, not by size place, but with a standard ruler, for example, we would typically assign a value of 0 on the number scale to "not any" height and assign the other numbers according to the rules of the interval scale. The scale that would be produced in this case would be a ratio scale of measurement, and ratio or multiplicative statements (such as "John, who is 5 feet tall, is *twice* as tall as Jimmy, who is 2.5 feet tall") would be meaningful. It should be pointed out that for variables to be considered to be measured on a ratio level, "not any" of the underlying characteristic only needs to be meaningful theoretically. Clearly, no one has zero height, yet using zero as an anchor value for this scale to connote "not any" height is theoretically meaningful.

CHOOSING A SCALE OF MEASUREMENT

Why is it important to categorize the scales of measurement as nominal, ordinal, interval, or ratio? If we consider college students and assign a 1 to those who are male college students, a 2 to those who are female college students, and a 3 to those who are not college students at all, it would not be meaningful to add these numbers nor even to compare their sizes. For example, two male college students together do not suddenly become a female college student, even though their numbers add up to the number of a female college student (1 + 1 = 2). And a female college student who is attending school only half-time is not suddenly a male college student, even though half of her number is the number of a male college student (2/2 = 1). On the other hand, if we were dealing with a ratio-leveled height scale, it would be possible to add, subtract, multiply, or divide the numbers on the scale and obtain results that are meaningful in terms of the underlying trait, height. In general, and as noted earlier, the scale of measurement determines which numerical

TABLE 1.1 Hierarchy of scales of measurement
1. Ratio
2. Interval
3. Ordinal
4. Nominal

operations, when applied to the numbers of the scale, can be expected to yield results that are meaningful in terms of the underlying trait being measured.

Said differently, any numerical operation can be performed on any set of numbers; whether the resulting numbers are meaningful, however, depends on the particular level of measurement being used.

Note that the four scales of measurement exhibit a natural hierarchy, or ordering, in the sense that each level exhibits all the properties of those below it (see Table 1.1). Any characteristic that can be measured on one scale listed in Table 1.1 can also be measured on any scale below it in that list. Given a precise measuring instrument, such as a perfect ruler, we can measure a person's height, for example, as a ratio-scaled variable, in which case we could say that a person whose height is 5 feet has twice the height of a person whose height is 2.5 feet. Suppose, however, that no measuring instrument were available. In this situation, we could, as we have done before, "measure" a person's height according to size place or by categorizing a person as tall, average, or short. By assigning numbers to these three categories (such as 5, 3, and 1, respectively), we would create an ordinal level of measurement for height.

In general, it may be possible to measure a variable on more than one level. The level that is ultimately used to measure a variable should be the highest level possible, given the precision of the measuring instrument used. A perfect ruler allowed us to measure heights on a ratio level, while the eye of the observer allowed us to measure height only on an ordinal level. If we are able to use a higher level of measurement but decide to use a lower level instead, we would lose some of the information that would have been available to us on the higher level. We would also be restricting ourselves to a lower level of permissible numerical operations.

EXAMPLE 1.3 Identify the level of measurement (nominal, ordinal, interval, or ratio) most likely to be used to measure the following variables:

1. Ice cream flavor
2. The speed of five runners in a one-mile race, as measured by the runners' order of finish, first, second, third, and so on.
3. Temperature measured in degrees Celsius.
4. The annual salary of individuals.

Solution
1. The variable ice cream flavor is most likely measured at the nominal level of measurement because the flavors themselves may be categorized simply as being the same or different and there is nothing inherent to them that would lend themselves to a ranking. Any ranking would have to depend on some extraneous property such as, say, taste preference. If numbers were assigned to the flavors as follows,

Flavor	Number
Vanilla	0
Chocolate	1
Strawberry	2
etc.	etc.

meaningful numerical comparisons would be restricted to whether the numbers assigned to two ice cream flavors are the same or different. The fact that one number on this scale may be larger than another is irrelevant.

2. This variable is measured at the ordinal level because it is the order of finish (first, second, third, and so forth) that is being observed and not the specific time to finish. In this example, the smaller the number the greater the speed of the runner. As in the case of measuring height via a size place ranking, it is not necessarily true that the difference in speed between the runners who finished first and second is the same as the difference in speed between the runners who finished third and fourth. Hence, this variable is not measured at the interval level. Had time to finish been used to measure the speed of the runners, the level of measurement would have been ratio for the same reasons that height, measured by a ruler, is ratio-leveled.

3. Temperature measured in degrees Celsius (centigrade) is at the interval level of measurement because each degree increment, no matter whether from 3 to 4 °C or from 22 to 23 °C, has the same physical meaning in terms of the underlying characteristic, heat. In particular, it takes 1 calorie to raise the temperature of 1 gram of water by 1 degree Celsius, no matter what the initial temperature reading on the Celsius scale. Thus, equal differences along the Celsius scale correspond to equal increments in heat, making this scale interval-leveled. The reason this scale is not ratio-scaled is because 0 degrees Celsius does not correspond to "not any" heat. The 0 degree point on the Celsius scale is the point at which water freezes, but even frozen water contains plenty of heat. The point of "not any" heat is at −273 degrees Celsius. Accordingly, we cannot make meaningful ratio comparisons with respect to amounts of heat on the Celsius scale and say, for example, that at 20 degrees Celsius there is twice the heat than at 10 degrees Celsius.

4. The most likely level of measurement for annual salary is the ratio level because each additional unit increase in annual salary along the numerical scale corresponds to an equal additional one dollar earned no matter where on the scale one starts, whether it be, for example, at $10,000 or at $100,000; and, furthermore, because the numerical value of 0 on the scale corresponds to "not any" annual salary, giving the scale a true or absolute zero. Consequently, it is appropriate to make multiplicative comparisons on this scale, such as "Sally's annual salary of $100,000 is twice Jim's annual salary of $50,000."

DISCRETE AND CONTINUOUS VARIABLES

As we saw in the last section, any variable that is not intrinsically numerically valued, such as the ice cream flavors in Example 1.3, may be converted to a numerically valued variable. Once a variable is numerically valued, it may be classified as either discrete or continuous.

Although there is really no exact statistical definition of a discrete or a continuous variable, the following usage generally applies. A numerically valued variable is said to be *discrete* (or *categorical* or *qualitative*) if the values it takes on are integers or can be thought of in some unit of measurement in which they are integers. A numerically valued variable is said to be *continuous* if, in any unit of measurement, whenever it can take on the values a and b, it can also theoretically take on all the values between a and b. The limitations of the measuring instrument are not considered when discriminating between discrete and continuous variables. Instead, it is the nature of the underlying variable that distinguishes between the two types.

☞ **Remark.** As we have said, there is really no hard and fast definition of discrete and continuous variables for use in practice. The words discrete and continuous do have precise mathematical meanings, however, and in more advanced statistical work, where more mathematics and mathematical theory are employed, the words are used in their strict mathematical sense. In this text, where our emphasis is on statistical practice, the usage of the terms discrete and continuous will not usually be helpful in guiding our selection of appropriate statistical methods or graphical displays. Rather, we will generally use the particular level of measurement of the variable, whether it is nominal, ordinal, interval, or ratio.

EXAMPLE 1.4 Let our population consist of all eighth grade students in the United States, and let X represent the region of the country in which the student lives. X is a variable, because there will be different regions for different students. X is not naturally numerically valued, but because X represents a finite number of distinct categories, we can assign numbers to these categories in the following simple way: 1 = Northeast, 2 = North Central, 3 = South, and 4 = West. X is a discrete variable, because it can take on only four values. Furthermore, because X is a nominal-leveled variable, the assignment of 1, 2, 3, and 4 to Northeast, North Central, South, and West, respectively, is arbitrary. Any other assignment rule would have been just as meaningful in differentiating one region from another.

EXAMPLE 1.5 Consider that we repeatedly toss a coin 100 times and let X represent the number of heads obtained for each set of 100 tosses. X is naturally numerically valued and may be considered discrete because the only values it can take on are the integer values 0, 1, 2, 3, and so forth. We may note that X is ratio-leveled in this example because 0 on the numerical scale represents "not any" heads.

EXAMPLE 1.6 Consider a certain hospital with 100 beds. Let X represent the percentage of occupied beds for different days of the year. X is naturally numerically valued as a proportion of the number of occupied beds. Although X takes on fractional values, it is considered discrete because the proportions are based on a count of the number of beds occupied, which is an integer value.

EXAMPLE 1.7 Let our population consist of all college freshmen in the United States, and let X represent their heights, measured in inches. X is numerically valued and is continuous because all possible values of height are theoretically possible. Between any two heights exists another theoretically possible height. For example, between 70 and 71 inches in height, exists a height of 70.5 inches and between 70 and 70.5 exists a height of 70.25 inches, and so on.

☞ **Remark.** Even if height in Example 1.7 were reported to the nearest inch (as an integer), it would still be considered a continuous variable because all possible values of height are theoretically possible. Reporting values of continuous variables to the nearest integer is usually due to the lack of precision of our measuring instruments. We would need a perfect ruler to measure the exact values of height. Such a measuring instrument does not, and probably cannot, exist. When height is reported to the nearest inch, a height of 68 inches is considered to represent all heights between 67.5 and 68.5 inches. While the precision of the measuring instrument determines the accuracy with which a variable is measured, it does not determine whether the variable is discrete or continuous. For that we need only to consider the theoretically possible values that a variable can assume.

☞ **Remark.** In addition to the problem of not being able to measure variables precisely, another problem that often confronts the behavioral scientist is the measurement of traits, such as intelligence, that are not directly observable. Instead of measuring intelligence directly, tests have been developed that measure it indirectly, such as the IQ test. While such tests report IQ, for example, as an integer value, IQ is considered to be a continuous trait or variable, and an IQ score of 109, for example, is thought of as theoretically representing all IQ scores between 108.5 and 109.5.

Another issue, albeit a more controversial one, related to the measurement of traits that are not directly observable, is the level of measurement employed. While some scientists would argue that IQ scores are only ordinal (given a good test of intelligence, a person whose IQ score is higher than another's on that test is said to have greater intelligence), others would argue that they are interval. Even though equal intervals along the IQ scale (say, between 105 and 110 and between 110 and 115) may not necessarily imply equal amounts of change in intelligence, a person who has an IQ score of 105 is likely to be closer in intelligence to a person who has an IQ score of 100 rather than to a person who has an IQ score of 115. By considering an IQ scale and other such psychosocial scales as ordinal only, one would lose such information that is contained in the data and the ability to make use of statistical operations based on sums and differences, rather than merely on rankings.

Another type of scale, widely used in attitude measurement, is the Likert scale, which consists of a small number of values, usually five or seven, ordered along a continuum representing agreement. The values themselves are labeled typically from strongly disagree to strongly agree. A respondent selects that score on the scale that corresponds to her or his level of agreement with a statement associated with that scale. For the same reasons noted earlier with respect to the IQ scale, for example, the Likert scale is considered by many to be interval rather than strictly ordinal.

EXAMPLE 1.8 For each variable listed, describe whether the variable is discrete or continuous. Also, describe the level of measurement for each variable. Use the following dataset excerpted from data analyzed by Tomasi and Weinberg (1999). The original study was carried out on 105 elementary school children from an urban area who were classified as learning disabled (LD) and who, as a result, were receiving special education services for at least three years. In this example, we use only the four variables described below.

Variable name	What the variable measures	How it is measured
SEX		0 = Male
		1 = Female
GRADE	Grade level	1, 2, 3, 4, or 5
AGE	Age in years	Ages ranged from 6 to 14
MATHCOMP	Mathematical comprehension	Higher scores associate with greater mathematical comprehension. Scores could range from 0 to 200.

Solution The variable SEX is discrete because the underlying construct represents a finite number of distinct categories (male or female). Furthermore, individuals may be classified as either male or female, but nothing in between. The level of measurement for SEX is nominal because the two categories are merely different from one another.

The variable GRADE is discrete because the underlying construct represents a finite number (five) of distinct categories and individuals in this study may only be in one of the five grades. The level of measurement for GRADE is interval because the grades are ordered and equal numerical differences along the grade scale represent equal increments in grade.

The variable AGE is continuous even though the reported values are rounded to the nearest integer. AGE is continuous because the underlying construct can theoretically take on any value between 5.5 and 14.5 for study participants. The level of measurement for AGE is ratio because higher numerical values correspond to greater age, equal numerical differences along the scale represent equal increments in age within rounding, and the value of zero is a theoretically meaningful anchor point on the scale representing "not any" age.

The variable MATHCOMP, like AGE, is continuous. The underlying construct, mathematical comprehension, theoretically can take on any value between 0 and 200. The level of measurement is at least ordinal because the higher the numerical value, the greater the comprehension in math, and it is considered to be interval because equal numerical differences along the scale are thought to represent equal or nearly equal increments in math comprehension. Because individuals who score zero on this scale do not possess a total absence of math comprehension, the scale does not have an absolute zero and is, therefore, not ratio-leveled.

DOWNLOADING AND INTERFACING WITH R

In order to access R, open your web browser and go to the URL **https://cran.r-project.org/**. Follow the download links for your Mac or PC computer, and install R using the instructions found on the website. We use version 3.5.3 in this textbook and suggest that readers download this version, even if newer updates are available.

When downloading R, two programs will be installed onto your computer: R and RStudio. RStudio provides a newer graphical user interface to access the R console, which is where you may type commands to perform analyses and see their output. Either R or RStudio may be used to carry out the analyses described in this textbook. Although RStudio has more advanced functionality, including R Markdown documents, we will not be taking advantage of that functionality in this textbook.

When interfacing with R, you may interact with four separate windows, not all of which appear simultaneously on a single screen. First, and as noted, the R console is where you may type commands to perform analyses and see their output. Figure 1.1 shows an R console window accessed through a Mac computer. Second, as described in further detail in Chapter 4, you may save the commands you type for use in later sessions in what is called a .R script file. Figure 1.2 shows a .R script file with some commands that will be used in Chapter 2. The third window is a plotting window that will pop up on your screen when a plotting command (such as one to make a histogram) is typed into the console. The fourth window is a help file window that may be accessed by preceding any command name you type into the console window with a **?**. For example, Figure 1.3 shows the help file for a histogram, accessed by typing **?hist** into the console and pressing **Enter**.

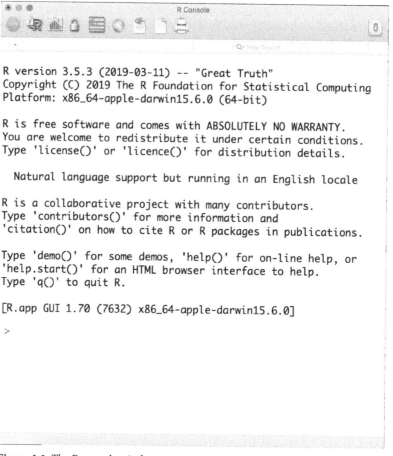

R version 3.5.3 (2019-03-11) -- "Great Truth"
Copyright (C) 2019 The R Foundation for Statistical Computing
Platform: x86_64-apple-darwin15.6.0 (64-bit)

R is free software and comes with ABSOLUTELY NO WARRANTY.
You are welcome to redistribute it under certain conditions.
Type 'license()' or 'licence()' for distribution details.

  Natural language support but running in an English locale

R is a collaborative project with many contributors.
Type 'contributors()' for more information and
'citation()' on how to cite R or R packages in publications.

Type 'demo()' for some demos, 'help()' for on-line help, or
'help.start()' for an HTML browser interface to help.
Type 'q()' to quit R.

[R.app GUI 1.70 (7632) x86_64-apple-darwin15.6.0]

  >

Figure 1.1 The R console window

When interfacing with RStudio, you also may interact with the same four windows as R, but unlike R, RStudio displays these four windows in a single screen as shown in Figure 1.4. In particular, the console window is on the bottom left, and the .R file, containing the set of commands from Chapter 2, is on the top left. In addition, the top right window provides three tabs (Environment, History, Connections) for displaying objects in working memory available within those tabs. For example, within the Environment tab, one may obtain a listing of the datasets you have loaded into working memory for that session. Finally, the bottom right window contains five tabs (Files, Plots, Packages, Help, Viewer) that when clicked displays the information relevant to that tab. In Figure 1.4, because the Help tab is shown to have been clicked and because **?hist** had been typed into the console during this R session, a description of the histogram command appears in this window.

It is important to note that R is case-sensitive, which means that R will interpret a lowercase m, for example, as different from an uppercase M. It also means that a variable name that contains only lower case letters must be typed into the console with lower case letters only; a variable name that contains only upper case letters must be typed into the console with only upper case letters; and a variable name that contains a combination of

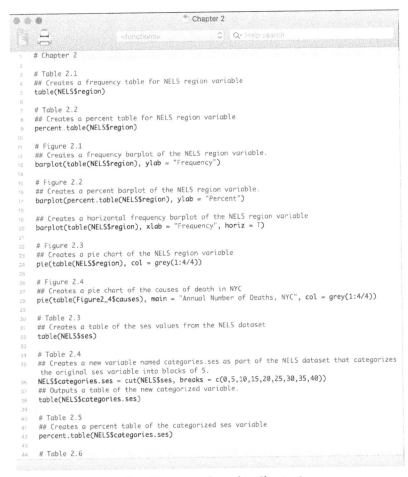

```
# Chapter 2

# Table 2.1
## Creates a frequency table for NELS region variable
table(NELS$region)

# Table 2.2
## Creates a percent table for NELS region variable
percent.table(NELS$region)

# Figure 2.1
## Creates a frequency barplot of the NELS region variable.
barplot(table(NELS$region), ylab = "Frequency")

# Figure 2.2
## Creates a percent barplot of the NELS region variable.
barplot(percent.table(NELS$region), ylab = "Percent")

## Creates a horizontal frequency barplot of the NELS region variable
barplot(table(NELS$region), xlab = "Frequency", horiz = T)

# Figure 2.3
## Creates a pie chart of the NELS region variable
pie(table(NELS$region), col = grey(1:4/4))

# Figure 2.4
## Creates a pie chart of the causes of death in NYC
pie(table(Figure2_4$causes), main = "Annual Number of Deaths, NYC", col = grey(1:4/4))

# Table 2.3
## Creates a table of the ses values from the NELS dataset
table(NELS$ses)

# Table 2.4
## Creates a new variable named categories.ses as part of the NELS dataset that categorizes
  the original ses variable into blocks of 5.
NELS$categories.ses = cut(NELS$ses, breaks = c(0,5,10,15,20,25,30,35,40))
## Outputs a table of the new categorized variable.
table(NELS$categories.ses)

# Table 2.5
## Creates a percent table of the categorized ses variable
percent.table(NELS$categories.ses)

# Table 2.6
```

Figure 1.2 A .R script file with commands used in Chapter 2

lower and upper case letters must be entered in the console with that exact combination of upper and lower case letters.

INSTALLING AND LOADING R PACKAGES

As an open-source software, R is a compilation of various packages, also referred to as libraries, that contain user-created functions for carrying out different tasks in data analysis. Said differently, each library may be thought of as a compilation of functions. Some libraries contain a diverse set of functions while others contain functions that are designed specifically to address a certain set of tasks. Many of the functions used in this textbook are part of what are called the "base" or "stats" libraries/packages. These are automatically installed and loaded when R is opened. There are several other functions, however, that we will be using in the textbook that are not part of the base libraries/packages, and we will need to install and then load them separately. Finally, there are still other functions that, at the time of writing this textbook, were not available as user-created functions, and we have taken it upon ourselves to develop our own package for these functions. You will need to install this package (which, as noted earlier, we are calling **sur**)

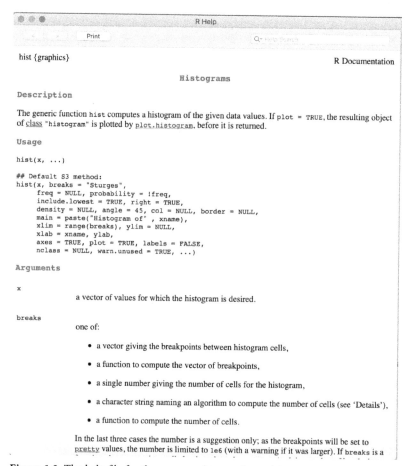

Figure 1.3 The help file for the command to produce a histogram

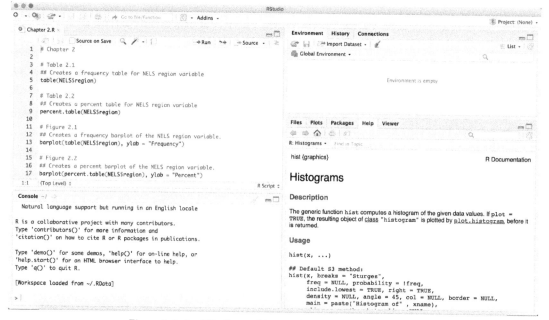

Figure 1.4 An RStudio working session

on each computer you will be using in connection with this textbook, and thereafter load this package at the beginning of every R session. In addition to functions contained in the **sur** package, as noted earlier, it also contains all the datasets that will be used in the textbook as well. Instructions for loading and then installing each package will be given at the time the functions in that package are needed. All instructions for using R will be presented for both Mac and PC users when there is a difference.[1]

MORE R: To install the **sur** package written for this textbook, once you have downloaded the R software onto your computer, type the following command into your R console and press **Enter**:

install.packages("sur")

Note: This has to be done only once on each computer you will be using in connection with this textbook.

To load the **sur** package, once you have installed it on your computer, type the following command *each time you begin an R session on your computer*:

library(sur)

To obtain a listing of the functions in the **sur** package, which include, for example, functions to create percentage tables, calculate the mode, and compute Levene's test for the equality of variances, type the following command into your R console and press **Enter**:

help(package = "sur")

Within the **sur** package, we have created a tutorial that teaches the user the basics of managing data frames within R. To access the tutorial, open RStudio and follow the set of instructions below.

MORE R: To access the tutorial on managing data frames, open RStudio, and type the following into the console window and press **Enter**:

library(sur)
learnr::run_tutorial("R_Basics", package = "sur")

The tutorial will then open in your default internet browser. To exit the tutorial, you must exit the tab in your browser, and also press **Escape** in the console Window of RStudio. For more details, see Appendix B.

SETTING A CONTEXT WITH REAL DATA

We turn now to some real data and gain familiarity with R. For this example and for others throughout the book, we have selected data from the National Educational Longitudinal Study begun in 1988, which we will refer to as the NELS dataset.

---

[1] For readers using a Mac computer, it may be necessary to download the newest operating system, as well as the newest version of XCode, in order for all the packages we reference to work.

In response to pressure from federal and state agencies to monitor school effectiveness in the United States, the National Center for Education Statistics (NCES) of the US Department of Education conducted a survey in the spring of 1988. The participants consisted of a nationally representative sample of approximately 25,000 eighth graders to measure achievement outcomes in four core subject areas (English, history, mathematics, and science), in addition to personal, familial, social, institutional, and cultural factors that might relate to these outcomes. Details on the design and initial analysis of this survey may be referenced in Horn, Hafner, and Owings (1992). A follow-up of these students was conducted during tenth grade in the spring of 1990; a second follow-up was conducted during the twelfth grade in the spring of 1992; and, finally, a third follow-up was conducted in the spring of 1994.

For this book, we have selected a sub-sample of 500 cases and 48 variables. The cases were sampled randomly from the approximately 5,000 students who responded to all four administrations of the survey, who were always at grade level (neither repeated nor skipped a grade) and who pursued some form of post-secondary education. The particular variables were selected to explore the relationships between student and home-background variables, self-concept, educational and income aspirations, academic motivation, risk-taking behavior, and academic achievement.

Some of the questions that we will be able to address using these data include: Do boys perform better on math achievement tests than girls? Does socioeconomic status relate to educational and/or income aspirations? To what extent does enrollment in advanced math in eighth grade predict twelfth grade math achievement scores? Can we distinguish between those who use marijuana and those who don't in terms of self-concept? Does owning a computer vary as a function of geographical region of residence (Northeast, North Central, South, and West)? As you become familiar with this dataset, perhaps you will want to generate your own questions of particular interest to you and explore ways to answer them.

A description of the NELS dataset may be found in Appendix A. This description can also be accessed by typing **?NELS** into the console and pressing **Enter**, after loading the **sur** package. Material for all appendices, including Appendix A, may be found online at the Cambridge University Press website for this textbook, www.cambridge.org/stats-r. Descriptions of the other real datasets we use throughout this text are also located in Appendix A.

Exercise 1.9 introduces you to some of the variables in the NELS dataset and does not require the use of R. Exercise 1.10 shows you how to open the NELS dataset in R and Exercise 1.13 shows you how to enter data using a program such as Excel and load it into R so as to create new datasets that are of interest to you that are not included as part of our **sur** package.

☞ **Remark.** There is an important distinction to be drawn between the numerical results of a statistical analysis and the *interpretation* of these results given by the researcher. Methods involved in the interpretation of results, such as researcher judgment, are not statistical operations. They are extra-statistical. For instance, to determine on the basis of having administered the same standardized test to a group of boys and girls that the girls attain, on average, higher scores than the boys is a statistical conclusion. However, to add that the reason for this difference is that the test is biased toward the girls is a researcher-based, not a statistically-based, conclusion. In offering such an interpretation, the researcher is drawing on non-statistical information. It is important to be able to separate statistical conclusions from researcher-inferred conclusions. The latter may not justifiably follow from the former; and unfortunately, the latter are the ones that are usually remembered and cited.

EXERCISES

The answers to all exercises may be found online in the textbook's website. We have included them to help you verify that the answers you obtain are correct and, if they are not correct, to help you figure out the correct solutions without spending inordinate amounts of time. Exercises 1.10–1.13 provide important foundational information on how to use R and we therefore highly recommend that they be among the exercises you complete in this chapter.

1.1 Suppose Julia is a researcher who is gathering information on the yearly income and number of years of experience of all female doctors practicing in the United States. Identify each of the following as either a constant or variable in this study. If your answer is variable, identify its most likely level of measurement (nominal, ordinal, interval, or ratio).

  (a) Sex
  (b) Yearly income as reported on one's tax return
  (c) Ethnicity
  (d) Profession (not specialty)
  (e) Number of years of experience

1.2 Given the population of all clowns in the Ringling Brothers, Barnum and Bailey Circus, identify the following as either constant or variable. If your answer is variable, identify its most likely level of measurement (nominal, ordinal, interval, or ratio).

  (a) Height
  (b) Profession
  (c) Age
  (d) Eye color

1.3 Identify each of the following numerical variables as either discrete or continuous and identify their most likely levels of measurement (nominal, ordinal, interval, or ratio).

  (a) Percentage of high school seniors each year who report that they have never smoked cigarettes
  (b) Annual rainfall in Savannah, Georgia, to the nearest inch
  (c) Number of runs scored in a baseball game
  (d) Weight
  (e) Verbal aptitude as measured by SAT verbal score
  (f) Salary of individual government officials

1.4 Identify the following numerical variables as either discrete or continuous and identify their most likely levels of measurement (nominal, ordinal, interval, or ratio).

  (a) Number of students enrolled at Ohio State University in any particular term
  (b) Distance an individual can run in five minutes
  (c) Hair length
  (d) Number of hot dogs sold at baseball games
  (e) Self-concept as measured by the degree of agreement with the statement, "I feel good about myself," on a five-point scale where 1 represents strongly disagree, 2 represents disagree, 3 represents neutral, 4 represents agree, and 5 represents strongly agree
  (f) Lack of coordination as measured by the length of time it takes an individual to assemble a certain puzzle

1.5 Identify the following numerical variables as either discrete or continuous and identify their most likely levels of measurement (nominal, ordinal, interval, or ratio).
- (a) Baseball jersey numbers
- (b) Number of faculty with PhDs at an institution
- (c) Knowledge of the material taught as measured by grade in course
- (d) Number of siblings
- (e) Temperature as measured on the Fahrenheit scale
- (f) Confidence in one's ability in statistics as measured by a yes or no response to the statement, "I am going to do very well in my statistics class this semester"

1.6 A survey was administered to college students to learn about student participation in university sponsored extracurricular activities. Identify the most likely level of measurement of each of the following variables taking into account the coding used.

Variable Name	Question asked	Coding (if any)
AGE	How old are you in years?	
EXTRAC	At which type of extracurricular activity do you spend most of your time?	1 = Sports 2 = Student government 3 = Clubs and organizations 4 = None
TIME	How much time do you spend weekly on university sponsored extracurricular activities?	0 = None 1 = 1–2 hours 2 = 3–5 hours 3 = 6–10 hours 4 = 11–20 hours 5 = More than 20 hours

- (a) AGE
- (b) EXTRAC
- (c) TIME

1.7 The Campus Survey of Alcohol and Other Drug Norms is administered to college students to collect information about drug and alcohol use on campus. Identify the most likely level of measurement of each of the following variables from that survey taking into account the coding used.

Variable name	Question asked	Coding (if any)
ABSTAIN	Overall, what percentage of students at this college do you think consume no alcoholic beverages at all?	
LIVING	Living arrangements	1 = House/apartment/etc. 2 = Residence Hall 3 = Other
STATUS	Student status:	1 = Full-time (12+ credits) 2 = Part-time (1–11 credits)

Variable name	Question asked	Coding (if any)
ATTITUDE	Which statement about drinking alcoholic beverages do you feel best represents your own attitude?	1 = Drinking is never a good thing to do. 2 = Drinking is all right but a person should not get drunk. 3 = Occasionally getting drunk is okay as long as it doesn't interfere with academics or other responsibilities. 4 = Occasionally getting drunk is okay even if it does interfere with academics or other responsibilities. 5 = Frequently getting drunk is okay if that's what the individual wants to do.
DRINK	How often do you typically consume alcohol (including beer, wine, wine coolers, liquor, and mixed drinks)?	0 = Never 1 = 1–2 times/year 2 = 6 times/year 3 = Once/month 4 = Twice/month 5 = Once/week 6 = 3 times/week 7 = 5 times/week 8 = Every day

(a) ABSTAIN
(b) LIVING
(c) STATUS
(d) ATTITUDE
(e) DRINK

*Exercise 1.8 includes descriptions of some of the variables in the Framingham dataset. The Framingham dataset is based on a longitudinal study investigating factors relating to coronary heart disease. A more complete description of the Framingham dataset may be found in Appendix A or by loading the **sur** package, and typing **?Framingham** into the console window and pressing **Enter**.*

1.8 For each variable described from the Framingham dataset, indicate the level of measurement.

(a) CURSMOKE1 indicates whether or not the individual smoked cigarettes in 1956. It is coded so that 0 represents no and 1 represents yes.

(b) CIGPDAY1 indicates the number of cigarettes the individual smoked per day, on average, in 1956.

(c) BMI1 indicates the body mass index of the individual in 1956. BMI can be calculated as follows $\text{BMI} = \left(\dfrac{\text{weight in pounds}}{(\text{height in inches}) \times (\text{height in inches})} \right) \times 703$.

(d) SYSBP1 and DIABP1 indicate the systolic and diastolic blood pressures, respectively, of the individuals in 1956. Blood is carried from the heart to all parts of your body in vessels called arteries. Blood pressure is the force of the blood pushing against the walls of the arteries. Each time the heart beats (about 60–70 times a minute at rest), it pumps out blood into the arteries. Your blood pressure is at its highest when the heart beats, pumping the blood. This is called systolic pressure. When the heart is at rest, between beats, your blood pressure falls. This is the diastolic pressure.

   Blood pressure is always given as these two numbers, the systolic and diastolic pressures. Both are important. Usually they are written one above or before the other, such as 120/80 mmHg. The top number is the systolic and the bottom the diastolic. When the two measurements are written down, the systolic pressure is the first or top number, and the diastolic pressure is the second or bottom number (for example, 120/80). If your blood pressure is 120/80, you say that it is "120 over 80." Blood pressure changes during the day. It is lowest as you sleep and rises when you get up. It also can rise when you are excited, nervous, or active. Still, for most of your waking hours, your blood pressure stays pretty much the same when you are sitting or standing still. Normal values of blood pressure should be lower than 120/80. When the level remains too high, for example, 140/90 or higher, the individual is said to have high blood pressure. With high blood pressure, the heart works harder, your arteries take a beating, and your chances of a stroke, heart attack, and kidney problems are greater.

The following exercises include descriptions and explorations of some of the variables in the NELS dataset. The NELS dataset is a subset of a dataset collected by the National Center for Education Statistics as part of a longitudinal study investigating factors relating to educational outcomes. A more complete description of the NELS dataset may be found in Appendix A or by loading the **sur** *package, and typing* **?NELS** *into the console window and pressing* **Enter**.

1.9 Read the description of the following variables from the NELS dataset. Then, classify them as either discrete or continuous and specify their levels of measurement (nominal, ordinal, interval, or ratio). The variable names are given in lowercase letters.

(a) gender. Classifies the student as either male or female, where 1 = "male" and 2 = "female."

(b) urban. Classifies the type of environment in which each student lives where 1 = "Urban," 2 = "Suburban," and 3 = "Rural."

(c) schtyp8. Classifies the type of school each student attended in eighth grade where 1 = "Public," 2 = "Private, Religious," and 3 = "Private, Non-Religious."

(d) tcherint. Classifies student agreement with the statement "My teachers are interested in students" using the Likert scale 1 = "strongly agree," 2 = "agree," 3 = "disagree," and 4 = "strongly disagree."

(e) numinst. Gives the number of post-secondary institutions the student attended.

(f) achrdg08. Gives a score for the student's performance in eighth grade on a standardized test of reading achievement. Actual values range from 36.61 to 77.2, from low to high achievement.

(g) ses. Gives a score representing the socio-economic status (ses) of the student, a composite of father's education level, mother's education level, father's occupation, mother's occupation, and family income. Values range from 0 to 35, from low to high ses.

(h) slfcnc12. Gives a score for student self-concept in twelfth grade. Values range from 0 to 43. Self-concept is defined as a person's self-perceptions, or how a person feels about himself or herself. Four items comprise the self-concept scale in the NELS questionnaire: I feel good about myself; I feel I am a person of worth, the equal of other people; I am able to do things as well as most other people; and, on the whole, I am satisfied with myself. A self-concept score, based on the sum of scores on each of these items, is used to measure self-concept in the NELS study. Higher scores associate with higher self-concept and lower scores associate with lower self-concept.

(i) schattrt. Gives the average daily attendance rate for the school.

(j) absent12. Classifies the number of times missed school. Assigns 0 to Never, 1 to 1–2 times, 2 to 3–6 times, etc.

Exercises 1.10–1.13 require the use of R and the NELS dataset. We highly recommend that these exercises be completed as they provide important foundational information on how to use R.

1.10 Follow the instructions given below to access the NELS dataset

Open R and load the **sur** package by typing **library(sur)**. (At this point, we are assuming that you have already installed the **sur** package on your computer.)

Type **str(NELS)** to view the *structure* (denoted **str** in R) of the dataset. (An excerpt of this output is given below.)

```
> str(NELS)
"data.frame" :   500 obs. of 48 variables:
$ id        :  num 1 2 3 4 5 6 7 8 9 10...
$ advmath8  :  Factor w/ 3 levels "No","Yes","Missing": 2 NA 1 1 2 1 2 2 2 1...
$ urban     :  Factor w/ 3 levels "Urban","Suburban": 1 1 2 1 1 1 1 1 1 1
$ region    :  Factor w/ 4 levels "Northeast","North Central",..: 1 1 2 2 2 2 2 2 2 2...
$ gender    :  Factor w/ 2 levels "Male","Female": 1 2 1 2 1 2 2 2 2 1...
$ famsize   :  num 4 7 4 3 4 4 4 3 5 5...
$ parmarl8  :  Factor w/ 6 levels "Divorced","Widowed",...4 4 4 4 4 4 4 4 4 4
$ homelang  :  Factor w/ 4 levels
$ slfcnc08  :  num 27 29 17 18 32 9 20 32 23 30...
$ slfcnclQ  :  num 22 23 19 21 35 16 26 28 21 33...
$ slfcncl2  :  num 36 22 33 29 41 27 33 43 29 41...
$ schtyp8   :  Factor w/ 3 levels "Public","Private","Religious",...:2 2 2 3 3 3 2 2 2
```

The first line of output in the console after **str(NELS)** tells us that the NELS dataset contains 500 observations and 48 variables. The lines following this first line contain the names of all of the variables in the NELS dataset. You may scroll down this list to confirm. You also will notice that each variable in the list has a $ preceding its name. The $ must be used in addition to each variable's name to access the variable. Because R allows more than one dataset to be in a computer's working memory per R session, in order to access a particular variable in a dataset, in addition to the $, we also would need to identify the dataset in which the variable belongs. Accordingly, since the variable id belongs to the NELS dataset, to access the variable id, for example, we would need to use its full name, **NELS$id**. Accordingly, if we were interested in printing out the list of id's in the NELS dataset, for example, we could do so by typing **NELS$id**. Typing id alone would not necessarily be sufficient.

Each line also contains each variable's data type, which is either continuous (numeric – num) or categorical (Factor). When a variable is a factor variable, the **str** command also displays the number of levels of that factor variable, as well as the coding value assigned to each level.

(a) What is the first variable in the NELS dataset?
(b) What is the second variable in the dataset and what is its variable type?
(c) How many variables are there in the NELS dataset? (Hint: Either look at the first line of output after **str(NELS)**, or type **dim(NELS)** to see how many rows and columns are in the dataset. Each row in the dataset represents an observation or case; each column represents a variable.)

1.11 In this question, we continue to explore the NELS dataset.
   (a) How many people are in the family (famsize) of the first student (id = 1) in the NELS dataset? To obtain this information, type **NELS$famsize[NELS$id == 1]** into the console and press **Enter**. Note that without the bracketed [NELS$id == 1], R would print out the values of famsize for all 500 cases. The [NELS$id == 1] limits the printing of famsize only to the case wherein id equals 1. We note that a double equal sign (==) is used to indicate "is equal to" in R.
   (b) Did the first student in the NELS dataset (id =1) take advanced math in eighth grade (advmath8)? To obtain this information, type **NELS$advmath8[NELS$id == 1]** into the console and press **Enter**.
   (c) Did the second student in the NELS dataset (id = 2) take advanced math in eighth grade (advmath8)? To obtain this information, type **NELS$advmath8[NELS$id == 2]** into the console and press **Enter**.
   (d) How many people are in the NELS dataset? To obtain this information, type **dim(NELS)** into the console and press **Enter**, or type **str(NELS)** and look at the information in the first line of output after **str(NELS)**.

1.12 The variable expinc30 gives, for each student in the NELS dataset, the expected income at age 30 in dollars. Identify the level of measurement used. Describe how the variable might have been measured using a lower level of measurement.

Exercise 1.13 provides a tutorial on data entry and requires the use of R.

1.13 In this exercise, we will enter data on 12 statisticians who each have contributed significantly to the field of modern statistics. We have provided a table of variable descriptions and a table of data values and detailed instructions on how to proceed. We will enter these data into R using the steps provided.

To enter data into R, open a spreadsheet editor, such as Microsoft Excel, and type in the following table into the spreadsheet.

Statistician	Gender	Birth	Death	AmStat
Sir Francis Galton	Male	1822	1911	7
Karl Pearson	Male	1857	1936	16
William Sealy Gosset	Male	1876	1937	0
Ronald Aylmer Fisher	Male	1890	1962	5
Harald Cramer	Male	1893	1985	0
Prasanta Chandra Mahalanobis	Male	1893	1972	0
Jerzy Neyman	Male	1894	1981	7
Egon S. Pearson	Male	1895	1980	1
Gertrude Cox	Female	1900	1978	6
Samuel S. Wilks	Male	1906	1964	1
Florence Nightingale David	Female	1909	1993	0
John Tukey	Male	1915	2000	12

Next, click **File > Save As** and save your dataset as Statisticians.csv in the comma separated values (csv) format. Make sure to save your dataset in a working directory that is easily accessed, such as your Desktop.

If you would like to read this dataset into R's working memory at some future time but do not know exactly where the dataset is located on your computer, you would need to browse to its location before reading it into R. To do so, type **Statisticians = read.csv (file.choose(), header = T)**. This command will open a browser window and allow you to navigate to select the Statisticians.csv dataset. The **header = T** argument tells R that the first line in the spreadsheet contains the names of each column. The **T** stands for True.

Alternatively, if you do know the path to the location of the dataset on your computer, you may specify that path directly in the read command. If, for example, your file, Statisticians.csv, had been saved on your computer's Desktop, you would include that path in quotes and type:

Statisticians = read.csv("~/Desktop/Statisticians.csv", header = T).

Now that the dataset is in working memory, you are ready to view the complete dataset through the **str** command, **str(Statisticians)**, or access each variable individually in that dataset using its full name. For example, the variable **Gender** would be referred to by its full name, **Statisticians$Gender**.

(a) Use the **str** command to identify the data type of each variable in this dataset.

(b) Print out the Gender of John Tukey by typing the following line of code into the console and pressing **Enter**. Note: We indicate that it is the Gender that we want to know by typing **Statisticians$Gender** first in the command. We then specify the name of the Statistician whose Gender it is we seek by qualifying the first part of the command and placing **Statisticians$Statistician** in brackets. We next specify the name of the Statistician whose Gender we seek by typing =="**John Tukey**". The reason that John Tukey is in quotes is because as we noted in part (a) of this exercise, Statistician is a string variable (its data type is designated as chr), as opposed to a numeric variable (num), and the values of a string variable need to be encased in quotes when referring to them.

Statisticians$Gender[Statisticians$Statistician == "John Tukey"]

(c) Print out the Birth Year of R. A. Fisher by typing the following line of code into the console and pressing **Enter**:

Statisticians$Birth[Statisticians$Statistician == "Ronald Aylmer Fisher"]

(d) Print out the number of AmStat publications of Gertrude Cox by typing the following line of code into the console and pressing **Enter**:

Statisticians$AmStat[Statisticians$Statistician == "Gertrude Cox"]

(e) In part (b) we sought to determine John Tukey's gender by typing, **Statisticians $Gender[Statisticians$Statistician == "John Tukey"]**

What results do you think you would obtain if you reversed the two parts of this command, and placed **Statisticians$Statistician** first and placed in brackets **Statisticians$Gender == 2**, as follows:

Statisticians$Statistician[Statisticians$Gender == 2].

Note that **== 2** is not in quotes because Gender is a numeric variable.

Hint: Recall that with respect to part (b), we placed **Statisticians$Gender** in the command first because we were seeking to find the Gender of one of the statisticians, whose name, John Tukey, was specified in the bracketed part. What does the new command suggest we are seeking to find and how does what it's in the bracketed part qualify that?

Run the command **Statisticians$Statistician[Statisticians$Gender == 2]** to see if you obtain the results you thought you would.

EXAMINING UNIVARIATE DISTRIBUTIONS

As noted in Chapter 1, the function of descriptive statistics is to describe data. A first step in this process is to explore how the collection of values for each variable is distributed across the array of values possible. Because our concern is with each variable taken separately, we say that we are exploring *univariate distributions*. Tools for examining such distributions, including tabular and graphical representations, are presented in this chapter along with R commands for implementing these tools.

MORE R: As discussed in Chapter 1, in order to access the datasets used in this textbook, and many of the functions used in this and subsequent chapters, you must first install the **sur** package (once per computer from which you are running R) and load it (once per R session) through the following commands:

install.packages("sur")
library(sur)

We recommend loading this package at the start of every R session you run.

COUNTING THE OCCURRENCE OF DATA VALUES

We again make use of the NELS dataset introduced in Chapter 1, by looking at various univariate distributions it includes. To begin our exploration, we ask the following questions about two of them. How many students in our sample are from each of the four regions of the country (Northeast, North Central, South, and West)? How are the students distributed across the range of values on socioeconomic status (ses)? By counting the number of students who live within a region, or who score within a particular score interval on the ses scale, we obtain the *frequency* of that region or score interval. When expanded to include all regions or all score intervals that define the variable, we have a *frequency distribution*. Frequency distributions may be represented by tables and graphs. The type of table or graph that is appropriate for displaying the frequency distribution of a particular variable depends, in part, upon whether the variable is discrete or continuous.

WHEN VARIABLES ARE MEASURED AT THE NOMINAL LEVEL

The variable region in the NELS dataset is an example of a discrete variable with four possible values or categories: Northeast, North Central, South, and West. To display the number of student respondents who are from each of these regions, we may use frequency and percent tables as well as bar and pie charts.

FREQUENCY AND PERCENT DISTRIBUTION TABLES

MORE R: To create a frequency table for the region variable from the NELS dataset, type the following command in the console and hit **Enter**:

table(NELS$region)

TABLE 2.1 Frequency table for region

Northeast	North Central	South	West
106	151	150	93

TABLE 2.2 Percent table for region

Northeast	North Central	South	West
21.2	30.2	30.0	18.6

The result, as given in Table 2.1, will appear on your screen in the console.

In Table 2.1, the first row lists the four possible categories of this variable. The second row presents the number of respondents from each region. From this row, we may note that the fewest number of respondents, 93, are from the West. Note that if we sum the frequency column we obtain 500, which represents the total number of respondents in our dataset. This is the value we should obtain if an appropriate category is listed for each student and all students respond to one and only one category. If an appropriate category is listed for each student and all students respond to one and only one category, we say the categories are *mutually exclusive and exhaustive*. This is a desirable, though not essential, property of frequency distributions.

While the frequency of a category is informative, so is also the *relative frequency* of the category; that is, the frequency of the category relative to (divided by) the total number of individuals responding. The relative frequency represents the *proportion* of the total number of responses that are in the category. The relative frequency of student respondents from the West, for example, is 93/500 or 0.186.

Relative frequencies can also be converted easily to percentages by multiplying the relative frequency by 100. Making this conversion, we find that 18.6 percent (0.186 x 100), or close to 20 percent, of our sample is from the West.

MORE R: To create a percent table for the region variable from the NELS dataset, type the following command in the console and hit **Enter**:

percent.table(NELS$region)

The result, as given in Table 2.2, will appear on your screen in the console.

The full percent distribution relative to all four regions may be found in the second row of Table 2.2. Note that the sum of values in this column equals 100 percent, as one would expect. In some cases, however, when round-off error is incurred in converting fractions to percentages, a sum slightly different from 100 percent may be obtained.

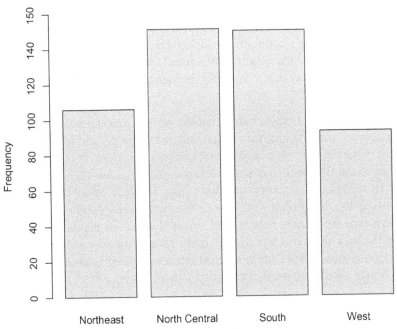

Figure 2.1 Bar chart of frequency distribution for region

BAR CHARTS

In addition to a tabular format, frequency and percent distributions of nominal data may be represented visually in the form of a bar chart. Figure 2.1 contains a bar chart depicting the frequency of each region.

MORE R: To generate the bar chart of Figure 2.1, type:

barplot(table(NELS$region), ylab = "Frequency")

in the console and hit **Enter**.

Note: The option **ylab = "Frequency"** labels the *y* (or vertical) axis with the word, Frequency.

As depicted in Figure 2.1, the values of the variable region are represented by points along the category (or horizontal or *x*) axis, whereas the frequencies (or counts) are represented by points along the vertical axis, labeled frequency. In other cases, relative frequencies or percentages are represented along the vertical axis. The ordering of the categories along the category axis follows the ordering of the numerical values assigned to the categories when the data were entered originally. Recall that as noted in Example 1.4 in Chapter 1, a 1 is assigned to the category Northeast, 2 to North Central, and so on. Because region is a nominal-leveled variable, this assignment of numbers to region categories is arbitrary.

Accordingly, in the case of Figure 2.1, the ordering of the regions along the category axis is arbitrary. For ordinal-, interval-, or ratio-leveled variables, however, the inherent ordering of the variable itself dictates the ordering of categories along the horizontal axis. The importance of this distinction will become clear when we discuss cumulative distributions.

A bar chart is characterized by *unconnected* bars or rectangles of equal width, each of whose height reflects the frequency of the category it represents. For example, the height of the bar labeled South reaches a count of 150, indicating that the frequency of that category is 150. Furthermore, because the heights of the bars labeled North Central and South are approximately equal we may infer that the frequencies for those two categories are approximately equal as well.

☞ **Remark** A nice property of this chart is that the vertical axis starts at 0. As discussed in Chapter 1, frequency, like height, may be considered to be a ratio-leveled variable. As a ratio-leveled variable, we may make multiplicative or ratio comparisons between different values along the frequency scale. Because height, as another ratio-leveled variable, is used to represent frequency in a bar chart, for such ratio comparisons to be meaningful using the heights of the bars, a bar with zero height should represent a category with zero frequency. Fortunately, this is the case in Figure 2.1. Before using the heights of the bars alone in a bar chart to make ratio comparisons between categories along the horizontal axis, check that the vertical axis actually begins at the value zero – that a bar of zero height would represent a category with zero frequency.

Although we have illustrated the use of bar charts to depict frequency distributions, we may also use bar charts to depict percent distributions.

MORE R: To generate a bar chart by percentages (Figure 2.2), we replace **table(NELS $region)** with **percent.table(NELS$region)**:

barplot(percent.table(NELS$region), ylab = "Percent")

Note again that the option **ylab = "Percent"** labels the *y* or vertical axis with the term "Percent."

To create a percent bar graph of a different nominal variable, simply substitute the name of that variable for the variable region whenever region appears in these commands.

You can run the command **?barplot** to learn more about the options available for constructing bar graphs.

Notice that the relative standing of the heights of the bars in Figure 2.2 is the same as that in the chart in Figure 2.1. This is because the percent scale differs from the frequency (or count) scale in terms of a constant of proportionality only. To obtain each percent value, we simply divide each frequency value by the sample size (500, in this case) and then multiply by 100. Effectively, then, each frequency value is multiplied by the constant of proportionality, one-fifth (100/500) to obtain the corresponding percent value, in this case.

MORE R: Orienting the direction of the bars.

To orient the bars horizontally, instead of vertically as has been shown, we use the command:

barplot(table(NELS$region), xlab = "Frequency", horiz = T)

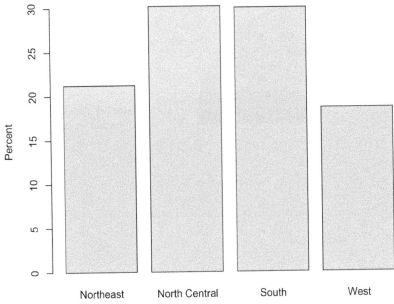

Figure 2.2 Bar chart of percent distribution for region

Note here that the option, **horiz = T**, orients the bar chart horizontally. **T** stands for the word **True**.

PIE CHARTS

Pie charts may be used to depict frequency and percent distributions in the discrete variable case as long as the categories are exhaustive. Pie charts are particularly useful for depicting each category relative to the entire set of categories. A pie chart of the frequency distribution for region is given in Figure 2.3.

MORE R: To create a pie chart of the variable region from the NELS dataset (denoted **NELS$region**), for example, type:

pie(table(NELS$region))

in the console and press **Enter**.

In a pie chart, the larger frequencies are indicated by larger slices. Notice that the two regions of approximately equal numbers of students, South and North Central, are represented by approximately equal-sized slices. And that these two regions account for more than half of the students who are in our sample. Just as bar charts may be misleading if their vertical axes do not start at zero, pie charts may be misleading if the categories they depict are not exhaustive. Consider the case illustrated in Figure 2.4 depicting the annual number of deaths in New York City: Tobacco vs. Other.

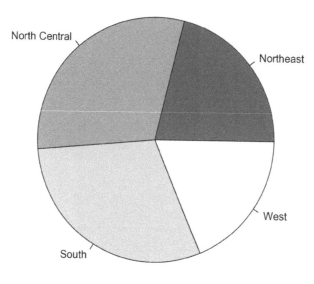

Figure 2.3 Pie chart of frequency distribution for region

MORE R: To create add a title to pie chart of the variable causes for the variable named causes from the Figure2_4 dataset (denoted **Figure2_4$causes**), for example, type:

pie(table(Figure2_4$causes), main = "Annual Number of Deaths, NYC")

in the console and press **Enter**.

The **main** option includes a main title for the plot.

Notice that this pie chart misleads the viewer into thinking that tobacco is the greatest cause of death. However, not included in the list of causes considered are, for example, heart disease and cancer unrelated to tobacco use, which are known leading causes of death. In this example, the categories are not exhaustive, and clearly for a reason. This pie chart was created as part of an anti-smoking campaign.

WHEN VARIABLES ARE MEASURED AT THE ORDINAL, INTERVAL, OR RATIO LEVEL

In the previous section we discussed ways to explore univariate distributions of variables that are measured at the nominal level. In this section, we present analogous tools for variables that are measured at the ordinal, interval, or ratio level.

FREQUENCY AND PERCENT DISTRIBUTION TABLES

Because a variable often has many distinct values in its distribution, a frequency distribution table with each category representing one value is often too unwieldy to be informative. Table 2.3 contains such a table generated by R for socioeconomic status (ses), a variable that is part of the NELS dataset. In this table, the ses values are in the first row; the corresponding frequencies are in the second row. ses ranges from 0 to 35 with higher scores associated with higher ses. ses is a composite of parents' education level, occupation, and family income.

TABLE 2.3 Frequency distribution for socioeconomic status (ses)

0	1	2	3	4	5	6	7	8	9	10	11	12	13	14	15	16	17	18	19	20	21	22	23	24	25	26	27	28	29	30	31	32	35
1	1	2	2	4	1	12	7	15	9	18	22	16	15	19	24	18	33	28	39	24	22	19	22	14	21	20	16	16	12	16	8	3	1

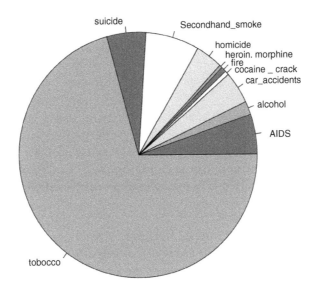

Figure 2.4 Annual number of deaths in NYC for different causes Data source: www.StopSmokingDoctors.com

Notice that while we have not lost any information contained in the original dataset with this tabular representation, the number of categories is too large for easy interpretation.

MORE R: To construct a frequency distribution table for the variable ses from the NELS dataset, for example, we type:

table(NELS$ses)

in the console and press **Enter**. The first row contains values and the second row contains their frequencies.

We can type **?table** to learn more about this command.

In Tables 2.4 and 2.5, the data have been grouped into categories defined by intervals of values, and the number of categories, therefore, has been reduced. Notice that unlike the frequency distribution for region, where each of the small number of categories contains a single value (Northeast, North Central, South, and West), each category for ses is actually a range of ses values represented by the lowest value in that range. For example, the first category, represented by the value 0, contains all ses values from 0 to 5, including the value 5. Ten students, representing 2.0 percent, have ses values within this range. Likewise, the second category, represented by the value 5, contains all ses values from just above 5 to the value 10 inclusive. Sixty-one students, representing 12.2 percent, have ses values within this range.

TABLE 2.4 Generation of the categories.ses variable and a grouped frequency distribution of socioeconomic status (ses)

(0,5]	(5,10]	(10,15]	(15,20]	(20,25]	(25,30]	(30,35]	(35,40]
10	61	96	142	98	80	12	0

TABLE 2.5 Percent table for ses

(0,5]	(5,10]	(10,15]	(15,20]	(20,25]	(25,30]	(30,35]	(35,40]
2.0	12.2	19.2	28.4	19.6	16.0	2.4	0.0

Because the ses scale is constructed so that a lower score corresponds to a lower socio-economic status, these students are the most socioeconomically disadvantaged in our sample.

Each ses category in Tables 2.4 and 2.5 defines an interval of the values in Table 2.3; the values are said to be grouped together. Accordingly, this type of frequency distribution is often referred to as a *grouped frequency distribution*.

MORE R: Grouped frequency distribution in tabular form.

To obtain the grouped frequency distribution in Tables 2.4 and 2.5, we use the **cut()** function to generate or create a new variable that contains the grouped frequencies at cut points (breaks) 0 to 40 by increments of 5. We then use the **table** and **percent.table** commands to display the values as a frequency distribution as follows:

```
NELS$categories.ses = cut(NELS$ses, breaks = c(0,5,10,15,20,25,30,35,40))
table(NELS$categories.ses)
percent.table(NELS$categories.ses)
```

In creating grouped frequency tables, in general, the following advice is offered. For variables that are at least ordinal and have many distinct values, grouped frequency tables should be created so that:

1. The number of categories is sufficiently small to reduce the data and make them more understandable, yet sufficiently large so as to retain much of the specific information contained in the data. Considering both clarity and retention of information, the number of categories typically is between 6 and 12 inclusive.
2. The categories are mutually exclusive and exhaustive (i.e., each piece of data must fall into one and only one category).
3. The categories are all of equal size so as to achieve a clear picture of the data.

Note that in Tables 2.4 and 2.5, there are eight mutually exclusive and exhaustive categories defined by intervals of equal size, beginning, respectively, at the values 0, 5, 10, and so on.

☞ **Remark** To uphold the principle that all categories should be mutually exclusive, we may consider the interval that begins with 5, for example, to include the values 5 up to just less than the value 10. The value 10 would be included in the next interval that begins with 10.

The grouped as opposed to the ungrouped frequency distribution often reflects more clearly the distribution's three major properties, its *level* (the magnitude of a "typical" value in the distribution), its *spread* (how far apart the values are from one another), and its *shape* (the extent to which the values of the distribution are balanced on either side of the typical value). The level of a distribution also may be viewed as a way of describing the *location* of the distribution relative to the entire set of values in the dataset.

In Chapter 3 and later in this chapter we elaborate on these three properties and provide ways for characterizing them statistically.

STEM-AND-LEAF DISPLAYS

An alternative technique for describing data that are at least ordinal is the stem-and-leaf display. In this display, the digits of each data value are separated into two parts, called a stem and a leaf. For distributions of values between 0 and 100, the stem contains all but the units (rightmost) digit of each data value, and the leaf contains only the units (rightmost) digit. The stems are ordered numerically in a column from smallest to largest and the leaves are listed to the right of their associated stems, also in increasing order from left to right.

Our first example of a stem and leaf will relate to the States dataset, which includes different educational measures of the 50 states. In this case, we will create a stem-and-leaf plot of pertak, a variable which gives, for each state, the percentage of high school seniors who took the SAT in that state in 2012. These data are from *The 2014 World Almanac and Book of Facts*.

MORE R: To obtain a stem-and-leaf display of pertak, for example, we type the following command in the console and hit **Enter**:

stem(States$pertak)

We may type **?stem** to learn more about this command and its options.

Table 2.6 contains a stem-and-leaf display of the variable pertak.

This stem and leaf sorts the 50 values into 11 groupings. The first grouping includes the values from 0 to 9 only, the second grouping includes the values from 10 to 19, the third grouping includes the values from 20 to 29, and so on. We know this to be the case because the heading of this plot notes that "the decimal point is 1 digit to the right of the |." Accordingly, in the first row, for example, we place the decimal point to the right of the 3 and read the value of 0 | 3 as 03 or, more simply, as 3. Likewise, 10 | 0 represents the number 100, and so on. We see that there are three instances of 0 | 6 or 06 or, more simply, 6 indicating that three states have only 6 percent of their high school seniors taking the SAT tests.

Because of the relatively small size of this dataset (50 cases), there is only one line per

TABLE 2.6 Stem-and-leaf display of pertak
The decimal point is 1 digit(s) to the right of the |
0 | 333444455555566789
1 | 03779
2 | 078
3 |
4 | 9
5 | 4578
6 | 2668999
7 | 234458
8 | 1389
9 | 03
10 | 0

stem. The first line contains the leaves for those states whose stem is 0, that is, whose percentage of high school seniors taking the SAT is less than 10. By counting the occurrences in that row, we see that there are 18 such states. The second line contains the leaves for those states whose stem is 1, that is, whose percentage of high school seniors taking the SAT is greater than or equal to 10, but less than 20. We see that there are five such states.

If we define the typical percentage of high school seniors who take the SAT per state as the most frequently occurring percentage of high school seniors who take the SAT per state, we may note that that value is 5 percent, according to the stem-and-leaf display. This is because the pertak value of 5 percent (appearing in row one of the display) occurs five times, more than any other percentage value in the distribution. Accordingly, using this definition of typical, we may say that the value 5 percent represents the level of the pertak distribution or its location relative to the entire set of pertak values in the distribution. Other, and perhaps better, ways of defining the level or location of a distribution are presented later in this chapter and in Chapter 3.

To determine how spread out the pertak values in this distribution are, we simply compute the range of percentage values in this distribution, obtained by subtracting the lowest (or minimum) value from the highest (or maximum) value, or $100 - 3 = 97$. In this case, a range of 97 suggests a large spread given that as percentages, the values in this distribution can range only from 0 to 100. Again, other, and perhaps better, ways of defining the spread of a distribution of values are presented later in this chapter and in Chapter 3.

Finally, we may note that the percentage values in this distribution do not appear to be balanced around the typical percentage value of 5. By contrast, the distribution of pertak values separates into two clusters of states, one cluster having fewer than 30 percent of its students taking the SAT and the other cluster having 49 percent or more of its students taking the SAT. Describing the shape of a distribution will be discussed in greater detail later in this chapter and in Chapter 3.

Another stem-and-leaf display is presented to exemplify a situation in which the values of the distribution are not between 0 and 100. This example also comes from the States dataset. In this case, we will create a stem-and-leaf plot of satm, a variable that gives, for each state, the average math SAT score of high school seniors in that state. If we were to type **stem(States$satm)**, the stems of the plot would contain only even numbers (e.g., 44, 46, 48, and so on). To have all the values appear as stems (not just the even values), we add the argument **scale = 2**. This will make the plot more precise and give it a length that is about twice as long as that of the default. In this case, the code is **stem(States$satm, scale = 2)**. Table 2.7 contains this stem-and-leaf plot.

In Table 2.7, as in Table 2.6, the stem (the value to the left of |) represents the beginning digits of the values in the distribution. For example, 61 | 7 represents the value 617, the highest satm average of all 50 states.

TABLE 2.7 Stem-and-leaf of satm

The decimal point is 1 digit(s) to the right of the |

```
45 | 79
46 | 67
47 |
48 | 77
49 | 0049
50 | 00114456
51 | 2249
52 | 023889
53 | 4
54 | 057
55 | 36
56 | 699
57 | 0
58 | 1348
59 | 55
60 | 11489
61 | 07
```

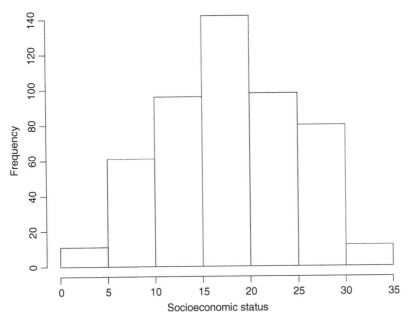

Figure 2.5 Default histogram of ses

HISTOGRAMS

Another graphic for representing data that are at least ordinal is the *histogram*. Figure 2.5 illustrates the use of a histogram to represent ses data from our NELS dataset. Along the horizontal axis of Figure 2.5 are the midpoints of the intervals whose frequencies are represented by the heights of the bars. The histogram differs from a bar chart in that no spaces appear between the bars unless categories with zero frequency occur. Eliminating the spaces between bars in a histogram makes the chart convey a feeling of continuity that reflects the ordinal nature of the variable. Bar charts, on the other hand, include spaces between the bars to avoid the interpretation of a trend in the case of nominal-leveled data. The ordering of categories from nominal-leveled data would be arbitrary along the horizontal axis.

MORE R: To generate a histogram of ses, for example, with frequencies on the *y*-axis, we type the following in the console and hit **Enter**:

hist(NELS$ses, main = "Histogram", xlab = "Socio-economic Status")

Note that the main = **"Histogram"** argument adds a main title to the graph, while the **xlab = "Socio-economic Status"** argument labels the *x*, or horizontal, axis.

We note that a histogram is affected by the number of bars (or bins) chosen. Figure 2.5 has a default number of bins determined by the spread of the distribution. This default value, creating Figure 2.5, appears to provide a good balance between summarizing the data and providing details about the distribution.

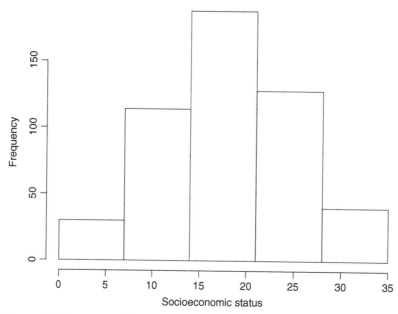

Figure 2.6 Histogram with 5 intervals

For those interested, in order to generate Figures 2.6 and 2.7, we must change the number of bins in the histogram, using the **breaks** argument. Code to generate these figures is provided below.

MORE R: To edit the number of bins of a histogram we use the **breaks** argument within the **hist** command and type the following to obtain Figure 2.6 with 5 bins:

hist(NELS$ses, breaks = seq(min(NELS$ses), max(NELS$ses), length.out = 6), main = "Histogram with 5 bins", xlab = "Socio-economic Status")

To obtain Figure 2.7 with 30 bins, we type:

hist(NELS$ses, breaks = seq(min(NELS$ses), max(NELS$ses), length.out = 31), main = "Histogram with 30 bins", xlab = "Socio-economic Status")

Notice that the **breaks** argument within the **hist** command requires four pieces of information. First, we ask R to create a sequence (using the **seq**) command, that ranges from the minimum value of ses (**min(NELS$ses)**) to the maximum value of ses (**max(NELS$ses)**) with a length of one more than the number of bins that we are looking to display in our histogram.

To generate a histogram with proportions rather than frequencies, we use the code provided below.

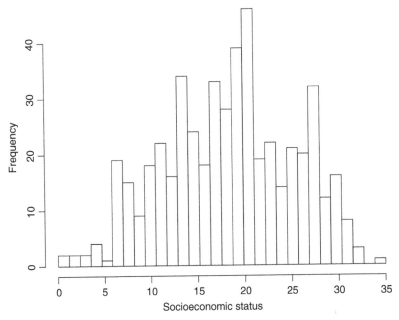

Figure 2.7 Histogram with 30 intervals

MORE R: To generate a histogram with proportion (or density) on the *y*-axis to obtain Figure 2.8, we include the **freq = F** argument within the **hist** command. The **F** stands for "False." We type:

hist(NELS$ses, freq = F, xlab = "Socio-economic Status", main = "Histogram")

The shape of the histogram in Figure 2.8 defined by percentages is identical to that of the default histogram in Figure 2.5. A histogram differs from a stem-and-leaf display in that the latter uses the leaf values themselves to create the bars of the display. As a result, the stem-and-leaf display provides more information about the original set of data than the histogram.

LINE GRAPHS

Another type of graph that is often used to represent data that are at least ordinal is the *line graph* or *polygon*. Figure 2.9 illustrates a density polygon for our socioeconomic status variable from the NELS dataset.

MORE R: To construct a line graph type:

line.graph(NELS$ses, main = "Line Graph", xlab = "Socio-economic Status", ylab = "Density")

The argument **ylab** includes a *y*-axis (or vertical axis) label.

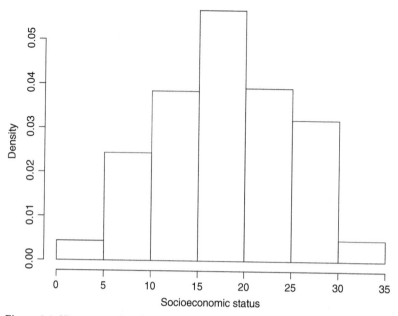

Figure 2.8 Histogram of ses by percentages

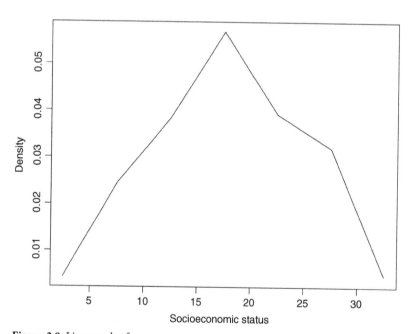

Figure 2.9 Line graph of ses

Figure 2.10 Default density graph

To obtain a smoothed version of the line graph type:

plot(density(NELS$ses), main = "Density Graph", xlab = "Socio-economic Status")

In the **density** command, the argument **bw** may be included to change the bandwidth (i.e., the width of the interval of ses values) used for obtaining the proportions. For less smoothing, we would use a smaller bandwidth value (e.g., **bw = 0.75**).

Figures 2.10 and 2.11 display two density graphs of the ses variable, with two different smoothing parameters. Figure 2.10 sets **bw = 1.80**, which is the default value of **bw** and therefore does not need to be included in the code; Figure 2.11 sets **bw = 0.75**.

As one would expect, the stem-and-leaf display, the histogram, the line graph, and density graphs all bear a strong resemblance to each other in their depiction of ses frequencies. While, as noted, there may be some advantages of one type of display over another, the ultimate choice of which display to use belongs to the researcher.

Line graphs are often used when we are depicting two variables, and one represents time. An example is given in Figure 2.12 that is taken from the Marijuana dataset. The figure shows, for the years 1987–2012, the percentage of high school seniors who said that they had ever used marijuana. These data are from *The 2014 World Almanac and Book of Facts* (2014).

MORE R: To create the two-variable line graph of Figure 2.12, type the following:

plot(Marijuana$MarijuanaUse~Marijuana$Year, type = "l", xlab = "Year", ylab = "Marijuana Use")

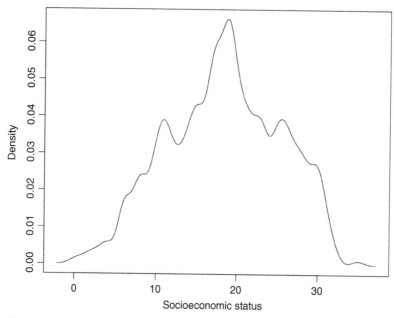

Figure 2.11 Less smooth density graph

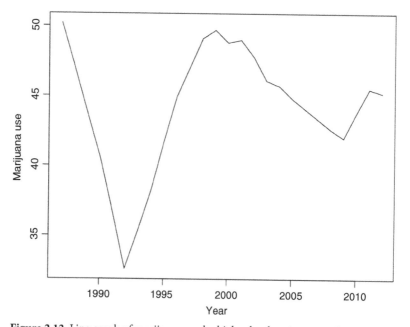

Figure 2.12 Line graph of marijuana use by high school seniors over time

In the plot command, the variable to be placed on the *y*-axis is listed before the ~; the variable to be placed on the *x*-axis is listed after the ~. Note that here we use the **plot** command with argument **type** = "**l**" (the letter l) to indicate that we would like a line graph rather than a graph with the individual year by use points plotted. Furthermore, we label the *x* and *y* axes using the **xlab** and **ylab** arguments, respectively.

MORE R: Line options to customize the line color, pattern, and width.

To customize Figure 2.12, we can make the line color blue, the line dashed, the line width medium, and also add a title to the graph itself, as follows:

plot(Marijuana\$MarijuanaUse~Marijuana\$Year, type = "l", xlab = "Year", ylab = "Marijuana Use", col = "blue", lwd = 2, lty = 2)

Here, **col = "blue"** indicates the line color, **lwd = 2** the line width, and **lty = 2** the line type. Given **lty = 2**, a dashed pattern is used. To learn more about the graphical parameters in R, use **?plot.** Notice that the options that relate to the line itself (**col, lwd, lty**) are placed within the parentheses since these options are modifying the line to be drawn.

DESCRIBING THE SHAPE OF A DISTRIBUTION

A curve is said to be *symmetric* if, when folded from left to right along its vertical axis of symmetry (its middle), one-half of the curve overlaps the other. Two symmetric curves are shown in Figure 2.13 and differ because the graph on the left is single-peaked (Figure 2.13a) and the one on the right is double-peaked (Figure 2.13b). In Chapter 3, we introduce other words to describe the shape of the curve based on its peaks. If, on the other hand, overlapping does not result, the curve is said to be *asymmetric*.

Another characteristic often used to describe the shape of a frequency or percent distribution graph is the *skewness*. For our purposes, the term skewness will refer to the distribution of the graph's area about its mean. For example, the histogram for self-concept in grade 12 (slfcnc12) from our NELS dataset (Figure 2.14) is asymmetric. The bulk of its scores ranges from 25 to 45 and its tail is to the left of this bulk (or in a negative direction). That is, the bulk of the data consists of relatively high scores, yet there are a few relatively low scores. Accordingly, we say that these data are *skewed to the left*, or *skewed negatively*. Thus, most students in our sample have higher values of self-concept and only relatively few have lower values of self-concept.

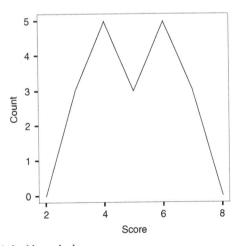

Figure 2.13 Symmetric curves (a) single-peaked and (b) double peaked

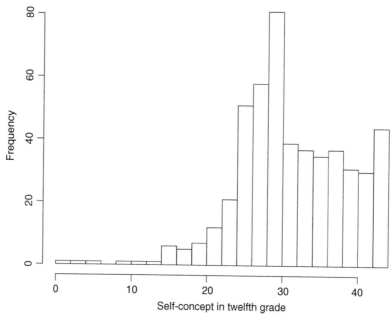

Figure 2.14 Histogram of slfcnc12

If the graph looked like Figure 2.15 instead, with its tail to the right of the main bulk (or in a positive direction from the main bulk), we would say that the graph is *skewed to the right*, or *skewed positively*. The skewness of a graph is the direction in which its tail lies relative to its main bulk. Figure 2.15 depicts for our sample the frequency distribution of responses to the question: "What annual income do you expect to have at the age of thirty?" Clearly, the bulk of students expect incomes less than or equal to $150,000 per year, while only a relative few expect incomes in excess of $150,000 and one student, in fact, expects an income of $1,000,000. Where would your response fit within this depiction, within the bulk of the responses, or in the tail?

☞ **Remark.** Extreme values, such as the $1,000,000 expected income, are called *outliers*. For reasons that will become clear in the next chapter, one of the key jobs of a data analyst is to learn how to identify and handle such outliers.

☞ **Remark.** Figure 2.15 is noticeably more skewed than Figure 2.14.

It is possible for a graph to be asymmetric without being noticeably skewed either to the left or to the right. In this case, we would simply say that the graph is asymmetric and leave it at that.

ACCUMULATING DATA

When data are at least ordinal, the inherent ordering of the values allows us to accumulate the data in ways that make sense. We can look at the percentage (or number) of scores below a given score. For example, we can find the percentage of students in the NELS

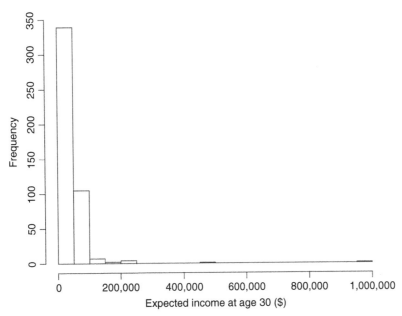

Figure 2.15 Histogram of expinc30

dataset who have socioeconomic status ratings of 9 or lower. We can also look at the score below which a certain percentage of scores fall. For example, we can ask what is the socioeconomic status score below which 25 percent of the students in the NELS dataset fall?

CUMULATIVE PERCENT DISTRIBUTIONS

Up to now, the vertical axis has represented either frequency or percent. There are other possibilities to be considered. Referring once again to the grouped frequency distribution of ses (Tables 2.4 and 2.5), suppose we want to know at a glance the percent of students in our sample who have socioeconomic status ratings of 9 or lower. While we could sum the percentages associated with the categories 0–3, 3–6, and 6–9 in Table 2.5, respectively, to obtain the sum 10.8 percent (1.2, 3.4, 6.2 percent), a more direct solution is available from the cumulative percent table in Table 2.8. This table contains the cumulative percent distribution for ses and may be used to obtain the percent of students whose ses values fall *at or below* a certain point in the distribution.

   Table 2.8 is useful in finding the cumulative percent of a value of 10, because 10 is the uppermost value of one of the categories, 5–10, contained in this table. Had we been interested in the cumulative percent of a value of 9, on the other hand, Table 2.8 would not have been useful because we do not know from this table how many of the 61 students with ses between 5 and 10 actually have an ses value at or below 9. By grouping the data into larger than unit intervals, we lose the specific information needed to answer this question exactly. Based on Table 2.8 alone, then, we do not know whether all, none, or some of the 61 students have ses values between 9 and 10 and should not be counted in answering this question. Because there is no way to determine the true situation from only the grouped

TABLE 2.8 Cumulative percent table for ses categories

(0,5]	(5,10]	(10,15]	(15,20]	(20,25]	(25,30]	(30,35]	(35,40]
2.0	14.2	33.4	61.8	81.4	97.4	99.8	99.8

TABLE 2.9 Cumulative percent distribution for ses

0	1	2	3	4	5	6	7	8	9	10	11	12	13	14	15	16
0.2	0.4	0.8	1.2	2.0	2.2	4.6	6.0	9.0	10.8	14.4	18.8	22.0	25.0	28.8	33.6	37.2

17	18	19	20	21	22	23	24	25	26	27	28	29	30	31	32	35
43.8	49.4	57.2	62.0	66.4	70.2	74.6	77.4	81.6	85.6	88.8	92.0	94.4	97.6	99.2	99.8	100.0

distribution given in Table 2.8, to determine the percent of students with ses values at or below 9, for example, we make use of the ungrouped ses data with cumulative percent table shown in Table 2.9. In doing so, we find that the percentage of students falling at or below a 9 is equal to 10.8.

Because ses is a many-valued variable, with values ranging from 0 to 35, R displays the table in four rows. Rows 1 and 3 contain the values of ses, while rows 2 and 4 contain the cumulative percentages associated with these ses values.

MORE R: To create the cumulative percent table in Table 2.8, type the following:

cumulative.table(NELS$categories.ses)

To create the cumulative percent table in Table 2.9, type the following:

cumulative.table(NELS$ses)

PERCENTILE RANKS

The *percentile rank* of a given raw score is the percent of scores falling below that raw score in a specified distribution. As discussed previously, the cumulative percent of a given raw score is the percent of scores falling at or below that raw score in a specified distribution. The difference between these two statistics, that one reports the percent *below* a given raw score, whereas the other reports the percent *at or below* a given raw score, rests in the distinction between continuous and discrete variables. Technically the percentile rank is more appropriate for variables that are continuous, and the cumulative percent is more appropriate for variables that are discrete.

Because many discrete variables, however, like income, property value, and frequency data, share many of the properties of a continuous variable, the percentile rank and the cumulative percent, when applied to such variables, will provide similar results. Likewise, when applied to continuous variables, in practice, the cumulative percent and the percentile rank will provide similar results. Given their respective definitions, the cumulative percent value will, in general, be larger than the percentile rank. In this book, for simplicity, we shall not compute the exact values of percentile ranks; rather we shall estimate them using cumulative percentages based on an ungrouped frequency distribution such as the one in Table 2.9.

EXAMPLE 2.1 Use the cumulative percent to estimate the percentile rank of an ses value of 13 for the sample of 500 students under study.

Solution We obtain an estimate of the percentile rank of 13 by using the cumulative percent distribution in Table 2.9. We find that one-fourth (25 percent) of the students in our sample have ses scores equal to or below 13; so that an estimate of the percentile rank of an ses score of 13 is 25th.

As the example illustrates, the percentile rank makes raw score data more meaningful by allowing us to know the relative standing of a single score within a set of scores. From another viewpoint, knowing that your raw score on an exam is 90, for example, has little meaning, because the exam could have been out of 100 points or it could have been out of 500 points. Knowing that your percentile rank on an exam is 90, however, means that 90 percent of the people taking the exam received scores below yours.

Often, we seek to know an individual's raw score corresponding to a particular percentile rank. For example, suppose you were told that your percentile rank on an exam was 90, and you wanted to find your raw score. In so doing, you would be finding the 90th percentile, or that raw score corresponding to the 90th percentile rank (that raw score with 90 percent of the scores below it).

PERCENTILES

In general, a percentile is that theoretical raw score that would correspond to a given percentile rank in a specified distribution. From Example 2.1, for example, we know that approximately one-fourth of these students' ses values are below the value of 13; that the value of 13 is at the 25 percentile in the ses distribution. Just as the value of 13 has approximately one-fourth of the distribution below it, it also has approximately three-fourths (75 percent) of the distribution above it. Accordingly, the value of 13 may be said to divide the ses distribution into two groups of students: one group that contains 25 percent or 125 students, and the other group that contain 75 percent or 375 students.

☞ **Remark** The percentile is often referred to as a centile and even more frequently as a quantile denoted by the letter Q. The 25th percentile, therefore, is denoted as Q_{25}.

For a fuller understanding of what centiles represent in terms of an underlying distribution, we shall examine the set of quantiles $Q_1, Q_2, Q_3, \ldots, Q_{99}$. These percentiles/quantiles are the 99 theoretically possible raw scores that divide a distribution into 100 equal parts. That is, between any two consecutive quantiles there will be 1 percent of all the scores in the distribution. For example, if, as in our ses distribution, there are 500 raw scores, then between any two consecutive quantiles, there will be 1 percent of the 500 scores, or (0.01)(500) = 5 scores.

☞ **Remark** Q_{100} is not necessary because only 99 points are needed to divide a set of scores into 100 intervals with equal frequencies. The scores from Q_{99} to the maximum value in the distribution define the 100th interval.

· ·

EXAMPLE 2.2 How many of the raw scores in a distribution made up of 500 raw scores will fall:

1. Between Q_{40} and Q_{41}
2. Between Q_{40} and Q_{50}
3. Below Q_{25}
4. Below Q_{10}

Solution

1. Because Q_{40} and Q_{41} are consecutive percentiles, there will be 1 percent of the total number of scores in the distribution, or $(0.01)(500) = 5$ scores between them.
2. Because Q_{40} and Q_{50} differ by 10 percentiles $(50 - 40 = 10$ percentiles), there will be (10) $(1\%) = 10\%$ of the total number of scores in the distribution between them. This would be $(0.10)(500) = 50$ scores.
3. Because Q_{25} is by definition the raw score having 25 percent of the total number of scores in the distribution below it, Q_{25} would have $(0.25)(500) = 125$ scores below it. Q_{25} is commonly referred to as the *1st quartile*. Q_{50} is commonly referred to as the *2nd quartile*, and Q_{75} is commonly referred to as the *3rd quartile*.
4. Because Q_{10} is by definition the raw score having 10 percent of the total number of scores in the distribution below it, Q_{10} would have $(0.10)(500) = 50$ scores below it. Q_{10} is commonly referred to as the *1st decile* and denoted by the symbol D_1. Similarly, Q_{20} is commonly referred to as the *2nd decile* and denoted by the symbol D_2, and so on. Therefore, $D_1 = Q_{10}$, $D_2 = Q_{20}$, $D_3 = Q_{30}$, $D_4 = Q_{40}$, $D_5 = Q_{50}$, $D_6 = Q_{60}$, $D_7 = Q_{70}$, $D_8 = Q_{80}$, and $D_9 = Q_{90}$. Because no reference is made to a 100th percentile, Q_{100}, we likewise make no reference to a 10th decile, D_{10}.

☞ **Remark.** We will make most use of quartiles. Another way of thinking of quartiles is that Q_{50} divides the entire distribution in half, Q_{25} divides the bottom half in half, and Q_{75} divides the top half in half.

☞ **Remark** Like percentile ranks, percentiles are appropriately defined on distributions of continuous variables, and may be thought of as cut points that divide a distribution into a given number of groups of equal frequency. The set of three quartiles represents the three cut points that will divide a distribution into four groups of equal frequency; the set of nine deciles represents the nine cut points that will divide a distribution into ten groups of equal frequency, and so on. To divide a distribution into a given number of groups of equal frequency, each cut point or percentile, by definition, is a theoretically possible value, which may or may not be one of the actual values from the scale of measurement used to measure the variable. Because for most applications, however, estimates of percentiles suffice, R does not calculate percentiles exactly; it only estimates them. As a result, the groups defined by these estimated percentiles will not necessarily have equal frequencies, although their frequencies will be approximately equal.

☞ **Remark** Be careful not to confuse the raw score with the percentile. For example, a person who gets a 75 percent on a test is probably not at the 75th percentile. For example, if 10 people took the test and 9 people get 100 percent and one person gets 75 percent, the percentile rank of the score of 75 percent is 0.

• •

EXAMPLE 2.3 Using R, find the three quartiles of the ses distribution – those values that divide the distribution into four (approximately) equal groups. Because there are 500 values in the ses distribution, each group should contain approximately 125 values. Use Table 2.2 to determine how many values are actually in each of the four groups.

Solution

MORE R: To find the quartiles of the ses distribution, type the following command in the console and press **Enter**:

quantile(NELS$ses, c(0.25, 0.5, 0.75))

Note the option **c(0.25, 0.5, 0.75)** in the command instructs R to find the first, second, and third quartiles, respectively. If other quantiles were desired, it would simply be necessary to change the values in this argument to reflect the quantiles of interest.

```
   25%    50%     75%
  13.75  19.00   24.00
```

The 25th, 50th, and 75th percentiles, corresponding to the first, second, and third quartiles, are given as 13.75, 19, and 24, respectively. If these percentiles were exact, then exactly 25 percent of the distribution (or 125 scores) would fall below 13.75, exactly 25 percent would fall between 13.75 and 19, exactly 25 percent would fall between 19 and 24, and, exactly 25 percent would fall at or above 24. But, these percentiles are not exact, and, as we shall see, the four groupings are only approximately equal to each other.

☞ **Remark.** By R convention, to determine how many scores fall between two percentiles, we include the frequency of the lower percentile, but not the frequency of the upper percentile.

Using Table 2.3 we find that 125 students (1 + 1 + 2 + 2 + 4 + 1 + 12 + 6 + 16 + 9 + 18 + 22 + 16 + 15) have ses ratings in the first quartile (below a score of 13.75), 122 students have ses ratings between the first and second quartiles (greater than or equal to 13.75 but less than 19), 126 students have ses ratings between the second and third quartiles (greater than or equal to 19 but less than 24), and finally, 127 students have ses ratings at or above a score of 24.

Notice that just as the three quartiles, as a set, divide the ses distribution into (approximately) equal quarters, the second quartile, labeled as the 50th percentile, divides the ses distribution into (approximately) equal halves. There are 247 scores below 19 and 253 scores at 19 or above. As such, the score of 19 is the middle score in the distribution, the score that locates the distribution's center.

Notice also that the middle 50 percent of the distribution is contained between the first and third quartiles, 13.75 and 24. Said differently, the middle 50 percent of this distribution lies between 13.75 and 24, and therefore, extends over 10.25 ses values (24 − 13.75). If the distribution were such that the value of 19 were again at its center, but the first and third quartiles were at 8 and 29, respectively, then the middle 50 percent of this distribution would extend over 21 ses values (29 − 8). We would say, in this case, that relative to the first distribution, the second distribution has a greater spread about its center, or a greater *interquartile range (IQR)* or *midspread*. We could say, equivalently, that the second distribution is less densely concentrated about its middle than the first distribution.

As this example illustrates, a lot can be learned about the location (level), shape, and form of a distribution by finding the quartiles of that distribution. The second quartile tells us something about its location, and the first and third quartiles tell us something about its spread. With the addition of two more points, the distribution's lowest value, its *minimum*, and its highest value, its *maximum*, a more complete picture may be obtained.

SIX-NUMBER SUMMARIES AND BOXPLOTS

In R, we may obtain a six-number summary of a distribution that includes the three quartiles, Q_{25}, Q_{50}, and Q_{75} as well as the minimum and maximum values, and the arithmetic mean (which will be discussed further in Chapter 3). While the three quartiles summarize distributional characteristics about the center, the minimum and maximum characterize the tails of the distribution. We may obtain the six-number summary by using the following command. Note that Q_{50} is often referred to as the *median* of the distribution.

MORE R: To find the six-number summary of the ses distribution, for example, type the following command in the console and press **Enter**:

summary(NELS$ses)

Using the **summary** command, we obtain Table 2.10.

From this six-number summary, we know that the ses distribution extends from a minimum value of zero to a maximum value of 35, with its center at 19 and its center bulk of 50 percent situated over the interval 13.75 to 24.

A graphical representation of five of this six-number summary is given by a *boxplot*, also called a *box-and-whiskers plot*. The mean is not represented in the boxplot. Figure 2.16 is a boxplot for our ses data. The box depicts the middle

TABLE 2.10 Six-number summary for ses					
Min.	1st quartile	Median	Mean	3rd quartile	Max.
0.00	13.75	19.00	18.43	24.00	35.00

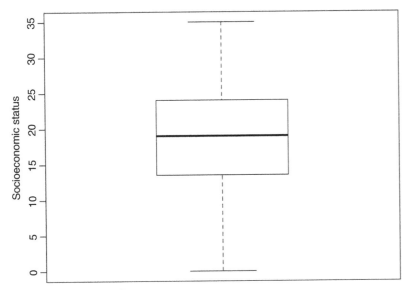

Figure 2.16 Boxplot of ses

50 percent of the distribution, which ranges from $Q_{25} = 13.75$ to $Q_{75} = 24$. The middle line in the box represents Q_{50}, the middle score of the distribution, which is equal to 19. The whiskers extend out from the box on both ends. From the end representing lower values, the whisker extends to the minimum value of 0 and from the end representing higher values, it extends to the maximum value of 35. The advantage of a boxplot is that it provides in one graphic information about the level (location), spread, and shape of a distribution.

The 50th percentile, or median, is another way of defining the typical score for the distribution. In this case, we see that the typical ses value in the NELS dataset is 19. There are two measures of spread easily obtained from the boxplot. The first, the range, is, as noted earlier, the maximum value minus the minimum value, or in this case, $35 - 0 = 35$. The range is often not the best measure of spread because it is based on only two values and they are the two most extreme or unusual values in the distribution. A better measure is the range of the middle 50 percent of the data, called the *interquartile* range. The interquartile range is the box height or $Q_{75} - Q_{25}$. In this case, we have $24 - 13.75$ or 10.25. In terms of the shape, notice in this representation, that the distance from Q_{75} to Q_{50} approximately equals the distance from Q_{50} to Q_{25}, and that the whiskers are of about equal length, suggesting that this distribution is reasonably symmetric, as we know it to be.

MORE R: To obtain a box-plot for ses, for example, type the following in the console:

boxplot(NELS$ses)

To learn more about this command, you can type **?boxplot**.

In comparing the boxplot to the histogram (Figure 2.5) of these data, we observe, that with only five numbers, the boxplot captures well the important features of this distribution. Characterizations that summarize data well with only a small number of values are called *parsimonious*. As you will learn, one of the goals of statistics is parsimony.

It is instructive to examine the boxplots for both self-concept in twelfth grade and expected income at age 30 that appear in Figures 2.17 and 2.18, respectively, and to compare these boxplots to the corresponding histograms of these variables that appear in Figures 2.14 and 2.15. Using R, we notice that in Figures 2.17 and 2.18 extreme values in the boxplots are shown.

Notice first, that like the boxplot of ses, depicted in Figure 2.16, the boxplots of self-concept and expected income capture the essential features of their corresponding

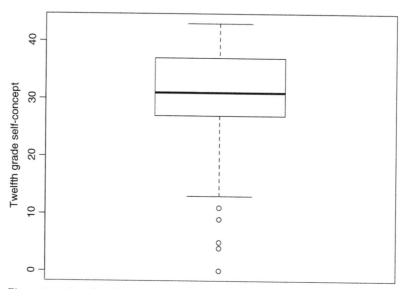

Figure 2.17 Boxplot of slfcnc12

Figure 2.18 Boxplot of expinc30

histograms. By looking at these boxplots alone, we should have no problem visualizing the complete distributions of these variables. In Figure 2.17, the several outliers, or extreme values, at the bottom of the plot (the lower tail of the distribution), suggest negative skewness. Add to that the fact that the distance between the end of the top whisker and Q_{50} is smaller than the distance between the end of the bottom whisker and Q_{50}, that is, that the bulk of the distribution of self-concept is relatively high, we have a rather full picture of the shape of the distribution of this variable.

There are four ways that the boxplot can indicate skewness of the distribution, listed from least serious, to most serious skew. First, the middle line, or 50th percentile, can be unevenly spaced within the box. Second, the box can be unevenly spaced between the whiskers. Third, there are asymmetric outliers, that is, points that lie beyond the whiskers on one side of the distribution, indicated by a circle on the boxplot.

Expected income at age 30 is more extremely skewed than self-concept. The greater concentration of values between 0 and 150,000 coupled with the larger number of more extreme outliers, located in the more positive direction, characterize this distribution as highly positively skewed. In fact, case number 102 is highly optimistic. He (this person actually is male) expects to earn \$1 million! Exercise 2.23 asks you to determine this individual's self-concept relative to the sample. Once again, we may notice that this boxplot summarizes well the histogram depicted in Figure 2.14.

The skew of the distributions of expected incomes (Figure 2.18) is considered to be more extreme than the skew of the distributions of self-concept (Figure 2.17), because there are more outliers on one side of the graph and they are further away from the bulk of the scores in terms of *IQR* units.

☞ **Remark.** To allow the full range of values to be displayed in the boxplot of Figure 2.18, the vertical scale must extend from the minimum of 0 to the maximum of 1,000,000, thanks to our optimist. Because of the presence of outliers, in this case, the bulk of the distribution, as depicted by the box, appears to be quite compact relative to the full range. To alleviate the influence of outliers on the graph, we may delete these cases from consideration, or we may change the scale of measurement from dollars to some other unit that preserves the ordinality of these data. Ordinality is an essential feature of these data, which makes the boxplot meaningful. Changing from one scale of measurement to another is called *transforming* or *re-expressing* the data. More will be said about this in Chapter 4.

☞ **Remark.** A distribution can be skewed even though no outliers are present, when the box is not centered between the whiskers or when the middle line is unevenly spaced within the box. In such cases, skewness tends not to be severe. We illustrate in Figure 2.19 with the variable educational expenditure per pupil, educexpe, from the States data, which gives the average educational expenditure per pupil by state. educexpe is positively skewed.

EXAMPLE 2.4 Use R to construct four side-by-side boxplots based on the States dataset showing the states' average educational expenditure per pupil by region. Use the graph to determine whether there are differences in:

1. the level of educational expenditures by region,
2. the spread of the educational expenditures by region, and
3. the shape of the educational expenditures by region.

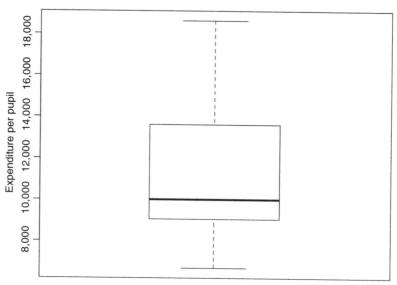

Figure 2.19 Boxplot of educexpe

Solution

MORE R: To obtain a single graphic that contains the boxplots of the educational expenditure by region, for example, type the following:

boxplot(States$educexpe~States$region)

The result is the following set of boxplots shown in Figure 2.20.

1. According to the heights of the 50th percentiles for the four regions, the Northeast has the highest overall level of educational expenditures per pupil, followed by the West, the Midwest, and the South.
2. According to the interquartile ranges, the educational expenditures are most spread out in the Northeast, followed by the West, the South, and the Midwest.
3. The distributions of educational expenditures are skewed in all regions. They are probably most skewed in the West because there are outliers that represent unusually high expenditures. In the Northeast the distribution is negatively skewed because the bottom whisker is longer than the top one. In the Midwest and South the distributions are positively skewed because the top whisker is longer.

☞ **Remark.** Both the stem-and-leaf display and the boxplot are inventions of John Tukey (1915–2000), which he described, along with other such novel and ingenious methods of data analysis, in his highly influential work *Exploratory Data Analysis* (1977). In this book, and elsewhere, Tukey promoted a very practical approach to data analysis, one that emphasizes an examination of the data themselves, rather than prior assumptions about the data, as the starting point for choosing an appropriate data analytic model. Because of his creative genius and versatility, demonstrated over a long and active career in statistics, Salsburg (2001) quite appropriately calls him "the Picasso of Statistics" (pp. 229–236).

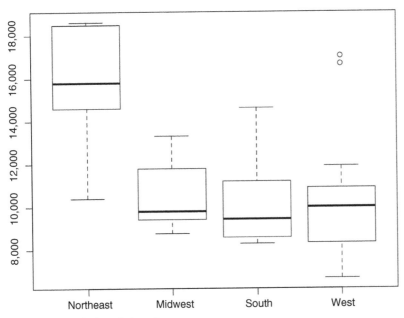

Figure 2.20 Side-by-side boxplots

SUMMARY OF GRAPHICAL SELECTION

You should know how to create each of the displays in this chapter and under what circumstances it is appropriate to use each of them.

If your variable is nominal or ordinal with only few categories, a frequency distribution table, bar graph, or pie graph (given that set of categories is exhaustive) are all appropriate methods for summarizing the data.

If your variable is ordinal with many categories or it is a scale variable, a frequency distribution table (unless there are too many values and the table becomes unwieldy), a stem-and-leaf plot, histogram, line graph, or boxplot are all appropriate methods for summarizing the data.

SUMMARY OF R COMMANDS

These are the command lines used to generate the tables and graphs in Chapter 2 and for some of the exercises. In Chapter 4, we will introduce .R, which provides another way to summarize all of the commands from each chapter.

Commands for frequency and percent distribution tables

Create	Command lines
Frequency table of region (Table 2.1)	table(NELS$region)
Percent table of region (Table 2.2)	percent.table(NELS$region)
Grouped frequency distribution for ses (Table 2.4)	NELS$categories.ses = cut(NELS$ses, breaks = c(0,5,10,15,20,25,30,35,40)) table(NELS$categories.ses)

Bar and pie graphs

Create	Command lines
Bar chart of region by counts (Figure 2.1)	barplot(table(NELS$region), ylab = "Frequency")
Bar chart of region by percentages (Figure 2.2)	barplot(percent.table(NELS$region), ylab = "Percent")
Bar chart with bars oriented horizontally	barplot(table(NELS$region), xlab = "Frequency", horiz = T)
Pie chart of region (Figure 2.3)	pie(table(NELS$region), col = grey(1:4/4))

Stem-and-leaf display

Create	Command lines
Stem-and-leaf of pertak (Table 2.6)	stem(States$pertak)

Histograms

Create	Command lines
Histogram of ses (Figure 2.5)	hist(NELS$ses, main = "Histogram", xlab = "Socio-economic Status")
Edit the scale of the horizontal axis of a histogram of ses (Figures 2.6 and 2.7)	hist(NELS$ses, breaks = seq(min(NELS$ses), max(NELS$ses), length.out = 6), main = "Histogram with 5 bins", xlab = "Socio-economic Status") for Figure 2.6 hist(NELS$ses, breaks = seq(min(NELS$ses), max(NELS$ses), length.out = 31), main = "Histogram with 30 bins", xlab = "Socio-economic Status") for Figure 2.7
Density histogram of ses (Figure 2.8)	hist(NELS$ses, freq = F, xlab = "Socio-economic Status", main = "Histogram")

Line graphs

Create	Command lines
Line graph of ses (Figure 2.9)	line.graph(NELS$ses, main = "Line Graph", xlab = "Socio-economic Status", ylab = "Density")
Smoothed line graph (Figure 2.10)	plot(density(NELS$ses), main = "Density Graph", xlab = "Socio-economic Status")
Line graph of marijuana use by year (Figure 2.12)	plot(Marijuana$MarijuanaUse~Marijuana$Year, type = "l", xlab = "Year", ylab = "Marijuana Use")

Create	Command lines
	OR
	plot(Marijuana$MarijuanaUse~Marijuana $Year, type = "l", xlab = "Year", ylab = "Marijuana Use", col = "blue", lwd = 2, lty = 2)

Percentiles

Create	Command lines
Quartiles of ses	quantile(NELS$ses, c(0.25, 0.5, 0.75))
Five-number summary of ses (Table 2.10)	summary(NELS$ses)

Boxplots

Create	Command lines
Boxplot of ses (Figure 2.16)	boxplot(NELS$ses)
Boxplots of educexpe by region (Figure 2.20)	boxplot(States$educexpe~States$region)

EXERCISES

Exercises 2.1–2.3 involve questions about frequency and percent distribution tables of variables in the NELS dataset.

2.1 Create a frequency distribution table and a percent table of the variable absent12, which gives the number of times a student was absent in twelfth grade and the proportion in each category, respectively. Use these tables to answer the following questions.

(a) How many students in the NELS dataset were absent 3–6 times in twelfth grade?

(b) How many students in the NELS dataset were absent exactly 3 times in twelfth grade?

(c) What percentage of students in the NELS dataset was absent 3–6 times in twelfth grade?

(d) What percentage of students in the NELS dataset was absent 6 or fewer times in twelfth grade?

(e) How would you describe the shape of the distribution of absences in twelfth grade – positively skewed, negatively skewed, or reasonably symmetric? Explain.

2.2 Create a frequency distribution table and a percent table of the variable parmarl8, which gives the marital status of the parents when the student was in eighth grade. Use these tables to answer the following questions.

(a) For how many students in the NELS dataset were parents separated?

(b) For what percent of students were parents separated?

(c) What is the most frequently occurring marital status for parents of students in the NELS?

2.3 Create a frequency distribution table and a percent table of the variable famsize, which represents the number of people in a student's household when the student was in eighth grade. Use the tables to answer the following questions.

(a) What was the greatest number of people in a household for all the students in the NELS dataset?

(b) How many students lived in households with only three members?

(c) How many students lived in households with at most three members?

(d) What percentage of the students lived in households with only three members?

(e) What percentage of the students lived in households with at most three members?

(f) Estimate Q_{50} for famsize.

Exercises 2.4–2.6 involve questions about bar graphs of variables in the NELS dataset.

2.4 Create a bar chart summarizing the variable gender with percentages. Use it to answer the following questions.

(a) Why is a bar chart an appropriate display in this case?

(b) Are there more males or females in the NELS?

(c) According to the graph, approximately what percentage of students is female?

(d) Would a pie chart be appropriate to depict these data?

2.5 In this exercise, we will make a bar graph of the variable, alcbinge, which indicates whether a student has ever binged on alcohol, first for females and then for males.

To create a frequency bar chart for females, we will specify that we only want to look at alcbinge for observations in which the variable gender is equal to "female." To do this, we put brackets next to our variable of interest, and indicate **NELS $gender=="Female"**. Note that we use two equal signs instead of one, as two equal signs means "exactly equal to." The full command is below.

barplot(table(NELS$alcbinge[NELS$gender=="Female"]), ylab="Frequency", main = "History of Alcohol Binging for Females")

To look at a bar graph of males, we type the following:

barplot(table(NELS$alcbinge[NELS$gender=="Male"]), ylab="Frequency", main = "History of Alcohol Binging for Males")

(a) What percentage of males in the NELS dataset has ever binged on alcohol?

(b) Which gender, males or females, has more of a tendency to have ever binged on alcohol?

2.6 Create a bar chart for average daily school attendance rate given by the variable schattrt in the NELS dataset. Use the bar chart to answer the following questions.

(a) What appears to be problematic with the way in which the values are set along the *x*-axis of the bar chart?

(b) What is a type of graph that could be selected to display schattrt that does not have that problem?

(c) What is the shape of the distribution of schattrt?

Exercise 2.7 involves questions about a pie chart of a variable in the NELS dataset.

2.7 Construct a pie chart of the variable urban, which indicates whether in eighth grade the student lived in an urban, suburban, or rural area in the United States.

 (a) Approximately what percentage of students come from an urban area?
 (b) Use R to construct the associated bar chart with percentages.
 (c) Compare the two charts. Which do you prefer? Why?
 (d) What have you learned about the distribution of students in this sample across urban, suburban, and rural areas?

Exercises 2.8–2.12 involve questions about stem-and-leaf graphs of variables from different datasets.

2.8 Create a stem-and-leaf of the variable mathcomp from the Learndis dataset. Use it to answer the following questions.

 (a) What is another type of graph that could be used to depict these data?
 (b) What is the total number of scores in this distribution?
 (c) How many scores are in the seventies?
 (d) Are there any outliers (i.e., extreme values) in this distribution?
 (e) How would you describe the shape of this distribution? Explain.
 (f) What is the 50th percentile?
 (g) What is/are the most frequently occurring score(s) in this distribution? How many times does it/do they occur?
 (h) What is the highest score in this distribution?
 (i) Can we use this stem-and-leaf to obtain the original set of values for this variable?

2.9 Create a stem-and-leaf of the variable Birth from the Statisticians dataset that you entered in Exercise 1.13. Use it to answer the following questions.

 (a) How many people in the dataset were born in 1900?
 (b) Are there any outliers (i.e., extreme values) in this distribution?
 (c) How would you describe the shape of this distribution? Explain.
 (d) What is/are the most frequently occurring score(s) in this distribution? How many times does it/do they occur?
 (e) What is the highest score in this distribution?
 (f) Can we use this stem-and-leaf to obtain the original set of values for this variable?

2.10 Create a stem-and-leaf of the variable total cholesterol, given by the variable TOTCHOL1 found in the Framingham dataset. Use it to answer the following questions.

 (a) What is the lowest score in this distribution?
 (b) Are there any outliers (i.e., extreme values) in this distribution? Describe them.
 (c) How would you describe the shape of this distribution? Explain.
 (d) What is the 50th percentile of these data?
 (e) What is the highest score in this distribution?
 (f) Can we use this stem-and-leaf to obtain the complete set of original values for this variable?

2.11 Create a stem-and-leaf of eighth grade math achievement scores given by the variable achmat08 in the NELS dataset. Use the stem-and-leaf to answer the following questions.

(a) According to the stem-and-leaf plot, what is the lowest eighth grade math achievement score?

(b) According to the stem-and-leaf graph, approximately how many students received the lowest eighth grade math achievement score?

(c) According to the stem-and-leaf plot, are there any outliers (extreme values) in this distribution?

(d) According to the stem-and-leaf plot, how would you characterize the shape of this distribution – negatively skewed, approximately symmetric, or positively skewed?

(e) According to the stem-and-leaf plot, which eighth grade math achievement score occurs most often?

(f) What type of question is better answered with a stem-and-leaf and what type of question is better answered by a frequency distribution table?

2.12 Follow the instructions to create separate stem-and-leaf graphs of sysbp1 (systolic blood pressure) for men and women (sex) using the Framingham dataset.

The following code creates a stem plot for all observations in which the variable sex is equal to men, as indicated in the square brackets. Note that we use two equal signs inside the brackets.

stem(Framingham\$SYSBP1[Framingham\$SEX=="Men"], scale = 2)

The following code creates a stem plot for all observations in which the variable sex is equal to women.

stem(Framingham\$SYSBP1[Framingham\$SEX=="Women"], scale = 2)

(a) In which distribution (male or female) do we find the lowest systolic blood pressure value? Explain.

(b) In which distribution is the most frequently occurring systolic blood pressure value higher? Explain.

(c) In which, if either, distribution does systolic blood pressure have a greater spread? Explain.

(d) In which, if either, distribution is systolic blood pressure more skewed? Explain.

Exercises 2.14–2.15 involve questions about histograms of variables in the NELS dataset.

2.13 Create a histogram of the twelfth grade math achievement given by the variable achmat12 in the NELS dataset. Use the histogram to answer the following questions.

(a) According to the histogram, what is the smallest twelfth grade math achievement score in the NELS dataset? Approximately how many times does that score occur?

(b) According to the histogram, what is the most frequently occurring twelfth grade math achievement score interval?

(c) According to the histogram, what is the shape of the distribution? Explain.

2.14 Follow the instructions to create two histograms for socioeconomic status, given by the variable ses in the NELS dataset. Let one histogram represent those who did not own a computer in eighth grade and the other histogram represent those who did own a computer in eighth grade (computer). Use it to answer the following questions.

To create a histogram of ses for eighth graders who did have a computer, the R code is:

hist(NELS$ses[NELS$computer=="Yes"], main = "Histogram of SES for Those Who Did Own a Computer", xlab = "ses", breaks = 20)

To create a histogram of ses for eighth graders who did not have a computer, the R code is:

hist(NELS$ses[NELS$computer=="No"], main = "Histogram of SES for Those Who Did Not Own a Computer", xlab = "ses", breaks = 20)

(a) Which computer group has the single highest ses score?
(b) Would you say that ses is higher for the group that owns a computer? Why or why not?
(c) Do the ses values have more spread for one group over another?

2.15 Create two histograms, one for a student's self-concept in eighth grade as given by the variable slfcnc08 in the NELS dataset and the other for a student's self-concept in twelfth grade as given by the variable slfcnc12 in the NELS dataset. Edit the histograms so that they each have the same scale and range of values on both the horizontal and vertical axes using the **xlim** and **ylim** arguments in the **hist** function, and use them to answer the following questions.
(a) For which grade (eighth or twelfth) is the overall level of self-concept higher?
(b) For which grade is the spread of self-concept scores less?
(c) For which grade is self-concept more skewed, and in which direction?

Exercises 2.16–2.18 involve questions about line graphs of variables in the NELS dataset.

2.16 Create a line graph for average daily attendance rate per school as given by the variable schattrt in the NELS dataset. According to the line graph, is schattrt negatively skewed? Explain.

2.17 Follow the instructions to create a cumulative plot for the distribution of schattrt. Use it to answer the following questions.

To create a cumulative plot of schattrt, we use the **ecdf** function, which stands for empirical cumulative distribution function, inside the **plot** function, as follows:

plot(ecdf(NELS$schattrt))

(a) Approximately how many students attend schools where the average daily attendance rate is less than 90 percent?
(b) Based on the cumulative plot, would you describe the distribution as positively skewed, negatively skewed, or symmetric?

2.18 In this exercise we will see that the interpretation of a line graph can change with a change in the scale of the vertical and horizontal axes.

(a) Use the Marijuana dataset and R to construct a line graph depicting the percentage of students who have ever tried marijuana by year.
(b) Use the following R code to change the range of the *y* axis.

Change the range of the *y*-axis by including the argument **ylim=c(0,60)** within the **plot** function as indicated below

plot(Marijuana$MarijuanaUse~Marijuana$Year, type = "l", xlab = "Year", ylab = "Marijuana Use", ylim=c(0,60))

What is the effect of this change on the interpretation of the graph?
(c) Restrict the range of values on the horizontal axis to 1992 through 1999 in the uncompressed graph using the argument **xlim=c(1992,1999)** . Provide an interpretation of the graph.

To limit the graph to show only the years 1992–1999 type in the R console:

plot(Marijuana$MarijuanaUse~Marijuana$Year, type = "l", xlab = "Year", ylab = "Marijuana Use", xlim=c(1992,1999))

Exercises 2.19–2.21 involve questions on percentiles and percentile ranks of variables in the NELS dataset. In these exercises, we use the cumulative percent to estimate the percentile rank.

2.19 Find the following values for a student's expected income at age 30 given by the variable expinc30 in the NELS dataset.
(a) What is the exact value of the 15th percentile, according to R? To answer this question, use the R command:

quantile(NELS$expinc30, .15, na.rm = TRUE)

(b) What is the exact value of the 50th percentile, according to R? To answer this question, use the R command:

quantile(NELS$expinc30, .5, na.rm = TRUE)

(c) What is the approximate percentile rank of an expected income of $50,000? To answer this question, use the R command:

ecdf(NELS$expinc30)(50000)

2.20 Why is the calculation of percentiles not appropriate for the variable parmarl8?

2.21 This question relates to the optimist who is expecting to earn $1,000,000 per year at age 30 (expinc30 = 1,000,000).
(a) What is this student's ID? We can find the answer by producing a table of values of ID for which expinc30 is 1,000,000 with the R code:

table(NELS$id[NELS$expinc30==1000000])

(b) What was this student's eighth grade self-concept score (slfcnc08)? This answer can be found by displaying the observation of slfcnc08 only for the student with the ID exactly equal to the ID found in part (a) with the R command:

NELS$slfcnc08[NELS$id==102]

(c) What is the percentile rank of his eighth grade self-concept score? Is it what you expected? You can calculate the percentile that 25, the answer found in part (b), is with the R command:

ecdf(NELS$slfcnc08)(25)

Use percentile ranks to determine the grade (eighth, tenth, or twelfth) in which this student was least self-confident relative to his peers. Follow steps taken in part (b) and part (c) for slfcnc10 and slfcnc12 to answer this question.

Exercise 2.22 deals with questions about a boxplot of a single variable from the NELS dataset.

2.22 Create a boxplot that shows the number of times a student in twelfth grade was recorded late for school as given by the variable late12. Note that the level of measurement of late12 is ordinal, so you can use the **as.numeric** argument within the **boxplot** function to plot the variable as though each factor were a number, with the R command:

boxplot(as.numeric(NELS$late12), ylab = "Number of times late for school in 12th grade")

Use the boxplot and the scoring information in the dataset to answer the following questions.

(a) Estimate and interpret the value of the 50th percentile for late12, represented by the line in the middle of the box.
(b) Estimate the *IQR* of this distribution.
(c) What is the shape of this distribution? Explain by referring to the boxplot.
(d) What is the significance of the fact that the graph has no bottom whisker?

Exercise 2.23 deals with questions about boxplots of more than one ordinal or scale variable constructed on the same axes.

2.23 Create three boxplots, one for each of the distributions of self-concept scores for eighth, tenth, and twelfth grades, respectively. Use these graphs to answer the following questions.

To obtain a boxplot for slfcnc08, slfcnc10, and slfcnc12, type in the R console:

boxplot(NELS$slfcnc08, main = "Self-concept, 8th Grade")
boxplot(NELS$slfcnc10, main = "Self-concept, 10th Grade")
boxplot(NELS$slfcnc12, main = "Self-concept, 12th Grade")

(a) How would you describe the shape of the distribution of self-concept in eighth grade?

(b) For which grade is the self-concept distribution most nearly symmetric?

(c) Overall, which of the three grades has the highest level of self-concept?

(d) Which of the three grades contains the highest single self-concept score? And, what is your estimate of that score?

(e) Based on the interquartile range, which distribution appears to have the highest spread?

Exercises 2.24 and 2.25 involve boxplots of a single variable for different subgroups.

2.24 Create four boxplots on the same axis, one for each region, that plots the number of years of math taken in high school as given by the variable unitmath of the NELS dataset. Use the graph to answer the following questions.

To create boxplots of unitmath by region, type in the R console:

boxplot(NELS\$unitmath~NELS\$region, main = "Years of Math Taken in High School by Region")

(a) Which region is most symmetric with respect to the distribution of units (years) of math taken in high school?

(b) In which of the four regions is the overall level of unitmath lowest?

(c) Which of the four regions contains the student with the single lowest number of units of math taken in high school? And, what is that number?

(d) In which region, if any, is the spread of unitmath smallest?

(e) How many of the 106 students in the Northeast have unitmath scores between Q_{25} and Q_{50}? Is this number confined to unitmath scores or does it generalize to all variables in this dataset?

2.25 Construct four side-by-side boxplots of the number of Advanced Placement (AP) classes offered at a student's school (apoffer), one for each of the four types of high-school programs (hsprog) represented in the NELS dataset.

(a) How might one explain that there are academic program schools that offer many AP courses, but not any rigorous academic program schools that offer more than 20?

(b) What would be a better way to represent AP courses offerings other than by their number per school?

Exercise 2.26 involves boxplots of more than one ordinal, interval, or ratio variable broken down by a grouping variable.

2.26 Make three side-by-side boxplots showing the distributions of slfcnc08, slfcnc10, and slfcnc12, the self-concept scores in eighth, tenth, and twelfth grades, respectively, by gender.

To obtain the boxplots for slfcnc08, slfcnc10, and slfcnc12 separated by gender, type in the R console:

boxplot(NELS\$slfcnc08~NELS\$gender, main = "Self-Concept in 8th Grade by Gender")

boxplot(NELS$slfcnc10~NELS$gender, main = "Self-Concept in 10th Grade by Gender")

boxplot(NELS$slfcnc12~NELS$gender, main = "Self-Concept in 12th Grade by Gender")

(a) Does self-concept generally appear to be increasing from eighth to twelfth grade for both sexes?

(b) What is most noticeable about these boxplots when comparing males to females?

(c) If not for the female outliers in twelfth grade, would you say that males and females are comparable in their homogeneity of self-concept in twelfth grade?

Exercises 2.27–2.29 involve a variety of boxplots.

2.27 In this exercise, we review the construction of the four different types of boxplots using the NELS dataset.

(a) Construct a boxplot of eighth grade reading achievement (achrdg08).

(b) Construct, within one set of axes, two boxplots of eighth grade reading achievement, one for males and the other for females using the variable gender.

(c) Construct two boxplots, respectively, of tenth and twelfth grade reading achievement.

(d) Construct, within one set of axes, boxplots of tenth and then twelfth grade reading achievement, separately for males and females.

2.28 Describe the shape of each the following distributions denoted a, b, c, d, e, and f.

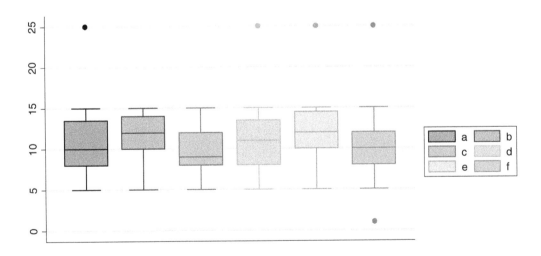

2.29 This exercise is based on the States dataset, but does not require the use of R. The boxplots below show, for each of the four regions, the average educational expenditure for the states in that region. The four stem-and-leaf displays, labeled (a), (b), (c), and (d) show the same. Match the letter associated with each stem-and-leaf to the appropriate boxplot.

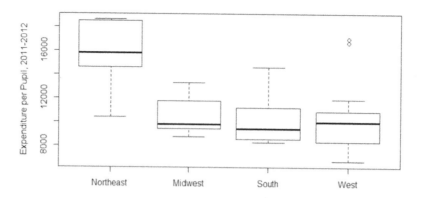

(a) The decimal point is 3 digit(s) to the right of the |

```
 8 |   3455668
 9 |   1468
10 |   0
11 |   28
12 |
13 |
14 |   046
```

(b) The decimal point is 3 digit(s) to the right of the |

```
10 |   4
11 |
12 |   9
13 |   69
14 |   8
15 |   7
16 |
17 |
18 |   566
```

(c) The decimal point is 3 digit(s) to the right of the |

```
 6 |   78
 8 |   231
10 |   002399
12 |
14 |
16 |   70
```

(d) The decimal point is 3 digit(s) to the right of the |

```
 8 |   8
 9 |   244
 9 |   588
10 |
10 |   8
11 |   4
11 |
12 |   2
12 |   5
13 |   3
```

Exercise 2.30 involves questions about selection of appropriate graphical displays.

2.30 For the following variables in the NELS dataset, indicate whether the most appropriate types of graphical displays are (1) bar chart or pie chart, or (2) histogram, line graph, stem-and-leaf plot, or boxplot.

  (a) gender
  (b) urban
  (c) schtyp8
  (d) tcherint
  (e) numinst
  (f) achrdg08
  (g) schattrt
  (h) absent12

Exercises 2.31–2.32 involve a number of different topics.

2.31 The following questions pertain to the tenth grade social studies achievement score for students as given by the variable achsls10 in the NELS dataset.

  (a) Calculate the highest tenth grade social studies achievement score in the NELS dataset using the R command:

   quantile(NELS$achsls10, 1, na.rm = TRUE)

  (b) Determine how many students obtained the highest score by using the R command:

   sum(NELS$achsls10==72.89, na.rm = TRUE)

  (c) Calcuate the most frequently occurring score in this distribution using the **the. mode** function.

  (d) Calculate the score that is the 50th percentile of the distribution with the R command:

   quantile(NELS$achsls10, .50, na.rm = TRUE)

  (e) Calculate the score that is the 67th percentile with the R command:

   quantile(NELS$achsls10, .67, na.rm = TRUE)

  (f) Calculate the percentage of students who scored 70 or below with the R command:

   ecdf(NELS$achsls10)(70)

  (g) What is the shape of the distribution? The R command to obtain the density histogram is:

   hist(NELS$achsls10, freq = F, main = "10th Grade Social Studies Achievement Scores", breaks = 20)

2.32 The following questions pertain to the amount of time spent weekly on extracurricular activities in twelfth grade as given by excurr12 in the NELS dataset.

  (a) How many students in the NELS dataset answered excurr12 that they spent 1–4 hours per week on extracurricular activities?

(b) What is the value at the 50th percentile? Because the quantile function requires numeric variables, the R code used to answer this question is:

quantile(as.numeric(NELS\$excurr12), .50, na.rm = TRUE)

(c) What is the shape of this distribution? This can be determined with the R code:

barplot(table(NELS\$excurr12), main = "Time Spent on Extracurriculars in 12th Grade", cex.names = .65, las=2)

To make the value labels fit on the plot, we use the **cex.names** argument to change the font size and the **las=2** argument to make the value labels perpendicular to the *x*-axis.

Exercises 2.33–2.35 involve reading and interpreting graphs.

2.33 The line graphs below show the number of jobs in thousands and the unemployment rate for part of the time president George W. Bush was in office. The graph was released on December 2, 2005 by the US Treasury Department and a good analysis of it may be found at www.brendan-nyhan.com/blog/2005/12/the_treasury_de.html. Answer the following questions.

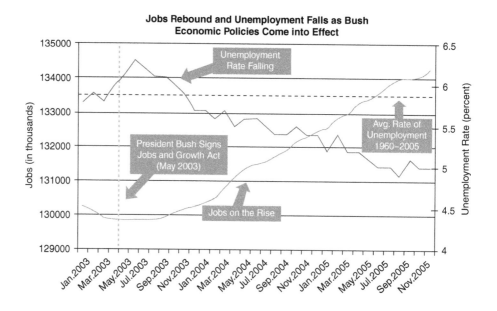

(a) The vertical line represents what month? Why is this month highlighted?
(b) What was the approximate number of jobs in March 2003? What was the approximate unemployment rate?
(c) Give the month and year of the lowest unemployment rate.
(d) Based on this graph, is it fair to say that President George W. Bush's Jobs and Growth Act helped create jobs and lower unemployment? Explain.

2.34 The following graph gives the hypothetical average speed of a professional baseball pitcher in 2016 and 2017. Comment upon the design of this graphic.

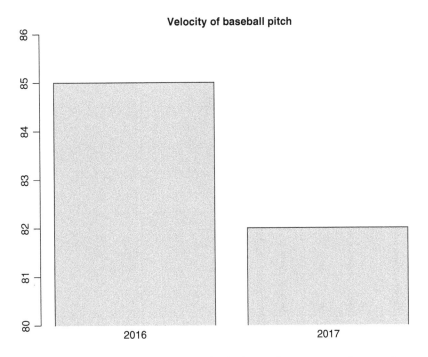

2.35 On June 3, 2014, H&R Block (www.businessinsider.com/worst-college-majors-2014-6) published pie and bar charts, indicating the best and worst college majors in terms of employment prospects.

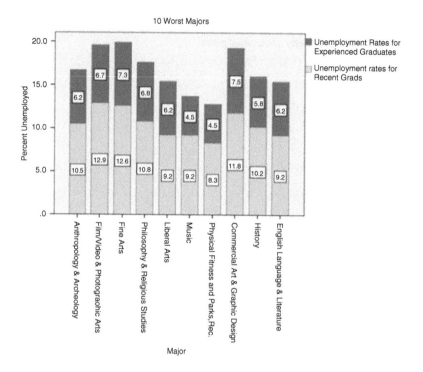

(a) In the pie chart, what is the interpretation of the 31 percent associated with the business major?

(b) What would be an advantage of using a bar chart instead of a pie chart to depict the most in-demand college majors?

(c) What percentage of recent grads who majored in anthropology and archeology are unemployed?

(d) Why does it make sense for this bar chart to be stacked?

Exercises 2.36–2.46 check your conceptual understanding of the material in this chapter, without the use of R.

2.36 Assuming the statistics are all calculated on the same set of data, rank the following from numerically smallest to numerically largest: C_{50} C_4 D_1 D_3 Q_{25} Q_{75}

2.37 Determine what, if anything, is wrong with the following statement: A raw score of 75 is always surpassed by 25 percent of the scores in the distribution from which it comes.

2.38 Determine what, if anything, is wrong with the following statement: A 90-item test was scored by giving one point for each correct answer so that possible scores ranged from 0 to 90. On this test, the highest percentile rank possible is 90.

2.39 Determine what, if anything, is wrong with the following statement: On a certain English exam, Alice's score is twice as high as Ellen's. Therefore, Alice's percentile rank on the exam must be twice Ellen's percentile rank.

2.40 Determine what, if anything, is wrong with the following statement: If it takes 10 raw score points to go from a percentile rank of 50 to a percentile rank of 58, then it must also take 10 raw score points to go from a percentile rank of 90 to a percentile rank of 98.

2.41 Determine what, if anything, is wrong with the following statement: Scott, who scored at the 85th percentile in a math achievement test given to everyone in his school, and at the 95th percentile in a science test given to all students in the city in which the school is located, is doing better in science than in math.

2.42 Determine what, if anything, is wrong with the following statement: In a recent door-to-door survey, only five of the people questioned said they were opposed to a proposed school bond issue. The local school board publicized the results of this survey as evidence of tacit approval of the proposal.

2.43 Are the following, possible values for percentiles: 50, −2, 512? Are they possible values for percentile ranks?

2.44 Explain how a symmetric distribution can have outliers in its boxplot.

2.45 Explain how a boxplot could have only one whisker.

2.46 Draw a picture of two side-by-side boxplots so that:
   (a) The one on the left clearly has scores that are typically at a higher level and the one on the right has scores that are clearly less consistent. The graphs you create indicate that higher scores do not necessarily mean more spread.
   (b) The one on the left is clearly less spread out and the one on the right is clearly less skewed. The graphs you create indicate that more skew does not necessarily mean more spread.

# CHAPTER THREE

MEASURES OF LOCATION, SPREAD, AND SKEWNESS

In our examination of univariate distributions in Chapter 2, three summarizing characteristics of a distribution were discussed. First, its shape (as denoted by its skewness or its symmetry, by how many peaks and/or outliers it has, and so on). Second, its location (as denoted by its middle score, the second quartile, Q_{50}). Third, its spread (as denoted by both the range of values and the interquartile range, which is the range of values within which its middle 50 percent falls). In this chapter, we will expand upon that discussion by introducing other summary statistics for characterizing the location, spread, and shape of a distribution.

CHARACTERIZING THE LOCATION OF A DISTRIBUTION

When we speak of the location of a univariate distribution, we mean the point or number between the smallest and largest values of the distribution that best represents the distribution's "center." It is a single value that connotes the typical or "average" value in the distribution, the point around which most values are centered. For this reason, measures of location are also known as measures of *central tendency*. In this section, we discuss three commonly used measures of location: mode, median, and mean. These measures can be used to answer questions like: "Do seniors typically have higher grade point averages than freshmen?"; "Do union workers have a higher overall income than non-union workers?"; and "Does female self-concept change, on average, from eighth grade to twelfth grade?"

THE MODE

The *mode* is that data value that occurs most often in a distribution and can be found for any distribution. The mode is easy to compute and simple to interpret. The mode of the distribution for homelang (home language background) for the 500 students in our NELS sample (see Table 3.1 for the frequency distribution) is English Only because that category occurs more often than any other in the distribution. That is, most students in our sample come from home backgrounds in which English is the only language spoken. Because relatively few students come from different home language backgrounds, the mode, English Only, best describes the typical home language background for this sample. As such, the category, English Only, is an effective measure of location for this distribution. In other situations, however, the mode is not so effective as a measure of a distribution's location.

Consider the frequency distribution of region presented in Table 2.1 of Chapter 2 and represented here as the bar graph of Figure 3.1. Notice that the frequencies of the

TABLE 3.1 Frequency distribution of home language background			
Non-English Only	**Non-English Dominant**	**English Dominant**	**English Only**
15	35	47	403

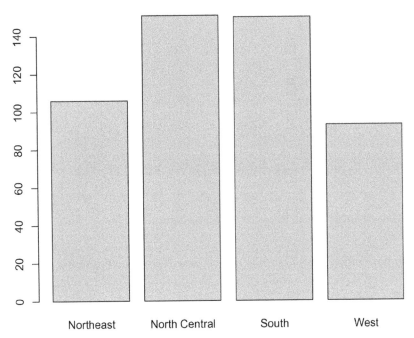

Figure 3.1 Bar graph of frequencies for region

categories North Central and South are approximately equal: North Central outnumbers South by only one case. Accordingly, it would be misleading to report North Central as the only mode of this distribution. A more appropriate characterization would be to report both North Central and South as modes in this case. Distributions that have two modes are called *bimodal.*

In Figure 3.1, the two peaks, one above each mode, are adjacent to each other. Because region is a nominal-leveled variable, and the order of categories in the distribution is arbitrary, the fact that the two modes are adjacent to each other is arbitrary as well.

When variables are ordinal-leveled or higher, however, and the order of categories in the distribution is not arbitrary, bimodal frequency distributions typically contain two peaks that are separated from each other by a gap in between. Figure 3.2 is an example of a bimodal distribution of 100 scores on a test of Spanish fluency.

Notice that most students either speak Spanish fluently (and receive very high scores on the test) or hardly at all (and receive very low scores on the test); a small number of students can speak some Spanish (and receive scores in the middle range).

Another distribution that has been suggested as being bimodal is that of the intelligence quotients (IQs) of viewers of the television show *Court TV*. Viewers of *Court TV* are

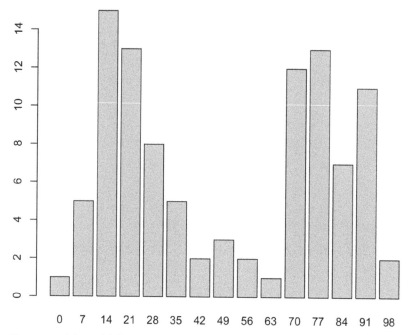

Figure 3.2 A bimodal distribution of test scores of Spanish fluency

purported to have either very high IQs or very low IQs; a small number of viewers are reported as having IQs in the middle range. Can you think of other examples of bimodal distributions?

Some distributions are trimodal (three modes), and by extension, it is possible to have a distribution in which every category has the same, and therefore the largest, frequency. Such distributions are called *uniform* or *rectangular* distributions and are not well characterized by the mode. Figure 3.3 is an example of a rectangular distribution. In this distribution, each score category contains exactly five cases.

While homelang was at least ordinal and region was nominal, and both had fewer than five categories, we may obtain the modes of distributions of any level of measurement which take on any number of possible values. As in the previous cases, however, the effectiveness of a mode as a measure of a distribution's location depends on the shape of the distribution itself. Where distributions are skewed or contain gaps in the middle, the effectiveness of the mode as a measure of location is diminished. Where the distribution is reasonably symmetric, and *unimodal* (one mode, or *single-peaked*), however, the mode is useful in characterizing the location, or center, of a distribution.

Recall that the frequency distribution of socioeconomic status, ses, presented in Table 2.3 of Chapter 2, and reproduced here as Figure 3.4 in its histogram form, is reasonably symmetric and unimodal. From the histogram, the mode of this distribution appears to be contained in the category with midpoint value 20 since that category occurs most often among the students in our sample of 500. Notice that because the distribution is reasonably symmetric and single-peaked, the mode is an effective numerical summary of the location of the ses distribution on the continuum from lowest to highest possible values.

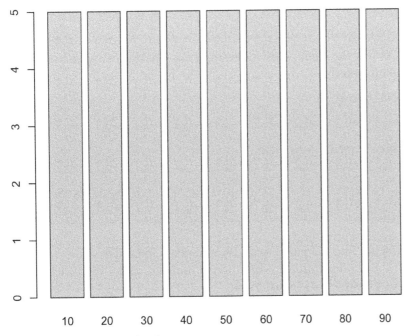

Figure 3.3 A rectangular distribution

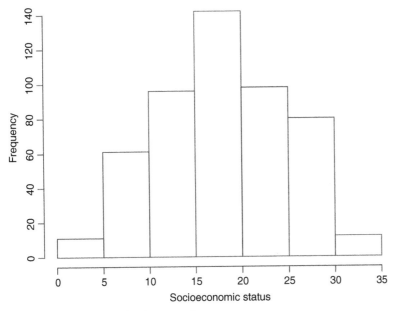

Figure 3.4 Histogram of socioeconomic status

The mode of a variable also may be obtained directly from R.

MORE R: To find the mode of ses, for example, we type the following command in the console and hit **Enter**:

the.mode(NELS$ses)

Using the **table** command, we obtain:

0	1	2	3	4	5	6	7	8	9	10	11	12	13	14	15	16	17	18	19	20	21	22	23	24	25	26	27	28	29	30	31	32	35
1	1	2	2	4	1	12	7	15	9	18	22	16	15	19	24	18	33	28	39	24	22	19	22	14	21	20	16	16	12	16	8	3	1

In so doing, we find the mode to be 19, since 19 is the single value that occurs most frequently in the ses distribution. Scanning the numbers under frequencies reveals that there are 39 cases where ses is equal to 19.

Using the **the.mode** command we obtain the same result.

THE MEDIAN

The *median* is defined as any theoretically possible data value in a distribution of a continuous variable below which 50 percent of all data values fall. Intuitively, then, the median may be thought of as the middle point in a distribution or as that point which divides a distribution into two equal halves. Since Q_{50} (the second quartile, or, equivalently, the 50th percentile) also is defined as the middle point in a distribution, the median is another name for Q_{50}.

To approximate the median of a variable in a small dataset, order the values in magnitude from lowest to highest. If the dataset contains an odd number of values, the median is simply the middle value. If, on the other hand, the dataset contains an even number of values, the median is the average of the two middle values obtained by summing the two middle values and dividing by 2.

. . . .

EXAMPLE 3.1 National data for the United States on the number of home accident deaths from firearms for years 1997 to 2003 are given in the *2006 World Almanac and Book of Facts*. Approximations to these data are given here by year. What is the median number of deaths?

Year	Number of accidental deaths due to firearms
1997	981
1998	866
1999	824
2000	776
2001	802
2002	800
2003	700

Solution To find the median number of home accident deaths in the United States due to firearms during the period from 1997 to 2003, we order the data from its lowest to highest value as follows:

700   776   800   802   824   866   981
                           ∧
                   median

Given that there are an odd number of values in this distribution, the median is simply the middle value, or 802. Notice that on both sides of this middle value, there is an equal number of values.

To find the median of a variable in a large dataset, like ses, for example, we make use of a software package, like R, and obtain Q_{50} as shown in Chapter 2.

MORE R: To find the median of ses, for example, we can type either of the following commands in the console and hit **Enter**:

median(NELS\$ses)
quantile(NELS\$ses, c(0.5))

The **quantile** command produces the following output. Both the **median** and **quantile** commands refer to the median as the 50th percentile or, in shortened form as p50. The median of ses is 19, which is the same value as the mode of ses:

50%
19

Recall that the median is defined as that point below which are half the values in the distribution and above which also are half the values in the distribution. As a result, the median is meaningful only when it makes sense to order the values in a dataset from low to high: that is, when the variable is at least ordinal-leveled. A median is not meaningful on data that are nominal-leveled because such data would be ordered arbitrarily and different orderings would give rise to different medians. For nominal-leveled data, the mode, then, is the only appropriate measure of location.

Suppose we are interested in knowing the incomes of three individuals, and we are told that one of these individuals has an income of $0, another has an income of $5,000, and the median income for all three individuals is also $5,000. Because the median can be thought of as the middle or central point in a distribution, it might seem reasonable to suppose that the third individual has an income of $10,000. In reality, the third individual's income could be any value at or above $5,000 and still be consistent with the given information. The third individual's income could, for example, be $1,000,000, and the three incomes of $0, $5,000, and $1,000,000 would still have a median of $5,000. Thus, because the total number of data values above the median equals the total number of data points below the median, the median is not particularly sensitive to the exact values of each data value in a distribution. Changing one of the data values may or may not have any effect on the value of the median.

THE ARITHMETIC MEAN

The *arithmetic mean* (or simply the *mean*) is the most frequently used measure of location and is especially useful in inferential statistics. If we denote the ith observation of the variable X by X_i, the mean (denoted $\overline{X}$) is the sum of all the data values of the distribution (Denoted $\sum X_i$, where the upper-case Greek letter sigma Σ represents the operation of summation) divided by N, the total number of data values in the distribution. The definition of the mean may be translated into the following mathematical equation:

$$\overline{X} = \frac{\sum X_i}{N}.$$

(3.1)

· ·

EXAMPLE 3.2 Find the mean number of home accident deaths due to firearms in the United States from the years 1997 to 2003.

Solution Following Equation 3.1, we obtain,

$$\frac{700 + 776 + 800 + 802 + 824 + 866 + 981}{7} = \frac{5749}{7} = 821.29.$$

The mean for these data equals approximately 821 deaths.

To find the mean using R, we can type the following command in the command window and then hit **Enter**:

MORE R: To find the mean of ses, for example, type:

mean(NELS$ses)

We find the mean ses to be 18.434. Recall that the median and mode for these data were both equal to 19.

Unlike the mode and the median, the mean is sensitive to any change in the data values of the distribution. Thus, if one value in the distribution is increased (or decreased), the mean of the distribution will increase (or decrease), but not by the same amount. If, for example, we increase one of the values in the ses distribution by 25 points, the new mean will equal 18.93, an increase of 0.5 points. Try it on your data, using any one of the values in the ses distribution. Be sure to replace the altered value by the original one once you have finished this check.

Of course, if more than one data value in a distribution is changed with some values increased and some values decreased, the changes can cancel out each other's effects on the mean and leave the mean unchanged.

There is another property of the mean worth mentioning. If for each X value in the distribution, X_i, we calculate its difference from the mean, $X_i - \overline{X}$, then these differences, summed across all data values, will be equal to zero. The difference, $X_i - \overline{X}$, also may be thought of as the deviation or distance of the value from the mean. This property may be expressed in terms of the following equation:

$$\sum (X_i - \overline{X}) = 0. \tag{3.2}$$

Equation 3.2 shows that when distance is measured from the mean, the total distance of points above the mean equals the total distance of points below the mean. As a result, a point that is far from the others in a distribution (e.g., an outlier) would pull the mean closer to it so as to balance the negative and positive differences about the mean. Further, because the mean relies on distances to find a distribution's center, means should be computed only on variables that are at least interval-leveled. A mean of region or home-lang (home language background), for example, would be meaningless.

EXAMPLE 3.3 Verify that $\sum (X_i - \overline{X}) = 0$ for the deaths due to firearms data.

Solution

(700 − 821.29) + (776 − 821.29) + (800 − 821.29) + (802 − 821.29) + (824 − 821.29) + (866 − 821.29) + (981 − 821.29)
= (−121.29) + (−45.29) + (−21.29) + (−19.29) + (2.71) + (44.71) + (159.71) = −207.16 + 207.13 = −0.03.

This value is within rounding of 0.

☞ **Remark.** Most statistical software packages will compute any measure of location on any set of numerical values, regardless of how meaningful or meaningless these values are in measuring the underlying trait in question. R, for example, will readily compute a mean of the variable region in the NELS dataset because numerical values have been assigned to the variable region's different categories, as long as one uses the **as.numeric()** wrapper on **NELS$region**. This wrapper tells R to treat region as a numeric variable and, in particular, to interpret each region as a value between 1 and 4. Using the R **mean** function, we see that the mean of region is 2.46, which is the average of all 500 values between 1 and 4. The value 2.46 does not have a meaningful interpretation because the variable region is measured at the nominal level with more than two categories. The onus is on the researcher, then, to know which summary measures are appropriate in which circumstances. Without good judgment and thought in data analysis, interpretations of results may often be meaningless.

MORE R: To find the mean of region, although meaningless, for example, we type:

mean(as.numeric(NELS$region))

Interpreting the Mean of a Dichotomous Variable

Although the mean is usually meaningless when calculated on a nominal-leveled variable, it is meaningful when calculated on a dichotomous variable (a variable with only two categories) when those categories are coded as 0 and 1. In particular, in this situation, the mean of the variable will be equal to the proportion of cases in the category assigned the value of 1.

· ·

EXAMPLE 3.4 Find the mean of gender in our NELS dataset of 500 cases.

Solution Recall that gender is a dichotomous variable with the two categories, male and female. In the NELS dataset, the category female is assigned the value of 2 while the category male is assigned the value of 1. Therefore, we first must create a new variable, which we name numeric_gender that takes on value 1 for female and 0 for male. We may do so simply by subtracting 1 from each of the values, 2 and 1. We may then take the mean of this new variable.

MORE R: To create a numeric gender variable, find its mean, and generate a percentage frequency distribution, type the following commands in the console, and hit **Enter** after each:

NELS$numeric_gender = as.numeric(NELS$gender) – 1
mean(NELS$numeric_gender)
percent.table(NELS$gender)

We obtain the following result:

0.546

Male	Female
45.4	54.6

Notice that the mean of gender equals 0.55 (rounded to two decimal places), which is equal to the proportion of females in our sample of 500 cases (the percentage divided by 100).

The Weighted Mean

In Example 3.2, each value (number of accidental deaths due to firearms) occurs once and therefore has a frequency equal to 1. If, instead, however, each value in the distribution occurred a different number of times, as in the case of the ses variable (see the frequency distribution for ses given in Table 2.3), we could use a modification of Equation 3.1 that takes into account the varying frequencies (f_i) of each value of ses (X_i) to represent the mean of the ses distribution. This equation is given by Equation 3.3:

$$\overline{X} = \frac{\sum_1^k X_i f_i}{N}.$$

(3.3)

In Equation 3.3, the value of k above the summation sign represents the number of distinct values in the distribution. In the ses example, $k = 36$, because as shown in Table 2.3, there are 36 distinct values (0 to 35) in the ses distribution (33 and 34 have 0 frequency), and $N = 500$, the number of individuals in the dataset with non-missing ses values. We know from our previous work that the mean of the ses distribution equals 18.43.

Suppose, instead, we were told that the ses distribution was divided into three mutually exclusive and exhaustive categories that represented low, middle, and high ses groupings, respectively. Suppose we also were told that the low ses category consisted of 168 individuals with ses mean equal to 10.6, the middle ses category consisted of 276 individuals with ses mean equal to 20.92, and the high ses category consisted of 56 individuals with ses mean equal to 29.55. If we did not already know that the overall mean of the ses distribution was 18.43, what procedure might we use to arrive at that value?

Because each ses category contains a different number of individuals, rather than add up the three means (10.6, 20.92, and 29.55) and divide by 3, our procedure would need to take into account the different sizes of each category and weight the means of the three categories accordingly. Because the middle ses group is largest, its mean should be weighted more heavily than the mean of the next largest group (the low ses group), which, in turn, should be weighted more heavily than the mean of the smallest group (the middle ses group).

Analogous to having weighted each X value (X_i) by its frequency (f_i) in Equation 3.3 to obtain the overall mean, we now weight each mean value $(\overline{X}_j)$ by the size of its group (n_j), to obtain what is called the *weighted mean*. Just as the sum of the frequencies (f_i) equals N, so does the sum of the group sizes n_j equal N. The resulting equation for the weighted mean is given by Equation 3.4:

$$\text{weighted mean} = \frac{\sum_1^k \overline{X}_j n_j}{N}. \tag{3.4}$$

Using Equation 3.4, we compute the weighted mean for ses as follows:

$$\text{ses weighted mean} = \frac{10.6 \times 168 + 20.92 \times 276 + 29.55 \times 56}{500} = 18.43.$$

COMPARING THE MODE, MEDIAN, AND MEAN

As we have noted in earlier sections of this chapter, the mode, median, and mean measure different aspects of the location of a distribution of data values. Depending upon the particular shape of a distribution, the numerical values of these three measures may be the same or different. Conversely, knowing the values of these three measures relative to one another can often provide us with a better understanding of the shape of the underlying distribution.

When a distribution is symmetric, the mean will be equal to the median (see Figure 3.5 (a) and (b)). When a distribution is symmetric and also unimodal, the mode will equal the mean and the median as well. The distribution of our data in Example 3.1 on home accident deaths due to firearms is symmetric and unimodal, which explains why the mode, median, and mean were all equal to each other.

If a distribution is highly negatively skewed, in general, the mean will be smaller than the median, because the value of the mean is more influenced than the value of the median by the extreme low values present in such a distribution. Analogously, for a distribution that is highly positively skewed, in general, the mean will be larger than the median, because it is more influenced than the median by the extreme high values present in such a distribution. Because of the differential influence of extreme scores on the mean and

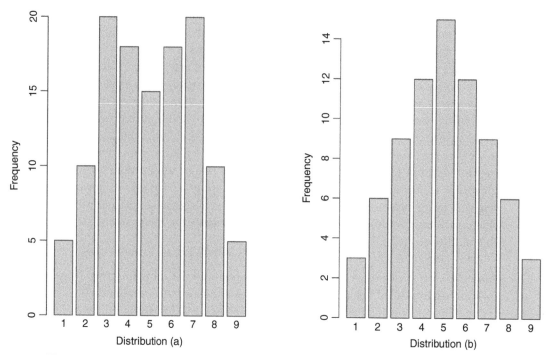

Figure 3.5 Histograms of two symmetric distributions.

median, the mean of a highly skewed distribution will lie in the direction of skewness (the direction of the tail) relative to the median. This relationship between the mean and the median is illustrated in Figures 3.6 and 3.7, which depict unimodal continuous distributions. Exercise 3.7 illustrates that in the case of discrete distributions or multimodal continuous distributions counter-examples exist. In fact, they are not uncommon in those circumstances. When, however, a distribution is severely skewed and unimodal continuous, we can expect the mean and median to differ in a predictable way.

☞ **Remark.** The converse is not true, however. That is, if the mean and the median are different from each other, the distribution need not be skewed. Analogously, if the mean is equal to the median, the distribution need not be symmetric.

• •

EXAMPLE 3.5 Compare the values of the mode, median, and mean for (1) ses; (2) expinc30 (expected income at age 30); (3) schattrt (school attendance rate, which measures the average daily attendance rate of the high school that each student attended); and (4) slfcnc08 (self-concept score in eighth grade). Explain the direction of difference that exists among these three measures of location. Note that by calculating the mean of these variables, we are treating them as at least interval-leveled.

Solution. We use the **mean()**, **median()**, and **the.mode()** commands for each of the four variables in question. The output is summarized below.

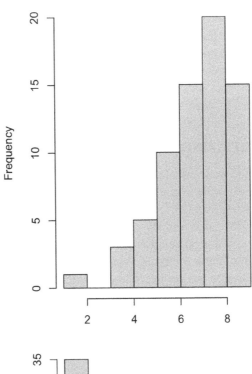

Figure 3.6 Severe
negative skew

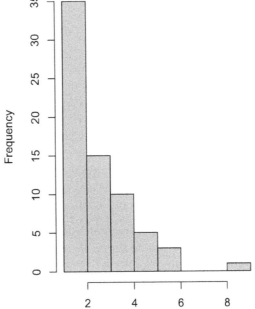

Figure 3.7 Severe
positive skew

	ses	expinc30	schattrt	slfcnc08
Mean	18.434	51574.73	93.65	21.06
Median	19	40000	95	21
Mode	19	50000	95	17

Recall that the distribution of ses is reasonably symmetric. We see that the two measures of location (central tendency) are approximately equal. On the other hand, we know from our earlier work that expected income at age 30 is highly positively skewed. Not surprisingly, the value of the mean is quite a bit higher than the value of the median. From Exercise 2.16, we know that average daily school attendance rate is highly negatively skewed, which explains why the mean is smaller than the median in this case.

CHARACTERIZING THE SPREAD OF A DISTRIBUTION

When we speak of the spread of a univariate distribution, we mean the extent to which the values in the distribution vary from its "average" and from one another. Instead of the word spread, we may use, equivalently, the words *variability*, *dispersion*, *heterogeneity*, *inconsistency*, and *unpredictability*. Several different summary statistics exist to measure spread: the range, interquartile range, variance, and standard deviation. As we shall see, each of these summary statistics taps a different aspect of spread. Measures of spread may be used to answer the following sample questions: "Are females more variable than males in their self-concept?"; "Are reading scores more homogeneous in private schools than in public schools?"; and "Are home insurance fees more consistent in California than in New York?"

We present a variation of an example from Burrill et al. (1993), to illustrate more clearly what it is that measures of spread capture about a set of numbers, as opposed to, for example, measures of location.

• •

EXAMPLE 3.6 Congratulations! You have just won a trip to one of two cities in the United States that have similar average annual temperatures (approximately 57 °F): San Francisco, CA or Springfield, MO. The prize also includes a wardrobe of clothes that would be suitable, from the point of view of warmth, for visiting the city of your choice any time during the year.

Would the same clothes be suitable for both cities at any time during the year? For which city would the wardrobe of clothing necessarily be more extensive? The average monthly temperatures (in Fahrenheit) for the two cities are given in Table 3.2 and are available by loading the Temp dataset located on the textbook's website or through the R package associated with the textbook, as described in Chapter 1.

Solution   Because a more extensive wardrobe would be required by the city that has a greater variability in temperature across the months of the year, we explore the relative variability in monthly temperature for the two cities using boxplots.

☞   **Remark.** There are two ways to enter these data as two variables. First, we could enter the data just as they are entered in the table naming the second two columns spring and sanfran. The first gives the Springfield temperature and the second the San Francisco temperature. Second the data could be reorganized. We could use two variables, city and temp. City is a dichotomous variable with two categories (Springfield, assigned the value of 1, and San Francisco, assigned the value of 2) while Temperature is a continuous variable of temperature in degrees Fahrenheit for each month. The second is the way the data are displayed in the data file Temp. An excerpt of the data file is presented.

TABLE 3.2 Average monthly temperature of Springfield and San Francisco		
Month	Springfield temperature (°F)	San Francisco temperature (°F)
Jan	32	49
Feb	36	52
Mar	45	53
Apr	56	55
May	65	58
Jun	73	61
Jul	78	62
Aug	77	63
Sep	70	64
Oct	58	61
Nov	45	55
Dec	36	49

City	Temperature (°F)
Springfield	32
SanFrancisco	49
Springfield	36
SanFrancisco	52
Springfield	45
SanFrancisco	53
etc.	etc.

The resulting graphs and statistics are the same regardless of the format of the data, but because the methods for obtaining them differ slightly, both are presented. For example, the way to create side-by-side boxplots giving the temperatures for the two cities differs depending on the layout of the dataset. The first is based on the first layout for the data.

MORE R: Constructing boxplots of different variables in one or more separate panels.

If the temperatures are given for the two cities, one column per city, each labeled spring and sanfran, for example, we would type:

boxplot(Temp$spring, Temp$sanfran)

If, instead, the values of the temperature for both cities are in one column labeled Temperature, and there is an associated column labeled City that is a grouping variable indicating from which city the corresponding temperature is from (San Francisco or

Springfield), to obtain the boxplots of the different groups (city, in this case), we would type:

boxplot(Temp$Temperature~Temp$City)

The command **boxplot(Temp$Temperature~Temp$City)** produces the following result:

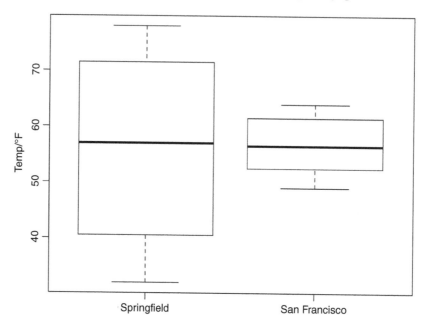

From the boxplot display, we may observe that while the cities share the same typical or "average" temperature across the twelve months of the year (the median is approximately 57 °F), they differ quite markedly in terms of the temperature spread. For Springfield, the temperature varies from a low of 32 °F to a high of 78 °F, whereas for San Francisco the temperature varies only from a low of 49 °F to a high of 64 °F. What this suggests is that while for San Francisco, middle-weight clothes would be suitable for all months of the year, for Springfield, light-, middle-, and heavy-weight clothes are necessary. Said differently, Springfield requires the more extensive wardrobe of the two cities.

☞ **Remark.** In addition to side-by-side boxplots, we may wish to view side-by-side histograms or bar plots when examining differences between two distributions. We can accomplish this in R by using the **par** command.

MORE R: Displaying multiple plots side by side in one frame.

If we want to display the histograms for the temperatures of Springfield and San Francisco next to each other for an easier comparison, we type the following commands:

par(mfrow=c(1,2))
hist(Temp$Temperature[Temp$City=="Springfield"],
main = "Springfield", xlab = "Temperature",

xlim = c(30,80), ylim = c(0,5), col = "grey")
hist(Temp$Temperature[Temp$City=="SanFrancisco"],
main = "San Francisco", xlab = "Temperature",
xlim = c(30,80), ylim = c(0,5), col = "grey")
par(mfrow=c(1,1))

The **par** command lets the user change graphical display parameters; the argument **mfrow** sets a "multi-frame" row with the specified number of rows and columns, which is one row and two columns in this case. We restore the original settings to a one-by-one display after rendering our histograms.

Note also that we gave the two histograms the same *x*- and *y*-axes for better comparison using the **xlim** and **ylim** arguments of hist.

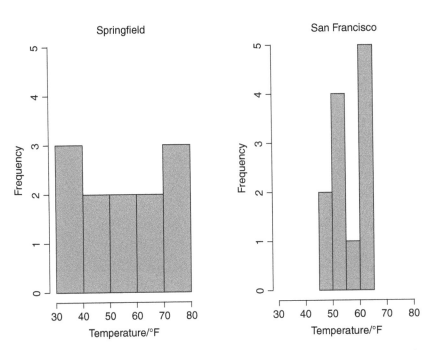

More formally, we may characterize the variability in temperature using one of several numeric summaries of spread.

THE RANGE AND INTERQUARTILE RANGE

The *range* of a distribution is simply the difference between the highest and lowest values in the distribution. The range is easy to compute and simple to interpret. For San Francisco, the range is 64 − 49 = 15 degrees Fahrenheit, while for Springfield, the range is 78 − 32 = 46 degrees Fahrenheit. As 46 °F is greater than 15 °F, the range correctly captures the relative spread for the data of these two distributions. However, because the range depends upon the highest and lowest values of a distribution, and because these values tend to be the least stable values of a distribution, the range is not usually the best measure of a distribution's spread.

For example, the interquartile range (*IQR*), introduced in Chapter 2, is less sensitive than the range to changes in the extreme values, or, more generally, to changes in the shape of the tails of a distribution. The *interquartile range* is the difference between the third quartile, Q_{75}, and the first quartile, Q_{25}, and as such, equals the distance covered by the middle 50 percent of the distribution.

Because the interquartile range is based on the values near the center of the distribution, it is not sensitive to the small number of values in the tails. Statistics, such as the interquartile range, which are not sensitive to changes in a small number of values within a distribution, are called *resistant statistics*. The median is another example of a resistant statistic because unlike the mean, the median is not sensitive to extreme values in either tail of the distribution.

To estimate the interquartile range for both cities, we first order the 12 temperature values from lowest to highest for each city.

For Springfield, the ordered temperature values are:

32   36   36   45   45   56   58   65   70   73   77   78
                              ^

The median is therefore 57. Because we may think of Q_{25} as that value that divides the lower half of the distribution in half, a good estimate for Q_{25} is the middle value of the six values, 32, 36, 36, 45, 45, 56, or that value that has three values below it and three values above it. An estimate of that value is halfway between 36 and 45, or 40.5. Likewise, a good estimate for Q_{75} is that value halfway between 70 and 73, or 71.5. An estimate of the interquartile range is therefore $Q_{75} - Q_{25} = 71.5 - 40.5 = 31$.

For San Francisco, the ordered temperature values are:

49   49   52   53   55   55   58   61   61   62   63   64
                              ^

The median for these data is 56.5, an estimate of $Q_{25} = 52.5$, and an estimate of $Q_{75} = 61.5$. Therefore, an estimate of the interquartile range is $Q_{75} - Q_{25} = 61.5 - 52.5 = 9$.

We may use R to obtain an estimate of the interquartile range that is based on a somewhat different set of assumptions about the data, as there are several ways to calculate the interquartile range. Therefore, the interquartile range from R will not necessarily be equal to the value obtained by our hand-calculated estimation procedure.

MORE R: To obtain the interquartile ranges for distributions of a single variable for different subgroups, defined in this case by the variable City, type the following in the console and hit **Enter**:

IQR(Temp$Temperature[Temp$City == "Springfield"])
IQR(Temp$Temperature[Temp$City == "SanFrancisco"])

Temp$City == " ... " within the square brackets [] allows us to compute the *IQR* on each city separately by creating two subsets of Temperature values, one for Springfield and the other for San Francisco. Without the square brackets, the *IQR* would be computed on all Temperature values from both cities combined. Said differently, the square brackets subset the variable Temperature by City.

In executing the two *IQR* commands, we obtain an *IQR* for Springfield of 28 and an *IQR* for San Francisco of 8.5.

THE VARIANCE

If we conceptualize the spread of a distribution as the extent to which the values in the distribution differ from the mean and from each other, then a reasonable measure of spread might be the average deviation, or difference, of the values from the mean. In notation form, this may be expressed as:

$$\frac{1}{N}\sum(X_i - \overline{X}). \tag{3.5}$$

Although at first glance, this might seem reasonable, using Equation 3.2, this expression always equals 0, regardless of the actual spread of the data values in the distribution. Recall that this occurs because the negative deviations about the mean always cancel out the positive deviations about the mean, producing a sum or average of 0.

To avoid this cancellation effect, one may simply drop any negative signs from the deviation values before averaging. In mathematical terminology, dropping the negative sign of a number is called taking that number's absolute value. The mean of the absolute values of the deviations is called the mean deviation. Although the mean deviation is a good measure for describing the spread of a given set of data, it is not often used because the concept of absolute value does not lend itself to the kind of advanced mathematical manipulation necessary for the development of inferential statistical equations.

The usual method for avoiding such cancellation is, therefore, to square the deviations rather than taking their absolute values. In so doing, we obtain a measure that is sensitive to differences in spread and is easy to work with mathematically in the development of inferential statistical equations. The average of the squared deviations about the mean is called the *variance*. It is denoted by the symbol SD^2 or *VAR* and is given by Equation 3.6.

$$VAR = SD^2 = \frac{\sum(X_i - \overline{X})^2}{N - 1}. \tag{3.6}$$

The variance of the distribution of Springfield temperatures is 282.99 while the variance of San Francisco temperatures is 29.06. These values are consistent with our observation that Springfield has a larger temperature spread than San Francisco, or that the distribution of Springfield temperatures is more variable (less homogeneous, or more heterogeneous) than the distribution of San Francisco temperatures.

While this book has a non-computational focus, we believe that seeing a worked-out example for computing the variance using Equation 3.6 will aid many of you in conceptualizing this statistic.

● ●

EXAMPLE 3.7 Use Equations 3.1 and 3.6 to find the mean and variance of the San Francisco monthly temperature.

Solution We denote the temperature variable as X.

X	$X-\bar{X}$	$(X-\bar{X})^2$
49	−7.83	61.31
52	−4.83	23.33
53	−3.83	14.67
55	−1.83	3.35
58	1.17	1.37
61	4.17	17.39
62	5.17	26.73
63	6.17	38.07
64	7.17	51.41
61	4.17	17.39
55	−1.83	3.35
49	−7.83	61.31
Total: 682		Total: 319.67

$$\text{Mean} = \bar{X} = \frac{\sum X_i}{N} = \frac{682}{12} = 56.83.$$

$$\text{Sum of squares} = SS = \sum (X_i - \bar{X})^2 = 319.67.$$

$$\text{Variance} = SD^2 = \frac{SS}{N-1} = \frac{\sum (X_i - \bar{X})^2}{N-1} = \frac{319.67}{11} = 29.06.$$

According to Equation 3.6, the more the values of the distribution tend to differ from the mean, the larger the variance. But, how large is a large variance? Unfortunately, there is no simple answer. Variances, like other measures of spread, are used primarily to compare the spread of one distribution to the spread of another and not to judge, offhand, whether or not a single distribution has a large spread. However, a variance of zero, the smallest possible value, indicates that there is no spread: that is, that all of the scores are the same.

The numerical value of a variance of a distribution also depends upon the unit of measurement used. As we will formalize in the next chapter, the variance of a distribution of heights measured in inches, for example, will be considerably larger than the variance of the same distribution of heights measured in feet. When comparing the variances of two or more distributions, therefore, for comparability, the unit of measurement should be the same for all distributions.

MORE R: To obtain the variances for distributions of a single variable for different subgroups, defined in this case by the variable city, type the following in the console and hit **Enter**:

var(Temp$Temperature[Temp$City == "Springfield"])
var(Temp$Temperature[Temp$City == "SanFrancisco"])

As before, the square brackets [] separate the variable Temp$Temperature into the subset of values for each city.

☞ **Remark.** We note that it may not be intuitive why the formula for the variance divides the sum of squared deviations by $N - 1$ instead of by N, as is the case when calculating the mean. The reason behind this difference has to do with what is known as *statistical bias*, which will be discussed in Chapter 9 in the context of inferential statistics.

☞ **Remark.** While the range and interquartile range for our temperature example are in terms of degrees Fahrenheit, the original units of measurement, this is not the case for the variance. The variance is expressed in terms of squared units as opposed to the original units of measurement. This means that for this example, the variance is expressed in terms of squared degrees Fahrenheit, rather than in degrees Fahrenheit. To see that this is the case we need only to review Example 3.7, in which the variance of the distribution of San Francisco temperatures is calculated. In Example 3.7, the mean (in degrees Fahrenheit) is subtracted from the value of each temperature to obtain a deviation, $X - \overline{X}$, in degrees Fahrenheit, for each month. But, then these deviations are squared. The squared deviations are in squared degrees Fahrenheit rather than in degrees Fahrenheit. The variance, which is the average of these squared deviations, is then also in squared degrees Fahrenheit.

THE STANDARD DEVIATION

Because the variance is expressed in squared units rather than in the original units of measurement, the variance value cannot meaningfully be related to the original set of data. The variance may be expressed in terms of the original units of measurement, however, if we take the positive square root of the variance. This new measure is called the *standard deviation*. It is denoted by the symbols SD or S, and is given by the following equation:

$$SD = \sqrt{VAR} = \sqrt{SD^2} \, . \tag{3.7}$$

Because the standard deviation is a measure of spread in terms of the original units of measurement, it may be directly related to the original set of data. The standard deviation of the San Francisco temperatures is 5.39. If we order the temperatures from lowest to highest, we have the following:

San Francisco temperatures in order of magnitude: 49, 49, 52, 53, 55, 55, 58, 61, 61, 62, 63, 64

The values within 57 ± 5.39 are the values within the interval 51.61 to 62.39. These are the values 52, 53, 55, 55, 58, 61, 61, and 62. Hence, 8 of the 12 values, or 67 percent, fall within one standard deviation of the mean. All values fall within two standard deviations of the mean for this distribution. The number of values that fall within one standard deviation of the mean in a distribution will vary somewhat from distribution to distribution, as will the number of standard deviations needed to capture all the values of a distribution.

☞ **Remark.** One may also describe the standard deviation as that distance from the mean (in both directions) within which the majority of values of a distribution fall. The distance will be shorter in distributions that are clustered tightly about the mean, and longer in distributions that are not clustered so tightly about the mean.

☞ **Remark.** While, as noted earlier, the interquartile range is a resistant statistic, the variance and standard deviation are not. The variance is conceptualized as the average of squared deviations about the mean and the standard deviation as the square root of that. Cases with extreme deviations, therefore, are highly influential as they enter the calculation as the deviation squared, rather than as the deviation itself. Because a deviation of 10 adds 100 points to the calculation while a deviation of 20 adds 400 points, for example, the more extreme the deviation, the greater the increase in its influence on the variance and standard deviation. As a result, the variance and standard deviation are especially sensitive to the influence of extreme values, and are considered to be highly non-resistant statistics.

MORE R: To find the standard deviation of the variable Temperature by city, we use the following commands:

sd(Temp$Temperature[Temp$City == "Springfield"])
sd(Temp$Temperature[Temp$City == "SanFrancisco"])

CHARACTERIZING THE SKEWNESS OF A DISTRIBUTION

In the previous chapter we described the shape of a distribution as symmetric or as positively or negatively skewed. Our description was based on "eyeballing" the data represented visually. Often one may be interested in a numerical summary of skewness for the purpose of comparing the skewness of two or more distributions or for evaluating the degree to which a single distribution is skewed. The *skewness statistic* is such a numerical summary. Equation 3.8 gives the expression for the skewness statistic, as calculated by R, and the standard error of the skewness:

$$\text{skewness} = \frac{\sum (X_i - \overline{X})^3 / N}{\left(\sqrt{\dfrac{\sum (X_i - \overline{X})^2}{N}} \right)^3}, \tag{3.8}$$

$$\text{standard error skewness} = \sqrt{\frac{6N(N-1)}{(N-2)(N+1)(N+3)}}.$$

While the variance is based on the sum of squared deviations about the mean, the skewness statistic is based on the sum of cubed deviations about the mean. And while the variance can only be positive or zero (since it is based on the sum of *squared* deviations), the skewness statistic may be either positive, zero, or negative (since it is based on the sum of *cubed* deviations). The skewness statistic is positive when the distribution is skewed positively, and it is negative when the distribution is skewed negatively. If the distribution is perfectly symmetric, the skewness statistic equals zero. The more severe the skew, the more the skewness statistic departs from zero.

To compare the skewness of two distributions of relatively equal size, one may use the skewness values themselves. To compare the skewness of two distributions that are quite unequal in size, or to evaluate the severity of skewness for a particular distribution when that distribution is small or moderate in size, one should compute a skewness ratio. The skewness ratio is obtained as the skewness statistic divided by the standard error of the skewness statistic. Although the meaning of the standard error will be discussed in Chapter 9, we note simply for now that the standard error is a function of the sample size.

. . . .

EXAMPLE 3.8 Use Equation 3.8 to calculate the skewness and standard error of the skew for the San Francisco monthly temperature.

Solution We denote the temperature variable as X. Recall that according to the output obtained using R, $\overline{X}=56.83$ and $SD = 5.39$ for San Francisco.

X	X−X̄	(X − X̄)³
49	−7.83	−480.05
52	−4.83	−112.68
53	−3.83	−56.18
55	−1.83	−6.13
58	1.17	1.60
61	4.17	72.51
62	5.17	138.19
63	6.17	234.89
64	7.17	368.60
61	4.17	72.51
55	−1.83	−6.13
49	−7.83	−480.05
	Total:	**−256.08**

$$\text{The skewness} = \frac{\sum (X_i - \overline{X})^3/N}{\left(\sqrt{\dfrac{\sum (X_i - \overline{X})^2}{N}}\right)^3} = \frac{-256.08/12}{\left(\sqrt{\dfrac{319.67}{12}}\right)^3} = \frac{-21.34}{5.16^3} = \frac{-21.34}{137.39} = -0.155.$$

$$\text{The standard error of the skewness} = \sqrt{\frac{6N(N-1)}{(N-2)(N+1)(N+3)}} = \sqrt{\frac{6(12)(11)}{(10)(13)(15)}} = 637.$$

And, the skewness ratio of Temperature for San Francisco is −0.155/0.637 = −0.243.

MORE R: To find the skew and standard error of skewness for San Francisco temperatures, type:

skew(Temp$Temperature[Temp$City == "SanFrancisco"])
se.skew(Temp$Temperature[Temp$City == "SanFrancisco"])

To find the standard error of the skew by hand, type:

sqrt((6*12*11)/(10*13*15))

To find the skewness ratio, defined as the skew divided by its standard error, type:

skew.ratio(Temp$Temperature[Temp$City == "SanFrancisco"])

Applying the same concept to Springfield, we obtain the following result:

For Springfield: skewness = −0.068, standard error of the skew = 0.637, and skewness ratio = −0.107.
   For San Francisco: skewness = −0.155, standard error of the skew = 0.637, and skewness ratio = −0.244.

By convention, when the skewness ratio exceeds 2.00 for small- and moderate-sized samples, one should consider the distribution to be highly skewed. In our case, these statistics corroborate our impressions from the boxplot that these distributions are not skewed.

   Because many summary statistics (e.g., the mean, variance, and standard deviation) are sensitive to extreme values, and because distributions which are skewed often contain extreme values, we routinely should check a distribution for the severity of its skewness. It is often possible to reduce the skewness of a distribution by expressing the data of that distribution in an alternative form. Ways for doing so are covered in the next chapter.

SELECTING MEASURES OF LOCATION AND SPREAD

Table 3.3 provides a summary of the relationship between the level of measurement of a variable and the generally appropriate measures of central tendency and spread. In the case of interval- or ratio-leveled variables, the shape of the distribution influences whether one chooses a resistant measure (i.e., median and interquartile range) or a non-resistant measure (i.e., mean, standard deviation, and range) to summarize the data. If a distribution is not severely skewed, either may be appropriate. If the distribution is severely

TABLE 3.3 Guidelines for selecting appropriate measures of location and spread based on a variable's level of measurement and other characteristics

Variable characteristics	Appropriate measures of	
	Location	Spread
Nominal with more than 2 categories	Mode	Frequency distribution table
Ordinal with fewer than 5 categories	Mode	Interquartile range
Ordinal with more than 5 categories	Median	Interquartile range
Scale (interval or ratio) and severely skewed	Median	Interquartile range
Scale (interval or ratio) and not severely skewed	Mean	Standard deviation

skewed, however, resistant measures are generally more appropriate. As discussed in this chapter, resistant measures are not as influenced by outliers as non-resistant measures and, therefore, will provide better summary characterizations of the data when data are severely skewed.

APPLYING WHAT WE HAVE LEARNED

Suppose we wish to know the extent to which eighth grade males expect larger incomes at age 30 than eighth grade females, and the extent to which there is lack of consensus among eighth grade males in their expectations of income at age 30 relative to females. We make use of the statistics presented thus far to find answers to our questions.

While quick answers might be obtained by comparing the numerical summaries of location and spread for expinc30 for both males and females, to be confident of their accuracy, we need first to examine the data that are being summarized. A good way to do so is with the help of two side-by-side boxplots, one for males and one for females.

MORE R: To obtain boxplots for each gender for the NELS expected income variable, type:

boxplot(NELS$expinc30~NELS$gender)

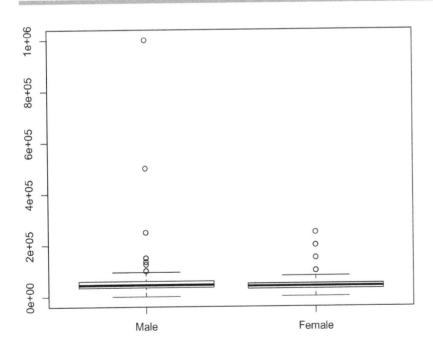

From the boxplots, we notice that with the exception of two outliers, the distributions of expinc30 are similar in shape for males and females. Because of the presence of many more extreme outliers in the male distribution, we can expect the male-to-female differences with respect to the mean, range, and standard deviation to be more pronounced than those based on the median and interquartile range, as these latter statistics are more resistant to being influenced by extreme values.

Using code similar to that presented earlier to obtain statistics for the temperature of each city, we may note that the skewness of the male distribution is approximately 8.801 whereas the skewness of the female distribution is approximately 3.792.

Because the NELS dataset has different numbers of males ($n = 215$) and females ($n = 244$):

For males: skewness = 8.801, standard error of the skew = 0.166, and skewness ratio = 53.051.
   For females: skewness = 3.792, standard error of the skew = 0.156, and skewness ratio = 24.333.

MORE R: To obtain the skew, standard error of the skew, and skewness ratio for each gender for the NELS expected income variable, type:

skew(NELS$expinc30[NELS$gender == "Male"])
se.skew(NELS$expinc30[NELS$gender == "Male"])
skew.ratio(NELS$expinc30[NELS$gender == "Male"])
skew(NELS$expinc30[NELS$gender == "Female"])
se.skew(NELS$expinc30[NELS$gender == "Female"])
skew.ratio(NELS$expinc30[NELS$gender == "Female"])

These summary statistics corroborate our graphical impressions that both distributions are severely positively skewed and that the male distribution is far more positively skewed than the female distribution.

MORE R: To obtain the mean and median for each gender for the NELS expected income variable, type:

mean(NELS$expinc30[NELS$gender == "Male"], na.rm = T)
median(NELS$expinc30[NELS$gender == "Male"], na.rm = T)
mean(NELS$expinc30[NELS$gender == "Female"], na.rm = T)
median(NELS$expinc30[NELS$gender == "Female"], na.rm = T)

In R, missing values are represented by the symbol **NA** (not available); the argument **na.rm = T** in these commands serves to remove any missing values from the expinc30 variable so that the mean (and median) can be computed. The **T** stands for "true" and can be replaced with the full word **TRUE** for the same result.

Notice that, as expected, the male mean is considerably higher than the female mean. On average, the 215 males who responded to this question expect an income at age 30 of $60,721, while the 244 females who responded to this question expect an income at age 30 of only $43,516. Notice also that the male median is $45,000 while the female median is $40,000. Thus, whether one uses the mean or the median, males are shown to have higher expected incomes at age 30 than females. However, the magnitude of difference is considerably greater between the sexes when one uses the mean rather than the median as a measure of location. This attests more to the fact that the distribution of expinc30 is more positively skewed for males than for females than to some essential truth about the difference in expected income between the majority of males and females.

MORE R: To obtain the variance, standard deviation, and *IQR* for each gender for the NELS expected income variable, type:

var(NELS$expinc30[NELS$gender == "Male"], na.rm = T)
sd(NELS$expinc30[NELS$gender == "Male"], na.rm = T)
IQR(NELS$expinc30[NELS$gender == "Male"], na.rm = T)
var(NELS$expinc30[NELS$gender == "Female"], na.rm = T)
sd(NELS$expinc30[NELS$gender == "Female"], na.rm = T)
IQR(NELS$expinc30[NELS$gender == "Female"], na.rm = T)

In order for the variance, standard deviation, and *IQR* to be calculated for expinc30 without interruption by the presence of missing values, we note that the argument **na.rm = T** is once again included. If, for example, at least one male and one female had a missing value on expinc30, and **na.rm = T** were not included as part of these commands, execution would stop prematurely before any of these statistics could be computed.

Comparing the spread of the male and female distributions, we find again that different summary statistics lead to different interpretations. The difference in expected income variability between males and females is most pronounced when non-resistant measures are used (e.g., the range, variance, and standard deviation) and less pronounced when more resistant measures of spread are used (e.g., the interquartile range). When a non-resistant statistic, like the standard deviation, is used to compare the spreads of the male and female distributions, males, with $SD = 79,259$, are shown to have much greater lack of consensus than females, with $SD = 26,965$. When a resistant statistic like the interquartile range is used, the degree of discrepancy between the genders is diminished. While males, with *IQR* of 25,000, are again shown to have a greater lack of consensus than females, with *IQR* of 20,000, the degree of difference in consensus is far smaller.

☞ **Remark.** Note that because the values of the variance are large for the two distributions, scientific notation was used by R to express some of these values. This is often the case when values are either very large or very small. To understand this format, we translate the value of the variance for males from scientific to standard notation. The value in scientific notation is 6.3E+09. This is equivalent to 6.3×10^9 or 6,300,000,000.

Because of the extreme outliers in the male distribution, the more resistant statistics, not being so influenced by these two extreme cases, are more accurate in describing the extent of difference between males and females relative to the bulk of the cases in our dataset. Had we not examined the data initially, we might have characterized the magnitude of the difference between the bulk of males and females as being greater than it actually is, both in terms of level and spread.

We might also explore the extent to which our summary statistics would change if these two male outliers were removed from the analysis. By eliminating these two outliers, we can expect our numerical summaries to represent with greater accuracy the bulk of cases in our sample. The two extreme outliers in the male group are cases 102 and 494.

MORE R: To exclude the two male outliers from our analyses, those with id values of 102 and 494, we would include the following in any of the above commands:

NELS\$expinc30[NELS\$gender == "Male" & NELS\$id != 102 & NELS\$id != 494]

Note that **!=** is a symbol for "not equal to" and **&** is a symbol for "and."
    In the case of the mean, the command would be:

mean(NELS\$expinc30[NELS\$gender == "Male" & NELS\$id != 102 & NELS\$id != 494], na.rm = T)

Notice that the skewness of this "new" male distribution is now quite similar to the skewness of the original female distribution. Notice also that the resistant statistics have not changed at all and that the non-resistant statistics all have moved quite a bit closer to the resistant statistics. In short, by eliminating 2 of the 500 cases, we have convergence in our results. We know now the extent to which males have higher expected incomes at age 30 and the extent to which they have less consensus on their income expectations relative to females. The reason why we know the extent of outlier influence in this example is because two separate analyses were carried out: one with and one without the outliers. Whenever outliers are eliminated from a dataset, standard practice should be to carry out one analysis on all data points, including outliers, and another analysis on the subset of data points excluding outliers. Then, the results of the original analyses can be reported along with the extent to which these results have been influenced by the outliers.

In practice, one should not eliminate data points indiscriminately to achieve a "better" result. One should not report that "the average expected income for the males in this sample is \$54,249," without adding that "two subjects with extremely high expected incomes were excluded."

If outliers are present, one needs to understand why they are there. Perhaps they represent errors in data entry, or perhaps they belong to persons who are not part of the population identified for study. Additionally, it may be that they represent a segment of the population underrepresented in your study and that through further sampling these cases will no longer be extreme. While we eliminated the two outliers in this example, other ways for reducing the effects of outliers are presented in the next chapter.

MORE R: Operators and expressions.

In addition to <, **&**, and **!=**, a more complete set of standard arithmetic, logical, and relational operators that may be used in expressions is given below:

Arithmetic: + (add); – (subtract); * (multiply); / (divide); ∧ (exponentiate)
Logical: ! (not); | (or); & (and)
Relational: == (equal to); != (not equal to); < (less than); > (greater than); <= (less than or equal to); >= (greater than or equal to)

SUMMARY OF R COMMANDS

Create	**Command lines**
Calculate the mode of ses	**the.mode(NELS$ses)**
Calculate the median of ses (Example 3.1)	**median(NELS$ses)** OR **quantile(NELS$ses, c(0.5))**
Calculate the mean of ses (Example 3.2)	**mean(NELS$ses)**
Find the mean of gender (Example 3.4)	**NELS$numeric_gender = as.numeric (NELS$gender) – 1** **mean(NELS$numeric_gender)**
Generate summary statistics for each of the three variables: ses, expinc30, and schattrt (Example 3.5)	**mean(NELS$ses)** **median(NELS$ses)** **the.mode(NELS$ses)** **mean(NELS$expinc30, na.rm = T)** **median(NELS$expinc30, na.rm = T)** **the.mode(NELS$expinc30)** **mean(NELS$schattrt, na.rm = T)** **median(NELS$schattrt, na.rm = T)** **the.mode(NELS$schattrt)**
Plot side-by-side histograms of Temperature in two cities.	**par(mfrow=c(1,2))** **hist(Temp$Temperature[Temp $City=="Springfield"],** **main = "Springfield", xlab = "Temperature",** **xlim = c(30,80), ylim = c(0,5), col = "grey")** **hist(Temp$Temperature[Temp $City=="SanFrancisco"],** **main = "San Francisco", xlab = "Temperature",** **xlim = c(30,80), ylim = c(0,5), col = "grey")** **par(mfrow=c(1,1))**
Obtain the interquartile ranges for distributions of the single	**IQR(Temp$Temperature[Temp$City == "Springfield"])**

Create	**Command lines**
variable Temperature for different subgroups for specified cities (Example 3.6) Obtain variances of Temperature for specified cities (Example 3.7)	IQR(Temp$Temperature[Temp$City == "SanFrancisco"]) var(Temp$Temperature[Temp$City == "Springfield"]) var(Temp$Temperature[Temp$City == "SanFrancisco"])
Obtain the standard deviations of Temperature for specified cities.	sd(Temp$Temperature[Temp$City == "Springfield"]) sd(Temp$Temperature[Temp$City == "SanFrancisco"])
Calculate the skew, standard error of skewness, and skewness ratio of Temperature for San Francisco (Example 3.8)	skew(Temp$Temperature[Temp$City == "SanFrancisco"]) se.skew(Temp$Temperature[Temp$City == "SanFrancisco"]) skew.ratio(Temp$Temperature[Temp$City == "SanFrancisco"])
Calculate the skew, standard error of skewness, and skewness ratio for the variable expinc30 broken down by the grouping variable gender	skew(NELS$expinc30[NELS$gender == "Male"]) se.skew(NELS$expinc30[NELS$gender == "Male"]) skew.ratio(NELS$expinc30[NELS$gender == "Male"]) skew(NELS$expinc30[NELS$gender == "Female"]) se.skew(NELS$expinc30[NELS$gender == "Female"]) skew.ratio(NELS$expinc30[NELS$gender == "Female"])
Obtain descriptive statistics for the variable expinc30 broken down by gender subgroups	mean(NELS$expinc30[NELS$gender == "Male"], na.rm = T) median(NELS$expinc30[NELS$gender == "Male"], na.rm = T) mean(NELS$expinc30[NELS$gender == "Female"], na.rm = T) median(NELS$expinc30[NELS$gender == "Female"], na.rm = T) var(NELS$expinc30[NELS$gender == "Male"], na.rm = T) sd(NELS$expinc30[NELS$gender == "Male"], na.rm = T) IQR(NELS$expinc30[NELS$gender == "Male"], na.rm = T) var(NELS$expinc30[NELS$gender == "Female"], na.rm = T)

Create	Command lines
	sd(NELS$expinc30[NELS$gender == "Female"], na.rm = T)
	IQR(NELS$expinc30[NELS$gender == "Female"], na.rm = T)
Obtain the mean of the variable expinc30 for males, omitting id values 102 and 494	mean(NELS$expinc30[NELS$gender == "Male" & NELS$id != 102 & NELS$id != 494])

EXERCISES

Exercises 3.1–3.7 involve measures of central tendency and require the use of R.

3.1 For the following variables from the NELS dataset, what are the appropriate measures of central tendency (mode, median, mean) and why? Use R to calculate the values of these measures and interpret the results.

   (a) gender
   (b) urban
   (c) schtyp8
   (d) tcherint
   (e) numinst
   (f) achrdg08
   (g) schattrt
   (h) absent12

3.2 These questions involve the variable late12 from the NELS dataset.

   (a) How many students in the dataset were never late to school?
   (b) How often was the first person in the dataset late to school?
   (c) What is a typical number of times students were late to school?

3.3 For the following variables in the NELS dataset, indicate the most appropriate set of summary statistics for summarizing the distribution: (1) frequencies or percentages and mode, (2) median and interquartile range, (3) median, interquartile range, and skewness ratio, (4) mean, standard deviation, and skewness ratio. Your answers should depend upon the level of measurement of the variable as well as the extent to which extreme values are present in the distribution to influence unduly the value of these summary statistics.

   (a) gender
   (b) urban
   (c) schtyp8
   (d) tcherint
   (e) numinst
   (f) achrdg08
   (g) schattrt
   (h) absent12

3.4 The variable cigarett is a dichotomous variable coded 1 for those who have not smoked and 2 for those who have.

(a) Compute the proportion of those that ever smoked based on the number from the percentage distribution.

(b) Compute the mean of cigarett after subtracting 1 from the variable (which recodes the variable from 1 and 2 to 0 and 1, respectively). Interpret the mean in view of the result of part (a).

(c) Do a greater proportion of males or females report having ever smoked?

3.5 In this exercise, we examine measures of central tendency for the variable CIGPDAY3 in the Framingham dataset.

(a) Create a boxplot showing the distribution of the number of cigarettes smoked per day (CIGPDAY3). Comment upon the presence of outliers in the distribution. Based on the graph, how many cigarettes per day do you think a typical person in the dataset smokes?

(b) Calculate and report the values for the mean and median of CIGPDAY3.

(c) Which measure of central tendency, mean or median, gives a better description of the number of cigarettes smoked per day by people in the Framingham dataset? Why do you suppose that is?

3.6 In this exercise, we examine the gender difference in the glucose levels of individuals in the Framingham dataset, taking into account the presence of one extreme male outlier.

(a) Create a boxplot showing the distribution of glucose levels (GLUCOSE3) by gender (SEX). Comment upon the presence of outliers in the two distributions.

(b) Are there gender differences in glucose levels within the Framingham dataset? Provide statistical support for your answer.

3.7 It was noted in this chapter that when a unimodal continuous distribution is positively skewed, the mean is generally larger than the median given that extreme values influence the value of the mean more than they do the value of the median. While there are rare exceptions to this rule in the case when a variable is many-valued, in other cases, as exemplified by this exercise, exceptions are more common.

(a) Create a bar plot of the numeric encoding of the variable tcherint from the NELS dataset, which contains only four possible values. According to the bar plot, what is the shape of the distribution?

(b) Which is larger, the mean of tcherint, or the median?

Exercise 3.8 involves measures of dispersion and the NELS dataset.

3.8 Which measure(s) of dispersion or variability (range, interquartile range, standard deviation, or variance), if any, may be used appropriately to measure the spread of the following variables from the NELS dataset? Report these values. In stating your answer, take into account both the level of measurement of the variable and whether there are extreme values in its distribution that could unduly influence the value of certain dispersion statistics, making them less representative of the distribution as a whole.

(a) gender

(b) urban

(c) numinst

    (d) achrdg08
    (e) schattrt
    (f) absent12

Exercises 3.9–3.14 involve selecting a relevant R procedure and calculating and interpreting a variety of appropriate summary statistics using variables from the NELS dataset.

3.9 Use R to find the following summary descriptive statistics for a student's self-concept in eighth grade (slfcnc08).
    (a) Minimum
    (b) Maximum
    (c) 40th percentile
    (d) 25th percentile
    (e) Mean
    (f) Median
    (g) Mode
    (h) Range
    (i) Interquartile range
    (j) Variance
    (k) Standard deviation
    (l) Skewness
    (m) Standard error of the skewness (seskew)

3.10 The following questions investigate how, among the students in the NELS dataset, tenth grade math achievement (achmat10) is related to whether or not the student's family owned a computer when he or she was in eighth grade (computer). Use R to generate the values of appropriate statistics to answer the related questions.
    (a) Compare the shape of the distributions of achmat10 for those who did and those who did not own a computer in eighth grade. Begin by constructing boxplots of achmat10, with one for each value of computer, and follow up by calculating skewness ratios.
    (b) Is tenth grade math achievement typically higher or lower for students whose families owned a computer when they were in eighth grade than for students whose families did not own a computer when they were in eighth grade? Explain and support your answer with the value of at least one appropriate descriptive statistic, indicating if any other statistics contradict your conclusion.
    (c) Among students in the NELS dataset, is tenth grade math achievement more or less variable for students whose families owned a computer when they were in eighth grade? Explain and support your answer with the value of at least one appropriate descriptive statistic, indicating if any other statistics contradict your conclusion.

3.11 This exercise addresses differences in socioeconomic status (ses) by urbanicity (urban) for students in the NELS dataset. Use R to generate the descriptive statistics that will be used for answering the following questions.
    (a) Describe the shape of ses for each of the three levels of urban.
    (b) Students from which type of urbanicity have the highest typical socioeconomic status: those from urban, suburban, or rural settings? Support your answer with appropriate descriptive statistics, indicating whether all such statistics support your conclusion.

(c) For what type of setting is the socioeconomic status of the students most dispersed: urban, suburban, or rural settings? Support your answer with appropriate descriptive statistics, indicating whether all such statistics support your conclusion.

(d) In what type of setting does the person with the highest socioeconomic status live, urban, suburban, or rural?

3.12 Answer the following questions to compare eighth grade self-concept (slfcnc08) to twelfth grade self-concept (slfcnc12) for students in the NELS dataset.

(a) Is the distribution of self-concept scores in the NELS dataset severely skewed in either eighth or twelfth grade? If the distribution is severely skewed, indicate the direction of the skew. If the distributions are severely skewed, indicate which is more skewed. Explain and support your answer using the value(s) of at least one appropriate statistic.

(b) Do students in the NELS dataset typically have higher self-concept scores in eighth or twelfth grade? Explain and support your answer with the value(s) of at least one appropriate statistic.

(c) Are the self-concept scores of students in the NELS dataset more heterogeneous in eighth or twelfth grade? Explain and support your answer with the value(s) of at least one appropriate statistic.

3.13 In this exercise, we explore differences between males and females on three variables in the NELS dataset: one affective, another cognitive, and the third behavioral.

(a) Are males and females similar in terms of the extent to which they believe teachers show an interest in them (tcherint)? Use R to obtain a comparison of measures of central tendency for these interest scores across gender.

(b) Do males and females display similar patterns of change in achievement in reading across eighth (achrdg08), tenth (achrdg10), and twelfth grades (achrdg12)? Use R to obtain a comparison of measures of central tendency for these achievement scores across grades.

(c) Do males and females have similar patterns of school attendance in grade 12 as measured by absent12, late12, and cuts12? Does one gender report greater incidents of absenteeism, lateness, or cutting than the other? Given the ordinal nature of these three variables, use R to calculate the median and interquartile range for all three variables by gender.

3.14 Taking advanced math in eighth grade is often thought to be a proxy for being a more serious student who is on a college-bound track. In this exercise, we explore differences on a number of academic and non-academic variables between those who did and did not take advanced math in eighth grade (advmath8).

(a) Do those who took advanced math in eighth grade report having spent more time per week on homework outside of school in twelfth grade (hwkout12) than those who did not take advanced math in eighth grade? Construct a boxplot for each group and follow-up with appropriate descriptive statistics for this ordinal variable.

(b) Do those who took advanced math in eighth grade report typically fewer incidents of absenteeism in twelfth grade (absent12) than those who did not take advanced math in eighth grade? Construct a boxplot for each group and follow-up with appropriate descriptive statistics for this ordinal variable.

(c) Is there a difference between those who took advanced math in eighth grade and those who did not in terms of the number of post-secondary institutions they attended (numinst). Recall that numinst is a ratio-leveled variable. Begin by constructing histograms and then follow-up with descriptive statistics.

Exercises 3.15–3.16 are based on datasets other than NELS and relate to a variety of summary statistics.

3.15 Create a stem-and-leaf plot of the variable readcomp from the Learndis dataset. Use it to answer the following questions.

(a) What term best describes the shape of this distribution: positively skewed, negatively skewed, or symmetric?

(b) What is the mode reading comprehension score for these students? If there is more than one mode, report them all.

(c) What is the maximum reading comprehension score for these students?

(d) Without calculating, which is probably larger for these students, the mean reading comprehension score or the median comprehension score? Explain.

(e) Without calculating it, which statistic would probably be best to summarize the spread of this distribution? Explain.

(f) Which boxplot below (A, B, or C) best describes the data in the stem-and-leaf plot?

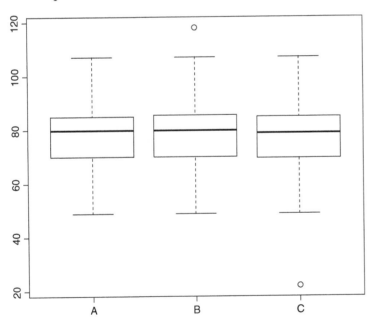

3.16 This question explores variables from the Framingham dataset. Provide a demographic assessment by sex of this sample of individuals at baseline with respect to the following variables.

(a) Age (AGE1)

(b) Total Serum Cholesterol (TOTCHOL1)

(c) Blood Pressure (Systolic and Diastolic) (SYSBP1 and DIABP1)

(d) BMI (BMI1)

(e) Current Cigarette Smoker (CURSMOKE1)

Exercises 3.17–3.19 require some computation by hand to reinforce your understanding of how the values provided by R are derived. In so doing, we believe that your conceptual understanding of these descriptive statistics will be enhanced.

3.17 Use the Statisticians dataset in this exercise.

(a) Calculate the mean, median, mode, range, interquartile range, variance, and standard deviation of the variable AmStat by hand.

(b) Use R to check your answers to part (a).

(c) Demonstrate that the sum of the deviations about the mean equals 0.

3.18 The following distribution of initial blood pressure values comes from the Blood dataset.

107	110	123	129	112	111	107	112	135	102	123
109	112	102	98	114	119	112	110	117	130	

(a) Calculate the mean, median, mode, range, interquartile range, variance, and standard deviation of the distribution by hand.

(b) Calculate the mean, median, mode, range, interquartile range, variance, and standard deviation of the distribution using R.

3.19 Create a frequency distribution table of the variable grade from the Learndis dataset. Use it to answer the following questions.

(a) Estimate Q_{25}, Q_{50}, and Q_{75} for this distribution based on the frequency distribution table.

(b) Estimate the interquartile range for this distribution.

(c) Suppose an error were found in the data, and two of the cases classified as second graders were really first graders. After the data is corrected, which of the mode, median, and mean will have changed, and in which direction?

Exercises 3.20–3.39 test your conceptual understanding and do not require the use of R.

3.20 For a sample of size 12, the mean is 4, the median is 5, and the mode is 6. Is it true that the sum of the raw scores is 36?

3.21 For each of parts (a)–(f), create a (possibly different) dataset with five numbers from −5 to 5 (with repeats allowed) for which:

(a) The mean, median, and mode are all equal.

(b) The mean is greater than the median.

(c) The mode is higher than the median or mean.

(d) The mean is 0.

(e) The standard deviation is as small as possible.

(f) The distribution is negatively skewed.

3.22 Three different people correctly report the typical wage of a group of five wage earners to be $5,000, $7,000, and $10,000. Explain how this is possible. Find a set of five wages that can correctly be said to have these three measures of location.

3.23 Show that a distribution with a higher mean does not necessarily have a higher standard deviation. Construct two distributions, X and Y, with two scores each, so that X has the larger mean and Y has the larger standard deviation.

3.24 Show that a distribution with a higher mean does not necessarily have a higher median. Construct two distributions, X and Y, so that X has the larger mean and Y has the larger median.

3.25 Show that a distribution with more values does not necessarily have a higher standard deviation. Construct two distributions, X and Y, so that X has more values in its distribution, but Y has the larger standard deviation.

3.26 Construct a distribution X for which the mode is not the majority response.

3.27 Is it possible for the standard deviation of a distribution to be more than half the range? Explain.

3.28 Show that a symmetric distribution exists for which the mean does not equal the mode, by sketching the graph of such a distribution.

3.29 Show that a distribution can have outliers and still be symmetric, by sketching the graph of such a distribution.

3.30 Show that a distribution with a higher maximum does not necessarily have a higher mean. Construct two distributions, X and Y, so that X has a higher maximum value, but Y has a higher mean.

3.31 Show that a skewed distribution can be consistent. Construct two distributions, X and Y, so that X is less skewed, but Y is more consistent.

3.32 Show that a skewed distribution can contain low typical scores. Construct two distributions, X and Y, so that X is more skewed, but Y has a larger mean.

3.33 Answer the following questions about statistics reported in the March 2013 article, "TheKnot.com and WeddingChannel.com Reveal Results of Largest Wedding Study of its Kind, Surveying more than 17,500 Brides." The relevant information is contained in the questions themselves, but the interested reader may look up the article at https://prn.to/3a5mn04.

    (a) According to the survey, the average wedding budget in 2012 was $28,427, excluding honeymoon. If someone wanted to encourage you to spend as much as possible on your wedding, which would be better to report, the mean or the median? Explain.

    (b) The average marrying age for brides in the US is 29. Do you think that the standard deviation is closer to 3 days, 3 months, or 3 years? Explain.

3.34 Consider the distribution, for all children in the United States, of the ages at which they enter kindergarten. Do you think that the standard deviation of this distribution is closer to 5 years or 5 months? Explain.

3.35 Assume that on a final exam, the raw scores for student performance were severely negatively skewed.

    (a) What is probably true about the performances of the students in the class on the exam?

    (b) If the exam were to be curved, which is preferable from a student perspective: that the median be set to a B− or that the mean be set to a B−?

3.36 Match each set of summary statistics (A, B, C, D, E) with the corresponding histogram (X1, X2, X3, X4, X5) below. Computations are not necessary to complete this exercise.

	A	B	C	D	E
Mean	4.5	5	5	5.5	6
Standard Deviation	1.96	1.23	82	1.96	1.23

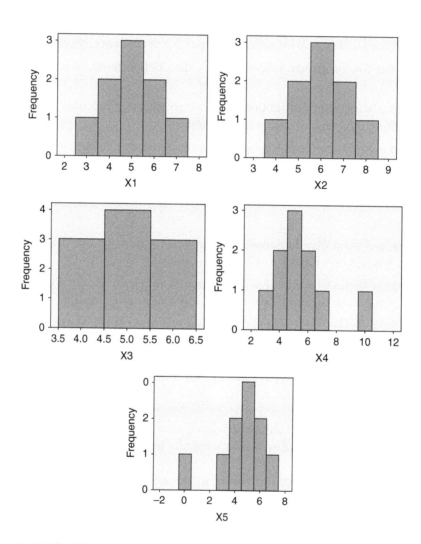

3.37 The following excerpt was taken from an editorial by Paul Krugman in the *New York Times* on January 21, 2003 (p. 23):

On Saturday, in his weekly radio address, George W. Bush declared that "the tax relief I propose will give 23 million small-business owners an average tax cut of $2,042 this year." That remark is intended to give the impression that the typical small-business owner will get $2,000. But as the Center on Budget and Policy Priorities points out, most small businesses will get a tax break of less than $500; about 5 million of those 23 million small businesses will get no break at all. The average is more than $2,000 only because a small number of very wealthy businessmen will get huge tax cuts.

(a) What is the shape of the distribution of tax cuts for small business owners?

(b) What would you guess is the value of the median of the distribution of tax cuts for small business owners?

(c) Would you suppose that the standard deviation is smaller or larger than $500? Explain.

3.38 Among women in the US aged 40–49, would you expect the mean number of living children per woman to be less than, greater than, or about the same as the median number of living children per woman? Explain your answer.

3.39 Assume your course average is based on a midterm exam worth 100 points and a final exam that also is worth 100 points. Assume also that the midterm exam counts for 40 percent of your course average and the final exam counts for 60 percent of your course average. If you scored 80 on the midterm exam and 85 on the final exam, what is your average grade for the course?

# CHAPTER FOUR

RE-EXPRESSING VARIABLES

Often, variables in their original form do not lend themselves well to comparison with other variables or to certain types of analysis. In addition, often we may obtain greater insight by expressing a variable in a different form. For these and other reasons, in this chapter we discuss four different ways to re-express or transform variables: applying linear transformations, applying nonlinear transformations, recoding, and combining. We also describe how to use syntax (.R) files to manage your data analysis.

LINEAR AND NONLINEAR TRANSFORMATIONS

In Chapter 1 we discussed measurement as the assignment of numbers to objects to reflect the amount of a particular trait such objects possess. For example, a number in inches may be assigned to a person to reflect how tall that person is. Of course, without loss of information, a number in feet or even in meters, can be assigned instead.

What we will draw upon in this section is the notion that the numbers themselves used to measure a particular trait, whether they be in inches, feet, or meters, for example, are not intrinsic to the trait itself. Rather, they are mere devices for helping us to understand the trait or other phenomenon we are studying. Accordingly, if an alternative numeric system, or *metric* (as a numeric system is called), can be used more effectively than the original one, then this metric should be substituted, as long as it retains whatever properties of the original system we believe are important. In making this change on a univariate basis, each number in the new system will correspond on a one-to-one basis to each number in the original system. That is, each number in the new system will be able to be matched uniquely to one and only one number in the original system.

The rule that defines the one-to-one correspondence between the numeric systems is called the *transformation*. Transformations may be classified according to the properties they retain of the original system. When transformations retain the order of data points in the original system, they are called *monotonic transformations*. In this chapter, we will confine discussion of transformations to monotonic transformations because, in the work we do in the behavioral and social sciences, ordinality is an important feature of a dataset worth retaining. This section is devoted to two types of monotonic transformation: *linear* and *nonlinear*. In short, a linear transformation preserves or reflects the shape of the original distribution, while a nonlinear transformation is often used to change the shape of the original distribution.

LINEAR TRANSFORMATIONS: ADDITION, SUBTRACTION, MULTIPLICATION, AND DIVISION

Linear transformations are defined by rules that include only a combination of multiplication, division, addition, and subtraction to set up the one-to-one correspondence between numeric systems. For example, suppose we are interested in studying the relative heights of professional basketball players in the United States and Italy. If we used the original numbers for measuring the players' heights in both countries, these numbers would not be comparable because of the different measurement systems used in the two countries. (In the United States, height is measured in inches or feet; in Italy, it is measured in centimeters or meters.) *To obtain comparability of measures*, a more appropriate approach might be to express the heights of the US players in centimeters rather than in inches. To do so, we need only multiply the values of height in inches by 2.54, since there are 2.54 centimeters per inch.

EXAMPLE 4.1 Use the Basketball dataset to re-express in centimeters the heights of the 20 scoring leaders, 10 each from the US Women's and Men's National Basketball Association, for the 2014–2015 season. Use the following arithmetic operation to do so.

height (in centimeters) = height (in inches) * 2.54

Solution The heights in inches and the heights re-expressed in centimeters are presented below.

Name	Height in inches (Heightin)	Height in centimeters (Height_cm)
Maya Moore	72	182.88
Skylar Diggins	69	175.26
Candace Parker	76	193.04
Angel McCoughtry	73	185.42
Tina Charles	76	193.04
Diana Taurasi	72	182.88
Seimone Augustus	72	182.88
Nneka Ogwumike	74	187.96
Odyssey Sims	68	172.72
Chiney Ogwumike	76	193.04
Kevin Durant	81	205.74
Carmelo Anthony	80	203.20
LeBron James	80	203.20
Kevin Love	82	208.28
James Harden	77	195.58
Blake Griffin	82	208.28
Stephen Curry	75	190.50
LaMarcus Aldridge	83	210.82
DeMarcus Cousins	83	210.82
DeMar DeRozan	79	200.66

We may use R to perform the computation to re-express the original values of height.

MORE R: To transform height in inches (Heightin) to height in centimeters (Height_cm), after opening the Basketball dataset, type:

Basketball$Height_cm = Basketball$heightin * 2.54

in the console and hit **Enter**.

The variable Height_cm will be added to your dataset as the last variable.

Because the rule for re-expressing inches as centimeters involves multiplying every value in the distribution by a positive constant, it is an example of a *linear transformation*. Notice that the order of data points has been retained under this transformation. Angel McCoughtry is taller than Diana Taurasi regardless of whether their heights are measured in inches or in centimeters.

While this linear transformation involves multiplication only, linear transformations may involve multiplication, addition, or a combination of multiplication and addition. The general form of a linear transformation may be expressed as:

$$X_{new} = K * X_{old} + C, \qquad\qquad (4.1)$$

where K and C are constants and $K \neq 0$. It is worth pointing out that K represents both multiplication and division. For example, when $K = 1/2$, multiplication by K is equivalent to division by 2. Also, C represents both addition and subtraction. For example, when $C = -4$, adding C units is equivalent to subtracting 4 units. K changes the scale of the original values, either by stretching (when K is less than -1 or greater than 1) or compressing (when K is between -1 and $+1$) the horizontal axis, while C translates the location of the original values either up (when C is positive) or down (when C is negative) along the horizontal axis. Figure 4.1 illustrates a linear transformation where $K = 2$ and $C = 10$. Notice that the scale of the new values is doubled (with each unit increase in X, there is a two-unit increase

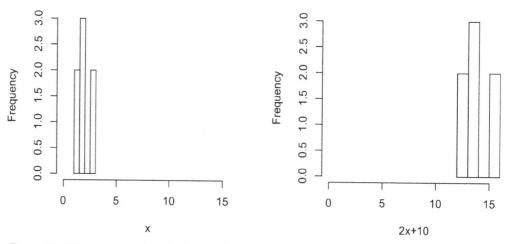

Figure 4.1 Histograms of original values and linearly transformed values ($2X + 10$).

in 2X + 10) and the location of the new values is shifted in a positive direction along the horizontal axis from 2 to 14 (2*2 + 10).

Linear transformations are so named because, as Equation 4.1 suggests, the new values are a linear function of the original values.

THE EFFECT ON THE SHAPE OF A DISTRIBUTION

Linear transformations not only retain the order of points in a distribution, but they also retain the relative distance between points in a distribution. That is, two points that are far from one another under the original numeric system will be as far from one another to the same relative extent under the new system. In our example, Diana Taurasi's height is closer to Angel McCoughtry's height than to Nneka Ogwumike's height to the same relative extent in both inches and centimeters. Because relative distance does not change under linear transformation, neither does the general shape of a distribution under linear transformation.

••

EXAMPLE 4.2 Construct boxplots of both distributions of height (in inches and in centimeters). Comment on the shape of these two distributions as represented by the histograms.

Solution Create boxplots of Heightin and Height_cm using R.

Clearly, the two boxplots shown in Figure 4.2 have the same shape. By transforming the data linearly from inches to centimeters, the general shape of a distribution remains the same, although the central tendency and spread can change, as they have in this example.

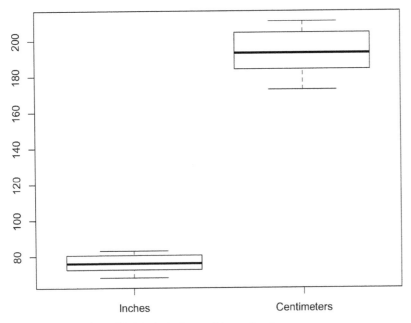

Figure 4.2 Boxplots of height in inches and in centimeters

MORE R: To generate the boxplots in Figure 4.2, including the addition of labels to each of the boxplots, type the following command into the console and press **Enter**:

boxplot(Basketball$heightin, Basketball$Height_cm, names = c("Inches", "Centimeters"))

Note that the first two arguments tell R which variables to plot, and the names argument labels each boxplot accordingly.

THE EFFECT ON SUMMARY STATISTICS OF A DISTRIBUTION

While under linear transformation, the general shape of a distribution remains the same, the summary characteristics of a distribution do not. Notice the difference in central tendency or level and spread values for the two boxplots pictured in Figure 4.2. More specifically, the mean height in centimeters (193.29) equals the mean height in inches (76.10) multiplied by 2.54, and the standard deviation of the height in centimeters (9.99) equals the standard deviation of the height in inches (3.93) multiplied by 2.54. In other words, both the mean and standard deviation are multiplied by 2.54, the value by which the heights themselves were multiplied.

While the new standard deviation is larger than the original standard deviation by a factor of 2.54, the new variance will be larger than the original variance by a factor of 2.54^2, or 6.45. Because the old variance was 3.93^2 or 15.44, the new variance, equals 6.45*15.44 or 99.61.

The boxplots depicted in Figure 4.3 give another example of a multiplicative transformation. In this case, we have created side-by-side boxplots of slfcnc12, the self-concept

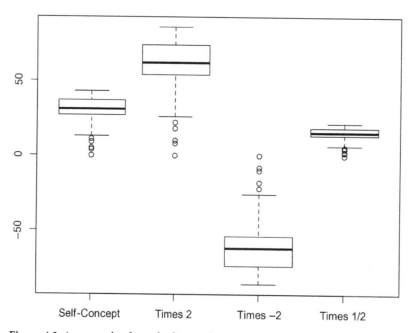

Figure 4.3 An example of a multiplicative linear transformation using the NELS dataset

scores of the students in the NELS dataset from twelfth grade, 2*slfcnc12, (−2)*slfcnc12, and (1/2)*slfcnc12. Looking at the level, spread, and shape of these boxplots, we can see certain patterns emerging. The level, or central tendency, of the distribution is given by the median of the boxplot. Here we see that the operation that was performed on every score was also performed on the median. So, the median of the original untransformed variable slfcnc12 is about 30. After multiplying every score in the distribution by two to obtain the second boxplot from the left, we see that the median is now around 60, which is twice what it was for the untransformed variable. Similarly, the median for the third boxplot from the left is approximately −60, or negative two times the untransformed median, and the median for the fourth boxplot is approximately 15, or one-half times the untransformed median. The spread is given by the interquartile range (IQR) of the distribution. Here we see that when multiplying every score by a number, the IQR is then multiplied by the absolute value of that number. In the case of the untransformed self-concept given in the leftmost boxplot, the IQR is approximately 10. When every score is multiplied by two, resulting in the second boxplot from the left, the IQR is approximately 20. In the third boxplot from the left, we note that the IQR is still positive, even though the distribution has been multiplied by a negative number. All measures of spread are always positive numbers. Even though every score was multiplied by negative 2, the resulting IQR is now 20, or twice what it was originally. Finally, the IQR for the fourth boxplot is 5, or one-half the untransformed value. We can look intuitively at the shape, because it is not possible to estimate the size of the skewness or skewness ratio from the boxplot. In this case we see that when K is positive, the direction of the skew is preserved, and when K is negative, the direction of the skew is reversed. In fact, the magnitude of the skew does not change under a linear transformation: only, potentially, the sign.

MORE R: There are three ways to generate the boxplots in Figure 4.3.

First, we can put the mathematical transformation of **NELS$slfcnc12** directly into the **boxplot** command, as follows:

boxplot(NELS$slfcnc12, NELS$slfcnc12*2, NELS$slfcnc12*(−2), NELS$slfcnc12*(1/ 2), names = c("Self Concept", "Times 2", "Times −2", "Times 1/2"))

However, if we would like to save these transformed variables in order to do further operations on them (e.g. calculate a mean or a median), we can save them *locally*, by creating three new variables. This can be done as follows:

times2 = NELS$slfcnc12*2
timesminus2 = NELS$slfcnc12*(−2)
timeshalf = NELS$slfcnc12*(1/2)
boxplot(NELS$slfcnc12, times2, timesminus2, timeshalf, names = c("Self Concept", "Times 2", "Times −2", "Times 1/2"))

Alternatively, we can add each of these variables to the NELS dataset by adding the prefix **NELS$** to each variable name as shown below:

NELS$times2 = NELS$slfcnc12*2
NELS$timesminus2 = NELS$slfcnc12*(−2)

NELS$timeshalf = NELS$slfcnc12*(1/2)
boxplot(NELS$slfcnc12, NELS$times2, NELS$timesminus2, NELS$timeshalf, names = c("Self Concept", "Times 2", "Times −2", "Times 1/2"))

However, even when using the **NELS$** prefix, the variables are not permanently saved to the dataset. When R is reopened, these variables would need to be regenerated. Therefore, at the end of this chapter we introduce the .R file, which allows us to keep track of all steps necessary to perform an analysis.

More generally, the effects on the measures of central tendency, spread, and shape of a distribution when multiplying all the values in a distribution by a nonzero constant, K, are summarized as follows.

When $X_{new} = K^*X_{old}$

1. For measures of central tendency:
    $Mode_{new} = K^*Mode_{old}$
    $Median_{new} = K^*Median_{old}$
    $Mean_{new} = K^*Mean_{old}$
2. For measures of spread:
    $IQR_{new} = |K|^*IQR_{old}$
    $SD_{new} = |K|^*SD_{old}$
    $Range_{New} = |K|^*Range_{old}$
    $Variance_{new} = K^2 *Variance_{old}$
3. For measures of shape the result depends on the sign of K:
    If K is positive:
    $Skewness_{new} = Skewness_{old}$
    $Skewness\ Ratio_{new} = Skewness\ Ratio_{Old}$
    If K is negative:
    $Skewness_{new} = (−1)^*Skewness_{old}$
    $Skewness\ Ratio_{new} = (−1)^*Skewness\ Ratio_{old}$

The boxplots depicted in Figure 4.4 give an example of an additive transformation. In this case, we have created side-by-side boxplots of slfcnc12, the self-concept scores of the students in the NELS dataset from twelfth grade, slfcnc12+5 and slfcnc12−5. Looking at the level, spread, and shape of these boxplots, we can see certain patterns emerging. The level, or central tendency, of the distribution is given by the median of the boxplot. Here we see that the operation that was performed on every score was also performed on the median. So, the median of the original untransformed variable slfcnc12 is about 30. After adding 5 to every score to obtain the second boxplot from the left, we see that the median is now around 35, which is five more than what it was for the untransformed variable. Similarly, the median for the third boxplot from the left is approximately 25, or five less than the untransformed median. The spread is given by the *IQR* of the distribution. Here we see that when adding or subtracting we do not change the spread of the distribution. In the case of the untransformed self-concept given in the leftmost boxplot, the *IQR* is approximately 10, and it is the same for both of the transformed boxplots as well. Similarly, the shape of the boxplot is unchanged by the transformation, and we see

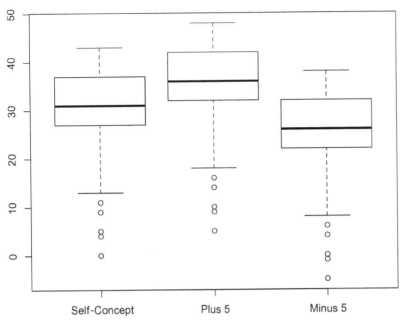

Figure 4.4 An example of an additive linear transformation using the NELS dataset

that both the skewness and skewness ratio of the transformed variables are the same as for the original.

We see that another type of linear transformation is adding a constant, C, to all values in a distribution. The effects on summary statistics of this type of transformation are summarized as follows.

When $X_{new} = X_{old} + C$
1. For measures of central tendency:
   $Mode_{new} = Mode_{old} + C$
   $Median_{New} = Median_{old} + C$
   $Mean_{New} = Mean_{old} + C$
2. For measures of spread:
   $IQR_{new} = IQR_{old}$
   $SD_{New} = SD_{old}$
   $Range_{new} = Range_{old}$
   $Variance_{New} = Variance_{old}$
3. For measures of shape:
   $Skewness_{new} = Skewness_{old}$
   $Skewness\ Ratio_{new} = Skewness\ Ratio_{old}$

COMMON LINEAR TRANSFORMATIONS

In this section, we present examples of three common types of linear transformation: Translation, reflection, and standard scores. Among standard scores, we will make the most use of z-scores.

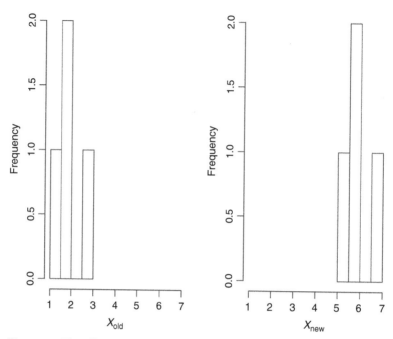

Figure 4.5 The effect of adding the value 4 to each data point in a distribution

● ●

EXAMPLE 4.3 Using the dataset 1, 2, 2, 3, show graphically and numerically the effects of adding 4 to all points in this dataset.

Solution Let X_{old} = 1, 2, 2, 3 and X_{new} = 5, 6, 6, 7. A graphical representation of the distributions of X_{old} and X_{new} are given in Figure 4.5.

Notice that the distributions are identical but for their location. In particular, the standard deviation, range, interquartile range, and variance of X_{new} equal the respective standard deviation and variance of X_{old}, but the mean, median, and mode of X_{new} are 4 points higher than the respective mean, median, and mode of X_{old}. In other words, X_{new} is X_{old} shifted along the axis 4 points to the right.

A linear transformation that shifts a distribution along the horizontal axis is called a *translation*. One type of translation that we will make use of in Chapter 17 is called *centering*, in which the mean of the distribution is subtracted from each of the scores.

● ●

EXAMPLE 4.4 Given that a survey was administered to 30 individuals that included the following as one of its items measuring assertiveness (the data for this item are contained in the dataset Likert):

Circle one value along the five-point scale below to indicate your degree of agreement with the statement: "I have the ability to stand up for my own rights without denying the rights of others."

strongly agree	agree	neutral	disagree	strongly disagree
1	2	3	4	5

Notice that on this scale, high scores are associated with low levels of assertiveness. This scoring could be considered to be illogical. Find a linear transformation that reverses the scores on this scale so that, instead, high scores associate with high levels of assertiveness, and low scores associate with low levels of assertiveness. Keep the range of values from 1 to 5.

Solution Multiplying all values in the distribution by −1 will convert the scale scores from 1 to 5 to −5 to −1 so that, now, the higher (the less negative) the value, the more assertive the response. Adding 6 to each value shifts the scale along the horizontal axis from −5 through −1 to 1 through 5, as desired. On this new scale, a value of 5 now corresponds to the response "strongly agree" and a response of 1 now corresponds to a response of "strongly disagree." On this new scale, the higher the score, the greater the assertiveness. Alternatively, we could have achieved the same result by subtracting each value in the scale from the value 6.

MORE R: To reflect the variable assert, type

Likert\$assertref = −1 * Likert\$Assertiveness + 6

in the console and press **Enter**.
    The new variable assertref will be added as a new variable to the Likert dataset until R is closed.

☞ **Remark.** Any time the values of a scale are multiplied by −1, the new values on the scale will be mirror images of the original values. As a result, this type of transformation is called a *reflection*. Values that were low on the original scale are now high on the new scale, and values that were high on the original scale are now low on the new scale. Because the values on the new scale are based on a reversed direction of scoring, caution must be exercised when interpreting results based on scales that have been reflected.

STANDARD SCORES

In addition to enhancing the comparability of values measured in different units, data are often linearly transformed to give meaning to individual scores within a distribution. For example, an SAT verbal score of 750 carries with it its own meaning relative to the distribution of individuals who have taken this test. Said differently, if you were told that on a recently administered SAT test you scored 750, you would not ask, "Is that a good score?" You would know already, by the score itself, that you performed better than the vast majority of other SAT test-takers. You would know this because SAT scores are an example of what are called *standard scores*. By contrast to raw scores that reveal nothing about the relative standing of a score within a distribution, standard scores convey meaning about relative standing because they are linked directly to the mean and standard deviation of the distribution of which they are a part.

TABLE 4.1 Means and standard deviations of commonly-used standard score systems

Standard score system	Mean	Standard deviation
Graduate Record Exam (GRE)	500	100
Intelligence Quotient (IQ)	100	15
Scholastic Aptitude Test (SAT)	500	100
T-scores	50	10
z-scores	0	1

In short, a standard score conveys how far above or below a raw score is from the mean of its distribution relative to the standard deviation of that distribution. Because the vast majority of scores of most distributions are clustered within two standard deviations of their means, scores that are approximately two standard deviations above the mean in a distribution are considered to be extremely high. Analogously, scores that are approximately two standard deviations below the mean in a distribution are considered to be extremely low. Scores that are at the mean fall zero standard deviations from the mean, and are considered to be average, or typical, scores in a distribution, and scores that fall between zero and two standard deviations away from the mean are considered to be somewhere between average and extreme.

Standard score systems, like the SAT, each have a specified mean and standard deviation. Table 4.1 provides the mean and standard deviation of each of several commonly used standard score systems.

To determine how many standard deviations from the mean the SAT score of 750 actually falls, we need to transform the SAT score linearly by performing a simple arithmetic operation. That is, we need to first subtract 500, the mean of the SAT score distribution, from 750 to find out how many SAT score units the score of 750 falls from the mean of 500. We then need to divide that difference by 100, the standard deviation of the SAT distribution, to determine how many standard deviations from the mean the score falls. This arithmetic operation is expressed as

$$\frac{750 - 500}{100} = \frac{250}{100} = 2.5. \tag{4.2}$$

According to Equation 4.2, an SAT verbal score of 750 is 2.5 standard deviations above the SAT verbal mean. A score that is 2.5 standard deviations above its mean surpasses the vast majority of scores in its distribution and is considered to be extremely high. This explains why, of course, a score of 750 would make some SAT test-taker quite happy.

Z-SCORES

Knowing the number of standard deviation distances a score is from the mean is quite informative and useful for locating a score within its distribution. Scores that have been re-expressed in terms of standard deviation distances from the mean are given a special name: *z-scores*. Because z-scores themselves convey the number of standard deviations a score is from the mean, a distribution of z-scores has, as Table 4.1 indicates, a mean of 0 and a standard deviation of 1. Any score may be re-expressed as a z-score by using Equation 4.3.

$$z = \frac{X - \overline{X}}{S}. \tag{4.3}$$

A comparison of Equation 4.3 with that of 4.2 suggests that in Equation 4.2 we converted the SAT verbal score of 750 to a z-score so that we could obtain the number of standard deviations the score was from the mean of 500. To convert an individual raw score to a z-score, one only needs the mean and standard deviation of the distribution of which the raw score is a part.

EXAMPLE 4.5 Determine the number of standard deviations away from the mean the following standard scores are:

1. an IQ score of 110;
2. a GRE score of 450;
3. a z-score of −2.

Solution

1. From Table 4.1, we know that the mean and standard deviation of an IQ scale are 100 and 15, respectively. We use Equation 4.3 to find that the z-score of an IQ score of 110 is

$$z = \frac{110 - 100}{15} = 0.67.$$

   In other words, an IQ score of 110 is 0.67 standard deviations above the IQ mean.
2. From Table 4.1, we know that the mean and standard deviation of the GRE scale are 500 and 100, respectively. We use Equation 4.3 to find that the z-score of a GRE score of 450 is

$$z = \frac{450 - 500}{100} = -0.50.$$

   In other words, a GRE score of 450 is one-half standard deviations below the GRE mean.
3. A z-score of −2 may be interpreted directly as being 2 standard deviations below the mean.

EXAMPLE 4.6 Determine the number of standard deviations away from the mean the following scores are:

1. a score of 90 on a test of Spanish fluency that has a mean of 85 and a standard deviation of 10;
2. a score of 30 on the ses scale from the NELS dataset;
3. all scores on the ses scale from the NELS dataset;
4. verify that the z-score distribution has mean 0 and standard deviation 1.

Solution

1. To find the number of standard deviations away from the mean a score of 90 is on a Spanish fluency test, we use Equation 4.3.

$$z = \frac{90 - 85}{10} = 0.50$$

A score of 90 on this test is one-half standard deviations above the mean in the distribution of Spanish fluency test scores.

2. Using R, we compute the mean and standard deviation of the ses distribution to be 18.43 and 6.92, respectively, when rounded to two decimal places. From Equation 4.3, we find the z-score equivalent of an ses score of 30 to be

$$z = \frac{30 - 18.43}{6.92} = 1.67$$

3. To transform all scores in the ses distribution to z-scores using R we use the **scale** command.

MORE R: Creating a standardized variable.

To standardize ses, for example, and to generate a new variable that contains the standardized values for ses, type:

NELS$zses = scale(NELS$ses)

in the console and press **Enter**.

---

4. To verify that zses has mean 0 and standard deviation 1, type: **mean(NELS$zses) and sd(NELS$zses)** in the console and press **Enter**. In the output, you see that the mean is given as $-1.476289e{-}16$, which is scientific notation for a number which is equal to zero when rounded to two decimal places. Also, the standard deviation is 1.00.

Thus, by transforming the scores of a distribution linearly into z-scores, we gain knowledge as to the placement of each score in that distribution relative to the mean and standard deviation of the scores in that distribution. Because conversion to z-scores involves a linear transformation, and because all linear transformations are monotonic, the order of scores in the original distribution is preserved in the z-score distribution. If Carolyn's score is higher than Allison's score in the original distribution, it will still be higher than Allison's score in the z-score distribution. In addition, because linear transformations preserve the relative distance between points in a distribution, the shape of a z-score distribution will be the same as that of the original distribution, except for possible stretching or shrinking along the horizontal axis.

Just as we can transform raw (or standard) scores to z-scores knowing the mean and standard deviation of the original distribution, we also can use Equation 4.3 to transform z-scores to raw (or standard scores) knowing the mean and standard deviation of the new distribution. Equation 4.3 can also be re-expressed so that it can be used directly to convert any z-score to its corresponding original score. Thus, any z-score may be converted to its corresponding raw score by using Equation 4.4.

$$X = Sz + \overline{X}. \tag{4.4}$$

EXAMPLE 4.7 Transform the following *z*-scores to raw scores within a distribution with a given mean and standard deviation:

1. a *z*-score of −2.5 on a test of Spanish fluency with mean 85 and standard deviation 10;
2. a *z*-score of −3 on the ses scale from the NELS dataset;
3. a *z*-score of 0 on the ses scale from the NELS dataset.

Solution

1. We use Equation 4.4 to find the Spanish fluency raw score equivalent of a *z*-score of −2.5 in a distribution with mean and standard deviation 85 and 10, respectively:

$$X = 10(-2.5) + 85$$
$$X = 60$$

2. We use Equation 4.4 to find the NELS ses raw score equivalent to a *z*-score of −3. Recall that the mean and standard deviation of the NELS ses distribution are 18.43 and 6.92, respectively.

$$X = 6.92(-3) + 18.43$$
$$X = -2.33$$

3. A *z*-score of 0 is at the mean of the *z*-score distribution. Therefore, the equivalent raw ses score would be equal to the mean of the ses distribution, 18.43. Of course, we could use Equation 4.4 to verify that this is the case.

Using z-Scores to Detect Outliers

In our discussion of boxplots in Chapter 2, we noted that R defines an outlier as a score that falls more than 1.5 *IQRs* beyond the 75th or 25th percentile. Because boxplots are based on resistant statistics, including the median, it makes sense to measure outliers in terms of *IQR* distances. In other contexts, when the location of a distribution is measured in terms of the mean, it makes sense to measure outliers in terms of standard deviation distances. Again, while there are no set conventions for defining outliers in terms of standard deviations, a reasonable approach is to call a score an outlier if it falls more than two standard deviations away from its distribution's mean; that is, if its *z*-score is greater than 2 in magnitude.

EXAMPLE 4.8 Using the variable slfcnc12 in the NELS dataset, which indicates the students' self-concept scores in twelfth grade, find the number of outliers in the distribution using:

1. the boxplot criterion (at least 1.5 *IQRs* above the 75th percentile or below the 25th percentile), and
2. the *z*-score criterion (at least two standard deviations away from the mean).

Solution

1. We create the boxplot depicted below using the command **boxplot(NELS$slfcnc12)** and count the number of circle outliers. In this case, we see that there are 5.

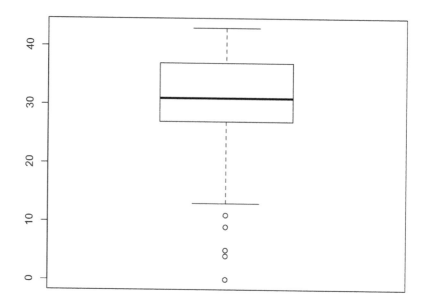

2. First we use the command **NELS\$zslfcnc12 = scale(NELS\$slfcnc12)** to convert all of the scores in the slfcnc12 distribution to z-scores and create a new variable (placed at the end of the dataset) called zslfcnc12 that contains these scores. We then perform an optional step to round each of the values in zslfcnc12 to three numbers after the decimal place, in order to make the following tables easier to read. To do this, we use the command:

NELS\$zslfcnc12 = round(NELS\$zslfcnc12,3)

We then create a frequency distribution of zslfcnc12 and add the frequencies for the entries that are less than −2 and greater than 2. In this case, we see that there are 17 (1 + 1 + 1 + 1 + 1 + 1 + 2 + 4 + 5). Alternatively, and more efficiently, we run the command:

table(NELS\$zslfcnc12[abs(NELS\$zslfcnc12) > 2])

Note that the **abs** function takes the absolute value of the variable in parentheses (namely, NELS\$zslfcnc12); the full command is instructing R to subset the original NELS\$zslfcnc12 down to those values that have an absolute value greater than 2 and then to create a frequency distribution table of these values.

Table of standardized slfcnc12 values:

−4.353	−3.8	−3.662	−3.109	−2.832	−2.556	−2.279	−2.141	−2.002	−1.726	−1.588
1	1	1	1	1	1	2	4	5	4	3
449	−1.311	−1.173	−1.034	−0.896	−0.758	−0.62	−0.481	−0.343	−0.205	−0.066
6	6	18	3	46	5	47	11	72	9	24
0.072	0.21	0.348	0.487	0.625	0.763	0.902	1.04	1.178	1.317	1.593
15	27	10	19	16	23	14	17	14	30	44

Table of zslfcnc12 values greater in absolute value than 2:

4.353	−3.8	−3.662	−3.109	−2.832	−2.556	−2.279	−2.141	−2.002
1	1	1	1	1	1	2	4	5

MORE R: Combining statements – using the relational operators & and | – we form expressions that combine statements using the relational operators & (and) and | (or). For example, instead of having used the command:

table(NELS$zslfcnc12[abs(NELS$zslfcnc12) > 2])

equivalently, we could have used the command:

table(NELS$zslfcnc12[NELS$zslfcnc12 > 2 | NELS$zslfcnc12 < −2])

Using z-Scores to Compare Scores in Different Distributions

In addition to using z-scores to determine the relative standing of a raw score within its own distribution, z-scores are often used to compare raw scores from different distributions. For such comparisons to be meaningful, however, the underlying raw score distributions must have similar shapes.

The boxplots in Figure 4.6, obtained using the command **boxplot(NELS$achrdg12~NELS$gender)**, show the distributions of twelfth grade reading achievement by gender. Notice both distributions are negatively skewed.

In order to find the means and standard deviations of a distribution broken down by subgroups, we may use the following summary statistics commands.

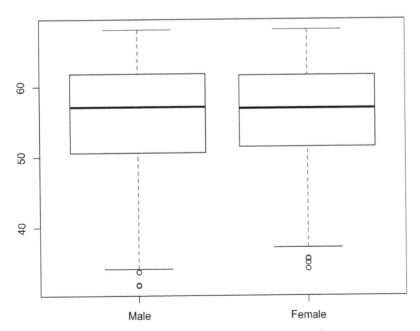

Figure 4.6 Boxplot of twelfth grade reading achievement by gender

TABLE 4.2 Means and standard deviations of twelfth grade reading achievement by gender		
Gender	Mean	Std. Dev.
Male	55.310352	8.560149
Female	55.844286	7.4803663

MORE R: To find means and standard deviations by subgroups, type the following commands into the console and press **Enter** after each:

mean(NELS$achrdg12[NELS$gender == "Male"])
sd(NELS$achrdg12[NELS$gender == "Male"])
mean(NELS$achrdg12[NELS$gender == "Female"])
sd(NELS$achrdg12[NELS$gender == "Female"])

The output from the above four commands is given in Table 4.2.

Consider Pat who scored 65. Did Pat score better relative to the males or the females in the dataset? Pat scored above the mean in both groups, and scored more points above the male mean than the female mean. However, when deciding in which group the score is further above the mean *relative to the scores in the group*, we should take into consideration the spread of the scores in the distributions. One way to do so is to calculate z-scores:

$$\text{relative to the males}: z = \frac{65 - 55.3104}{8.5601} = 1.13$$

$$\text{relative to the females}: z = \frac{65 - 55.8443}{7.4804} = 1.22.$$

Because 1.22 exceeds 1.13, we see that Pat performed better relative to the females. The score of 65 is 1.22 standard deviations above the mean for the females and only 1.13 standard deviations above the mean for the males.

Relating z-Scores to Percentile Ranks

In the previous section, we looked at the use of z-scores to compare scores in different distributions. Recall that for such comparisons to be meaningful, however, the underlying raw score distributions must have similar shapes. It is not even enough, as the following example illustrates, for the two raw score distributions to have the same mean and standard deviation. If the raw score distributions do not have similar shapes, the same z-scores may correspond to different percentile ranks, undermining the utility of z-scores in comparing raw scores from different distributions. Consider that two tests, math and English, have been administered to the same individuals and that their score distributions are as in Table 4.3.

These two distributions do not have similar shapes. The math distribution is

TABLE 4.3 Distributions of math and English achievement	
Math achievement	English achievement
2 3 3 3 4 4 4 8 9 10	0 1 2 6 6 6 7 7 7 8

positively skewed; the English distribution is negatively skewed. (You might want to construct a histogram for each distribution to convince yourself of this.) Both math and English distributions have means of 5 and standard deviations of 2.72. (You may want to convince yourself of this as well.) Therefore, in each distribution, a raw score of 8 corresponds to a z-score of

$$z = \frac{X - \overline{X}}{S} = \frac{8 - 5}{2.72} = \frac{3}{2.72} = 1.10.$$

But, in the math distribution, the percentile rank of a score of 8 is 70 (as estimated by the cumulative percentage), whereas in the English distribution the percentile rank of a score of 8 is 90. While a comparison based on z-scores suggests that an individual with a raw score of 8 on both math and English tests has the same performance on these exams relative to the two distributions, this is not the case. Because these two distributions are dissimilar in shape, the more appropriate comparison of performance is based on percentile ranks. Based on percentile ranks, a score of 8 represents a higher score in English than in math for this group of students.

In sum, when the shapes of distributions are not known to be similar, percentile ranks are a better scoring system than z-scores for comparing scores between distributions.

NONLINEAR TRANSFORMATIONS: SQUARE ROOTS AND LOGARITHMS

As we have seen, statistics, like the mean and standard deviation, do not characterize well the bulk of values in a highly skewed distribution. To remedy this situation, in the previous chapter, we eliminated the two extreme values in the right tail of the expected income at age 30 distribution. In so doing, we shortened the long right tail and made this once highly positively skewed distribution more symmetric. As a result, the mean and standard deviation corroborated with the other, more resistant numeric summaries of location and spread, making the job of describing the bulk of our data easier and more accurate.

By making a distribution more symmetric, we avoid the problem of having a small number of extreme values highly influence the numeric summaries that characterize a dataset. For this reason and others, it is advantageous to symmetrize distributions. But, as we have observed previously, we are often not justified in making distributions more symmetric by merely eliminating extreme values.

An approach that is preferred, because it does not entail the elimination of points from a distribution, is the *monotonic nonlinear transformation*. Like the linear transformation, the monotonic nonlinear transformation retains the order of values in a distribution. Unlike the linear transformation, however, the monotonic nonlinear transformation changes the relative distances between the values in a distribution, and in so doing, effects a desired change in the shape of the distribution. Two commonly used monotonic non-linear transformations are the square root and logarithm base 10.

☞ **Remark.** Logarithms are defined by exponents. The logarithm of the value 8 using the base 2 equals 3 since $2^3 = 8$. This statement can be expressed as $\log_2 8 = 3$. Likewise, the logarithm of 16 base 2 equals 4 since $2^4 = 16$, i.e., $\log_2 16 = 4$. And, the logarithm of 100 base 10 equals 2 since $10^2 = 100$, i.e., $\log_{10} 100 = 2$. What is $\log_{10} 1,000,000$?

☞ **Remark.** Examples of logarithmic scales used in practice are the Richter scale to measure the motion of the ground due to earthquakes, decibels to measure the energy intensity of sound, and pH to measure the acidity of a substance. For example, an earthquake that measures 4 on the Richter scale is 10 times more powerful than one that measures 3 and 100 times more powerful than one that measures 2. In other words, an increase in the Richter scale of k units indicates that the earthquake is more powerful by a factor of 10^k. Decibels compare the level of pressure from a sound (represented by p_1) to the level of pressure from the smallest noise audible to a person with normal hearing (represented by p_0). The decibel is then given by $D = 10\log\left(\dfrac{p_1}{p_0}\right)$. Finally, the acidity, or pH, of a substance is found by the formula pH $= -\log(H+)$ where $(H+)$ represents the concentration of the hydrogen ion. If the pH is less than 7, the solution is said to be acidic. If the pH equals 7, the solution is said to be neutral. If the pH is greater than 7, the solution is said to be basic.

Example 4.9 illustrates how a monotonic nonlinear transformation changes the relative distance between the values in a distribution and, in so doing, changes the shape of the distribution.

EXAMPLE 4.9 Given the following set of data points: 1 4 16 64 256:

1. Compute the distances between the adjacent points in the dataset. Would you say the distribution is skewed? Why? Compute the skewness of these data using R.
2. Transform the dataset linearly by multiplying each value by 1/2. Compute the distances between the adjacent points in the dataset. Compare the distances and skewness of the distribution to those obtained in part (1). What does this result imply about the effect of a linear transformation on the skewness and relative distances between points in a distribution?
3. Transform the dataset nonlinearly by taking the square root of each value. The command for calculating a new variable that is the square root of another variable stored locally as **x**, is **newvar = sqrt(x).**
4. Compute the distances between the adjacent points in the dataset. Have the relative distances between adjacent points changed? In what way? Is the square root–transformed dataset less positively skewed than the original dataset?
5. Transform the dataset nonlinearly by taking the logarithm (using base 2) of each value.
6. Compute the distances between the adjacent points in the dataset. Have the relative distances between adjacent points changed? In what way? Is the logarithmic-transformed dataset less positively skewed than the original dataset? Is it less positively skewed than the square root–transformed dataset?

Solution

1. The original values along with their adjacent distances are:

Values:	1		4		16		64		256
		V		V		V		V	
Adjacent distances:		3		12		48		192	

Because these distances between adjacent points increase as the values themselves increase, the distribution appears to be skewed positively. Using R, we find that the distribution is positively skewed with skew = 1.31.

2. The new values, linearly transformed by multiplication by 1/2, along with their adjacent distances are:

Values:	0.5		2		8		32		128
		V		V		V		V	
Adjacent distances:		1.5		6		24		96	

Notice that the transformed scores and their adjacent distances are both 1/2 as large as the original scores and their adjacent distances. Relative to the new scale then, the distances between points remain the same, and the skewness, therefore, remains the same. Using R, we find that the linearly transformed distribution has skew = 1.31, as before. What this implies is that linear transformations do not change the relative distances between points, and hence, do not change the shape of the distribution, including its skew.

3. The original distribution, transformed by its square root, is:

1   2   4   8   16.

4. The transformed values from part (3) along with their adjacent distances are:

Values:	1		2		4		8		16
		V		V		V		V	
Adjacent distances:		1		2		4		8	

The relative distances between the values have changed as a result of this square root transformation. In particular, the square root transformation has reduced the distances between adjacent values in a non-uniform way. The higher the value, the more the reduction in distance between it and its adjacent points. The most extreme distance of 192 units in the original distribution is reduced to a distance of only 8 units after square roots are taken; the next most extreme distance of 48 units in the original distribution is reduced to a distance of 4 units after square roots are taken. Because a nonlinear transformation, such as the square root transformation, reduces differentially the distances between points in a distribution, with greatest reduction occurring in the right tail, the shape of the distribution changes. Such a transformation has the effect of "bringing in" the right tail and making the distribution more symmetric as the new skew value of 0.89 (obtained from R) indicates.

5. The original distribution, transformed by the logarithm base 2, is: 0 2 4 6 8.

6. The log-transformed values along with their adjacent distances are:

Values:	0		2		4		6		8
		V		V		V		V	
Adjacent distances:		2		2		2		2	

Notice that, in contrast to the other cases in this example, the log-transformed distribution is symmetric about the value of 4, and the adjacent distances are all equal to one another. Using R, we find that the skew value for these log-transformed values is, in fact, 0. A log transformation will not usually make a distribution perfectly symmetric. Because the log transformation has a greater impact on extreme scores than the square root transformation, it is often the case that for highly skewed data, the log transformation will be more effective than the square root transformation for making a distribution more symmetric. It is often a good idea to try both types of transformation to see which of the two produces more symmetric results and to use the one that does.

☞ **Remark.** While we used a base 2 logarithm in Example 4.9, other positive values except 1 may be used as bases. A logarithmic transformation, whether its base is 2.7, 3, 4, 5, or 10, for example, will reduce the skewness of a distribution by the same amount and change the shape of the distribution to the same extent. Two commonly used logarithmic bases are e (approximated by 2.7), associated with what is called the natural logarithm, and 10, associated with what is called the common logarithm. R uses the logarithm command **log(x, base)** where **base** is the intended base for the logarithm. In this text, we make use of **log(x, 10)**.

☞ **Remark.** For the type of data we encounter in the behavioral and social sciences, square roots are defined only on values greater than or equal to 0, while logarithms are defined only on values greater than 0. Thus, to apply a square root transformation to data that ranges from −12 to 5 we would first add 12, for example, to all values in the distribution, so that the values are all greater than or equal to 0. Likewise, to apply a logarithmic transformation to data that ranges from −12 to 5, we would first need to add 13, for example, to all values in the distribution so that the values are all greater than 0.

In Example 4.10, we illustrate with NELS data the effects on the shape and skewness of a distribution of using the square root and common logarithms. Through this example, you will learn that we may often need to apply a combination of transformations in our efforts to reduce the skew of a distribution. In this example, the square root and log transformations are used in conjunction with a reflection and a translation.

· ·

EXAMPLE 4.10 As we have observed, and as is indicated in Figures 4.7 and 4.8, the distribution of expected income at age 30 is positively skewed, and the distribution of self-concept in grade 12 is negatively skewed. Use appropriate transformations to make both distributions more symmetric.

Solution The descriptive statistics for these two variables are as follows. They are generated using the R commands:

summary(NELS$expinc30)

and

summary(NELS$slfcnc12)

Figure 4.7 Boxplot for expected income

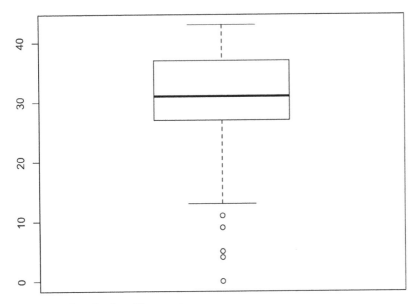

Figure 4.8 Boxplot for self-concept

Summary statistics for expected income:

Min.	1st Qu.	Median	Mean	3rd Qu.	Max.	NAs
0	30000	40000	51575	55000	1000000	41

Summary statistics for self-concept:

Min.	1st Qu.	Median	Mean	3rd Qu.	Max.
0.00	27.00	31.00	31.48	37.00	43.00

In symmetrizing the income at age 30 distribution, which is positively skewed, we try both the square root and logarithm (base 10) transformations. Because the minimum value of expected income is 0, and because the logarithm of 0 is undefined, we first add some small quantity, like 1, to each value, and then we take the logarithm of each value. The numeric expression for carrying out the logarithm transformation is $\log_{10}(\text{expinc30} + 1)$. Although it would be meaningful to take the square root of 0, for consistency, we also compute the square root of the translated expected income.

MORE R: Transforming a variable (expinc30) using logs and square roots.

To add 1 to each value and take the log transformation, we type:

NELS\$expinclg = log(NELS\$expinc30+1, 10)

in the console and press **Enter**.

For the square root transformation, we type:

NELS\$expincsq = sqrt(NELSexpinc30+1)

in the console and press **Enter**.

Descriptive statistics for the $\log_{10}$- and square-root-transformed variables are output as follows.

Summary statistics for log of expected income plus 1:

Min.	1st Qu.	Median	Mean	3rd Qu.	Max.	NAs
0.000	4.477	4.602	4.590	4.740	6.000	41

Summary statistics for square root of expected income plus 1:

Min.	1st Qu.	Median	Mean	3rd Qu.	Max.	NAs
1.0	173.2	200.0	214.5	234.5	1000.0	41

Notice that the log transformation over-compensates for the positive skew as it results in a highly negatively skewed distribution. In this case, the square root transformation is the better of the two as Figure 4.9 illustrates.

As we have seen, the logarithm and square root transformations may be used to symmetrize a positively skewed distribution. If the logarithm or square root transformation is applied to a negatively skewed distribution, however, the effect will be to make that distribution even more negatively skewed. Accordingly, when a distribution is negatively skewed, a first step in symmetrizing such a distribution would be to reflect it so that it becomes positively skewed. Because the square root is not defined on negative values, and the logarithm is not defined on negative or zero values, if there are negative or zero values in the distribution, the next step would be to add a constant to each value in the distribution to eliminate such negative or zero values. The third step would be to apply the logarithm or square root transformation as before. Self-concept in grade 12 (slfcnc12) is an example of a negatively skewed distribution.

In preparation for taking the logarithm and square root transformations, we want all the values of slfcnc12 to be greater than 0. To accomplish this, we add 44 to each value of

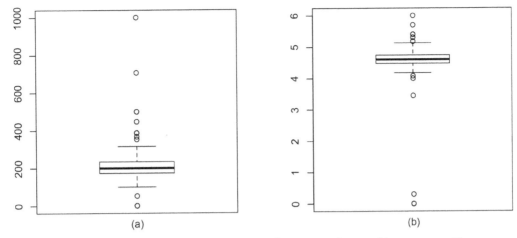

Figure 4.9 Boxplots of square root (a) and $\log_{10}$ (b) transformations of expected income at age 30

slfcnc12 because 44 equals 1 more than the maximum value of slfcnc12. This type of variable transformation is called a **translation**.

MORE R: To translate the variable slfcnc12, type:

NELS\$slfcnc12reftr = (−1)*NELS\$slfcnc12 + 44

in the console and press **Enter**:
A new variable called slfcnc12reftr will appear as the last variable in your dataset.

☞ **Remark.** Through this numeric operation, on this new scale, scores that were originally high are now low, and scores that were originally low are now high. As a consequence, higher self-concept is represented by lower scores, and lower self-concept is represented by higher scores.

The distribution of slfcnc12 is presented on the left-hand side of Figure 4.10, with slfcnc12reftr on the right-hand side.

The distributions of the square root and log transformed variables are shown in Figure 4.11 on the left- and right-hand sides, respectively. The skewness of these two new variables are −0.4953 and −1.3196, respectively.

Because the two new variables are more negatively skewed than the original slfcnc12 variable (original skew = −0.383), neither transformation serves to improve symmetry. Accordingly, the best course of action, in this case, would be to leave slfcnc12 in its original form.

NONLINEAR TRANSFORMATIONS: RANKING VARIABLES

Sometimes we may be interested in knowing the ranking of scores in a distribution and working with those rather than the scores themselves. For example, while we may have information on each student's grade point average in a particular graduating class, we also

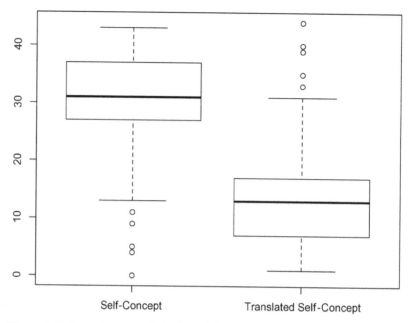

Figure 4.10 Preparing a negatively skewed distribution for a square root and logarithmic transformation (from left to right)

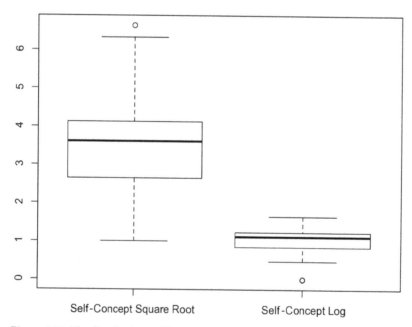

Figure 4.11 The distributions of the square-root- (left) and log-transformed (right) variables.

may be interested in their class ranking; that is, we may be interested in whether they placed 1st, 50th, or in some other position. To transform scores to ranks, we shall assign a 1 to the highest score, a 2 to the next highest, and so on. In the case of tied scores, each score is assigned the mean of the ranks that would have been assigned those scores had they not been tied. We illustrate the ranking procedure in Example 4.11 with the Hamburger dataset from McDonald's on the number of grams of fat and calories contained in each of five types of hamburger sold.

EXAMPLE 4.11 Rank the five hamburgers by their (a) fat content and (b) calorie content using R. In both instances, assign the value 1 to the hamburger with the lowest value. Assign the mean ranking in the case of ties.

MORE R: Transforming scores to ranks.

To transform the variables fat and calories into new variables whose scores are now ranks, we use the **rank** function, as follows:

Hamburger$rfat = rank(Hamburger$fat)
Hamburger$rcalories = rank(Hamburger$calories)

The **rank** function assigns a rank of 1 to the variable's lowest value. If, instead, we want the variable's highest value to be assigned a rank of 1, we would subtract the ranked values from one more than the number of values in the dataset as follows:

Hamburger$rkfat = 6 – Hamburger$rfat
Hamburger$rkcalories = 6 – Hamburger$rcalories

The two new ranked variables, named rkfat and rkcalories, will appear in your dataset as shown below. Notice that in the case of fat, where there are no ties (each hamburger has a unique fat content), the rankings are the whole numbers 1 to 5. From this ranking we know, for example, that a Quarter Pounder™ with Cheese ranks number 1 in fat relative to the other hamburgers and that a Hamburger ranks last. In the case of calories, there is a tie between the Quarter Pounder™ with Cheese and the Big Mac™. Accordingly, these two types of hamburger share the 1st and 2nd place rank and so are assigned the mean of 1 and 2, which is, of course, 1.5.

name	fat	calories	rkfat	rkcalories
Hamburger	10	270	5.0	5.0
Cheeseburger	14	320	4.0	4.0
Quarter Pounder™	21	430	3.0	3.0
Quarter P. ™ w/ c	30	530	1.0	1.5
Big Mac™	28	530	2.0	1.5

We may note that a rank transformation preserves the ordinality of the values, but that is all. The interval or ratio properties that might have existed in the original data are now lost.

☞ **Remark.** Rankings provide the ordinal position of a value in a distribution. From rankings we may know, for example, that a value is 100th in a distribution, but from that rank alone, we do not know how many other, or what percentage of, values are below that value. For this information, we use the percentile ranking introduced in Chapter 2.

OTHER TRANSFORMATIONS: RECODING AND COMBINING VARIABLES

RECODING VARIABLES

Variables may be recoded for at least two reasons: to transform variables and to collapse or combine categories. In Example 4.4, we reflected the Likert scale used to measure assertiveness so that lower scores no longer associated with agreement, but rather with disagreement, and higher scores no longer associated with disagreement, but rather with agreement. In particular, we applied the linear transformation (6 − assert) to achieve the desired transformation of this five-point scale. In Example 4.12 we provide an example that shows how to collapse categories of a variable.

••

EXAMPLE 4.12 In the frequency distribution of eighth grade school type, schtyp8, given below, we may note that school type is described as: 1 = public, 2 = private (religious), and 3 = private (non-religious). If we are interested in distinguishing between 1 = public and 2 = private types only, then we may use the ifelse procedure to collapse these three categories into two in the following way.

Solution

MORE R: Reducing the number of categories of a variable by collapsing some.

To collapse the three categories of schtyp8 into two categories: public and private, we type the following **ifelse** command into the console, and press **Enter**:

NELS$schtypre = ifelse(NELS$schtyp8 == "Public", "Public", "Private")

Note that the **ifelse** command takes three arguments. First, we set a condition to test, specifically if schtyp8 is equal to Public in the NELS dataset, then we follow the second argument, which sets the new variable, schtypre, equal to Public. Otherwise, we set the new variable, schtypre, equal to Private.

Whenever a variable is treated as if it were continuous, it is preferable to retain as much of the variability in the scores as possible, which implies continuing to measure the variable on a many-valued scale. Sometimes, however, researchers choose to dichotomize such variables to simplify interpretation, among other reasons, using a *median split*. The *Bem Sex-Role Inventory* (Bem, 1977), for example, uses two median splits, one on each of two continuous variables, Masculinity and Femininity, to divide the scores on each into two categories: low and high Masculinity and low and high Femininity. The low Femininity–low Masculinity category is labeled Undifferentiated, the low Femininity–high Masculinity category is labeled Masculine, the high Femininity–low Masculinity category is labeled Feminine, and the high Femininity–high Masculinity category is labeled Androgynous.

Simply stated, a median split transforms a many-valued variable into two categories, one that includes all scores above the median and the other that includes all scores below the median. The scores at the median typically are assigned arbitrarily to one of the two categories. Note that if the variable is skewed originally, in taking a median split, the new variable will be symmetric. Although we do not recommend the median split, the next example describes how to split a variable at its median to create a dichotomous variable from one that is originally continuous.

EXAMPLE 4.13 Find the median of self-concept in eighth grade, slfcnc08, and transform this variable using a median split procedure.

Solution The median of slfcnc08 is 21, obtained using **median(NELS$slfcnc08)**.

MORE R: Obtaining a median split of a variable.

To obtain the median split of slfcnc08, we once again use the **ifelse** command as follows:

NELS$slfcnc08ms = ifelse(NELS$slfcnc08 <= 21, 1, 2)

We begin by creating a new variable to assign values to, slfcnc08ms, on the left-hand side of the equation. We then assign to this new variable the value 1 for values of slfcnc08 less than or equal to the median, 21, and the value 2 for values of slfcnc08 greater than the median.

The frequency distribution of slfcn8ms, obtained by using the command **table(NELS$slfcnc08ms)** is given below.

1	2
266	234

The decision of whether to lump all scores that equal the median value in the lower or upper category needs to be made by the researcher. Because there are 30 individuals who scored at the median of 21, the two categories do not each constitute 50 percent of the distribution. In this case, the median value of 21 was placed in the lower category. The upper category started at 22 because the distribution takes on only integer values.

COMBINING VARIABLES

While variables may be combined in a variety of ways, in this book we will be concerned with combining variables using the operations of addition, subtraction, multiplication, and division. For example, using the NELS dataset, suppose we wished to construct a variable that represented the combined number of years of math and English courses the student took in high school. The NELS dataset has two variables that are relevant: the number of years of math taken, unitmath, and the number of years of English taken, unitengl. In Example 4.14 we construct a new variable that represents the combined number of years of math and English.

EXAMPLE 4.14 Construct a new variable, sumunits, which represents the combined number of years of math and English taken in high school.

Solution

MORE R: Creating a new variable as the sum of two variables.

The following command will create the new variable, sumunits, as the sum of the unitmath and unitengl:

NELS$sumunits = NELS$unitmath + NELS$unitengl

DATA MANAGEMENT FUNDAMENTALS: THE .R FILE

One of the most important tasks as a data analyst is to keep a permanent and detailed record of the steps you take in carrying out the data analysis portion of your project, including documentation on how variables were re-expressed and created, which specific analyses were carried out, and the order in which they were carried out. The final product of such documentation should be so detailed that if we were to lose the entire set of output in connection with your project, we could, with a click or two, reproduce what was done in a matter of minutes, if not seconds.

To keep a permanent and detailed record of such documentation, we need to create and save a file, called a .R file or R Script, that contains all the commands we executed, whether they relate to variable creation or modification, data selection, graphical display, or to the analyses themselves. These commands include those we type directly into the console.

To create a new .R file, on the main menu bar, we would click, **File>New Document** (we need to further select **R Script** if working in RStudio). In each case, a new .R window will appear, and you may begin typing your commands directly into that window. Periodically, and certainly when you are finished typing your commands into the .R file, you will need to save the file to a location and name of your choosing. To do so, on the main menu, click **File>Save as**, browse to a location of your choosing on your computer, give your file a name, and click **Save**. The .R file will have the extension **.R** to distinguish it from other file types.

To open an existing .R file, on the main menu bar, we would click **File>Open Document**, browse to the location of the file, highlight the filename, and click **Open.**

To execute the commands in your .R file, whether all, or a selection of them, highlight the chosen commands and we would press **command+enter** on our computer keyboard (for a Mac computer) or **control+enter** (for a Windows computer).

Comments that describe the work we are undertaking are critical components to a .R file. Without them, we would most certainly not remember, by the next time we opened the .R file, which might not happen for several weeks, why we included the commands we did. To create such descriptive comments, we may type one or more number signs, **#**, at the beginning of a line. The following illustrates how to include comments in a .R file.

 # The following syntax generates descriptive statistics for temp.
summary(temp)

MORE R: A .R file for each of the chapters in this text has been created that contains the R commands used to execute the analyses and construct the figures of that chapter. Once you have had a chance to create your own .R file in Example 4.15, it would be a good idea to open the .R file associated with this chapter and run the commands contained in it so that you can see first-hand how to reproduce the R output we obtained in this chapter. You also may wish to go back to Chapters 2 and 3 and do the same thing with respect to those chapters.

Going forward, we recommend that you adopt a more interactive way of reading this text by opening the .R file associated with the chapter you are currently reading and executing, in order, the R commands in that .R file so as to reproduce the R output contained in the text of the chapter itself.

EXAMPLE 4.15 Consider the situation of Example 4.14 in which we were interested in creating a new variable, sumunits as the sum of the two variables, unitmath and unitengl. Compute summary statistics on that new variable and create a boxplot. Rather than typing each of the necessary commands into the console directly and pressing **Enter** at the end of each line, in this example, carry out this work using a .R file.

Solution

MORE R: To create and save a .R file, open a .R file using

File>New Document

Type and execute the loading of the package associated with this textbook using **library(sur)**, which would automatically load the NELS dataset (as well as all the other datasets used in this textbook).

We are now ready to type the remaining commands into our .R file to carry out what we wish to do. We type the following lines as shown, which includes both documentation and commands:

```
## Create the variable sumunits
NELS$sumunits = NELS$unitmath + NELS$unitengl
## Create a box plot of sumunits
boxplot(NELS$sumunits)
## Generate summary statistics for the variable sumunits
summary(NELS$sumunits)
```

Save the .R file to a location and filename of your choosing. Highlight the commands in the file you want to execute, starting with the **library(sur)** command. Execute these commands from the .R file by pressing **Command+Enter** or **Control+Enter** depending upon whether you are working on a Mac or Windows computer, respectively.

The boxplot will pop up on the screen and the summary statistics will be printed in the console, as usual.

As you continue to work through this text, it will become increasingly clear how the ability to create, modify, and save .R files provides flexibility and power in carrying out the work of a data analyst.

SUMMARY OF R COMMANDS

(See also the .R file for Chapter 4.)

Create	Command lines
Perform a multiplicative linear transformation to convert height from inches to centimeters (Example 4.1)	Basketball$Height_cm = Basketball$heightin * 2.54
Reflect and translate the variable assert on a 1 to 5 scale (Example 4.4)	Likert$assertref = −1 * Likert$Assertiveness + 6
Create the standardized variable for ses (Example 4.6)	NELS$zses = scale(NELS$ses)
List all outliers in the dataset according to the z-score criterion (Example 4.8)	table(NELS$zslfcnc12[abs(NELS$zslfcnc12) > 2]) OR table(NELS$zslfcnc12[NELS$zslfcnc12 > 2 | NELS$zslfcnc12 < −2])
Calculate summary statistics (mean and standard deviation) of achrdg12 by gender	mean(NELS$achrdg12[NELS$gender == "Male"]) sd(NELS$achrdg12[NELS$gender == "Male"]) mean(NELS$achrdg12[NELS$gender == "Female"]) sd(NELS$achrdg12[NELS$gender == "Female"])
Take the log of the variable expinc30, but first add 1 to each value (Example 4.10)	NELS$expinclg = log(NELS$expinc30 +1, 10)
Take the square root of the variable expinc30, but first add 1 to each value (Example 4.10)	NELS$expincsq = sqrt(NELS$expinc30+1)
Rank a variable assigning 1 to the highest value (Example 4.11)	Hamburger$rfat = rank(Hamburger$fat) Hamburger$rkfat = 6 − Hamburger$rfat
Recode school type to collapse the two types of private school to one (Example 4.12)	NELS$schtypre = ifelse(NELS$schtyp8 == "Public", "Public", "Private")
Perform a median split on slfcnc08 (Example 4.13)	NELS$slfcnc08ms = ifelse(NELS$slfcnc08 <= 21, 1, 2)
Create a new variable that is the sum of existing variables (Example 4.14)	NELS$sumunits = NELS$unitmath + NELS$unitengl
Create and save a .R file (Example 4.15)	See the text for this example.

EXERCISES

Create a .R file for each exercise that requires the use of R. Run code from the .R file by highlighting or having the cursor on the line of code and hitting **control+enter** on a PC computer keyboard or **command+enter** on a Mac computer keyboard. Save each .R file using a name associated with the Exercise for which it was created. It is recommended that you review the .R file for Chapter 4 located on the textbook's website before completing these exercises. To facilitate doing each exercise, it may be helpful to copy and paste relevant code from the .R file for Chapter 4 into your own .R file and modify them as needed.

Exercises 4.1–4.8 involve the effects of linear transformations on the summary statistics of a distribution.

4.1 In this series of exercises, we find the summary statistics of distributions that are linear transformations of original distributions. These exercises do not require the use of R.

(a) If each value in a distribution with mean equal to 5 has been tripled, what is the new mean?

(b) If each value in a distribution with standard deviation equal to 5 has been tripled, what is the new standard deviation?

(c) If each value in a distribution with skewness equal to 1.14 has been tripled, what is the new skewness?

(d) If each value in a distribution with mean equal to 5 has the constant 6 added to it, what is the new mean?

(e) If each value in a distribution with standard deviation equal to 5 has the constant 6 added to it, what is the new standard deviation?

(f) If each value in a distribution with skewness equal to 1.14 has the constant 6 added to it, what is the new skewness?

(g) If each value in a distribution with mean equal to 5 has been multiplied by –2, what is the new mean?

(h) If each value in a distribution with standard deviation equal to 5 has been multiplied by –2, what is the new standard deviation?

(i) If each value in a distribution with skewness equal to 1.14 has been multiplied by –2, what is the new skewness?

(j) If each value in a distribution with mean equal to 5 has had a constant equal to 6 subtracted from it, what is the new mean?

(k) If each value in a distribution with standard deviation equal to 5 has had a constant equal to 6 subtracted from it, what is the new standard deviation?

(l) If each value in a distribution with skewness equal to 1.14 has had a constant equal to 6 subtracted from it, what is the new skewness?

4.2 Consider a situation in which you would like to measure the amount of time it takes children in grades 4 and 6 to complete a task. This exercise does not require R.

(a) The grade 4 teacher found that the average time to complete a task was 20 minutes with a standard deviation of 7 minutes. The grade 6 teacher found that the average time was 0.25 hours to complete a task with a standard deviation of 0.09 hours. In which grade were the students faster? In which grade were the students more similar in the amount of time taken to complete the task?

(b) The grade 4 teacher found that the average time was 20 minutes with a standard deviation of 7 minutes, and the grade 6 teacher found that the average time was 22 minutes with a standard deviation of 5 minutes. The grade 6 teacher had included reading the instructions, which took four minutes, in his calculation of the time to complete the task. After adjusting for this additional time to make the two classes comparable, in which grade were the students faster? In which grade were the students more similar in the amount of time taken to complete the task?

4.3 Assume that you are studying college students and have measured a variable called credits that gives the number of credits taken by a part-time or full-time student during the current semester. For the individuals you are studying, the number of credits taken ranges from 4 to 26, with a mean of 16.26, a standard deviation of 2.40, and a skewness ratio of −12.05. This exercise does not require R.

(a) Assuming that, on average, each class is worth 3 credits, define an R command to create a variable called classes as a linear transformation of credits that estimates the average number of classes taken during the current semester.

(b) What is the mean of classes?

(c) What is the standard deviation of classes?

(d) What is the shape of the distribution of classes? Explain and support your answer with an appropriate descriptive statistic. Be sure to indicate whether or not the distribution is *severely* skewed.

(e) Why do you suppose the skewness is so severe in the negative direction?

4.4 The variable schattrt in the NELS dataset gives the average daily attendance rate for the school that the student attends.

(a) What are the mean, median, standard deviation, variance, range, interquartile range, and skewness of schattrt?

(b) Compute a new variable schattpp that expresses the average daily attendance as a decimal instead of as a percentage, i.e., that gives the average daily attendance proportion for the school that the student attends. What is the command you used?

(c) Based on the summary statistics for schattrt that you generated in part (a), find the mean, median, standard deviation, variance, interquartile range, and skewness of schattpp.

(d) Use R to calculate the mean, median, standard deviation, variance, range, interquartile range, and skewness of schattpp.

4.5 The variable expinc30 in the NELS dataset measures the expected annual income at age 30 of students in the eighth grade.

(a) What are the mean, median, standard deviation, variance, range, interquartile range, and skewness of expinc30?

(b) Compute a new variable, expcents, which gives the expected income at age 30 in terms of pennies, not dollars. What is the command you used?

(c) Based on the summary statistics for expinc30 that you generated in part (a), find the mean, median, standard deviation, variance, interquartile range, and skewness of expcents.

(d) Use R to calculate the mean, median, standard deviation, variance, range, interquartile range, and skewness of expcents.

4.6 The variable computer in the NELS dataset indicates whether the student's family owned a computer when the student was in eighth grade. The variable is coded so that 1 = No and 2 = Yes.
  (a) Use R to compute the mean and standard deviation of the variable computer.
  (b) What is the linear transformation to convert computer into comp1, which is coded 0 for No and 1 for Yes?
  (c) What is the linear transformation to convert comp1 into comp2, which is coded 0 for Yes and 1 for No?
  (d) Use the rules for the effects of linear transformations on summary statistics to determine the means and standard deviations of the variables comp1 and comp2. Verify that in using this coding, the mean equals the proportion of "1"s, which is the proportion of Yes responses for comp1 and the proportion of No responses for comp2.

4.7 The variable CIGPDAY3 from the Framingham dataset gives the number of cigarettes smoked per day by the respondents at third examination. Assume that the values of CIGPDAY3 are then multiplied by negative 2 and then 3 is added to each value to create the variable CIGTRANS.
  (a) What are the values of the mean, standard deviation, and skewness of CIGPDAY3?
  (b) What is the value of the mean of CIGTRANS?
  (c) What is the value of the new SD?
  (d) What is the value of the new skewness statistic?

4.8 In the Framingham dataset, SEX is coded so that 1 = Men and 2 = Women. What is the mean of SEX? Apply appropriate linear transformations to interpret the mean of SEX as a proportion of women.

Exercises 4.9–4.17 involve z-scores.

4.9 Consider the variable for family size, or the number of members in a student's household, given by the NELS variable famsize.
  (a) If a student has a z-score of −1.28, how many members are in her household?
  (b) What is the z-score for a student with 6 members in her household?
  (c) Using the z-score criteria for outliers, that is, that a score is an outlier if its associated z-score is less than −2 or greater than 2, how many outliers are in this distribution?

4.10 Consider the variable for self-concept in eighth grade given by the NELS variable slfcnc08.
  (a) Find the mean and standard deviation of slfcnc08.
  (b) Write an R command that uses the mean and standard deviation of slfcnc08 to calculate the z-score distribution for slfcnc08, and call the variable zslfcnc08ver1.
  (c) Use the R command **scale** to create the z-score distribution for slfcnc08. Call this variable zslfcnc08ver2.
  (d) Without computing, what are the means and standard deviations of zslfcnc08ver1 and zslfcnc08ver2?

(e) If a new variable, slf08p5, were created by adding 5 points to the eighth grade self-concept score for each student in the NELS dataset, what would be the mean and standard deviation of slf08p5?

4.11 The variable unitengl in the NELS dataset gives the number of years of English taken in high school. The variable unitmath gives the number of years of math taken in high school. Advanced coursework enabled some of the recorded values of these two variables in the dataset to exceed four.

(a) What is the z-score of a student who took 5.5 years of high school English?

(b) How many years of high school English did a student with a z-score of -1.71 take?

(c) Using the z-score criteria for outliers (that is, that a score is an outlier if its associated z-score is less than -2 or greater than 2), how many outliers are in the distribution unitengl?

(d) According to cumulative percentages, obtained using the **cumulative.table** command, if a student took 5.5 years of each of math and English, relative to their classmates, is that more unusual for English or math?

(e) According to z-scores, if a student took 5.5 years of both math and English, relative to his classmates, is that more unusual for English or math?

4.12 The variables slfcnc08, slfcnc10, and slfcnc12 in the NELS dataset measure self-concept in eighth, tenth, and twelfth grade, respectively. A self-concept score of 25 is relatively highest in which of these distributions?

(a) Base your answer on cumulative percentages.

(b) Base your answer on z-scores.

4.13 Does an eighth grade self-concept (slfcnc08) score of 25 represent a higher level of eighth grade self-concept for males or for females? Use as criteria (a) cumulative percentages and (b) z-scores. Create separate cumulative percentage distributions and mean and standard deviation statistics for male and female students in the NELS dataset using the following commands:

cumulative.table(NELS$slfcnc08[NELS$gender=="Female"])
cumulative.table(NELS$slfcnc08[NELS$gender=="Male"])
mean(NELS$slfcnc08[NELS$gender=="Female"])
sd(NELS$slfcnc08[NELS$gender=="Female"])
mean(NELS$slfcnc08[NELS$gender=="Male"])
sd(NELS$slfcnc08[NELS$gender=="Male"])

4.14 Who scores higher in science achievement in eighth grade (achsci08) relative to his or her gender, a female who scores 58 or a male who scores 63? Use as criteria (a) cumulative percentages and (b) z-scores. As in 4.13, create separate cumulative percentage distributions for male and female students in the NELS dataset.

4.15 Determine the number of standard deviations away from the mean a score of 89 is on a test with mean 92 and variance 4.

4.16 If Steve's z-score on a test is $+1.5$, what is his raw score if the mean of the test is 75 and the standard deviation is 10?

4.17 Given a unimodal, symmetric distribution, rank from numerically smallest to numerically largest the following values from that distribution: a z-score of $+1$, $\overline{X}$, and Q_{25}.

Exercises 4.18–4.20 involve a mixture of topics about linear transformations and some review topics.

4.18 The following questions involve the variable grade from the Learndis dataset.

   (a) What are the mean, standard deviation, and skewness ratio of the variable grade?

   (b) Assume that students start first grade at age 6 and go up one grade each year. Use a linear transformation to convert grade to age, the approximate age of the student in that grade.

   (c) Use the information about the distribution grade to find the mean age for students in the dataset.

   (d) Use the information about the distribution grade to find the standard deviation for age.

   (e) Use the information about the distribution grade to find the skewness ratio for age. How would you describe the shape of the age distribution?

4.19 Compare the distribution of reading comprehension scores (readcomp) in the Learndis dataset by whether the student was assigned part time to the resource room for additional instruction (placemen = 1 or "RR") or full time in a self-contained classroom (placemen = 2 or "MIS").

   (a) Is either of the two distributions severely skewed? If so, which one(s) and what is the direction of the skew? Explain and support your answer with appropriate descriptive statistics.

   (b) In which type of placement do students have a higher overall level of reading comprehension? Explain and support your answer with an appropriate descriptive statistic taking into account the varying degrees of skewness in the two distributions. Is there another statistic that suggests an alternative conclusion?

   (c) For which type of placement are the reading comprehension scores more consistent? Explain and support your answer with an appropriate descriptive statistic taking into account the varying degrees of skewness in the two distributions. Is there another statistic that suggests an alternative conclusion?

   (d) Does the student with the highest reading comprehension score in the dataset have a resource room or a self-contained classroom placement? Provide statistical support your answer.

   (e) What is the z-score corresponding to a reading comprehension score of 75 for a student with a resource room placement?

   (f) What is the reading comprehension score corresponding to a z-score of 2 for a student with a resource room placement?

   (g) Would a student with a reading comprehension score of 75 be more unusual (further from the bulk of the scores in standard deviation units) relative to the resource room students or to the self-contained classroom students? Explain and support your answer.

   (h) Can a percentile in the distribution of reading comprehension scores for the students with a resource room placement have the value 103? Explain.

4.20 Consider the variable AGE1 in the Framingham dataset, which gives a respondent's age in 1956, the first year of the study.

   (a) How many people in the dataset were 40 years old in 1956?

   (b) What percentage of people in the dataset were younger than or equal to 40 in 1956?

(c) Is 40 years old above or below the median in this dataset? Explain.

(d) Is 40 years old above or below the mean in this dataset? How many standard deviations is 40 years old above or below the mean?

(e) If we consider a score to be an outlier if its associated z-score is less than -2 or greater than 2, how many outliers are there in the AGE1 distribution?

(f) What is the breakdown of outliers by men and women?

(g) Write the command for linearly transforming the variable AGE1 to the new variable BIRTHYR, which gives the year in which the person was born.

(h) What is the median of the variable BIRTHYR?

(i) What is the standard deviation of the variable BIRTHYR?

Exercises 4.21–4.23 involve square root and logarithmic transformations.

4.21 Consider the two achievement measures in the tenth grade, achmat10 and achrdg10, in the NELS dataset. Determine their skewness, standard error of skewness, and skewness ratio. Then find a nonlinear transformation (e.g., log, square root) that will be useful in symmetrizing the variable if it is highly skewed.

4.22 For each of the following variables from the NELS dataset, determine whether the variable is skewed, and, if so, whether a log or square root transformation is effective in symmetrizing the variable.

(a) apoffer

(b) famsize

(c) schattrt

(d) What would be the effect, if any, of a nonlinear transformation on a dichotomous variable, such as cigarett?

4.23 For each of the following variables from the Learndis dataset, determine whether the variable is skewed, and, if so, whether a log or square root transformation is effective in symmetrizing the variable.

(a) grade

(b) mathcomp

(c) readcomp

Exercises 4.24–4.28 involve recoding and combining variables.

4.24 In the NELS dataset, unitmath represents the total number of units (in years) of mathematics taken in high school, while unitcalc represents the number of units (in years) of calculus taken.

(a) Create the variable unitmnc to represent the number of units of non-calculus mathematics taken.

(b) What is the largest number of units of non-calculus math taken by a student in the NELS dataset? How many student(s) took that amount of non-calculus math?

4.25 There are four variables in the NELS dataset that describe different types of achievement in twelfth grade: achmat12, achrdg12, achsci12, and achsls12.

(a) Create a composite variable, achtot12 that represents the sum of a student's achievement on all four tests.

(b) Describe the shape of the distribution of achtot12.

(c) On average, do boys score higher on achtot12 than girls? Support your answer with appropriate descriptive statistics and indicate if different statistics lead to different conclusions.

4.26 The variable apoffer gives the number of Advanced Placement (AP) courses offered by the school that the student attends in the NELS dataset.

(a) Create a new variable, apoffyn, that indicates whether a school offers any AP courses. First, write an **ifelse** command that sets apoffyn to "yes" if apoffer is greater than 0 and "no" otherwise. Next, we will ensure that missing values of apoffer are counted in apoffyn as missing values (and not as "no") using the following command:

NELS$apoffyn = ifelse(is.na(NELS$apoffer), NA, NELS$apoffyn)

(b) How many schools in the NELS dataset do not offer AP courses?

(c) If we were to code apoffyn as 0 = no and 1 = yes, how might we interpret the mean of this variable?

4.27 Using the variables in the Statisticians dataset, create the following new variables and answer related questions about them.

(a) Create the variable alive, representing how long each statistician lived. Who lived the longest?

(b) Create the variable old, that indicates how old each statistician would be now, if they were still living. Who is the "youngest" statistician in the dataset?

4.28 Use the Framingham dataset to determine if after experiencing a coronary heart disease event (CHD), individuals have reduced weight (as measured by BMI) and total cholesterol (as measured by TOTCHOL). Consider the initial period as period 1 (1956) and the final period as period 3 (1968). The variable ANYCHD4 indicates whether a person in the study experienced a CHD during the study.

(a) Create two new variables that reflect the difference in BMI and TOTCHOL from period 1 to period 3; e.g., BMIDIFF = BMI3 – BMI1 and CHOLDIFF = TOTCHOL3 – TOTCHOL1. Looking at the cumulative percentage distribution of these two variables, how many individuals lost weight? How many had reduced total cholesterol?

(b) What is the change in BMI, on average, from period 1 to period 3 for those who experienced a CHD event during this time period as compared to those who did not experience a CHD event during this time period?

(c) What is the change in total cholesterol, on average, from period 1 to period 3 for those who experienced a CHD event during this time period as compared to those who did not experience a CHD event during this time period?

Exercises 4.29–4.32 make use of the .R files for Chapters 2 and 3.

4.29 Use the .R file for Chapter 2 to reproduce Table 2.1 and Figures 2.1, 2.2, 2.3, and 2.4 in the text by highlighting the relevant command lines in the .R file and pressing **command (or control) + enter.**

4.30 Use the .R file for Chapter 2 to obtain the results of Example 2.3 and to reproduce Figures 2.15, 2.16, and 2.17 in the text by highlighting the relevant command lines in the .R file and pressing **command (or control) + enter.**

4.31 Use the .R file for Chapter 3 to reproduce the mean and median results of Example 3.5 in the text by highlighting the relevant command lines in the .R file and pressing **command (or control) + enter**.

4.32 Use the .R file for Chapter 3 to duplicate the analysis described under the section, "Applying What We Have Learned" as it regards the variable expinc30 from the NELS dataset by highlighting the relevant command lines in the .R file and pressing **command (or control) + enter**.

# CHAPTER FIVE

EXPLORING RELATIONSHIPS BETWEEN TWO VARIABLES

Up to this point, we have been examining data univariately: that is, one variable at a time. We have examined the location, spread, and shape of several variables in the NELS dataset, such as socioeconomic status, mathematics achievement, expected income at age 30, and self-concept. Interesting questions often arise, however, that involve the relationship between two variables. For example, using the NELS dataset we may be interested in knowing if self-concept relates to socio-economic status; if gender relates to science achievement in twelfth grade; if sex relates to nursery school attendance; or if math achievement in twelfth grade relates to geographical region of residence.

When we ask whether one variable relates to another, we are really asking about the shape, direction, and strength of the relationship between the two variables. We also find it useful to distinguish among the nature of the variables themselves: that is, whether the two variables in question are both measured either, at least, at the interval level, or are both dichotomous, or are a combination of the two. For example, when we ask about the relationship between socio-economic status and self-concept, we are asking about the relationship between two at least interval-leveled variables. When we ask about whether sex relates to nursery school attendance, we are asking about the relationship between two dichotomous variables. And, when we ask about whether sex relates to twelfth grade science achievement, we are asking about the relationship between one dichotomous variable and one at least interval-leveled variable.

WHEN BOTH VARIABLES ARE AT LEAST INTERVAL-LEVELED

While the questions posed in the introductory paragraph of this chapter are motivated by our familiarity with the NELS dataset, for heuristic reasons, we have chosen much smaller, yet real, datasets to introduce the important ideas associated with the concept of relationship between two continuous variables.

Do hamburgers that have more fat tend to have more calories? Table 5.1 contains the fat grams and calories associated with the different types of hamburger sold by McDonald's. The data are from McDonald's Nutrition Information Center and are saved in the Hamburger dataset.

Does a state's average SAT Critical Reading score relate to the percentage of students who have taken the SAT in that state? Data on the percentage of students who took the SAT in 2012 in each state along with the average SAT Critical Reading score is taken from the States dataset. The source for these data is *The World Almanac and Book of Facts 2014*.

For bills of $20 or lower, is there an association between the value of the bill and the total number in circulation? Table 5.2 contains for the smaller bill denominations, the value

TABLE 5.1 Fat grams and calories by type of McDonald's hamburgers

Type of McDonald's hamburger	Grams of fat (X)	Calories (Y)
Hamburger	10	270
Cheeseburger	14	320
Quarter Pounder™	21	430
Quarter Pounder™ w/ cheese	30	530
Big Mac™	28	530

TABLE 5.2 Value and total circulation of United States currency

Denomination	Total circulation ($)	Number in circulation
$1	10,334,000,000	10,334,000,000
$2	2,009,000,000	1,004,500,000
$5	12,025,000,000	2,405,000,000
$10	17,332,000,000	1,733,200,000
$20	148,219,000,000	7,410,950,000

of the bill, and the total circulation in dollars. These values are saved in the Currency dataset. We use the methods of Chapter 4 to calculate the total number of bills in circulation by dividing the total circulation in dollars by the bill value, given as the last column in Table 5.2. The source for these data is *The World Almanac and Book of Facts 2014*.

Finally, what is the pattern of marijuana use by twelfth graders from 1987 through 1996? We answer this question using data from the Marijuana dataset, which gives the year and the percentage of twelfth graders who report that they have ever used marijuana. The source for these data is *The World Almanac and Book of Facts 2014*.

SCATTERPLOTS

With any of these datasets, a natural question is, how may we describe the relationship between the two variables? While the relationship may often be grasped by inspecting the table of pairs of data values, a better approach is to use a graphic that depicts each pair of (X,Y) values as a separate point in an (X,Y) coordinate plane. Such a graphic is called a *scatterplot*. The scatterplots for the data in our four examples are given in Figures 5.1–5.4, respectively.

MORE R: To obtain the scatterplot in Figure 5.1, for example, type the following in the console and press **Enter**:

```
plot(Hamburger$calories~Hamburger$fat, xlab = "Fat", ylab = "Calories")
```

Figure 5.1 McDonald's hamburgers

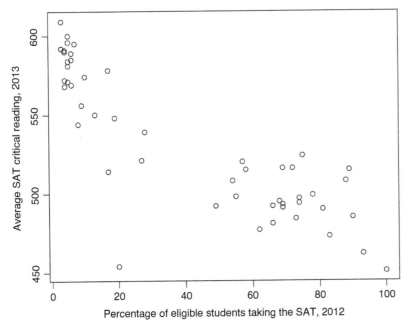

Figure 5.2 The SAT in the states

MORE R: To obtain a scatterplot on a restricted set of data as in Figure 5.4, we use square brackets to subset our data, as was done previously in Chapter 3. This has the effect of limiting the values of both variables to the years 1987 through 1996: that is, to

Figure 5.3 United States currency

Figure 5.4 Marijuana use

the years greater than or equal to 1987 and less than or equal to 1996. The first variable listed in the plot command (MarijuanaUse, in this case) defines the *y*-axis and the second defines the *x*-axis (Year, in this case).

plot(Marijuana$MarijuanaUse[Marijuana$Year <= 1996 & Marijuana$Year >= 1987]~Marijuana$Year[Marijuana$Year <= 1996 & Marijuana$Year >= 1987], xlab = "Year", ylab = "Marijuana Use")

MORE R: Customizing our graphic.

A title may be added to a graph as an argument in the plot command (**main**). We also could customize the symbol, color, and size of the points in the scatterplot by including **pch** (plot character), **col** (color), and **cex** (character expansion) in our command. To learn more about the different aspects of a plot that you can customize, type **?par**. Because these options relate to the scatter itself, they must be placed within the parentheses that define the scatterplot of marijuana vs. year:

plot(Marijuana$MarijuanaUse[Marijuana$Year <= 1996 & Marijuana$Year >= 1987]~Marijuana$Year[Marijuana$Year <= 1996 & Marijuana$Year >= 1987], xlab = "Year", ylab = "Marijuana Use", main = "Marijuana Use Over the Years", pch = 16, col = "red", cex = 2)

An important feature of a relationship is its *shape*. Notice that in the scatterplots of Figures 5.1 and 5.2, although all points do not exactly fall along a single straight line, the points are represented well by a straight line. Accordingly, the relationships between fat content and calories and between the percentage of students taking the SAT exam and the average SAT Critical Reading score for the United States are said to be linear. By contrast, the variables of the scatterplot of Figure 5.3 are not systematically related because the points follow neither a single straight line nor a simple curve. We say that there is no relationship between the denomination of the bill and the number of such bills in circulation. In Figure 5.4, on the other hand, the variables are systematically related because the points of this scatterplot are best represented by a simple curve, not by a single straight line. Marijuana use is relatively high in the late 1980s and early 1990s, decreases until 1992 and then increases again through 1996. This particular type of curvilinear relationship is called *quadratic* because it has an approximately parabolic shape, and parabolic curves are represented by quadratic functions.

Another important feature of a relationship is its *direction*. Because the straight line representing the points of Figure 5.1 has positive slope, the linear relationship is said to be positive: that is, the higher the fat content, the higher the number of calories (and the lower the fat content, the lower the number of calories). On the other hand, because the straight line representing the points of Figure 5.2 has negative slope, the linear relationship is said to be negative. That is, the states with higher percentages of students taking the SAT tend to have lower average SAT Critical Reading scores (and the states with lower percentages of students taking the SAT tend to have higher average SAT Critical Reading scores). Because Figure 5.3 suggests no simple systematic relationship between the two variables in question (currency value and number in circulation), the notion of a direction of relationship is not meaningful. Finally, in the quadratic relationship of Figure 5.4 the direction of the relationship changes from negative to positive. For years 1988 through 1992, the earlier years are associated with higher marijuana use while the later years are associated with lower marijuana use. For years 1992 through 1996, the earlier years are associated with lower marijuana use while the later years are associated with higher marijuana use.

Relationships also may be characterized by their *strength*. Simply stated, the closer the points in the scatterplot are to the straight line (or curve) that best represents the points, the stronger the relationship between the two variables. If all the points in the scatterplot fall exactly on the line (or curve) that best represents the points, we would say that a perfect linear (or nonlinear) relationship exists between the two variables. The farther the points in the scatterplot are from the line (or curve), the weaker the linear (or nonlinear) relationship between the two variables.

Figures 5.5(a) through (i) provide a series of scatterplots varying in the direction and strength of the linear relationships they depict. They also include fit lines superimposed on the graphs to accentuate the strength and direction of the relationship.

The data for Figure 5.5(a) through Figure 5.5(i) are located in the file, Figures5_5.rda.

MORE R: To superimpose a fit line on a scatterplot as illustrated in Figure 5.5(a):

plot(Figure5_5\$ay~Figure5_5\$ax, xlab = "Days elapsed in a given year", ylab = "Days remaining in that same year")
abline(lm(Figure5_5\$ay~Figure5_5\$ax), col = "red")

Note that **abline()** plots a straight line, and **lm()** instructs R to draw as the straight line, the *line of best fit*, known as the *regression line* which will be described in greater detail in Chapter 6.

The .R file associated with this chapter and located on the text's website contains the code used to generate Figures 5.5(a) through 5.5(i) with the superimposed fit lines.

Figures 5.5 (a–d) depict increasingly weaker negative linear relationships because the points in these figures depart increasingly from the straight line that best represents them. While Figure 5.5(a) represents a perfect negative linear relationship because all points fall exactly on the straight line, Figures 5.5 (b–d) do not. Figure 5.5 (e) depicts no relationship between the two variables and Figures 5.5 (f–i) depict increasingly stronger positive linear relationships.

A scatterplot may be used to depict the shape, direction, and, to a lesser extent, the strength of the relationship between two variables, but summary statistics may also be used to quantify the strength and direction of relationships. In the case of two continuous variables, when both are on at least interval scales of measurement, the direction and strength of the linear relationship between them may be characterized by what is called the *Pearson product-moment correlation coefficient*.

☞ **Remark.** The Pearson correlation coefficient is named after Karl Pearson, who in 1896 published the first mathematically rigorous treatment of this index. However, it was Sir Francis Galton, a cousin of Charles Darwin, who first conceptualized the notion of correlation and regression (to be covered in the next chapter) in the 1870s through his work in genetics and, in particular, by examining two-dimensional scatterplots of the relationship between the sizes of sweet pea plants of mother–daughter pairs (Stanton, 2001).

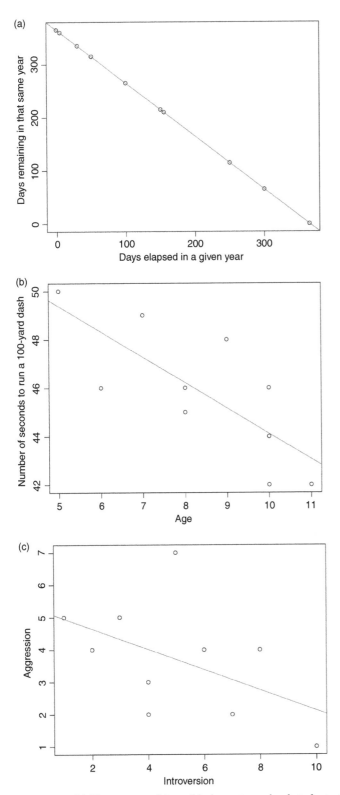

Figure 5.5 (a) The passage of time; (b) elementary school students; (c) adolescent boys; (d) college freshmen; (e) male college students; (f) college students; (g) children in grades K–3; (h) elementary school students; (i) dimensions of a tree

Figure 5.5 (*continued*)

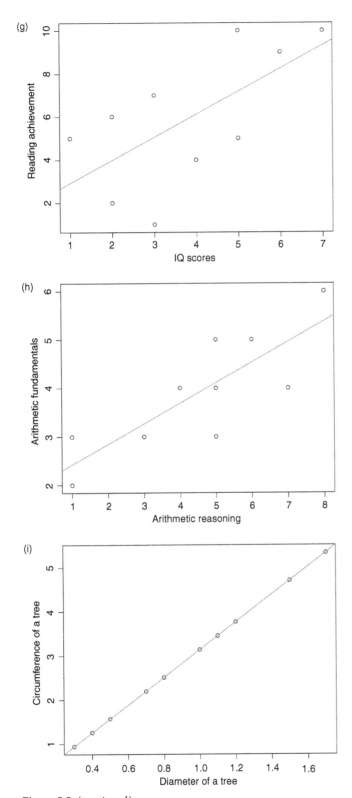

Figure 5.5 (*continued*)

While indices exist to represent the strength of nonlinear relationships, these are beyond the scope of our discussion, which, in this section, is confined to linear relationships only. For a more advanced treatment of correlation, including nonlinear relationships, the interested reader is referred to Cohen et al. (2003).

THE PEARSON PRODUCT-MOMENT CORRELATION COEFFICIENT

The strength of a linear relationship is characterized by the extent to which a straight line fits the data points. In the case of a *positive*, or *direct*, linear relationship, this is the extent to which high scores on one variable are paired with high scores on the other, and low scores on one variable are paired with low scores on the other. In the case of a *negative*, or *indirect*, linear relationship, this is the extent to which high scores on one variable are paired with low scores on the other, and vice versa.

To illustrate, we refer to the fat-content (X) and calorie (Y) values of the five types of hamburger given in Table 5.1 that we have observed to have a positive linear relationship. For convenience, as shown in Table 5.3, we index the values by a subscripting letter rather than by the type of hamburger itself.

We may determine whether high scores on fat content are paired with high scores on calories and whether low scores on fat content are paired with low scores on calories by first determining if each type of hamburger's fat-content value is high or low *within the set of fat-content values*. And we can do likewise for each type of hamburger's value for calories. Once we have labeled each fat-content value and calorie value as either high or low within its own distribution, we can compare one to the other for each type of hamburger. In so doing, we may determine the extent to which high fat-content values tend to be paired with high calorie values and low fat-content values tend to be paired with low calorie values.

In order to label a particular fat-content value as either high or low within its own distribution, we calculate the z-scores for each fat and calorie value within its own distribution. These z-scores, as calculated using the R commands **Hamburger\$zfat = scale(Hamburger\$fat)** and **Hamburger\$zcalories = scale(Hamburger\$calories)**, are shown in Table 5.4 for both X and Y.

To determine whether a high fat content is paired with a high calorie count, and whether a low fat content is paired with a low calorie count, we form the product of the two z-scores for each hamburger type. If both X and Y scores are high with regard to their respective distributions, then both terms in the product will be positive and the product itself will be positive. Likewise, if both the X and Y scores are low with regard to their respective distributions, then both terms in the product will be negative and the product will again be positive.

TABLE 5.3 Fat content and calories of five hamburger types		
Type of McDonald's hamburger (indexed)	**Grams of fat (X)**	**Calories(Y)**
1	$X_1 = 10$	$Y_1 = 270$
2	$X_2 = 14$	$Y_2 = 320$
3	$X_3 = 21$	$Y_3 = 430$
4	$X_4 = 30$	$Y_4 = 530$
5	$X_5 = 28$	$Y_5 = 530$

TABLE 5.4 Difference about the mean for grams of fat content and calories

Type of McDonald's hamburger (indexed)	fat (X)	calories (Y)	zfat	zcalories
1	$X_1 = 10$	$Y_1 = 270$	−1.226	−1.226
2	$X_2 = 14$	$Y_2 = 320$	−0.763	−0.806
3	$X_3 = 21$	$Y_3 = 430$	0.046	0.118
4	$X_4 = 30$	$Y_4 = 530$	1.087	0.957
5	$X_5 = 28$	$Y_5 = 530$	0.856	0.957

TABLE 5.5 Taking the product of the difference terms

Fat (X)	Calories (Y)	z_x	z_y	$z_x z_y$
$X_1 = 10$	$Y_1 = 270$	−1.226	−1.226	1.503
$X_2 = 14$	$Y_2 = 320$	−0.763	−0.806	0.615
$X_3 = 21$	$Y_3 = 430$	0.046	0.118	0.005
$X_4 = 30$	$Y_4 = 530$	1.087	0.957	1.041
$X_5 = 28$	$Y_5 = 530$	0.856	0.957	0.819

Notice that all the products in Table 5.5 are positive. A positive product results when either both terms are positive or both terms are negative.

☞ **Remark.** When one (but not both) of the differences is negative, signifying either a high X value paired with a low Y value or a low X value paired with a high Y value, a negative product results.

In order to obtain a summary measure that incorporates all types of hamburger and all types of fat-content and calorie values, we can approximate the *average* tendency of the values to have positive (or negative) products by dividing the sum of the products by $N-1$:

$$r = \frac{\sum z_x z_y}{N - 1}. \tag{5.1}$$

Equation 5.1 is called the *Pearson product-moment correlation coefficient*, denoted by the symbol r_{xy} or the letter r. Here, N represents the number of pairs of fat content and calorie count values in the dataset. In the McDonald's example, N equals 5 because there are 5 pairs of values. For these data, $r = 0.996$, rounded to three numbers after the decimal place.

MORE R: Using R to compute r as given by Equation 5.1, we first transform the fat and calorie values to *z*-scores:

Hamburger$zfat = scale(Hamburger$fat)
Hamburger$zcalories = scale(Hamburger$calories)

We then generate the product terms **zfat*zcalories**:

Hamburger$prod = Hamburger$zfat*Hamburger$zcalories

We then obtain the sum of the products:

prod_sum = sum(Hamburger$prod)

and the number of data points, N:

N = length(Hamburger$prod)

Note that the length command returns the number of values in the variable Hamburger
$prod, which is the sample size of the dataset. In R, a variable is arranged as a column of
values, called a *vector*, and the number of values in that vector is called the *length of the
vector*.

Finally, we calculate and display the results of Equation 5.1 in the console:

r = prod_sum/(N−1)
r

Note that the first line, **r = prod_sum/(N−1)**, stores the value of the Pearson product-
moment correlation coefficient in the local variable, r. The second line, **r**, displays this value.

The sign of the correlation indicates the direction of the relationship; the magnitude of
the correlation indicates the strength. The correlation is bounded between −1.00 and
+1.00 inclusive. A correlation value of −1.00 indicates a *perfect negative linear relationship*,
while a Pearson correlation value of +1.00 indicates a *perfect positive linear relationship*. A
correlation value of 0 indicates no linear relationship.

As expected, the sign of the correlation between fat and calories is positive, suggesting
that hamburgers with low fat content tend to have low calorie counts, and hamburgers
with high fat content tend to have high calorie counts. Furthermore, because the magnitude of this correlation is so close to 1.00, we may infer that the relationship between fat
content and calorie count is very strong.

☞ **Remark.** The calculation of *z*-scores for the numerator of Equation 5.1 requires that
we divide by both S_x and S_y. Because division by 0 is not defined, we must impose the
restriction that whenever either $S_x = 0$ or $S_y = 0$ (all the X values are the same or all the Y
values are the same) or both, the Pearson correlation coefficient will be undefined.
Conceptually, the Pearson correlation coefficient should not be defined in this case. For
example, suppose we wanted to determine the relationship between age rounded to the
nearest year (X) and income (Y), and the data consisted only of 25 year olds. Because there
is no variability in age for such data, the standard deviation of age would be zero, and there
would be no way to determine whether in fact income varies with age.

MORE R: To obtain the correlation coefficient between two variables (fat and calories), use either of the following commands:

cor(Hamburger$calories, Hamburger$fat)

or

cor.test(Hamburger$calories, Hamburger$fat, method = "Pearson")

Note that the **cor.test** function provides other information, including results from hypothesis tests and a confidence interval, which will be discussed in Chapter 15. For now, we focus on the output at the bottom, which displays the correlation coefficient as described above.

The output from the **cor** command is reproduced below:

0.9957418

The output from the **cor.test** command is reproduced below:

Pearson's product-moment correlation		
data: Hamburger$calories and Hamburger$fat		
$t = 18.709$, $df = 3$		p-value = 0.0003333
alternative hypothesis: true correlation is not equal to 0		
95 percent confidence interval:	0.9340276	0.9997331
sample estimates:	cor	0.9957418

Note that reversing the order of the variables in the **cor** command has no effect on the output because the bivariate correlation is a symmetric measure of a linear relationship. That is, $r_{xy} = r_{yx}$.

EXAMPLE 5.1 Given the data corresponding to Figures 5.2 through 5.4, find and interpret the correlations between (1) the percentage of students taking the SAT and the average Critical Reading SAT score in the United States; (2) the currency value of a bill and the total number of such bills in circulation; (3) percentage of marijuana use among twelfth graders and year, from 1987 through 1996.

Solution Using R, we obtain the following results (see the .R file for this chapter for commands).
1. $r = -0.86$, suggesting that states with larger percentages of students taking the SAT tend to have lower average Critical Reading SAT scores, and vice versa.
2. $r = 0.13$, suggesting that the currency value of a bill is only weakly positively linearly related to the total number of such bills in circulation. From the scatterplot of Figure 5.3, we may conclude further that knowing the currency value of a bill tells us almost nothing about how many such bills are in circulation.
3. $r = -0.42$, suggesting that percentage of marijuana use is negatively linearly related to the year of observation, from 1987 to 1996. However, we know from looking at the scatterplot of Figure 5.4, that correlation, which measures the strength and direction of the linear relationship, is not a good statistic to use to describe the relationship between these two variables. Over the entire span of years measured, the relationship is better described as quadratic, not linear. Alternatively, one could compute two correlations, one based on the data from 1992 and earlier, and the other on the data from 1992 and later. These two

correlations would better reflect the strong relationship between marijuana use and year of use, negative before 1992 and positive after 1992.

☞ **Remark.** When describing the nature of the linear relationship between two variables, you need to be careful to avoid causal language. For example, when we are looking at the positive relationship between weight and height among adults, it might be tempting to write, "As weight goes up, height goes up." However, that statement is not correct because plenty of adults gain weight as they age and their height does not change. A correct statement is, "Adults who are heavier tend to be taller, and adults who weigh less tend to be shorter." When writing up these descriptions, we recommend that you start the sentence with the unit of analysis of the dataset. So, for the Hamburger dataset we write, "Hamburgers with low fat content tend to have low calorie counts, and hamburgers with high fat content tend to have high calorie counts." For the States dataset we write, "States with larger percentages of students taking the SAT tend to have lower average Critical Reading SAT scores, and vice versa."

● ●

EXAMPLE 5.2 The following table gives the correlation coefficient for each of the scatterplots depicted in Figures 5.5(a–i). Do the magnitude and direction of these relationships corroborate the impressions obtained from the scatterplots?

Figure letter	Correlation, r
a	−1.00
b	−0.76
c	−0.50
d	−0.20
e	0.00
f	+0.32
g	+0.65
h	+0.82
i	+1.00

Solution The correlations (a) through (d) are increasingly less negative and corroborate the fact that the points in these figures depart increasingly from the negatively sloped straight line that best represents them. As expected, the correlation of Figure 5.5(e) is zero, and the correlations (f) through (i) are increasingly more positive.

INTERPRETING THE PEARSON CORRELATION COEFFICIENT

Judging the Strength of the Linear Relationship

Whether a Pearson correlation coefficient value r is to be judged unusually strong or unusually weak depends on the situation in which the correlation has been computed. For example, if we administered the Stanford–Binet intelligence test to a group of elementary school children and then re-administered the test to these same children a week later, the correlation value we would expect to obtain between the two administrations of the test is approximately $r = 0.90$. Under these circumstances, the correlation value of $r = 0.90$ would not be considered unusually strong; it would be considered typical. This is because, given the relatively short time between tests, it is unlikely that anything has happened to alter substantially the responses to the test.

Under different circumstances, a correlation value of $r = 0.90$ might be considered unusually strong. If, for example, two different tests had been used instead of only one (a test of intelligence and a test of creativity, for example), then a correlation of $r = 0.90$ might be considered unusually strong. Thus, the terms *strong* and *weak* are used to compare descriptively the obtained correlation value to the value we would expect under the given circumstances.

Within an applied psychology framework, specific criteria for categorizing the magnitude of linear relationships as strong, moderate, and weak were first introduced by Cohen (1988) and are now widely used in behavioral science research. The strength of the correlation also is known as its *effect size*.

According to an often-cited publication by Cohen (1988), Pearson correlation values approximately equal to:

$r = \pm 0.50$ are considered strong;
$r = \pm 0.30$ are considered moderate;
$r = \pm 0.10$ are considered weak.

Cohen's classification of a correlation of ± 0.50 as strong, comes from his assertion that "workers in personality-social psychology, both pure and applied (i.e., clinical, educational, personnel), normally encounter correlation coefficients above the 0.50–0.60 range only when the correlations are measurement reliability coefficients" (1988, p. 75).

Based on these criteria, case (h) of Example 5.2 ($r = 0.82$) indicates a *very strong* linear relationship between the two variables, whereas case (f) ($r_{xy} = 0.32$) indicates only a *moderate* linear relationship between the two variables. However, both are examples of typical correlation values within their respective contexts.

Because the sign of the correlation value indicates only the nature of the relationship between the two variables (whether it is positive or negative) and not its magnitude, a Pearson correlation value of +0.50 indicates a linear relationship of the same strength as a Pearson correlation coefficient value of −0.50. Likewise, a correlation of −0.76 represents a stronger linear relationship than a correlation of 0.65.

To get a sense of some of the correlation values that appear in the literature, Table 5.6 gives correlation coefficients for selected variables (Thorndike and Hagen, 1969).

The Correlation Scale Itself Is Ordinal

One may ask whether an increase in correlation values of 0.10 units represents a constant increase in the strength of the relationship regardless of the values of the correlations themselves. Because the Pearson correlation coefficient as a measure of linear relationship is on an ordinal level of measurement, it does not. Whereas a correlation value of +0.50 represents a stronger relationship between two variables than a correlation value of +0.30, and a correlation value of +0.30 represents a stronger relationship between two variables than a correlation value of +0.10, the increase in strength from +0.10 to +0.30 is not the same as (and is actually smaller than) the increase in strength from +0.30 to +0.50.

TABLE 5.6 Correlation coefficients for selected variables

Variables	Correlation coefficient
Heights of identical twins	0.95
Intelligence test scores of identical twins	0.88
Reading test scores grade 3 vs. grade 6	0.80
Rank in high school class vs. teachers' rating of work habits	0.73
Height vs. weight of 10-year-olds	0.60
Arithmetic computation test vs. nonverbal intelligence test (grade 8)	0.54
Height of brothers, adjusted for age	0.50
Intelligence test score vs. parental occupational level	0.30
Strength of grip vs. speed of running	0.16
Height vs. Binet IQ	0.06
Ratio of head length to width vs. intelligence	0.01
Armed Forces Qualification Test scores of recruits vs. number of school grades repeated	−0.27
Artist interest vs. banker interest	−0.64

Correlation Does Not Imply Causation

Another important consideration in interpreting a Pearson correlation coefficient value is that, in general, the existence of a correlation between two variables does not necessarily imply the existence of a causal link between these two variables.

For example, suppose we obtain a correlation of $r = +0.60$ between the number of television sets in various countries at a particular time and the number of telephones in the same countries at the same time. This correlation does not necessarily imply that a causal relationship exists between the number of televisions and the number of telephones in a country. For example, importing a million television sets into a country will not automatically increase that country's number of telephones. Similarly, importing a million telephones into a country will not automatically increase that country's number of television sets.

It is possible that the values of both of these variables are due to a common third variable (such as the industrial level of the country or its gross national product) and that this third variable causes both the other two variables. If this is true, an artificial increase in either the number of television sets or the number of telephones will not cause a change in the other variable, because the real cause of normal changes, the third variable, has remained the same. In general, causal links cannot be deduced merely from the existence of a correlation between two variables. All that can justifiably be said is that the two variables are related. We need more information than the existence of a correlation to establish a cause-and-effect relationship.

The Effect of Linear Transformations

Another important point in interpreting a Pearson correlation coefficient relates to the units of measurement employed. Suppose you compared the heights of individuals measured in inches to the weights of the same individuals measured in pounds and found a Pearson correlation value of $r = 0.30$. Would you expect the correlation value to change if you re-computed the correlation, measuring the heights of the individuals in feet and the weights of the individuals in ounces, and could get all measurements perfectly? We do not suppose you would. If a person's height is high relative to that of others in the group when the heights are measured in inches, it should be just as high relative to the others when the heights are measured in feet. That is, the position of an individual relative to his or her group will remain the same, despite the fact that the scores of the group are transformed into some other scale or frame of reference. In this example, each original height score, measured in inches, was converted to feet by dividing by 12. In addition, each original weight score, measured in pounds, was converted to ounces by multiplying by 16.

Had a constant value been added to either height or weight or both, in addition to the multiplication or division that was done, the relative standing of individuals within each group would still have been the same, and the correlation value would have remained the same. Thus, linear transformations of the X variable and/or Y variable do not change the magnitude (size) of the Pearson correlation coefficient. The sign of the coefficient will be reversed only if one but not both of the sets of scores (X or Y) is multiplied or divided by a negative number. For example, if the correlation between X and Y is $r_{xy} = 0.70$, and if all the X scores are multiplied by -2, the new correlation coefficient will have the same magnitude but a reversed sign. That is, the new correlation coefficient value will be $r_{xy} = -0.70$.

Restriction of Range

When a correlation is computed on a subset of the natural range of one or both variables, the magnitude of the correlation may be either smaller or larger than the correlation computed on the entire range.

Suppose, for example, that we are interested in the correlation coefficient between Age X and Weight Y for a group of individuals whose ages range from 1 year to 15 years. A correlation coefficient calculated on only the very youngest and the very oldest of the individuals (say, on only those individuals who are 3 or younger or 12 or older), will result in a stronger correlation than one based on the entire set of data. This is because, in this subset, there is a greater tendency for the younger group to have lower weight and for the older group to have higher weight than for the entire set of individuals taken as a whole.

Analogously, if we calculate the correlation coefficient on a restricted, more homogeneous subset of the entire range (such as on only those individuals with ages between $X = 9$ and $X = 11$ years of age), then we can expect the correlation to be weaker (closer to 0) than if it were calculated on the entire set of data. This is because, with all the individuals in this subset being so similar to each other in age relative to the entire group, there will be less of a tendency for differences in age among the individuals to correspond to systematic differences in weight.

We present another example of restriction of range that involves the elimination of the middle values of the distribution. The Brainsz dataset, taken from the DASL (Datasets and Stories Library) website, is based on a study by Willerman et al. (1991) in which such a method was used. The purpose of the study was to examine the relationships between brain size, gender, and intelligence. The research participants consisted of 40 introductory psychology students who were selected from a larger pool of psychology students with total Scholastic Aptitude Test scores higher than 1,350 or lower than 940, where these scores were used to measure intelligence. In other words, students with moderate intelligence scores were omitted from the study. The result was that the correlations between gender and intelligence and brain size and intelligence were inflated.

The conclusion to be drawn from this discussion is that you should not expect the correlation between two variables to be the same in a large group as it is in a subset of that group if the subset is either more or less homogeneous than the larger group in one or both of the variables under study. By eliminating the middle group, the subset becomes less homogeneous than the original, larger group.

The Shape of the Underlying Distributions

Another factor that affects the size of a correlation is the relative similarity or dissimilarity of the shapes of the X and Y distributions. Simply stated, a perfect positive correlation between X and Y ($r = +1$) can only occur when the X and Y distributions have exactly the same shape. For example, if X were positively skewed and Y were negatively skewed, we would expect this difference in shape to result in a weaker positive correlation than if the two distributions had the same shape. If one or both of the variables is skewed, one should consider applying a nonlinear transformation (e.g., square root or logarithm) to symmetrize the distribution(s) prior to calculating r.

The Reliability of the Data

Yet another factor that affects the size of r concerns the reliability of the X and Y values or, in other words, the extent to which the X and Y values consistently reflect the amounts of the characteristics they are supposed to represent. The less reliable a measure, the greater the amount of error in each of its observed values. Because error, by definition, is random and does not correlate with anything, the more error a variable contains, the less we can expect that variable to correlate with any other variable. Consequently, it is important to check the reliability of any measuring instruments used and to employ those instruments with a high reliability. A more complete discussion of reliability is beyond the scope of this book. The interested reader should consult a text on tests and measurement. One such example is Cohen and Swerdlik (2005).

WHEN AT LEAST ONE VARIABLE IS ORDINAL AND THE OTHER IS AT LEAST ORDINAL: THE SPEARMAN RANK CORRELATION COEFFICIENT

The Spearman rank correlation coefficient measures the strength of the linear relationship between two variables when the values of each variable are rank-ordered from 1 to N, where N is the number of pairs of values. The formula for the Spearman correlation coefficient, given as Equation 5.2 and denoted by r_s, may be obtained as a special case of the Pearson correlation coefficient when the N cases of each variable are assigned the integer values from 1 to N, inclusive, and no two cases share the same value:

$$r_s = 1 - \frac{6 \sum d_i^2}{N^3 - N},$$

(5.2)

where d_i represents the difference between ranks for each case. As a special case of the Pearson correlation coefficient, r_s is interpreted in the same way as the Pearson. For example, notice that when the ranks for the two variables being correlated are identical, the differences between them will be zero, and the Spearman correlation coefficient will be 1.00, indicating a perfect positive correlation between the variables.

EXAMPLE 5.3 Consider the McDonald's hamburger data. Suppose we are not convinced that our measure of fat is interval-leveled. That is, while we believe that the Quarter Pounder™, with 21 grams of fat, has more fat than the Cheeseburger, with 14 grams of fat, and less fat than the Big Mac™, with 28 grams of fat, we are not convinced that, in terms of fat, the Quarter Pounder™ is midway between the other two types of hamburger. Accordingly, we decide to consider the fat scale as ordinal, and transform the original data to ranked data. To find the relationship between fat and calories, we compute the Spearman correlation coefficient on the ranked data instead of the Pearson correlation coefficient on the original data.

☞ **Remark.** The formula for the Spearman is derived as a special case of the Pearson formula by taking advantage of the fact that the data are rankings from 1 to N. We may note that the Spearman correlation coefficient on the ranked data will give the identical result as the Pearson correlation coefficient on the ranked data.

Solution To obtain the ranked data by hand, we simply rank order the five types of hamburger in terms of fat and assign a value from 1 to 5 to each hamburger to denote its place in that ranking. Then, we assign ranked values to the five types of hamburger in terms of calories. The original data, together with their rankings, are provided in the first five columns of Table 5.7. The last two columns contain the difference and squared difference between the ranks for each hamburger, respectively.

Notice that the Quarter Pounder with Cheese™ and the Big Mac™ have the same original calorie count of 530. Accordingly, they are tied for first and second place in the rankings. We, therefore, assign the average of these two ranks, 1.5, to each of them. The same procedure is used whenever ties occur.

The Spearman correlation coefficient equals, in this case, $r_s = 1 - 6(0.50)/(125 - 5) = 0.975$, suggesting that there is a very strong linear relationship between fat and calories expressed in ranked form. Notice that this value is slightly different from the Pearson correlation coefficient of $r = 0.996$, because the Quarter Pounder with Cheese™ and the Big Mac™ are tied in their numbers of calories.

TABLE 5.7 Original and ranked data for hamburger fat and calories

Hamburger type	Grams of fat (X)	Ranked fat	Calories (Y)	Ranked calories	d_i	d_i^2
Hamburger	$X_1 = 10$	5	$Y_1 = 270$	5	0	0
Cheeseburger	$X_2 = 14$	4	$Y_2 = 320$	4	0	0
Quarter Pounder™	$X_3 = 21$	3	$Y_3 = 430$	3	0	0
Quarter Pounder w/cheese™	$X_4 = 30$	1	$Y_4 = 530$	1.5	−0.5	0.25
Big Mac™	$X_5 = 28$	2	$Y_5 = 530$	1.5	0.5	0.25

MORE R: To obtain the Spearman correlation coefficient (between calories and fat), type the following command:

cor.test(Hamburger$calories, Hamburger$fat, method = "spearman")

☞ **Remark.** The Pearson correlation coefficient measures the direction and strength of the linear relationship between the *numerical values* assigned to the variables in question. Because these numerical values may take on many forms, including rankings and dichotomies, we need to be sensitive to the nature of these numerical values when interpretations are made.

WHEN AT LEAST ONE VARIABLE IS DICHOTOMOUS: OTHER SPECIAL CASES OF THE PEARSON CORRELATION COEFFICIENT

In measuring the correlation between two variables when one is at least interval and the other is dichotomous or when both are dichotomous, we may use the Pearson correlation coefficient. In these cases, however, the Pearson correlation coefficient is often given a different name to reflect the type of data being analyzed.

The *point biserial correlation coefficient* is the name given to the special case of the Pearson for measuring the direction and strength of the linear relationship between two variables when one is dichotomous and the other is at least interval. The *phi coefficient* is the name given to the special case of the Pearson for measuring the direction and strength of the linear relationship between two dichotomous variables.

THE POINT BISERIAL CORRELATION COEFFICIENT: THE CASE OF ONE AT LEAST INTERVAL AND ONE DICHOTOMOUS VARIABLE

EXAMPLE 5.4 Use the McDonald's dataset to perform a correlation analysis to determine whether there is a relationship between the calorie count of a burger and whether or not it comes with cheese and, if there is one, to describe it. In other words, we will perform a correlation analysis to determine whether there is a difference in the average number of calories between those hamburgers with and those without cheese. Table 5.8 contains, for each of the five types of hamburger, the calories and whether or not the burger has cheese.

TABLE 5.8 Calories and cheese for McDonald's hamburgers

Hamburger type	Calories (Y)	Cheese (0 = "no" 1 = "yes")
Hamburger	270	0
Cheeseburger	320	1
Quarter Pounder™	430	0
Quarter Pounder w/cheese™	530	1
Big Mac™	530	1

Solution Cheese is a dichotomous variable as it takes on two values (no, yes) while the variable calories is measured at the ratio level. We use R to obtain the Pearson correlation coefficient because we know that the Pearson will give the identical numerical result as the point biserial correlation coefficient, the special case of the Pearson when one variable is at least interval and the other is dichotomous.

As in the case of two at least interval variables, we first depict the relationship between these two variables using a scatterplot. If we proceed to obtain the scatterplot, as shown earlier, with cheese as the *X* variable and calories as the *Y* variable, the result appears as in Figure 5.6. Recall that for these data, hamburgers without cheese are assigned the value 0 on cheese, and hamburgers with cheese are assigned the value 1.

Because cheese is dichotomous, the scatterplot does not appear as a cloud of points as it does in Figures 5.1 through 5.4, but rather, as two vertical columns of points centered, respectively, over 0 (for no cheese) and 1 (for cheese). By inspecting the scatterplot and, in particular, the locations of the two vertical columns relative to the calorie scale (the *y*-axis), we may infer that, for these McDonald's hamburgers, hamburgers with cheese have more calories, on average, than those without cheese.

MORE R: To create a variable for cheese content on each hamburger, we type:

Hamburger$cheese = c(0,1,0,1,1)

Furthermore, because hamburgers without cheese are assigned a value of 0 and hamburgers with cheese a value of 1, we may note that low scores on cheese (no cheese) associate with low scores on calories, and high scores on cheese (cheese) associate with high scores on calories. Given the coding of our variables, then, we should expect to obtain a positive correlation between calorie and cheese content for these hamburgers. Using R, we find the correlation between cheese and calories is $r = 0.506$, a strong positive correlation.

☞ **Remark.** Had the coding scheme been reversed for the variable cheese so that hamburgers with no cheese were assigned a 1 and hamburgers with cheese a 0, the sign of the correlation coefficient would have changed from positive to negative, leaving the interpretation of the direction of the relationship unchanged. While the coding reversal changes the sign of the correlation, it does not affect the magnitude.

Notice that the horizontal axis of the scatterplot given in Figure 5.6 is treating cheese as if it were continuous. It makes more sense to have a discrete horizontal axis with two categories representing the two types of cheese content. Such a graph is provided as Figure 5.7.

EXAMPLE 5.5 Use the NELS dataset to determine the correlation for students in the West between (1) gender and achievement in science in twelfth grade, and (2) gender and achievement in reading in twelfth grade. Our focus on the students in the West in this example is for heuristic reasons.

Solution
1. Gender is a dichotomous variable as it takes on two values (male, female) while achievement in science in twelfth grade is a continuous variable. We use R to obtain the Pearson

Figure 5.6 Scatterplot of calorie and cheese content for McDonald's hamburgers

Figure 5.7 Scatterplot of calorie and cheese content for McDonald's hamburgers

correlation coefficient because we know that the Pearson will give the identical numerical result as the point biserial correlation coefficient, the special case of the Pearson when one variable is continuous and the other is dichotomous.

Given our question, we first need to select the students in the West so that our analysis will be confined to those students only.

MORE R: To obtain a correlation on a subset of the data, we use square brackets as part of the command to select the subset of students in the West:

cor(NELS\$achsci12[NELS\$region == "West"], as.numeric(NELS\$gender)[NELS\$region == "West"])

The **as.numeric** function surrounding **NELS\$gender** tells R to treat gender as a numeric variable.

Note that **cor.test** would have given the same result as **cor**.

By inspecting the scatterplot in Figure 5.8 and, in particular, the locations of the two vertical columns relative to the achievement in science scale (the y-axis), we may infer that, for students in the West, males do slightly better in science achievement in twelfth grade than females.

Furthermore, because males are assigned a value of 1 and females a value of 2, we may note that low scores on gender (Males) associate with high scores on achievement in science and high scores on gender (Females) associate with low scores on achievement in science. Given the coding of our variables, then, we should expect to obtain a negative correlation between gender and achievement in science in twelfth grade. Using R, we find that for the 93 students in the West, the correlation between gender and achievement in science in twelfth grade is $r = -0.395$, a moderately strong negative correlation.

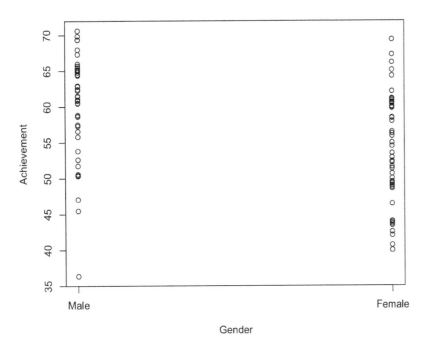

Figure 5.8 Scatterplot of gender and twelfth grade science achievement for students in the West

☞ **Remark.** Notice the outlier in the distribution of male science achievement scores in Figure 5.8. Checking further, we find that this outlier score belongs to case number 194.

MORE R: To find the row number of the outlier, we type:

which(NELS\$achsci12==min(NELS\$achsci12[NELS\$region   ==   "West"   &   NELS \$gender=="Male"]))

This command looks for the row number of the achsci12 score that is the minimum score of males in the West. Note that the **min** command finds the minimum value of a variable, while the **max** command can be used to find the maximum value. Since row number is the same as the value of the id variable, we can use **which** to find the id number we seek.

To see to what extent score 194 influences the result, we re-compute the correlation between gender and achievement in science on these data, but without the score for this individual. The result is $r = -0.443$, suggesting an even stronger relationship between gender and science achievement in twelfth grade for students in the West without this outlier.

Solution

2. We plot reading achievement against gender. The commands for this plot are available in the accompanying .R file for this chapter.

Notice that in Figure 5.9, the locations of the two vertical columns relative to the achievement in reading scale (y-axis) are not as different from one another as they are in Figure 5.8

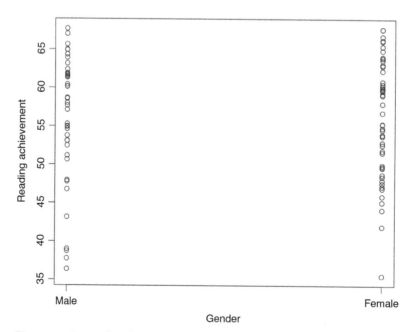

Figure 5.9 Scatterplot of gender and reading achievement in twelfth grade for students in the West

(relative to science achievement). In fact, they are hardly different from one another at all, suggesting that there is little or no relationship between gender and achievement in reading in twelfth grade for students in the West. That is, boys do not appear to do better or worse than girls in reading achievement in the twelfth grade. Using R, we find that for the 93 students in the West, the Pearson correlation coefficient between sex and reading achievement in the twelfth grade is $r = -0.021$, confirming our impressions of little or no relationship.

☞ **Remark.** From the above two results, we may infer that the stronger the correlation between a dichotomous variable and a continuous one, the greater the separation between the two groups, designated by the dichotomous variable, in terms of the values on the continuous measure. On average, the reading achievement distributions for boys and girls were quite similar, whereas the science achievement distributions for boys and girls were not. Conceptually, therefore it should make sense that a point biserial correlation reflects the degree to which the means of the two groups on the continuous measure are different. The formula for the point biserial correlation coefficient, given as Equation 5.3, makes this interpretation clear:

$$r_{pb} = \frac{(\bar{Y}_1 - \bar{Y}_0)S_X}{S_Y}, \tag{5.3}$$

where $\bar{Y}_1$ and $\bar{Y}_0$ are the Y means of the groups designated by the dichotomous variable. S_X and S_Y represent the standard deviations of X and Y, respectively. Note that because X is dichotomous and takes on the values 0 and 1, S_X can be expressed as $\sqrt{pq}$, where p and q are the respective proportions of the total for each of the two groups. From Equation 5.3, we realize that when there is no separation between the two groups on the continuous measure, Y, (i.e., when $\bar{Y}_1 = \bar{Y}_0$), r_{pb} will equal zero. Likewise, the larger the separation between the two groups relative to the spread (i.e., the more discrepant and are relative to the spread), the stronger the correlation, r_{pb}, will be.

THE PHI COEFFICIENT: THE CASE OF TWO DICHOTOMOUS VARIABLES

As noted earlier, when both variables are dichotomous the Pearson correlation coefficient may be expressed in a simplified, numerically equivalent form, called the phi coefficient.

EXAMPLE 5.6 Use the NELS data to determine the correlation between (1) nursery school attendance and gender for students in the South and (2) nursery school attendance and computer ownership for students in the West.

Solution (1) To select students from the South only, we must use square brackets; and, in particular, set **NELS$region == "South"**. We then proceed with the solution to the problem.

MORE R: To obtain the correlation in question, we must add an argument to the **cor** command to account for the fact that there are missing values in the variables we are working with:

cor(as.numeric(NELS$nursery[NELS$region == "South"]), as.numeric(NELS$gender[NELS$region == "South"]), use = "complete.obs")

In this case, the **use = "complete.obs"** argument tells R to use only complete observations; that is, R should remove cases that have missing values on region or gender before computing the correlation. To learn more about the **cor** command, type **?cor** into the console and press **Enter**.

While scatterplots were useful in depicting the types of bivariate relationship discussed earlier in this chapter, as Figure 5.10 illustrates, they are not useful when the two variables in question are both dichotomous.

If there were a relationship between gender and nursery school attendance, then the pattern of frequencies of the four cells, represented by the four points in Figure 5.10, would vary in a systematic way. That is, a relationship would be suggested if, for example, the relative frequency of girls who attended nursery school were different from the relative frequency of boys who attended nursery school. Said differently, if the likelihood of attending nursery school varied as a function of gender, then a relationship between the two variables would be said to exist. To obtain information on the frequencies, an alternative graphic is the clustered bar graph.

MORE R: To obtain a clustered bar graph (as shown in Figure 5.11), type:

barplot(table(NELS$nursery[NELS$region == "South"], NELS$gender[NELS$region == "South"]), beside = T, legend.text = c("No", "Yes"), args.legend = list(x = 3, y = 50, bty = "n"))

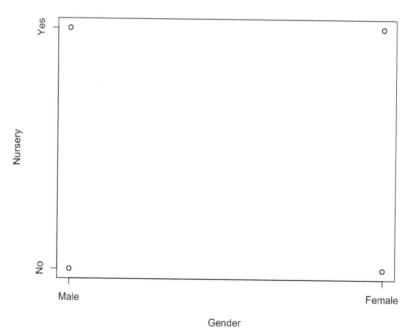

Figure 5.10 Scatterplot of nursery school attendance by gender for students in the South

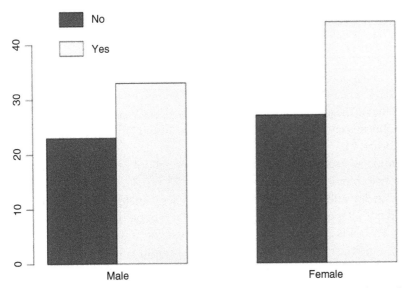

Figure 5.11 Clustered bar graph of nursery school attendance and gender for students in the South

Note that the variable nursery will have two boxes, one labeled "No" and the other labeled "Yes," and these boxes will have different colors. The argument **legend.text** creates a legend to indicate which color has been assigned to "No" and which to "Yes." In addition, each pair of boxes will be grouped by gender so that one pair will be grouped together for Males and the other for Females. Furthermore, **beside = T** tells R to plot the bars side-by-side rather than stacked on top of each other, and **args.legend** repositions the legend box to the given x- and y-coordinates and **bty = "n"** removes the outline around the legend box.

Notice that each bar represents one of the four points of the scatterplot depicted in Figure 5.10 and that the heights of the bars represent the corresponding frequencies. The relative difference in bar heights between those who have attended nursery school and those who have not is similar for males and females in both direction and magnitude. This similarity in profiles suggests little or no relationship between nursery school attendance and gender for these students in the South.

MORE R: To obtain a crosstab table (as given in Figure 5.12), instead of a clustered bar graph, of the frequencies of each of the four cells represented by nursery attended and gender, we type:

table(NELS$nursery[NELS$region == "South"], NELS$gender[NELS$region == "South"])

To understand whether nursery school attendance varies as a function of gender, we compare the pattern of the total counts either for gender or for nursery school to the pattern of cell counts by

	Male	Female
No	23	27
Yes	33	44

Figure 5.12 Cross-tabulation of nursery school attended by gender for students in the South

either row or column. The total counts are called *marginals* since they appear in the margins of the crosstabs table. The nursery school (or row) marginals are 50 and 77 while the gender (or column) marginals are 56 and 71.

The proportion of males who did attend nursery school relative to the total number of individuals who did attend nursery school is $33/77 = 0.43$. That is, 43 percent of the individuals who did attend nursery school are males. Analogously, the proportion of males who did not attend nursery relative to the total number of individuals who did not attend nursery school is $23/50 = 0.46$. That is, 46 percent of the individuals who did not attend nursery school are males. Because these proportions are nearly equal, we may conclude that there is little or no relationship between gender and nursery school attendance. An analysis based on a comparison between those who did and did not attend nursery school for males and females separately would have led to the same result.

An alternative analysis of the relationship may be based on a comparison of the ratio of frequencies that appear in the column marginals (e.g., 56 to 71) to the ratio of frequencies that appear in the columns within each row of the table. That is, we would expect the same ratio of column marginals between males and females (e.g., 56 to 71) to be replicated in each row if there were no relationship. The ratio of males to females overall is 56 to 71 (equivalently, 1 to 1.27); the ratio of males to females for those who attended nursery school is 33 to 44 (equivalently, 1 to 1.33); and, the ratio of males to females for those who did not attend nursery school is 23 to 27 (equivalently, 1 to 1.17). These ratios are not identical, but they are close in value, suggesting, once again, little or no relationship between gender and nursery school attendance.

We may measure the magnitude of this relationship by computing the phi coefficient. To do so, we calculate the Pearson correlation coefficient as before, since the phi coefficient is a special case of the Pearson. The result of this calculation is that $r = 0.031$, suggesting that, as expected, little or no relationship exists between these variables. Based on our earlier interpretation of the results of the crosstabs, you should be able to justify the positive sign associated with this correlation value.

☞ **Remark.** The cross-tabulation of Figure 5.12 also is called a *contingency table* because the entries in each cell are contingent upon the row and column of each cell.

☞ **Remark.** The phi coefficient may be expressed as a special case of the Pearson correlation coefficient that relates to the entries in the contingency table. In particular, if we label the cells

A	B
C	D

then the phi coefficient is given by Equation 5.4,

$$\phi = \frac{AD - BC}{\sqrt{(A+B)(C+D)(A+C)(B+D)}} \tag{5.4}$$

In the case of the data of Figure 5.12, we obtain the following result:

$$\phi = \frac{44 \times 23 - 33 \times 27}{\sqrt{77 \times 50 \times 56 \times 71}} = \frac{121}{3912.5} = 0.031,$$

which agrees with our earlier result when using the Pearson correlation coefficient.

We now return to solving the second part of Example 5.6.

Solution (2)

MORE R: To plot a clustered bar graph (Figure 5.13) and a crosstab (Figure 5.14) between computer and gender for those in the West, type:

barplot(table(NELS\$computer[NELS\$region == "West"],NELS\$nursery[NELS\$region == "West"]), beside = T, legend.text = c("No Computer", "Yes Computer"), xlab = "Nursery Attendence", args.legend = list(x = 5, y = 40, bty = "n"))
table(NELS\$computer[NELS\$region == "West"],NELS\$nursery[NELS\$region == "West"])

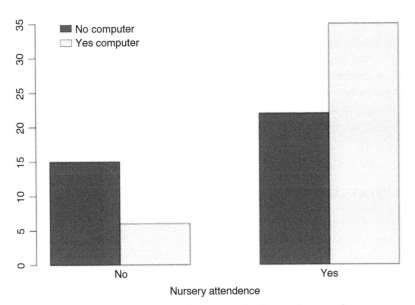

Figure 5.13 Clustered bar graph of nursery school attendance and computer ownership for students in the West

	No	Yes
No	15	22
Yes	6	35

Figure 5.14 Cross-tabulation of computer ownership by nursery school attendance for students in the West. The rows represent whether a computer was owned by the family in eighth grade, and the columns represent whether the child attended nursery school.

The bar graph of Figure 5.13 suggests a relationship between eighth grade computer ownership and past nursery school attendance. The relative difference in bar heights between those who owned computers in eighth grade and those who did not is strikingly different in both magnitude and direction for those who attended nursery school and those who did not. In particular, those who attended nursery school were more likely to own a computer in eighth grade whereas those who did not attend nursery school were more likely not to own a computer in eighth grade.

As one would expect, Figure 5.14 also suggests a relationship between these two variables. Among students who had attended nursery school, 39 percent did not own a computer while among students who had not attended nursery school, 71 percent did not own a computer.

Alternatively, the ratio of non-computer ownership to computer ownership for those who attended nursery school is 22 to 35 (equivalently, 1 to 1.59), while the ratio for those who did not attend nursery school is 15 to 6 (equivalently, 1 to 0.4). Because the individual row ratios differ from the marginal ratio of 1 to 1.11 (and from each other), a systematic relationship appears to exist between these two dichotomous variables for the West. In particular, the likelihood of computer ownership is greater for those families who sent their children to nursery school (1.59 versus 1.11) than for those who did not (0.4 versus 1.11).

To measure the magnitude of this relationship using a single summary statistic, we compute the Pearson correlation coefficient using R and find the correlation for **region == "West"** to be moderate in size ($r = 0.292$). The positive direction of the correlation tells us that low values on computer ownership (noes) associate with low values on attended nursery school (noes) and vice versa, thus corroborating our conclusions based on either the clustered bar graph of Figure 5.13 or contingency table of Figure 5.14.

OTHER VISUAL DISPLAYS OF BIVARIATE RELATIONSHIPS

In the foregoing sections of this chapter, we discussed the quantification of linear relationships between two variables in the case where (1) both variables are at least interval, (2) both are dichotomous, (3) one is at least interval and the other is dichotomous, and (4) both are ranked. We also discussed ways to visually represent the relationships contained within these four cases. In this section we revisit the boxplot and clustered bar graph and show their versatility in representing relationships that arise from (2) and (3) and variations of (2) and (3) that involve nominal-

and ordinal-leveled variables that are not necessarily dichotomous. We present these graphics without corresponding indices for quantifying the nature and magnitude of the relationships represented.

EXAMPLE 5.7 Use a boxplot to depict for students in the West the relationships between (1) gender and achievement in science in twelfth grade and (2) gender and achievement in reading in twelfth grade. This question was addressed earlier in Example 5.5.

Solution Notice that the boxplot in Figure 5.15 resembles closely the scatterplot of Figure 5.8 and offers the same interpretation – males tend to score higher than females on science achievement in twelfth grade for students in the West.

The boxplot depicting reading achievement in twelfth grade by gender appears in Figure 5.16 and also resembles closely the scatterplot of Figure 5.9.

Although we have used the boxplot to compare the distributions of a continuous measure for two groups, we may also use boxplots to compare the distributions of a continuous measure for any (reasonably small) number of groups, and in so doing, look for a relationship between group membership and the continuous measure.

☞ **Remark.** Because group membership typically is nominal-leveled, with more than two groups, the relationship between group membership and a continuous measure cannot be described meaningfully as linear. From this it follows that one would not want to compute a Pearson correlation coefficient on nominal data with more than two categories because its interpretation, as a measure of linear relationship, would be

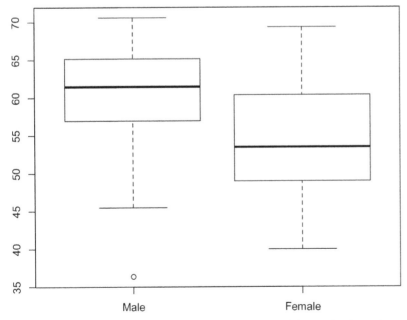

Figure 5.15 Boxplot of science achievement in twelfth grade by gender for students in the West

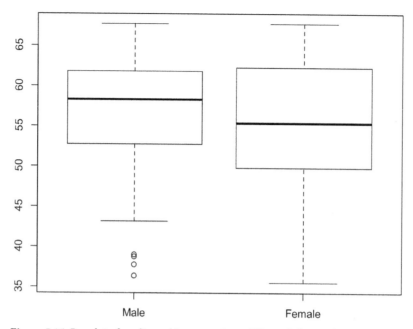

Figure 5.16 Boxplot of reading achievement in twelfth grade by gender for students in the West

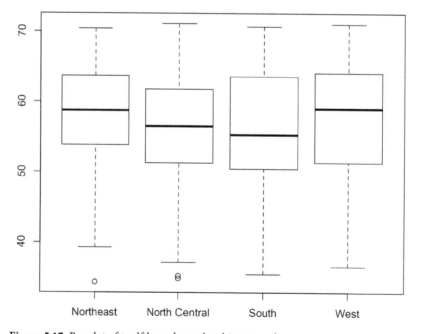

Figure 5.17 Boxplot of twelfth grade math achievement by region

meaningless. The type of relationship that can be explored with such data is simply whether the groups, on average, differ from one another on the continuous measure. An index for measuring the strength of this type of relationship will be discussed in a later chapter.

. . . .

EXAMPLE 5.8 Construct a boxplot of twelfth grade math achievement by region and use it to determine whether there appears to be a relationship between the two variables (Figure 5.17).

Solution Because region is a nominal-leveled variable, the order of the four region categories (Northeast, North Central, South, and West) on the x-axis is arbitrary. As a result, it would not be meaningful to attempt to interpret the relationship between region and mathematics achievement in twelfth grade as linear. The best we can do is to define the relationship between these two variables in terms of the extent to which the four regions, on average, differ from one another on mathematics achievement in twelfth grade.

Given that the medians for the four groups are different from one another, we say that there appears to be a relationship between region and twelfth grade math achievement for the students in our NELS dataset. The highest level of math achievement is in the West, while the lowest is in the South, with the other regions being intermediate.

As we have seen, when both variables are dichotomous, an appropriate visual display is the *clustered bar graph,* and an appropriate statistical indicator of the relationship is the contingency table and the associated percentages. The clustered bar graph, the contingency table, and percentages may be used also when one or both variables have more than two, yet a reasonably small number of categories.

. . . .

EXAMPLE 5.9 Do families in the NELS dataset differ on computer ownership by the region of the country in which they reside?

Solution The contingency table generated using the command **table(NELS$computer, NELS $region)** is reproduced below:

	Northeast	North Central	South	West
No	46	89	86	42
Yes	60	62	64	51

The results in the contingency table indicate that there is a relationship between computer ownership and region. Students in the Northeast and West were more likely to own a computer than not, with 56.6 percent and 54.8 percent, respectively, owning a computer. Students in the North Central and South were less likely to own a computer than not, with 41.1 percent and 42.7 percent, respectively, owning a computer.

The clustered bar graph is given below using the command:

barplot(table(NELS$computer, NELS$region), beside = T, legend.text = c("No", "Yes"), args. legend = list(x = 14, y = 100, bty = "n"))

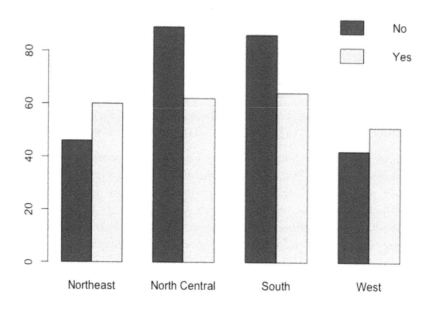

SELECTION OF APPROPRIATE STATISTIC OR GRAPH TO SUMMARIZE A RELATIONSHIP

The table below provides guidelines for selecting appropriate graphs and statistics for describing bivariate relationships. Other choices may also be correct.

Levels of measurement	Nominal with two categories	Nominal with more than two categories or ordinal with more than two categories but not more than five categories	Ordinal with five or more categories	Scale
Nominal with two categories	Pearson correlation or percentages from cross-tabulation and clustered bar graph	Percentages from cross-tabulation and clustered bar graph	Spearman correlation and interactive scatterplot or boxplot	Pearson correlation and interactive scatterplot or boxplot
Nominal with more than two categories or ordinal with more than two categories but not more than five categories	Percentages from cross-tabulation and clustered bar graph	Percentages from cross-tabulation and clustered bar graph	Spearman correlation (if both ordinal) or medians and interactive scatterplot or boxplot	Means or medians (depending on skew) and interactive scatterplot or boxplot
Ordinal with five or more categories	Spearman correlation and interactive scatterplot or boxplot	Spearman correlation (if both ordinal) or medians and interactive scatterplot or boxplot	Spearman correlation and scatterplot	Spearman correlation and scatterplot
Scale	Pearson correlation and interactive scatterplot or boxplot	Means or medians (depending on skew) and interactive scatterplot or boxplot	Spearman correlation and scatterplot	Pearson correlation and scatterplot. Correlation should not be used if scatterplot is well fit by a simple curve

SUMMARY OF R COMMANDS

(See also the .R file for Chapter 5.)

Create	Command lines
Create a scatterplot (Figure 5.1)	plot(Hamburger$calories~Hamburger$fat, xlab = "Fat", ylab = "Calories")
Create a scatterplot with values restricted on an axis (Figure 5.4)	plot(Marijuana$MarijuanaUse[Marijuana$Year <= 1996 & Marijuana$Year >= 1987]~Marijuana$Year[Marijuana$Year <= 1996 & Marijuana$Year >= 1987], xlab = "Year", ylab = "Marijuana Use")
Create a scatterplot with title and customized points (customization of Figure 5.4)	plot(Marijuana$MarijuanaUse[Marijuana$Year <= 1996 & Marijuana$Year >= 1987]~Marijuana$Year[Marijuana$Year <= 1996 & Marijuana$Year >= 1987], xlab = "Year", ylab = "Marijuana Use", main = "Marijuana Use Over the Years", pch = 16, col = "red", cex = 2)
Create a scatterplot with fit line added (Figures 5.5 (a–i); code for Figure 5.5 (a) shown to the right)	plot(Figure5_5$ay~Figure5_5$ax, xlab = "Days elapsed in a given year", ylab = "Days remaining in that same year") abline(lm(Figure5_5$ay~Figure5_5$ax), col = "red")
Create a scatterplot with points adjusted slightly to avoid clumping (Figure 5.6)	plot(Hamburger$calories~jitter(Hamburger$cheese,0.25), xlab = "Cheese", ylab = "Calories")
Create a scatterplot with value labels on one axis (Figure 5.7)	plot(Hamburger$calories~jitter(Hamburger$cheese, 0.25), axes = F, xlab = "Cheese", ylab = "Calories") box() axis(2) axis(1, at = c(0,1), labels = c("No", "Yes"))
Create a clustered bar graph (Example 5.6/Figure 5.11)	barplot(table(NELS$nursery[NELS$region == "South"], NELS$gender[NELS$region == "South"]), beside = T, legend.text = c("No", "Yes"), args.legend = list(x = 3, y = 50, bty = "n"))
Compute a Pearson correlation (see also: Example 5.1 code in .R file)	cor(Hamburger$fat, Hamburger$calories) OR

Create	Command lines
	cor.test(Hamburger$calories, Hamburger$fat, method = "pearson")
Compute a Pearson correlation on a subsample (Example 5.5)	cor(NELS$achsci12[NELS$region == "West"], as.numeric(NELS$gender)[NELS$region == "West"])
Compute a Spearman correlation (Example 5.3)	cor.test(Hamburger$calories, Hamburger$fat, method = "spearman")
Obtain a cross-tabulation or contingency table (Example 5.6/Figure 5.12)	table(NELS$nursery[NELS$region == "South"], NELS$gender[NELS$region == "South"])
Find the row number of an outlier (Example 5.5)	which(NELS$achsci12==min(NELS$achsci12[NELS$region == "West" & NELS$gender=="Male"]))

EXERCISES

Create a .R file for each exercise that requires the use of R. Run code from the .R file by highlighting or having the cursor on the line of code and hitting **control+enter** on a PC computer keyboard or **command+enter** on a Mac computer keyboard. Save each .R file using a name associated with the Exercise for which it was created. It is recommended that you review the .R file for Chapter 5 located on the textbook's website before completing these exercises. To facilitate doing each exercise, it may be helpful to copy and paste relevant code from the .R file for Chapter 5 into your own .R file and modify them as needed.

Exercises 5.1–5.4 involve scatterplots.

5.1 Use the States dataset to create a scatterplot to depict the relationship between the percentage of students taking the SAT (pertak) and the average SAT Writing score (satw). Use it to explain why a correlation will capture one aspect of the relationship, but that it is probably not the most appropriate technique to use for measuring this relationship.

5.2 Use the States dataset to create a scatterplot to depict the relationship between the average teacher salary (teachpay) and the average SAT Math score (satm). Use it to determine whether states that pay their teachers better tend to have higher SAT Math scores, on average.

5.3 Use the States dataset and scatterplots to investigate the relationships between the average SAT Critical Reading score for the state (satcr) and the following three variables: average SAT Math score for the state (satm), percentage of eligible students taking the SAT for the state (pertak), and the average student–teacher ratio for the state (stuteach). Create three separate bivariate graphs, and use these graphs to answer the following questions.

(a) Rank these linear relationships from strongest to weakest.

(b) Describe the nature of the linear relationship, or indicate that little or no linear relationship exists, between the average SAT Critical Reading score for the state and the average SAT Math score for the state.

(c) Describe the nature of the linear relationship, or indicate that little or no linear relationship exists, between the average SAT Critical Reading score for the state and the percentage of eligible students taking the SAT for the state.

(d) Describe the nature of the linear relationship, or indicate that little or no linear relationship exists, between the average SAT Critical Reading score for the state and the average student–teacher ratio for the state.

5.4 In Example 5.5, using the NELS dataset, we selected cases to investigate students from the West and identified the outlier for the relationship between achsci12 and gender as id number 194. This exercise asks you to perform a similar analysis using the Framingham dataset.

(a) Using complete pairs of observations, report and interpret the correlation between the total cholesterol at time 3 (TOTCHOL3) and the body mass index at time 3 (BMI3).

(b) Create a scatterplot between these two variables and add a line of best fit in blue.

(c) Find the ID number of the outlier that appears most extreme in the scatterplot. Note that the **min** and **max** commands may take the argument **na.rm** = **T** when used with variables that have missing (NA) values.

(d) Calculate the correlation between these two variables without this person in the dataset using the following command:

cor(Framingham$TOTCHOL3[Framingham$ID!=205], Framingham$BMI3[Framingham$ID!=205], use = "complete.obs")

Does the correlation value change as a result of omitting this person from the dataset?

Exercises 5.5–5.7 involve Pearson correlation between two scale variables.

5.5 Conduct a correlation analysis using the States dataset to determine whether various factors are associated with educexpe, the average educational expenditure per pupil. These factors are stuteach, student–teacher ratio; satcr, average SAT Critical Reading score for the state; and teachpay, the average salary of public school teachers in the state.

(a) Create three separate bivariate graphs that compare educexpe to each of the three variables named above. Determine whether a linear model is an appropriate representation of the relationships between all pairs of these variables.

(b) Calculate the correlation between all pairs of these variables. This can be done in one step by creating a correlation matrix using the following command:

cor(States[,c("educexpe","stuteach","satcr","teachpay")])

(c) Do states in which expenditures per pupil are higher tend to pay their teachers more?

(d) Do states in which expenditures per pupil are higher tend to have higher SAT Critical Reading scores, on average?

(e) Do states in which expenditures per pupil are higher tend to have lower student–teacher ratios?

(f) Of the three variables, student–teacher ratio, average SAT Critical Reading scores, and teacher salary, which is most strongly correlated with expenditure per pupil?

5.6 For each of the following variables in the NELS dataset, indicate whether you think their correlations with mathematics achievement in grade 12 (achmat12) is positive, negative, or near zero. Use R to determine if your thinking is correct.

(a) Socioeconomic status (ses).

(b) The extent to which students agree with the statement, "My teachers are interested in their students" (tcherint), where 1 represents "Strongly Agree" and 4 represents "Strongly Disagree."

(c) Family size (famsize).

5.7 The following questions, using the NELS dataset, show how both linear and nonlinear transformations can affect the value of a correlation coefficient.

(a) Find and interpret the correlation between schattrt, the average daily school attendance rate (as a percentage) of the school the student attends, and slfcnc08, the student's eighth grade self-concept score.

(b) In Exercise 4.4 (b), the variable schattpp was created to give the average daily school attendance rate as a proportion (rather than as a percentage) for the school that the student attends. Based only on your answer to 5.7 (a), and without using R, what is the correlation between schattpp and slfcnc08?

(c) In general, do children who have higher socioeconomic status expect to have greater incomes by age 30? Construct the scatterplot and determine the correlation coefficient between expinc30 and ses. Interpret the results.

(d) Rather than simply eliminating the most extreme value in the scatterplot, we reduce its undue influence on the value of the correlation by following the methods in Chapter 4 and creating a new variable that represents the square root of expinc30. Label this new variable expincsq. Construct the scatterplot and determine the correlation coefficient between expincsq and ses. Do children who have higher ses expect to have higher incomes by age 30?

(e) What is the correlation between expincsq and expinc30? Under what circumstance would the correlation be equal to 1.00?

(f) For students in the Northeast, find the Pearson correlation coefficient between slfcnc12 and expinc30.

(g) Using the procedures described in Chapter 4, create a new variable that is the logarithm of the reflection of slfcnc12. For students in the Northeast, find the Pearson correlation coefficient between the transformed version of slfcnc12 and expincsq from part (d).

(h) Which is stronger, the correlation between the original or transformed variables?

(i) Why are the signs of the correlations between the transformed and untransformed variables different?

(j) Has the general interpretation of the relationship changed now that the sign is negative?

Exercises 5.8–5.13 involve using the Pearson correlation when at least one of the variables is dichotomous.

5.8 In this exercise, we use the NELS dataset to look at the relationship of socioeconomic status (ses) with eighth grade computer ownership (computer), a dichotomous variable. Do students whose families owned a computer when they were in eighth grade tend to have higher socioeconomic statuses than those whose families did not own a computer when they were in eighth grade?

    (a) Create a scatterplot between computer and ses. Use it to describe whether students whose families owned a computer when they were in eighth grade tend to have higher socioeconomic statuses than those whose families did not own a computer when they were in eighth grade.

    (b) Calculate the correlation between these variables to determine the extent to which there is a relationship as described.

5.9 Use the Learndis dataset to investigate whether different variables are associated with reading achievement. The following questions examine the correlations between the following variables: reading achievement (readcomp), grade level (grade), intellectual ability (iq), and whether the student was placed in the resource room for part of the day or in a full-time self-contained classroom (placemen, where 1 = resource room and 2 = self-contained classroom).

    (a) Determine and interpret the correlation between reading comprehension and intellectual ability.

    (b) Based on the correlation between readcomp and placemen, which group, on average, has higher reading comprehension: those in the resource room or those in a self-contained classroom? Explain.

    (c) Determine and interpret the correlation between type of placement and grade level.

    (d) Determine and interpret the correlation between grade level and reading comprehension for these students.

5.10 In this exercise, you are asked about the relationship between pairs of variables in the Framingham dataset.

    (a) Compute the correlation (r) between the initial diastolic blood pressure at time 1 (DIABP1) and whether or not the person was taking anti-hypertensive (blood pressure) medication at time 1 (BPMEDS1). Interpret your result.

    (b) What is another name for the special case of the Pearson correlation coefficient calculated between DIABP1 and BPMEDS1?

    (c) In part (a), a positive, yet weak, correlation was noted between the taking of blood pressure medication and blood pressure level. That is, the correlation indicates that those who take blood pressure medication have higher blood pressure levels, on average, than those who do not. What is a likely explanation for this relationship?

    (d) Which gender (SEX) is more likely to have developed coronary heart disease (CHD) by the end of the study (ANYCHD4)? Explain and support your answer with appropriate statistic(s).

    (e) What is another name for the special case of the Pearson correlation coefficient calculated between SEX and ANYCHD4?

(f) Explain why correlation is not the most appropriate way to statistically describe the relationship between the initial glucose level (GLUCOSE1) and the initial number of cigarettes smoked per day (CIGPDAY1).

5.11 According to the data in the Framingham dataset, what evidence is there in these data to suggest that HDL is "good" cholesterol and LDL is "bad" cholesterol? Hint Compute the correlation between HDL3 and ANYCHD4 and between LDL3 and ANYCHD4.

5.12 In the NELS dataset, the variable computer indicates whether the student's family owned a computer when the student was in eighth grade. In this question, we will look at the effect that the coding of this variable has on the correlation.
(a) Compute and interpret the correlation between ses and computer.
(b) Recode the variable computer into comp1 so that 0 = No and 1 = Yes. Write the equation representing this linear transformation. Does this transformation include a reflection of the original variable computer? Recall that the original coding is: 1 = No and 2 = Yes.
(c) What is the correlation between computer and comp1?
(d) Recode the variable computer into comp2 so that 0 = Yes and 1 = No. Write the equation representing this linear transformation. Does this transformation include a reflection of the original variable computer?
(e) What is the correlation between computer and comp2?
(f) Without using R, what is the correlation between ses and comp1? Between ses and comp2?

5.13 The median split, discussed in Chapter 4, is a type of nonlinear transformation that serves to symmetrize the distribution of a continuous variable into two equal halves. The resulting variable is dichotomous since all values below the median are assigned one code, and all values above the median are assigned a different code. Depending upon the nature of the underlying distribution of the continuous variable, the correlation between the newly formed dichotomous variable (via the median split transformation) and another variable may be stronger or weaker in magnitude than the correlation based on the original continuous variable and that other variable. This example illustrates the case, using the NELS dataset, in which the resulting correlation becomes weaker in magnitude.
(a) Find and interpret the correlation between ses and slfcnc12.
(b) Create new variables sesdi and slfcnc12di that are the median splits of ses and slfcnc12, respectively. Find and interpret the correlation between sesdi and slfcnc12.
(c) Comment on the effect of using the median split transformation in this case given that one of the continuous variables (slfcnc12) is skewed negatively.

Exercise 5.14 involves Spearman correlation.

5.14 In this exercise, we investigate the relationship of two variables with excurr12, participation in extracurricular activities in twelfth grade in the NELS dataset. Note that this variable is measured using an ordinal level of measurement.
(a) Is there a correlation between smoking cigarettes (cigarett) and participation in extracurricular activities in twelfth grade (excurr12)? If so, describe the nature of the correlation. Provide statistical support for your answer.

(b) Is there a correlation between missing school in twelfth grade (absent12) and participation in extracurricular activities in twelfth grade (excurr12)? If so, describe the nature of the correlation. Provide statistical support for your answer.

(c) Is there a correlation between socioeconomic status (ses) and participation in extracurricular activities in twelfth grade (excurr12)? If so, describe the nature of the correlation. Provide statistical support for your answer.

Exercises 5.15–5.16 involve contingency tables (cross-tabulations).

5.15 Use cross-tabulations applied to two variables from the NELS dataset (advmath8 and urban) to obtain a summary of who took advanced math in eighth grade by type of environment. Use the resulting summary to answer the following, related questions.

(a) What proportion of students took advanced math in eighth grade from each of the three environments: urban, suburban, and rural?

(b) What proportion of students took advanced math in eighth grade over all environments?

(c) Which environment has the largest proportion of advanced math takers: urban, suburban, or rural?

(d) Is there a relationship between urbanicity and enrollment in advanced math in eighth grade? Explain.

5.16 In this exercise, we make use of the Framingham dataset to explore the relationship between gender and cigarette use at time 1 and at time 3.

(a) Create a contingency table of cigarette use at time 1 (CURSMOKE1) by sex and, use it to determine whether the two variables are related.

(b) Create a contingency table on cigarette use at time 3 (12 years into the study) (CURSMOKE3) by sex, and use it to determine whether the two variables are related.

(c) Calculate the correlation between cigarette use at time 1 (CURSMOKE1) and sex, and use it to confirm that the two variables are not related.

(d) Calculate the correlation between cigarette use 12 years into the study (CURSMOKE3) and sex, and use it to determine whether the two are related.

Exercise 5.17 requires you to select an appropriate statistic for answering the question asked and to analyze the NELS dataset using that statistic.

5.17 Select an appropriate statistic that conveys the magnitude and nature of the relationship that exists between pairs of variables in the NELS dataset. When describing that relationship, use terms that someone who has not taken statistics could understand (for example, positive correlation is not sufficient).

(a) Is there a relationship between years of math taken in high school (unitmath) and math achievement in twelfth grade (achmat12)? If so, describe that relationship.

(b) Is there a relationship, between the number of times the student is late to school in twelfth grade (late12) and the number of times the student skipped/cut classes in twelfth grade (cuts12)? If so, describe that relationship.

(c) Is there a relationship between the school type attended in eighth grade (schtyp8) and whether or not the student took any Advanced Placement classes in high school (approg)? If so, describe that relationship.

(d) Is there a relationship between family size (famsize) and self-concept in twelfth grade (slfcnc12)? If so, describe that relationship.

(e) Is there a relationship between socioeconomic status (ses) and science achievement in twelfth grade (achsci12)? If so, describe that relationship.

(f) Is there a relationship between region of the country (region) and whether or not a student took advanced math in eighth grade (advmath8)? If so, describe that relationship.

(g) Is there a relationship between number of classes cut in twelfth grade (cuts12) and whether or not the student took advanced math in eighth grade (advmath8)? If so, describe that relationship.

(h) Is there a relationship between cigarette use (cigarett) and urbanicity (urban)? If so, describe that relationship.

(i) Is there a relationship between whether or not students took advanced math in eighth grade (advmath8) and whether or not they took an AP class (approg) in high school? If so, describe that relationship.

(j) Is there a relationship between the frequency of cutting class in twelfth grade (cuts12) and being absent from school in twelfth grade (absent12)? If so, describe that relationship.

(k) Is there a relationship between twelfth grade self-esteem (slfcnc12) and socioeconomic status (ses)? If so, describe that relationship.

(l) Is there a relationship, between socioeconomic status (ses) and nursery school attendance (nursery)? If so, describe that relationship.

(m) Is there a relationship between socioeconomic status (ses) and urbanicity (urban)? If so, describe that relationship.

Exercises 5.18–5.23 include a variety of topics. The exercises are based on the Impeach dataset, created by Professor Alan Reifman of Texas Tech University in response to a US Senate vote taken on February 12, 1999 on whether to remove a president from office, based on impeachment articles passed by the US House of Representatives. This was only the second time in US history that such a vote took place. The data contain descriptions of each senator as a way to try to understand each senator's voting behavior.

5.18 The questions in this exercise relate to a correlation analysis between all pairs of the following variables: the vote on perjury (vote1), the degree of conservatism of the senator (conserva), the state voter support for Clinton (supportc), and whether or not the senator was first-term (newbie). Compute a correlation between each pair of variables as needed to answer the following questions.

(a) Is it appropriate to compute a correlation between conserva and supportc? Why or why not?

(b) Describe the magnitude and nature of the linear relationship between these two variables, the degree of conservatism of the senator and the state voter support for Clinton.

(c) Based on the results of a correlation analysis, can you determine whether conservative senators were more likely to vote guilty or not guilty on perjury? Explain.

(d) Based on the results of a correlation analysis, can you determine whether senators from states that supported Clinton in 1996 were more likely to vote guilty or not guilty on perjury? Explain.

(e) Based on the results of a correlation analysis, can you determine whether first-term senators were more likely to vote guilty or not guilty on perjury? Explain.

(f) If you were looking for one variable to statistically discriminate between those senators who voted guilty and those who voted not guilty on perjury, which variable (conserva, supportc, newbie) would you choose? Explain.

(g) Explain why it would not be appropriate to calculate the correlation between the region of the country that the senator is from (region, where 1 = Northeast, 2 = Midwest, 3 = South, and 4 = West) and the vote on perjury. Give the name of an alternative analysis that could be used to analyze the relationship between these two variables.

5.19 Create two scatterplots, one to depict the relationship between conservatism (conserva) and the vote on perjury (vote1) and the other to depict the relationship between conservatism and the vote on obstruction of justice (vote2). Use them to answer the following questions.

(a) Describe the nature of the relationship between the vote on obstruction of justice and conservatism. Use language that someone who has never taken statistics could understand.

(b) Based on your political knowledge, explain why your answer to part (a) makes sense.

(c) According to the scatterplots, which pair of variables has the stronger correlation? Explain.

5.20 Create a contingency table that gives the breakdown of the vote on perjury (vote1) by region. Use it to answer the following questions.

(a) How many senators voted not guilty on perjury?

(b) What percentage of senators voted not guilty on perjury?

(c) Of all not guilty votes, what percentage (or proportion) came from the South?

(d) Of all votes from the South, what percentage (or proportion) were not guilty votes?

(e) According to the contingency table, are there differences in the vote on perjury depending on the region from which the senator comes? Explain in a way that someone with no background in statistics could understand and support your answer with the values of relevant statistics.

(f) What type of graph is best used to display the relationship between the vote on perjury and region? Create this graph.

(g) Explain why a contingency table should not be used to analyze the relationship between region and conservatism.

5.21 Create a clustered bar graph that gives the number of guilty and not guilty votes on perjury (vote1) for both first-term and more senior senators (newbie). Use it to answer the following questions.

(a) Is there a relationship between the vote on perjury and whether or not the senator is first term? Explain.

(b) Without calculating, what is the sign of the Pearson correlation between vote1 and newbie? Explain.

5.22 Create two clustered bar graphs that depict the relationships between whether or not the senator was first term (newbie) and how the senator voted on obstruction of justice (vote2). Let one graph represent those senators who were up for re-election in 2000 and the other graph represent those who were up for re-election in 2002. Use them to answer the following questions.

(a) For those senators up for re-election in 2000, describe the nature of the relationship between seniority status as a senator (whether the senator was first term or not) and voting behavior on the issue of obstruction of justice. Explain.

(b) Is the Pearson correlation coefficient that may be calculated to describe the relationship noted in part (a) positive, negative, or near zero? Explain.

(c) According to these clustered bar graphs, is the correlation between whether or not the senator was first term and his or her vote on obstruction of justice stronger for senators up for re-election in 2000 or in 2002? Explain.

5.23 In order to determine whether the relationship between state voter support for Clinton (supportc) and conservatism (conserva) varies as a function of how the senator voted on perjury (vote1), create two scatterplots of supportc by conserva: one for those senators that voted guilty on vote1 and one for those who voted not guilty on vote1. Use your scatterplots to answer the following questions. Follow up by calculating separate correlation coefficients for those senators who voted guilty and for those who voted not guilty, and use them to corroborate the answers based on the scatterplot.

(a) Describe the nature of the relationship, or indicate that there is not one, between state voter support for Clinton and conservatism for those senators who voted guilty on perjury.

(b) Describe the nature of the relationship, or indicate that there is not one, between state voter support for Clinton and conservatism for those senators who voted not guilty on perjury.

Exercises 5.24–5.33 test conceptual understanding and do not require the use of R.

5.24 The correlation between manual dexterity (X) and age from 2 years to 80 years (Y) is $r = 0.08$. Nevertheless, the investigator was able to make reasonably accurate predictions of a person's manual dexterity score on the basis of his or her age. Explain how this could be possible.

5.25 What (if anything) is wrong with the following statement? "A Pearson correlation coefficient value of $r = 0.8$ between two variables represents twice the linear relationship that a Pearson correlation coefficient value of $r = 0.4$ represents."

5.26 Read the following excerpt from the article "TV, video games at night may cause sleep problems in kids," by Amanda Gardner on June 27, 2011. You do not need to read the entire article to answer the related questions, but it may be found online at: https://bit .ly/2Ry47UX. Use it to answer the related questions.

Watching television or playing video games close to bedtime can act like a jolt of caffeine to young children, making them more likely to experience difficulty falling asleep, nightmares, and daytime fatigue, a new study in the journal *Pediatrics* suggests.

In the study, 28% of preschoolers who watched TV or played video games for at least 30 minutes after 7 p.m. had sleep problems most nights of the week, versus 19% of children whose TV and video-game use took place only before 7 p.m.

The study included 612 children ages 3 to 5. [Lead author] Garrison and her colleagues asked the parents to keep a detailed diary of their child's media consumption over the course of one week, including the title, timing, and duration of each show or game. (To determine the level of violence, researchers consulted parental guidance ratings and actually analyzed specific shows and games.)

On average, the kids spent 73 minutes per day in front of a TV or computer. The more time they spent watching TV or playing video games in the evening, the more likely they were to experience a sleep problem.

(a) According to the results of this study, if you had a much younger brother or sister, should you limit television and video-game time after 7 p.m. in order to ensure a good night's sleep? Explain. Be as detailed as you can.

(b) Create the clustered bar graph depicting the relationship between whether or not the child watched television or played video games for at least 30 minutes after 7 p.m. and whether or not the child had sleep problems most nights of the week as described in the article. Make sure to label your axes and the bars.

(c) Based on the information in the excerpt from the article, is it fair to conclude that the number of children who watch TV after 7 p.m. and have sleep problems is more than the number of children who don't watch TV after 7 p.m. and have sleep problems? Why or why not?

5.27 Read the following excerpt of the article, "Pain pills add cost and delays to job injuries" by Barry Meier in the *New York Times* on June 2, 2012. Use the excerpt to answer the following questions.

Workers who received high doses of opioid painkillers to treat injuries like back strain stayed out of work three times longer than those with similar injuries who took lower doses, a 2008 study of claims by the California Workers Compensation Institute found. When medical care and disability payments are combined, the cost of a workplace injury is nine times higher when a strong narcotic like OxyContin is used than when a narcotic is not used, according to a 2010 analysis by Accident Fund Holdings, an insurer that operates in 18 states.

(a) What is the sign (positive or negative) of the correlation between dose of opioid painkillers and number of days out of work?

(b) According to the results of this article, should doctors stop prescribing painkillers to people with workplace injuries? Explain.

5.28 What (if anything) is wrong with the following statement? "A Pearson correlation coefficient value of $r = 1.05$ was found between two variables X and Y. This represents a very strong linear relationship between the two variables."

5.29 What (if anything) is wrong with the following statement about the NELS data? "The correlation between region and the number of Advanced Placement classes offered is $r = 0.11$ indicating that the higher the region, the more Advanced Placement courses offered, on average."

5.30 What (if anything) is wrong with the following statement: "If the correlation between X and Y is $r = .50$, then you can perform any linear transformation on the variable X and the correlation between the transformed X and Y will still be $r = 0.50$."

5.31 What (if anything) is wrong with the following statement? "If the correlation between average math SAT and average verbal SAT for all 50 states is $r = 0.97$, that implies that the scores on the verbal portion are higher than the scores on the math portion."

5.32 Draw a scatterplot for which the Pearson product-moment correlation would not capture the true magnitude and nature of the relationship between the two variables.

5.33 The following questions relate to the scatterplot below, which shows the relationship between X and Y for four different subgroups.

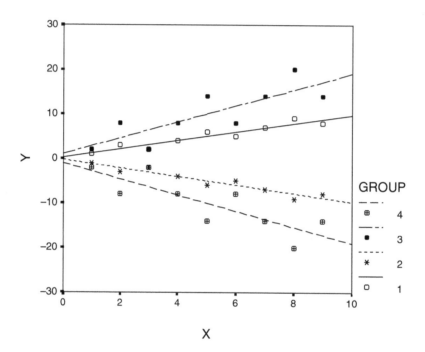

For each subgroup, select the Pearson correlation coefficient, r, from the column on the right that best represents the relationship between X and Y for the subgroup. You may select a value more than once.

Group 1: _____   (a) $r = 1.25$
                        (b) $r = -1.25$
Group 2: _____   (c) $r = 0.95$
                        (d) $r = -0.95$
Group 3: _____   (e) $r = 0.82$
                        (f) $r = -0.82$
Group 4: _____   (g) $r = 0$

# CHAPTER SIX

SIMPLE LINEAR REGRESSION

In the previous chapter, we remarked that even when a strong linear correlation exists between two variables, X and Y, it may not be possible to talk about either one of them as the cause of the other. Even so, there is nothing to keep us from using one of the variables to *predict* the other. In making predictions from one variable to another, the variable being predicted is called the *outcome variable*, and the variable predicting the outcome variable is called the *predictor variable*. The outcome variable may also be referred to as the *dependent variable*, while the predictor variable may also be referred to as the *independent* or *criterion variable*. One way of facilitating such predictions is to obtain a linear equation that somehow fits, or represents, the available data. This equation can then be used to predict the variable Y from the variable X. It can also be used to *explain* the relationship between Y and X in more detail than correlation alone provides. In particular, the equation can be used to study how a change in one variable, X, relates to a change in the other variable, Y.

In this chapter, we introduce a technique for finding such a linear equation, called the *regression equation*, and measuring the extent to which it describes the data. As we will see, the stronger the correlation between X and Y, the more accurately Y can be predicted from X; the weaker the correlation, the less accurately Y can be predicted from X.

THE "BEST-FITTING" LINEAR EQUATION

If the linear relationship between X and Y were perfect so that all points of the dataset fell along a single straight line, the task of finding a linear equation that fits the given data exactly would be quite straightforward. With the help of some coordinate geometry, we could find the equation of the single straight line passing through all the points.

In behavioral and social research, however, it is extremely unlikely to encounter data that are perfectly linearly related. The question we would like to investigate in this section is: "How do we find the best-fitting line to predict one variable from another when the two variables are not perfectly linearly related?" Let us return to the data from our McDonald's example reproduced here as Table 6.1. Recall that the Pearson correlation coefficient between fat and calories for these is 0.996.

Although $r = 0.996$ implies an extremely strong positive linear relationship between fat and calories, the fact that it is not a perfect linear relationship means that no one line passes exactly through all five points of the scatterplot. However, because such a strong correlation value implies that the relationship between fat (X) and calories (Y) is *almost* perfectly

TABLE 6.1 Fat grams and calories by type of McDonald's hamburgers

Type of McDonald's hamburger	Grams of fat (X)	Calories (Y)
Hamburger	10	270
Cheeseburger	14	320
Quarter Pounder™	21	430
Quarter Pounder™ w/ cheese	30	530
Big Mac™	28	530

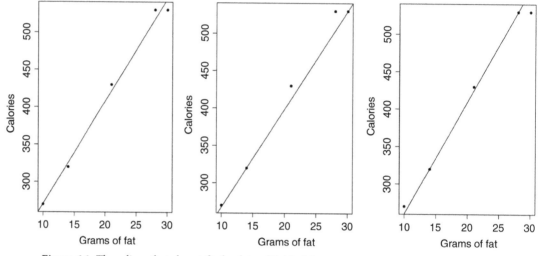

Figure 6.1 Three lines that almost fit the data of Table 6.1

linear, there should be many lines that almost work. Three such lines are illustrated in Figure 6.1 with the scatterplot of our data.

Because all three lines in Figure 6.1 (as well as many others) almost fit the data of Table 6.1, they would all seem reasonable to use for prediction purposes. But which one is the best-fitting line, and how do we find its equation? The question of which line is best fitting is subjective and depends to a large extent on what we mean by "best." We might, for example, select the line that actually goes through as many of the points of the scatterplot as possible. But if we do this, the line might turn out to be very far from the points it does not pass through. The usual way of choosing a best-fitting line, and the one we will use, is to take one that, on the average, comes "closest" in terms of squared deviations to *all* the points of the scatterplot. Such a line is called a (least squares) *regression line* or (least squares) *prediction line*, and its equation is called a (least squares) *linear regression equation*. Let us now see what is meant by a *deviation* and how we find the equation of the best-fitting line.

Suppose we have a line L that we think of using to predict calories (Y) from fat (X) for the data of Table 6.1 (see Figure 6.2). For each of our given X_i values ($i = 1$, 2, 3, 4, 5), let $\hat{Y}_i$ be the Y value that the equation of line L predicts from X_i (i.e., the value that is obtained when X_i is substituted into the equation of line L; or,

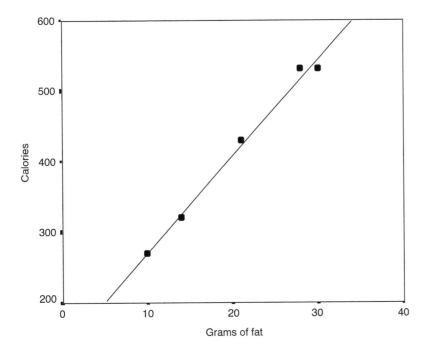

Figure 6.2 The regression line for the data of Table 6.1

equivalently, the value that when paired with X_i gives a point (X_i, Y_i) on line L). Then, because Y_i is the actual Y value paired with X_i, and $\hat{Y}_i$ is the Y value predicted by L to pair with X_i, their difference (or deviation) $d_i = Y_i - \hat{Y}_i$ is just the error of prediction (or error of estimate) at X_i when using L. While we have been referring to errors of prediction as deviations, they are also, more commonly, referred to as *residuals*, since they represent that part of the actual Y score that is *left over* after taking into account the predicted Y score. Figure 6.3 zooms in on three pairs of (X,Y) values to provide a magnified view of their residuals.

Note that for the three points of Figure 6.3, two residuals (d_i) are positive, whereas one is negative. Positive residuals indicate that the predicted Y value, $\hat{Y}$, is less than the actual Y value, whereas negative residuals indicate that the predicted Y value, $\hat{Y}$, is greater than the actual Y value. If we obtained the sum of the residuals for all five pairs of values in our dataset based on the regression line, the negative residuals would cancel out the positive residuals, resulting in a false impression that there is no error of prediction. To obtain a valid measure of error of prediction (one that avoids cancellation of positive with negative error terms), we could either take the absolute value of each term before summing, or we could square each error term before summing. These are exactly the two alternatives we faced in Chapter 3 when defining a measure of variability. As before, we choose to square each of the individual error terms d_i to obtain d_i^2 before summing. To make this squared index of error independent of the number of pairs of data values, we divide the sum of the d_i^2 by N to obtain what is called the *average squared deviation* (or *average squared error*) D^2. Finally, to bring the measure back to the original units of the data, we take the square root of D^2, and obtain D, the *standard error of estimate* or *prediction*:

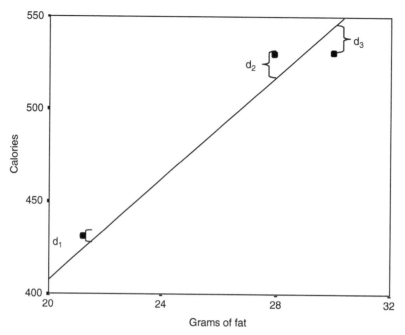

Figure 6.3 Residuals from the regression line: a magnified view using three points

$$D = \sqrt{\frac{\sum di^2}{N}}.$$

(6.1)

We see that D is approximately the average vertical distance to the regression line in the same way that the standard deviation is approximately the average distance to the mean. We will use D as our index of error of prediction for a given prediction line on a given set of data.

We now can define what we mean by the best-fitting line for a given set of data. The best-fitting line is the line that minimizes (or gives the smallest possible number for) the value of D for the given data. It is called the (least squares) *regression line* or (least squares) *prediction line.* The equation of the regression line is called the *linear regression equation,* and the criterion we use to define it (that of minimizing the value of D) is called the *least squares criterion.* Although the actual derivation of the equation for the regression line is beyond the scope of this book, the equation itself is really quite simple. Given a set of paired data (X, Y) with N pairs, the equation of the regression line (the linear regression equation) for predicting Y from X is

$$\hat{Y} = a + bX$$

(6.2)

where

$$b = r\frac{S_Y}{S_X}$$

(6.3)

$$a = \overline{Y} - b\overline{X}.$$

(6.4)

In Equation 6.2, $\hat{Y}$ represents the predicted value for Y. The value of b for use in the linear regression equation to predict Y from X is called the *regression coefficient*. In Equation 6.2 the regression coefficient, b, represents the slope of the linear regression equation, and the constant, a, represents the Y-intercept.

While the regression equation, Equation 6.2, can be used to find the predicted Y for a given value of X, the values of b and a can be used to explain the relationship between X and Y.

Equation 6.3 shows the relationship between the slope, b, of the regression equation and the value of the Pearson correlation coefficient, r. Because standard deviation is always positive, we see that b and r always have the same sign. That is, if b is positive, then Y will increase with an increase in X, whereas if b is negative, then Y will decrease with an increase in X. Moreover, b can always be interpreted as the amount of change in $\hat{Y}$, on average, for each unit increase in X.

Equation 6.4 shows the relationship between the Y-intercept of the regression line, a, and the means of both X and Y. In particular, a is defined so that an X value equal to the mean of X would be predicted to have a Y value equal to the mean of Y. That is, so that $(\overline{X}, \overline{Y})$ lies on the regression line. The value of a can be interpreted as the predicted Y for the value $X = 0$. Such an interpretation makes sense only when 0 is a reasonable value for the variable X and when data close to $X = 0$ have been collected.

☞ **Remark.** According to Equation 6.3, when $r = 0$, that is, the two variables are not linearly associated, $b = 0$. In this case, we see that $\hat{Y}$ is just the constant, $\overline{Y}$. Said differently, if X and Y are not linearly related, then given any X value, the predicted Y value is simply the mean of Y.

☞ **Remark.** Suppose you were told that the mean height of 10-year-old girls is 4 feet 1 inch and that the mean weight for 10-year-old girls is 82 pounds. Alice is a 10-year-old girl who is 4 feet 1 inch tall. Based on this information alone, what would you predict Alice's weight to be? If you said 82 pounds, the mean weight for 10-year-old girls, you would agree with the prediction that would be obtained from the linear regression equation for predicting weight from height for 10-year-old girls.

Regression to the mean: How regression got its name. In the previous Remark, it was noted that a least squares regression equation will predict the weight of a 10--year-old girl who is at the mean height of all 10-year-old girls in that sample (4 feet 1 inch tall) to be equal to 82 pounds, the mean weight of all 10-year-old girls in that sample. That is, given the correlation between height and weight for these 10-year-old girls, the regression equation will predict the weight of a girl whose height equals the mean height for that sample to be equal to the mean weight for that sample.

It is also true that if we select a subsample of 10-year-old girls from that sample who are extremely tall (whose height is much greater than the overall mean height of 4 feet 1 inch), then that subsample's predicted mean weight will tend to be less extreme on weight than it was on height. The same can be said for a subsample selected from that sample to be extremely short (whose height is much lower than the overall mean height for the overall sample); namely, its predicted mean weight will tend to be less extreme on weight than it was on height. That is, in both cases, their predicted means on weight will tend to *regress toward the mean* weight of the total sample.

This phenomenon was first noticed by Sir Francis Galton (1886) in the late nineteenth century in his use of linear modeling to study the heights of a large sample of fathers and their adult sons. He called the phenomenon *regression to the mean*, and the linear models that produced these results, *regression models*.

In particular, Galton found that the fathers who were above average in height tended to have sons who were shorter than they; and, the fathers who were below average in height tended to have sons who were taller than they. But, he also found the reverse to be true. Most of the tallest sons had fathers shorter than they, and most of the shortest sons had fathers taller than they. Furthermore, because Galton found that, overall, the standard deviation of the sons' heights was just about equal to the standard deviation of their fathers' heights, he realized that the heights of the younger generation of sons were not becoming more homogeneous in height.

In its most general form, when there is an imperfect correlation between X and Y (as there is between height and weight), subsamples that are more extreme on X will tend to be less extreme on Y: i.e., their means will be regressed to the mean of the overall sample, and we will have regression to the mean.

As will be noted in Chapter 12, because regression to the mean can impact the interpretation of research results, it must be considered in the design of research studies. The reader who is interested in learning more about the history of this phenomenon is referred to Stigler (1997), and in learning more about the phenomenon itself is referred to Darlington (1990).

EXAMPLE 6.1 Given the data of Table 6.1, use R to obtain the linear regression equation for predicting calories (Y) from fat content (X) in two ways, using the following:

1. Derive the regression equation from Equations 6.2 through 6.4 using R to obtain the required values.
2. Derive the equation directly using R.
3. Interpret the slope, and if meaningful, the intercept of the regression equation.
4. Create a scatterplot and edit it in R to include the regression line.
5. Use the regression line found in parts (1) and (2) and the graph of the regression line found in part (4) to find the predicted number of calories for a McDonald's hamburger with fat content of 28 grams.

Solution

1. Using the R commands:

   mean(Hamburger$calories), mean(Hamburger$fat)
   cor(Hamburger$calories, Hamburger$fat)

   or

   cor.test(Hamburger$calories, Hamburger$fat),

   we find that $\overline{Y} = 416$ calories, $S_Y = 119.08$ calories, $\overline{X} = 20.6$ fat grams, $S_X = 8.65$ fat grams, and $r_{XY} = .996$. We need to use these values to find a and b.

Using Equation 6.3, we find that $b = r\dfrac{S_Y}{S_X} = 0.996\dfrac{119.08}{8.65} = 13.71$.

Using Equation 6.4, we find that $a = \overline{Y} - b\overline{X} = 416 - (13.71)(20.6) = 133.57$.

Equation 6.2 gives the general form of the regression equation:

$\hat{Y} = bX + a$.

Substituting for a and b, we have $\hat{Y} = 133.57 + 13.71X$ or

$\hat{Y} = 133.57 + 13.71(\text{fat})$.

2.

MORE R: To obtain a regression analysis using calories and fat, type:

model = lm(Hamburger$calories~Hamburger$fat)
summary(model)

Note that **lm** stands for linear model, another name for the regression model. Here, we create a local variable, named **model**, that stores the results of the regression analysis. We may then use the **summary** command to print as output the coefficients of our model.

The above commands only will output the unstandardized regression coefficients. In order to obtain the standardized regression coefficients (the beta weights) as well, we would need to standardize our variables as shown below:

model2 = lm(scale(Hamburger$calories)~scale(Hamburger$fat))
summary(model2)

In order to not overwrite our first model, we name this second model **model2**.

That part of the output relevant to finding the unstandardized regression equation is reproduced in Figure 6.4.

In this output, "Estimate" refers to the unstandardized regression coefficients. Note that the regression coefficient for fat, b, equals approximately 13.71. The value of the constant, a, also appears under the column labeled Estimate in the row labeled (Intercept). The constant equals approximately 133.58. These values agree, within rounding, with the values obtained in part (1).

Coefficients:

	Estimate	Std. error	t-value	Pr(>|t|)	
(Intercept)	133.5762	16.1251	8.284	0.003685	**
Hamburger$fat	13.7099	0.7328	18.709	0.000333	***

Signif. codes: 0 "***" 0.001 "**" 0.01 "*" 0.05 "." 0.1 " " 1

Figure 6.4 Coefficient information for the simple linear regression equation

As before, we write the regression equation using Equation 6.2.

$$\hat{Y} = 133.58 + 13.71X \text{ or } \hat{Y} = 133.58 + 13.71(\text{fat}).$$

3. The slope of 13.71 tells us that each additional gram of fat is associated with 13.71 additional calories, on average. More specifically, we can interpret this coefficient to mean that if we compare two types of hamburgers that differ in their fat content by one gram, then, on average, these two types of hamburgers will differ in their caloric level by 13.71 calories. The intercept of 133.57 is not meaningful because none of the hamburgers in the dataset had close to 0 grams of fat, so that the value $X = 0$ is beyond the range of the data.

4.

MORE R: To obtain the scatterplot with the regression line superimposed, type:

plot(Hamburger$calories~Hamburger$fat, xlab = "Fat", ylab = "Calories", pch = 16)
abline(lm(Hamburger$calories~Hamburger$fat))

or

plot(Hamburger$calories~Hamburger$fat, xlab = "Fat", ylab = "Calories", pch = 16)
abline(model)

Note that the **plot** command with its arguments in parentheses will produce the scatterplot for these variables with calories on the y-axis and fat on the x-axis. The **abline** command with its argument in parentheses will superimpose the fitted regression line onto the scatterplot.

The regression line should appear as it does in Figure 6.2.

---

5. To find the predicted calorie content of a hamburger with 28 grams of fat using the regression equation, we substitute the value $X = 28$ into $133.57 + 13.71X$.

$$\hat{Y} = 133.57 + (13.71)(28) = 517.45.$$

Thus, we predict that a hamburger with 28 grams of fat will have approximately 517 calories.

To estimate the predicted calorie content of a hamburger with 28 grams of fat using the scatterplot of the regression equation, we approximate the location of $X = 28$ on the horizontal axis, read up to the regression line, and then read across to the predicted number of calories. We get the less accurate estimate of approximately 520 calories.

Note in Table 6.1 that there actually *was* a hamburger in our original dataset for which the fat content was 28 grams, and for that amount of fat, there is 530 calories. According to Example 6.1, however, we would predict the number of calories to be approximately 517. Because of this discrepancy between actual and predicted Y values, a question arises. In which of these two values (517 or 530) can we place more confidence when making predictions about different types of hamburger at McDonald's for which the fat content is 28 grams?

Recall that our interest was in developing a *general* prediction model based on the available data – a model that could then be used to make predictions in similar situations occurring in the future. By making the simplifying assumption that our prediction model should be linear and by *making use of all the available data*, we were able to develop the linear regression equation that is just such a general prediction model. Clearly, predictions made using the linear regression equation (which is based on *all* the available data) can be made with more confidence than predictions made using other prediction systems that are *not* based on all the available data. It follows, therefore, that we can place more confidence in the prediction based on the linear regression equation than on a prediction based on a single observation.

THE ACCURACY OF PREDICTION USING THE LINEAR REGRESSION MODEL

Our goal in this section is to show the relationship between the Pearson correlation coefficient, r, and the standard error of estimate or prediction, D.

Recall that r was introduced in Chapter 5 as a measure of the linear relationship between two variables and that the more the points of the scatterplot conform to a straight line, the closer the value of r will be to a perfect correlation of either -1 or $+1$. Recall further that D was introduced as a measure of how well a given linear equation fits a set of data and that the linear regression equation was then defined as the particular linear equation that minimized D. From now on we will reserve the symbol D to indicate the standard error of estimate based on the linear regression equation, not on just any linear equation. Because the linear regression equation is the best-fitting line for the points of the scatterplot and D is the measure of error of fit for this best-fitting line, it is clear that when r is close to a perfect correlation value of $+1$ or -1, the regression line should fit the scatterplot almost perfectly and consequently the value of D should be close to zero. Thus, an inverse relationship between D and the magnitude of r is suggested. Namely, when the magnitude of r is small (r near 0), D should be large, and when the magnitude of r is large (r near $+1$ or -1), D should be small. Because it is the magnitude (not the sign) of r that is apparently inversely related to D, we might obtain a better indication of this relationship by comparing D with r^2 rather than with r. There is, in fact, a simple equation that relates the values of D and r^2 for a given set of (X,Y) data pairs, it is:

$$D = \sqrt{S_Y^2(1 - r_{XY}^2)}, \tag{6.5}$$

where S_Y^2 is the variance of the given Y values.

From Equation 6.5, it should now be clear that, in general, the closer r is to a perfect correlation, the more accurate the prediction equation will be for the data on which it is based. It is tempting to infer that the more accurate the prediction equation is for the data on which it is based (the closer r is to a perfect correlation), the more accurate we can expect it to be when we are using it to make predictions in the future under similar circumstances. Although this inference is usually a valid one, many factors (such as the number of pairs of data values on which the linear regression equation is based) influence the relationship between the magnitude of r and the accuracy of prediction in the future. These factors involve an understanding that we have not as yet acquired of the basic concepts of inferential statistics. We must therefore postpone a more complete discussion of linear regression analysis until Chapter 15.

THE STANDARDIZED REGRESSION EQUATION

When the regression analysis is computed on the standardized variables (the z-score transformations of X and Y), z_X and z_Y, the resulting equation takes the form:

$$\hat{z}_Y = r z_X. \tag{6.6}$$

Equation 6.6 is a simplification of Equation 6.2 because for standard scores, $\bar{z}_X = \bar{z}_Y = 0$ and $S_{z_X} = S_{z_Y} = 1$. The slope of the standardized regression equation is denoted as β.

As shown in Equation 6.6, $\beta = r$ in the case where there is only one predictor variable (simple linear regression). The value of r between X and Y is also 0.996.

The standard score regression equation is not particularly useful for making predictions because generally scores are given in raw form. When we study multiple regression in Chapter 16, we will see how β may be used to assess the relative importance of the predictor variables in the equation.

R AS A MEASURE OF THE OVERALL FIT OF THE LINEAR REGRESSION MODEL

As part of the regression output, R provides a model summary, including R-squared. For now, we will limit our discussion of that summary to the value of R, which is the correlation between the actual and predicted values of Y, and may be obtained as the positive square root of R-squared. For the McDonald's example, the summary is provided in Figure 6.5, from which we may compute R to equal $\sqrt{0.9915} = 0.996$.

In the McDonald's example, $R = r$. That is, in this example, the correlation between Y and $\hat{Y}$ is the same as the correlation between Y and X. We will see that this is also the case in Example 6.4. However, as we shall see in Example 6.3, it is not true in general in simple linear regression that $R = r$. Because R is always positive, $R = r$ only when r is positive. When r is negative, then $R = -r$. In general, we may say that $R = |r|$, the absolute value of r.

● ●

EXAMPLE 6.2
1. Use R to find the predicted values, $\hat{Y}$, for the McDonald's example.
2. Find the correlation between predicted calories ($\hat{Y}$) and calories (Y) and compare this value to the correlation between fat content (X) and calories (Y).
3. Construct a scatterplot of Y and $\hat{Y}$ and of X and $\hat{Y}$.

Residual standard error: 12.68 on 3 degrees of freedom

Multiple R-squared: 0.9915	Adjusted R-squared: 0.9887
F-statistic: 350 on 1 and 3 DF	p-value: 0.0003333

Figure 6.5 Model summary for simple linear regression

Solution

1.

MORE R: To obtain the predicted values, $\hat{Y}$ (Yhat), type:

model = lm(Hamburger\$calories~Hamburger\$fat)
yhat = predict(model)
yhat

Note, the **predict** command is an example of what R refers to as a post-estimation command (as opposed to a post-estimation statistic). That is, once the regression equation is estimated, we can derive other estimates based on that equation. Predicting yhat is the default option for the **predict** command, the option being defined by **a + bX**.
   To predict the residual values (y – yhat) we would use the command:

YminusYhat = model\$residual

or

YminusYhat = model\$res
YminusYhat

Note that after we create a local variable named YminusYhat, we must type its name into the console to display the values stored in that variable.

The predicted yhat values are provided in Table 6.2.

2. Using the R commands **cor(Hamburger\$calories,Hamburger\$fat)** and **cor(Hamburger \$calories, yhat)**, we find that the correlation between fat and calories $r_{XY} = 0.996$ and that the correlation between predicted calories and calories $r_{Y\hat{Y}} = 0.996$.

☞ **Remark.** In the McDonald's example, the correlation between fat content (X) and calories (Y) is equal to the correlation between predicted calories ($\hat{Y}$) and calories (Y). In general, that is not true. Because, in simple linear regression, $R = |r|$, R and r will have the same magnitude, but they may not have the same sign.

3. The scatterplot between Y and $\hat{Y}$ is given below.

TABLE 6.2 Predicted values for the McDonald's example

Type	Fat	Calories	yhat
Hamburger	10	270	270.68
Cheeseburger	14	320	325.52
Quarter Pounder^{TM}	21	430	421.48
Quarter Pounder^{TM} with cheese	30	530	544.87
Big Mac^{TM}	28	530	517.45

Conceptually, it makes sense that the correlation between the actual and predicted values of Y is always positive. It is desirable for high actual values to be associated with high predicted values and for low actual values to be associated with low predicted values. Hence, the correlation between Y and $\hat{Y}$ will always be positive.

The scatterplot of X (grams of fat) and $\hat{Y}$ is given below.

Notice that the points fall along a perfect straight line with positive slope, indicating that the correlation between X and $\hat{Y}$ is +1. This is because $\hat{Y}$ is defined as a linear transformation of X (a + bX) for which b is positive. If b were negative, the line would have a negative slope, and the correlation would be −1.

R does not enhance our understanding of the overall fit of our regression equation to our data over and above *r* in the case of simple regression. The situation is different in multiple regression, as we shall see in Chapter 16.

• •

EXAMPLE 6.3 In Chapter 5, using the States data, we performed a correlation analysis to determine that in the United States, the average SAT Critical Reading score of a state (satcr) is inversely related to the percentage of students who have taken the SAT in that state (pertak). In this example, we perform a regression analysis to predict the average SAT Critical Reading score for these states, and use it to answer the following questions.

1. Why is a regression analysis appropriate for these data?
2. Write down the regression equation for predicting the SAT Critical Reading score from the percentage of students who have taken the SAT in the state.
3. What is the value of the intercept of this regression equation, and what is its interpretation within the context of this problem?
4. What is the value of the slope of this regression equation, and what is its interpretation within the context of this problem?
5. Use the regression equation to predict the average SAT Critical Reading score for a state with 25 percent of the students taking the SAT.
6. Construct a scatterplot of Y and $\hat{Y}$, and compare that scatterplot to the scatterplot constructed in the solution to part (1). What does this comparison imply about the relationship between R and r?

Solution

1. To determine whether regression analysis is appropriate, we construct the scatterplot, add the fit line, and note that the pattern of the points is linear, confirming that regression analysis is appropriate for these data. The scatterplot is produced below. We also note that both variables are measured at the scale or ratio level, which is appropriate for regression.

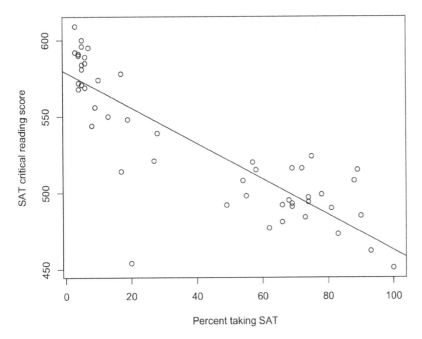

Percent taking SAT

2. We use the R regression procedure. We see from the coefficients table, reproduced below, that the regression equation is

$\hat{Y} = 578.975 - 1.163(\text{pertak})$, where $\hat{Y}$ = predicted satcr.

Coefficients:

	Estimate	Std. Error	t-value	Pr(> |t|)	
(Intercept)	578.97456	5.18885	111.6	< 2e−16	***
States$pertak	−1.16287	0.09936	−11.7	8.43e−16	***

Signif. codes: 0 "***" 0.001 "**" 0.01 "*" 0.05 "." 0.1 " " 1

3. The value of the intercept is 578.97. The intercept indicates the predicted average satcr score when a state has no students taking the SAT. In this case, it is impossible for a state to have an average of no students take the SAT, so the value of the intercept is not meaningful to interpret.
4. The value of the slope is −1.16. The slope indicates that every additional 1-point increase in the percentage of students taking the SAT in the state is associated with a 1.16-point decrease in the average satcr score for the state.
5. $\hat{Y} = 578.975 - 1.163(25) = 549.90$.
6. The scatterplot of Y and $\hat{Y}$ is given below. It suggests a positive relationship between Y and $\hat{Y}$ in contrast to the scatterplot given in part (1), which suggests a negative relationship between X and Y. Hence, while R, a measure of the relationship between Y and $\hat{Y}$ is positive, r, a measure of the relationship between X and Y, is negative in this case. We can show that $r = -0.86$. Because $R = |r|$, we know that $R = 0.86$, as expected from the positive linear shape of the scatterplot.

SIMPLE LINEAR REGRESSION WHEN THE PREDICTOR VARIABLE IS DICHOTOMOUS

In this section, we present an example of simple linear regression when the predictor variable is dichotomous and highlight the connection between the strength of a correlation and the difference between the means on the continuous variable of the two groups represented by the dichotomy.

EXAMPLE 6.4 In Example 6.1 we were concerned with obtaining a regression equation that predicts calories from fat content. In this example, we wish to predict calories from whether or not the hamburger contains cheese. Table 6.3 contains the data for our example. Notice that variable X, representing the presence of cheese, equals 1 when cheese is present and 0 otherwise. Variable X is therefore a dichotomous variable.

A regression analysis is performed to predict the number of calories based on whether or not the hamburger contains cheese. The Coefficients Table from the R output is provided below.

Coefficients:	Estimate	Std. error	*t*-value	Pr(>|*t*|)	
(Intercept)	350.00	83.86	4.173	0.0251	*
Hamburger$cheese	110.00	108.27	1.016	0.3844	

Signif. codes: 0 "***" 0.001 "**" 0.01 "*" 0.05 "." 0.1 " " 1
Unstandardized regression

Coefficients:	Estimate	Std. error	*t*-value	Pr(>|*t*|)
(Intercept)	0.0000	0.4454	0.000	1.000
Scale(Hamburger$cheese)	0.5060	0.4980	1.016	0.384

Standardized regression

Use the Coefficients Table to respond to the following items:
1. What is the correlation between calories and cheese?
2. Write down the regression equation for predicting the calories from the presence of cheese. How well does the model fit the data?

TABLE 6.3 Calories and cheese content by type of McDonald's hamburgers

Type of McDonald's hamburger	Cheese? (X)	Calories (Y)
Hamburger	0	270
Cheeseburger	1	320
Quarter Pounder^{TM}	0	430
Quarter Pounder^{TM} w/ cheese	1	530
Big Mac^{TM}	1	530

3. What is the value of the intercept of this regression equation and what is its interpretation within the context of this problem?
4. What is the value of the slope of this regression equation and what is its interpretation within the context of this problem?
5. Compute the mean number of calories for hamburgers with cheese.
6. Use the regression equation to predict the calorie content of a burger with cheese.
7. Compute the mean number of calories for hamburgers without cheese.
8. Use the regression equation to predict the calorie content of a burger without cheese.
9. What is the difference in calorie content between a burger with cheese and one without cheese? How is this reflected in the regression equation?

Solution

1. $r = 0.506$.
2. $\hat{Y} = 350 + 110(\text{cheese})$, where $\hat{Y}$ = predicted calories. Note that cheese takes on the values 0 and 1. The correlation of $r = 0.506$ is strong, indicating that the model fits the data well.
3. The value at the intercept is 350. The intercept indicates the predicted Y value when $X = 0$. In this case, it indicates that when cheese = 0, that is, the burger does not have cheese, the predicted number of calories is 350.
4. The value of the slope is 110. The slope indicates the change in the predicted Y value for a one-unit increase in the X value. In this case, it indicates that a one-unit increase in the value of cheese is associated with a 110-calorie increase; that is, a burger with cheese is predicted to have 110 more calories than a burger without cheese, on average.
5. The mean number of calories for hamburgers with cheese $(320 + 530 + 530)/3 = 460$.
6. Using the regression equation, we may find the predicted number of calories for hamburgers with cheese (cheese = 1) as $\hat{Y} = 350 + 110(1) = 460$, which equals the mean number of calories for hamburgers with cheese. The predicted value is the mean or expected value for the number of calories in a burger with cheese.
7. The mean number of calories for hamburgers without cheese is $(270 + 430)/2 = 350$.
8. The predicted number of calories for hamburgers without cheese may be found using the regression equation with cheese = 0 as $\hat{Y} = 350 + 110(0) = 350$. This is the mean or expected value of the number of calories for hamburgers without cheese.
9. The difference in calories between a burger with cheese and one without is $460 - 350 = 110$. This is the value of the slope of the regression equation as explained in part (4).

☞ **Remark.** We should point out that as reflected by the equation for the point biserial correlation coefficient (Equation 5.3), the stronger the correlation between the dichotomous variable (cheese, in this case) and the predictor variable (calories, in this case), the greater the separation between the means on the outcome variable for the two groups represented by the dichotomous variable (relative to the spread). Here the means of the two groups are 460 and 350. If the spread of the calories in each group stayed the same, but the mean of 460 was now 500, the correlation between cheese and calories would be even stronger than what it is now.

USING *r* AND *R* AS MEASURES OF EFFECT SIZE

The *effect size* of the simple linear regression model refers to the strength of the linear relationship between the two variables. As we have seen, one measure of effect size for the linear relationship is *r*, the Pearson correlation coefficient between the variables, and we have used Cohen's scale to evaluate the size of the effect. We also have noted that when the predictor variable is dichotomous, the difference between means on the continuous outcome variable relative to the spread may be expressed as a correlation coefficient. Accordingly, the correlation coefficient is a good measure of effect size for simple linear regression, whether it is used to assess the strength of a linear relationship between two variables or the difference between the means of two groups relative to spread. Because *r* and *R* always have the same magnitude, either may be used to express the size of the effect.

EMPHASIZING THE IMPORTANCE OF THE SCATTERPLOT

Throughout this book we have made the point that summary statistics may be misleading if the data they are purported to characterize are anomalous (if, for example, they contain outliers or are skewed in other ways). The linear regression model is no exception. Because the regression model serves to characterize, in summary form, the linear relationship between two variables as a line with intercept and slope, it too may be misleading, or in some way, fail to capture the salient features of the data. The use of graphical displays is critical in the process of assessing how appropriate a given model is for describing a set of data.

To illustrate, we consider the four panels of (X, Y) pairs located in Table 6.4 (Anscombe, 1973). For all panels, the respective X and Y means, X and Y standard deviations, and correlations, slopes, intercepts, and standard errors of estimate are equal. In particular, for each of the four panels, using R, $\overline{X} = 9.0$, $\overline{Y} = 7.5$, $S_X = 3.32$, $S_Y = 2.03$, the equation of regression line is $\hat{Y} = 0.5X + 3$, and $r_{XY} = 0.82$. Accordingly, without a visual representation of these four panels, one might assume that the statistics from all four panels summarize the same dataset. Yet, if we look at the four scatterplots of Figures 6.6(a–d), we see to what extent these datasets are different from one another.

TABLE 6.4 Anscombe's data in four panels

I		II		III		IV	
X	Y	X	Y	X	Y	X	Y
10.0	8.04	10.0	9.14	10.0	7.46	8.0	6.58
8.0	6.95	8.0	8.14	8.0	6.77	8.0	5.76
13.0	7.58	13.0	8.74	13.0	12.74	8.0	7.71
9.0	8.81	9.0	8.77	9.0	7.11	8.0	8.84
11.0	8.33	11.0	9.26	11.0	7.81	8.0	8.47
14.0	9.96	14.0	8.10	14.0	8.84	8.0	7.04
6.0	7.24	6.0	6.13	6.0	6.08	8.0	5.25
4.0	4.26	4.0	3.10	4.0	5.39	19.0	12.50
12.0	10.84	12.0	9.13	12.0	8.15	8.0	5.56
7.0	4.82	7.0	7.26	7.0	6.42	8.0	7.91
5.0	5.68	5.0	4.74	5.0	5.73	8.0	6.89

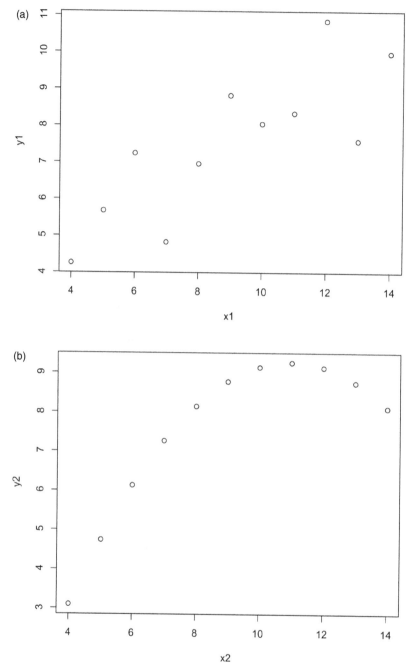

Figure 6.6 (a) Scatterplot of panel I; (b) Scatterplot of panel II; (c) Scatterplot of panel III; (d) Scatterplot of panel IV

Figure 6.6 (*continued*)

In only one case, that of panel (a), is the linear model a good characterization of the underlying data. In panel (b) nonlinearity is a salient feature, yet that feature is not captured by the linear regression model. In panel (c), the presence of the outlier, perhaps due to an error in data entry, unduly influences the result of the analysis, and in so doing, compromises what otherwise would have been a perfectly fitting model. Finally, the regression model in panel (d) exists only because of the single outlier. Without this outlier, we would have been unable to fit a non-vertical line to these data at all.

Although the correlation coefficient in all four panels is $r = 0.82$, which, by itself, suggests a strong linear relationship between the X and Y pairs, and a good-fitting linear model, our visual displays tell us otherwise. The moral of this story is to beware of summary statistics without accompanying visual representations!

SUMMARY OF R COMMANDS

(See also the .R file for Chapter 6.)

Create	Command lines
Run a regression analysis, save the results to a local variable, and print a summary of the results (Example 6.1)	**model = lm(Hamburger$calories~ Hamburger$fat)** **summary(model)**
Run a regression analysis with standardized coefficients (Example 6.1)	**model2 = lm(scale(Hamburger$calories)~scale (Hamburger$fat))** **summary(model2)**
Obtain the predicted and residual values for each observation after running a regression analysis (Example 6.2)	**model = lm(Hamburger$calories~ Hamburger$fat)** **yhat = predict(model)** **YminusYhat = model$residual**
Create a scatterplot with a regression line superimposed (Example 6.1)	**plot(Hamburger$calories~Hamburger$fat, xlab = "Fat", ylab = "Calories", pch = 16)** **abline(lm(Hamburger$calories~ Hamburger$fat))**

EXERCISES

Create a .R file for each exercise that requires the use of R. Run code from the .R file by highlighting or having the cursor on the line of code and hitting **control+enter** on a PC computer keyboard or **command+enter** on a Mac computer keyboard. Save each .R file using a name associated with the Exercise for which it was created. It is recommended that you review the .R file for Chapter 6 located on the textbook's website before completing these exercises. To facilitate doing each exercise, it may be helpful to copy and paste relevant code from the .R file for Chapter 6 into your own .R file and modify them as needed.

Exercises 6.1–6.7 involve simple linear regression models between variables that are interval or ratio.

6.1 In Exercise 5.5, we used the States dataset to determine that there was a positive linear relationship between educexpe, the average educational expenditure per pupil, and teachpay, the average salary of public school teachers in the state. In this exercise, we expand on that relationship to create and interpret a model to predict educexpe from teachpay.

(a) Verify that regression is appropriate in this case.
(b) Find the regression equation for predicting educexpe from teachpay.
(c) Interpret the value of the slope of the regression equation in the context of this exercise using language that someone who has not taken statistics would understand.
(d) Interpret the value of the intercept in the context of this exercise using language that someone who has not taken statistics would understand or indicate why it is not meaningful.
(e) What is the predicted educational expenditure for a state with teacher pay of $40,000?
(f) Is it appropriate to use the regression equation to find the predicted educational expenditure for a state with teacher pay of $80,000?
(g) Report the value of R and interpret it in the context of this analysis.

6.2 In this exercise, we use the States dataset to find the variables that are the best predictors, in a linear sense, of the variable teachpay, which gives the average salary of public school teachers in the state. The possible predictor variables are pupils per teacher (stuteach), average SAT Critical Reading (satcr), and expenditure per pupil (educexpe).

(a) Is linear regression appropriate for these three models? Explain.
(b) Of the three variables, pupils per teacher, average SAT verbal, and expenditure per pupil, which would be the best predictor of teacher salary using the technique of simple linear regression?
(c) Explain why it would not be appropriate to use region as a predictor variable for the prediction of teachpay.

6.3 Using the NELS dataset, can twelfth grade math achievement (achmat12) be predicted by eighth grade socioeconomic status (ses) for students in the NELS dataset? Perform a regression analysis using R and use the results to answer the questions that follow.

(a) Create a scatterplot of achmat12 by ses and superimpose the regression line. Determine that regression is an appropriate technique to use for predicting achmat12 from ses.
(b) What is the regression equation for predicting achmat12 from ses?
(c) Is there a way to interpret the slope that is meaningful in the context of this analysis? If so, explain what additional information it provides.
(d) Is there a way to interpret the y-intercept that is meaningful in the context of this analysis? If so, explain what additional information it provides.
(e) What is the predicted twelfth grade math achievement score of a student with ses = 20?
(f) For the first student in the NELS dataset (id = 1), what is the value of the *actual* twelfth grade math achievement score?

(g) For the first student in the NELS dataset (id = 1), what is the value of the *predicted* twelfth grade math achievement score?

6.4 Use the Impeach dataset to perform a simple linear regression analysis to predict the conservatism of the senator (conserva) based on his or her state's voter support for Clinton (supportc). Use it to answer the following questions.

(a) Create a scatterplot with a superimposed regression line and use it to verify that the data have an approximately linear shape.

(b) What is the correlation, r, between conservatism and state voter support for Clinton?

(c) What is the value of R, a measure of the goodness of fit of the regression model to the data? Describe the goodness of fit for this example.

(d) Write down the linear regression equation for predicting conservatism (Y) from the state voter support for Clinton (X).

(e) What is the interpretation of the slope of the regression equation in the context of this analysis?

(f) Interpret the y-intercept or constant within the context of this analysis, or explain why it is not meaningful.

(g) Use the regression equation to predict the conservatism score for a senator with voter support (the percentage of the vote Clinton received in the 1996 presidential election in the senator's state) of 50.

6.5 The following scatterplot, created using variables from the Framingham dataset, shows the relationship between initial body mass index (BMI1) and initial diastolic blood pressure (DIABP1). Use the scatterplot to answer the following questions.

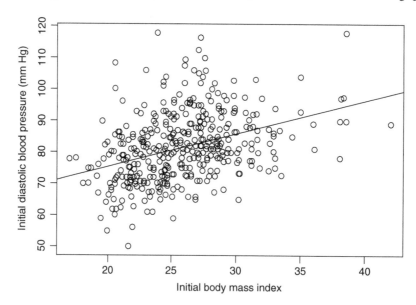

(a) Is linear regression appropriate to analyze the relationship between these variables? Explain.

(b) Is the slope of the regression line positive, negative, or near 0? What does that tell you about the relationship between the variables involved?

(c) Use the regression line in the scatterplot to estimate the initial diastolic blood pressure of a person with an initial body mass index of 19.

(d) Explain why the regression model should not be used to estimate the initial diastolic blood pressure of a person with an initial body mass index of 50.

6.6 In this exercise, we use scatterplots created using the Framingham dataset to compare the relationship between initial body mass index (BMI1) with initial diastolic blood pressure (DIABP1) to the relationship between initial body mass index (BMI1) with initial heart rate (HEARTRTE1)

(a) Create two scatterplots, one depicting the relationship between BMI1 and DIABP1 and the other depicting the relationship between BMI1 and HEARTRTE1. Add the regression line to both scatterplots.

(b) Based on the scatterplots, which relationship with BMI1 has the stronger Pearson's *r* value, diastolic blood pressure or heart rate? Explain.

(c) On average, is a one-unit increase in BMI1 associated with a greater increase in diastolic blood pressure or heart rate?

6.7 Examine by gender the relationship between systolic blood pressure and age for those in the Framingham dataset.

(a) Construct two scatterplots of SYSBP1 by AGE1, one for each level of the variable SEX.

(b) Construct, for each sex, a regression equation to predict systolic blood pressure (SYSBP1) from age (AGE1).

(c) Interpret the results.

(d) Comment on the goodness of fit of each regression line.

(e) Use the respective regression lines to predict the systolic blood pressure for a woman and a man who are each 50 years old.

Exercise 6.8 involves residual analysis for simple linear regression.

6.8 In Exercise 6.1, we used the States dataset to create and interpret a model to predict educexpe from teachpay. In this exercise, we examine and interpret some of the residuals. Run a regression analysis predicting educexpe from teachpay. Then, save to the States dataset the predicted *Y* values as a variable called yhat and the residuals as a variable called res.

(a) For Alabama, the first state in the dataset, what is the *predicted* average educational expenditure for the state?

(b) For Alabama, the first state in the dataset, what is the *actual* average educational expenditure for the state?

(c) For Alabama, the first state in the dataset, what is the value of the residual?

(d) Does the model over- or under-predict the value of educexpe for Alabama?

(e) Was there a larger residual (in magnitude) for the first state in the dataset, or for the second?

Exercises 6.9– 6.10 involve the use of linear transformations.

6.9 Perform a simple linear regression analysis using the Learndis dataset with reading comprehension score (readcomp) as the outcome variable and grade level (grade) as the predictor variable.

    (a) What is the regression equation to predict the reading comprehension score from the grade level of the student?

    (b) Recall that in Exercise 4.18 (b) you created a linear transformation to convert grade to age: **Learndis$age = Learndis$grade + 5**. Use the variable age that you created to find the regression equation to predict the reading comprehension score from the age of the student.

    (c) Why do you suppose that the slope of the regression line does not change in this case?

    (d) Why do you suppose that the intercept is 16.726 points larger for the model with age as the predictor variable?

6.10 The variable schattrt in the NELS dataset gives the average daily attendance percentage for the school that the student attends.

    (a) Find the regression equation to predict slfcnc08 from schattrt. Find also the means and standard deviations of slfcnc08 and schattrt.

    (b) If we were to transform schattrt by dividing its values by 100 we would create a variable schattpp that gives the average daily attendance proportion for the school that the student attends. Using the information obtained in part (a), find the regression equation to predict slfcnc08 from schattpp.

Exercise 6.11 involves the use of nonlinear transformations in simple linear regression.

6.11 In this exercise, we create a model to predict socioeconomic status (ses) from expected income at age 30 (expinc30) in the NELS dataset.

    (a) Conduct initial univariate and bivariate analyses of the variables involved in the multiple regression model.

    (b) Use the square root and log transformations to diminish the severe negative skew in the variable expinc30. Which, if any, are effective?

    (c) Perform a correlation analysis to determine the variable that is most highly correlated with socioeconomic status, the untransformed expected income or the log or square root transformation of the variable.

    (d) Of the three expected income variables correlated with socioeconomic status in part (c), select the one that will give the best-fitting regression model for predicting socioeconomic status and construct that model.

    (e) Use your regression equation to predict the socioeconomic status of a student who predicted that he or she would earn $75,000 a year at age 30.

Exercises 6.12–6.13 involve simple linear regression when the predictor variable is dichotomous.

6.12 In this exercise, we use the NELS dataset to create a model to predict socioeconomic status (ses) from eighth grade computer ownership (computer), a dichotomous variable.

    (a) Create a scatterplot between ses and computer, customize the *x*-axis labels so that the computer axis is nicely labeled (refer to Figure 5.8 of Chapter 5 for a review of creating a scatterplot with a dichotomous variable and customizing axis labels).

(b) What is the regression equation for predicting ses from computer ownership? Note that even though the computer variable is coded as 1 = "No" and 2 = "Yes," when included as a variable in a regression equation, only one of these categories appears in the output (in this case, NELS$computerYes). A preferable approach for use in regression is to assign 1 to computer if the student belongs to this category and 0 if they do not.

(c) Interpret the slope of the regression equation in the context of this analysis.

(d) Interpret the intercept of the regression equation in the context of this analysis or indicate why it would not be meaningful to do so.

(e) Use the regression equation to predict the ses of those who owned a computer in eighth grade.

(f) Use the regression equation to predict the ses of those who did not own a computer in eighth grade.

(g) Use R to find the mean ses of those who did and those who did not own a computer in eighth grade.

6.13 Students in an introductory college statistics course took the SATS (Survey of Attitudes Toward Statistics (Schau et al., 1995)), a regression model was conducted to predict VALUE (attitudes about the usefulness, relevance, and worth of statistics in personal and professional life, rated on the average of several 1–7 Likert scale items) from GENDER (coded with 1 representing male and 2 representing female). The regression equation is $\hat{Y}= 0.573(GENDER) + 4.059$. You do not have this dataset, so you must use the given regression equation and the coding to answer the following questions.

(a) What is the sign of the correlation between GENDER and VALUE?

(b) Which gender tended to give a higher rating to the value of the course?

(c) What is the predicted VALUE score for females?

(d) What is the average VALUE score for males?

Exercises 6.14–6.24 are on a variety of regression topics. For each question, select the most appropriate answer from among the response alternatives.

6.14 If r is 0, and one were asked to predict Y for a given value of X, the best prediction of Y, in a least squares sense, would be:

(a) The mean of all the X values.

(b) The mean of all the Y values.

(c) The given X value.

(d) None of the above.

6.15 If there is a positive linear correlation between X and Y, then we know that the regression equation for predicting Y from X will have a:

(a) positive slope

(b) negative slope

(c) positive y-intercept

(d) negative y-intercept

6.16 The degree to which the points of a scatterplot cluster about the regression line predicting Y from X is reflected by:

(a) The correlation between X and Y.
(b) The standard error of prediction.
(c) The slope of the regression equation, b.
(d) Both (a) and (b).
(e) Both (a) and (c).
(f) Both (b) and (c).
(g) (a), (b), and (c).

6.17 A regression line for predicting Y from X always:
(a) Passes through the origin (0,0).
(b) Passes through $(\overline{X}, \overline{Y})$.
(c) Has a positive slope, b.
(d) Has a positive y-intercept, a.

6.18 If the correlation coefficient between X and Y is $r = 0.60$, and the standard deviations of the Y scores and the X scores are 8 and 4, respectively, then the slope of the regression line for predicting Y from X must be:
(a) 1.20
(b) 0.60
(c) 0.30
(d) 1.00
(e) One cannot determine from the data

6.19 During the semester, the students in a statistics class provided their average weekly study time and their course grade (on a scale from 0.0 to 4.0) for purposes of analysis. The regression equation for predicting grade from the number of hours studied was found to be $\hat{Y} = 1.2X + 0.3$. If a student studies 3 hours per week on average, what is her predicted numerical grade in the course?
(a) 2.25
(b) 3.90
(c) 3.60
(d) One cannot determine from the data

6.20 Given the scenario in Exercise 6.19, which of the following conclusions is warranted?
(a) For each additional hour of study per week, the predicted grade increases by 1.2 on average.
(b) For each additional hour of study per week, the predicted grade increases by 0.3 on average.
(c) For each additional hour of study per week, the predicted grade decreases by 1.2 on average.
(d) For each additional hour of study per week, the predicted grade decreases by 0.3 on average.

6.21 The correlation between exhaustion level and performance on an essay exam was found to be $r = -0.90$. If Alejandro scores below the mean on exhaustion level, it is likely that he will score:
(a) above the mean on the essay exam;
(b) below the mean on the essay exam;

(c) on the mean on the essay exam;

(d) in an unpredictable way on the essay exam.

6.22 We know that unless certain restrictions are placed on a regression model, such models may not be used to make causative claims. Give a concrete example to illustrate a situation in which prediction makes sense, but causation does not.

6.23 The following questions relate to the scatterplot below, which shows the relationship between X and Y for four different subgroups.

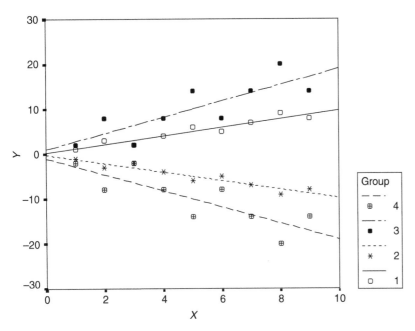

For each subgroup, select the slope of the regression line, b, from the column on the right that best represents the relationship between X and Y for the subgroup. You may select a value more than once.

Group 1: _____   (a) $b = 0.95$
Group 2: _____   (b) $b = -0.95$
Group 3: _____   (c) $b = 1.80$
Group 4: _____   (d) $b = -1.80$
                      (e) $b = 0$

6.24 It is known that the correlation between X and Y is $r = -0.46$.

(a) Find the correlation between X and X.

(b) Find the correlation between Y and $\hat{Y}$.

(c) Find the correlation between X and $\hat{Y}$.

Exercises 6.25–6.28 involve the use of formulas to enhance understanding of regression analysis.

6.25 Use Equations 6.2 and 6.4 to show that the regression line always passes through the point $(\overline{X}, \overline{Y})$.

6.26 Use Equations 6.3 and 5.3 to show that in the case where one variable is dichotomous and one is continuous that $b = \overline{Y}_0 - \overline{Y}_1$. Hint: you will need to use the fact that $S_x = \sqrt{pq}$, assuming that X is the dichotomous variable.

6.27 Use Equations 6.2 and 6.4 to show that the mean of the predicted values is $\overline{Y}$.

6.28 Use the regression equation to show that $R = |r|$.

# CHAPTER SEVEN

PROBABILITY FUNDAMENTALS

In Chapter 1, we made a distinction between descriptive and inferential statistics. We said that when the purpose of the research is to describe the data that have been (or will be) collected, we are in the realm of descriptive statistics. In descriptive statistics, because the data are collected on *all* the individuals about whom a conclusion is to be drawn, conclusions can be drawn with 100 percent certainty. In inferential statistics, on the other hand, the purpose of the research is not to describe the set of data that have been collected, but to generalize or make inferences based on them to a larger group called the *population*. Because data are not available on the entire population, however, we cannot draw conclusions about the population with 100 percent certainty. One of the questions that confronts us in inferential statistics is therefore: "What degree of certainty do we have that our inferred conclusions about the population are correct, and how can we quantify this degree of certainty?" The quantification of degree of certainty is defined in terms of basic probability.

While the concepts of probability apply to variables that are either discrete or continuous, for ease of understanding, in this chapter we illustrate our discussion of probability with examples based on variables that are discrete. In the next chapter, we introduce the continuous case and describe how the fundamentals introduced in this chapter are modified for the continuous case.

THE DISCRETE CASE

We begin the topic of basic probability with the definition of a (*simple*) *experiment*. A (*simple*) *experiment* is defined as any action (such as tossing a coin or answering an item on a test) that leads to one of several possible observable outcomes, without complete certainty as to which outcome will be observed in any given implementation of the experiment. The observable outcomes of any experiment, or any combinations of observable outcomes, are called *events*. If our experiment is to take a die and roll it once, we can observe six possible outcomes {1, 2, 3, 4, 5, 6}, and any one or any combination of these six outcomes can be classified as an event. For example, "The die comes up 6" is an event; "The die comes up 4 or 6" is also an event; and "The die comes up odd" is a third example of an event.

EXAMPLE 7.1 Take a fair coin and toss it once.

1. List all the possible outcomes of this simple experiment.
2. State some examples of events for this simple experiment.

Solution

1. The outcomes of this simple experiment are: {Head (H), Tail (T)}.
2. Some examples of events for this simple experiment are:

"The coin comes up heads"
"The coin comes up tails"

EXAMPLE 7.2 Take a fair coin and toss it twice.

1. List all the possible outcomes of this simple experiment.
2. State some examples of events for this simple experiment.

Solution

1. The possible outcomes of this experiment are: {HH, HT, TH, TT}.
2. Some examples of events for this experiment are:

"The coin comes up first H and then T"
"The coin comes up HH"
"The coin comes up with an H and a T in any order"
"The coin comes up TT"

How can we determine the *probability*, or degree of certainty, that a particular event will occur when an experiment is actually carried out? *If we assume that all outcomes of an experiment are equally likely* (that they all have the same chance of occurring), then we can define the probability of an event E, P(E), as the number of outcomes that satisfy the event E divided by the total number of outcomes of the experiment.

$$P(E) = \frac{\text{number of outcomes satisfying E}}{\text{total number of outcomes of the experiment}}. \tag{7.1}$$

For example, in terms of the die experiment mentioned at the beginning of this section, we obtain the probability of the event E: "The die comes up 6" as $P(E) = \frac{1}{6}$ because only one outcome of the six possible outcomes (the outcome "6") satisfies the event E.

EXAMPLE 7.3 In the experiment of taking a fair coin and tossing it twice, what is the probability of the event E: "HH"? (Said differently, "What is the probability of obtaining two heads?")

Solution Because there are four possible equally likely outcomes for this experiment {HH, HT, TH, TT} and only of them, HH, satisfies the event E, Equation 7.1 gives $P(E) = \frac{1}{4}$.

EXAMPLE 7.4 In the NELS dataset, there are 227 males and 273 females. If the experiment consists of selecting one individual from this dataset at random,

1. What is the probability that the individual is a female?
2. What is the probability that the individual is a male?
3. What is the probability that the individual is a toddler?
4. What is the probability that the individual is either a female or a male?

Solution There are 500 possible outcomes for this experiment: 227 outcomes are male and 273 outcomes are female. Because we are selecting one of these individuals at random, we can assume that all 500 possible outcomes are equally likely. Therefore, we use Equation 7.1.

1. P(individual is a female) $= \dfrac{273}{500} = 0.546$

2. P(individual is a male) $= \dfrac{227}{500} = 0.454$

3. P(individual is a toddler) $= \dfrac{0}{500} = 0.00$, because there are no toddlers in the NELS dataset.

4. P(individual is either a female or a male) $= \dfrac{500}{500} = 1.00$, because all 500 individuals are either female or male.

☞ **Remark.** From part (3) of Example 7.4, we note that the probability of an event that has no chance of occurring in the given experiment is 0, whereas, from part (4), we note that the probability of an event that occurs with certainty in the given experiment is 1.00. In general, the probability of an event is a number between 0 and 1 inclusive. We may also note from parts (1) and (2) that events that are more likely to occur have higher probabilities. If you were asked to bet on whether a randomly sampled individual from the NELS dataset were male or female, the better choice would be female since there is a greater probability of selecting a female from this dataset than a male. Keep in mind that only within the context of a well-defined experiment are events and their probabilities of occurrence defined.

☞ **Remark.** Notice that the probability of an event is its relative frequency. As such, probability values are often reported as percentages.

THE COMPLEMENT RULE OF PROBABILITY

Let us take another look at parts (1) and (2) of Example 7.4. Because males and females have no possible outcomes in common (in other words, a female individual cannot also be male and vice versa), we call these two events *mutually exclusive* or *disjoint*. In addition, because there are only two categories, the event "The individual selected is male" may also be described as "The individual selected is *not* female." Accordingly, we say that the event "The individual selected is male" is the *complement* of the event "The individual selected is female."

Complement rule of probability: If two events E_1 and E_2 are complements of each other, then

$$P(E_1) = 1 - P(E_2). \tag{7.2}$$

Given that the probability is 0.546 that the individual selected is a female, we could have obtained the answer to part (2) of Example 7.4 as $1 - 0.546 = 0.454$.

☞ **Remark.** We often denote the complement of E_1 as E_1^c. The superscript c denotes that we are interested in the complementary event (to be described in more detail in a later section of this chapter).

THE ADDITIVE RULES OF PROBABILITY

In part (4) of Example 7.4, we sought the probability of occurrence for the event: "The individual selected is *either* male *or* female," which, in this case, equals 1.00 because all individuals in our sample are either male or female. We can approach the solution to this problem in a slightly different way. Because this event consists of a combination of two types of outcome (selecting a male, selecting a female), we can consider each of these types of outcome as separate events and recast the problem as *finding the compound probability of the two events*, E_1 : "The person selected is a male" and E_2: "The person selected is a female." We are now seeking the probability of the combined event "E_1 *or* E_2," labeled $P(E_1$ or $E_2)$. Because E_1 and E_2 have no possible outcomes in common (in other words, the outcomes that satisfy E_1 do not also satisfy E_2, and vice versa, because a male cannot also be a female), we call these two events *mutually exclusive* or *disjoint*. In this case, we can find $P(E_1$ or $E_2)$ by simply adding together the simple probabilities, $P(E_1)$ and $P(E_2)$. Using this new approach, we find that for Example 7.4 (4):

$$P(\text{individual is female}) + P(\text{individual is male}) =$$

$$P(\text{individual is either a female or a male}) = \frac{273}{500} + \frac{227}{500} + \frac{500}{500} = 1.00.$$

We may state this more formally as the *first additive rule of probability*.

FIRST ADDITIVE RULE OF PROBABILITY

When two events E_1 and E_2 of the same experiment are mutually exclusive (or disjoint) and we seek to find the probability of the event "E_1 or E_2," we can do so by adding $P(E_1)$ and $P(E_2)$ together. In other words,

$$P(E_1 \text{ or } E_2) = P(E_1) + P(E_2). \tag{7.3}$$

This rule also holds for more than two events if they are all *pairwise disjoint*, which means that no two of them can occur at the same time.

EXAMPLE 7.5 The number of students in the NELS dataset by region is given below based on having used the command **table(NELS\$region)**.

Northeast	North Central	South	West
106	151	150	93

If a student is selected at random from this dataset, find the probability that:

1. The student is from the Northeast.
2. The student is from the South.
3. The student is from either the Northeast or South.
4. The student is not from the South.

Solution Because we are selecting randomly one of the students from the dataset, we can reasonably assume that all 500 students are equally likely to be chosen.

1. $P(\text{Northeast}) = \dfrac{106}{500} = 0.21.$

2. $P(\text{South}) = \dfrac{150}{500} = 0.30.$

3. If we define the events, E_1 and E_2 as

    E_1: "The student is from the Northeast"
    E_2: "The student is from the South"

    then, E_1 and E_2 are mutually exclusive events: they cannot both occur at the same time. Therefore, we can use the first additive rule of probability. Accordingly,

    $$P(\text{Northeast or South}) = P(E_1 \text{ or } E_2) = P(E_1) + P(E_2) = 0.21 + 0.30 = 0.51.$$

4. We may calculate the probability of the event E: "The student is not from the South," in two ways, either through the first additive rule or through the complement rule. Using the first additive rule,

    $P(E) = P(\text{Northeast or North Central or West})= P(\text{Northeast}) + P(\text{North Central}) + P(\text{West}) = 0.21 + 0.30 + 0.19 = 0.70.$

Using the complement rule,

$$P(E) = 1 - P(\text{South}) = 1 - 0.30 = 0.70.$$

In part (3) of Example 7.5, we were able to determine the probability of the event "The student is from the Northeast *or* South" as the sum of the probabilities of the two mutually disjoint events "The student is from the Northeast" and "The student is from the South." If, however, the two were *not* mutually exclusive, we would not have been able to use the first additive rule of probability to find the answer. A more general rule is the *second additive rule of probability* which applies to whether the events are either mutually exclusive or not.

SECOND ADDITIVE RULE OF PROBABILITY

Given two events E_1 and E_2 of the same experiment, if we seek to find the probability of the event "E_1 or E_2," we can do so by using the equation:

$$P(E_1 \text{ or } E_2) = P(E_1) + P(E_2) - P(E_1 \text{ and } E_2), \tag{7.4}$$

where $P(E_1 \text{ and } E_2)$ represents the probability of the outcomes that E_1 and E_2 have in common.

☞ **Remark.** If, in the second additive rule of probability, the events E_1 and E_2 are disjoint, then they have no outcomes in common and $P(E_1 \text{ and } E_2) = 0$. Consequently, when the events are mutually disjoint, the second additive rule gives the same answer as the first additive rule. The second additive rule may, therefore, be considered the more general of the two, and may be used in either case.

EXAMPLE 7.6 A cross-tabulation of the number of students in the NELS dataset by region and whether or not the family owned a computer when the student was in eighth grade is given below based on having used the command **table(NELS$computer, NELS$region)**. Note that the rows of the table represent whether a student's family owned a computer, while the columns of the table represent the region that the student is from. If a student is selected at random from this dataset, determine the probability of selecting a student who is from the South or whose family owned a computer.

	Northeast	North Central	South	West
No	46	89	86	42
Yes	60	62	64	51

Solution The events "Student is from the South" and "Student's family owned a computer" are not mutually exclusive because they have 64 outcomes in common: students who are from the South and whose family owned a computer. Therefore, we use the more general second additive rule with E_1 = "Student is from the South" and E_2 = "Student's family owned a computer" to find:

$$P(E_1 \text{ or } E_2) = P(E_1) + P(E_2) - P(E_1 \text{ and } E_2) = \frac{86 + 64}{500} + \frac{60 + 62 + 64 + 51}{500} - \frac{64}{500}$$

$$= \frac{150}{500} + \frac{237}{500} - \frac{64}{500} = \frac{323}{500} = 0.65.$$

Note that to find the $P(E_1)$ from the table, we must add the number of students in the South whose families did not own a computer with the number of students in the South whose families did own a computer, and divide by the total number of students, 500. Similarly, to find $P(E_2)$ from the table, we have to add the number of students whose families did own a computer across each of the four regions. We can use R to simplify this task by using an additional command to compute marginal sums when we create our table.

MORE R: To add marginal sums to a table, we can use the **addmargins()** command, placing the original table command within the ()s of the **addmargins** command:

addmargins(table(NELS$computer, NELS$region))

	Northeast	North Central	South	West	Sum
No	46	89	86	42	263
Yes	60	62	64	51	237
Sum	106	151	150	93	500

Using the table with marginal sums, we see the total number of students from the South is 150, making $P(E_1)$= 150/500. Likewise, we can see that the total number of students whose family owned a computer is 237, making $P(E_1)$= 237/500. Since the column sum for South and the row sum for Yes both include the 64 students from the South whose family owned a computer, the probability of being in this group must be subtracted out to avoid double counting. This is the probability of both events occurring, $P(E_1$ *and* $E_2)$, that is subtracted out at the end of Equation 7.4. Thus, by the *second additive rule of probability*, we again find the probability of selecting a student who is from the South or whose family owned a computer to be:

$$P(E_1) + P(E_2) - P(E_1 \text{ } and \text{ } E_2) = 150/500 + 237/500 - 64/500 = 323/500 = 0.65.$$

THE MULTIPLICATIVE RULE OF PROBABILITY

Suppose, in an experiment involving the toss of a single fair coin twice, we are interested in finding the probability of obtaining a head on the first toss and a head on the second toss. That is, we want the probability that the events E_1: "Head on first toss" and E_2: "Head on second toss" will both occur. This is denoted by $P(E_1$ and $E_2)$. One way of proceeding is simply to enumerate all possible outcomes of the experiment and then find the desired probability by inspection. The possible outcomes of this experiment are: {HH, HT, TH, TT}.

The only outcome of this experiment that satisfies *both* E_1 and E_2 is {HH}. Accordingly,

$$P(E_1 \text{ and } E_2) = P(HH) = \frac{1}{4} = 0.25.$$

In more complex situations, the job of enumerating such probabilities becomes rather tedious. In some problems, it may actually be impossible to enumerate a set of equally likely outcomes. In such cases, the following rule, called the *multiplicative rule of probability*, can sometimes be used.

Multiplicative rule of probability: Suppose E_1 and E_2 are independent events of the same experiment. (E_1 and E_2 are said to be *independent* events if they have no effect on each other; that is, the occurrence of E_1 has no effect on the probability of E_2.) Then,

$$P(E_1 \text{ and } E_2) = P(E_1) \cdot P(E_2). \tag{7.5}$$

This result also holds for more than two events as long as they are mutually independent. It is worth emphasizing that if the events are not *mutually independent*, they are said to be *dependent*, and Equation 7.5, or a generalization of it to more than two events, will not hold.

We can use the multiplicative rule of probability to obtain the answer to our last problem of finding $P(E_1$ and $E_2)$, where E_1 is "Head on first toss" and E_2 is "Head on second toss," because, in this case, E_1 and E_2 are independent events. Simply,

$$P(E_1 \text{ and } E_2) = P(E_1) \cdot P(E_2) = P \text{ (Head on first toss)} \cdot P(\text{Head on second toss})$$

$$= \frac{1}{2} \cdot \frac{1}{2} = \frac{1}{4} = 0.25.$$

EXAMPLE 7.7 We select, at random, a student from the entire NELS dataset and note whether that student ever smoked marijuana. Then, we select again, at random, from the entire NELS dataset and note again whether the newly selected student (which, according to our sampling scheme, may be the same student that was selected first) ever smoked marijuana. What is the probability that neither student smoked marijuana?

☞ **Remark.** The type of sampling scheme used in Example 7.7 is called *sampling with replacement* because the student selected on the first draw was replaced before the second draw was made. When sampling with replacement, the entire dataset is available for selection at each draw and, therefore, the probability of drawing any student from the dataset (e.g., one who has ever smoked marijuana) remains constant from one draw to the next. The topic of sampling will be covered in more detail later in this chapter.

Solution We first obtain the frequency distribution for marijuana use by students in the NELS dataset using the command **table(NELS$marijuan)**.

Never	Yes
408	92

We define E_1 as: "The first student selected never smoked marijuana" and E_2 as: "The second student selected never smoked marijuana." We want the probability of the event E_1 and E_2. At each stage of the selection process, the probability of selecting a student who never smoked is $\frac{408}{500} = 0.816$. In addition, because we used sampling with replacement, E_1 and E_2 are independent of each other. Therefore, we can use the multiplicative rule of probability:

$$P(\text{neither student ever smoked marijuana}) = P(\text{first student never smoked marijuana and the second student never smoked marijuana})$$
$$= P(E_1 \text{ and } E_2) = P(E_1) \bullet P(E_2)$$
$$= 0.816 \bullet 0.816 = 0.67.$$

EXAMPLE 7.8 Three students are randomly selected with replacement from the NELS dataset. What is the probability that:

1. the first two students never smoked marijuana while the third student did?
2. the first and third students never smoked marijuana while the second student did?
3. the second and third students never smoked marijuana while the first student did?
4. exactly two of the three students never smoked marijuana?

Solution
1. Letting the events E_1, E_2, and E_3 be defined as
   E_1: "The first student never smoked marijuana"
   E_2: "The second student never smoked marijuana"
   E_3: "The third student smoked marijuana"

We are looking for the probability of the event "E_1 *and* E_2 *and* E_3." For each student selected, the probability that the student never smoked marijuana is 0.816, and the probability that the student smoked marijuana is 0.184. Furthermore, because E_1, E_2, *and* E_3 all refer to a different stage of the selection process and because sampling is with replacement, the student selected at any one stage will not affect who is selected at any other stage, these three events are independent of each other. Therefore, we can use the multiplicative rule of probability:

$$P(E_1 \text{ and } E_2 \text{ and } E_3) = P(E_1) \bullet P(E_2) \bullet P(E_3) = 0.816 \bullet 0.816 \bullet 0.184 = 0.1225.$$

2. Letting the events E_1, E_2, and E_3 be defined as;
   E_1: "The first student never smoked marijuana"
   E_2: "The second student smoked marijuana"
   E_3: "The third student never smoked marijuana"

Once again, we are looking for the probability of the event "E_1 *and* E_2 *and* E_3" and we can use the multiplicative rule of probability.

$$P(E_1 \text{ and } E_2 \text{ and } E_3) = P(E_1) \bullet P(E_2) \bullet P(E_3) = 0.816 \bullet 0.184 \bullet 0.816 = 0.1225.$$

3. Letting the events E_1, E_2, and E_3 be defined as:
   E_1: "The first student smoked marijuana"
   E_2: "The second student never smoked marijuana"
   E_3: "The third student never smoked marijuana"

Once again, we are looking for the probability of the event "E_1 *and* E_2 *and* E_3" and we can use the multiplicative rule of probability.

$$P(E_1 \text{ and } E_2 \text{ and } E_3) = P(E_1) \bullet P(E_2) \bullet P(E_3) = 0.184 \bullet 0.816 \bullet 0.816 = 0.1225.$$

4. If we define the events F, G, and H as:
   F: "The first two students never smoked marijuana while the third student did"
   G: "The first and third students never smoked marijuana while the second student did"
   H: "The second and third students never smoked marijuana while the first student did"

Then, we can think of the event "Exactly two of the three students never smoked marijuana" as F *or* G *or* H because these three combinations are the only ways in which the event "Exactly two of the three students never smoked marijuana" can occur. As we have seen in parts (1), (2), and (3) of this example, P(F) = 0.1225, P(G) = 0.1225, *and* P(H) = 0.1225. The three events, F, G, and H, are mutually disjoint, because no two of them can occur at the same time. Therefore, we can use the first additive rule of probability:

P(Exactly two of the three students never smoked marijuana)
= P(F *or* G *or* H)
= P(F) + P(G) + P(H)
= 0.1225 + 0.1225 + 0.1225
= 0.3675.

CONDITIONAL PROBABILITY

As we have mentioned already, when two events E_1 and E_2 are independent, they have no effect on each other, and the probability of each event does not depend upon whether or not the other event has occurred. When two events are not independent, however, the probability of one event does depend upon whether or not the other has occurred. To denote the probability of an event E_1 given that an event E_2 has occurred, we write $P(E_1|E_2)$.

EXAMPLE 7.9 We know from Example 7.7 that the probability that a randomly selected student from the NELS dataset has never smoked marijuana is $0.816 \left(\frac{408}{500} \right)$. Is this probability the same for males and females? That is, is the probability of never having smoked marijuana *given* that the student is male equal to the probability of never having smoked marijuana *given* that the student is female?

Solution We obtain, as shown below, the cross-tabulation of gender by marijuana use for the NELS dataset based on having used the command **addmargins(table(NELS\$gender, NELS\$marijuan))**.

	Never	Yes	Sum
Male	185	42	227
Female	223	50	273
Sum	408	92	500

1. To find the probability that a randomly selected student from the NELS dataset never smoked marijuana *given that the student is male*, we need only consult the first row of the table. By limiting to the first row, we are looking at only the 227 male students since that is the given event of interest. Now we look for the number of those 227 male students who never smoked marijuana, and we find that

$$P(\text{student never smoked marijuana} \mid \text{student is male}) = \frac{185}{185 + 42} = \frac{185}{227} = 0.815.$$

2. To find the probability that a randomly selected student from the NELS dataset never smoked marijuana *given that the student is female*, we need only consult the second row of the table because that row limits us to looking at marijuana use for only the 273 females. From the second row, we find that

$$P(\text{student never smoked marijuana} \mid \text{student is female}) = \frac{223}{223 + 50} = \frac{223}{273} = 0.817.$$

According to these results, the probability of never smoking marijuana is effectively the same for males and females.

EXAMPLE 7.10 Find the probability that a randomly selected student is male given that the student never smoked marijuana.

Solution Using the table associated with Example 7.9, we refer to column one so that we are limited to just those 408 students who have never smoked to find that
$$P(\text{student is male} \mid \text{student never smoked marijuana}) = \frac{185}{185 + 223} = \frac{185}{408} = 0.453.$$

☞ **Remark.** Because P(student never smoked marijuana | student is male) does not equal P(student is male | student never smoked marijuana), we may note that $P(E_1|E_2)$ and $P(E_2$

$|E_1)$ do not have to be equal to each other. In fact, they will be equal to each other only when $P(E_1) = P(E_2)$.

To find a conditional probability, as we have done in Examples 7.9 and 7.10, we may use Equation 7.6 as an alternative approach.

$$P(E_1|E_2) = \frac{P(E_1 \text{ and } E_2)}{P(E_2)}. \tag{7.6}$$

In applying Equation 7.6 to the problem of Example 7.9 (a), we let E_1 = "The student never smoked marijuana" and E_2 = "The student is male." Then, $P(E_1 \text{ and } E_2)$ $= \frac{185}{500} = 0.370$, $P(E_2) = \frac{227}{500} = 0.454$. Substituting these values into Equation 7.6, we obtain

$$P(E_1|E_2) = \frac{P(E_1 \text{ and } E_2)}{P(E_2)} = \frac{0.370}{0.454} = 0.815,$$

the same result as before.

☞ **Remark.** By the multiplicative rule of probability, if events E_1 and E_2 are independent, then $P(E_1 \text{ and } E_2) = P(E_1) \cdot P(E_2)$. Consequently, by Equation 7.6,

$$P(E_1|E_2) = \frac{P(E_1 \text{ and } E_2)}{P(E_2)} = \frac{P(E_1) \cdot P(E_2)}{P(E_2)} = P(E_1).$$

In other words, if E_1 and E_2 are independent, the probability of E_1 is the same whether or not we know that E_2 has occurred, which goes back to the definition of independence.

Sometimes we are interested in the complement of a conditional probability. For example, we may know the probability that a pregnancy test comes back negative given that a woman is actually pregnant (known as a false negative), and we are interested in knowing the probability that the pregnancy test comes back positive given that a woman is actually pregnant (known as a true positive). Equation 7.7 provides us with a method of calculating this probability.

$$P(E_1^c|E_2) = 1 - P(E_1|E_2). \tag{7.7}$$

. . . .

EXAMPLE 7.11 Suppose that the probability that a pregnancy test comes back negative given that a woman is actually pregnant is 0.05. Find the probability of the test coming back positive given that a woman is actually pregnant.

Solution If we let E_1 be the event that the pregnancy test comes back positive, then the complement of this event, E_1^c, is that the pregnancy test comes back negative. Furthermore, if we let E_2 be the event that the woman is actually pregnant, we are interested in finding $P(E_1|E_2)$. Since we are given that $P(E_1^c|E_2) = 0.05$, by Equation 7.7, we know that $P(E_1|E_2)$ must be 0.95.

. . . .

EXAMPLE 7.12 Calculate the probability that a student from the NELS dataset has smoked marijuana given that the student is male.

Solution We refer back to the notation used in Example 7.9. In this case, we are interested in finding $P(E_1^c|E_2)$. By Equation 7.7, we calculate that the probability that a student has smoked marijuana given that the student is male is $1 - 0.815$ or 0.185.

We may confirm this answer using the table provided in the solution to Example 7.9 (part 1) and obtain $\frac{42}{185 + 42} = \frac{42}{227} = 0.185$.

THE RELATIONSHIP BETWEEN INDEPENDENCE, MUTUAL EXCLUSIVITY, AND CONDITIONAL PROBABILITY

The multiplicative rule of probability can be used only when the two events, E_1 and E_2, are independent of one another, whereas the first additive rule of probability can be used only when the two events, E_1 and E_2, are mutually exclusive, or disjoint from one another. Because confusion often arises over the distinction between independence and mutual exclusivity, we include the following statement to clarify the relationship between these two concepts:

Given two events, E_1 and E_2, of the same experiment, E_1 and E_2 cannot be both independent of one another and mutually exclusive of one another, unless one of the events has a zero probability of occurring.

Why is this true? By definition, to be mutually exclusive is to be inherently dependent: if E_1 occurs, then E_2 cannot occur. Said differently, the occurrence of E_1 affects the probability of E_2 occurring by entirely precluding E_2 from happening. We illustrate this concept in the following example.

EXAMPLE 7.13 Given the experiment of rolling a fair die once, let event E_1 be rolling a 2 and event E_2 be rolling a 6. Thus, $P(E_1)$ and $P(E_2)$ are each equal to 1/6, or about 0.167. Are these events mutually exclusive? Are they independent?

Solution The two events are mutually exclusive because the die cannot come up as both a 2 and a 6 on a single roll. Mathematically, $P(E_1 \text{ and } E_2) = 0$.

By our previous definition of independence, if the two events were independent, the occurrence of either event would not change the probability of the other occurring. Mathematically, as shown earlier by Equation 7.6, this would mean $P(E_2 \mid E_1) = P(E_2)$; regardless of whether E_1 occurs, E_2 occurs with the same probability. However, this is not the case with our roll of the die. Say the die is rolled and comes up a 2 (E_1 occurs). Given that the roll is a 2, there is a probability of zero that this roll is a 6. That is, $P(E_2 \mid E_1) = 0$. Since $P(E_2) = 0.167$, the probability of E_2 occurring is not equal to the conditional probability of E_2 occurring given that E_1 occurs, so the two events are not independent.

While two events of the same experiment cannot be both independent and mutually exclusive, they can be (1) independent and not mutually exclusive, (2) not independent and mutually exclusive, or (3) not independent and not mutually exclusive. We return to this point in Exercises 7.9–7.11.

THE LAW OF TOTAL PROBABILITY

The law of total probability provides an expression for calculating an *unconditional* probability from a set of *conditional* probabilities. Let A be some event, say that a pregnancy test comes back positive, and let E_1 and E_1^c be complementary events, say that a woman is either pregnant or not pregnant, respectively. Suppose we are given the true positive rate $(P(A|E_1) = 0.95)$ and false positive rate $(P(A|E_1^c) = 0.01)$ for a given pregnancy test. Further suppose that we know that 75 percent of women who take the pregnancy test are actually pregnant. How do we find the probability the test would come back positive, regardless of whether the woman is pregnant or not? Equation 7.8, known as the law of total probability, provides such an expression:

$$P(A) = P(A|E_1)P(E_1) + P(A|E_1^c)P(E_1^c). \tag{7.8}$$

EXAMPLE 7.14 Use the information provided in the above paragraph to calculate the probability that a test would come back positive regardless of whether the woman is pregnant or not.

Solution Using Equation 7.8, we note that $P(E_1) = 0.75$ and therefore $P(E_2) = 0.25$. Substituting the appropriate values into Equation 7.8, we obtain:

$$P(A) = P(A|E_1)P(E_1) + P(A|E_1^c)P(E_1^c) = 0.95*0.75+0.01*0.25 = 0.715.$$

EXAMPLE 7.15 The cross-tabulation below shows the number of students of the NELS dataset by number of times the student was absent in twelfth grade and high school program type taken. The table was produced with marginal sums using the R command **addmargins(table (NELS$absent12,NELS$hsprog))**.

	Rigorous Academic	Academic	Some Vocational	Other	Sum
Never	21	26	6	2	55
1–2 times	61	110	12	12	195
3–6 times	54	99	17	10	180
7–9 times	9	33	7	2	51
10–15 times	3	8	1	0	12
Over 15 times	1	3	0	3	7
Sum	149	279	43	29	500

First, use the table to find the probability that a randomly selected student from the NELS dataset took a rigorous academic program. Then, verify that this matches the result obtained using the law of total probability by using the table to complete parts (1)–(4) below and substituting the results into Equation 7.8. If a student from the NELS dataset is randomly selected, what is the probability that

1. the student was absent at least 7 times during twelfth grade.
2. the student was absent 6 or fewer times during twelfth grade; that is, find the complement of part (1).

3. the student took a rigorous academic program, given that the student was absent at least 7 times in twelfth grade.

4. the student took a rigorous academic program, given that the student was absent 6 or fewer times in twelfth grade.

Solution If a student is randomly selected from the NELS dataset, let A be the event that the student took a rigorous academic program and let E_1 be the event that the student was absent at least 7 times during twelfth grade. Then, from the table, the number of students who took a rigorous academic program is 149, the sum of the first column. This means $P(A) = 149/500$, or 0.298.

Next, we obtain the components of the law of total probability by completing parts (1)–(4).

1. This is the unconditional probability $P(E_1)$. The last three groups of the variable absent12 – "7–9 times," "10–15 times," and "Over 15 times" – constitute the total number of students absent at least 7 times. The row sums tell us that the number of students absent 7–9 times is 51, 10–15 times is 12, and over 15 times is 7. Thus, the $P(E_1)$ is $(51+12+7)/500 = 70/500 = 0.14$.

2. This is $P(E_1^c)$, the complement of $P(E_1)$, which can be found by adding the remaining row sums and dividing by 500 total students. This probability can also be found using Equation 7.2, the complement rule of probability:

   $$P(E_1^c) = 1 - P(E_1) = 1 - 0.14 = 0.86.$$

3. This is the conditional probability $P(A|E_1)$. Since we know the student was absent at least 7 times, we look at just rows 4–6. Adding up the sums in the last column for rows 4–6, we get $51 + 12 + 7 = 70$ students absent at least 7 times. Next, we find how many of those 70 students took a rigorous academic program by looking at the Rigorous Academic column for rows 4–6 to find the total to be $9 + 3 + 1 = 13$ students. Then, $P(A|E_1)$ is 13/70, or about 0.1857.

4. This is the conditional probability $P(A| E_1^c)$. The event that the student was absent 6 times or fewer, E_1^c, is represented in the table by the first three rows. Similar to what we did in part (3), we add the row sums for rows 1–3 to get the total number of students for which E_1^c occurred to get $55 + 195 + 180 = 430$ students. Then we sum the entries of the Rigorous Academic column for rows 1–3 to get $21 + 61 + 54 = 136$ students. So, $P(A|E_1^c) = 136/430$, or about 0.3163.

Finally, we substitute our results back into Equation 7.8 to verify the result we obtained for $P(A)$ from the table:

$$P(A) = P(A|E_1)P(E_1) + P(A| E_1^c)P(E_1^c)$$
$$P(A) = 0.1857*0.14 + 0.3163*0.86$$
$$P(A) = 0.298.$$

BAYES' THEOREM

Bayes' theorem, named after Reverend Sir Thomas Bayes (1702–1761), an English theologian and mathematician, provides an expression for flipping around the events inside of a conditional probability expression. That is, if you are provided with $P(A|E_1)$ and are interested in $P(E_1|A)$, then Bayes' theorem as given by Equation 7.9 may be used.

$$P(E_1|A) = \frac{P(A|E_1)P(E_1)}{P(A|E_1)P(E_1) + P(A|E_1^c)P(E_1^c)}. \tag{7.9}$$

Bayes' theorem may appear complicated at first, but it is actually an application of both the formula for computing conditional probability presented earlier (Equation 7.6) and the law of total probability (Equation 7.8) from the last section. We can show how we arrive at Bayes' theorem by applying Equation 7.6 to write $P(E_1|A) = P(E_1 \text{ and } A)/P(A)$.

First, we change the numerator to match that of Bayes' theorem. Again by Equation 7.6, the flipped conditional probability, $P(A|E_1)$, is equal to $P(E_1 \text{ and } A)/P(E_1)$. Rearranging this equation shows us that $P(E_1 \text{ and } A)$ is equivalent to $P(A|E_1)P(E_1)$, which can then be substituted in as the numerator. Next, we can easily substitute $P(A)$ in the denominator with $P(A|E_1)P(E_1) + P(A|E_1^c)P(E_1^c)$ by Equation 7.8, the law of total probability. Thus, in only two steps we arrive at Bayes' theorem.

EXAMPLE 7.16 Suppose as given above, the probability that a woman's pregnancy test comes back positive (A) given that she is pregnant (E_1) is $P(A|E_1) = 0.95$, and we are interested instead in the probability that a woman is pregnant (E_1) given that her pregnancy test comes back positive (A). That is, we are interested in $P(E_1|A)$. We also know, as given above, that 75 percent of women who take the pregnancy test are actually pregnant and that the probability that a woman's pregnancy test comes back positive (A) given that she is not pregnant (E_1^c) is $P(A|E_1^c) = 0.01$. To find $P(E_1|A)$, we apply Bayes' theorem (Equation 7.9).

Solution Substituting the appropriate probability values into Equation 7.9, we obtain the following probability that a woman is pregnant given her pregnancy test comes back positive:

$$P(E_1|A) = \frac{P(A|E_1)P(E_1)}{P(A|E_1)P(E_1) + P(A|E_1^c)P(E_1^c)} = \frac{0.95 \times 0.75}{0.95 \times 0.75 + 0.01 \times 0.25} = 0.997.$$

EXAMPLE 7.17 Suppose for a given year, 14 of the top 250 grossing films were directed by women. Of those films directed by a woman, approximately 78.6 percent feature a female protagonist. In contrast, about 22.2 percent of the films directed by a man feature a female protagonist. Say we are watching a randomly selected film from the top 250 films, and the protagonist is female. What is the probability that the film was directed by a woman? Assign a letter to represent each event, and then use Bayes' theorem (Equation 7.9) to find the solution. Assume that for the top 250 films, every director is either a woman or a man, and every protagonist is either female or male.

Solution First, we assign each of the two events a letter: let D be the event that a film was directed by a woman and let F be the event that a film featured a female protagonist. Then we are being asked to find $P(D|F)$. Then, by Equation 7.9,

$$P(D|F) = \frac{P(F|D)P(D)}{P(F|D)P(D) + P(F|D^c)P(D^c)}.$$

Since 14 of the top 250 films were directed by women, P(D)=14/250, or 0.056. Then, by the complement rule of probability (Equation 7.2), the probability that a film was directed by a man, $P(D^c)$, is $1 - P(D) = 1 - 0.056 = 0.944$. And, P(F|D) is the probability that a film has a female protagonist given that the film was directed by a woman, or 0.786, and $P(F|D^c)$ is the probability that a film has a female protagonist given that the film was directed by a man, or 0.222. Substituting these values back into our equation, we obtain

$$P(D|F) = \frac{0.786 * 0.056}{0.786 * 0.056 + 0.222 * 0.944},$$

or approximately 0.174. Thus, the probability that the film was directed by a woman given that the protagonist is female is approximately 0.174.

THE LAW OF LARGE NUMBERS

So far we have been interested in probabilities simply as a way of determining the likelihood of events when an experiment is performed once. The theory of probability is even more useful, however, when an experiment is repeated several times. This fact is illustrated by the following law, which provides the basic link between the theoretical notion of probability and the applied, empirical one. It is known as the *law of large numbers*.

In the law of large numbers, suppose E is an event in an experiment and the probability of E is p ($P(E) = p$). If the experiment is repeated n independent and identical times (each repetition may be called a trial), then the relative frequency of E occurring in these n trials will be approximately equal to p. In general, the larger the number of trials, the better p is as an approximation of the relative frequency of E actually obtained.

☞ **Remark.** We can therefore think of p, the probability of event E, as the relative frequency with which E will occur "in the long run" (i.e., for an infinite number of trials). A value of $p = 0.75$ would then mean that in the long run, event E will occur 75 percent of the time. Because we never actually do any of our experiments an infinite number of times, all we can expect, as stated in the law of large numbers, is for p to approximate the relative frequency of E, with the approximation generally becoming better as the number of trials n increases.

One concrete example of the law of large numbers can be seen through the experiment of flipping a fair coin many times. When a coin is only flipped 10 times, then it is possible that we will obtain an outcome of exactly 5 heads out of the 10 coin flips. However, it is also possible that we will obtain 4 or 6 heads instead, for a relative frequency of 0.4 or 0.6. If the coin is flipped 1,000,000 times instead, then the relative frequency of the number of heads out of the total number of trials will get closer to the true probability of heads, 0.5.

SUMMARY OF R COMMANDS

(See also the .R file for Chapter 7.)

Create	Command lines
Table of NELS region (Example 7.5)	**table(NELS$region)**
Table with marginal sums (Example 7.6)	**addmargins(table(NELS$computer, NELS$region))**
Table of proportions with marginal sums (Exercise 7.14)	**addmargins(percent.table(Wages$ed, Wages$marr))/100**

EXERCISES

Create a .R file for each exercise that requires the use of R. Run code from the .R file by highlighting or having the cursor on the line of code and hitting **control+enter** on a PC computer keyboard or **command+enter** on a Mac computer keyboard. Save each .R file using a name associated with the exercise for which it was created. It is recommended that you review the .R file for Chapter 7 located on the textbook's website before completing these exercises. To facilitate doing each exercise, it may be helpful to copy and paste relevant code from the .R file for Chapter 7 into your own .R file and modify them as needed.

Exercises 7.1–7.5 relate to the NELS dataset.

7.1 Create frequency and percent distribution tables of the variable edexpect, which indicates the highest level of education the students in eighth grade expect to achieve eventually. If one student is selected at random from the NELS dataset, what is the probability that:
   (a) The student anticipates earning a bachelor's degree?
   (b) The student anticipates earning a master's degree?
   (c) The student anticipates earning either a bachelor's or master's degree?
   (d) The student anticipates earning something other than a bachelor's degree?

7.2 Create a cross-tabulation of edexpect by gender, including marginal sums. Use it to find the following probabilities if one student is selected at random from the NELS dataset.
   (a) The student expects to earn less than a college degree.
   (b) The student is female.
   (c) The student expects to earn less than a college degree and is female.
   (d) The student expects to earn less than a college degree or is female.
   (e) The student does not expect to earn less than a college degree.
   (f) The student is female given that the student expects to earn less than a college degree.
   (g) The student expects to earn less than a college degree given that the student is female.
   (h) The student is female given that the student does not expect to earn less than a college degree.

7.3   Use the frequency and percent distribution tables you created in Exercise 7.1 to find the following probabilities. One student is selected at random from those in the NELS dataset. This student is then replaced and a second student is selected at random. What is the probability that:

(a) The first student anticipates earning a bachelor's degree?
(b) The second student anticipates earning a master's degree?
(c) The first student anticipates earning a bachelor's degree and the second student anticipates earning a master's degree?
(d) Can you use the multiplicative rule of probability to answer part (c) of this exercise? Explain why or why not.

7.4   Use the frequency and percent distribution tables you created in Exercise 7.1 to find the following probabilities. One student is selected at random from those in the NELS dataset. Without replacement, a second student is selected at random. What is the probability that:

(a) The first student anticipates earning a bachelor's degree?
(b) The first student anticipates earning a bachelor's degree and the second student anticipates earning a master's degree?
(c) Can you use the multiplicative rule of probability to answer part (b) of this exercise? Explain why or why not.

7.5   Use the frequency and percent distribution tables you created in Exercise 7.1 to find the following probabilities. One student is selected at random from those in the NELS dataset. If this experiment is repeated 1,000 times, approximately how many times of the 1,000 do you expect to select:

(a) A student who anticipates earning a bachelor's degree?
(b) A student who anticipates earning a master's degree?
(c) A student who anticipates earning either a bachelor's or master's degree?
(d) A student who anticipates earning something other than a bachelor's degree?

7.6 The numbers 1–10 inclusive are written on pieces of paper and the pieces of paper are put in a bowl. If one of them is drawn at random, what is the probability that the number selected is

(a) even?
(b) odd?
(c) either even or odd?
(d) either less than 5 or even?
(e) either greater than 2 or odd?

7.7 What (if anything) is wrong with the following statement? Consider the events:
E_1: "Before finishing this book you will inherit \$1 million"
E_2: "Before finishing this book you will not inherit \$1 million"

Because these two events are mutually exclusive and exhaustive (one of them must occur and both of them cannot occur at the same time), $\text{Prob}(E_1) = \text{Prob}(E_2) = \frac{1}{2}$.

7.8   What (if anything) is wrong with the following statement? "We are given an urn containing white and black marbles in equal numbers. It is impossible to determine the probability that one marble selected at random from this urn is white, because we do not know how many marbles there are in the urn to begin with."

7.9   In this exercise, we see that two events of the same experiment, E_1 and E_2, can be independent and not mutually exclusive. Suppose we toss a fair coin twice. Let E_1 and E_2 be defined as

E_1: "The first toss is a head"

E_2: "The second toss is a head"

   (a) Show that E_1 and E_2 are *not* mutually exclusive.
   (b) Show that E_1 and E_2 are independent of each other.

Hint for part (b): To show that E_2 is independent of E_1, show that the probability of E_2 occurring is not influenced by whether or not E_1 occurs. This can be done in two steps. First, find the probability of E_2 assuming we have no information about whether E_1 occurred. Second, determine the probability of E_2 assuming we know that E_1 has occurred. Because these two values are equal, we may conclude that the occurrence E_1 has no effect on the probability of E_2, and thus that E_2 is independent of E_1.

7.10   In this exercise, we see that two events of the same experiment, E_1 and E_2, can be dependent and mutually exclusive. Suppose we toss a fair coin once. If it comes up heads, we stop. If it comes up tails, we toss it again. Let E_1 and E_2 be defined as

E_1: "The first toss is a head"

E_2: "The second toss is a head"

   (a) Show that E_1 and E_2 are mutually exclusive.
   (b) Show that E_1 and E_2 are dependent.

7.11   In this exercise, we see that two events of the same experiment, E_1 and E_2, can be dependent and not mutually exclusive. Suppose we toss a fair coin once. If it comes up heads, we stop. If it comes up tails, we toss it again. Let E_1 and E_2 be defined as:

E_1: "The first toss is a tail"

E_2: "The second toss is a tail"

   (a) Show that E_1 and E_2 are not mutually exclusive.
   (b) Show that E_1 and E_2 are dependent.

7.12 Let E_1 have probability 0.6. Let $A|E_1$ have probability 0.5 and $A|E_1^c$ have probability 0.7.
   (a) Find the probability of A.
   (b) Find the probability of $E_1|A$.

7.13 John is a very forgetful person, especially when it comes to his umbrella. Suppose that in the town where John lives, the probability that it is raining on any given day is 0.6. Furthermore, suppose that on 40 percent of all days, it is both raining and John has forgotten his umbrella at home.
   (a) Calculate the probability that on a rainy day, John will forget his umbrella at home.
   (b) Suppose John realizes that given it is not raining, he has not forgotten his umbrella 80 percent of the time. Find the probability that, regardless of the weather, John forgets his umbrella.
   (c) On his way to work, John realizes that he has forgotten his umbrella. Knowing this, what is the probability that it is raining outside?

7.14 This exercise uses the Wages dataset, which contains a random subsample of the 1985 Current Population Survey. Create a cross-tabulation of proportions with marginal sums for the highest education level attained (ed) and marital status (marr) variables. This can be done by using the command **percent.table(Wages$ed,Wages$marr)**, wrapping this command within the **addmargins()** command, and finally dividing the entire line by 100 in order to express the relative frequencies (percentages) as proportions (decimals). The result is the following table of proportions:

x	y		
	Not married	Married	Sum
Less than high school degree	0.070	0.130	0.200
High school degree	0.080	0.120	0.200
Some college	0.095	0.105	0.200
College degree	0.045	0.155	0.200
Graduate school	0.070	0.130	0.200
Sum	0.360	0.640	1.000

Each cell in the table represents the proportion of all individuals who have the characteristics of the corresponding row and column, with marginal sums of proportions in the last row and last column. Thus, the cell in the first row, first column indicates that 0.070 of the total individuals in the dataset have less than a high school degree and are not married. As noted earlier in the chapter, the relative frequency of an event is equal to the probability that the event will occur, and since a proportion is just the relative frequency expressed as a decimal, each cell of the table also represents the probability of the event occurring for a randomly selected individual. Thus, 0.070 is the probability that a randomly selected individual from the Wages dataset has less than a high school degree and is not married.

Using the law of total probability (Equation 7.8) and the computational formula for conditional probability (Equation 7.6), show that the marginal sum of the fifth row of the table (0.200) is equal to the probability that a randomly selected individual from the Wages dataset has completed graduate school.

7.15 Andrea has a diverse sock collection: three pairs are purple (one pair with polka dots, one pair with argyle, and one pair with stripes); three pairs are green (one pair with polka dots, one pair with argyle, and one pair with stripes); three pairs are blue with stripes; and one pair is black with rainbows. Andrea dislikes spending time folding her socks, so all her socks remain unpaired and mixed up in her sock drawer. Every day she selects each of two socks. Assuming that each sock is selected randomly from the drawer and that all socks of the same color and pattern are identical, compute the following probabilities:

(a) Starting with a full set of socks, what is the probability that the first sock selected of the two socks to be selected has polka dots?

(b) Starting with a full set of socks, given that the first sock selected of the two socks to be selected has stripes, what is the probability that it is purple?

(c) Starting with a full set of socks, if the first sock selected of the two socks to be selected is green with argyle, what is the probability that the second sock is also green?

(d) Starting with a full set of socks, how much greater is the probability of getting a perfectly matched pair of socks if the first sock selected of the two socks to be selected is blue than if the first sock selected of the pair is black?

(e) If four individual socks already have been tried on and not returned to the drawer (purple with argyle, blue with stripes, green with argyle, and black with rainbows), what is the probability that a sock selected from the drawer is a match for one of the previously tried-on socks?

7.16 About 22 percent of dog owners adopt their dog from a shelter. About 75 percent of dogs adopted from shelters are mixed breed, and about 53 percent of dogs adopted from places other than a shelter are purebred. Given a person's dog is purebred, and assuming no other information about the person or dog, find the probability that the dog came from a shelter.

# CHAPTER EIGHT

THEORETICAL PROBABILITY MODELS

A theoretical probability model is a mathematical representation of a class of experiments having certain specified characteristics in common, and from which we may derive the probabilities of outcomes of any experiment in the class. The extent to which the probabilities derived from the theoretical model are correct for a particular experiment depends on the extent to which the particular experiment possesses the characteristics required by the model. In most cases, the match between the theoretical model and a specific experiment will not be perfect, and the answer we obtain using the model will be only an approximation of the true answer. The advantage of using a theoretical model, however, is that it enables us to answer questions about all the experiments that have the specified characteristics of the model without having to treat each experiment as a completely new and unique situation. Theoretical probability models are applicable when all possible outcomes of an experiment, taken together, follow a pattern of regularity that may be described by the model. As a result, they enable us to obtain the probability of any single outcome or combination of outcomes for that experiment.

In this chapter we present two theoretical probability models that have widespread applicability: the binomial probability model and the normal probability model. The binomial probability model answers questions about a particular type of discrete variable, whereas the normal probability model answers questions about a particular type of continuous variable. Of the two models, the normal is more widely used. In fact, the normal is perhaps the most widely used of all theoretical probability models.

THE BINOMIAL PROBABILITY MODEL AND DISTRIBUTION

In general, the binomial probability model applies to experiments that consist of *a fixed number of independent* and *identical* trials, the outcomes of which on any one trial may be thought of as *dichotomous* (as either success or failure), with the same probability of success across each trial. This dichotomy is the reason for the name *binomial*; there are two outcomes (such as head/tail, pass/fail, or absent/present).

Recall Example 7.8 (part 4) in which we sought the probability that exactly two of three students selected randomly with replacement from the NELS dataset never smoked marijuana. Using the language of the binomial model, we define a trial as the selection of one student from the dataset and recognize that, for this example, there are three trials. As we shall see, the three trials satisfy the assumptions of the binomial probability model in that they are independent and identical and their outcomes are each dichotomous.

The trials are *independent* because each student is selected at random with replacement; knowing who is selected at one trial tells us nothing about who will be selected at subsequent trials. The trials are *identical* because each and every trial consists of selecting one student at random from the 500 students of the NELS dataset. And finally, because the outcome of each trial may be categorized as either "student has smoked marijuana" or "student has never smoked marijuana," each outcome is *dichotomous*.

In Example 7.8 (part 4), we are interested in the probability that two of the three students never smoked marijuana. In the language of the binomial model, we may say that we are interested in the probability of obtaining two "successes" in three trials. A *success*, in this case, therefore means *the student never smoked marijuana*.

Of course, given that there are three trials in this example, a *complete* description of the probabilities associated with each possible result would include knowing the probabilities of observing 0 successes, 1 success, 2 successes, and 3 successes in the three trials. These probabilities, obtained "by hand" using the approach of Example 7.8 (part 4), are given in Table 8.1 and displayed as a bar graph in Figure 8.1. Taken together, these probabilities define what is called the *binomial probability distribution* for this case. That is, the number of trials (denoted by n) equals 3, the probability of a success on any one trial (denoted by p) equals 0.816, and the number of successes (denoted by k) takes on the values 0, 1, 2, 3, in turn. Then, the binomial probability distribution consists of the probabilities associated with each possible number of successes and is given numerically in Table 8.1 and graphically in Figure 8.1.

Notice that the probabilities associated with obtaining either 2 or 3 successes are much greater

TABLE 8.1 Binomial probability distribution for $n = 3$ and $p = 0.816$

k	Probability of k successes
0	0.006
1	0.083
2	0.368
3	0.543

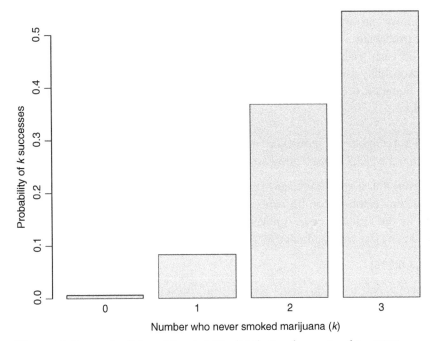

Figure 8.1 Bar graph of binomial probability distribution for $n = 3$ and $p = 0.816$

than the probabilities associated with obtaining either 0 or 1 success. In other words, this discrete distribution is skewed negatively. Can you explain why this distribution is skewed negatively? Hint: Recall that it is quite likely (with probability 0.816) that a randomly selected student never smoked marijuana.

☞ **Remark.** In defining a complete binomial probability distribution, we need to specify the values of n and p and allow k, the number of successes, to vary from 0 (no successes) to n (all successes). If we do this, we can evaluate the probability for each possible value of k individually and construct a corresponding probability distribution and probability bar graph for the given experiment.

☞ **Remark.** Two interesting observations may be made concerning the bars in the binomial distribution bar graph of Figure 8.1. First, the probability of each of the individual events (0 students never smoked marijuana, 1 student never smoked marijuana, 2 students never smoked marijuana, 3 students never smoked marijuana) is just the height of the corresponding bar in the bar graph. Therefore, we can obtain any desired probability by summing the heights of the appropriate bars in the bar graph. But moreover, because each bar has the same width, and the sum of the areas of all the bars is 1, we can also obtain any desired probability by summing the areas of the appropriate bars in the bar graph. In general, whenever we are using a probability distribution in which the total area of the graph is 1, we can obtain the probability of any event by finding the proportion of the area under the graph corresponding to that event. Thinking of probabilities as proportions of area under the relevant probability graph (or curve) will be extremely useful in solving problems for situations in which only areas are available, such as those involving continuous variables, as opposed to discrete ones.

While we computed the probabilities in Table 8.1 by hand, using the approach of Example 7.8 (part 4), there are three other approaches we can take. Given a binomial distribution, we can use R's binomial probability distribution function, **dbinom(k,n,p)**, to obtain the probability of obtaining k successes in n trials, where p equals the probability of a success on each trial; or we can use Table C.4 in Appendix C, which summarizes the binomial probability distribution to approximate this particular binomial distribution; or we can solve Equation 8.2 directly with help from R. We illustrate all three approaches in Example 8.1.

EXAMPLE 8.1 Obtain the probability that exactly 2 students out of 3, who are randomly selected from the NELS dataset, never smoked marijuana.

Solution Using R Using the language of the binomial probability model, we may rephrase this problem in terms of the probability of obtaining $k = 2$ successes in $n = 3$ trials, where a success is defined as the "student never smoked marijuana" and $p = 0.816$ is the probability of a success on any one trial, and run the command:

dbinom(2,3,0.816)

The console window will contain the value 0.368, which is the probability of obtaining $k = 2$ students who smoked marijuana out of $n = 3$ students randomly selected from the NELS dataset. This is the value we calculated by hand.

MORE R: Finding probabilities in the binomial model and graphing them.

To create the list of probabilities given in Table 8.1 and the bar graph of Figure 8.1, we use the following series of R commands that are in the .R file associated with Chapter 8.

```
probs = dbinom(c(0, 1, 2, 3), 3, 0.816)
barplot(probs, names.arg = c(0,1,2,3), xlab = "Number who never smoked marijuana (k)")
```

Solution Using Table C.4 in Appendix C To obtain this distribution using Table C.4, we have $n = 3$ and $p = 0.816$. The box associated with $n = 3$ contains many columns, each representing the binomial distribution for fixed values of p. Note that the highest value of p given is $p = 0.5$. In our case, we have defined "success" to be "the student never smoked marijuana," and for a single randomly selected student the probability of "success" is 0.816. However, because the table is made to approximate distributions with $p \leq 0.5$, we redefine "success" as "the student smoked marijuana at least once." Because the probability is 0.816 that the student never smoked marijuana, then $1 - 0.816$, or 0.184, is the probability that the student smoked marijuana at least once. Also, because $n = 3$, the event "0 students never smoked marijuana" is equivalent to the event "3 students smoked marijuana at least once."

Because there is no value of p equal to 0.184 exactly, we use the closest tabled value, which is $p = 0.20$. From the table, we see that the probability that 0 students smoked marijuana is approximately 0.512, that 1 student smoked marijuana is approximately 0.384, that 2 students smoked marijuana is approximately 0.096, and that 3 students smoked marijuana is approximately 0.008. Accordingly, the probability that 0 students never smoked marijuana is approximately 0.008, the probability that 1 student never smoked marijuana is 0.096, and so on. These values are close to the ones provided by R in Table 8.1 based on the more precise $p = 0.816$.

Alternatively, the individual probability also may be estimated using Table C.4 in Appendix C by looking up $n = 3$, $k = 1$, and $p = 0.20$. We use $k = 1$ because the probability that 2 students of 3 never smoked marijuana is the same as the probability that 1 student of 3 smoked marijuana at least once. The individual value is 0.384.

Solution Using Equation 8.2 The binomial formula, which gives the probability of obtaining k successes in n trials, where p is the probability of success and q is the probability of failure, involves notation that we have not used before. Before presenting the binomial equation itself, we provide a discussion of factorial notation and combinations.

We introduce the new notation, *factorial notation*, to help us more conveniently denote the operation of sequential multiplication. The mathematical symbol $n!$ (read "n factorial") is defined, for the positive integer n, as the ordered product of all the positive integers from 1 up to and including n: $n! = 1 \times 2 \times 3 \times \cdots \times (n-1) \times (n)$. For example, $5! = 1 \times 2 \times 3 \times 4 \times 5 = 120$.

☞ **Remark.** It would be meaningless to try to use the equation $n! = 1 \times 2 \times 3 \times \cdots \times (n-1) \times (n)$ to evaluate $0!$ because we could not start at 1 and multiply "up to" 0, since 0 is less than 1. Because there are formulas involving factorial notation in which we may want to use this notation for all the nonnegative integers including 0, we now define the symbol $0!$ as $0! = 1$.

We also introduce combination notation. Given n objects, the number of ways in which k of these objects (k between 0 and n inclusive) can be combined, or selected, without regard to order of selection is denoted by the symbol $_nC_k$ or the symbol $\binom{n}{k}$ and is given by Equation 8.1:

$$\binom{n}{k} = \frac{n!}{k!(n-k)!}.$$ (8.1)

We can now express the binomial equation that gives the probability of obtaining k successes in n trials, where p is the probability of success and q is the probability of failure ($q = 1 - p$).

$$\text{Pr}(k \text{ successes in } n \text{ trials}) = \binom{n}{k}p^k q^{n-k}.$$ (8.2)

Applying Equation 8.2 to the example at hand, we have $n = 3$, $p = 0.816$, and $q = 1 - 0.816 = 0.184$.

For $k = 0$, Pr(0 students ever smoked marijuana) $= \binom{3}{0}0.816^0(0.184)^3 = 0.006$.

For $k = 1$, Pr(1 student ever smoked marijuana) $= \binom{3}{1}0.816^1(0.184)^2 = 0.083$.

For $k = 2$, Pr(2 students ever smoked marijuana) $= \binom{3}{2}0.816^2(0.184)^1 = 0.368$.

For $k = 3$, Pr(3 students ever smoked marijuana) $= \binom{3}{3}0.816^3(0.184)^0 = 0.543$.

☞ **Remark.** Of course, we did not need to generate the complete distribution to answer the particular question of Example 8.1. We did so to describe how to generate an entire binomial distribution. With that knowledge in hand, we can suggest a more simple and straightforward solution to Example 8.1.

☞ **Remark.** The complete binomial distribution may be described in summary statistic form like any other distribution. Fairly simple equations are available for both the mean and the standard deviation. For the case of the binomial, these summary statistics are in terms of number of successes. The equations, presented without derivation, are:

$$\text{mean} = np; \text{standard deviation} = \sqrt{npq},$$ (8.3)

where n = number of trials, p = probability of success on any one trial, and q = probability of failure on any one trial. Note that for Example 8.1, the mean and standard deviation of the binomial distribution equal $(3)(0.816) = 2.45$ and $\sqrt{(3)(0.816)(0.184)} = 0.67$, respectively. Both Table 8.1 and Figure 8.1 indicate that these values are reasonable for this distribution. Notice that this binomial distribution is negatively skewed. Because the probability of a success, p, on any one trial is large ($p = 0.816$), it is unlikely that we would observe a relatively small number (near zero) of successes and likely that we would observe a relatively large number of successes. In general, when $p > 0.5$ the binomial distribution is skewed negatively, when $p < 0.5$ it is skewed positively, and when $p = 0.5$, it is symmetric.

THE APPLICABILITY OF THE BINOMIAL PROBABILITY MODEL

We were able to use the binomial probability model to solve the problem of Example 8.1 because, as we noted, this problem satisfied the assumptions of this model. In this section we seek to clarify the criteria an experiment must meet to be considered a binomial experiment by examining situations to which the model does and does not apply.

To review, the criteria an experiment must meet to be considered a binomial experiment are:

1. The experiment consists of n identical trials ($n \geq 1$).
2. The trials are independent of each other.
3. On each trial, the outcomes can be thought of in a dichotomous manner as Success and Failure, so that the two events Success and Failure are mutually exclusive (cannot both happen at the same time) and exhaustive (each trial must result in either a Success or a Failure).
4. If $\Pr(\text{Success}) = p$ and $\Pr(\text{Failure}) = q$, then p and q do not change their values from trial to trial, and (by criterion 3) $p + q = 1$ on each trial.

EXAMPLE 8.2 Does the binomial model apply to the following situation: In randomly sampling with replacement 10 students from the NELS dataset, what is the probability that 5 are from the Northeast, 3 from the South, 1 from the West, and 1 from the North Central regions?

Solution No, the binomial model does not apply to this situation because the outcomes of the experiment on any one trial are not dichotomous. In particular, four events are specified on each trial: obtaining a student from the Northeast, obtaining a student from the South, obtaining a student from the West, and obtaining a student from the North Central region.

EXAMPLE 8.3 Does the binomial model apply to the following situation: In randomly sampling with replacement 10 students from the NELS dataset, what is the probability that 5 are from the Northeast, and 5 from the South?

Solution No, the binomial model does not apply to this situation. Although only two events are specified on each trial, the sum of the probabilities, p and q, for these two events does not equal 1.00. The probability, p, of obtaining a student from the Northeast is $106/500 = 0.21$ and the probability, q, of obtaining a student from the South is $150/500 = 0.30$. Therefore, $p + q = 0.51$, not 1.00. The reason $p + q$ is not equal to 1 in this example is that the events "the student is from the Northeast" and "the student is from the South" are not exhaustive. That is, it is possible for an outcome of a trial to be neither a student from the Northeast nor a student from the South; for example, the student could be from the West.

EXAMPLE 8.4 Does the binomial model apply to the following situation: Ten students are randomly selected from the NELS dataset *without* replacement. What is the probability that exactly ten students are from the South?

Solution No. The binomial model does not apply to this situation because by sampling without replacement, we caused the values of p and q to change from one trial to the next. On the first trial, the probability, p, that the student is from the South is $150/500$ or 0.30 and the probability, q, that the student is not from the South is 350/500 or 0.70. On the second trial, however, the probabilities of p and q depend on the outcome of the first trial. If, on the first trial, the student selected is from the South, then on the second trial, the probability of selecting a student from the South is 149/499 or 0.299. On the other hand, if, on the first trial, the student selected is not from the South, then on the second trial, the probability of selecting a student from the South is 150/499 or 0.301. In either case, the values of p and q will have changed from the first trial to the second (and will continue to change in each subsequent trial). Because p and q change from one trial to the next, these trials may not be considered to be either identical or independent.

EXAMPLE 8.5 Does the binomial model apply to the following situation: Ten students are randomly selected from the NELS dataset *with* replacement. What is the probability that exactly five students are from the South?

Solution Yes! The binomial model does apply to this situation. Because we are explicitly interested in obtaining students from the South, we can define Success as "selecting a student from the South" and Failure as "not selecting a student from the South." In each trial, the probability of Success is 0.30, whereas the probability of Failure is 0.70, and p and q do not change from trial to trial. Because the events defined as Success and Failure are mutually exclusive and exhaustive, $p + q = 1.00$.

Given that this example satisfies the binomial probability model, let's find the answer to the question posed using R, approximate it using Table C.4 in Appendix C, and calculate it using Equation 8.2.

MORE R: The binomial probability distribution function, **dbinom**.
We use the following to obtain the binomial probability when $n = 10$, $k = 5$, and $p = 0.30$:

dbinom(5, 10, .30)

We obtain as our answer, probability = 0.103. Using Table C.4, we look up $n = 10$, $k = 5$, and $p = 0.30$. We find that the probability is 0.1029, or 0.103 when rounded to three decimal places. Computing the probability directly from Equation 8.2 by solving:

$$\Pr(5 \text{ successes in } 10 \text{ trials}) = \binom{10}{5} 0.30^5 (0.70)^5,$$

with the help of R, we multiply $(0.30^5)*(0.70)^5$ by the number of combinations of taking $n = 10$ things $k = 5$ at a time, $(1*2*3*4*5*6*7*8*9*10)/(1*2*3*4*5*1*2*3*4*5)$ as follows:

((1*2*3*4*5*6*7*8*9*10)/ (1*2*3*4*5*1*2*3*4*5))* (.30^5)*(.70)^5

MORE R: The combinations or *choose* command **choose(n,k)**.
To find the number of combinations of $n = 10$ things taken $k = 5$ at a time, we can more simply make use of the combinations command, **choose(n,k)**.

choose(10,5) * (.30^5)*(.70^5)

As before, the probability of obtaining five students from the South in a sample of 10 students randomly selected with replacement from the NELS dataset is found to be 0.103.

By the law of large numbers, we may interpret this result to mean that if we repeated this experiment 1,000 times, then our sample of 10 will contain exactly 5 students from the South approximately 103 times.

Following are some other examples to which the binomial model applies that do not rely on the NELS dataset.

• •

EXAMPLE 8.6 Jill is taking a 10-question multiple-choice examination on which there are four possible answers to each question. Assuming that Jill just *guesses* the answer to each question, what is the probability of her getting exactly four of the questions correct?

Solution Let Success on each question (or trial) be "getting the correct answer" and Failure be "getting an incorrect answer." Because these two events are mutually exclusive and exhaustive on each trial, and because Jill is *guessing* on each question, so that $p = 1/4$ and $q = 3/4$ (there are four possible answers to each question and only one of them is correct), the binomial model is applicable to this situation ($k = 4$, $n = 10$, $p = 0.25$).

Using R's **dbinom(k,n,p)** function, we obtain Pr(4 successes in 10 trials) = **0.1460:**

dbinom(4,10,.25)

Using Table C.4 in Appendix C we find also that the probability is 0.1460. Computing the probability directly from Equation 8.2:

$$\text{Pr(4 successes in 10 trials)} = \binom{10}{4} 0.25^4 (0.75)^6,$$

using **choose(10,4)*(.25^4)*(.75^6),** we obtain a probability = 0.1460.

By the law of large numbers, we can interpret this result in the following way: If a large number of people take this 10-question exam and guess on each of the questions, we can expect approximately 15 percent of them to get exactly 4 of the 10 questions correct.

• •

EXAMPLE 8.7 Erie Pharmaceutical Company manufactures a drug for treatment of a specific type of ear infection. They claim that the drug has probability 0.40 of curing people who suffer from this ailment. Assuming their claim to be true, if the treatment is applied to 50 people suffering from this ailment, what is the probability that exactly 25 of these 50 people will be cured?

Solution If we consider the treatment of each person with this ailment to be a trial, we can define Success and Failure on each trial as "the person's ailment is cured" and "the person's ailment is not cured," respectively. These two events are mutually exclusive and exhaustive for each trial (each person being treated). Because the claim is that the long-run probability of this treatment working is 0.40 (and we are accepting this claim as true), we can take this value as the probability of success on each trial. Therefore, the binomial probability model is applicable to this situation ($k = 25$, $n = 50$, $p = 0.40$).

Using R, we run the command **dbinom(25, 50, .40)** to find that Pr(25 successes in 50 trials) = 0.0405.

Because the maximum value of n given in Table C.4 is 20, we cannot use Table C.4 to find a solution to this problem. For those interested, an alternative approach is discussed in Exercise 8.32 using the normal distribution to approximate the binomial.

Computing the probability directly from Equation 8.2,

$$\Pr(25 \text{ successes in } 50 \text{ trials}) = \binom{50}{25} 0.4^{25}(0.6)^{25} = 0.0405.$$

using **choose(50, 25)*(.4^25)*(.6^25)**, we obtain a probability = 0.0405.

By the law of large numbers, we may say that if the company's claim is true, and a large number of groups of 50 people are each treated with this drug, then we should expect to see exactly 25 people cured in approximately 4 percent of these groups.

• •

EXAMPLE 8.8 Using the same situation as in Example 8.7, what is the probability of obtaining:

1. at most 15 Successes (cures)?
2. at least 20 Successes (cures)?

Solution As we saw in Example 8.7, the binomial model is applicable to this situation with $n = 50$, and $p = 0.40$.

1. "At most 15 Successes" is the same as "15 or fewer Successes" and can be expressed as $k \leq 15$. The answer may be obtained directly using the cumulative binomial probability distribution function available in R.

MORE R: The cumulative binomial probability function.

Given the binomial probability distribution, we may find the probability that the number of successes *is less than or equal to* some value, say k, by using R's cumulative binomial probability function:

pbinom(k, n, p)

replacing **n** with the value equal to the number of trials, **k** with the value equal to the number of successes, and **p** with the value equal to the probability of a success on each trial.

For this problem, we use the command **pbinom(15, 50, .40)** to obtain a probability = 0.0955.

By the law of large numbers, we may say that if a large number of groups of 50 people each are treated with this drug, we should expect to see at most 15 people cured in approximately 10 percent of these groups.

2. "At least 20 Successes" is the same as "20 or more Successes" and can be expressed as $k \geq 20$.

MORE R: The complement of the cumulative binomial probability function.

Given the binomial probability distribution, we may find the probability that the number of successes *is greater than but not equal to* some value, say k, by using the **lower.tail = F** argument (recall that **F** in this case refers to the word **False**).

pbinom(k, n, p, lower.tail = F)

where **n** = the number of trials, **k** = the number of successes, and **p** = the probability of a success on each trial. Because the **pbinom** function with the **lower.tail = F** argument does not include the value **k** in its summation, we must use **k−1** instead if we want **k** to be included in the calculation.

To find the probability that *at least* 20 of the 50 people will be cured we use the following command:

pbinom(19, 50, .40, lower.tail = F)

and obtain the value 0.5535.

By the law of large numbers, we may say that if a large number of groups of 50 people are each treated with this drug, then we should expect to see at least 20 people cured in approximately 55 percent of these groups.

In summary, in a binomial experiment with n trials, where p equals the probability of a success on each trial:

- To find the probability of exactly k successes, we use R's **dbinom** function:

  dbinom(k,n,p)

- To find the probability of at most k successes (which equals the probability of k or fewer successes), we use R's cumulative binomial function, **pbinom**:

  pbinom(k, n, p)

- To find the probability of at least k successes (which equals the probability of $k + 1$ or more successes), we use R's **pbinom** function with the **lower.tail = F** argument:

  pbinom(k, n, p, lower.tail = F)

THE NORMAL PROBABILITY MODEL AND DISTRIBUTION

The importance of the normal probability model lies in the fact that in the real world many traits – such as height, weight, IQ scores, and the like – have relative frequency curves that are closely approximated by this model. Moreover, as we shall see, throughout the course of this book, many problems in mathematical statistics either are solved, or can be solved, by using the normal probability model or a probability model based on the normal.

The normal probability model was developed by one of the greatest mathematicians of all time, Johann Carl Friedrich Gauss (1777–1855). Most mathematicians of Gauss' period were interested in applying mathematics to real-world problems, such as astronomy and navigation. Knowing that data obtained through observation and measurement contained errors due to the imprecision of the measuring instruments employed, Gauss studied many different sets of such data and noticed that they all possessed certain common characteristics. In general, each set of observations was symmetric about some central value and the farther from this central value, the fewer and fewer such observations there were. Based on such studies, Gauss was able to develop a mathematical model that could be used to describe the distribution of errors contained in these sets of data. Gauss called the mathematical model *the normal probability model*, and the distribution of errors the normal probability distribution.

We will use the normal probability model descriptively, to describe real variables. Further, we will use it when we introduce inferential statistics, to describe the sampling distribution of the mean when the standard deviation of the population is known.

Although the normal probability model is given by a mathematical equation, we will not present that equation here. Instead, we will list three characteristics of the distributions described by the normal probability model. The model is used to find the probabilities of certain score ranges by finding the corresponding areas under the normal curve.

1. A normal distribution is symmetric about its mean, μ (read: mu).
2. A normal distribution extends indefinitely to the right and to the left of the mean, always getting closer and closer to the horizontal axis but never quite reaching it. (That is, observations that are farther from the mean have smaller relative frequencies than observations that are closer to the mean.)
3. The total area under the normal distribution is 1. By symmetry, this means that one-half of the area is to the right of the mean, and one-half is to the left.

In general, all normal distributions have the same bell-shape appearance and differ from each other only in their particular mean and standard deviation values. The mean indicates where the distribution is located on the horizontal axis, whereas the standard deviation indicates the extent to which the scores tend to cluster about the mean. Figure 8.2 shows a general normal distribution curve with mean μ and standard deviation σ (read: sigma) and indicates what proportion of the distribution can be expected to lie within one and two standard deviations of the mean.

MORE R: To create the graph of the standard normal distribution of Figure 8.2:

```
x  = seq–4, 4, length=100)
hx = dnorm(x, 0, 1)
plot(hx ~ x, type="l", xlab="z scores",
ylab="Density", main="Standard Normal Distribution")
```

Note that the first line of code creates a sequence of 100 values that spans from the minimum of –4 to a maximum of 4. The second line (**hx**) calculates the height of the standard normal curve (mean = 0; sd = 1) across this sequence of *x* values. The third line plots the *hx* values for the sequence of *x* values; the letter l in **type="l"** specifies the plot as a line graph; titles are added to the *x*-axis, the *y*-axis, and to the plot overall. Additional details about this command may be found in the .R-file associated with Chapter 8.

The normal probability model describes the entire family of normal probability distributions, each with its own mean and standard deviation. The particular normal

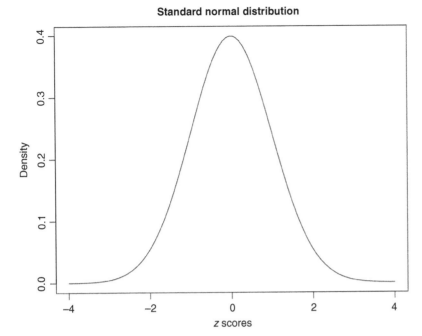

Figure 8.2 The standard normal distribution

distribution with mean 0 and standard deviation 1 is called the *standard normal distribution*. Standard normal distributions are usually denoted with the letter *Z*, while *arbitrary normal distributions*, those with different means or standard deviations, are denoted with other letters, such as *Y*. However, if *Y* is a normal distribution with mean μ and standard deviation σ, then we can generate a standard normal distribution through the equation:

$$Z = \frac{Y - \mu}{\sigma}. \tag{8.4}$$

The family of normal probability distributions may be used to answer probability questions about sets of data that are either known, or assumed, to be normally distributed. In general, probabilities can be obtained as proportions of area under the appropriate normal curve.

Because the probabilities are found as areas, all probability values in the continuous case are between 0 and 1 inclusive.

The probability that a single randomly selected score will be lower than a particular score, *x*, is found by calculating the area under the normal distribution curve to the left of *x*. The probability that a single randomly selected score will be higher than a particular score, *x*, is found by calculating the area under the normal distribution curve to the right of *x*.

Alternatively, by the complement rule, the probability that a single score selected at random from a normal distribution is higher than the score *x* may be calculated as 1 – the probability that the score selected is lower than the score *x*.

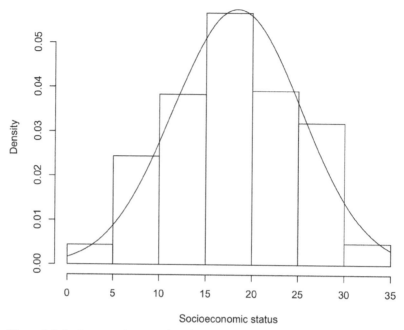

Socioeconomic status

Figure 8.3 Socioeconomic status distribution with normal curve overlay

Because the normal distribution is symmetric, with area under the curve equal to 1, the probability that a single randomly selected score is above the mean equals 0.5, and the probability that the score is below the mean equals 0.5.

Because the distribution is continuous rather than discrete, the probability that a randomly selected score will have a particular value is 0. As a result, the probability that a single randomly selected score is greater than a particular value, x, is the same as the probability that the single randomly selected score is greater than or equal to x.

We illustrate finding probabilities under the normal curve using R and Table C.1 in Appendix C, which contains areas under the standard normal curve.

Recall the histogram of the ses distribution from the NELS dataset illustrated in Chapter 2 as Figure 2.5 and reproduced here as Figure 8.3. You will note that in Figure 8.3 a normal curve is superimposed on the histogram.

MORE R: To create the ses histogram of Figure 8.3 with normal curve overlay, type:

```
x  = seq(0, 35, length = 100)
hx = dnorm(x, 18.40, 6.92)
hist(NELS$ses, freq = F, xlab = "Socio-economic status", main = "")
lines(hx~x)
```

In this case, the first line of code creates a sequence of 100 values that spans from the minimum to the maximum NELS ses score. The second line (**hx**) calculates the height of the normal curve with mean = 18.40 and sd = 6.92 across this sequence of x values. The third line plots a density (as opposed to frequency) histogram, and the fourth line overlays the normal curve onto the histogram using the **lines** command.

While the ses distribution is not exactly normally distributed, it may be considered to be approximately so with mean 18.40 and standard deviation 6.92, and we may use the normal probability distribution to estimate areas under the ses curve.

••

EXAMPLE 8.9 Use the normal distribution with mean 18.40 and standard deviation 6.92 to approximate the proportion of students in the NELS dataset with ses values *less than or equal to* 26.

Solution Using R To find the area under the normal curve to the left of $X = 26$ (see Figure 8.4), we use the following cumulative distribution function command:

pnorm(26, mean = 18.40, sd = 6.92)

or

pnorm(z, mean = 0, sd = 1)

where z is replaced with either the z-score value itself or the expression for computing the z-score value given by Equation 4.4.

For this problem, we simply would use the following command:

pnorm((26–18.40)/6.92, mean = 0, sd = 1)

to obtain the result 0.86 in the console. This result means that the area under this normal curve to the left of the value of 26 equals 0.86, or that, if you were to randomly select a score from a normal distribution with mean 18.4 and standard deviation 6.92, the probability is 0.86 that it would fall below the value of 26. In the context of our example, this means that approximately 86 percent of the individuals in our NELS dataset have ses scores at or below the value 26.

Of course, rather than include the expression for the calculation of the z-score within the parentheses following the command **pnorm**, as we have done in this example, we first could have calculated the z-score using the following command:

(26–18.40)/6.92

to obtain the result that $z = 1.10$ and then used:

pnorm(1.10, mean = 0, sd = 1)

MORE R: To plot a histogram with a shaded normal curve overlay as in Figure 8.4, type:

```
x = seq(0, 35, length = 100)
hx = dnorm(x,18.434, 6.925)
hist(NELS$ses, freq = F, xlab = "Socio-economic status", main = "")
lines(hx~x)
cord.x = c(0,seq(0,26,length = 100),26)
cord.y = c(0,dnorm(seq(0,26,length = 100), 18.434, 6.925),0)
polygon(cord.x, cord.y, col="grey")
```

cord.x and **cord.y** are the coordinates for the area shaded under the normal curve. The **cord.x** values are a sequence from 0 to 26, the values on the x-axis that are shaded. The **cord.y** values are the corresponding heights of the normal curve for the x-axis values. Therefore, drawing a polygon on these **cord.x** and **cord.y** values shades underneath the normal curve.

Figure 8.4 The area under the normal curve with $\mu = 18.40$ and $\sigma = 6.92$ to the left of 26

Solution Using Table C.1 in Appendix C To use Table C.1 in Appendix C to find the proportion of students in the NELS dataset with ses values less than or equal to 26 in a distribution with mean 18.40 and standard deviation 6.92, we also would first need to convert the value 26 to a z-score using Equation 4.4. We need to do so because Table C.1 only gives areas under the standard normal curve with mean 0 and standard deviation 1.

$$z = \frac{X - \mu}{\sigma} = \frac{26 - 18.40}{6.92} = 1.10.$$

This z-score may be decomposed as 1.1 + 0.00. According to Table C.1, the area to the right of this z-score is 0.1357. To find the area to the left of the z-score, we use the complement rule and compute $1 - 0.1357 = 0.8643$, which is the proportion we seek.

We may see how far this estimate departs from the actual percentage of cases at or below an ses score of 26 to assess the accuracy of our approximation. To do so, we use R to find the percentile rank of the value 26, estimated from the command **cumulative.table**, the cumulative percent of scores at or below a score of 26 is 85.6, suggesting that the approximation using the normal curve is a good one in this case.

☞ **Remark.** Because ses is a continuous variable, when we ask about the proportion of cases at or below an ses value of 26, it is equivalent to ask about the proportion of cases below an ses value of 26. This is because, for truly continuous variables, the value of exactly 26 has zero probability of occurring.

In inferential statistics, for reasons that will become clear in the next chapter, we focus on the upper and lower tails of a probability distribution, as opposed to its mid area. Hence, the next example has as its focus the area in the right tail of a normal distribution.

EXAMPLE 8.10 Determine how likely it is to select a value at random from a set of scores known to be normally distributed that is two or more standard deviations above the mean.

Solution Using R This is equivalent to finding the area under the standard normal curve to the right of a z-score of 2. This area is shaded in Figure 8.5. Although we will use the same R cumulative distribution function (**pnorm()**) as before, because we now want the area to the *right* of the z-score and the **pnorm** function gives us areas to the left by default, we can either use the complement rule to find the area we want, or use the option **lower.tail = F**. We run the following commands:

pnorm(2, 0, 1)

to obtain the probability value 0.977.

And, then, subtract this probability value from 1 using the following command:

1 − .977

to obtain the probability value we seek. The area to the right of a z-score of 2 is 0.023.
Alternatively, we type the command:

pnorm(2, 0, 1, lower.tail = F)

to obtain the probability value of 0.023.

MORE R: To plot a normal curve with shading as in Figure 8.5, type:

curve(dnorm, c(−4, 4), xlim = c(−4,4), main = "Area under the curve to the right of a z-score of 2", ylab = "Density", xlab = "z")
cord.x = c(2,seq(2,4,length = 100),4)
cord.y = c(0,dnorm(seq(2,4,length = 100), 0, 1),0)
polygon(cord.x, cord.y, col="grey")

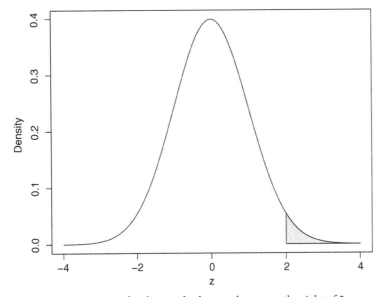

Figure 8.5 The area under the standard normal curve to the right of 2

Solution Using Table C.1 in Appendix C To use Table C.1 in Appendix C to find the area under the standard normal curve to the right of $z = 2.00$, we decompose 2.00 as 2.0 plus 0.00 and find the area under the curve to the right of this value to be 0.0228.

That is, the probability is only 0.023 of randomly selecting a score from a normal distribution that is 2 or more standard deviations above the mean. Said differently, only 2.3 percent of scores fall in this range.

EXAMPLE 8.11 Assuming that ses has a normal distribution with mean 18.4 and standard deviation 6.92, find the ses value that has an area of 0.025 to its right.

Solution Using R In contrast to the two earlier problems wherein we sought an area corresponding to a given score, in this problem we seek a score corresponding to a given area. To do so, we make use of R's inverse normal probability function as shown below. In this command, p represents the area under the curve to the left and the output from this command provides the z-score corresponding to this area:

qnorm(p, 0, 1)

In our example, we want the score that marks off 0.025 of the area to its right, which is equivalent to the score that marks off 0.975 of the area to its left. Accordingly, we run this command with $p = 0.975$, as follows:

qnorm(.975, 0, 1)

to obtain the following result in the console: 1.96.

Alternatively, we can use the **lower.tail = F** argument and type:

qnorm(0.025, 0, 1, lower.tail = F)

We see from this result that the z-score that marks off 0.975 of the area under a normal curve to its left (or equivalently 0.025 of the area to its right) is approximately 1.96.

To convert the z-score of 1.96 into a value within the ses metric, we flip around Equation 4.4 to obtain $X = \sigma z + \mu$ and type the following:

6.92*1.96+18.40

The ses score we obtain in the console is 31.96.

This result tells us that under the normally distributed ses curve, 0.025 of the area falls to the right of an ses value equal to 31.96.

Solution Using Table C.1 in Appendix C To use Table C.1 in Appendix C to find the z-score that has an area of 0.025 to its right under the standard normal curve, we look for 0.0250 in the body of the table and see what its corresponding z-score is. We find 0.0250 in the row labeled 1.9 and column labeled 0.06. Accordingly, the z-score we seek is 1.9 plus 0.06 equals 1.96, and convert to a score within the ses metric as before.

EXAMPLE 8.12 Find the left-tailed area from a standard normal distribution corresponding to a z-score of −2.45.

Solution Using R We use the following:

pnorm(−2.45, 0, 1)

and obtain 0.0071 as the result.

Solution Using Table C.1 in Appendix C To use Table C.1 in Appendix C to find the area to the left of $z = -2.45$, we use symmetry to see that it is the same as the right-tailed area for $z = 2.45$. The right-tailed area corresponding to $z = 2.45$ is 0.0071. Thus, the left-tailed area corresponding to $z = -2.45$ equals 0.0071.

USING THE NORMAL DISTRIBUTION TO APPROXIMATE THE BINOMIAL DISTRIBUTION

As n, the number of trials in a binomial experiment, increases, the binomial distribution more closely resembles, or approaches, the normal distribution. In fact, as long as both products np and nq are greater than or equal to 5, the approximation of the binomial by the normal is quite good. The values p and q, in addition to n, are important as conditions for this approximation because a larger value of n is needed to compensate for the skewness introduced whenever $p \neq q$. Exercise 8.28 illustrates how to compute an approximation of a binomial probability using the normal distribution.

SUMMARY OF R COMMANDS

(See also the .R-file for Chapter 8.)

Create	Command lines
Calculate the probability of obtaining $k = 2$ successes in $n = 3$ trials, with the probability of success, $p = 0.816$ (Example 8.1)	**dbinom(2,3,0.816)**
Calculate the probabilities of obtaining all possible number of successes in $n = 3$ trials, with the probability of success, $p = 0.816$, and create the associated bar graph (Table 8.1 and Figure 8.1)	**probs = dbinom(c(0, 1, 2, 3), 3, 0.816)** **barplot(probs, names.arg = c(0,1,2,3),** **xlab = "Number who never smoked** **marijuana (k)")**
Calculate the probability when $n =10$, $k = 5$, and $p = 0.30$ using the combinations formula applied to $n =10$ things taken $k = 5$ at a time (Example 8.5)	**choose(10, 5)*(.30^5)*(.70^5)**
Calculate the probability of at most $k = 15$ successes in $n = 50$ trials, with the probability of success, $p = 0.40$ (Example 8.8)	**pbinom(15, 50, .40)**

Create	Command lines
Plot the graph of the standard normal distribution (Figure 8.2)	x = seq−4, 4, length=100) hx = dnorm(x, 0, 1) plot(hx ~ x, type="l", xlab="z scores", ylab="Density", main="Standard Normal Distribution")
Create the histogram of ses with normal curve overlay (Figure 8.3)	x = seq(0, 35, length = 100) hx = dnorm(x,18.434, 6.925) hist(NELS$ses, freq = F, xlab = "Socio-economic status", main = "") lines(hx~x)
Calculate the area under the normal curve with mean 18.40 and standard deviation 6.92 to the left of 26 (Example 8.9)	pnorm(26, mean = 18.40, sd = 6.92)
Plot the histogram of ses with shaded normal curve overlay (Figure 8.4)	x = seq(0, 35, length = 100) hx = dnorm(x,18.434, 6.925) hist(NELS$ses, freq = F, xlab = "Socio-economic status", main = "") lines(hx~x) cord.x = c(0,seq(0,26,length = 100),26) cord.y = c(0,dnorm(seq(0,26,length = 100), 18.434, 6.925),0) polygon(cord.x, cord.y, col="grey")
Plot a normal curve with shading to the right of $z = 2$ (Figure 8.5)	curve(dnorm, c(−4, 4), xlim = c(−4,4), main = "Area under the curve to the right of a z-score of 2", ylab = "Density", xlab = "z") cord.x = c(2,seq(2,4,length = 100),4) cord.y = c(0,dnorm(seq(2,4,length = 100), 0, 1),0) polygon(cord.x, cord.y, col="grey")
Calculate the area under the standard normal curve to the left of $z = 2$ (Example 8.10)	pnorm(2, 0, 1, lower.tail = F)
Calculate the z-score with area 0.975 below it (Example 8.11)	qnorm(0.975, 0, 1)

EXERCISES

Create a .R file for each exercise that requires the use of R. Run code from the .R file by highlighting or having the cursor on the line of code and hitting **control+enter** on a PC computer keyboard or **command+enter** on a Mac computer keyboard. Save each .R file using a name associated with the exercise for which it was created. It is recommended that you review the .R file for Chapter 8 located on the textbook's website before completing these exercises. To facilitate doing each exercise, it may be helpful to copy and paste relevant code from the .R file for Chapter 8 into your own .R file and modify them as needed.

Exercises 8.1–8.8 involve the binomial probability model. First, decide whether the given problem satisfies the conditions of a binomial experiment. Only if it does, solve the exercise.

8.1 A person taking a 15-item true/false examination has studied the material to be covered on the exam. What is the probability that this person will get exactly 10 of the 15 items correct?

8.2 A new drug is being tested, and the results of treatment with this drug are being categorized as full recovery, partial recovery, and additional treatment required. The probabilities of these three possible outcomes are 1/3, 1/3, and 1/3, respectively. If this drug is used on 100 patients, what is the probability that exactly 40 of the patients will have full recovery, 20 will have partial recovery, and 40 will need further treatment?

8.3 It is known that the toys produced by a certain toy manufacturer have a 1-in-10 chance of containing imperfections. What is the probability that in a day's production of 500 of these toys, exactly 50 will have imperfections?

8.4 Suppose giving birth to a girl and giving birth to a boy are equally likely, and Mrs. Fecund is due to give birth to triplets. What is the probability that exactly one of the three children born will be a girl?

8.5 A 10-item multiple-choice test is given with four possible answers on each item. If a student guesses on each item, what is the probability that she will get:
  (a) None of the 10 items correct?
  (b) Exactly 3 of the 10 items correct?
  (c) All of the 10 items correct?
  (d) At least 8 of the 10 items correct?
  (e) At most 4 of the 10 items correct?
  (f) Between 2 and 5 of the 10 items (inclusive) correct?

8.6 Use the percent distribution table provided below to find the probability that if 10 students are selected at random from the NELS dataset with replacement that exactly 5 are from the Northeast.

Percentage of Students by Region in the NELS Dataset	
Region	**Percentage**
Northeast	21.2
North Central	30.2
South	30.0
West	18.6
Total	100.0

8.7 Suppose that a certain automobile manufacturing company has a problem installing airbags. Usually, these are installed correctly 95 percent of the time. However, on Friday afternoons, these are installed correctly only 90 percent of the time. Assuming that the company manufactures 1,000 cars per week, what is the probability that exactly 950 of these will have correctly installed airbags?

8.8 Women over 50 are advised to get a mammogram every year, so there is a need to be aware of the prevalence of false-positive results. A false-positive is defined as a mammogram that is interpreted as indicative of cancer, indeterminate, or prompts recommendations for additional tests in a woman who is not diagnosed with breast cancer within a year. Assuming that the risk of a false-positive result is constant from year to year, the probability of a false-positive result from a single mammogram is $p = 0.0653$. Given that, find the probability of at least one false-positive result in 10 mammograms. The information in this exercise is based on Elmore et al. (1998).

Exercise 8.9 requires the use of R, the NELS dataset and the binomial distribution.

8.9 If one student is selected at random from the NELS dataset, use the variable urban to determine the probability that:
- (a) The student is from an urban environment.
- (b) The student is from a suburban environment.
- (c) The student is not from a rural environment.
- (d) The student is from a rural or a suburban environment.

If five students are selected at random with replacement from the NELS dataset, determine the probability that:
- (e) At most 3 of them are from urban environments.
- (f) Exactly 3 of them are from urban environments.
- (g) At least 3 of them are from urban environments.
- (h) No more than 3 of them are from urban environments.

8.10 An individual tosses a fair coin 10 times. Find the probability of getting:
- (a) Heads on the first five tosses and tails on the second five tosses.
- (b) Five heads and five tails in any order.

8.11 Suppose you are going to toss a fair coin three times and want to determine the probability of obtaining exactly two heads in the three tosses. Why do the following two methods of solving this problem give different answers?

Solution 1 In terms of numbers of heads obtained, the possible outcomes of the experiment are:

    0 heads   1 head   2 heads   3 heads

Because only one of the four outcomes listed satisfies the given condition (2 heads), the probability of this event is 1/4 = 0.25.

Solution 2 In terms of the way each toss comes out, the possible outcomes of the experiment are:

    HHH   HTH   HTT   TTH
    HHT   THH   THT   TTT

Because three of the eight outcomes listed satisfy the given condition (HHT, HTH, THH), the probability of this event is 3/8 = 0.375.

8.12 Is the following statement true or false? "By the law of large numbers, you are much more likely to obtain 5 heads in 10 tosses of a fair coin than to obtain 2 heads in 4 tosses of a fair coin."

8.13 Given a binomial experiment with $n = 6$ and $p = 0.5$:
  (a) Determine the probability distribution for this experiment.
  (b) Construct the corresponding probability bar graph and describe the shape of the distribution.
  (c) Use Equation 8.3 to find the mean and the standard deviation of the binomial distribution.

Exercises 8.14–8.18 involve the standard normal probability model.

8.14 If a single score is selected at random from a standard normal distribution, find the probability that:
  (a) The score is above $z = 1.36$.
  (b) The score is above $z = -2.08$.
  (c) The score is below $z = 1.36$.
  (d) The score is below $z = -2.08$.
  (e) The score is between $z = -2.08$ and $z = 1.36$.
  (f) The score is between $z = 0.40$ and $z = 1.36$.
  (g) The score is between $z = -0.40$ and $z = -1.36$.
  (h) The score is less than $z = -0.40$ or greater than $z = 0.40$.

8.15 If a single score is selected at random from a standard normal distribution:
  (a) What is the value of the score, z, such that the probability of selecting a score greater than or equal to z is approximately 30 percent?
  (b) What is the value of the score, z, such that the probability of selecting a score greater than or equal to z is approximately 65 percent?
  (c) What is the value of the score, z, such that the probability of selecting a score less than or equal to z is approximately 30 percent?
  (d) What is the value of the score, z, such that the probability of selecting a score less than or equal to z is approximately 65 percent?

8.16 If a distribution is normally distributed, what proportion of the scores fall:
  (a) At least two standard deviations below the mean?
  (b) At least two standard deviations above the mean?
  (c) At least two standard deviations away from the mean?
  (d) Between $z = -2$ and $z = 2$?

8.17 Find the area under the standard normal curve and
  (a) to the right of $z = 2.15$
  (b) more extreme than $z = \pm 0.85$, that is, more than 0.85 standard deviations away from the mean
  (c) to the left of $z = -1.63$
  (d) to the left of $z = 1.3$

8.18 Find the following z-scores.
  (a) What z-score on the standard normal curve has an area of 0.1151 to its right?
  (b) What z-score on the standard normal curve has an area of 0.6446 to its right?
  (c) What z-score on the standard normal curve has an area of 0.3372 to its left?

Exercises 8.19–8.27 involve the use of the normal probability model. In some cases, we assume a normal distribution and find probabilities related to that distribution. In other cases, we look to see the extent to which the normal distribution gives a good approximation to the distribution of the observed data.

8.19 If a single score is selected at random from a normal distribution with mean 50 and standard deviation 10, find the probability that:
  (a) The score is above 70.
  (b) The score is above 40.
  (c) The score is below 70.
  (d) The score is below 40.
  (e) The score is between 40 and 70.
  (f) The score is between 60 and 70.
  (g) The score is between 30 and 40.
  (h) The score is 10 or more points away from the mean.

8.20 If a single score is selected at random from a normal distribution with mean 50 and standard deviation 10:
  (a) What is the value of the score, X, such that the probability of selecting a score greater than or equal to X is 10 percent?
  (b) What is the value of the score, X, such that the probability of selecting a score greater than or equal to X is 90 percent?
  (c) What is the value of the score, X, such that the probability of selecting a score less than or equal to X is 90 percent?
  (d) What is the value of the score, X, such that the probability of selecting a score less than or equal to X is 10 percent?

8.21 Suppose a distribution is normally distributed with mean 75 and standard deviation 10.
  (a) What is the value of the score, X, such that the probability of selecting a score less than or equal to X is 5 percent?
  (b) What is the value of the score, X, such that the probability of selecting a score greater than or equal to X is 5 percent?
  (c) If a single score is selected at random from the distribution, what is the probability that the score falls above 90?
  (d) If a single score is selected at random from the distribution, what is the probability that the score falls at 90 or above?
  (e) If a single score is selected at random from the distribution, what is the probability that the score falls between 70 and 80?
  (f) If a single score is selected at random from the distribution, what is the probability that the score falls below 50?
  (g) If a single score is selected at random from the distribution, what is the probability that the score falls between 70 and 90?

8.22 Find the z-score that has the following percentages of area under the standard normal curve contained between $-z$ and z:

(a) 90 percent
(b) 95 percent
(c) 99 percent

8.23 Given a set of scores that is normally distributed with mean 90 and standard deviation 8, what proportion of individuals will score:

(a) Between 92 and 96 inclusive?
(b) At least 94?
(c) At most 98?

8.24 One way to qualify to join Mensa, a high IQ society, is to score in the top 2 percent on a standardized IQ test such as the Wechsler Adult Intelligence Scales Full Scale IQ Test. The scores on the Full Scale IQ test are normally distributed and standardized to have a mean of 100 and a standard deviation of 15. What score is necessary on this test to qualify for Mensa?

8.25 Suppose the distribution of maximum daily temperatures for a 1,000-day period in a certain tropical area is normal in shape with a mean of 87 degrees Fahrenheit and a standard deviation of 3 degrees Fahrenheit.

(a) How many of these days had maximum daily temperatures above 80 degrees Fahrenheit?
(b) What would be the percentile rank in this distribution for a day that had a maximum temperature of 80 degrees Fahrenheit?

8.26 Suppose you are told that 1,000 scores from a nationally administered achievement test are normally distributed with mean 50 and standard deviation 5.

(a) How many people would you expect to score greater than 57?
(b) What is the percentile rank of a score of 52?
(c) What raw score would you expect 10 percent of the scores to fall above?

8.27 Suppose you are told that the distribution of weights for all 12-month-old males in the United States is normally distributed with a mean of 18 pounds and a standard deviation of 3 pounds. If your son is 12 months old and weighs 22.5 pounds:

(a) What proportion of the 12-month-old male population weighs less than your son?
(b) What is your son's percentile rank relative to this population?

Exercises 8.28–8.30 involve the NELS dataset and require the use of R.

8.28 Use the normal distribution to approximate the percentage of students in the NELS dataset with eighth grade math achievement scores (achmat08) less than or equal to 72. Then, find the actual percentile rank of 72. How do these two values compare and what does this comparison suggest about the appropriateness of using the normal curve to approximate the distribution of eighth grade math achievement scores?

8.29 Use the normal distribution to approximate the number of students in the NELS dataset with eighth grade math achievement scores (achmat08) that are within one standard deviation of the mean. How does the estimate based on the normal probability model compare to the actual number of scores in the NELS dataset that are so extreme?

8.30 While some distributions of observed data, especially those based on the sum or average of many items, are approximately normal, others are not. In this exercise, we look at an instance where the normal distribution does not give a good approximation of a distribution. Use the normal distribution to approximate the number of students in the NELS dataset coming from a school in which 6 or more AP classes are offered (apoffer). Compare the estimate based on normal distribution to the actual number of students coming from a school in which 6 or more AP classes are offered. Speculate on the reason for the discrepancy.

Exercise 8.31 involves the Impeach dataset and requires the use of R.

8.31 Consider the variable supportc which gives the distribution of the percentages of the voter support for Clinton. Unless otherwise specified, use the *normal curve* to approximate the distribution of supportc in order to answer the following questions.
   (a) Create a histogram with a normal curve overlay of the variable supportc. Describe the shape of the distribution.
   (b) What supportc score has $z = 1.3$?
   (c) If supportc = 35 percent what is z?
   (d) Use the normal curve to estimate the proportion of states with voter support for Clinton at or below 35 percent.
   (e) Use a frequency distribution table to find the actual proportion of states with voter support for Clinton at or below 35 percent.
   (f) What is the approximate percentile rank of a score of 35 percent in supportc?
   (g) What proportion or percent of senators score above supportc = 55 percent for their states?
   (h) What proportion or percent of senators score below supportc = 55 percent for their states?
   (i) What proportion or percent of senators score between supportc = 35 percent and supportc = 55 percent for their states?
   (j) What supportc score cuts off the bottom 30 percent of supportc values?
   k) What supportc score would place you in the top 5 percent of scores?
   (l) Use the normal curve to estimate the state voter support for Clinton percentage that would place a state at the 50th percentile for these states.

Exercise 8.32 involves normal approximations to the binomial.

8.32 Given a binomial experiment with number of trials n, probability of success p, and probability of failure q, if both the products np and nq are greater than or equal to 5, we may use a normal curve with mean $\overline{X} = np$ and standard deviation SD = $\sqrt{nqp}$ to approximate the binomial distribution. This exercise demonstrates how.
   (a) We take a fair coin and toss it 20 times. What is the probability of obtaining between 10 and 15 heads inclusive? Answer this question using the binomial distribution.
   (b) Demonstrate that the criterion for a normal approximation to the binomial is satisfied.
   (c) What are the mean and standard deviation of the normal distribution that we will use to approximate this binomial distribution?

(d) It is not quite so simple as to approximate the area under this normal curve between 10 and 15 because the normal distribution is continuous and the binomial distribution is discrete. We need to use a continuity correction. We accomplish this by thinking of the binomial distribution as if it were really continuous with all scores being reported to the nearest integer value. Therefore, the event "between 10 and 15 successes inclusive" should be thought of as if it were really "between 9.5 and 15.5 inclusive." Note that all we have done is to extend the original interval (10 to 15 inclusive) by 0.5 in each direction. This extension of the real interval by 0.5 in each direction is called a correction for continuity and is employed whenever a (continuous) normal distribution is used to approximate a (discrete) binomial distribution for calculating binomial probabilities. Find the area under the normal curve with mean and standard deviation specified in part (c) between 9.5 and 15.5 inclusive. This number is the normal approximation to the answer you obtained in part (a).

# CHAPTER NINE

THE ROLE OF SAMPLING IN INFERENTIAL STATISTICS

As noted at the beginning of Chapter 7, a distinction exists between descriptive and inferential statistics. Whereas descriptive statistics are used to describe the data at hand, inferential statistics are used to draw inferences from results based on the data at hand to a larger *population* from which the data at hand have been selected. The data at hand form what is called a *sample*. In this chapter we discuss some fundamental components of inferential statistics, including sampling, sampling distributions, and characteristics of estimators.

SAMPLES AND POPULATIONS

Why, you may ask, should we study a sample at all if what we are really interested in is the population? Why not just study the population itself and be done with it? The answer to this question is that in actual research situations, it is often not possible, in terms of both time and resources, to obtain the desired data from the entire population.

For example, suppose we wanted to know, in a particular election year, how people were going to vote in the upcoming presidential election. The population, in this case, consists of all the people eligible to vote in the general election. Clearly, it would be enormously expensive and time-consuming to gather and tabulate data from each person in the population. Instead, we would select a sample that is somehow representative of the entire population, poll the sample on how they will vote, and then draw conclusions about the population from the sample. Though we are studying the sample, our real interest in inferential statistics is the population, and the conclusions we will draw are always about it.

We can describe measures taken on populations of things in the same ways that we can describe measures taken on samples of things. For example, if we could get data from the entire population, we could compute all measures of location, variability, and relationship (e.g., the mean, standard deviation, and correlation) just as we can on a sample taken from that population. When computed for populations, the values of such descriptive measures are called *parameters*; when computed for samples, they are called *statistics*. In inferential statistics, we use statistics computed on a sample to draw conclusions about unknown parameters in the population. In order to make it clear whether we are talking about a measure taken on a sample or on a population, we denote statistics by Roman letters and parameters by Greek letters. Table 9.1 contains examples of these symbols.

As another example, consider that we want to find the mean (average) number of hours eighth graders in the United States spend watching television per week. In order to find exactly what we want, the population mean, μ, we would somehow have to obtain the number of hours of television viewing for each member of the population. This is

TABLE 9.1 Symbols for common statistics and parameters	
Statistics	**Parameters**
$\overline{X}$ = sample mean	μ = population mean
S^2 = sample variance	σ^2 = population variance
S = sample standard deviation	σ = population standard deviation
r = sample correlation	ρ = population correlation

obviously impractical. Instead we might pick a sample of, say, 1,000 eighth graders in the New York metropolitan area, find the mean number of hours of television watched in the sample, and then use our calculated value of the sample mean, $\overline{X}$, as an estimate of the unknown population mean μ.

Do you think the procedure we have just outlined is a good one for estimating the mean number of hours of television viewing, μ, of the population described? Actually, there are several things wrong with it. First, we have not explained how our sample is to be picked or why we want it to be of size $N = 1,000$. Do we just walk into the nearest middle school and pick the first 1,000 eighth graders we see? If we are going to draw valid conclusions about the population from calculations made on the sample, we want the sample to be representative of the population. Second, can we expect the sample mean $\overline{X}$ to be a good estimator of the population mean μ? Analogously, can we expect the sample mode to be a good estimator of the population mode and the sample variance to be good estimator of the population variance? After all, the sample size N is not a good estimator of the population size, is it? Considerations like these are crucial for the correct use and understanding of inferential statistics. Before proceeding, let us take a closer look at them.

RANDOM SAMPLES

In order for conclusions about our population to be accurate, the sample we use must be a subset of the population. For example, if we were interested in estimating the median income for all practicing attorneys in the United States (the population), it would make no sense to select a sample of medical doctors on which to base the estimate. Obviously, our sample should be comprised of attorneys from the population. That is, we would, in some way, select a sample of attorneys from our population of all practicing attorneys in the United States and compute the median income of the sample. We might then be able to use this sample median as an estimator of the median of the population. Many samples could be picked from this population; however, each sample would differ somewhat from all the other samples, even though they all come from the same population. The accuracy of our estimate will therefore depend, among other things, on how representative our sample is of the population. If our sample is truly representative of the population, we can expect our estimate of the population median to be accurate. On the other hand, if our sample deviates to some extent from being truly representative of the population, we would expect our estimate to be inaccurate to some extent.

The question that naturally arises in this connection is whether it is possible to determine just how representative a particular sample is and, therefore, how accurate the corresponding estimate is. The answer to this question is that in most cases we cannot make such a determination with a particular sample, but that we can do so in the long run if we use specific sampling procedures in selecting our sample, called *probability sampling*. If we follow the procedure known as *simple random sampling* (or just *random sampling*) to select our sample, we can often determine probabilistically just how representative or non-representative our sample can be expected to be. This is not possible or feasible with many other types of sampling procedures, which is why much of inferential statistics is based on the assumptions of random sampling from populations.

Suppose, for example, we wish to estimate the proportion of students enrolled in fifth grade throughout the state of Idaho who are female. Suppose too that somehow we are able to determine that if we use simple random sampling to select a sample of size $N = 25$, the probability of selecting a representative sample is high. We then go ahead and select a random sample of 25 fifth graders in Idaho and find that our sample consists of 25 males and no females. Our estimate of the proportion of students enrolled in the fifth grade who are female would therefore be 0/25, or 0.

In this example, we know enough about the characteristics of the population under study (all fifth graders in Idaho) to realize that the sample we have selected, by virtue of the fact that it contains no females, is not representative of the population. In most cases, however, we will simply not know enough about the characteristics of the population to determine whether the sample actually selected is representative. (If we knew so much about the population, we probably would not be using inferential statistics on it in the first place.) *Before selecting our sample*, we will know only what the *chances* are of obtaining a sample with a given degree of representativeness. All we can do is set up our sampling procedures so as to ensure that the probabilities of obtaining representative samples are large and the probabilities of obtaining non-representative samples are small. And we must be aware that either type of sample *could* occur. We will then be able to answer such questions as: "What is the probability that a random sample of 200 practicing lawyers in the United States will have a median income that differs from the median income of all practicing lawyers in the United States by less than $1,000?" If that probability is high and the sample median turns out to be $25,000, we can be reasonably sure that the population median is somewhere between $24,000 ($25,000 − $1,000) and $26,000 ($25,000 + $1,000). With this introduction, we turn to a discussion of simple random sampling.

OBTAINING A SIMPLE RANDOM SAMPLE

Once we have decided we want to use random sampling, the question becomes: "What is a random sample and how do we get one?" Simply stated, a simple *random sample* is a sample chosen from a given population in such a way as to ensure that each person or thing in the population has an equal and independent chance of being picked for the sample. To understand what we mean by the words *equal and independent*, think of the selection of a sample as picking a first object from the population to be in the sample, then picking a second object from those remaining in the population, and so on. *Equal* means that at each stage of the selection process, all the objects remaining in the population are equally likely to be picked for the sample. *Independent* means that no pick has any effect on any other pick. Violating either one of these conditions results in a nonrandom sample.

Let us illustrate what can go wrong in selecting a random sample. Suppose you are the president of the local Democratic Club and you want to get some indication of how the registered Democrats in your district feel about a certain bill. You plan to select a random sample of size 20 from the population of registered Democrats in your district and ask the people in the sample their opinion of the bill. After randomly selecting 19 registered Democrats, you suddenly notice that all 19 are female, so you decide to pick your 20th member of the sample from among the male registered Democrats only. Is your sample a random one? It is not, because at the last stage (the 20th selection), all the people remaining in the population *did not have an equal chance of being picked*. In fact, the women remaining at the last stage had no chance of being picked.

As another example, suppose you want some information about all the students in the local high school. To save time, you are going to select a random sample of 25 students from this population, find out from the sample what you want to know, and then infer from the sample to the population. You also decide, however, that you do not want more than one student from any one family in the sample. Is this a random sample of your population? It is not if the population contains any brother–brother, sister–sister, or brother–sister pairs. If such pairs exist, the different stages of the selection process *might not be independent of each other*. In other words, each selection of a member of the sample disqualifies all that student's brothers and sisters from selection in later stages of the selection process.

The actual selection of a random sample can be accomplished through the use of a uniform random-number generator available in most statistical software packages, including R. The important properties of a uniform random-number generator are: (1) each digit generated is independent of all other digits; and (2) in the long run, each digit occurs with equal frequency. For example, one million digits generated by a uniform random-number generator should contain approximately 100,000 zeros, 100,000 ones, ..., and 100,000 nines.

More R: Suppose you have 5,000 cases in your population from which you would like to select a simple random sample of size 50 and collect data on these 50. Number the objects in your population from 1 to 5,000. We perform the selection using R by typing:

x = sample(1:5000, 50, replace = F)
x

The 50 random IDs are now stored in the local variable named x. The argument **replace=F** stipulates that the cases are drawn without replacement as defined in the next section.

SAMPLING WITH AND WITHOUT REPLACEMENT

Simple random sampling is an example of what is called *sampling without replacement*. That is, once an object from the population has been selected to be included in the sample, it is removed from consideration in all remaining stages of the selection process. In sampling with replacement, *every* object in the population is available for selection to the sample at every stage of the selection process, regardless of whether it has already been selected. Note that one consequence of sampling with replacement is that the same object may be picked more than once. Because simple random sampling is sampling without replacement, this cannot happen in our sampling procedure. The following example illustrates some of the differences between these two sampling procedures.

EXAMPLE 9.1 We have a deck of 52 playing cards consisting of 4 suits (clubs, diamonds, hearts, and spades), with 13 cards per suit (Ace, 2, 3, 4, 5, 6, 7, 8, 9, 10, jack, queen, and king). We want to select a sample of size 2 from this population. Describe both sampling with and without replacement in this context and the probabilities of selection associated with each.

Solution

1. *With replacement.* One of the 52 cards is selected to be in the sample. Then this card is replaced in the deck and a second card is selected to complete the sample. Because the card that is picked first is replaced before the second card is selected, the same card can be selected both times, and the probability of any particular card being picked does not change from the first selection to the second. (The probability of any particular card being picked is 1/52 on the first selection and 1/52 on the second selection.)

2. *Without replacement.* One of the 52 cards is selected to be in the sample. Then, without this card being replaced, a second card is selected from the remaining 51 to complete the sample. In this case, the same card *cannot* be selected both times, and the probability of any particular card being picked *does* change from the first selection to the second. (For the first selection, each card has a probability of 1/52 of being picked. For the second selection, the card that was picked the first time has a probability of 0 of being picked, while all the other cards have a probability of 1/51 of being picked.)

Why have we gone to the trouble of discussing and comparing these two types of sampling? Although random sampling is sampling *without* replacement, many of the techniques we will want to use in inferential statistics hold only when sampling with replacement is being used. Somehow we must reconcile this apparent conflict of interest. We can do this by introducing the concept of an infinite population.

A population is said to be *infinite* if it has at least as many objects in it as there are positive integers (1, 2, 3, . . .). If we draw a finite sample from an infinite population, then sampling with and without replacement are essentially the same because discarding a few objects will not appreciably alter the relative occurrence of objects in the population. Most realistic applications of inferential statistics involve very large, but still finite, populations. When our population size is very large relative to the sample size N, then *for all practical purposes* it can be thought of as an infinite population, in which case sampling with and without replacement are essentially the same. For most statistical purposes, this is the case when the population size *is at least 100 times* as large as the sample size. To illustrate, let us return to the example of selecting a sample of size 2 from a deck of playing cards. If the first card selected were the ace of hearts, the probabilities for selecting the second card are as given in Table 9.2.

Note how different the probabilities are with and without replacement. This is because the population is only 26 times as large as the sample being drawn from it (52 compared to 2). If, on the other hand, we take one hundred decks of cards as our population, the proportions are still the same (each type of card makes up 100/5200 or 1/52 of the

TABLE 9.2 Probabilities of selecting the second card (population size = 52; sample size = 2)

	With replacement	Without replacement
Probability of ace of hearts	$\frac{1}{52} = 0.0192307$	$\frac{0}{52} = 0.0$
Probability of all other cards	$\frac{1}{52} = 0.0192307$	$\frac{1}{51} = 0.0196078$

TABLE 9.3 Probabilities of selecting the second card (population size = 5,200; sample size = 2)

	With replacement	Without replacement
Probability of ace of hearts	$\frac{100}{5200} = 0.0192307$	$\frac{99}{5199} = 0.0190421$
Probability of all other cards	$\frac{100}{5200} = 0.0192307$	$\frac{100}{5199} = 0.0192344$

population), but now the population is 2,600 times as large as the sample (5,200 compared to 2). If we again assume that the first card selected was an ace of hearts, the probabilities for selecting the second card are as given in Table 9.3.

The probabilities for sampling with and without replacement are much closer to each other in Table 9.3 than in Table 9.2. In other words, when the population is at least 100 times as large as the sample being drawn from it, we can assume that, for all practical purposes, sampling with and without replacement are essentially the same.

☞ **Remark.** The inferential statistical techniques we will present from this point on are really appropriate only for sampling with replacement. However, by assuming that all populations are at least 100 times as large as the samples being drawn from them, we will be able to use sampling without replacement and obtain quite accurate results.

SAMPLING DISTRIBUTIONS

Now that we are somewhat more familiar with what a random sample is and how one is selected, we will turn to the question of how it is used in inferential statistics.

As mentioned previously, the basic idea in inferential statistics is to use a statistic calculated on a sample in order to estimate a parameter of a population. This procedure is made difficult by the unavoidable fact that in most cases, the value we get for any statistic will vary somewhat from sample to sample, even when all the samples are randomly selected from the same "parent" population.

DESCRIBING THE SAMPLING DISTRIBUTION OF MEANS EMPIRICALLY

Imagine the process of deciding on a particular sample size N to use, randomly choosing and listing all possible samples of size N from the parent population, and for each sample, recording the value of the statistic we are interested in. (Of course, each *sample* of size N is replaced in the population before the next sample of size N is selected.) If we then take all the values we have obtained for this statistic, we can construct a frequency distribution of them just as we can construct a frequency distribution of any collection of numbers. Such a distribution is called an *empirical* (or observed) *sampling distribution* for the given statistic.

EXAMPLE 9.2 Use the following population of 10 scores and compute by hand the *sampling distribution of means* for samples of size $N = 2$ drawn from it. Use the sampling distribution of means to determine the probability that when a single sample of size $N = 2$ is selected from the population, its mean will be within 2 points of the actual population mean. (We really should not use a population that is only five times as large as the sample being drawn from it, but doing so makes the sampling distribution easier to enumerate.)

Population: 0 1 3 3 5 7 7 7 8 10

Note that the population mean is 5.1 and the population standard deviation is 3.25.

Solution In the following table, we list all possible random samples of size $N = 2$ that could possibly be drawn from this population, and for each one, we calculate its sample mean, $\overline{X}$.

Sample	Mean	Sample	Mean	Sample	Mean	Sample	Mean	Sample	Mean
0,0	0.0	3,0	1.5	5,0	2.5	7,0	3.5	8,0	4.0
0,1	0.5	3,1	2.0	5,1	3.0	7,1	4.0	8,1	4.5
0,3	1.5	3,3	3.0	5,3	4.0	7,3	5.0	8,3	5.5
0,3	1.5	3,3	3.0	5,3	4.0	7,3	5.0	8,3	5.5
0,5	2.5	3,5	4.0	5,5	5.0	7,5	6.0	8,5	6.5
0,7	3.5	3,7	5.0	5,7	6.0	7,7	7.0	8,7	7.5
0,7	3.5	3,7	5.0	5,7	6.0	7,7	7.0	8,7	7.5
0,7	3.5	3,7	5.0	5,7	6.0	7,7	7.0	8,7	7.5
0,8	4.0	3,8	5.5	5,8	6.5	7,8	7.5	8,8	8.0
0,10	5.0	3,10	6.5	5,10	7.5	7,10	8.5	8,10	9.0
1,0	0.5	3,0	1.5	7,0	3.5	7,0	3.5	10,0	5.0
1,1	1.0	3,1	2.0	7,1	4.0	7,1	4.0	10,1	5.5
1,3	2.0	3,3	3.0	7,3	5.0	7,3	5.0	10,3	6.5
1,3	2.0	3,3	3.0	7,3	5.0	7,3	5.0	10,3	6.5
1,5	3.0	3,5	4.0	7,5	6.0	7,5	6.0	10,5	7.5
1,7	4.0	3,7	5.0	7,7	7.0	7,7	7.0	10,7	8.5
1,7	4.0	3,7	5.0	7,7	7.0	7,7	7.0	10,7	8.5
1,7	4.0	3,7	5.0	7,7	7.0	7,7	7.0	10,7	8.5
1,8	4.5	3,8	5.5	7,8	7.5	7,8	7.5	10,8	9.0
1,10	5.5	3,10	6.5	7,10	8.5	7,10	8.5	10,10	10.0

For example, the first pair listed in the table, (0,0), represents the sample of size 2 containing the values 0 and 0. Its corresponding sample mean is $(0 + 0)/2 = 0.0$.

We can now enter these sample mean values into R to create a frequency distribution table (using the **table** command) and a corresponding frequency histogram (using the **hist**

TABLE 9.4 Frequency distribution table for the sampling distribution of means for samples of size $N = 2$

0	0.5	1	1.5	2	2.5	3	3.5	4	4.5	5	5.5	6	6.5	7	7.5	8	8.5	9	10
1	2	1	4	4	2	6	6	12	2	15	6	6	6	9	8	2	6	1	1

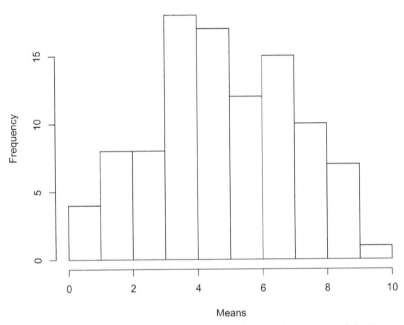

Figure 9.1 Histogram of sampling distribution of means for samples of size $N = 2$

command) as shown in Table 9.4 and Figure 9.1, respectively. (The specific code is given in the .R file associated with this chapter.)

The histogram depicts the way in which the process of sampling at random from a population produces a distribution of mean values. It is an example of what we have called an empirical sampling distribution – in this case, a sampling distribution of means from samples of size $N = 2$.

To use the sampling distribution of means to determine the probability that a sample mean selected at random will be within 2 points of the actual population mean, we find the proportion of sample means that are between 3.5 and 7 inclusive. According to the frequency distribution table, 62 of the 100 equally likely sample means fall within that range, so that we conclude that the probability that a randomly selected sample mean will be within 2 points of the actual population mean is 0.62.

EXAMPLE 9.3 Compare the graph of Figure 9.2, the sampling distribution of means from the population {0, 1, 3, 3, 5, 7, 7, 7, 8, 10} based on 10,000 samples of size 8 randomly selected with replacement from this population of 10 scores, with that of Figure 9.1. This procedure is known as the *bootstrap*, where sampling the original dataset with replacement creates B re-samples of a certain size, N.

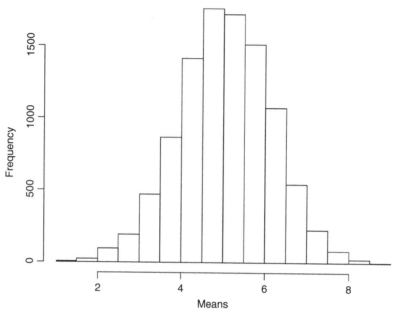

Figure 9.2 Sampling distribution of means, $N = 8$

MORE R: Using the **boot.mean** command to generate the sampling distribution of means of Figure 9.2 with $N = 8$ and $B = 10,000$ replications, begin by creating a vector, **y**, that contains these 10 values:

y = c(0, 1, 3, 3, 5, 7, 7, 7, 8, 10)

Next, you will need to create a dataset that contains the 10,000 samples of size 8 randomly selected with replacement from this population of 10 scores by typing the following:

b.mean = boot.mean(y, B = 10000, n = 8)$bootstrap.samples

The **boot.mean** command will randomly sample with replacement a sample of size 8 from our dataset of size 10, compute the mean of these 8 randomly selected values, and save that mean to the local variable, b.mean.

To construct a histogram of these data, we type:

hist(b.mean, xlab = "means", main = "")

Because the mean values plotted in Figure 9.2 are based on sets of 8 values that have been randomly selected from the 10 values in our dataset, each time we run this command, a different set of mean values will be generated. Accordingly, the histogram based on the means generated from your execution of this command will be similar, but not necessarily identically equal, to Figure 9.2.

☞ **Remark.** If you would like the same random values to be selected each time you run the bootstrap procedure, you should insert the command **set.seed(1234)** directly before the **boot.mean** command. The number 1234 may be any number you choose.

Solution. We can use Figures 9.1 and 9.2 to compare how much we can expect our sample statistic value to vary from sample to sample depending upon the size of the sample. For example, Figure 9.1 reveals that if we were to select at random a sample of size $N = 2$ with replacement from the given population, the mean value for this sample would most likely fall somewhere between 3 and 8. Notice that sample mean values down to 0.0 and up to 10 would also be possible but less likely. Figure 9.2 reveals that if we were to select at random, and with replacement, a sample of size $N = 8$ from the given population, the mean value for this sample would most likely fall somewhere between the narrower interval of 4.0 to 6.5. Sample mean values below 2 and above 8 would also be possible, but far less likely.

Based on this comparison, we find that the range of mean values *most likely* to be obtained decreases as the sample size increases. We also note that the population mean for our 10 scores is $\mu = 5.1$, which falls within both intervals, 3 and 8, and 4.5 and 6.0, the sample mean values most likely to be obtained in the two cases, respectively. Thus, we find that as we increase the size of our sample, we can expect to obtain a more accurate estimate of the population mean. As a general rule, when we are using sample statistics to estimate population parameters, the larger the sample we use, the more accurate we can expect the estimate to be.

Figures 9.1 and 9.2 not only illustrate that the larger the sample size the more accurately we may estimate the population parameter, but they also illustrate that the larger the sample size, the more the shape of the sampling distribution resembles the normal distribution. Notice that Figure 9.2 looks much more like a normal distribution than Figure 9.1. The population we used in these examples (9.2 and 9.3) consists of a particular set of 10 scores with a particular distribution. It can be shown, however, that if we had begun with a different population of scores with a different distribution (and, of course, there are an infinite number of distributions that we could have chosen), we would have obtained a similar result. That is, regardless of the population distribution of scores, as the sample size increases, the estimate of the population mean becomes more accurate and the shape of the sampling distribution of means becomes much more like that of a normal distribution. This is what is called the *central limit theorem* (CLT), which is more formally stated in the next section.

DESCRIBING THE SAMPLING DISTRIBUTION OF MEANS THEORETICALLY

Using the methods of mathematical statistics, it is often possible to determine *theoretically* what the sampling distribution of a particular sample statistic should look like. While the previous example was concerned with the mean, theoretical sampling distributions may be obtained for other common sample statistics as well, including, for example, the variance and correlation coefficient. As noted in the previous section, the sampling distribution of means becomes more normal in shape as the sample size increases. As we will see in later chapters, the theoretical sampling distributions of many of the other common statistics covered in this book (e.g., the variance) approach a different set of shapes as the sample size increases. Regardless of their eventual shape, however, these theoretical sampling distributions provide the foundation for drawing inferences about the population by making explicit the relationship that exists between the parameters of that population and those of the sampling distribution.

We now present a more formal statement of the *central limit theorem*, which specifies the shape, mean, and standard deviation of a sampling distribution of means in terms of the parameters μ and σ, the mean and standard deviation of the population from which these samples have been derived.

THE CENTRAL LIMIT THEOREM

Given a population of values with no specified distribution, and a sample size N that is sufficiently large, the *sampling distribution of means* for samples drawn from this population with replacement can be described as follows:

1. Its shape is *approximately* normally distributed.
2. Its mean, $\mu_{\bar{x}}$, is equal to μ.
3. Its standard deviation, $\sigma_{\bar{x}}$, is equal to $\sigma \big/ \sqrt{N}$.

☞ **Remark.** Notice that we denote the mean of the sampling distribution of means as $\mu_{\bar{x}}$ because it is the mean of means. Furthermore, we denote the standard deviation of the sampling distribution of means as $\sigma_{\bar{x}}$ because it is the standard deviation of means. The standard deviation of the sampling distribution of means, $\sigma_{\bar{x}}$, is also referred to as the *standard error of the mean.*

Note that the CLT requires that the samples be drawn from the population with replacement. However, as long as the population being considered is relatively large compared to the sample being drawn from it (for our purposes, at least 100 times as large), sampling with and without replacement will give approximately equivalent results, so the CLT will hold approximately. One of the statements in the CLT is that if the sample size N being used is sufficiently large, then certain results will be true. Just what is meant here by "sufficiently large"? This is a subjective question. The answer will vary from one situation to another and from one researcher to another. In general, the larger the sample size N being used, the closer the approximation will be, and it is up to the researcher to decide just how good an approximation is desired. By empirical observation, for our purposes in this book, we will consider that the distribution of means based on samples of size N greater than or equal to 30 ($N \geq 30$) gives a good enough approximation to a normal distribution.

☞ **Remark.** Notice that Figure 9.2 looks quite normal in shape despite the fact that the conditions of the CLT are not met. That is, the parent population is not normally distributed and $N = 8$. It is likely that Figure 9.2 looks quite normal in shape because the distribution of the population from which the samples have been randomly selected is approximately symmetric. When distributions are known to be symmetric or approximately so, a minimum N value of 30 is rather conservative. When distributions are known to be nearly normal, sample sizes as low as 10 or even 8 may be appropriate, and when distributions are known to be exactly normal, any size sample will yield a normally distributed sampling distribution.

The central limit theorem was first proved by Abraham de Moivre (1756) in connection with his interest in developing techniques for the calculation of gamblers' odds that emerged from his frequent visits to London coffeehouses. The proof, along with the techniques he developed, was first published in 1716 in his book *The Doctrine of Chances* (Stigler, 1986; Salsburg, 2001).

The CLT is a powerful and extremely useful statement of probability theory that underlies why the normal distribution commonly is used to model (or approximate the distribution of) observed data.

Let us look at some examples of how to use the CLT to determine, for given populations and sample sizes, what sampling distributions of means should look like.

● ●

EXAMPLE 9.4 Suppose we are given a normally distributed population of 5,000 scores with mean equal to 15 and standard deviation equal to 3. (1) What will the corresponding sampling distribution of means for samples of size $N = 16$ (with replacement) look like? (2) If we were to select a single sample of size $N = 16$ at random from this population of scores, what is the probability that the mean for this sample will fall between 13 and 17?

Solution

1. Because the parent population is normally distributed, the sampling distribution of means will also be normally distributed. Its mean, $\mu_{\bar{x}}$, will be equal to the mean of the population, 15, and its standard deviation, $\sigma_{\bar{x}}$, will be given by $\sigma_{\bar{x}} = \sigma/\sqrt{N} = 3/4 = 0.75$. The parent population and the corresponding sampling distribution of means based on 1,000 samples, each of size 16, randomly drawn from the population with replacement are shown in Figures 9.3 and 9.4, respectively. Notice that while the means are the same in both figures, the range of scores on the horizontal axis in Figure 9.3 is from 6 to 24, while in Figure 9.4 it is only from 12 to 18.

2. Because we are making a statement about the sampling distribution of means, which is known to be normally distributed with mean 15 and standard deviation 0.75, we use the following R syntax:

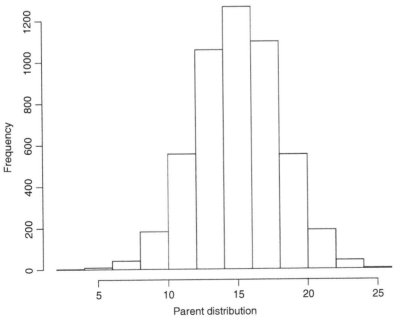

Figure 9.3 Normally distributed population of 5,000 scores with $\mu = 15$ and $\sigma = 3$

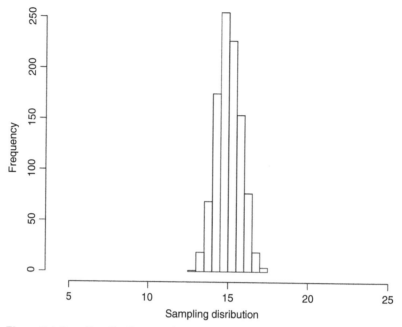

Figure 9.4 Sampling distribution of 1,000 means with $N = 16$, $\mu_{\bar{x}} = 15$, and $\sigma_{\bar{x}} = 0.75$

pnorm((17 – 15)/.75) – pnorm((13 – 15)/.75)

The value obtained is 0.99, indicating that almost all such sample means fall within the specified range.

EXAMPLE 9.5 Suppose we are given an arbitrarily distributed (say, positively skewed as in the distribution given in Figure 9.5) population of 1,000 scores with mean equal to 8 and standard deviation equal to 4. What will the corresponding sampling distribution of means for samples of size $N = 100$ (with replacement) look like?

Solution Because the sample size ($N = 100$) is sufficiently large, we know from the CLT that the sampling distribution of means will be approximately normally distributed; that its standard deviation will be equal to $\sigma_{\bar{x}} = \sigma/\sqrt{N} = 4/10 = 0.4$; and that its mean, $\mu_{\bar{x}}$, will be equal to the mean of the parent population, 8. Figure 9.5 shows what the parent population might look like, and Figure 9.6 shows what the corresponding sampling distribution of means based on 10,000 re-samples, each of size 100, randomly selected from the positively skewed parent population with replacement will look like.

Recall that because the means are generated by this program through a random process, one that relies on randomly selecting samples from the positively skewed parent population, the histogram you obtain on re-running this program will be similar, but not necessarily identical, to the histogram of Figure 9.6.

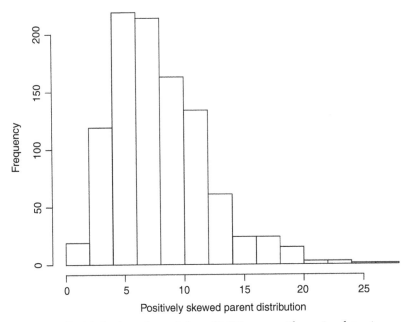

Figure 9.5 Positively skewed population of 1,000 scores with $\mu = 8$ and $\sigma = 4$

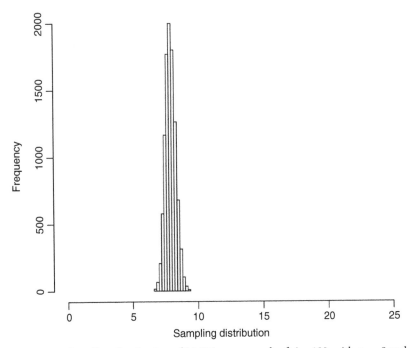

Figure 9.6 Sampling distribution of 10,000 means, each of size 100, with $\mu_{\bar{x}} = 8$ and $\sigma_{\bar{x}} = 0.4$

MORE R: Using the CLT to generate and plot the sampling distribution of means of Figure 9.6.

To generate the 10,000 normally distributed values with mean 8 and standard deviation 0.4 and to plot Figure 9.6, we use the following commands based on the central limit theorem:

```
sampling_distribution = rnorm(10000, 8, 0.4)
hist(sampling_distribution, xlim = c(0, 25))
```

One of the things the CLT tells us is that as long as sampling with replacement is used and the other conditions specified are satisfied, the sampling distribution of means will have its mean equal to the mean of the parent population. As a matter of fact, this result is exactly true even if sampling is without replacement, even if the sample size is not sufficiently large, and even if the population is not at least 100 times as large as the sample being drawn from it. In other words, given any size population and any sample size N, and whether we are sampling with or without replacement, the sampling distribution of means of size N from this population will have its mean equal to the mean of the parent population. We will use this fact in the next section on estimators and bias.

Another immediate consequence of the CLT is that whenever its conditions are satisfied, we can, by increasing the sample size N, make the sampling distribution of means cluster as closely as we want around its mean μ. (Look again at the formula for the standard deviation of the sampling distribution given in the CLT. Because the denominator is just the square root of N, we can make $\sigma_{\bar{x}}$ as small as we like by making N sufficiently large, and a small standard deviation implies that the scores are all clustered about the distribution's mean.) Because the mean of the sampling distribution is also the mean of the parent population, we can conclude once again, that as the sample size we are using increases, we can expect our sample means $\overline{X}$ to become more and more accurate as estimators of the population mean, μ.

ESTIMATORS AND BIAS

Suppose that we have a population with an unknown mean μ and that we want to use a random sample to estimate μ. It seems reasonable to expect that the sample mean $\overline{X}$ should be a better estimator of μ than either the sample mode or sample median. But just what is it that makes an estimator good or bad? One important property, and the one we will discuss in this section, is what is called "unbiasedness."

A sample statistic is said to be an *unbiased estimator* for a population parameter if the sampling distribution for this statistic has mean value equal to the parameter being estimated. In other words, the statistic is an unbiased estimator if the values of the statistic obtained from sampling are, on average, equal to the parameter. As we mentioned earlier, the sample mean $\overline{X}$ has exactly this property as an estimator of the population mean μ. Therefore, we can say that $\overline{X}$ is an unbiased estimator of μ.

One might wonder why the formula for the sample variance presented in Chapter 3 involved dividing the sum of squared deviations from the mean by $N - 1$ instead of N, given that N is used in the denominator to calculate the sample mean. This is because if we had defined the sample variance to be $\dfrac{\sum(X_i - \overline{X})^2}{N}$, it would *not* be an unbiased estimator of the population variance σ^2. It would be a biased estimator. In particular, the mean of all these variances calculated on samples of a given sample size, N, would always be smaller than the value of σ^2, the variance of the population from which these samples have been selected. If, however, we replace N in the denominator of the variance formula with $N - 1$, as presented in Chapter 3, it can be shown mathematically that the resulting formula would be an unbiased estimator of σ^2. For the purpose of estimating the variance of the population, we use the *variance estimator, $\hat{\sigma}^2$*, which entails dividing the sum of squared deviations from the mean by $N - 1$.

If we take the positive square root of the variance estimator, we obtain $\hat{\sigma}$, which is referred to as the *square root* of the variance estimator. We do not call $\hat{\sigma}$ the standard deviation estimator because, even though $\hat{\sigma}^2$ is an unbiased estimator of σ^2, $\hat{\sigma}$ is *not* an unbiased estimator of σ.

SUMMARY OF R COMMANDS

(See also the .R-file for Chapter 9.)

Create	Command lines
Enter a dataset (Example 9.3)	y = c(0, 1, 3, 3, 5, 7, 7, 7, 8, 10)
Create distribution of 10,000 bootstrapped means of size 8 from dataset (Example 9.3)	set.seed(1234) b.mean = boot.mean(y, B = 10000, n = 8) $bootstrap.samples
Create histogram of sampling distribution of bootstrapped means (Figure 9.2)	hist(b.mean, xlab = "means", main = "")
Given a sampling distribution of the mean with population mean 15 and standard error 0.75, find the probability of extracting a single sample mean between 13 and 17 (Example 9.4)	pnorm((17 – 15)/.75) – pnorm ((13 – 15)/.75)
Create and graph a positively skewed distribution with mean 8 and standard deviation 4 (Figure 9.5)	set.seed(1234) x = rchisq(1000, 8) hist(x, xlab = "positively skewed parent distribution", main = "")
Create a set of 10,000 normally distributed values with mean 8 and standard deviation 0.4 (used in Figure 9.6)	set.seed(1234) rnorm(10000, 8, 0.4)

EXERCISES

Create a .R file for each exercise that requires the use of R. Run code from the .R file by highlighting or having the cursor on the line of code and hitting **control+enter** on a PC computer keyboard or **command+enter** on a Mac computer keyboard. Save each .R file using a name associated with the Exercise for which it was created. It is recommended that you review the .R file for Chapter 9 located on the textbook's website before completing these exercises. To facilitate doing each exercise, it may be helpful to copy and paste relevant code from the .R file for Chapter 9 into your own .R file and modify them as needed.

9.1 Given the following population of values: {0, 1, 2, 3, 4, 5, 6, 7, 8, 9}.
  (a) Describe the shape of the distribution of the population scores.
  (b) Make a list of all the samples of size $N = 2$ that could be selected with replacement from this population.
  (c) Enter the list of the means of these samples into a new R dataset. Create a frequency and percent distribution table.
  (d) Construct a histogram for the distribution of sample means found in part (b). This graph depicts the sampling distribution of means for samples of size $N = 2$ from our population. Describe the shape of this distribution.
  (e) Find the mean and standard deviation of both the population and the sampling distribution of means. How do they compare?
  (f) If we were to use the mean of a randomly selected sample of size $N = 2$ to estimate the population mean in this exercise, what would be the probability of getting an estimate within two points of the exact answer?

9.2 Adapt the R instructions for Example 9.3 to generate an approximation to the sampling distributions of means from the population {0, 1, 2, 3, 4, 5, 6, 7, 8, 9}, based on 10,000 samples of size 9. Construct a histogram of the distribution. Compare the actual mean and standard deviation for the sampling distribution of means to those based on the central limit theorem.
  (a) Describe how one obtains the sampling distribution of means for samples of size $N = 8$.
  (b) If a certain population is normally distributed with mean 70 and standard deviation of 2.5, give the mean and the standard deviation of the sampling distribution of means of size $N = 8$.
  (c) Describe the effect on your answer to part (b) of increasing the sample size.
  (d) If we were to select a single sample of size $N = 8$, what is the probability that the mean of this sample will be two or more points higher than the actual population mean?

9.3 Suppose we are given a normally distributed population of scores with mean equal to 500 and standard deviation equal to 100.
  (a) Describe the shape of the sampling distribution of means of size $N = 30$ (with replacement).
  (b) What is the mean of the sampling distribution of means of size $N = 30$ (with replacement)?
  (c) What is the standard deviation of the sampling distribution of means of size $N = 30$ (with replacement), also called the standard error of the mean?

(d) If we were to select a single sample of size $N = 30$ at random from this population of scores, what is the probability that the mean for this sample will be more than two standard errors away from the actual population mean?

(e) What will the sampling distribution of means of size $N = 9$ (with replacement) look like?

9.4 Suppose we are given a uniformly distributed population of scores with mean equal to 500 and standard deviation equal to 100.

(a) Describe the shape of the sampling distribution of means of size $N = 50$ (with replacement).

(b) What is the mean of the sampling distribution of means of size $N = 50$ (with replacement)?

(c) What is the standard deviation of the sampling distribution of means of size $N = 50$ (with replacement), also called the standard error of the mean?

(d) If we were to select a single sample of size $N = 50$ at random from this population of scores, what is the probability that the mean for this sample will be more than two standard errors away from the actual population mean?

(e) What will the sampling distribution of means of size $N = 9$ (with replacement) look like?

9.5 Suppose we are given a negatively skewed population with mean 100 and standard deviation 10.

(a) Describe or give the value of the following characteristics of the sampling distribution of means of size $N = 64$ (with replacement): Shape, mean, and standard error.

(b) What proportion of sample means falls below 98?

9.6 Suppose that a certain population is normally distributed with $\mu = 500$ and $\sigma = 100$. Indicate whether each statement is true or false.

(a) The standard deviation of the population is also called the standard error.

(b) The mean of a sample of size 16 is the same as the population mean.

(c) An increase in sample size from $N = 16$ to $N = 25$ will produce a sampling distribution with a smaller standard deviation.

(d) The mean of a sampling distribution of means is equal to the population mean divided by the square root of the sample size.

(e) The larger the sample size, the more the sample resembles the shape of the population.

(f) The larger the sample size, the more the sampling distribution of means resembles the shape of the population.

(g) The sampling distribution of means is a normal distribution.

(h) The mean of the sampling distribution of means for samples of size $N = 15$ will be the same as the mean of the sampling distribution for samples of size $N = 100$.

9.7 In order to get some idea of what television programs people in New York City watch, we hand out a questionnaire to the members of all statistics classes at New York University and then tabulate the answers we receive. Is this a random sample of the population in which we are interested? Why or why not?

9.8 What (if anything) is wrong with the following statement: "A sampling distribution of means is always normally distributed."

9.9 What (if anything) is wrong with the following statement: "In order to obtain a sampling distribution of means for use in inferential statistics, one must empirically draw many samples of size N from the population of interest and record the corresponding sample mean values obtained."

9.10 Suppose researchers want to estimate the IQ of children who have a twin brother or twin sister. Assume that 100 children (50 pairs of twins) constitute the available population and that the researchers can administer intelligence tests to 30 children. Each time the researchers choose a child at random, they also select that child's twin. Using this procedure, will the researchers obtain a simple random sample of children who have a twin brother or twin sister? Why or why not?

9.11 Given the population of 5,000 scores with $\mu = 8$ and $\sigma = 4$ as shown below:

(a) If a researcher randomly draws a single sample of 300 values from this population, what is the likely shape of the distribution of sample scores: negatively skewed, positively skewed, approximately normal, or exactly normal?

(b) If a researcher randomly draws 200 samples, each containing 300 values, from this population and computes the sample mean for each of the 200 samples, what is the likely shape of the distribution of sample means: negatively skewed, positively skewed, approximately normal, or exactly normal?

(c) What is an appropriate label for the horizontal axis of the distribution described in part (a)?

(d) What is an appropriate label for the horizontal axis of the distribution described in part (b)?

# CHAPTER TEN

INFERENCES INVOLVING THE MEAN OF A SINGLE POPULATION WHEN σ IS KNOWN

One population parameter that is of particular interest to the behavioral scientist is the mean μ of a population. In this chapter, we will discuss two approaches to statistical inference involving the mean of a population: interval estimation and hypothesis testing. Although these approaches are both carried out using samples and give essentially equivalent results, there is a basic difference between them, and it is important to know what this difference is.

In interval estimation of the population mean μ, we begin with no a priori belief about the value of μ. We select at random a sample from the population of interest, compute its sample mean $\overline{X}$, and then use this sample value $\overline{X}$ to construct an interval centered at $\overline{X}$ that will contain μ with a known degree of confidence. In hypothesis testing, we start with an a priori belief about the value of the population mean μ. We select at random a sample from the population of interest, compute its sample mean $\overline{X}$, and then use this sample value $\overline{X}$ to decide whether this belief about the value of μ is plausible.

For example, inference concerning the average amount of some trait possessed by the people or objects of a particular population, where "average" is generally construed to be the arithmetic mean, could be concerned with the mean height of all American males, the mean number of cavities of all children aged 7–8 years in Los Angeles in a particular year, or the mean annual rainfall in inches in Chicago for each year since 1925. Although our discussion of statistical inference in this chapter will be confined to examples concerning the mean μ, it applies equally well to many of the other parameters we will encounter later in the book.

ESTIMATING THE POPULATION MEAN, μ, WHEN THE POPULATION STANDARD DEVIATION, σ, IS KNOWN

The use of a single sample value such as $\overline{X}$ to estimate a population value is known as *point estimation*, because the single value $\overline{X}$ represents one point (or one number) on the real-number line. Referring to the task of trying to estimate the mean height of all American males, we might select a random sample of 25 American males, calculate the sample mean height $\overline{X}$, and then use this sample-mean value as our *point estimate* of the population mean μ.

Although the technique of point estimation is often employed in inferential statistics, it has some serious drawbacks that we should know. One of the drawbacks is illustrated by Example 9.3 in the previous chapter in the section on sampling distributions. In this example, we were given the following population of 10 values: {0, 1, 3, 3, 5, 7, 7, 7, 8, 10}.

From this population, we constructed the sampling distribution of means for all possible samples of size $N = 2$. If we look at the list of all possible sample means that could occur from samples of this size taken from this population, we see that the only values $\overline{X}$ could take on are the following:

Sample means that could be observed

0.0	0.5	1.0	1.5	2.0	2.5	3.0	3.5	4.0	4.5
5.0	5.5	6.0	6.5	7.0	7.5	8.0	8.5	9.0	10.0

But the real mean of this population is $\mu = 5.1$, and none of the sample means listed is exactly equal to 5.1. In other words, in this example it would have been impossible, using point estimation with samples of size 2, to obtain a perfectly accurate estimate of μ.

Suppose, however, that around each sample mean $\overline{X}$ on the list we had constructed an interval of length 6 centered at the sample mean. Considering the intervals rather than just the sample points themselves, we find from Table 10.1 that 79 of the 100 intervals (or 79 percent) actually contain the population mean 5.1.

This result leads us to consider using intervals centered at the sample statistic, rather than just the sample statistic points themselves, to estimate the population parameter. While for this example we chose an interval length of 6, as we shall see later in this chapter, it is always possible to choose an interval length for which some nonzero percent of intervals contain (or "capture") the population mean μ. Furthermore, in most cases, it is possible to determine just what length interval should be used to give exactly any desired percent of intervals that work to capture μ.

TABLE 10.1 Intervals of length 6 constructed about sample means

Sample mean value $\overline{X}$	Frequency of $\overline{X}$	Interval of length 6 centered around $\overline{X}$	Contains $\mu = 5.1$?
0.0	1	(−3.0, 3.0)	No
0.5	2	(−2.5, 3.5)	No
1.0	1	(−2.0, 4.0)	No
1.5	4	(−1.5, 4.5)	No
2.0	4	(−1.0, 5.0)	No
2.5	2	(−0.5, 5.5)	Yes
3.0	6	(0.0, 6.0)	Yes
3.5	6	(0.5, 6.5)	Yes
4.0	12	(1.0, 7.0)	Yes
4.5	2	(1.5, 7.5)	Yes
5.0	15	(2.0, 8.0)	Yes
5.5	6	(2.5, 8.5)	Yes
6.0	6	(3.0, 9.0)	Yes
6.5	6	(3.5, 9.5)	Yes
7.0	9	(4.0, 10.0)	Yes
7.5	8	(4.5, 10.5)	Yes
8.0	1	(5.0, 11.0)	Yes
8.5	6	(5.5, 11.5)	No
9.0	2	(6.0, 12.0)	No
10.0	1	(7.0, 13.0)	No

INTERVAL ESTIMATION

Interval estimation involves the estimation of a population parameter by means of a line segment (or interval) on the real-number line within which the value of the parameter is thought to fall. For example, we might estimate the mean height (to the nearest inch) of all American males by using the interval 65–71 inches centered at the sample-mean value $\overline{X} =$ 68 inches rather than by using the sample-mean value, $\overline{X} = 68$ inches, itself. We could then say we believe μ to be one of the numbers within the interval 65–71 or, equivalently, that we believe the interval 65–71 contains μ. Of course, this is not as precise a statement as saying that we believe $\mu = 68$ inches exactly. But because both statements are statements of belief, we may ask: "In which of the two statements (the interval statement or the point statement) do we have more confidence that our belief is true?"

In general, we can place more confidence in interval estimations than in point estimations and, by extension, more confidence in interval estimation using longer intervals than in interval estimation using shorter intervals. There is a trade-off between the precision of an estimate and our confidence that the estimate is true.

If we develop a procedure for constructing intervals of estimation that has a prescribed probability of giving an interval that contains μ, then we can use this probability as our measure of confidence that the population mean falls within the interval. Such procedure is based on the central limit theorem.

Recall that under the conditions of the central limit theorem, the sampling distribution of means calculated on samples of size N drawn at random from a population with mean μ and standard deviation σ, is either exactly or approximately normally distributed, with mean μ and standard error $\sigma_{\overline{X}} = \sigma/\sqrt{N}$. Also recall from Example 8.11 that 95 percent of the area under any normal curve lies within 1.96 standard deviations of its mean (within $z = \pm 1.96$ of its mean). Using these two pieces of information, as Figure 10.1 illustrates, 95 percent of the sample means fall within 1.96 standard errors of the population mean;

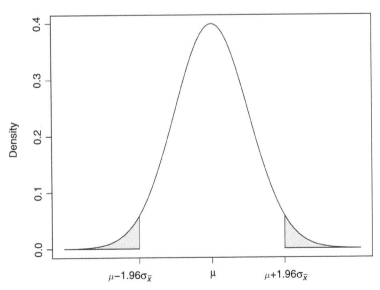

Figure 10.1 Sampling distribution of means: 95 percent of the sample means should fall between the points $\mu - 1.96\ \sigma_{\overline{X}}$ and $\mu + 1.96\ \sigma_{\overline{X}}$

that is, from $\mu - 1.96\sigma_{\overline{X}}$ to $\mu + 1.96\sigma_{\overline{X}}$. Said differently, the probability of selecting at random a sample of size N whose mean $\overline{X}$ lies between $\mu - 1.96\sigma_{\overline{X}}$ and $\mu + 1.96\sigma_{\overline{X}}$ is 0.95, or the probability that $\overline{X}$ lies within a distance of $1.96\sigma_{\overline{X}}$ from μ is 0.95. By this we mean that if we were to construct infinitely many intervals of this form from different samples randomly selected from this population, then 95 percent of them would capture the true mean, μ.

But, if $\overline{X}$ lies within a distance of $1.96\sigma_{\overline{X}}$ from μ, then μ must lie within a distance of $1.96\sigma_{\overline{X}}$ from $\overline{X}$, and μ must lie within the interval $\overline{X} - 1.96\sigma_{\overline{X}}$ to $\overline{X} + 1.96\sigma_{\overline{X}}$. Because 95 percent of all sample means *will* fall within a distance $1.96\ \sigma_{\overline{X}}$ from μ, it follows that 95 percent of all intervals $\overline{X} - 1.96\sigma_{\overline{X}}$ to $\overline{X} + 1.96\sigma_{\overline{X}}$ will capture μ.

Instructions for creating several of the figures in the chapter are available in a table at the end of the chapter, as well as in the .R file associated with Chapter 10 located online.

Figure 10.2 shows graphically that when $\overline{X}$ is within $1.96\sigma_{\overline{X}}$ of μ (as it will be 95 percent of the time), the resulting interval around $\overline{X}$ will capture μ. Figure 10.3 shows graphically that when $\overline{X}$ is farther than $1.96\sigma_{\overline{X}}$ from μ (as it will be 5 percent of the time), the resulting interval around $\overline{X}$ will not capture μ.

The interval $(\overline{X} - 1.96\sigma_{\overline{X}}, \overline{X} + 1.96\sigma_{\overline{X}})$ is called a *confidence interval* (CI) *for* μ, and its confidence level is defined as the proportion of such intervals that can be expected to capture μ, in this case 0.95, or 95 percent. Although any level of confidence may be used, three that are most commonly employed are 90 percent, 95 percent, and 99 percent.

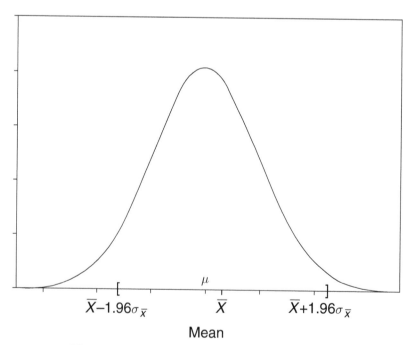

Figure 10.2 $\overline{X}$ falls within $1.96\sigma_{\overline{X}}$ of μ

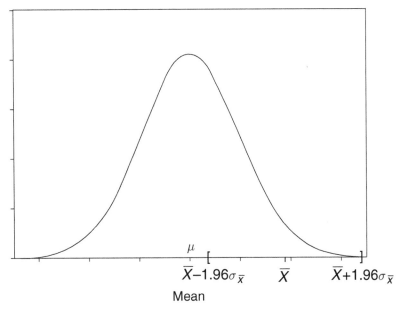

Figure 10.3 $\overline{X}$ does not fall within $1.96\sigma_{\overline{X}}$ of μ

A general equation for the confidence interval for estimating μ is:

$$\text{upper limit} = \overline{X} + z_c\sigma_{\overline{X}} = \overline{X} + z_c\frac{\sigma}{\sqrt{N}} \qquad (10.1)$$

$$\text{lower limit} = \overline{X} - z_c\sigma_{\overline{X}} = \overline{X} - z_c\frac{\sigma}{\sqrt{N}}$$

$$\text{Or, equivalently,} \quad \overline{X} - z_c\frac{\sigma}{\sqrt{N}} \leq \mu \leq \overline{X} + z_c\frac{\sigma}{\sqrt{N}}$$

$$\text{or, equivalently,} \, \overline{X} \pm z_c(\text{s.e.})$$

where
   $z_c = 1.645$ for a 90 percent confidence interval
          1.960 for a 95 percent confidence interval
          2.576 for a 99 percent confidence interval

and (s.e.) is the standard error of the mean defined in Chapter 9.

☞ **Remark.** Because these confidence intervals require the value of $\sigma/\sqrt{N}$ in their construction, they are based on the assumption that σ, the population standard deviation, is known – that it does not need to be estimated. In practice, this assumption is not tenable, and one would normally need to estimate σ. We make this assumption here for heuristic reasons and will present a more realistic approach in the next chapter.

EXAMPLE 10.1 Never Ready Flashlight Company has just invented a new, longer-lasting flashlight. Company analysts believe the life expectancy of this new model to have the same variance as the old model, $\sigma^2 = 16$, but they do not know the mean life expectancy, μ. (Keep in mind that μ represents the *population* mean, and in this example, the population consists of *all* these new flashlights.) To estimate μ, they take a random sample of size $N = 100$ flashlights and run them until they die out. If the sample mean turns out to be $\overline{X} = 150$ hours, find a 95 percent CI for μ.

Solution. Because $N = 100$ is large enough to permit us to use the central limit theorem, and we know that $\sigma = \sqrt{16} = 4$, we can use Equation 10.1 with $\overline{X} = 150$, $\sigma_{\overline{X}} = \sigma/\sqrt{N} = 4/10 = 0.4$, and $z_c = 1.960$.

Thus, our 95 percent CI for μ is (149.216, 150.784) hours.

☞ **Remark.** Keep in mind that the procedure and equation given in this chapter for the construction of confidence intervals rests on the assumption that the sampling distribution of means is normally or approximately normally distributed. If this were not true, the z-values provided in Equation 10.1 would not be accurate. Thus, either the population must be known to be normally distributed or the sample must be large enough ($N \geq 30$) to invoke the central limit theorem to be sure that the sampling distribution of means is normally or approximately normally distributed.

☞ **Remark.** Contrary to what you might believe, the CI constructed in Example 10.1 does not have a 95 percent chance of containing the true average lifetime of these new flashlights, μ. Said differently, we are not 95 percent confident or certain that the true average lifetime of these new flashlights is between 149 and 151 hours. Once we have selected our sample, calculated $\overline{X}$, and found the corresponding confidence interval, either μ, the true average lifetime of these new flashlights, is in this interval or it is not, and the probability that the interval contains that true mean is either 1 (if it contains μ) or 0 (if it does not contain μ), not 0.95. What we can say about Example 10.1 is that if we repeated the *process* of sampling 100 flashlights randomly and computing their average lifetimes, then 95 percent of all the intervals we would construct about these sample means would contain μ. The particular interval that we have constructed (149, 151) may be either one of the 95 percent that do contain the true average lifetime of these new flashlights or one of the 5 percent that do not. However, because such a large proportion of all the intervals would contain μ, the true average lifetime of these new flashlights, we cannot help but believe that this particular interval is one of those that does.

☞ **Remark.** Based on the above discussion, the reader should be convinced that the 95 percent confidence interval (149, 151) also does NOT imply, for example, that 95 percent of all of such new flashlights will last between from 149 to 151 hours, nor that 95 percent of the particular new flashlights in our sample of 100 flashlights will last between from 149 to 151 hours, nor that there is a 95 percent probability that each of the flashlights in our sample of 100 will last between from 149 to 151 hours. Said simply, the level of confidence (in this case 95 percent) is a statement about the likely true *average* lifetime of such flashlights, and not about the lifetime of individual flashlights themselves.

☞ **Remark.** The notion of the confidence interval was first introduced by Jerzy Neyman, another giant in the development of the history of modern statistics, in 1934 in a talk before the Royal Statistical Society entitled "On the Two Different Aspects of the Representative Method" (Salsburg, 2001, p. 120).

RELATING THE LENGTH OF A CONFIDENCE INTERVAL, THE LEVEL OF CONFIDENCE, AND THE SAMPLE SIZE

Based on Equation 10.1, we may note that:

1. If we increase the confidence level, say from 90 percent to 95 percent, and keep the sample size the same, the resulting confidence interval will be longer. Our estimate of μ will then be less precise, but we will be more confident that it is accurate.
2. If we increase the sample size N and keep the confidence level the same, the resulting confidence interval will be shorter.
3. If we decrease the length of the confidence interval and keep the sample size N the same, then the confidence level will decrease.

In actual research situations employing interval estimation, it is often possible to specify a desired precision of estimation (i.e., a desired confidence interval length). Because a direct relationship exists between the precision of estimation and the sample size N, as we will discuss in a later section on power, it should be possible to obtain any desired precision of estimation by simply selecting an appropriate sample size N.

HYPOTHESIS TESTING

By contrast to interval estimation, where we do not need to begin with an a priori belief about the population parameter of interest (e.g., μ), in hypothesis testing we do. We usually make hypotheses based on our own past experiences and any other available information and then act on these hypotheses. To take an example from everyday life, we take aspirin when we have a headache because we hypothesize, from what we read, from what other people say, and from our own experiences that aspirin helps to relieve headaches. But, if the headache gets better some of the time and other times it gets worse, then these experiences are inconsistent with our original hypothesis, and so we may decide that our original hypothesis is not plausible. As another example, we pay for the privilege of using certain credit cards because we hypothesize, from their advertisements, that using them will make our shopping and traveling easier. If it turns out, however, that many of the stores in which we shop do not honor these credit cards, then these experiences are inconsistent with our original hypothesis, and so we may decide that our hypothesis is not plausible. How then, do we decide whether data we have obtained are consistent or inconsistent with our hypothesis; that is, how do we decide whether a hypothesis we have made is plausible? One way is to use the method of hypothesis testing.

Suppose, based on past observation and theory, you believe that the average mathematics aptitude of first-year college students in California is better than that of the country at large, and you would like to test your belief. You decide to use the Scholastic Aptitude Test in Mathematics (SAT-M) to measure mathematics aptitude. You know that the mean score for the national population on which the test was standardized is known to be 500, but you believe that the mean score for California students is higher. Because you have limited funds, you are able to collect data on only a sample of students from the population of 160,000 first-year college students in California and you randomly select a sample of 1,600 from this population. For the time being, assume that you do not have any reason to believe that the variability of the population of California students is different from that of the national standardization population for which the standard deviation is known to be 100.

When stated formally, your belief (that, on average, California students perform better than the country at large on the SAT-M) is called a *hypothesis*. Because your hypothesis challenges conventional wisdom, that California students do not score higher than the country at large in terms of mathematics aptitude, your hypothesis is called the *alternative hypothesis*, denoted in this book by the symbol H_1. The hypothesis that represents current thinking and that will be believed true until you demonstrate that it is implausible (or nullifies it), is called the *null hypothesis*, denoted in this book by the symbol H_0. By contrast, the alternative hypothesis is the statement we would switch to if, through your experiment or study, H_0 were shown to be implausible and H_1 plausible – that is, if the observed results were inconsistent with H_0.

The null hypothesis, in this case, states that the mean of the population of California first-year college students is 500 and may be expressed symbolically as:

H_0: μ = 500.

The alternative hypothesis, in this case, states that the mean of the population of California first-year college students is *greater than* 500 and may be expressed symbolically as:

H_1: μ > 500.

In sum, the null hypothesis is the hypothesis of no difference (that, in this case, California is no different from the rest of the country in its SAT-M performance); it is also the hypothesis we would like to nullify, or cast doubt on. The alternative hypothesis, on the other hand, is the hypothesis of an effect; it is the hypothesis that we would like to support. H_0 and H_1 represent two different statements about the state of the California population in this case. The purpose of hypothesis testing is to determine which one of the two is the more plausible.

The outcome of the hypothesis test will be determined by the data you obtain on your random sample of size $N = 1,600$. In particular, if your data are consistent with H_0 (i.e., if $\overline{X}$ is close to or less than 500), then you should conclude that H_0 is a plausible hypothesis. If, on the other hand, your data are not consistent with H_0 (i.e., if $\overline{X}$ is far larger than 500) then you should conclude that H_0 is an implausible hypothesis and that H_1 is a plausible one. Notice, that as constructed, the focus of the hypothesis test is on H_0, the null hypothesis, because this is the hypothesis that represents what is believed currently and what will be believed in the future unless something or someone casts doubt upon it through some experiment or study.

In determining which sample outcomes are likely and which are not, we assume that H_0 is true (that $\mu = 500$) and use the CLT to provide us with information concerning the distribution of all possible sample means that could be obtained. In this example, we know from the CLT that the sampling distribution of means is approximately normally distributed with mean $\mu_{\overline{X}} = 500$, and standard deviation $\sigma_{\overline{X}} = \sigma/\sqrt{N} = 100/\sqrt{1600} = 100/40 = 2.5$. From this information we can assess, under the assumption that H_0 is true, the probabilities of obtaining all possible sample means. Let's consider two possible sample means, $\overline{X} = 505$ and $\overline{X} = 502$, and find the probabilities associated with them (or a value larger than them) given that H_0 is true. The shaded areas of Figures 10.4 and 10.5 represent these respective probabilities. The .R file associated with this chapter, as well as the summary table at the end of this chapter, contain the syntax for creating these and many of the remaining figures in this chapter.

The shaded area in both cases represents the probability of obtaining a result (e.g., sample mean) that is as or more extreme than the actual result (e.g., sample mean) observed, given that the null hypothesis is true. This probability is called the *p-value* of the test.

First we consider the case where $\overline{X} = 505$. To obtain the *p*-value, or probability of obtaining a mean of 505 or more, we may use either R or Table C.1 in Appendix C.

To use R, you may simply input and execute the following command in your .R file:

pnorm(505, mean = 500, sd = 2.5, lower.tail = F)

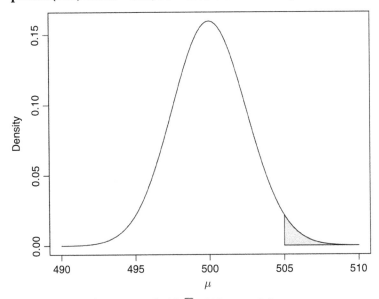

Figure 10.4 *p*-value associated with $\overline{X} \geq 505$ or $z \geq 2.0$

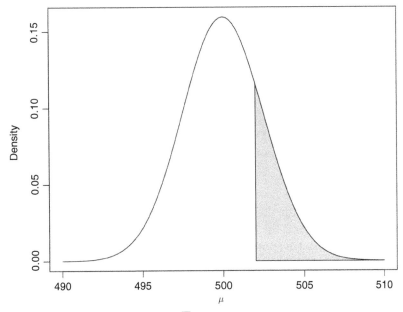

Figure 10.5 *p*-value associated with $\overline{X} \geq 502$ or $z \geq 0.8$

The *p*-value returned in the console is 0.0228.

To use Table C.1, we need to first convert the mean of 505 to a *z*-score to find the number of standard errors $\overline{X} = 505$ is away from $\mu = 500$. To do so we adapt Equation 4.3, the *z*-score formula, as Equation 10.2. Equation 10.2 gives the number of standard errors ($\sigma_{\overline{X}}$) the observed mean ($\overline{X}$) is away from the null hypothesized mean (μ) under the sampling distribution of means:

$$z = \frac{\overline{X} - \mu}{\sigma_{\overline{X}}}. \tag{10.2}$$

According to Equation 10.2, the obtained *z*-score is $z = \dfrac{505 - 500}{2.5} = 2.0$, which also may be obtained using R's built-in calculator (**pnorm(2.0, mean = 0, sd = 1, lower.tail = F)**). We may then consult Table C.1 to find the area under the curve to the right of $z = 2.0$. Whether we use R or Table C.1, we find that the *p*-value associated with $\overline{X} \geq 505$ is roughly 0.023.

Given that this probability of occurrence is so small, if the null hypothesis were true, we could hardly expect to obtain a sample of 1,600 first-year college students with a mean mathematics aptitude score that would be so much greater than 500. Accordingly, we would have to question the truth of the null hypothesis. In fact, if we were to obtain a sample with such a large mean value, we would have evidence to support our belief in the alternative hypothesis. Based on this evidence we would decide to reject the null hypothesis in favor of the alternative.

☞ **Remark.** Because this test is based on a variation of the *z*-score formula (Equation 10.2), in general, a hypothesis test of the parameter μ when σ is known is called a *z-test*.

Now we consider the case where $\overline{X} = 502$. To obtain the *p*-value, or probability of obtaining a mean of 502 or more, we may, once again, use either R or Table C.1 in Appendix C. Either we input and execute the following R syntax:

pnorm(502, mean = 500, sd = 2.5, lower.tail = F)

Or we calculate a *z*-value using Equation 10.2 and R's built-in calculator to obtain $z = 0.8$ and consult Table C.1 in Appendix C. In either case, we find the *p*-value to be approximately 0.212.

Given that, in this case, the probability is large (there is one chance in five of obtaining 502 or more), the result is consistent with the null hypothesis, casting doubt on our belief in the alternative hypothesis. Based on this result we would decide not to reject the null as implausible.

☞ **Remark.** The *p*-value may be viewed as the degree to which the observed result or one more extreme is consistent with the null hypothesis. The less consistent the observed result is with the null hypothesis, the lower the *p*-value. In our example, a result of 505 or more is less consistent with a true population mean of 500 than is a result of 502 or more. Accordingly, *p*-values provide an indication of the strength of evidence to reject or not to reject the null hypothesis in favor of the alternative.

While we have categorized 0.023 as a probability associated with an unlikely event and 0.21 as a probability associated with a likely one, it is up to the researcher to decide, *when setting up the hypothesis test*, the probability level that distinguishes between likely and unlikely outcomes. The probability level that the researcher chooses to distinguish an unlikely outcome from a likely one is called the *significance level* of the test, and is denoted by α. While p-values depend on the particular result observed, significance levels do not. A significance level may be considered a standard or criterion from which to judge the strength of evidence against the null hypothesis. Commonly used significance levels are $\alpha = 0.10$, $\alpha = 0.05$, and $\alpha = 0.01$. When a significance level is set at 0.01, for example, stronger evidence is required to reject the null hypothesis than when either 0.05 or 0.10 is used. Accordingly, $\alpha = 0.01$ is considered to be a more stringent criterion than $\alpha = 0.05$ or 0.10.

While the commonly used significance levels in the behavioral and social sciences are 0.10, 0.05, and 0.01, a range of reasonable values should be considered before one is chosen. Significance levels greater than 0.10, however, are generally not used because they allow too great a chance of incorrectly rejecting H_0. Significance levels less than 0.01 are also generally not used because they tend to make the test so conservative that we run a large risk of failing to reject H_0 when we should not have done so (we will talk more about this type of error later in this chapter). The significance level α is set as the largest risk of incorrectly rejecting the null hypothesis that the researcher is willing to make in a particular situation. According to Fisher (1959), the individual who introduced the hypothesis testing procedure in the 1920s, "no scientific worker has a fixed level of significance at which, from year to year, and in all circumstances, he rejects [null] hypotheses; he rather gives his mind to each particular case in the light of his evidence and his ideas" (p. 42).

In our example, we implicitly used 0.05 as our significance level, and as a result, judged the p-value of 0.023 as providing sufficiently strong evidence to reject the null hypothesis in favor of the alternative. In the first case, therefore, we concluded that, on average, first-year college students in California score statistically significantly higher on the SAT-M than the country as a whole ($\overline{X} = 505$, $\sigma = 100$, $p = 0.023$). Analogously, using a 0.05 significance level, or even a 0.10 significance level, a p-value of 0.21 does not provide sufficiently strong evidence to reject the null hypothesis in favor of the alternative. In the second case, therefore, we concluded that, on average, first-year college students in California do not score statistically significantly higher on the SAT-M than the country as a whole ($\overline{X} = 502$, $\sigma = 100$, $p = 0.212$).

In general, if the p-value is less than α, we reject the null hypothesis as implausible in favor of the alternative and say that the result is statistically significant. Alternatively, if the p-value is greater than α, we fail to reject the null hypothesis as plausible and say that the result is not statistically significant.

We remarked at the beginning of Chapter 9 that when we work in the area of inferential statistics, we can never be 100 percent certain of our conclusions. We should note here that whenever a hypothesis is tested, the decision to reject or not to reject H_0 is always made with some degree of uncertainty. In other words, the possibility always exists that the decision made is, in fact, the wrong decision.

Suppose that, with respect to our example, we did observe a mean of 505. While the p-value of 0.023 associated with a mean of 505 or greater renders this event *unlikely* if H_0 is true, it does not render this event *impossible*. There is still a possibility, albeit small ($p = 0.023$), that we would have observed a mean of 505 or greater in a sample selected randomly from a population whose true mean is 500.

Analogously, suppose we did observe a mean of 502. While the *p*-value of 0.212 associated with a mean of 502 or greater renders this event likely if H_0 is true, this *p*-value does not prove that H_0 is true. There is still an unknown possibility that we would have observed a mean of 502 or greater in a sample selected randomly from a population whose true mean is greater than 500.

Thus, while rejection of a null hypothesis does not, by itself, say a lot about the truth of that null hypothesis, neither does non-rejection. By failing to reject a null hypothesis, one cannot conclude that the null hypothesis is true; all that one can conclude is that one cannot conclude that the null hypothesis is false (Cohen, 1990). However, the null hypothesis testing procedure provides a way to make sense of the observed result in terms of whether it is real or merely apparent (due to sampling error).

☞ **Remark.** As mentioned earlier, Sir Ronald A. Fisher introduced the null hypothesis testing procedure in the 1920s. In his approach, one states a hypothesis that describes in null form the state of affairs in a population with regard to the value of some parameter, such as a mean. Through the collection of data, randomly sampled from that population, one then seeks to nullify that hypothesis with some degree of probability, and in so doing, engage in a scientific process of proof through disproof. Jerzy Neyman and Egon Pearson, Karl Pearson's son, later expanded Fisher's approach by incorporating an alternative hypothesis and by forcing a choice between the null and its alternate. In the Neyman and Pearson approach, which is the one currently used today, one does not simply reject the null hypothesis, but, rather, rejects the null *in favor of the alternative*.

The Neyman and Pearson null hypothesis testing procedure is further illustrated in Example 10.2.

EXAMPLE 10.2 Suppose Write-On Pen Company manufactures a pen that has a mean and a standard deviation, measured in hours of continuous writing, of $\mu = 100$ and $\sigma = 9$, respectively. To increase its sales, the company has slightly modified the manufacturing process to produce a pen that it claims will last longer than the old pens. It has no reason to believe, however, that the new process alters the variability of these pens in terms of hours of continuous writing. To test this claim, the company selects at random $N = 400$ pens manufactured under the new process and uses them continuously until they no longer work. If the sample mean in terms of hours of continuous writing turns out to be $\overline{X} = 101$, and the significance level selected is $\alpha = 0.05$, what conclusion can the company draw about this new pen?

Solution. The company would like to claim that its new pen is an improvement (in terms of hours of continuous writing) over its old pen, that the mean writing time of the new pen is greater than that of the old pen. However, until evidence is provided to the contrary, the company must assume that the mean writing time of the new pen is 100 hours, the same as the mean writing time of the old pen. These hypotheses may be stated symbolically as:

H_0: $\mu = 100$
H_1: $\mu > 100$,

where μ represents the mean continuous writing time (in hours) of the population of all pens manufactured using the new process.

☞ **Remark.** While expressed as H_0: $\mu = 100$ versus H_1: $\mu > 100$, there are two reasons why a more logical rendition of these hypotheses would be H_0: $\mu \leq 100$ versus H_1: $\mu > 100$. First, it would be in the company's best interests to nullify the hypothesis that the mean writing time of its new pen is *at most* 100 hours (not simply *equals* 100 hours), in favor of the hypothesis that the mean writing time of its new pen is greater than 100 hours. Second, the hypotheses, H_0: $\mu \leq 100$ versus H_1: $\mu > 100$, account for *all* possible values of μ, not just those equal to or greater than 100. Why then do we express the hypotheses as H_0: $\mu = 100$ versus H_1: $\mu > 100$? Simply stated, the CLT requires a single-valued null hypothesis (e.g., H_0: $\mu = 100$) to describe the sampling distribution of means upon which the hypothesis test rests; the single value used (100 in this case) is most reasonable because any sample result that would cause us to reject H_0: $\mu = 100$ in favor of H_1: $\mu > 100$ would also cause us to reject any other single value of μ less than 100.

Because the null hypothesis specifies a particular (single) value for μ (i.e., 100), we can use the CLT to describe the sampling distribution of means. If we assume H_0 true, the sampling distribution of means for samples of size $N = 400$ from this population should be approximately normal with mean $\mu_{\overline{X}}$, and standard deviation $\sigma_{\overline{X}} = \sigma/\sqrt{N} = 9/\sqrt{400} = 9/20 = 0.45$. Using the **pnorm(101, mean = 100, sd = 0.45, lower.tail = F)** command in R or by calculating a z-score and using Table C.1 in Appendix C we determine the p-value, the probability of observing a mean of 101 hours or greater given the null hypothesis is true, to be $p = 0.013$ (see Figure 10.6).

Because the significance level for this test has been set at $\alpha = 0.05$, and because p is less than α in this case, we reject the null hypothesis as implausible in favor of the alternative. That is, the new pen lasts statistically significantly longer than the old pen ($\overline{X} = 101$, $\sigma = 9$, $p = 0.013$).

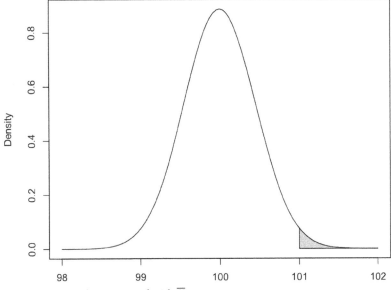

Figure 10.6 p-value associated with $\overline{X} \geq 101$

☞ **Remark.** In our example, we were able to reject the null in favor of the alternative that the new pen lasts longer than the old pen because the observed sample mean was sufficiently *greater than* 100. Had the sample mean been *less than* 100, no matter how much less, logically, we would not have been able to reject the null hypothesis in favor of the alternative because, under this circumstance, the alternative would have been even less plausible than the null. Because the alternative hypothesis stipulates a direction of difference from the null, as illustrated in Figure 10.6, only one-tail under the normal curve would yield an appropriate p-value. As illustrated in Figure 10.6, for this example, the one tail that will yield an appropriate p-value is the right tail. Had the alternative hypothesis been of the form $H_1: \mu < 100$, the left tail would have been the one to yield an appropriate p-value. Directional alternative hypotheses always give rise to *one-tailed tests*.

The alternative hypotheses in both the SAT-M and Write-On Pen situations were directional and hence required one-tailed tests. In the next example, we present a scenario where the alternative hypothesis is non-directional and the hypothesis test is *two-tailed*.

• •

EXAMPLE 10.3 P. Ahjay, a well-known researcher in learning theory, would like to determine whether a particular type of preconditioning affects the time it takes individuals to solve a given set of anagram problems. In the past, individuals without such preconditioning have solved the set of problems in an average of 280 seconds with a standard deviation of 20 seconds. For her study, Ms. Ahjay selects a random sample of $N = 100$ individuals, gives them the preconditioning, and then computes the time it takes them to solve the set of problems. While she expects the preconditioning to affect mean performance, she has no reason to believe that it will affect performance variability. Accordingly, she assumes that the standard deviation of the population with preconditioning is the same as the standard deviation of the population without preconditioning, $\sigma = 20$ seconds. (In the next chapter, we will discuss more fully the reasonableness of this assumption about the standard deviation, but for the time being we need to make such an assumption to use the central limit theorem.) If she finds the mean time for solving this set of problems for her sample to be $\overline{X} = 276$ seconds, determine, using the null hypothesis testing procedure and $\alpha = 0.05$, whether preconditioning affects the mean time for solving this set of problems.

Solution Because preconditioning may have the effect of increasing or decreasing the time it takes to solve the set of anagram problems, P. Ahjay would like to support the hypothesis that mean time to complete the set of anagrams is *different* (either more or less) with preconditioning than without. However, until evidence is provided to the contrary, she must assume that the mean time to solve this set of problems is 280 seconds, the same as without preconditioning. Therefore, our null and alternative hypotheses are:

H_0: $\mu = 280$
H_1: $\mu \neq 280$,

where μ represents the mean time (in seconds) for the population to solve the anagram task with preconditioning.

Because the null hypothesis specifies a particular value for μ (i.e., 280), we can use the CLT to describe the sampling distribution of means. If we assume H_0 true, the sampling distribution of means for samples of size $N = 100$ from this population should be approximately normal with mean $\mu_{\bar{X}} = \mu = 280$, and standard deviation $\sigma_{\bar{X}} = \sigma/\sqrt{N} = 20/\sqrt{100} = 20/10 = 2$.

☞ **Remark.** Recall that when the alternative hypothesis is directional and we are using a one-tailed test, we find the *p*-value by finding the probability of obtaining the observed result or one that is more extreme in the direction of the tail that will allow us to reject the null in favor of the alternative. If the alternative hypothesis is of the form: H_1: $\mu >$ some value, then the appropriate tail is on the right. On the other hand, if the alternative hypothesis is of the form: H_1: $\mu <$ some value, then the appropriate tail is on the left. In the case of a non-directional alternative hypothesis, we find the *p*-value by finding the probability of obtaining the observed result or one that is more extreme in the direction of *both tails* because an extreme value in either tail would logically allow us to reject the null hypothesis in favor of the alternative. See Figure 10.7.

Because the observed result in our example is 276 seconds, a difference of 4 from the hypothesized population mean μ of 280 seconds, a result more extreme than 276 seconds is defined as 276 or fewer seconds *or* 284 or more seconds. Figure 10.7 illustrates the two areas under the normal curve that, when combined, yield the *p*-value we seek: The probability of observing a mean result of 276 seconds or fewer, or 284 seconds or more, given the null hypothesis is true. Using the command **2*pnorm(276, mean = 280, sd = 2)** in R we determine this *p*-value to be 0.046.

Alternatively, we could have found the *p*-value associated with $\overline{X} \leq 276$ or $\overline{X} \geq 284$ relative to a mean of 280 and a standard error of 2 as the area associated with $z \leq -2$ or $z \geq 2$ relative to a mean of 0 and a standard deviation of 1 using Table C.1 in Appendix C. (Note that from Equation 10.3, $z = \dfrac{276 - 280}{2} = -2$, and that $z = \dfrac{284 - 280}{2} = 2$). In this case, as well, the *p*-value equals 0.046.

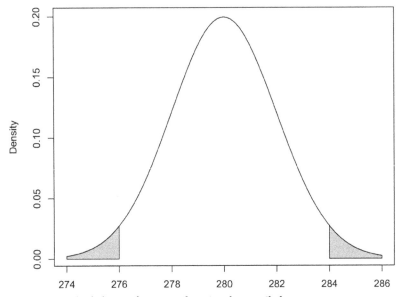

Figure 10.7 Shaded areas for a non-directional two-tailed test

Because the significance level for this test has been set at $\alpha = 0.05$, and because p is less than α in this case, we reject the null hypothesis as implausible in favor of the alternative. That is, the preconditioning statistically significantly affects the time it takes to complete the anagram task. Furthermore, because the observed result of 276 seconds is below 280 seconds, we may conclude that preconditioning statistically significantly decreases the amount of time it takes to complete the anagram task ($\overline{X} = 276$, $\sigma = 20$, $p = 0.046$).

THE RELATIONSHIP BETWEEN HYPOTHESIS TESTING AND INTERVAL ESTIMATION

In the introduction to this chapter, we noted that interval estimation and hypothesis testing of the mean μ give essentially equivalent results. We explore this more closely in relation to Example 10.3.

Recall that in Example 10.3, P. Ahjay hypothesized that a certain type of preconditioning affects the time it takes individuals to solve a given set of anagram problems. In particular, she hypothesized that with preconditioning the population mean time to complete the anagram task would be different from 280 seconds, the known time to complete this task without preconditioning. Using a random sample of $N = 100$ individuals, she found the mean time, with preconditioning, to be $\overline{X} = 276$ seconds. She set $\alpha = 0.05$ and found the probability to be only $p = 0.046$ of observing this mean, or one more extreme in either direction, in a random sample selected from a population whose true mean is $\mu = 280$. Accordingly, she concluded that preconditioning statistically significantly affects the mean time for solving this set of problems, and, in fact, decreases it.

Suppose, that instead of running a hypothesis test of H_0: $\mu = 280$ versus H_1: $\mu \neq 280$, P. Ahjay decided to use her sample result to construct a 95 percent CI for μ. Using Equation 10.1, the 95 percent CI she would have constructed is ($276 - 1.96(2)$, $276 + 1.96(2)$), or equivalently, (272.08, 279.92). Given this interval, she would have confidence that μ is equal to one of the values within the interval 272.08 to 279.92, and that μ is *not* equal to any of the values outside the interval 272.08 to 279.92.

Because $\mu = 280$ is *not* within the confidence interval, she would conclude that it is unlikely that 280 is a plausible value of μ. In hypothesis test terms this would imply a rejection of H_0: $\mu = 280$ in favor of H_1: $\mu \neq 280$. Because in this case $\mu = 280$ falls above the upper limit of the CI, she would conclude that preconditioning statistically significantly decreases the mean time for solving this set of problems, which is exactly the conclusion she reached on the basis of her earlier hypothesis test.

In general, given a $(1 - \alpha) \times 100$ percent CI estimate of μ:

1. The values that fall within the confidence interval are exactly those values of μ that would be retained as plausible in a non-directional hypothesis test at significance level α.
2. The values that fall outside the confidence interval are exactly those values of μ that would be rejected as implausible in a non-directional hypothesis test at significance level α.

Constructing a $(1 - \alpha) \times 100$ percent confidence interval estimate of μ may be viewed as the equivalent of running non-directional hypothesis tests at significance level α simultaneously on all possible values of μ from negative infinity to positive infinity.

Because confidence intervals capture the magnitude of the difference between the observed and null hypothesized values, they provide more meaningful information as to the magnitude of the treatment effect than just whether the difference is likely to be zero in the population.

EFFECT SIZE

From Equation 10.2, we may note that the size of the z-value, representing the degree to which the observed mean deviates from the null hypothesized mean, depends not only on $\overline{X}$, μ, and σ, but also on the sample size, N. When N is large, even when the difference between $\overline{X}$ and μ is small, z will be large because the standard error of the mean, $\sigma_{\overline{X}} = \sigma/\sqrt{N}$, which is the denominator of the z-ratio, will be small. As a result, even trivially small deviations from the null hypothesized mean can be statistically significant. While the hypothesis test tells us how likely the observed sample result is given the null hypothesis is true, it tells us nothing about *the degree to which* the null hypothesis is false: that is, the degree to which the observed result departs from the value of the null hypothesis. To be useful in helping us discover truths about phenomena of interest, the null hypothesis test must be supplemented by other forms of analysis that are independent of sample size to determine the nature and magnitude of the result obtained. Knowing the magnitude of the result obtained, called the *effect size*, allows us to determine whether our statistically significant result is also *practically significant*.

In Example 10.3, the test result was statistically significant, indicating that $H_1: \mu \neq 280$ was a more plausible statement about the true value of the population mean μ than $H_0: \mu = 280$. Taking this result literally, all we have shown is that there is reason to believe that μ differs from 280. The amount by which μ differs from 280 is not specified by our conclusion. That is, our conclusion could imply that μ differs from 280 by a great deal or by a trivially small amount. If trivially small, the difference is likely not to have practical significance or importance, and would render inconsequential the fact of having achieved statistical significance.

In our example, preconditioning resulted in a 4-second reduction in the solution time for the sample. Whether this reduction is deemed to be trivially small must rely on the content area experience and best judgment of the researcher carrying out this study. Of course, the researcher may gain insight into the importance of her finding by constructing a confidence interval to consider the range of plausible values for μ, so that she can determine how close the boundaries of the interval are to the null hypothesized value of 280, in this case. That the upper limit to the CI in this case is 279.92 suggests a potential population mean difference of only 0.08 seconds (from 280), which one could assume is small. She may also gain insight by computing Cohen's d, one of many possible measures of effect size that are independent of sample size (Cohen 1988).

In this situation, d is computed by taking the difference between the observed mean and null hypothesized mean, μ, and dividing that difference by the population standard deviation, σ, assumed to be known. An algebraic expression for Cohen's d is given by Equation 10.3:

$$d = \frac{\overline{X} - \mu}{\sigma}. \qquad (10.3)$$

For Example 10.3, $d = \dfrac{276 - 280}{20} = \dfrac{-4}{20} = -0.20$. The sign indicates the direction of the effect (it is negative in this example because the observed mean falls below the null hypothesized mean), while the absolute value indicates the magnitude of the effect (0.20 standard deviations). Thus, Cohen's d tells our researcher that the observed result falls only 0.20 standard deviations below the null hypothesized mean of 280. This finding would appear to corroborate the CI estimate of a small effect and suggest that preconditioning has limited utility in altering the time to solve such anagram problems. In the final analysis, however, judgments about the magnitude of effect size are subjective and must be based ultimately on the content area knowledge of the researcher. In the absence of such knowledge, Cohen (1988) offers the following guidelines for evaluating effect sizes in terms of d:

$d = 0.20$ represents a "small" effect size
$d = 0.50$ represents a "medium" effect size
$d = 0.80$ represents a "large" effect size.

These guidelines suggest the effect of preconditioning to be small in the case of these anagrams.

TYPE II ERROR AND THE CONCEPT OF POWER

When a decision is made based on a hypothesis test, four different situations can result:

1. H_0 is true but we reject it.
2. H_0 is true and we fail to reject it.
3. H_0 is false and we reject it.
4. H_0 is false but we fail to reject it.

These outcomes and their probabilities of occurrence are displayed in Figure 10.8. Notice that while situations 1 and 4 represent incorrect decisions, situations 2 and 3 represent correct decisions.

The incorrect decision of situation 1 is what we have called a Type I error. The risk of committing a Type I error equals the α level of the test, the level at which we would regard an observation to be unlikely to occur by chance. The incorrect decision of situation 4 is

	Reject H_0	Fail to Reject H_0
H_0 is true	Incorrect decision: Type I error Probability = α	Correct decision Probability = $1 - \alpha$
H_0 is false	Correct decision Probability = $1 - \beta$	Incorrect decision: Type II error Probability = β

Figure 10.8 The four possible outcomes of a hypothesis test.

what is called a Type II error. The risk of committing a Type II error equals the β (beta) level of the test. Unfortunately, we never know if we have, in fact, committed a Type I or Type II error, since which hypothesis is true can never be known. Instead, we try to minimize the probability of making one of these errors.

When we conduct a hypothesis test, we want to minimize the probability of making either a Type I error or a Type II error. Unfortunately, these two types of errors are, in a sense, inversely related. The typical research situation of concern in this book is one in which H_0 represents some established procedure and H_1 represents a deviation from it. A decision to reject H_0 in favor of H_1 might therefore result in further expenditures, further testing, and possibly even in some basic changes in the established procedure.

Accordingly, if we are to reject H_0, we certainly do not want to reject it falsely (commit a Type I error), so we generally try to set our test so that the significance level α is the one that is kept small at the possible expense of having a relatively large β.

The correct decision of situation 2 arises when the test does not detect a difference from the null hypothesis when the null hypothesis is in fact true. The probability of this correct decision is represented by the complement of α, $1 - \alpha$. Finally, the correct decision of situation 3 arises when the test does detect a difference from the null hypothesis when the null hypothesis is in fact false (when the alternative hypothesis is true). The probability of this correct decision is represented by the complement of β, $1 - \beta$, and because of its importance within the null hypothesis test procedure, this probability is called the *power* of the test.

The power of a hypothesis test may be likened to the power of magnification used to view a cell under a microscope (Hays, 1973). Suppose, for example, a particular cell in which we are interested has a break in its cell wall that we cannot observe with the naked eye. If we place the cell under the microscope and use a low power setting, we still do not detect the break in the cell wall. In this case, we say that the microscope lacks sufficient power to detect the difference or break in the cell wall that exists. When we increase the microscope power setting to high we detect the difference in the cell wall. In this case, the power of the microscope is sufficiently high to detect the break in the cell wall.

Without sufficient power in the microscope, we are not likely to detect the difference that exists in the cell wall. So, it is the same for the hypothesis test. Without sufficient power in the hypothesis test, we are not likely to detect a difference from the null hypothesis even when such a difference exists. Hence, when we set up a hypothesis test, we want to maximize the power of the test, $1 - \beta$. We also want to minimize the risk of making a Type I error, α. As noted earlier, an α level greater than 0.10 is seldom used. Likewise, a power level less than 0.80 is also seldom used. When conducting a hypothesis test, researchers like to have a probability of at least 0.80 of detecting a difference where one exists. In that case, if no difference were detected, and the null hypothesis were retained, the researcher would be reasonably confident that a difference did *not* exist rather than that a difference did exist and that the test had insufficient power to detect it.

A good way to understand power is through its graphic representation as shown in Figure 10.9. In Figure 10.9, the curve labeled "H_0 true" represents the sampling distribution of means given that H_0 is true.

We know by the central limit theorem that this curve is normal in shape. We also know by the central limit theorem that the mean of the means, $\mu_{\overline{X}}$, under this distribution equals

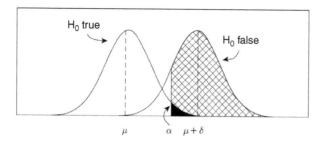

Figure 10.9 Sampling distributions of means under H_0 true and H_0 false with α, δ, and $\sigma_{\overline{X}}$ shown

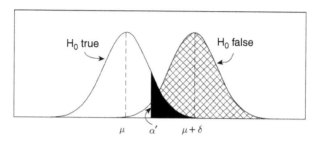

Figure 10.10 Sampling distributions of means under H_0 true and H_0 false with $\alpha' > \alpha$, δ, and $\sigma_{\overline{X}}$

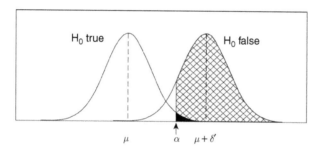

Figure 10.11 Sampling distributions of means under H_0 true and H_0 false with α, $\delta' > \delta$, and $\sigma_{\overline{x}}$

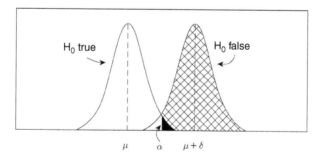

Figure 10.12 Sampling distributions of means under H_0 true and H_0 false with α, δ, and $\sigma'_{\overline{X}} < \sigma_{\overline{X}}$

μ and that the standard deviation of the means, $\sigma_{\overline{X}}$, under this distribution equals $\sigma/\sqrt{N}$, where N equals the size of the sample randomly selected from the population of interest. The shaded area under the curve in the right tail depicts α; that is, if $\alpha = 0.05$, for example, then the shaded area represents 5 percent of the area under that curve. The z-value that marks off this shaded area to its right is labeled z_c. Whenever the observed sample mean $\overline{X}$ exceeds z_c, our decision is to reject H_0 as implausible. Hence, the shaded area (to the right of z_c) represents the probability of rejecting H_0 as implausible when in fact H_0 is true.

The curve labeled "H$_0$ false (H$_1$ true)" represents the sampling distribution of means given that H$_0$ is false by a difference of δ units. Once again, we know by the central limit theorem that this curve is normal in shape. We also know by the central limit theorem and the rules of transformation, that the mean of the means, $\mu_{\overline{X}}$, under this distribution equals $\mu + \delta$ and that the standard deviation of the means, $\sigma_{\overline{X}}$, under this distribution equals $\sigma/\sqrt{N}$, where N equals the size of the sample randomly selected from the population of interest. (We assume that the curves differ only in their means, by an amount δ, and that their standard deviations are the same.) The cross-hatched area under this curve depicts 1 $- \beta$, the power of the test, because in this area H$_0$ is false and our decision is to reject H$_0$ as implausible since in this area, the observed $\overline{X}$ exceeds z_c. If $1 - \beta = 0.80$, for example, then the shaded area represents 80 percent of the area under that curve.

☞ **Remark.** By separating the two curves by an amount equal to δ units, we are indicating that we wish to find the power associated with this hypothesis test for detecting a difference of δ units from the null hypothesized mean μ. When units are expressed in terms of standard deviation units, the difference of δ units is the effect size. In practice if the effect size is set equal to the minimum-sized difference that the researcher would like to detect as meaningful, and if the power of the hypothesis test is adjusted to detect that effect size as statistically significant, then only meaningful or important effects, as judged by the researcher, should be declared statistically significant. In general, such practice will avoid the problem of detecting trivially important effects to be statistically significant. Effects that are trivially important are just that, even in the face of statistical significance. Hence, effects that are statistically significant but trivially important should not be declared significant in the broad sense of the term. To be truly significant, an effect should be both statistically and practically significant.

If we wish to adjust power to detect differences that are deemed to be important, we must understand the factors that influence power. Using Figures 10.10 through 10.12 in conjunction with Figure 10.9 we shall illustrate that the size of the cross-hatched area, the area that represents the power of the test, will vary as a function of α, δ, and $\sigma_{\overline{X}}$. That is, we shall illustrate that, all things being equal, if the value of any one of the parameters, α, δ, or $\sigma_{\overline{X}}$, changes, the result will be a change in the proportion of the cross-hatched area under the curve: that is, the power of the test.

INCREASING THE LEVEL OF SIGNIFICANCE, α

If we hold δ and $\sigma_{\overline{X}}$ to be the same as in Figure 10.9, but we increase α, the level of significance, to α', then the shaded area associated with the level of significance in Figure 10.10 exceeds that of Figure 10.9. If we compare Figure 10.9 with Figure 10.10, we may note that an increase in the level of significance, while keeping δ and $\sigma_{\overline{X}}$ the same, increases the proportion of cross-hatched area under the H$_0$ false curve. Said differently, *an increase in the level of significance of a hypothesis test, with δ and $\sigma_{\overline{X}}$ held constant, will increase the power of that test.* Because, as noted earlier, however, levels of significance greater than 0.10 are seldom used, an increase in α to achieve greater power is self-limiting.

INCREASING THE EFFECT SIZE, δ

If we hold α and $\sigma_{\overline{X}}$ to be the same as in Figure 10.9, but we increase δ, the effect size to δ', then in Figure 10.11, the cross-hatched area associated with the power of the test will increase. Said differently, *an increase in the minimum effect size, the minimum difference in population means that we would like to detect by a hypothesis test, with α and $\sigma_{\overline{X}}$ held constant, will increase the power of that test.* Because there are specific, minimum-sized differences in population means that a researcher would like to detect as meaningful, the effect size, like the level of significance, cannot be set to be arbitrarily large for the sake of increasing power.

DECREASING THE STANDARD ERROR OF THE MEAN, $\sigma_{\overline{X}}$

If we hold α and δ to be the same as in Figure 10.9, but decrease $\sigma_{\overline{X}}$, the standard error of the means, to $\sigma'_{\overline{X}}$ then in Figure 10.12, the cross-hatched area associated with the power of the test will increase. Said differently, *an increase in the standard error of the means, $\sigma_{\overline{X}}$, with α and δ held constant, will decrease the power of the test.* Furthermore, because $\sigma_{\overline{X}} = \sigma/\sqrt{N}$, a simple way to decrease $\sigma_{\overline{X}}$ is by increasing the sample size, N. Thus, *an increase in sample size N, with α and δ held constant, will increase the power of the test.*

Of the three factors shown to affect the power of a test, the level of significance α, the effect size δ, and the standard error of the means, $\sigma_{\overline{X}} = \sigma/\sqrt{N}$, an increase in sample size, N, is usually the most viable in producing an increase in power.

In practice, given a specified α-value, one should set the power of the test to detect a difference from the null hypothesis that is of practical importance. As noted earlier, this approach can avoid detecting trivially small departures from the null hypothesis as statistically significant. The usual procedure is to set α, to decide on the appropriate effect size worth detecting, and to find the sample size N that will decrease the standard error of the means sufficiently to achieve the desired power. A number of computer programs are available both commercially and from the Internet that are designed to help researchers find the sample size required to achieve a desired power with specified α and δ. In the next chapter, we will show how this may be accomplished using R commands. Before the availability of such computer programs, Cohen's (1988) book of power tables was a popular reference for making these determinations.

To give some perspective on the sample size required to obtain a power of 0.80, the customary value used for power analyses, to detect a small, medium, and large effect given $\alpha = 0.05$, two-tailed, we present Table 10.2.

TABLE 10.2 Approximate sample sizes required to obtain a power of 0.80 for different effect sizes when $\alpha = 0.05$

Effect size (Cohen's d)	Sample size (N)
0.20	196
0.50	31
0.80	12

☞ **Remark.**

For other values of Cohen's d, when $\alpha = 0.05$ and the alternative hypothesis is non-directional, we may use the following equation to find N to achieve a power of 0.80:

$$\sqrt{N} = \frac{2.80}{d}. \tag{10.4}$$

TABLE 10.3 Effect size indices and guidelines for judging their magnitudes

	Index	Small	Medium	Large
t-test for means	d	0.20	0.50	0.80
t-test for correlations	r	0.10	0.30	0.50
F-test for regression	f^2	0.02	0.15	0.35
F-test for ANOVA	f	0.10	0.25	0.40
chi-square	w	0.10	0.30	0.50

In succeeding chapters, as we learn about additional tests of inference for testing hypotheses, different effect size indices other than the one discussed in this chapter will be appropriate. These are given in Table 10.3 (Cohen, 1988) along with guidelines that may be useful for evaluating their magnitude.

CLOSING REMARKS

This chapter has been concerned with inferences involving the population mean based on interval estimation and the null hypothesis testing procedure. For some time now, and with greater frequency more recently, the null hypothesis testing procedure has been the subject of much scrutiny and public debate (Bakan, 1966; Carver, 1978; Cohen, 1990, 1994; Falk & Greenbaum, 1995; Hagen, 1997; Harlow, Mulaik, & Steiger, 1997; Kaplan, 1964; Kirk, 1996; Lykken, 1968; Meehl, 1967; Rosnow & Rosenthal, 1989; Rozeboom, 1960; Thompson, 1994, 1996).

Intended as a method of ruling out chance as an explanation of observed results, the null hypothesis testing procedure has become, since its introduction by Fisher in the 1920s, a ubiquitous technique in the behavioral sciences. Not only is it "identified with 'scientific method,' but it is so mechanically applied that it undermines the very spirit of scientific inquiry" (Kaplan, 1964, p. 29). For this reason, in this chapter we have taken care to point out some of the pitfalls associated with using the null hypothesis testing procedure in so purely a mechanical way.

We reiterate that statistical significance without practical significance does not advance our knowledge regarding the truths concerning phenomena of interest, and that practical significance may be established only through an interplay of strong theories, critical thinking, and subjective judgment. To have greatest impact on a field of inquiry, the research process must be a process in the true sense of the word. It must rely on scientific principles and formulations, but it must also engage the researchers with all their good judgment, creative energies, and content area expertise. As Kaplan (1964) suggests, "Electronic computers, game-theoretic models, and statistical formulas are but instruments after all; it is not *they* that produce scientific results but the investigator who uses them scientifically" (p. 29; italics in original).

In the remainder of this book we present some of the instruments of scientific inquiry and rely upon you, our reader, to provide your own good judgment, creative energies, and content area expertise to use these instruments scientifically.

SUMMARY OF R COMMANDS

(See also the .R-file for Chapter 10.)

Create	Command lines
Figure 10.1	curve(dnorm, c(−4, 4), xlim = c(−4,4), main = "Critical Values for the Standard Normal Distribution", ylab = "Density", xlab = "", axes = F) box() axis(2) axis(1, at = c(−1.96, 0, 1.96), labels = c(expression (paste(mu,"−1.96",sigma[xbar])), expression(mu), expression(paste(mu,"+1.96",sigma[xbar])))) cord.x = c(1.96,seq(1.96,4,length = 100),4) cord.y = c(0,dnorm(seq(1.96,4,length = 100), 0, 1),0) polygon(cord.x, cord.y, col="grey") cord.x2 = c(−4,seq(−4,−1.96,length = 100),−1.96) cord.y2 = c(0,dnorm(seq(−4,−1.96,length = 100), 0, 1),0) polygon(cord.x2, cord.y2, col="grey")
Figure 10.4	curve(dnorm(x, mean = 500, sd = 2.5), c(490, 510), xlim = c(490,510), main = "Area under the curve to the right of a mean of 505", ylab = "Density", xlab = "") cord.x = c(505,seq(505,510,length = 100),510) cord.y = c(0,dnorm(seq(505,510,length = 100), 500, 2.5),0) polygon(cord.x, cord.y, col="grey")
Figure 10.5	curve(dnorm(x, mean = 500, sd = 2.5), c(490, 510), xlim = c(490,510), main = "Area under the curve to the right of a mean of 502", ylab = "Density", xlab = "") cord.x = c(502,seq(502,510,length = 100),510) cord.y = c(0,dnorm(seq(502,510,length = 100), 500, 2.5),0) polygon(cord.x, cord.y, col="grey")
Figure 10.6	curve(dnorm(x, mean = 100, sd = .45), c(98, 102), xlim = c(98,102), main = "Area under the curve to the right of a mean of 101", ylab = "Density", xlab = "") cord.x = c(101,seq(101,102,length = 100),101) cord.y = c(0,dnorm(seq(101,102,length = 100), 100, .45),0) polygon(cord.x, cord.y, col="grey")
Figure 10.7	curve(dnorm(x, mean = 280, sd = 2), c(274, 286), xlim = c(274, 286), main = "Critical areas under the curve in both tails", ylab = "Density", xlab = "")

Create	Command lines
	cord.x = c(284,seq(284,286,length = 100),286)
	cord.y = c(0,dnorm(seq(284,286,length = 100), 280, 2),0)
	polygon(cord.x, cord.y, col="grey")
	cord.x2 = c(274,seq(274,276,length = 100),276)
	cord.y2 = c(0,dnorm(seq(274,276,length = 100), 280, 2),0)
	polygon(cord.x2, cord.y2, col="grey")
Calculate the one-tailed *p*-value associated with sample mean 505 in a distribution with $\mu = 500$ and standard error = 2.5	**pnorm(505, mean = 500, sd = 2.5, lower.tail = F)**
Calculate the two-tailed *p*-value associated with sample mean 276 in a distribution with $\mu = 280$ and standard error = 2 (Example 10.3)	**2*pnorm(276, mean = 280, sd = 2)**

EXERCISES

Create a .R file for each exercise that requires the use of R. Run code from the .R file by highlighting or having the cursor on the line of code and hitting **control+enter** on a PC computer keyboard or **command+enter** on a Mac computer keyboard. Save each .R file using a name associated with the Exercise for which it was created. It is recommended that you review the .R file for Chapter 10 located on the textbook's website before completing these exercises. To facilitate doing each exercise, it may be helpful to copy and paste relevant code from the .R file for Chapter 10 into your own .R file and modify them as needed.

10.1 Suppose we want to estimate the mean height μ for American males and we know that the standard deviation σ, for the entire population is 3 inches. We take a random sample of American males of sample size $N = 100$ from this population and find that its sample mean is $\overline{X} = 68$.
  (a) Explain why the normal curve gives a good approximation of the sampling distribution of means.
  (b) Use this information to construct a 90 percent CI for μ.
  (c) To what does the 90 percent refer?
  (d) Can we conclude that 90 percent of the males from this population have heights within the interval of values obtained in part (b)?
  (e) Would the 95 percent CI be longer or shorter?

10.2 Suppose we know that the standard deviation for the IQ of all Americans is $\sigma = 15$ but we do not know the mean IQ score μ. To estimate μ we select a random sample of size $N = 225$ and find that the sample has mean $\overline{X} = 105$.

(a) Use this information to construct a 99 percent CI for μ.

(b) To what does the 99 percent refer?

(c) Can we conclude that 99 percent of the 225 individuals from this sample have IQ's within the interval of values obtained in part (b)?

(d) Can we conclude that we are 99 percent certain that each individual from this population of Americans has an IQ within the interval of values obtained in part (b)?

10.3 Given that $N = 100$, $\sigma = 15$, and $\overline{X} = 92$ for a random sample selected from a given population of values:

(a) Construct a 90 percent CI for the population mean μ.

(b) Using the result of part (a), what would your decision be if you were to run the following hypothesis test at $\alpha = 0.10$?

H_0: $\mu = 96$
H_1: $\mu \neq 96$

(c) Using the result of part (a), what would your decision be if you were to run the following hypothesis test at $\alpha = 0.10$?

H_0: $\mu = 91.5$
H_1: $\mu \neq 91.5$

10.4 In order to estimate the mean air-pollution index μ for Pittsburgh, Pennsylvania, over the past 5 years, we randomly select a sample of $N = 64$ of those days and compute the mean air-pollution index for this sample. Assuming that the sample mean is found to be $\overline{X} = 15$ and the population is known to have a standard deviation of $\sigma = 4$, find a 95 percent CI for μ. Use the confidence interval to determine whether the air-pollution index for the past 5 years is statistically significantly different from 14.

10.5 The Weston, Massachusetts Postal Service is thinking of introducing a training program for their employees on how to sort mail by zip code number in order to increase sorting speed. They know that without any such training their employees sort an average of 600 letters per hour with a standard deviation of 20. A random sample of $N = 400$ postal employees is selected and given the training program. Their average mail-sorting speed at the end of training is recorded as 603. Assume that the standard deviation is no different with training from without training.

(a) State the null and alternative hypotheses in terms of specific values for the population mean for determining whether the training program increases the sorting speed.

(b) Explain why the z-distribution may be used as a basis of the hypothesis test, in this instance, by explaining why the sampling distribution of means is normally or approximately normally distributed.

(c) Calculate the observed z-statistic.

(d) Is the test one- or two-tailed?

(e) Find the p value for conducting a hypothesis test at significance level 0.10 on whether training increases mail-sorting speed.

(f) What can you conclude based on your results in part (e)?

(g) If the result of the hypothesis test is statistically significant, find and interpret an appropriate effect size.

(h) Would you recommend that the town endorse such training? Why or why not?

(i) Could a 90 percent confidence interval have been used to determine whether training increases mail-sorting speed?

10.6 Children graduating from a particular high school district in a disadvantaged area of New York City have on average scored 55 on a standard college-readiness test with a standard deviation of 12. A random sample of 36 students from this district is selected to participate in Project Advance, a special program to help high school students prepare for college. At the end of the project, the 36 students are given the college-readiness test. They obtain a sample mean of $\overline{X} = 56$. Assume that the standard deviation for the population of all students in this district who might participate in Project Advance is no different from that for all those who would not participate ($\sigma = 12$). Conduct a hypothesis test at significance level $\alpha = 0.05$ to determine whether students in this district who participate in Project Advance in general score *higher* on the college-readiness test than those who do not participate. State your conclusions clearly in the context of the problem.

10.7 The average cholesterol level for adults in the United States is known to be 200 mg dl^{-1}. A group of 50 randomly selected adults in the United States participated in a study on the efficacy of diet in reducing cholesterol. They ate a low-fat diet (less than 30 percent of their total daily calories came from fat) for 6 months. After 6 months, their average serum cholesterol level was 185 mg dl^{-1}. Assume that the standard deviation for the population of cholesterol levels for adults in the United States following the diet is the same as it is for all adults in the United States, $\sigma = 50$, and that the distribution of cholesterol levels for the population of adults in the United States following the diet is normally distributed.

(a) Conduct a hypothesis test at significance level $\alpha = 0.05$ to determine whether adults following the diet have significantly *lower* cholesterol levels than 200 mg dl^{-1}, on average. State your conclusions clearly in the context of the problem.

(b) If the result in part (a) is statistically significant, find and interpret the effect size, classifying its magnitude according to Cohen's scale. Does the effect size indicate that the result is practically significant?

10.8 You are dean of a college that has just admitted 1,000 first-year students, and you want to know whether these students have a scholastic aptitude (as measured on a standard scholastic aptitude test) *different* from that of previous first-year classes. You pick a random sample of size $N = 81$ from the new class and give them the scholastic aptitude test on which previous first-year classes scored a mean of 100. Assume that this entire first-year class would have a standard deviation of $\sigma = 9$ on this test if they all took it.

(a) Construct a 95 percent CI for the mean scholastic aptitude for all 1,000 current first-year students if the sample mean is 101.5.

(b) Use the confidence interval to determine whether the current first-year students, on average, have a scholastic aptitude *different* from that of previous first-year classes. If their average is statistically significantly different from that of previous first-year classes, determine whether it is statistically significantly higher or lower.

(c) If the result is statistically significant, approximate and describe the effect size.

(d) The 90 percent confidence interval for the mean scholastic aptitude for all 1,000 current first-year students would be:
1. longer (wider) than the 95 percent confidence interval,
2. shorter (narrower) than the 95 percent confidence interval,
3. the same as the 95 percent confidence interval.

(e) If the sample selected had been smaller, but with the same mean and standard deviation as in the original analysis, the 95 percent confidence interval for the mean scholastic aptitude for all 1,000 current first-year students would be:
1. longer
2. shorter
3. the same

(f) If everything had been the same as in the original analysis, except that the standard deviation had been 10 instead of 9, then the 95 percent confidence interval for the mean scholastic aptitude for all 1,000 current first-year students would have been:
1. longer
2. shorter
3. the same

10.9 A test of general intelligence is known to have a mean of 100 and a standard deviation of 15 for the population at large. You believe that students at the university where you teach have a *different* mean on this test. To test this belief, you randomly select a sample of 36 students at your university and give them this test of general intelligence. Assume that the standard deviation of your university's students is no different from that of the population at large and that your sample result is $\overline{X} = 106$. Construct a 90 percent confidence interval and use it to test your belief. State your conclusions clearly in the context of the problem. If the result is statistically significant, calculate and interpret the effect size.

10.10 Curriculum planners decided to determine whether a curriculum change should be instituted to increase the reading comprehension of eighth graders in Seattle, Washington. The mean reading-comprehension score under the old curriculum was 92 on the Stanford Secondary School Comprehension Test. After the new curriculum was used for one term, the mean of a sample of 400 students was 95. Assume that the standard deviation for the entire population of eighth graders in Seattle is the same under the new curriculum as under the old ($\sigma = 10$). Test at significance level 0.01 whether there would be an *improvement* in reading comprehension in general if the entire population of eighth graders in Seattle were taught using the new curriculum. State your conclusions clearly in the context of the problem. If the result is statistically significant, calculate and interpret the effect size. Could a confidence interval have been used to answer the research question? Explain.

10.11 A publishing company has just published a new college textbook. Before the company decides to charge $79 for the textbook, it wants to know the average price of all such textbooks in the market, to determine whether it is statistically significantly different from $79. The research department at the company takes a random sample of

40 such textbooks and collects information on their prices. This information produced a mean price of $76.40 for the sample. Assume that the standard deviation of the prices of all such textbooks is $7.50. Test at a significance level of 0.05 whether the mean price of all such textbooks is different from $79. State your conclusions clearly in the context of the problem. If the result is statistically significant, calculate and interpret the effect size.

10.12 Explain why $z_c = 1.96$ for a 95 percent CI.

10.13 Given the scenario of Exercise 10.9, assume that the students at the university where you teach have a higher mean on this test. Would the *power* of the test have been less, the same, or greater had you wanted to determine whether the students had a higher mean on this test, instead of whether the students had a different mean on this test? Explain.

10.14 If you want to conduct a test with power approximately 0.80 on a single population mean using $\alpha = 0.05$, what is the sample size you need under the following conditions?

(a) Based on a review of the literature, you decide to set up your study to detect (with probability 0.80) an effect size equal to $d = 0.50$.

(b) What would be the sample size needed if instead you set the effect size to be detected equal to $d = 0.30$?

INFERENCES INVOLVING THE MEAN WHEN σ IS NOT KNOWN: ONE- AND TWO-SAMPLE DESIGNS

In the previous chapter, we presented a statistical model for answering questions about a single population mean μ when σ was known. Because σ usually is not known in practice, we present in this chapter a statistical model that is appropriate for answering questions about a single population mean when σ is not known. We also present two other statistical models that are appropriate for answering questions about the equality of two population means. In one model the groups representing the two populations are related to each other and in the other they are not. In later chapters, we consider different research questions that involve different designs and different parameters of interest (including, for example, the mean, variance, and correlation), and we present statistical models appropriate to each situation. In general, you will find that by knowing the features of a particular design as well as the parameter of interest, you will be able to make sense of the array of statistical models presented and choose one or more that are appropriate to a given situation.

SINGLE SAMPLE DESIGNS WHEN THE PARAMETER OF INTEREST IS THE MEAN AND σ IS NOT KNOWN

As you should have noted in Chapter 10, which, in part, dealt with questions about the mean of a single population, a wide range of questions may be addressed by studies that are carried out to estimate or test the value of a single population mean. While the type of questions we will address in this section are like those addressed in Chapter 10, different, and more realistic, assumptions are made in this section about the nature of our data. These different assumptions change the procedures for estimating or testing the value of the single population mean.

In Chapter 10 we assumed that σ, the standard deviation of the population, was known so that we could use the central limit theorem to justify the use of the normal distribution of the sampling distribution of means and to compute the standard error, $\sigma_{\overline{X}} = \dfrac{\sigma}{\sqrt{N}}$.

We used the z-test, $z = (\overline{X} - \mu)/\left(\dfrac{\sigma}{\sqrt{N}}\right)$, provided in Equation 10.2 of Chapter 10 to determine how deviant a particular sample mean $\overline{X}$ is from the population mean μ. Because, in most cases, however, the value of σ is not known, in this chapter we introduce another way to describe the sampling distribution of means, one that does not rely on knowledge of σ. As we shall see, when the parent population is normally distributed, but when σ is not known, we can use what is called *Student's t-* (or just *t-*) *distribution* to describe the sampling distribution of means.

In this section we will use the t-distribution to determine whether adult African American males, on average, have a systolic blood pressure that is different from the general population of adult American males; whether college-bound females from the South who have always been at grade level take three years of mathematics in high school, on average; and, whether college-bound males from the South who have always been at grade level take more than three years of mathematics in high school, on average.

For all questions regarding a single population mean, we can represent the null and alternative hypotheses as follows:

H_0: $\mu = c$
H_1: $\mu \neq c$ or H_1: $\mu < c$ or H_1: $\mu > c$

where c is a specified number.

THE t-DISTRIBUTION

From Chapter 9 we know that $\hat{\sigma}^2$ calculated from sample data is an unbiased estimator of σ^2, the population variance for the distribution underlying the data. If we substitute $\hat{\sigma}$ for σ in the z-test equation, we obtain a new statistic called Student's t, or simply t, as our measure of sample mean deviation from μ. Equation 11.1 displays the equation for the t-statistic for the one-sample t-test:

$$t = (\overline{X} - \mu) \left/ \left(\frac{\hat{\sigma}}{\sqrt{N}} \right) \right. = \frac{\overline{X} - \mu}{\hat{\sigma}_{\overline{X}}} \tag{11.1}$$

Although the t statistic resembles the z statistic in form, there is an important difference between them. In the z statistic, the numerator $\overline{X} - \mu$ depends on the particular sample selected, because $\overline{X}$ is the sample mean. Hence, the value of $\overline{X} - \mu$ will in general vary from one sample to another. The denominator $\frac{\sigma}{\sqrt{N}}$ of the z-statistic, however, depends only on the population parameter σ and the sample size N and, therefore, will stay constant from sample to sample. By contrast, both numerator $\overline{X} - \mu$ *and* denominator $\frac{\hat{\sigma}}{\sqrt{N}}$ of the t-statistic depend on the particular sample selected, and therefore, in general, both will vary from sample to sample.

Because the t-statistic appears to be a reasonable measure of sample-mean deviation that may be used in place of the z-statistic when σ is not known, we should be interested in knowing the shape of the t-distribution. Because of the differences between the z- and t-statistics, we should not expect the t-distribution to have exactly the same shape as the z. In fact, as discovered by a young chemist named William Sealy Gosset in the early twentieth century, they do not. His results appeared in a short paper entitled "The probable error of the mean," published in the journal, *Biometrika* in 1908 (Salsburg, 2001). Because the company he worked for, the Guinness Brewing Company of Dublin, Ireland, prohibited its employees from publishing, Gosset published under the pseudonym "Student." He chose that pseudonym because he considered himself to be a student of statistics: hence the name given to this distribution.

Gosset set up a normal parent population, empirically selected random samples of size N from this population, and computed a t-statistic as given in Equation 11.1 for each sample selected. He then constructed a distribution of these t-statistics and found it to be generally similar in shape to the standard normal curve distribution but flatter at its center and taller in its tails. When different sample sizes N were used, he obtained distributions with slightly different shapes, indicating that there are really many t-distributions, one for each sample size N. He also found that the family of t-distributions varies not by their sample size N but, rather, as a function of their sample size, called their degrees of freedom, symbolized by df or by the Greek letter v (read: nu).

DEGREES OF FREEDOM FOR THE ONE-SAMPLE t-TEST

The number of degrees of freedom of a statistic not only depends on the number of observations in the sample (N), but also considers other factors that tend to affect the sampling distribution. The number of degrees of freedom of a statistic is the number of *independent pieces* of information used in computing that statistic.

The t-statistic, as given in Equation 11.1, relies on the square root of the variance estimator, $\hat{\sigma}$, which was presented in Chapter 3, and reproduced here as Equation 11.2:

$$\hat{\sigma} = \sqrt{\frac{\sum (X_i - \overline{X})^2}{N - 1}}. \tag{11.2}$$

From Equation 11.2 it appears at first glance that the value of $\hat{\sigma}$ depends on N independent pieces of information: $d_1 = X_1 - \overline{X}, d_2 = X_2 - \overline{X}, d_3 = X_3 - \overline{X}, ..., d_N = X_N - \overline{X}$. Recall, however, that the sum of all deviations about the mean must equal 0 ($\sum d_i = 0$), so that if we know $N - 1$ of the d_is, then the Nth, or last one, must be completely determined by them.

For example, suppose you are told to make up a set of five scores using any numbers you desire, provided that the scores have a mean of 3. Suppose that as your first four numbers you freely and arbitrarily select the numbers 4, 2, 7, and 1. Accordingly, $d_1 = X_1 - \overline{X} = 4 - 3 = 1, d_2 = -1, d_3 = 4, d_4 = -2$. Do you now have the same freedom of choice in selecting the fifth score to complete the set? Clearly you do not. The only score that will be consistent with $\sum d_i = 0$, is $X_5 = 1$, making $d_5 = -2$. In short, you had no freedom in selecting the fifth, or last, score; the choice was determined by the fact that the mean had been specified. Thus, with a specified mean, required for the estimation of the variance, there are only four degrees of freedom for selecting a set of five scores. In general, with a specified mean, there are only $N - 1$ degrees of freedom for selecting a set of N scores.

When σ is not known, the number of degrees of freedom associated with the one-sample t-statistic for μ is $df = N - 1$ when either constructing a confidence interval or carrying out a hypothesis test.

☞ **Remark.** In general, t-distribution curves resemble the standard normal curve in that they are symmetric and unimodal, but they are flatter at the middle and taller in the tails. The mean of a t-distribution with any number of degrees of freedom df is

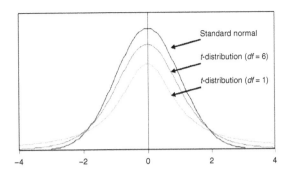

Figure 11.1 Comparison of two t-curves with the standard normal curve

0, the same mean as in the standard normal curve. The variance of t-distribution, however, is not always 1, as it is in the standard normal curve. For a t-distribution with more than two degrees of freedom ($df > 2$), the variance is $\dfrac{df}{df - 2}$. The smaller the value of df, the larger the variance; and as df becomes large, the variance of the t-distribution approaches 1, the variance of the standard normal curve. As a matter of fact, as the number of degrees of freedom df increases, the t-distribution itself approaches the standard normal curve; that is, the t-distribution has the standard normal curve as a limiting curve (see Figure 11.1).

In addition to R, we may use Table C.2 in Appendix C to obtain t-distribution values for right-tail areas. That is, the t-value that has 0.05 of the area to its right under a distribution with 10 degrees of freedom, for example, may be found in Table C.2 at the intersection of the row labeled $df = 10$ and column labeled 0.05. This t-value is 1.812. With an infinite number of df, the t-value with 0.05 of the area to its right is 1.645, which, as you will recall, equals the z-value with 0.05 of the area to its right under the standard normal distribution, thus confirming that as the degrees of freedom increase, the t-distribution approaches the standard normal distribution. Table C.2 may also be used to find approximate p-values corresponding to approximate t-values.

VIOLATING THE ASSUMPTION OF A NORMALLY DISTRIBUTED PARENT POPULATION IN THE ONE-SAMPLE t-TEST

The t-distribution defines a sampling distribution of means when the parent population, that is, the distribution underlying the data, is normally distributed and when σ needs to be estimated from sample data. If Gosset had not placed a restriction of normality on the parent population, however, he would not have been able to determine the distribution of t-statistics in a simple form. Although the requirement of normality in the parent population may seem too limiting to be useful in practice, it is often actually a reasonable assumption to make. As we mentioned in our discussion of normal curves, many natural occurrences due to chance give rise to normally distributed probability curves. In addition, even when the parent population is not normally distributed, it can be shown mathematically that for a sufficiently large sample size N, the t-distribution will not be affected appreciably by violations of the normality assumption.

In general, the more the parent population deviates from normality, the larger the sample size must be to apply the t-distribution to determine sample-mean deviation. For this reason, there is no specific sample size above which deviation from normality in the parent population can always be ignored. It has been found, however, that unless the parent population deviates radically from normality, a sample of size 30 or larger will be sufficient to compensate for lack of normality in the parent population. It is therefore a good idea in general to use samples of size 30 or larger. In practice, however, this is not a real restriction because the sample size necessary to obtain reasonably high power when using the null hypothesis test procedure almost always exceeds 30, as does the sample size necessary to obtain reasonably high precision when constructing a confidence interval.

CONFIDENCE INTERVALS FOR THE ONE-SAMPLE t-TEST

We may construct confidence intervals about μ using the t-distribution when the parent population is known to be normally distributed (or the sample size is sufficiently large) and when σ needs to be estimated using sample data. We could use Equation 11.3 to find the confidence intervals by hand:

$$\begin{aligned}\text{upper limit} &= \overline{X} + t_c\hat{\sigma}_{\overline{X}} \\ \text{lower limit} &= \overline{X} - t_c\hat{\sigma}_{\overline{X}}\end{aligned} \tag{11.3}$$

☞ **Remark.** The confidence interval based on the t-distribution is obtained by hand using Equation 11.3 instead of Equation 10.1. You will note that by contrast to Equation 10.1, Equation 11.3 uses t_c, the critical value from the t-distribution, instead of z_c, the critical value from the standard normal distribution, and $\hat{\sigma}_{\overline{X}}$ instead of $\sigma_{\overline{X}}$.

To find the value of t_c using R we can use the functions called **pt**, and **qt**. As shown in Example 11.1, by specifying the degrees of freedom and the p-value, we may use **qt** to obtain the critical t-value of interest.

EXAMPLE 11.1 Construct a 95 percent confidence interval using the data given below to determine whether adult African American males, on average, have a systolic blood pressure that is different from the general population of adult American males, which is known to be 120 mmHg. The data are based on a sample of 21 African American adult males selected randomly from the population of African American adult males. These data come from the Data and Story Library (DASL) website.

Systolic blood pressure (mmHg)

| 107 | 110 | 123 | 129 | 112 | 111 | 107 | 112 | 135 | 102 | 123 |
| 109 | 112 | 102 | 98 | 114 | 119 | 112 | 110 | 117 | 130 | |

Solution If we knew σ, the standard deviation of the parent population, we would use the central limit theorem and proceed as we did in Chapter 10, using Equation 10.1, to construct the desired 95 percent confidence interval. Because we do not know σ, however, we estimate it as $\hat{\sigma}$ using Equation 11.2. We then construct the 95 percent confidence interval based on the t-distribution using Equation 11.3.

For these data,

$$\overline{X} = (107 + 110 + 123 + 129 + 112 + 111 + 107 + 112 + 135 + 102 + 123 + 109$$
$$+112 + 102 + 98 + 114 + 119 + 112 + 110 + 117 + 130)/21 = 114$$

$$\hat{\sigma}^2 = [(107 - 114)^2 + (110 - 114)^2 + (123 - 114)^2 + (129 - 114)^2 + \cdots$$
$$+ (112 - 114)^2 + (110 - 114)^2 + (117 - 114)^2 + (130 - 114)^2]/(21 - 1)$$
$$= 92.16$$

$$\hat{\sigma} = \sqrt{92.16} = 9.60; \; \hat{\sigma}_{\overline{X}} = \frac{\hat{\sigma}}{\sqrt{N}} = \frac{9.60}{\sqrt{21}} = 2.10.$$

To find the critical t-value, t_c, we make use of either R or Table C.2 from Appendix C.

To use R, we use the **qt(p, df, lower.tail = F)** function, where p is the proportion of area (or probability) to the right of the t-value. Because we want the 95 percent CI, we need the t values that mark off 0.025 area in each of the two tails.

MORE R: To calculate the t-value with 0.025 area to its right, type the following syntax into your .R file, and press **command+enter** (on a Mac) or **control-R** (on a PC) or type directly into the console:

qt(0.025, 20, lower.tail = F)

The console will list the t-value with 0.975 area to its left (or 0.025 of its area to the right) as 2.086.

To use Table C.2 in Appendix C to find the critical t-value, we refer to the value at the intersection of the row labeled $df = 20$ and the column labeled 0.025. Like the **qt** function in R, the p-value in Table C.2 marks off that proportion of area (or probability) under the t-distribution to its right. The t-value from Table C.2 that marks off 0.025 area to its right is 2.086, which agrees with the value obtained from R. Because of symmetry we know that the t-value that marks off 0.025 of the area under the t-distribution to its left is –2.086. To calculate upper and lower limits we use only the positive t-value:

lower limit = $\overline{X} - t_c\hat{\sigma}_{\overline{X}} = 114 - t_c(2.10) = 114 - (2.086)(2.10) = 114 - 4.38 = 109.62$,

upper limit = $\overline{X} + t_c\hat{\sigma}_{\overline{X}} = 114 + t_c(2.10) = 114 + (2.086)(2.10) = 114 + 4.38 = 118.38$.

Accordingly, the 95 percent confidence interval for μ in this case is (109.62, 118.38). Because $\mu = 120$ does not fall within this interval, it is not a plausible value of the population mean systolic blood pressure for adult African American males, at an α equal to 0.05. Based on the interval, plausible population mean values fall in the range from 109.62 to 118.38, and suggest that the mean systolic blood pressure for adult African American males is statistically significantly lower than 120, at an α equal to 0.05.

Alternatively, we may use R to obtain the confidence interval directly. These data may be found in the Blood dataset. First, we run the following syntax to examine the descriptive statistics for the variable systolc1, including its skewness ratio. To keep a record of the steps we are taking for this analysis, and to facilitate being able to run these steps again in the future, we continue to input the syntax into our .R file:

mean(Blood$systolc1)
sd(Blood$systolc1)
skew(Blood$systolc1)
se.skew(Blood$systolc1)
skew.ratio(Blood$systolc1)

The output for this analysis is as follows:

mean	=	114
sd	=	9.596874
skewness	=	0.56760552
seskew	=	0.50119474
skewness ratio	=	1.1325049

As expected, the mean and standard deviation values are the same as calculated by hand.

The skewness is less than 1 in magnitude and the skewness ratio is less than 2 in magnitude, suggesting that the normality assumption is tenable. To examine, more specifically, the extent to which the systolc1 distribution departs from that of a normal curve, we use graphical methods, and, in particular, the **qqnorm**, **qqline**, and **hist** commands.

Running the syntax **qqnorm(Blood$systolc1)** and **qqline(Blood$systolc1)** from our .R file, we obtain a plot of the quantiles (percentiles) of systolc1 against the theoretical quantiles of the normal distribution (q–q plot) (see Figure 11.2). In general, if our variable of interest is normally distributed, the quantiles of that variable will equal the quantiles of a

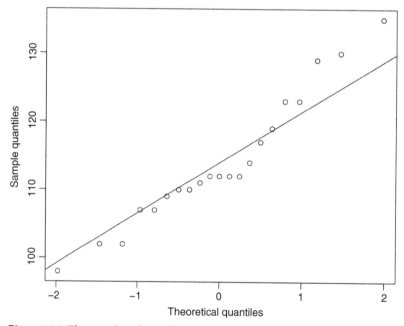

Figure 11.2 The q–q plot of initial blood pressure

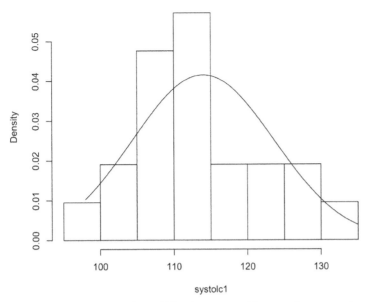

Figure 11.3 Histogram of initial blood pressure with normal curve overlay

normal distribution and the points of the plot will fall along a straight line. Examining the nature of the departure of points from a straight line will allow us to identify the source of our variable's non-normality (e.g., whether it is due to a few or many outliers).

Plotting a histogram with a normal curve, we obtain Figure 11.3.

The slight concave (u-shape) form of the q–q plot and the appearance of the histogram both suggest the slight positive skew of systolc1 as measured by its skewness of 0.57 and skewness ratio of 1.13.

MORE R: To generate the histogram of Figure 11.3, type into the .R file the following commands:

```
hist(Blood$systolc1, freq=F, main = "", xlab = "systolc1")
x = seq(min(Blood$systolc1), max(Blood$systolc1), length = 100)
hx = dnorm(x, mean(Blood$systolc1), sd(Blood$systolc1))
lines(hx~x)
```

In the **hist** command, **freq=F** specifies that we want the scale of the *y*-axis of the histogram not to be a frequency, but rather a density. The F stands for "False." The argument **main = ""** sets the main title of the plot to blank, while **xlab = "systolc1"** sets the *x*-axis label to be systolc1. The **seq** command in the second line generates a sequence of 100 values from the minimum value of systolc1 to the maximum value of systolc1. The **dnorm** command in the third line calculates the height of a normal density curve (with mean and standard deviation equal to the respective mean and standard deviation of systolc1) at each of the sequence of values just generated. The **lines** command in the fourth line of code plots the normal density across the sequence of values with a smooth line.

Based on these graphical and statistical analyses, we conclude that the assumption of the normality of systolc1 underlying the one-sample t-test is tenable, and we continue to construct the desired confidence interval using R.

MORE R: Constructing the 95 percent confidence interval.

To obtain the 95 percent CI for μ when σ is not known for a one-sample design, we type the following command into our .R-file and run:

t.test(Blood$systolc1)

or

t.test(Blood$systolc1)$conf.int

The use of the one-sample test is dictated by the fact that our design contains only one sample in this case. We obtain the R output in the console:

One sample t-test		
data: Blood$systolcl		
$t = 54.436$	$df = 20$	p-value < 2.2e-16
alternative hypothesis: true mean is not equal to 0		
95 percent confidence interval:	109.6316	118.3684
sample estimates:	mean of x	114

The 95 percent confidence interval from R (109.6316, 118.3684) agrees within rounding error with the interval we obtained by hand.

• •

EXAMPLE 11.2 Use R to construct a 95 percent CI to estimate the population mean number of units (years) of mathematics taken in high school by females who live in the South. Recall that the population of such students is defined as those who responded to all four administrations of the NELS survey, who were always at grade level, and who pursued some form of post-secondary education. Assume that σ is not known and that it needs to be estimated from the sample data. Note that the data on math units taken were collected originally by the National Assessment of Educational Progress (NAEP) and then incorporated into the NELS dataset.

Solution If we knew σ, the standard deviation of the parent population, we would use the central limit theorem and proceed as we did in Chapter 10, using Equation 10.1, to construct the desired 95 percent confidence interval. Because we do not know σ, however, we construct the 95 percent confidence interval based on the t-distribution. This construction is readily performed using R.

To get a sense of our data, and to check on the tenability of the underlying normality assumption, we obtain descriptive statistics for our variable, unitmath, using the commands:

mean(NELS$unitmath)
sd(NELS$unitmath)
skew(NELS$unitmath)
se.skew(NELS$unitmath)
skew.ratio(NELS$unitmath)

To obtain the descriptive statistics only for girls in the South, we include the syntax **[NELS $gender == "Female" & NELS$region == "South"]** when we refer to the variable NELS $unitmath as follows:

mean(NELS$unitmath[NELS$gender == "Female" & NELS$region == "South"])
sd(NELS$unitmath[NELS$gender == "Female" & NELS$region == "South"])
skew(NELS$unitmath[NELS$gender == "Female" & NELS$region == "South"])
se.skew(NELS$unitmath[NELS$gender == "Female" & NELS$region == "South"])
skew.ratio(NELS$unitmath[NELS$gender == "Female" & NELS$region == "South"])

The following are the summary statistics for gender=="Female" & region=="South":

> mean = 3.664048

> sd = 0.7225592

> skewness = 0.11980437

> seskew = 0.26265054

> skewness ratio = 0.45613602.

Recall that the standard deviation given in the R output is $\hat{\sigma}$. Thus, we know that $N = 84$, $\overline{X} = 3.66$, $\hat{\sigma} = 0.72$, and skewness = 0.12. Using the commands:

qqnorm(NELS$unitmath[NELS$gender == "Female" & NELS$region == "South"])

and

qqline(NELS$unitmath[NELS$gender == "Female" & NELS$region == "South"])

the skewness statistic, as well as the q–q plot in Figure 11.4, suggest that our normality assumption for this sample of unitmath scores is tenable. Furthermore, the sample of size 84 is sufficiently large to warrant the use of the t-distribution in this case.

The q-q plot looks the way it does in Figure 11.4 because unitmath is a ratio-level variable consisting only of integers.

We use R to construct the 95 percent confidence interval as before. Once again, the use of the one-sample t-test is dictated by the fact that our design contains only one sample in this case. From the command:

t.test(NELS$unitmath[NELS$gender == "Female" & NELS$region == "South"])

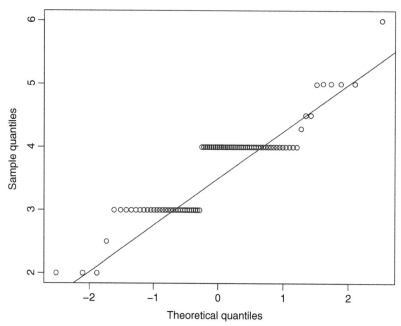

Figure 11.4 The q–q plot (using the commands **qqnorm** and **qqline**) of unitmath

we obtain the following output:

One sample *t*-test
data: NELS$unitmath[NELS$gender == "Female" & NELS$region = "South"]
$t = 46.476$ $df = 83$ *p*-value < 2.2e-16
alternative hypothesis: true mean is not equal to 0
95 percent confidence interval: 3.507243   3.820853 sample estimates: mean of x   3.664048

Of interest in this example is the 95 percent CI, (3.51, 3.82). In other words, it is plausible that the mean number of years of math taken in high school for the population of Southern girls represented by our sample falls between 3.51 and 3.82. Said differently, this result means that if we were to construct an interval estimate of μ for all possible random samples of size 84 from this population, exactly 95 percent of all these interval estimates would in fact contain μ and only 5 percent would not. Does this estimate surprise you? Would you have expected college-bound females from the South to take fewer or more years of math in high school?

EXAMPLE 11.3 Use the same data as in Example 11.2 to construct a 99 percent CI about μ.

MORE R: To obtain the 99 percent confidence interval about μ for the variable unitmath, type the following command into your .R file and run:

t.test(NELS$unitmath[NELS$gender == "Female" & NELS$region == "South"], conf.level = 0.99)

In so doing, we obtain the following results:

One sample *t*-test

---

data: NELS$unitmath[NELS$gender == "Female" & NELS$region == "South"]

t = 46.476   df = 83   p-value < 2.2e-16

alternative hypothesis: true mean is not equal to 0

99 percent confidence interval: 3.456202   3.871893
sample estimates: mean of x   3.664048

Notice that the 99 percent CI (3.46, 3.87) is longer than the 95 percent CI. As noted in the previous chapter, if we increase the confidence level, say from 95 percent to 99 percent, and keep the sample size the same, the resulting CI will be longer. Our estimate of μ will then be less precise, but we will be more confident that it is accurate.

HYPOTHESIS TESTS: THE ONE-SAMPLE *t*-TEST

When the parent population is known to be normally distributed (or the sample size is sufficiently large) and when σ is not known and needs to be estimated using sample data, we may conduct hypothesis tests of μ by carrying out a *t*-test (as opposed to the *z*-test described in the previous chapter). A *t*-test is based on the *t*-distribution while the *z*-test is based on the normal distribution. We may ask, as we have done previously, whether adult African American males, on average, have a systolic blood pressure that is different from the general population of adult American males, which is known to be 120 mmHg. In reference to our NELS data, we may ask, for example, whether college-bound females from the South who have always been at grade level take an average of three years of math in high school. We may also ask, among other questions, whether college-bound males from the South who have always been at grade level take an average of more than three years of math in high school. We use R to carry out these tests, but we also carry out the systolic analysis by hand.

••

EXAMPLE 11.4 Use the same data as in Example 11.1 to test, using a one-sample *t*-test, whether adult African American males, on average, have a systolic blood pressure that is different from the general population of adult American males, which is known to be 120 mmHg. Use $\alpha = 0.05$. Carry out the analysis by hand and also by using R.

Solution If we knew σ, the standard deviation of the parent population, we would use the central limit theorem and proceed as we did in Chapter 10 to test these hypotheses. Because we do not know σ, however, we use the *t*-distribution as the basis for the null hypothesis testing procedure in this case. We are warranted to do so because from Example 11.1, we know that our sample is sufficiently symmetric to assume normality.

The null and alternative hypotheses are:

H_0: $\mu = 120$ versus H_1: $\mu \neq 120$.

Based on our earlier calculations in connection with Example 11.1, we know that:

$$\overline{X} = 114; \hat{\sigma}^2 = 92.16; \hat{\sigma} = \sqrt{92.16} = 9.60; \hat{\sigma}_{\overline{X}} = \frac{\hat{\sigma}}{\sqrt{N}} = \frac{9.60}{\sqrt{21}} = 2.10.$$

Using the t-ratio of Equation 11.1, we may determine the number of standard errors the observed sample mean of 114 is from the population mean of 120 as follows:

$$t = (\overline{X} - \mu)/\left(\frac{\hat{\sigma}}{\sqrt{N}}\right) = \frac{\overline{X} - \mu}{\hat{\sigma}_{\overline{X}}} = \frac{114 - 120}{2.10} = -2.86.$$

The t-ratio tells us that the observed mean of 114 is 2.86 standard errors below the hypothesized mean of 120.

To find the p-value associated with this t-ratio, we use R and Table C.2 in Appendix C. In both cases we need the value of the t-ratio and its associated degrees of freedom. We have $t = -2.86$. Given this is a one-sample t-test, $df = N - 1 = 21 - 1 = 20$.

MORE R: To obtain the area to the left of an observed t-value, type **pt(t,df)**, with appropriate values substituted for t and df. This function returns the cumulative (lower or left tail) Student's t-distribution with df degrees of freedom.

Because, for this problem, the degrees of freedom are 20 and the observed t-value is -2.86, we input and run the following command:

pt(−2.86, 20)

The p-value, listed in the console as 0.0048, is a one-tailed value because it represents the area in the left tail only. To find the two-tailed p-value, we multiply 0.0048 by 2 to obtain 0.0096.

To use Table C.2 in Appendix C to find this p-value, we make use of the symmetry of the t-distribution. Because the t-distribution is symmetric, we may ignore the negative sign and look for the printed value closest to 2.86 in Table C.2 to approximate the obtained p-value. We scan the row labeled $df = 20$ in Table C.2 and find that the closest printed t-value to 2.86 is 2.845. This value has 0.005 of the area under the t-distribution to its right. Because the alternative hypothesis is non-directional (H$_1$: $\mu \neq 120$), we multiply this value by 2 to obtain the approximate two-tailed p-value, which is $p = 0.005 \times 2 = 0.010$.

That is, the probability that we have observed a mean at least as extreme as 114 that comes from a population with mean equal to 120 is only 0.01. Because this probability is so small (it is smaller than 0.05), we conclude that it is likely that the population mean is not equal to 120, and we reject the null hypothesis in favor of the alternative. Because the sample mean of 114 is smaller than the null hypothesized value of 120, we conclude that the systolic blood pressure of African American males ($M = 114$, $SD = 9.6$) is statistically significantly lower than 120, the mean for the general population of adult American males, $t(20) = -2.86$, $p = 0.01$.

We now carry out the analysis for this example using R.

MORE R: To find the *p*-value associated with a one-sample *t*-test, type and highlight the command in the .R-file and run:

t.test(Blood$systolc1, mu = 120)

We obtain the following results:

One sample t-test		
data: Blood$systolcl		
t = −2.865 df = 20		p-value = 0.009571
alternative hypothesis: true mean is not equal to 120		
95 percent confidence interval: 109.6316		118.3684
sample estimates: mean of x		114

The observed *t*-value of −2.87 matches the one we obtained by hand within rounding error, and the two-tailed *p*-value of 0.0096 associated with the non-directional alternative hypothesis H_1: $\mu \neq 120$ also agrees with our earlier result. Recall that ≠ stands for "not equal to."

☞ **Remark.** The 95 percent CI does not include the null hypothesis test value of 120. Because the CI contains all values of the null hypothesis that would not be rejected at the 0.05 two-tailed level of significance, the fact that the value of 120 falls outside this CI, we should not be surprised that the hypothesis test, H_0: $\mu = 120$ was rejected in favor of the alternative that H_1: $\mu \neq 120$.

MORE R: To obtain the area to the right of an observed *t*-value.

If our alternative hypothesis were H_1: $\mu \geq 120$, to find the area to the right of the observed *t*-value, we would use R's **pt(t,df, lower.tail = F)** function, which returns the reverse cumulative (upper or right tail) Student's *t*-distribution with *df* degrees of freedom, and input the observed *t*-value and its associated degrees of freedom.

☞ **Remark.** As indicated by Equation 11.1, a *t*-value is simply the ratio of a statistic divided by the standard error of that statistic. In Equation 11.1, that statistic is the mean; however, it need not be. In the case of skewness, by dividing the skewness statistic by its standard error, we are forming a *t*-ratio as well. The skewness ratio (*t*-value) in this case is 1.13, which is not considered to be large given that we typically consider *t*-ratios greater than 2 to be large.

EFFECT SIZE FOR THE ONE-SAMPLE *t*-TEST

In terms of *d*, the effect size for a one-sample *t*-test equals:

$$d = \frac{\overline{X} - \mu}{\hat{\sigma}}.$$

(11.4)

The effect size for the result in Example 11.4 is $d = \dfrac{114 - 120}{9.60} = -0.625$, which indicates that the mean systolic blood pressure of adult African American males is 0.625 standard deviations below 120. This is a moderate to large effect in this case according to Cohen's rule-of-thumb guidelines.

EXAMPLE 11.5 Suppose that a recent survey conducted in the southern region of the United States indicates that college-bound females who have always been at grade level take an average of three years of math in high school. Based on your own personal knowledge and what you have read in the literature, you believe that this is not the case, although you do not know whether the number of years is more or less than 3. Accordingly, you wish to carry out a test to nullify the hypothesis that $H_0: \mu = 3$ in favor of the alternative hypothesis that $H_1: \mu \neq 3$. Use the NELS dataset and set $\alpha = 0.05$.

Solution If we knew σ, the standard deviation of the parent population, we would use the central limit theorem and proceed as we did in Chapter 10 to test these hypotheses. Because we do not know σ, however, we use the t-distribution as the basis for the null hypothesis testing procedure in this case. We are warranted to do so because of the size of our sample ($N = 84$) and the fact that, from Example 11.2, we know that our sample is sufficiently symmetric to assume normality.

We select cases as in Example 11.2. Because the dataset is large, we do not carry out the computations by hand; rather, we use R.

MORE R: To find the p-value associated with the t-test for a subset of cases, type and run the following syntax in the .R file:

t.test(NELS$unitmath[NELS$gender == "Female" & NELS$region == "South"], mu = 3)

We obtain the following results:

One sample t-test		
data: NELS$unitmath[NELS$gender == "Female" & NELS$region == "South"]		
t = 8.423 df = 83		p-value = 9.32e-13
alternative hypothesis: true mean is not equal to 3		
95 percent confidence interval: 3.507243		3.820853
sample estimates: mean of x		3.664048

The t-value is 8.42 with 83 degrees of freedom ($df = N - 1 = 84 - 1 = 83$, in this case) and the p-value (for a two-tailed test) is given in the output as 9.32e-13, which uses scientific notation because the p-value is so small. This value may be re-written as 9.32×10^{-13}, which also may be re-written as 0.000000000000923, obtained by moving the decimal point 13 places to the left. Our conclusion then is to reject the null hypothesis in favor of the alternative that the mean number of units of math taken in high school by southern females is indeed different from 3. Furthermore, because the obtained sample mean is $\overline{X} = 3.66$, we may conclude that the mean number of units of math taken in high school is statistically significantly *higher* than 3.

In terms of d, the effect size equals $d = \dfrac{\overline{X} - \mu}{\hat{\sigma}} = \dfrac{3.66 - 3}{0.72} = 0.92$, which indicates that the mean number of years of math taken by college-bound females from the South who have always stayed on grade level is 0.92 standard deviations larger than 3 and which suggests a large effect in this case according to Cohen's rule-of-thumb guidelines.

☞ **Remark.** If we had used the 95 percent CI that we constructed in Example 11.2 to test H_0: $\mu = 3$ versus H_1: $\mu \neq 3$, we would have arrived at the same conclusion to reject H_0 in favor of H_1 that we did in Example 11.5. That 95 percent CI so constructed in Example 11.2 equals (3.51, 3.82). By the definition of a CI we know that the values falling within the CI (from 3.51 to 3.82) are exactly those values of μ that would *not* be rejected as implausible in a non-directional hypothesis test at significance level 0.05. We also know that the values of μ falling outside the CI are the ones that would be rejected in a non-directional hypothesis test at significance level 0.05. Because the null-hypothesized value of 3 does not fall within the CI, it is not considered to be a plausible value of μ and so must be rejected in the context of a hypothesis test.

· ·

EXAMPLE 11.6 Suppose that a recent survey conducted in the southern region of the United States indicates that college-bound males who have always been at grade level take an average of three years of math in high school. Based on your own personal knowledge and what you have read in the literature, you believe that this is not the case, that, in fact, they take more than 3 years of math in high school. Accordingly, you wish to carry out a test to nullify the hypothesis that H_0: $\mu = 3$ in favor of the alternative hypothesis that H_1: $\mu > 3$. You use the NELS dataset and set $\alpha = 0.05$.

Solution Using the command:

length(NELS\$unitmath[NELS\$gender == "Male" & NELS\$region == "South"])

we find that there are $N = 66$ males in the South, which suggests that the dataset is sufficiently large to justify our use of the t-distribution in this case to test the null hypothesis of interest.

We do not use the z-test because σ is not known and needs to be estimated from the data. We carry out the test to determine whether the amount by which 3.9, the sample mean, exceeds 3 is significant of a real difference or is due only to sampling error. Had the obtained value been less than 3, there would have been no reason to carry out the hypothesis test at all because the null hypothesis would be more plausible than the alternative.

We proceed as in Example 11.5 to find the p-value associated with the t-test (syntax is **t.test(NELS\$unitmath[NELS\$gender == "Male" & NELS\$region == "South"], mu = 3, alternative = "greater")**) and obtain the following results. Note that we now include the argument **alternative = "greater"** to tell R that we are interested in the one-sided alternative hypothesis representing values of μ that are greater than 3.

```
One sample t-test
_____
data: NELS$unitmath[NELS$gender == "Male" & NELS$region == "South"]

t = 10.107          df = 65                      p-value = 2.918e-15

alternative hypothesis: true mean is greater than 3

95 percent confidence interval:   3.765321                    Inf
sample estimates:                  mean of x                  3.916667
```

For this example, we expect the degrees of freedom to be $N - 1 = 66 - 1 = 65$, which is the value reported in the output. The t-value of 10.11 with 65 degrees of freedom has an associated two-tailed p-value of 2.918e-15. Because, in this case, the alternative hypothesis is directional, a one-tailed p-value is most appropriate. Given that the p-value is less than 0.05, we know that our result is statistically significant: that the population of college-bound males in the southern region of the United States takes more than 3 years of math in high school on average.

We could not have used a two-sided confidence interval to determine whether college-bound males from the South take more than 3 years of high school math because two-sided confidence intervals are only equivalent to two-sided hypothesis tests. However, R does output a one-sided confidence interval in its output. Since 3 is not included in this one-sided confidence interval, we may reject the null hypothesis in favor of the alternative at the $\alpha = 0.05$ significance level.

Given that the results of the one-sample t-test are statistically significant, they should be further analyzed for practical significance, using a measure of the magnitude of the effect.

In terms of d, the effect size is $\dfrac{\overline{X} - \mu}{\hat{\sigma}} = \dfrac{3.92 - 3}{0.74} = 1.24$, which indicates that the mean number of years of math taken by college-bound males from the South who have always stayed on grade level is approximately 1.24 standard deviations larger than 3, a very large effect, according to Cohen's rule-of-thumb guidelines, in this case.

TWO-SAMPLE DESIGNS WHEN THE PARAMETER OF INTEREST IS μ, AND σ IS NOT KNOWN

In this section, we expand the number of groups in the design from one to two, and in so doing allow for the possibility of answering a whole different set of questions. As related to the various populations represented by the NELS dataset, we may ask, for example:

1. On average, do college-bound males from the South who have always been on grade level differ in the number of years of math in high school from females from the South?
2. On average, do college-bound females from the Northeast who have always been on grade level who own a computer score higher in twelfth grade math achievement than those who do not own a computer?
3. On average, do college-bound females from the South who have always been on grade level change in self-esteem from eighth grade to twelfth grade?

Each of these questions is concerned with estimating the means of two populations, μ_1 and μ_2, for the purpose of comparing them to each other. In question 1, we may define μ_1 as the mean number of years of math taken in high school by females from the South and μ_2 as the mean number of years of math taken in high school by males from the South. In question 2, we may define μ_1 as the mean math achievement score in twelfth grade for those who own a computer and μ_2 as the mean math achievement score in twelfth grade for those who do not own a computer. Finally, in question 3, we may define μ_1 as the mean self-esteem score of females in eighth grade and μ_2 as the mean self-esteem score of the same females, now in twelfth grade. In each case, we are concerned with knowing whether a difference between the two population means exists; that is, whether it is plausible that the difference between population means is zero. If the difference is not zero, then we would be interested in knowing the magnitude of the difference that exists.

To test whether in fact the two population means μ_1 and μ_2 differ from each other, we begin by estimating μ_1 and μ_2 by $\overline{X}_1$ and $\overline{X}_2$, respectively, where we calculate each sample mean on a sample randomly selected from the appropriate population. We then compute the difference between $\overline{X}_1$ and $\overline{X}_2$. Because our interest is not with the sample mean difference per se, but rather with the population mean difference, we need a procedure for judging whether the sample mean difference is real or merely apparent (due to sampling error). In the last section, when the design involved only one sample and σ was unknown, we used the one-sample t-distribution, the sampling distribution of means when σ is unknown, to determine whether the observed sample mean was statistically significantly different from the hypothesized value, μ. In the present case, our design involves two samples, and we assume that $\sigma_1 = \sigma_2 = \sigma$ and that σ is not known. By analogy, we turn to the sampling distribution of differences between means $\overline{X}_1$ and $\overline{X}_2$ calculated on samples of size N_1 and N_2, respectively, to determine whether the observed difference between sample means is statistically significantly different from the hypothesized difference $\mu_1 - \mu_2$.

INDEPENDENT (OR UNRELATED) AND DEPENDENT (OR RELATED) SAMPLES

To determine whether an observed difference in sample means is large enough to cause us to infer a difference in population means we need first to consider another aspect of study design: the degree to which factors extraneous to the main variable of interest are controlled. We may think of the observed difference in sample means as comprised of two components: a *signal* component that reflects the true difference between sample means in terms of the variable under study (e.g., the number of years of math taken during high school) and a *noise* component that reflects the difference between sample means due to extraneous and random factors (e.g., educational aspirations, academic interests, and career goals). By analogy, we may think of the signal as a radio broadcast and the noise as static in the airwaves. Just as our ability to detect a particular radio signal will depend upon the amount of static present, so our ability to detect a statistical difference will depend upon the degree to which extraneous and random factors have not been controlled.

In question 1 above, if all variables that might impact on the number of years of math taken in high school were the same for males and females (e.g., educational aspirations, academic interests, career goals, and so on), we would say that the system contained little or no noise. In this case, we would have little difficulty detecting the signal, the true difference, no matter how small. On the other hand, if none of the variables that might impact on number of years of math taken in high school were controlled, we would say that the system contained a great deal of noise. In this case, we might have great difficulty detecting the signal, the true difference, no matter how large. In general, the more control we exercise over extraneous factors, the smaller the difference between $\overline{X}_1$ and $\overline{X}_2$ that we will be able to detect as statistically significant (i.e., as significant of a difference between population means).

If, with respect to question 1, a random sample of males were selected and a random sample of females were selected *independently*, extraneous factors such as educational aspirations, academic interests, career goals and the like would not be controlled for explicitly. Any or all of these factors would be considered as noise in the system and they could contribute to the observed difference between $\overline{X}_1$ and $\overline{X}_2$. Explicit control over extraneous factors may be achieved if a random sample of males were selected and a sample of females were then selected in such a way that each female *matched* each male on a one-to-one, pairwise basis with respect to as many of the extraneous factors as possible. A result of such control is a reduction in the noise component and a consequent expectation of smaller differences between means. Accordingly, decisions as to whether a statistical difference is real or apparent (merely due to sampling error) must depend, at least, in part, upon whether the design of the study controls for extraneous factors or not. When the selection of subjects for one sample has no effect whatsoever on the selection of subjects for the second sample (as when the females were selected independently of the males), the two samples are said to be *independent*, or *unrelated*. When the samples are selected in such a way as to allow individual matching into pairs on extraneous factors across samples (as when individuals are matched on educational aspirations, academic interests, career goals, etc.), the two samples are said to be *dependent*, *paired*, or *related*.

A particular case of related samples arises when *the same individuals* are tested twice with an intervening treatment or interval of time (as in question 3). Because measures are taken repeatedly on the same individuals, this type of design is often called a *repeated-measures design*. Although repeated-measures designs do, in general, afford more control than unrelated-samples designs, repeated-measures designs are usually employed to comply with the theoretical framework of the research problem rather than for explicit control.

Because the size of sample mean differences $\overline{X}_1 - \overline{X}_2$ depends in part on whether the design controls for extraneous factors or not (i.e., whether it is based on related or unrelated samples), we must treat the cases of related and unrelated samples separately in our discussion of sampling distributions. We first consider designs that use independent samples.

TABLE 11.1 Descriptive statistics for units of math taken by males and females in the southern region

Gender	N	Mean	SD	Min.	Max.
Male	66	3.9167	0.7368	2	6
Female	84	3.6640	0.7336	2	6

INDEPENDENT SAMPLES *t*-TEST AND CONFIDENCE INTERVAL

In the previous section on the one-sample *t*-test, we determined that southern US college-bound males and females who have always been at grade level each take an average of more than 3 years of math in high school. But, does the population of males differ from the population of females in terms of the number of years of math taken in high school? Questions like these imply a comparison of one group mean to the other, rather than a separate comparison of each group mean to a specified value, three in this case. Furthermore, because the males and females are each selected independently of each other, the appropriate test to answer this question is the independent samples *t*-test.

The sample means and standard deviations of the number of years of high school mathematics taken by both males and females from the South are given in Table 11.1. The R commands to obtain these values are displayed in the Summary of R Commands at the end of this chapter, within the table of independent samples *t*-test commands, and are also available in the .R file for this chapter.

As with the one group *t*-test, our question concerns whether the observed mean difference between males and females (3.92 − 3.66 = 0.26) is large enough to conclude that a real difference exists between males and females in the population. To determine whether it is large enough, we need to extend the procedure we used in relation to the one-sample *t*-test to incorporate the fact that we are now interested in making judgments about differences between means rather than about means alone. Recall that the one-sample *t*-ratio is described by Equation 11.1, as:

$$t = \frac{\overline{X} - \mu}{\hat{\sigma}_{\overline{X}}}.$$

In extending this ratio to the case of mean differences, we simply substitute a mean difference quantity for every instance of a mean. We thus obtain Equation 11.5 as the *t*-ratio that is used to test hypotheses about mean differences on independent samples:

$$t = \frac{(\overline{X}_1 - \overline{X}_2) - (\mu_1 - \mu_2)}{\hat{\sigma}_{\overline{X}_1 - \overline{X}_2}}. \tag{11.5}$$

While the computation of the numerator of this ratio contains no new notation, the denominator requires some explanation. In short, $\hat{\sigma}_{\overline{X}_1 - \overline{X}_2}$ is the standard deviation of the sampling distribution of sample mean differences, also called the standard error of the difference in means. The equation for determining $\hat{\sigma}_{\overline{X}_1 - \overline{X}_2}$ when the variances for the two populations from which the samples are drawn are equal is given as

$$\hat{\sigma}_{\overline{X}_1-\overline{X}_2} = \sqrt{\frac{(N_1-1)\hat{\sigma}_1^2 + (N_2-1)\hat{\sigma}_2^2}{N_1+N_2-2}\left(\frac{1}{N_1}+\frac{1}{N_2}\right)}. \tag{11.6}$$

Equation 11.6 is based on a weighted average of the two variance estimators, $\hat{\sigma}_1^2$ and $\hat{\sigma}_2^2$. Notice that $\hat{\sigma}_1^2$ is weighted by the degrees of freedom of sample one, $N_1 - 1$, and $\hat{\sigma}_2^2$ is weighted by the degrees of freedom of sample two, $N_2 - 1$. The degrees of freedom, $N_1 - 1$ and $N_2 - 1$, for each group respectively is a function of its size. Because, in general, estimators from larger samples are more accurate, Equation 11.6 weights more heavily the estimate that comes from the larger sample.

Substituting Equation 11.6 into Equation 11.5, we present an alternate version of the t-statistic for the two-population, unrelated-samples case with homogeneous variances as

$$t = \frac{(\overline{X}_1 - \overline{X}_2) - (\mu_1 - \mu_2)}{\sqrt{\frac{(N_1-1)\hat{\sigma}_1^2 + (N_2-1)\hat{\sigma}_2^2}{N_1+N_2-2}\left(\frac{1}{N_1}+\frac{1}{N_2}\right)}}. \tag{11.7}$$

The number of degrees of freedom for this t-statistic may be determined by recalling that we are using both sample variance estimators $\hat{\sigma}_1^2$ and $\hat{\sigma}_2^2$ to obtain the denominator of this statistic and that $\hat{\sigma}_1^2$ has $N_1 - 1$ degrees of freedom associated with it, whereas $\hat{\sigma}_2^2$ has $N_2 - 1$ degrees of freedom associated with it. Because $\hat{\sigma}_1^2$ and $\hat{\sigma}_2^2$ come from independent samples, the total number of independent pieces of information contained in the data, and therefore the number of degrees of freedom for this t-statistic, is:

$$v = v_1 + v_2 = (N_1 - 1) + (N_2 - 1) = N_1 + N_2 - 2 \tag{11.8}$$

To estimate the mean difference between populations, we construct a confidence interval using Equation 11.9.

$$\begin{aligned} \text{upper limit} &= (\overline{X}_1 - \overline{X}_2) + (t_{\text{crit}})(\hat{\sigma}_{\overline{X}_1-\overline{X}_2}) \\ \text{lower limit} &= (\overline{X}_1 - \overline{X}_2) - (t_{\text{crit}})(\hat{\sigma}_{\overline{X}_1-\overline{X}_2}). \end{aligned} \tag{11.9}$$

where $\hat{\sigma}_{\overline{X}_1-\overline{X}_2}$, the standard error of the mean difference, is given in Equation 11.6 and t_{crit} is found as before using the function **qt** with *df* equal to $N_1 + N_2 - 2$.

Notice that Equation 11.9 is an extension of Equation 11.3 for constructing confidence intervals in the one-sample design when σ is not known.

THE ASSUMPTIONS OF THE INDEPENDENT SAMPLES t-TEST

Although the t-test procedure just outlined results in a sample statistic, there is in general no guarantee that this procedure will yield a *t-statistic* with a corresponding *t-distribution*. If certain conditions are satisfied by our two populations, however, then the statistic will be a *t-statistic*, and therefore follow a *t-distribution*. These conditions are as follows:

1. The null hypothesis is true.
2. Both parent populations are normally distributed.
3. The two populations have equal variances (this is called homogeneity of variance).

If any of these three conditions is not met, then the statistic obtained may not be distributed as a t-distribution with hypothesized mean difference $\mu_1 - \mu_2$ and estimated variance $\hat{\sigma}^2_{\bar{X}_1 - \bar{X}_2}$. Specifically, condition 1 highlights the fundamental purpose of hypothesis testing. If under the assumption that the null hypothesis is true, an unusual sample outcome is observed, then we must call into question the assumption that the null hypothesis is true, in favor of some alternative hypothesis. However, in order to test condition 1, we must ensure that the subsequent two conditions are met, otherwise the p-values calculated based on the *t-distribution* would be invalid. In testing the difference between population means, if conditions 2 and 3 are known to be satisfied and an unusual sample outcome is observed, then the plausibility of the remaining condition, condition 1, becomes questionable, and one would decide to reject H_0 as implausible.

Thus, it appears that conditions 2 and 3 need to be satisfied in order to test condition 1, using the t-statistic provided in Equation 11.7, that H_0 is true. For this reason, conditions 2 and 3 are usually referred to as the underlying assumptions of this t-test. In actual research situations, we cannot always be certain that either or both conditions 2 and 3 hold, and we must expend some effort to investigate the tenability of these assumptions and use alternative statistical approaches if they are not tenable.

Because the t-distribution is based on the assumptions of normality and homogeneity of variance, there has been much research on the effect of violations of these assumptions on the t-test. Based on the results of such research, we know that, under certain conditions, the t-test can withstand a great deal of deviation from its underlying assumptions. In statistical terms, we say that the t-test is *robust*. For an extensive review of research related to the consequences of violating the assumptions of the t-test on the probability statements of the t-test, the interested reader is referred to Glass, Peckham, and Sanders (1972).

Violations of the second condition, normality of the two parent populations, may be assessed qualitatively by constructing either boxplots or histograms and quantitatively by the skewness ratio. Sometimes violations of the normality assumption may be corrected using nonlinear transformations as discussed in Chapter 4. However, violations of the normality assumption may be essentially ignored if the sample from the non-normal parent population is sufficiently large (30 or larger will usually suffice, as in the statement of the central limit theorem). Or, if the sample cannot be large, then if the distribution of the non-normal parent population is approximately symmetric.

Violations of the third condition assumption, equality of the two parent population variances, may be assessed by Levene's test. As we shall see, results from this test are not provided in R in the output of an independent samples t-test, but we may obtain results from this test as well as those from other robust tests for the equality of variances using the command **levenes.test**.

For now, it is enough to know that the null hypothesis tested by Levene's test is that the two population variances are equal (H_0: $\sigma_1^2 = \sigma_2^2$), and the alternative hypothesis is that the two population variances are not equal (H_1: $\sigma_1^2 \neq \sigma_2^2$). If the p-value associated with Levene's test is less than α, following usual procedure, we reject H_0

in favor of H_1 that the two population variances are not equal and conclude that the third assumption is not tenable. On the other hand, if the p-value associated with Levene's test is greater than α, we conclude that the homogeneity of variance assumption is tenable.

Violations of the homogeneity of variance assumption may be essentially ignored as long as the samples being used have equal or approximately equal sizes. If, however, Levene's test indicates that the assumption of equal population variances is not tenable, and the samples are of unequal size, it would be incorrect to pool the two variance estimates using Equation 11.5. The assumption of equal variances can be avoided by using an estimate of variance proposed by Satterthwaite (1946),

$$\hat{\sigma}_s^2 = \frac{\hat{\sigma}_1^2}{N_1} + \frac{\hat{\sigma}_2^2}{N_2}. \tag{11.10}$$

The degrees of freedom associated with Equation 11.10 are not $N_1 + N_2 - 2$, but are given by the following, much more complicated, expression that does not necessarily result in an integer value:

$$df = \nu = \frac{\left(\dfrac{\hat{\sigma}_1^2}{N_1} + \dfrac{\hat{\sigma}_2^2}{N_2}\right)^2}{\left(\dfrac{1}{N_1 - 1}\right)\left(\dfrac{\hat{\sigma}_1^2}{N_1}\right)^2 + \left(\dfrac{1}{N_2 - 1}\right)\left(\dfrac{\hat{\sigma}_2^2}{N_2}\right)^2}. \tag{11.11}$$

A good rule of thumb, therefore, is that if both sample sizes are large and equal (or approximately equal), then violations of either or both underlying assumptions, normality and homogeneity of variance, will not seriously affect the applicability of the t-test for unrelated samples. If the samples are not equal, then Levene's test should be used to test for the assumption of homogeneity of variance. If, according to Levene's test, we find that the homogeneity of variance assumption is not tenable, we should use the t-statistic based on separate sample variances to estimate the two different population variances with degrees of freedom given by Equation 11.11.

For heuristic reasons, we begin by illustrating by hand the tests of inference described in this section using an extended dataset from Example 11.1 that incorporates another feature of this study.

· ·

EXAMPLE 11.7 To determine whether an increase in calcium intake reduces blood pressure, 10 of the 21 men in Example 11.1 were randomly assigned to a treatment condition that required them to take a calcium supplement for 12 weeks. The remaining 11 men received a placebo for the 12 weeks. Conduct an analysis to determine whether there is a mean difference in the initial systolic blood pressure readings between the men assigned to the treatment and placebo conditions before they begin the experimental protocol. The data are provided below and are also available online under the filename Blood. Those in the placebo condition are coded as 0. Those in the treatment condition are coded 1. Systolic has been renamed systolc1 to underscore the fact that these data are *initial*, pretreatment measures of systolic blood pressure. Use $\alpha = 0.05$.

Treatment condition	Systolic blood pressure (mmHg)
1	107
1	110
1	123
1	129
1	112
1	111
1	107
1	112
1	135
1	102
0	123
0	109
0	112
0	102
0	98
0	114
0	119
0	112
0	110
0	117
0	130

Solution In statistical terms, the null and alternative hypotheses for this test are:

$H_0: \mu_T = \mu_P$,   or equivalently, $H_0: \mu_T - \mu_P = 0$

$H_1: \mu_T \neq \mu_P$,   or equivalently, $H_1: \mu_T - \mu_P \neq 0$.

As usual, we begin the analysis by reviewing the descriptive statistics for each group.

MORE R: To obtain summary statistics by treatment group (treatmen), type and run the following syntax:

```
mean(Blood$systolc1[Blood$treatmen == "Calcium"])
sd(Blood$systolc1[Blood$treatmen == "Calcium"])
skew(Blood$systolc1[Blood$treatmen == "Calcium"])
se.skew(Blood$systolc1[Blood$treatmen == "Calcium"])
skew.ratio(Blood$systolc1[Blood$treatmen == "Calcium"])
mean(Blood$systolc1[Blood$treatmen == "Placebo"])
sd(Blood$systolc1[Blood$treatmen == "Placebo"])
skew(Blood$systolc1[Blood$treatmen == "Placebo"])
se.skew(Blood$systolc1[Blood$treatmen == "Placebo"])
skew.ratio(Blood$systolc1[Blood$treatmen == "Placebo"])
```

Descriptive statistics requested for systolc1 will be printed for each of the separate treatment groups. Descriptive statistics are shown below. We arbitrarily label the Calcium Group, Group 1 and the Placebo Group, Group 0.

For the Calcium Condition (Group 1):

$$
\begin{aligned}
N1 &= 10 \\
\overline{X}_1 &= 114.8 \\
\hat{\sigma}_1^2 &= 112.78 \\
\hat{\sigma}_1 &= \sqrt{112.78} = 10.62 \\
\text{skew} &= 0.8208 \\
\text{SE(skew)} &= 0.6870 \\
\text{skew ratio} &= 1.1947
\end{aligned}
$$

For the Placebo Condition (Group 0):

$$
\begin{aligned}
N2 &= 11 \\
\overline{X}_2 &= 113.27 \\
\hat{\sigma}_2^2 &= 81.36 \\
\hat{\sigma}_2 &= \sqrt{81.36} = 9.02 \\
\text{skew} &= 0.1040 \\
\text{SE(skew)} &= 0.6606 \\
\text{skew ratio} &= 0.1574
\end{aligned}
$$

We use these descriptive statistics to provide an initial review of t-test assumptions. The skewness value for each group is lower than 1.00 (and the skewness ratios of both groups are less than 2 in magnitude), suggesting that the normality assumption is reasonable. The sample standard deviations, however, are not approximately equal, leaving open the possibility that the population variances are not equal either and that the assumption of homogeneity of variances is not met for these data. For now, we assume that this assumption is met, and therefore the differences we observe in the sample statistics are not reflective of differences in the true population parameters, and continue with the independent samples t-test by hand to determine whether initial systolic blood pressure differs, on average, between those assigned to the calcium condition and those assigned to the placebo condition. We will use R in a later analysis to formally test the homogeneity of variance assumption, and we shall see that it is a reasonable assumption for these data.

Substituting these values into Equation 11.7, we obtain the following result:

$$
\begin{aligned}
t &= \frac{(\overline{X}_1 - \overline{X}_2) - (\mu_1 - \mu_2)}{\sqrt{\dfrac{(N_1 - 1)\hat{\sigma}_1^2 + (N_2 - 1)\hat{\sigma}_2^2}{N_1 + N_2 - 2}\left(\dfrac{1}{N_1} + \dfrac{1}{N_2}\right)}} \\[2em]
&= \frac{114.80 - 113.27}{\sqrt{\dfrac{(10 - 1)(112.78) + (11 - 1)(81.36)}{10 + 11 - 2}\left(\dfrac{1}{10} + \dfrac{1}{11}\right)}} \\[2em]
&= \frac{1.53}{\sqrt{\dfrac{9(112.78) + 10(81.36)}{19}}(.10 + .09)} = \frac{1.53}{4.29} = 0.356
\end{aligned}
$$

To find the p-value associated with this t-ratio, we use R and Table C.2 in Appendix C. In both cases we need the value of the t-ratio and its associated degrees of freedom. We have $t = 0.356$ and given that this t-value is from an independent samples t-test, $df = N_1 + N_2 - 2 = 10 + 11 - 2 = 19$.

To obtain the one-tailed p-value using R, we run the following command:

pt(.356, 19, lower.tail = F)

The resulting one-tailed p-value is 0.363. The two-tailed p-value is obtained by multiplying 0.363 by 2, yielding $p = 0.726$.

We may use Table C.2 to approximate the obtained p-value. In this case, we scan the row labeled $df = 19$ to find that the closest printed t-value to 0.356 is 0.688. From this poor approximation, we can say that the area to the right of 0.356 is greater than 0.25. We multiply 0.25 by 2 because the null hypothesis is non-directional, and obtain the result that $p > 0.5$. The large discrepancy between $p = 0.726$ and $p > 0.5$ is due to the fact that Table C.2 provides only a limited set of p-values relative to the t-distribution. The p-values provided are only those associated with the commonly used definitions of statistical significance. The t-distribution given by R, however, is complete, and may be relied upon to provide accurate estimates of p-values for associated t-values. Therefore, using statistical software provides a more accurate result than Table C.2 in Appendix C.

From the more accurate R p-value we know that the probability of observing a mean difference of, or more extreme than, 1.53 coming from two populations with a mean difference of zero is 0.726. Because this probability is so large, we conclude that the obtained result is consistent with the statement of the null hypothesis that $\mu_P = \mu_C$. We therefore do not reject the null hypothesis in favor of the alternative hypothesis and conclude, based on this p-value, that those assigned to the Calcium Condition are no different, on average, from those assigned to the Placebo Condition in terms of their initial, pre-treatment systolic blood pressure.

To estimate the population mean difference in initial systolic blood pressure between Groups 1 and 2, we may construct a 95 percent CI for $\mu_P - \mu_C$. To do so we substitute the earlier values we calculated by hand for this example into Equation 11.9.

To find the t_c value we may use either R or Table C.2 in Appendix C.

To find t_c using R, we use the syntax **qt(.025, 19, lower.tail = F)** and obtain $t_c = 2.09$.

To find t_c using Table C.2, we find the value at the intersection of the row labeled $df = 19$ and the column labeled 0.025. The t-value that has area 0.025 to its right is 2.09,

$$\text{upper limit} = (\overline{X}_1 - \overline{X}_2) + (t_c)(\hat{\sigma}_{\overline{X}_1 - \overline{X}_2}) = (114.80 - 113.27) + t_c(4.29)$$

$$= 1.53 + 2.09(4.29) = 1.53 + 8.97 = 10.50,$$

$$\text{lower limit} = (\overline{X}_1 - \overline{X}_2) - (t_c)(\hat{\sigma}_{\overline{X}_1 - \overline{X}_2}) = (114.80 - 113.27) - t_c(4.29)$$

$$= 1.53 - 2.09(4.29) = 1.53 - 8.97 = -7.45.$$

Accordingly, we estimate the mean difference in systolic blood pressure between the Calcium and Placebo populations to be between −7.45 and 10.50. Because 0 falls within this interval, it is plausible that the mean difference between populations is 0, or that the null hypothesis of a zero population mean difference is true, which is the conclusion we reached from the earlier t-test.

We now carry out the analysis for this example using R.

MORE R: To perform an independent samples t-test, followed by Levene's test, type and run the following two commands:

t.test(Blood$systolc1[Blood$treatmen == "Placebo"], Blood$systolc1[Blood$treatmen == "Calcium"], var.equal = T)
levenes.test(Blood$systolc1, Blood$treatmen)

This syntax assumes a 95 percent confidence interval in the **t.test** output. The command in the first line runs the independent samples t-test. The command in the second line runs a Levene's test for equality of variances.

We obtain the results shown below:

Two sample t-test			
data: Blood$systolcl[Blood$treatmen == "Placebo"]			
and Blood$systolcl[Blood$treatmen == "Calcium"]			
$t = -0.35619$ $df = 19$ p-value = 0.7256			
alternative hypothesis: true difference in means is not equal to 0			
95 percent confidence interval: −10.50178 7.44723			
sample estimates: mean of x 113.2727 mean of y 114.8000			
Levene's test for homogeneity of variance			
	df	F-value	Pr(>F)
group	1	0.5584	0.464
	19		

Levene's test for equality of variances is provided in the output above. Because $p = 0.464$ and $\alpha = 0.05$ for this example, we conclude that the population variances are not different and that the assumption of homogeneity of variance is met for these data.

According to the independent groups t-test results, $t(19) = 0.356$, $p = 0.726$, suggesting that there is no difference in mean initial systolic blood pressure between the calcium and placebo groups. These are the hypothesis tests results we obtained in our hand calculation. The mean difference and standard error of the mean difference (1.53 and 4.29, respectively) are given as well. These also agree with our hand calculations, as does the 95 percent CI of the population mean difference given as −10.50 to 7.45.

EXAMPLE 11.8 Does the population of college-bound males from the southern United States who have always been on grade level differ from the corresponding population of females in terms of the number of years of math in high school? Conduct the significance test at $\alpha = 0.05$.

Solution In statistical terms, the null hypothesis for this test is $H_0: \mu_M = \mu_F$, or equivalently, H_0: $\mu_M - \mu_F = 0$ and the alternative hypothesis is $H_1: \mu_M \neq \mu_F$, or equivalently, $H_1: \mu_M - \mu_F \neq 0$. As before, we begin with an evaluation of the underlying assumptions of this t-test. From the earlier descriptive statistics given for females and males, in Examples 11.2 and 11.3, respectively, we know that both assumptions, normality and homogeneity of variance, appear to be met. Boxplots of the variable, number of years in math in high school, for males and females from the South visually confirm these impressions.

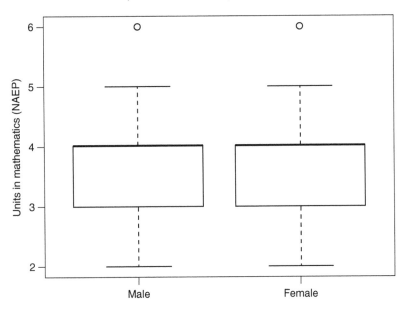

The output of the t-test and Levene's test are as follows:

Two sample t-test			
data: NELS$unitmath[NELS$region == "South" & NELS$gender == "Male"] and NELS$unitmath[NELS$region == "South" & NELS$gender == "Female"]			
t = 2.1071	df = 148	p-value = 0.0368	
alternative hypothesis: true difference in means is not equal to 0			
95 percent confidence interval:	0.0157010	0.4895371	
sample estimates:	mean of x 3.916667	mean of y 3.664048	
Levene's test for homogeneity of variance			
	Df	F value	Pr(>F)
Group	1	1.1087	0.2941
	148		

Because $p = 0.294$ is greater than $\alpha = 0.05$, the results of Levene's test indicate that the two samples are from populations with equal variances. Hence the results from the t-test with equal variances are relevant ($t(148) = 2.107$, $p = 0.04$).

☞ **Remark.** If Levene's test were statistically significant, suggesting that the homogeneity of variance assumption is not met for these data, we would drop the option, **var. equal = T** in the **t.test** command to obtain the results for the two-sample t-test with unequal variances. In particular, the command we would type is:

t.test(NELS$unitmath[NELS$region == "South" & NELS$gender == "Male"], NELS$unitmath [NELS$region == "South" & NELS$gender == "Female"])

Because $p < 0.05$, we reject the null hypothesis in favor of the alternative and conclude that there is a statistically significant difference in terms of the mean number of years of math taken in high school between college-bound males and females from the South who have always stayed on track. Based on the means given in the group statistics output, we may further conclude that this population of males appears to take statistically significantly more years in math in high school than this population of females.

The 95 percent confidence interval can also be used to determine whether the population of college-bound males from the southern United States who have always been on grade level differs from the corresponding population of females in terms of the number of years of math in high school. Because 0 is not contained in the 95 percent confidence interval, $(0.02, 0.49)$, we may conclude that the difference $\mu_M - \mu_F$ is not likely to be 0, and may be as great as one-half year. That is, as observed in connection with the null hypothesis test, the two group means are statistically significantly different from each other. Based on the means given in the group statistics output, we may further conclude that this population of males appears to take statistically significantly more years of math in high school than this population of females.

Note that in the case of a non-directional alternative hypothesis, we can base our conclusion on either a p-value or a confidence interval.

EFFECT SIZE FOR THE INDEPENDENT SAMPLES t-TEST

In addition to the confidence interval, we may extend Cohen's index of effect size, d, to the present case to obtain another estimate of the magnitude of the difference between population means.

Assuming the null hypothesis to be $H_0: \mu_1 = \mu_2$, Cohen's d, expressed as the difference between the two group means relative to the common standard deviation, is given by Equation 11.12:

$$d = \frac{\overline{X}_1 - \overline{X}_2}{\sqrt{\dfrac{(N_1 - 1)\hat{\sigma}_1^2 + (N_2 - 1)\hat{\sigma}_2^2}{N_1 + N_2 - 2}}}. \tag{11.12}$$

The effect size, d, for the case of Example 11.8, which may be obtained using R, is equal to:

$$d = \frac{3.917 - 3.664}{\sqrt{\dfrac{(65)(0.737)^2 + (83)(0.723)^2}{66 + 84 - 2}}} = \frac{0.253}{0.729} = 0.35.$$

That is, the number of years of math, on average, taken by college-bound southern males exceeds that for college-bound southern females by 0.35 standard deviations, a small to moderate effect size, further corroborating the results supported by the confidence interval.

EXAMPLE 11.9 Among college-bound students in the northeastern United States who have always been on grade level, do those who own a computer score higher in math achievement in twelfth grade than those who do not? Conduct the significance test at $\alpha = 0.05$.

Solution For this question, the null and alternative hypotheses are, respectively: $H_0: \mu_C = \mu_{NC}$ and $H_1: \mu_C > \mu_{NC}$. To inspect visually the math achievement distributions for both groups, we obtain the following boxplot. We also obtain the corresponding descriptive statistics for each group separately.

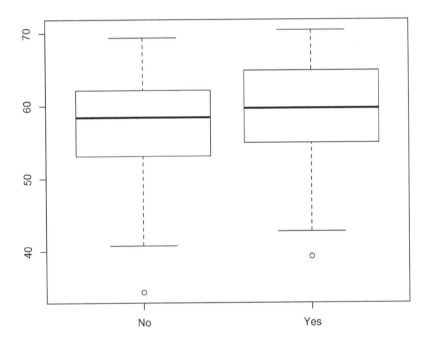

Both distributions have outliers, suggesting some negative skew for each; however, the samples are large enough to ignore the normality assumption. According to the boxplot, the variances appear to be homogeneous. Because the two samples are not equal in size, $N_C = 60$ and $N_{NC} = 46$, we will rely on Levene's test to evaluate the tenability of this assumption.

The syntax to run this analysis is:

t.test(NELS$achmat12[NELS$region == "Northeast" & NELS$computer == "No"], NELS $achmat12[NELS$region == "Northeast" & NELS$computer == "Yes"], var.equal = T)
levenes.test(NELS$achmat12[NELS$region == "Northeast"], NELS$computer[NELS$region =="Northeast"])

Two sample *t*-test

---

data: NELS$achmat12[NELS$region == "Northeast" & NELS$computer == "No"]
and NELS$achmat12[NELS$region == "Northeast" & NELS$computer == "Yes"]

$t = -1.0911$ $df = 104$ p-value = 0.2778

alternative hypothesis: true difference in means is not equal to 0

95 percent confidence interval: −4.534594   1.315725
sample estimates: mean of x 57.33457   mean of y 58.94400

Levene's test for homogeneity of variance

	df	F-value	Pr(>F)
group	1	0.7758	0.3805
	104		

Because Levene's test is not statistically significant ($p = 0.38$), the homogeneity of variance assumption is met for these data. The *t*-test results suggest that the observed difference in means is not statistically significant (note that we adjust the *p*-value by dividing by 2 to obtain the one-tailed test result: $p = 0.278/2 = 0.14$). Hence, we conclude that students who own a computer do not score statistically significantly higher in twelfth grade math than those who do not, $t(104) = -1.09$, $p = 0.14$.

PAIRED SAMPLES *t*-TEST AND CONFIDENCE INTERVAL

Earlier in this chapter we posed three questions, each involving a comparison of two means. We asked: whether, on average, males and females from the South differ in the number of years of math taken in college; whether, on average, those who own computers from the Northeast show greater achievement in twelfth grade math than those who do not; and whether, on average, college-bound females from the South change in self-esteem from eighth grade to twelfth grade. While the first two questions make use of an independent or unrelated samples design, the third question makes use of a dependent or related groups design because the same individuals are measured twice, in eighth grade and again in twelfth. Because the same individuals are measured twice, this design controls for several factors including socioeconomic status, peer group, physical appearance, and so on that may be related to self-concept.

The names *repeated measures* or *longitudinal* are used to describe this type of design, in which observations are taken on the same objects across time. With only two sets of observations, one at time 1 and the other at time 2, we have, in this case, what is also called a *pre-post* design. Had we chosen, instead, to answer the third question using a *cross-sectional* design, we would have studied simultaneously a sample of females from eighth grade and an independently selected sample of females from twelfth grade, and we would have used the independent samples *t*-test to analyze our data. Because the scores in our two groups of data are matched pairwise, we select a method of analysis that exploits the particular paired or dependent structure of the data: the paired samples *t*-test.

The paired samples *t*-test capitalizes on the dependent structure of the data by basing its calculations on the difference scores computed for each matched pair. As such, the paired samples *t*-test may be viewed simply as a one-sample *t*-test on the difference scores, D, calculated on each matched pair and may be expressed as Equation 11.13, which is an adaptation of Equation 11.1, the one-sample *t*-test:

$$t = \frac{\overline{D} - \mu_D}{\hat{\sigma}_{\overline{D}}}, \tag{11.13}$$

$df = N - 1 =$ number of pairs $- 1$.

The standard error of the mean difference, $\hat{\sigma}_{\overline{D}}$, is given by Equation 11.14:

$$\hat{\sigma}_{\overline{D}} = \frac{\hat{\sigma}_D}{\sqrt{N}}. \tag{11.14}$$

Because difference scores form the basis of the paired samples *t*-test, the null hypothesis for this test is expressed as H_0: $\mu_D = 0$, which is equivalent to H_0: $\mu_1 - \mu_2 = 0$ because the difference of the sample means, $\overline{X}_1 - \overline{X}_2$, equals the mean of the paired differences, $\overline{D}$.

To estimate the mean difference between populations in a paired samples design, we construct a confidence interval using Equation 11.15:

$$\begin{aligned} \text{upper limit} &= \overline{D} + (t_c)(\hat{\sigma}_{\overline{D}}) \\ \text{lower limit} &= \overline{D} - (t_c)(\hat{\sigma}_{\overline{D}}), \end{aligned} \tag{11.15}$$

where $\hat{\sigma}_{\overline{D}}$, the standard error of the mean difference is given by Equation 11.14, and t_c is found as before using the R syntax for **qt(p, df, lower.tail = F)** or by using Table C.2 in Appendix C, both with *df* equal to $N - 1$.

THE ASSUMPTIONS OF THE PAIRED SAMPLES *t*-TEST

The underlying assumptions of the paired samples *t*-test and confidence interval are the same as those for the independent samples *t*-test: normality and homogeneity of variance of the two parent populations. While the normality assumption requires some investigation in the case of the paired samples *t*-test, the homogeneity of variance assumption does not. The two groups are, by design, equal in size, and as noted earlier with respect to the independent samples *t*-test, violations of the homogeneity of variance assumption may be ignored when this is the case. Hence, Levene's test of homogeneity of variance is unnecessary.

For heuristic reasons, we extend the situation described in Example 11.7 to illustrate how a paired samples t-test may be carried out by hand. Recall that these data may be found in the file Blood on the text's website, or in our R package.

EXAMPLE 11.10 The 10 men in the Calcium Condition group are given calcium supplements for the next 12 weeks, while the 11 men in the Placebo Condition group are given a placebo for the next 12 weeks. At the end of this time period, systolic blood pressure readings of all men are recorded. Use the paired samples t-test to test whether there is a mean reduction in blood pressure from pretest to posttest based on the entire group of 21 men. Use $\alpha = 0.05$. The data occupy the first three columns of the table provided below. The variable systolc2 contains the posttest measures of systolic blood pressure.

Treatment condition	systolc1 (mmHg)	systolc2 (mmHg)	d = systolc1 − systolc2
1	107	100	7
1	110	114	−4
1	123	105	18
1	129	112	17
1	112	115	−3
1	111	116	−5
1	107	106	1
1	112	102	10
1	135	125	10
1	102	104	−2
0	123	124	−1
0	109	97	12
0	112	113	−1
0	102	105	−3
0	98	95	3
0	114	119	−5
0	119	114	5
0	112	114	−2
0	110	121	−11
0	117	118	−1
0	130	133	−3

Solution The null and alternative hypotheses for this test are

$$H_0: \mu_{\overline{D}} = 0 \text{ and } H_1: \mu_{\overline{D}} > 0.$$

Because we wish to test whether there is a reduction in blood pressure, we expect the mean of the difference scores, assuming we subtract systolc2 from systolc1, to be positive. Hence this test is a directional, one-tailed paired samples t-test.

We compute the difference scores using the R command **Blood$d = Blood$systolc1 −Blood$systolc2**. These appear in the fourth column of the previous table. The skew of d, systolc1 and systolc2 are provided below.

Skew of systolc1:	0.5676
Skew of systolc2:	0.1128
Skew of d:	0.6725

Because the skewness values are low, we may assume that the normality assumption is tenable for these data. We note that the difference of blood pressure means (114 − 112) equals the mean of the difference (2). However, the standard deviation of the difference, d, is lower than the standard deviation of either systolc1 or systolc2. This is because the two samples are paired, and systolc1 and systolc2 are positively related. The paired samples design, in this case, provides a more powerful hypothesis test than would an independent samples test carried out on the same data. Can you figure out why?

Given the D values, which are, incidentally, easily computed by hand, we now compute $\overline{D}$ and $\hat{\sigma}_{\overline{D}}$.

$$\overline{D} = (7 - 4 + 18 + 17 - 3 - 5 + 1 + 10 + 10 - 2 - 1$$
$$+ 12 - 1 - 3 + 3 - 5 + 5 - 2 + 11 - 1 - 3)/21 = 42/21 = 2.$$

$$\hat{\sigma}_D = \sqrt{\frac{(7 - 2)^2 + (-4 - 2)^2 + (18 - 2)^2 + \cdots + (11 - 2)^2 + (-1 - 2)^2 + (-3 - 2)^2}{21 - 1}}$$

$$= \sqrt{\frac{1182}{20}} = \sqrt{59.1} = 7.69$$

$$\hat{\sigma}_{\overline{D}} = \frac{\hat{\sigma}_D}{\sqrt{N}} = \frac{7.69}{\sqrt{21}} = \frac{7.69}{4.58} = 1.68.$$

Substituting these values into Equation 11.13, we obtain:

$$t = \frac{\overline{D} - \mu_{\overline{D}}}{\hat{\sigma}_{\overline{D}}} = \frac{2 - 0}{1.68} = 1.19$$

and $df = N - 1 =$ number of pairs $- 1 = 21 - 1 = 20$.

We find p either by using R or by using Table C.2 in Appendix C. To use R, we use the syntax **pt(1.19, 20, lower.tail = F)** and obtain $p = 0.12$. To use Table C.2, we look at the row with $df = 20$ and find that the closest t value is 1.064. The associated p-value, located at the top of the column, is $p = 0.15$, which we use as our estimate.

We conclude that there is not a mean reduction in blood pressure from pretest to posttest, $t(20) = 1.19$, $p = 0.12$.

While ordinarily we would not compute a 95 percent CI for this one-tailed test, we do so here for heuristic purposes. Substituting the values calculated by hand into Equation 11.15, we obtain:

upper limit $= \overline{D} + (t_c)(\hat{\sigma}_{\overline{D}}) = 2 + t_c (1.68) = 2 + 2.086(1.68) = 2 + 3.47 = 5.47$
lower limit $= \overline{D} - (t_c)(\hat{\sigma}_{\overline{D}}) = 2 - t_c(1.68) = 2 - 2.086(1.68) = 2–3.47 = -1.47.$

The critical t value ($t_c = 2.086$) was obtained either by computing **qt (0.025,20, lower. tail = F)** or from Table C.2 in the row labeled $df = 20$ and the column labeled 0.025.

Accordingly, the 95 percent CI ranges from −1.47 to 5.47. We obtain the same results using the paired samples t-test in R (within rounding error).

MORE R: To perform a paired samples t-test, type the following syntax into your .R file and run:

t.test(Blood\$systolc1, Blood\$systolc2, paired = T)

By default, this test computes a 95 percent confidence interval. The T in **paired = T** stands for True, indicating that the test being performed is a paired t-test.

The output will appear as such:

Paired t-test		
data: Blood\$systolcl		
and Blood\$systolc2		
$t = 1.1922$ $df = 20$		p-value = 0.2471
alternative hypothesis: true difference in means is not equal to 0		
95 percent confidence interval: −1.499377		5.499377
sample estimates: mean of the differences		2

We employ the paired samples t-test in Example 11.11 to answer the third question posed in this section related to self-esteem.

EXAMPLE 11.11 Do college-bound females from the South who have always been on grade level change in self-esteem from eighth grade to twelfth grade on average? Conduct the significance test at $\alpha = 0.05$.

Solution In statistical terms, the null hypothesis for this test is H_0: $\mu_D = 0$ and the alternative hypothesis is H_1: $\mu_D \neq 0$. We begin with an evaluation of the underlying assumption of normality using a boxplot from the following command:

boxplot(NELS\$slfcnc08[NELS\$gender == "Female" & NELS\$region == "South"], NELS \$slfcnc12[NELS\$gender == "Female" & NELS\$region == "South"], names = c("8th grade", "12th grade"))

Then we conduct the paired t-test using the command:

t.test(NELS\$slfcnc08[NELS\$gender == "Female" & NELS\$region == "South"], NELS \$slfcnc12[NELS\$gender == "Female" & NELS\$region == "South"], paired = T)

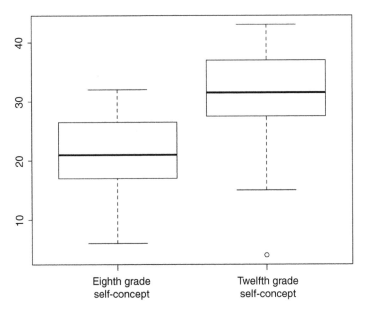

From visual inspection of the boxplots, we see that while the eighth grade distribution of self-concept is approximately symmetric, the twelfth grade distribution is negatively skewed. Because the sample size of $N = 84$ for each sample is large, however, we are not concerned about the possible deviation of the population distributions from normality. We may note also the large increase in female self-concept from eighth to twelfth grade among the students in the dataset.

Results of this t-test are given below.

Paired t-test		
data: NELS\$slfcnc08[NELS\$gender == "Female" & NELS\$region == "South"] and NELS\$slfcnc12[NELS\$gender == "Female" & NELS\$region == "South"]		
$t = -14.586$ $df = 83$	p-value < 2.2e-16	
alternative hypothesis: true difference in means is not equal to 0		
95 percent confidence interval: −11.945283		−9.078526
sample estimates:	mean of the differences	−10.5119

From the results of the t-test shown above, we see that the difference of 10.51 points in self-concept may not be attributable to chance, that it indicates a statistically significant increase in self-concept in the population ($t = -14.59$, $p < 0.0005$).

Furthermore, this output also contains the confidence interval. It informs us that it is likely that the self-concept mean difference between grades 8 and 12 falls between −11.95 and −9.08. Because 0 is not contained in this interval, it is indicative of a statistically significant increase in self-concept in the population.

EFFECT SIZE FOR THE PAIRED SAMPLES t-TEST

In the situation of the paired samples t-test, the effect size is measured relative to the standard deviation of the paired differences, $\hat{\sigma}_D$, and is given by Equation 11.16:

$$d = \frac{\overline{D}}{\hat{\sigma}_D}.$$ (11.16)

For Example 11.11, we may find the descriptive statistics necessary for this equation through R by typing the following commands:

diffs = NELS\$slfcnc12[NELS\$gender == "Female" & NELS\$region == "South"] –
** NELS\$slfcnc08[NELS\$gender == "Female" & NELS\$region == "South"]**
mean(diffs)
sd(diffs)

In this example, $\hat{\sigma}_D$ equals 6.61, and the effect size is $d = \dfrac{31.81 - 21.30}{6.61}$ $= \dfrac{10.51}{6.61} = 1.59$, suggesting that twelfth grade self-concept among females in the South is 1.59 standard deviations (of the paired differences) higher than it was in eighth grade, a large effect.

Given the paired nature of the data, we may compute the correlation between self-concept scores measured in eighth and twelfth grades to determine to what extent those who score low on self-concept in eighth grade tend to score low on self-concept in twelfth grade, and so forth. In an independent groups design, we would expect this correlation to be 0. If, by matching, one or more sources of variability have been controlled, as intended, then we would expect a positive correlation between pairs. The positive correlation represents the degree to which the matched pairs design improves the power of the analysis. By contrast, a negative correlation implies that we have compromised the power of our analysis by matching on the particular values we have. While negative correlations typically do not arise in the context of repeated measures designs, they sometimes do arise when subjects are sampled in pairs (e.g., husbands and wives, fathers and sons) or when subjects are matched by pairs on some basis by the researcher (e.g., on age and education level).

Pearson's product-moment correlation

---

data: NELS\$slfcnc12[NELS\$gender == "Female" & NELS\$region == "South"]
and NELS\$slfcnc08[NELS\$gender == "Female" & NELS\$region == "South"]

$t = 5.8386$ $df = 82$ p-value = 1.019e-07

alternative hypothesis: true correlation is not equal to 0

95 percent confidence interval: 0.3705426   0.6775655
sample estimates: cor   0.5418888

The correlation value of 0.542 given in the last line of output is positive and moderately strong. It suggests that by utilizing before–after matching we have removed one or more sources of variability related to self-concept and thereby improved the power of our analysis relative to a cross-sectional, independent samples design.

CONDUCTING POWER ANALYSES FOR *t*-TESTS ON MEANS

In the previous chapter, we noted that without sufficient power in conducting a hypothesis test, we are not likely to detect a difference from the null hypothesis even when such a difference exists. Accordingly, in conducting such tests, we not only want to minimize the risk of making a Type I error by setting α no greater than 0.10, but we also want to maximize the power of the test, $1 - \beta$, by typically setting it to be no less than 0.80. With a probability of at least 0.80 of detecting a difference where one exists, if a difference were not detected, and the null hypothesis were retained, we could be reasonably confident that a difference did *not* exist rather than that a difference did exist and that the test had insufficient power to detect it.

In practice, to avoid detecting trivially small departures from the null hypothesis as statistically significant, the usual procedure before embarking on a study is to set α, decide on an effect size that is worth detecting from a practical perspective, and find the sample size N that will decrease the standard error sufficiently to achieve the desired power.

We shall demonstrate how we may use R's **pwr** library to find the sample size, N, necessary to achieve a power of 0.80 given a specified α and effect size for the *t*-tests on means covered in this chapter. Note that the commands used in the next section require a separate library to be loaded that contains the set of commands needed to carry out a power analysis. As discussed in Chapter 1, many of the more advanced R functions are not included in the "base" package and require user-written libraries to be loaded. To load the library that contains the commands needed to carry out a power analysis, type:

install.packages("pwr")
library(pwr)

The first line of code only needs to be run once for each computer you are using, while the second line of code needs to be run each time you re-open R to run a new session and plan to carry out a power analysis as one of the analyses in that session.

• •
EXAMPLE 11.12 In this example, we illustrate R's power library (named **pwr**) as it applies to a one group *t*-test situation, using the following null and alternative hypotheses: H_0: $\mu = 100$ vs. H_1: $\mu \neq 100$. We use R's **pwr.t.test** command to find the sample size necessary to achieve a power of 0.80 to detect a minimum mean difference of 0.20 standard deviations, equivalent to Cohen's small effect size, $d = 0.20$, from the null hypothesis value of 100 with α set to 0.05.

Solution Because the test of this null hypothesis is a two-tailed, one-sample *t*-test on means, we obtain the sample size required using the following R command:

pwr.t.test(d = 0.2, sig.level = 0.05, power = 0.8, type = "one.sample", alternative = "two.sided")

where the value **d = 0.2** represents the effect size for the alternative hypothesis, **sig.level = 0.05** represents the α set to 0.05, **power = 0.8** represents the desired power, and **type = "one.sample"** and **alternative = "two.sided"** describe the type of test that we are looking to run.

The obtained results are as follows:

One-sample t-test power calculation		
n	=	198.1508
d	=	0.2
sig.level	=	0.05
power	=	0.8
alternative	=	two.sided

Based on these results, for this two-tailed test, we would need a sample of size 199, rounding up from $n = 198.1508$, to obtain a power of 0.80 to detect a small effect size of 0.2 standard deviations with $\alpha = 0.05$.

EXAMPLE 11.13 In this example, we keep all parameters the same as in the previous example and investigate the effect on the required sample size by having an alternative hypothesis that is directional rather than non-directional.

Solution Because the default for this command is a two-sided test, we change the argument alternative from **"two.sided"** to **"greater"** (since the alternative hypothesis is directional and in the positive direction) to find the desired sample size.

pwr.t.test(d = 0.2, sig.level = 0.05, power = 0.8, type = "one.sample", alternative = "greater")

We obtain the following results:

One-sample t-test power calculation		
n	=	155.9256
d	=	0.2
sig.level	=	0.05
power	=	0.8
alternative	=	greater

Notice with all things being equal, the required sample size to detect a small effect size with power equal to 0.80 and α equal to 0.05 is only 156 individuals for the one-tailed test as opposed to 199 for the two-tailed test. This is because with a two-tailed test, the area representing α is divided in half, with one-half in each tail. With a one-tailed test, the area representing α is not divided in half, but is located instead in one of the tails. Assuming the researcher's hypothesized direction of difference is correct, all things being equal, this is tantamount to increasing the α level, as illustrated in the last chapter in Figures 10.9 and 10.10. As shown in these figures, an increase in the area representing the α level results in an increased shaded area under the H_1 curve, and a resulting increase in power. But, if we were not interested in increasing the power of the test, but rather in keeping it at say, 0.80, we could, as the results of this power analysis suggest, achieve a power of 0.80 to detect a small effect size at α equal to 0.05 with the reduced sample size of 156 as opposed to 199.

☞ **Remark.** In general, all things being equal, one-tailed (one-sided) tests are more powerful than two-tailed (two-sided) tests and therefore typically require smaller sample sizes to achieve a desired level of power, as long as the direction of the difference is specified correctly in the alternative hypothesis.

EXAMPLE 11.14 In this example, we illustrate R's **pwr.t.test** command as it applies to a two-tailed independent samples *t*-test situation. In particular, we seek to find the sample size necessary to achieve a power of 0.80 to detect a minimum difference between population means of 0.50 standard deviations, equivalent to Cohen's medium effect size $d = 0.50$, with α set to 0.05. For this example, the null and alternative hypotheses are: H_0: $\mu_1 = \mu_2$ versus H_1: $\mu_1 \neq \mu_2$.

Solution Given the appropriate test for this situation is a two-tailed independent groups *t*-test, we use the following command:

pwr.t.test(d = 0.5, sig.level = 0.05, power = 0.8, type = "two.sample", alternative = "two. sided")

We obtain the following results:

Two-sample t-test power calculation		
n	=	63.76561
d	=	0.5
sig.level	=	0.05
power	=	0.8
alternative	=	two.sided
NOTE: n is number in *each* group		

Had the alternative hypothesis been directional, and the test one-tailed, the N per group would be 51, rather than 64, in keeping with the notion that, all things being equal, one-tailed tests are more powerful than two-tailed tests.

EXAMPLE 11.15 In this example, we illustrate R's **pwr.t.test** command as it applies to a two-tailed paired samples *t*-test situation. We keep the situation the same as in Example 11.14, but for the fact that instead of two independent groups, our two groups are now paired. As before, we seek to find the sample size necessary to achieve a power of 0.80 to detect a minimum difference between population means of 0.50 standard deviations, equivalent to Cohen's medium effect size $d = 0.50$, with α set to 0.05. Recall that in the case of a paired groups design, a difference in the means between groups is equivalent to the mean of the difference scores computed on the paired scores from the two groups. If we assume the population standard deviation of difference scores to be 20, then the effect size in terms of a difference in population means is 10 points. For this example, the null and alternative hypotheses are: H_0: $\mu_D = 0$ versus H_1: $\mu_D \neq 0$.

Solution Given that the appropriate test for this situation is a two-tailed paired samples t-test, we type the following:

pwr.t.test(d = 0.5, sig.level = 0.05, power = 0.8, type = "paired", alternative = "two.sided")

We obtain the following results:

Paired t-test power calculation		
n	=	33.36713
d	=	0.5
sig.level	=	0.05
power	=	0.8
alternative	=	two.sided
NOTE: n is number of *pairs*		

Notice that the required sample size is reduced to $N = 34$ (rounding up from the $n = 33.36$ displayed in the output above) in this paired groups design from $N = 64$ in the independent groups design. This is because, as noted in an earlier section of this chapter, by matching the individuals in the two groups on a pairwise basis, we are controlling for a number of factors extraneous to the main variable of interest, and in so doing, we are increasing our signal to noise ratio. Simply stated, an increased signal to noise ratio allows a true difference between means to be more easily detected as statistically significant, which means greater power.

SUMMARY

Table 11.2 below contains a summary of the equations for the different hypothesis tests based on the t-distribution given in this chapter. Table 11.3 contains a summary of the equations for the confidence intervals based on the t-distribution given in this chapter. Table 11.4 contains a summary of the equations for the effect sizes for the different hypothesis tests given in this chapter. Figures 11.5–11.7 contain flow charts for the one sample, independent samples, and paired samples t-tests, respectively.

TABLE 11.2 Equations for obtaining observed t-test values

Test	Obtained statistic using the notation in the book	Obtained statistic using the notation from the R output
One-sample t-test	$t = (\overline{X} - \mu)/\left(\dfrac{\hat{\sigma}}{\sqrt{N}}\right) = \dfrac{\overline{X} - \mu}{\hat{\sigma}_{\overline{X}}}$ $df = N - 1$	$t = \dfrac{\text{mean} - \text{test value}}{\text{std. error mean}}$ $df = N - 1$ The test value is the null hypothesized value for the population mean
Independent samples t-test	$t = \dfrac{(\overline{X}_1 - \overline{X}_2) - (\mu_1 - \mu_2)}{\sqrt{\dfrac{(N_1 - 1)\hat{\sigma}_1^2 + (N_2 - 1)\hat{\sigma}_2^2}{N_1 + N_2 - 2}\left(\dfrac{1}{N_1} + \dfrac{1}{N_2}\right)}}$ $df = N_1 + N_2 - 2$	$t = \dfrac{\text{mean difference}}{\text{std. error difference}}$ $df = N_1 + N_2 - 2$
Paired samples t-test	$t = \dfrac{\overline{D} - \mu_D}{\hat{\sigma}_{\overline{D}}}$ $df = N - 1$	$t = \dfrac{\text{paired differences mean}}{\text{paired differences std. error mean}}$

TABLE 11.3 Equations for obtaining confidence intervals based on the t-distribution. To find t_c, use the equations for the degrees of freedom found in Table 11.2

Test	Confidence interval using the notation in the book	Confidence interval using the notation from the R output
One-sample t-test	Upper Limit $= \overline{X} + t_c\hat{\sigma}_{\overline{X}}$ Lower Limit $= \overline{X} - t_c\hat{\sigma}_{\overline{X}}$	U.L. $=$ mean $+ (t_c)(\text{std. error mean})$ L.L. $=$ mean $- (t_c)(\text{std. error mean})$
Independent samples t-test	Upper Limit $= (\overline{X}_1 - \overline{X}_2) + t_c \bullet \hat{\sigma}_{\overline{X}_1 - \overline{X}_2}$ Lower Limit $= (\overline{X}_1 - \overline{X}_2) - t_c \bullet \hat{\sigma}_{\overline{X}_1 - \overline{X}_2}$	U.L. = mean difference $+$ $(t_c)(\text{std. error difference})$ L.L. = mean difference $-$ $(t_c)(\text{std. error difference})$
Paired samples t-test	Upper Limit $= \overline{D} + t_c \bullet \hat{\sigma}_{\overline{D}}$ Lower Limit $= \overline{D} - t_c \bullet \hat{\sigma}_{\overline{D}}$	U.L. = paired differences mean $+$ $(t_c)(\text{paired differences std.}$ error mean$)$ L.L. = paired differences mean $-$ $(t_c)(\text{paired differences std.}$ error mean$)$

TABLE 11.4 Effect size equations associated with t-tests

Test	Approximate effect size using the notation in the book	Approximate effect size using the notation from the R output
One-sample t-test	$d = \dfrac{\overline{X} - \mu}{\hat{\sigma}}$	$d = \dfrac{\text{mean } - \text{ test value}}{\text{std. deviation}}$
Independent samples t-test	$d = \dfrac{(\overline{X}_1 - \overline{X}_2)}{\sqrt{\dfrac{(N_1 - 1)\hat{\sigma}_1^2 + (N_2 - 1)\hat{\sigma}_2^2}{N_1 + N_2 - 2}}}$	$d = \dfrac{\text{mean difference}}{\sqrt{\dfrac{(N_1 - 1)SD_1^2 + (N_2 - 1)SD_2^2}{N_1 + N_2 - 2}}}$
Paired samples t-test	$d = \dfrac{\overline{D}}{\hat{\sigma}_D}$	$t = \dfrac{\text{paired differences mean}}{\text{paired differences std. deviation}}$

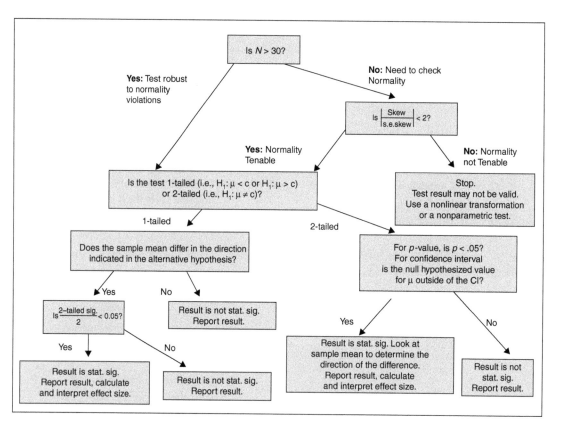

Figure 11.5 Flow chart for one-sample t-test

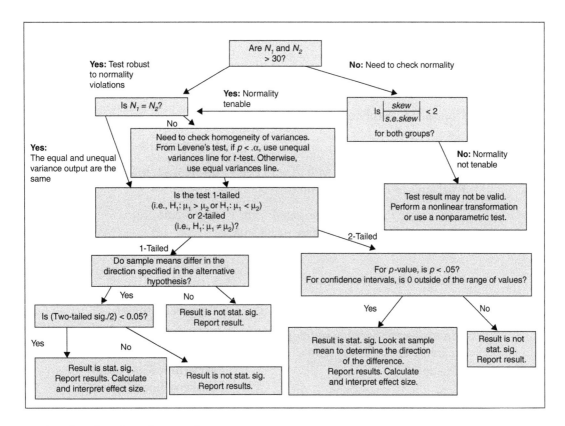

Figure 11.6 Flow chart for independent samples t-test

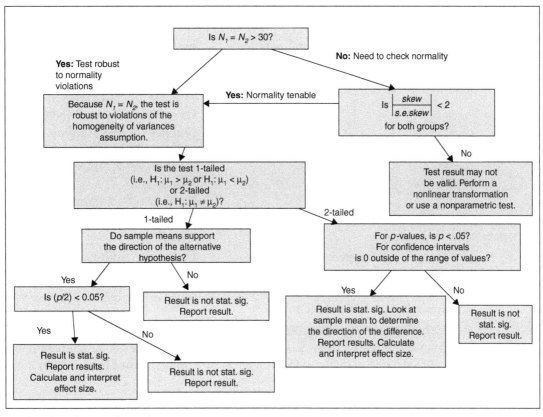

Figure 11.7 Flow chart for paired samples t-test

SUMMARY OF R COMMANDS

(See also the .R-file for Chapter 11)

Commands involving the *t*-distribution

Create	Command lines
To calculate the *t*-value with *df* = 20 and 0.025 area to its right (Example 11.1)	**qt(.025, 20, lower.tail = F)**
To calculate the *p*-value associated with the two-tailed test with *t*-value −2.86 with *df* = 20 (Example 11.4)	**2*pt(−2.86, 20)**

One-sample *t*-test commands

Create	Command lines
Summarize the variable systolc1 including the skewness ratio (Example 11.1)	**mean(Blood$systolc1)** **sd(Blood$systolc1)** **skew(Blood$systolc1)** **se.skew(Blood$systolc1)** **skew.ratio(Blood$systolc1)**
Create a q-q plot of the variable systolc1 (Example 11.1)	**qqnorm(Blood$systolc1)** **qqline(Blood$systolc1)**
Compute the 95 percent confidence interval for systolc1 (Example 11.1)	**t.test(Blood$systolc1)$conf.int**
Summarize the variable unitmath for a subset of the NELS dataset, in this case for women from the South (Example 11.2)	**mean(NELS$unitmath[NELS$gender == "Female" & NELS$region == "South"])** **sd(NELS$unitmath[NELS$gender == "Female" & NELS$region == "South"])** **skew(NELS$unitmath[NELS$gender == "Female" & NELS$region == "South"])** **se.skew(NELS$unitmath[NELS$gender == "Female" & NELS$region == "South"])** **skew.ratio(NELS$unitmath[NELS$gender == "Female" & NELS$region == "South"])**
Compute the 95 percent confidence interval for unitmath for a subset of the NELS dataset, in this case for women from the South (Example 11.2)	**t.test(NELS$unitmath[NELS$gender == "Female" & NELS$region == "South"])**
Compute the 99 percent confidence interval for unitmath for a subset of the NELS dataset, in this case for women from the South (Example 11.3)	**t.test(NELS$unitmath[NELS$gender == "Female" & NELS$region == "South"], conf.level = 0.99)**

Create	Command lines
Perform the one-sample *t*-test to determine whether the average initial systolic blood pressure in the population is 120 (Example 11.4)	**t.test(Blood$systolc1, mu = 120)**
Conduct a power analysis to determine the sample size needed for a power of 0.80 for a two-tailed one-sample *t*-test using α = 0.05, *SD* = 10, and *d* = 0.20, given the effect size (Example 11.12)	**pwr.t.test(d = 0.2, sig.level = 0.05, power = 0.8, type = "one.sample", alternative = "two.sided")**
Conduct a power analysis to determine the sample size needed for a power of 0.80 for a one-tailed one-sample *t*-test using α = 0.05 with *d* = 0.20 given the effect size (Example 11.13)	**pwr.t.test(d = 0.2, sig.level = 0.05, power = 0.8, type = "one.sample", alternative = "greater")**

Independent samples *t*-test commands

Create	Command lines
Generate descriptive statistics for units of math taken by males and females in the southern region (Table 11.1)	**length(NELS$unitmath[NELS$gender == "Male" & NELS$region == "South"])** **mean(NELS$unitmath[NELS$gender == "Male" & NELS$region == "South"])** **sd(NELS$unitmath[NELS$gender == "Male" & NELS$region == "South"])** **min(NELS$unitmath[NELS$gender == "Male" & NELS$region == "South"])** **max(NELS$unitmath[NELS$gender == "Male" & NELS$region == "South"])** **length(NELS$unitmath[NELS$gender == "Female" & NELS$region == "South"])** **mean(NELS$unitmath[NELS$gender == "Female" & NELS$region == "South"])** **sd(NELS$unitmath[NELS$gender == "Female" & NELS$region == "South"])** **min(NELS$unitmath[NELS$gender == "Female" & NELS$region == "South"])** **max(NELS$unitmath[NELS$gender == "Female" & NELS$region == "South"])**
Obtain summary statistics by treatment group (treatmen) (Example 11.7)	**mean(Blood$systolc1[Blood$treatmen == "Calcium"])** **sd(Blood$systolc1[Blood$treatmen == "Calcium"])**

Create	Command lines
	skew(Blood$systolc1[Blood$treatmen == "Calcium"])
	se.skew(Blood$systolc1[Blood$treatmen == "Calcium"])
	skew.ratio(Blood$systolc1[Blood$treatmen == "Calcium"])
	mean(Blood$systolc1[Blood$treatmen == "Placebo"])
	sd(Blood$systolc1[Blood$treatmen == "Placebo"])
	skew(Blood$systolc1[Blood$treatmen == "Placebo"])
	se.skew(Blood$systolc1[Blood$treatmen == "Placebo"])
	skew.ratio(Blood$systolc1[Blood$treatmen == "Placebo"])
Perform the independent samples *t*-test of systolc1 by treatmen (Example 11.7)	t.test(Blood$systolc1[Blood$treatmen == "Placebo"],Blood$systolc1[Blood$treatmen == "Calcium"], var.equal = T)
Perform the independent samples *t*-test of unitmath by gender for students in the South when the homogeneity of variances assumption is not tenable (Example 11.8) Conduct a power analysis to find the sample size necessary to achieve a power of 0.80 in a two-tailed independent samples *t*-test with equal sample sizes for both groups, *d* = 0.50, and α = 0.05 (Example 11.14)	t.test(NELS$unitmath[NELS$region == "South" & NELS$gender == "Male"], NELS$unitmath[NELS$region == "South" & NELS$gender == "Female"]) pwr.t.test(d = 0.5, sig.level = 0.05, power = 0.8, type = "two.sample", alternative = "two.sided")

Paired samples *t*-test commands

Create	Command lines
Perform the paired samples *t*-test of systolc1 and systolc2 (Example 11.10) Conduct a power analysis to find the sample size necessary to achieve a power of 0.80 in a two-tailed paired samples *t*-test with equal sample sizes for both groups, *d* = 0.50, and α = 0.05 (Example 11.15)	t.test(Blood$systolc1, Blood$systolc2, paired = T) pwr.t.test(d = 0.5, sig.level = 0.05, power = 0.8, type = "paired", alternative = "two.sided")

EXERCISES

Create a .R file for each exercise that requires the use of R. Run code from the .R file by highlighting or having the cursor on the line of code and hitting **control+enter** on a PC computer keyboard or **command+enter** on a Mac computer keyboard. Save each .R file using a name associated with the Exercise for which it was created. It is recommended that you review the .R file for Chapter 11 located on the textbook's website before completing these exercises. To facilitate doing each exercise, it may be helpful to copy and paste relevant code from the .R file for Chapter 11 into your own .R file and modify them as needed.

Exercises 11.1–11.2 involve one-sample t-*tests using variables from the Learndis dataset. For inferential purposes, we consider the children in the dataset to be a random sample of all children attending public elementary school in a certain city who have been diagnosed with learning disabilities. Use* α = 0.05 *for all significance tests.*

11.1 The mean intellectual ability (iq) score for all children attending public elementary school in the city is 100 with standard deviation, $\sigma = 15$. The children in our sample are a random subset of the population of all children attending public elementary school in this city who are diagnosed with learning disabilities. Use R to construct a 95 percent confidence interval to estimate the mean iq score for this population. We do not want to assume that the standard deviation of the population of learning disabled children is the same as for all children attending public elementary school in this city, but instead want to use the sample to obtain an estimate of the standard deviation. Answer the related questions.

(a) Address the reason for choosing a *t*-test over a *z*-test, in this case.
(b) Evaluate the tenability of the normality assumption or indicate why the assumption is not an issue for this analysis, that the results of the *t*-test would not be compromised by a failure to meet this assumption.
(c) What is the 95 percent confidence interval for the mean iq score of all children attending public elementary school in this city who have been diagnosed with learning disabilities?
(d) State the null and alternative hypotheses for determining whether or not children attending public elementary school in this city who are diagnosed with learning disabilities have a mean iq score of 100.
(e) Using the results of the 95 percent CI, can the null hypothesis be rejected? Why or why not?
(f) State the results of the hypothesis test in context.

11.2 Find the *p*-value associated with the one-sample *t*-test to determine whether the mean reading comprehension score (readcomp) of children attending public elementary school in this city who are diagnosed with learning disabilities is 75. Answer the related questions.

(a) Evaluate the tenability of the normality assumption or indicate why the assumption is not an issue for this analysis, that the results of the *t*-test would not be compromised by a failure to meet this assumption.
(b) What are the null and alternative hypotheses?

(c) What is the p-value associated with the one-sample t-test for testing these null and alternative hypotheses?

(d) Use the p-value to determine whether or not the null hypothesis can be rejected in favor of the alternative.

(e) State the results of the hypothesis test in context.

(f) What is the 95 percent confidence interval for the mean reading comprehension score of children attending public elementary school in this city who are diagnosed with learning disabilities?

(g) Using the results of the 95 percent CI, can the null hypothesis be rejected? Why or why not?

(h) Would the test have been more or less powerful if the sample size had been larger than 76, say 300? Explain.

Exercises 11.3–11.4 involve one-sample t-tests using variables from the Framingham dataset. For inferential purposes, we consider the people in the Framingham dataset to be a random sample of the population of all non-institutionalized adults. Use $\alpha = 0.05$ for all significance tests.

11.3 A person with body mass index higher than 25 is classified as overweight. In this exercise, we will determine whether the mean body mass index of the population of non-institutionalized adults as measured during the first examination (BMI1) is greater than 25.

(a) Evaluate the tenability of the normality assumption or indicate why the assumption is not an issue for this analysis, that the results of the test would not be compromised by a failure to meet this assumption.

(b) State the null and alternative hypotheses for determining whether the mean body mass index of the population of non-institutionalized adults as measured during the first examination is greater than 25.

(c) Conduct the one-sample t-test and determine, based on the resulting p-value, whether the mean body mass index of the population of non-institutionalized adults as measured during the first examination is greater than 25.

(d) Calculate and interpret Cohen's d as a measure of effect size for the analysis.

(e) Why is the confidence interval provided in the one-sample t-test output not appropriate for determining whether the mean body mass index of non-institutionalized adults at first examination is greater than 25?

11.4 Normal systolic blood pressure is less than 120 mmHg. In this exercise we will determine whether the mean systolic blood pressure of non-institutionalized adults at first examination (SYSBP1) is less than 120 mmHg.

(a) State the null and alternative hypotheses for determining whether the mean systolic blood pressure of the population of non-institutionalized adults as measured during the first examination is less than 120 mmHg.

(b) Explain why it is not necessary to carry out a test of these hypotheses in this case.

Exercises 11.5–11.11 involve one-sample t-tests using variables from the NELS dataset. For inferential purposes, we consider the students in the dataset to be a random sample of the population of all college-bound students who have always been at grade level. Use $\alpha = 0.05$ for all significance tests.

11.5 Use the variable famsize, which gives the number of people in a household, to construct a 95 percent CI to determine whether the average family size is 4.5 (two parents and 2.5 kids) for college-bound high school students who are always at grade level.

(a) Evaluate the tenability of the normality assumption or indicate why the assumption is not an issue for this analysis, that the results of the *t*-test would not be compromised by a failure to meet this assumption.

(b) What is the 95 percent confidence interval for the average family size?

(c) Use the confidence interval to determine whether the average family size for this population is 4.5. If it is not 4.5, indicate whether it is higher or lower than 4.5.

(d) Calculate and interpret the value of Cohen's *d* as a measure of the effect size.

11.6 Use a 95 percent confidence interval to estimate the average twelfth grade self-concept score (slfcnc12) of the population of college-bound students who have always been at grade level. Use this interval to determine whether the average twelfth grade self-concept score is different from 32 for the population of college-bound students who have always been at grade level.

11.7 Use the *p*-value derived from an appropriate test of inference to determine whether the average twelfth grade self-concept score (slfcnc12) is different from 32 for the population of college-bound students who have always been at grade level.

11.8 Use the *p*-value derived from an appropriate test of inference to determine whether the population of college-bound students who have always been at grade level on average take more than 3.6 units of mathematics in high school (unitmath).

11.9 For the population of college-bound students from the Northeast (region = "Northeast") who have always been at grade level, use a 95 percent confidence interval to estimate the average number of years of English taken in high school (unitengl).

(a) Restrict the sample to students from the Northeast.

(b) Evaluate the tenability of the normality assumption or indicate why the assumption is not an issue for this analysis, that the results of the *t*-test would not be compromised by a failure to meet this assumption.

(c) What is the 95 percent confidence interval for the average number of years of English taken in high school?

(d) According to the 95 percent confidence interval, is the estimate for the average number of years of English taken in high school by this population of college-bound students from the Northeast equal to 3?

(e) Calculate and interpret the value of Cohen's *d* as a measure of the effect size.

11.10 Does the population of college-bound twelfth graders who have always been at grade level and who attend rigorous academic schools (hsprog = "Rigorous Academic") have a mean social studies achievement score (achsls12) larger than 55?

(a) Evaluate the tenability of the normality assumption or indicate why the assumption is not an issue for this analysis, that the results of the test would not be compromised by a failure to meet this assumption.

(b) State the null and alternative hypotheses.

(c) Verify that the sample mean supports the hypothesized direction of the difference.

(d) Find the *p*-value associated with the appropriate test of inference for determining whether the mean social studies achievement score for this population is greater than 55.

(e) Is this result statistically significant?

(f) State the conclusion in context.

(g) Calculate and interpret the value of Cohen's *d* as a measure of the effect size.

(h) Conceptually, not computationally, what is the difference between what the standard deviation value of 8.56 represents and what the standard error of the mean value of 0.70 represents?

(i) If the standard deviation had been 20 instead of 8.56, and the mean and sample size remained the same, would the *p*-value have been smaller or larger? Explain.

11.11 For the population of college-bound students who were always at grade level and whose parents were divorced when they were in eighth grade (parmarl8 = "Divorced"), use a 95 percent confidence interval to estimate the mean twelfth grade self-concept score (slfcnc12).

(a) Evaluate the tenability of the normality assumption or indicate why the assumption is not an issue for this analysis, that the results of the test would not be compromised by a failure to meet this assumption.

(b) What is the 95 percent confidence interval for the mean twelfth grade self-concept score for college-bound students who were always at grade level and whose parents were divorced when they were in eighth grade?

Exercises 11.12–11.13 involve independent samples t-tests using variables from the Learndis dataset. For inferential purposes, we consider the children in the dataset to be a random sample of all children attending public elementary school in a certain city who have been diagnosed with learning disabilities. Unless otherwise specified, use $\alpha = 0.05$ for all significance tests.

11.12 Conduct an independent samples *t*-test to determine whether there are gender (gender) differences in average math comprehension (mathcomp) among children attending public elementary school in a certain city who have been diagnosed with learning disabilities. Answer the following related questions. Note that there is missing data in the Learndis dataset. To get the sample size, use the command **na.omit** before **length**. For mean and standard deviation, add the argument **na.rm = T** after the variable in each command. Below is an example of how to get descriptive statistics on mathcomp for females:

length(na.omit(Learndis$mathcomp[Learndis$gender == "female"]))
mean(Learndis$mathcomp[Learndis$gender == "female"], na.rm=T)
sd(Learndis$mathcomp[Learndis$gender == "female"], na.rm=T)

(a) Evaluate the tenability of the normality assumption or indicate why the assumption is not an issue for this analysis, that the results of the test would not be compromised by a failure to meet this assumption.

(b) According to Levene's test of equality of variances, should the *t*-ratio be calculated using equal or unequal variances, in this case?

(c) State the null and alternative hypotheses.

(d) According to the p-value associated with this test, are there statistically significant gender differences in average math comprehension for this type of student? If so, describe the nature of the differences.

(e) Calculate and interpret the value of Cohen's d as a measure of the effect size.

11.13 Conduct an independent samples t-test to determine whether there are differences in mean intellectual ability (iq) by the type of placement (placemen: "RR" for resource room or "MIS" for self-contained classroom) among children attending public elementary school in a certain city who have been diagnosed with learning disabilities. Answer the following related questions.

(a) Evaluate the tenability of the normality assumption or indicate why the assumption is not an issue for this analysis, that the results of the test would not be compromised by a failure to meet this assumption.

(b) According to Levene's test of equality of variances, should the t-ratio be calculated using equal or unequal variances, in this case?

(c) According to the 95 percent confidence interval, are there statistically significant differences in mean intellectual ability by type of placement? If so, describe the nature of the differences.

(d) Calculate and interpret the value of Cohen's d as a measure of the effect size.

Exercises 11.14–11.18 involve independent samples t-tests using variables from the Framingham dataset. For inferential purposes, we consider the people in the Framingham dataset to be a random sample of the population of all non-institutionalized adults. Use α = 0.05 for all significance tests. Note that there is missing data in the Framingham dataset; see the instructions for Exercise 11.12 for help getting descriptive statistics on variables with missing values.

11.14 Use the independent samples t-test to investigate whether on average there are initial differences in age (AGE1) between the sexes (SEX) for the population of non-institutionalized adults represented in the Framingham dataset. Use R to create boxplots of AGE1 by SEX.

(a) Based on the boxplots, do the assumptions underlying the independent samples t-test appear tenable? What do you anticipate the result of the independent samples t-test to be? Explain.

(b) Evaluate further the tenability of the normality assumption or indicate why the assumption is not an issue for this analysis, that the results of the test would not be compromised by a failure to meet this assumption.

(c) According to Levene's test of equality of variances, should the t-ratio be calculated using equal or unequal variances, in this case?

(d) According to the p-value, are there initial differences in age on average between the sexes of all non-institutionalized adults? If so, describe the nature of the differences.

(e) Use the 95 percent CI to estimate the average difference in age between males and females at initial examination, which we know from the hypothesis is not statistically significant.

(f) Under what circumstances can we expect the results of the independent samples t-test based on the p-value to be consistent with those based on the confidence interval, as they relate to this hypothesis test?

11.15 Is the mean body mass index (BMI3) of smokers (CURSMOKE3) lower than that for non-smokers as measured at the third and final examination time among the population of non-institutionalized adults? Assume that both the normality and equality of variance assumptions are tenable.

(a) What is the p-value derived from the independent samples t-test for determining whether, on average, the body mass index of smokers is lower than that for non-smokers among the population represented by the Framingham data and what does it convey?

(b) If the question had been whether among the population of non-institutionalized adults the mean BMI of smokers is different (instead of lower) than it is for non-smokers, would the independent samples t-test have been more or less powerful?

11.16 While one can expect initial differences in body mass index (BMI1) between males and females, we may question whether there are differences between males and females in their changes in BMI from 1956 to 1968 (BMI3 – BMI1). In this exercise, we will investigate the change in body mass index for both males and females. You will need to compute a new variable that captures these change values.

(a) Create a new variable BMIDIFF that captures the change in body mass index. Report and interpret BMIDIFF for the first person in the dataset (ID = 1).

(b) Create an associated boxplot, one for males and one females on the same axes. Describe the nature of this new variable for the two groups.

(c) Evaluate the tenability of the normality assumption or indicate why the assumption is not an issue for this analysis, that the results of the test would not be compromised by a failure to meet this assumption.

(d) According to Levene's test of equality of variances, should the t-ratio be calculated using equal or unequal variances, in this case?

(e) According to the p-value derived from the appropriate test of inference, are there differences, on average, in the change in body mass index between males and females for this population of non-institutionalized adults? If so, describe the nature of the differences.

(f) Calculate and interpret the value of Cohen's d as a measure of the effect size.

11.17 In this exercise, we use a nonlinear transformation in conjunction with the independent samples t-test in order to determine, using the Framingham dataset, whether there are differences in average systolic blood pressure (SYSBP3) between those who were and those who were not taking anti-hypertensive (blood pressure) medication at time 3 (BPMEDS3).

(a) Evaluate the tenability of the normality assumption or indicate why the assumption is not an issue for this analysis, that the results of the test would not be compromised by a failure to meet this assumption.

(b) Demonstrate that the log transformation is effective in normalizing the distribution of SYSBP3 for both groups.

(c) Conduct an independent samples t-test on the log transformed systolic blood pressure at time 3 between those who did and did not take anti-hypertensive medication at time 3. Report and interpret the results.

(d) Is it fair to conclude that taking anti-hypertensive medication appears to increase systolic blood pressure? Explain.

11.18 Use an independent samples t-test to determine whether, among the population of non-institutionalized adults, there are differences in total serum cholesterol (TOTCHOL3) by sex (SEX). Be sure to address the underlying assumptions. Interpret the results using either a p-value (with $\alpha = 0.05$) or a 95 percent confidence interval. If the result is statistically significant, report and interpret a measure of effect size.

Exercises 11.19–11.20 involve independent samples t-tests using variables from the NELS dataset. For inferential purposes, we consider the students in the dataset to be a random sample of the population of all college-bound students who have always been at grade level. Use α = 0.05 for all significance tests. Note that there is missing data in the NELS dataset; see the instructions for Exercise 11.12 for help getting descriptive statistics on variables with missing values.

11.19 Among the population of college-bound students who have always been at grade level, do students whose families owned a computer in eighth grade (computer) score differently in twelfth grade math achievement (achmat12), on average, than those whose families did not own a computer?

(a) Explain why an independent samples t-test is more appropriate than a one-sample or paired samples test to answer this question.

(b) Evaluate the tenability of the normality assumption or indicate why the assumption is not an issue for this analysis, that the results of the test would not be compromised by a failure to meet this assumption.

(c) According to Levene's test of equality of variances, is there reason to believe that a violation of the homogeneity of variances assumption would compromise the validity of the t-test results?

(d) State the null and alternative hypotheses regarding whether among this population, students whose families owned a computer in eighth grade score, on average, differently in twelfth grade math achievement than those whose families did not own a computer.

(e) Find the p-value for determining whether among the population of college-bound students who have always been at grade level, students whose families owned a computer in eighth grade score differently in twelfth grade math achievement, on average, than those whose families did not own a computer.

(f) Interpret the results of the hypothesis test using the context of the problem.

(g) Find the 95 percent confidence interval for the mean difference in twelfth grade math achievement between those whose families owned a computer in eighth grade and those whose families did not.

(h) According to the 95 percent confidence interval, among the population of college-bound students who have always been at grade level, do students whose families owned a computer in eighth grade score differently in twelfth grade math achievement, on average, than those whose families did not own a computer?

(i) Calculate and interpret the value of Cohen's d as a measure of the effect size.

(j) Which is longer, the 99 percent CI of the difference or the 95 percent CI of the difference? Use R to confirm your answer.

11.20 Use an independent samples t-test to answer the following questions or indicate why it is not appropriate to do so. In each case, the population is comprised of college-bound students who have always been at grade level and the data are from the NELS dataset. Be sure to address the underlying assumptions. Interpret the results using either a hypothesis test with $\alpha = 0.05$ or a 95 percent confidence interval. If the result is statistically significant, report and interpret a measure of effect size.

(a) Among college-bound students who are always at grade level, is the average twelfth grade self-concept score (slfcnc12) different for smokers and non-smokers (cigarett)?

(b) Among college-bound students who are always at grade level, do students who take advanced math in eighth grade (advmath8) have different expectations for future income (expinc30) than students who do not?

(c) Among college-bound students who are always at grade level, do students who take advanced math in eighth grade (advmath8) have better eighth grade self-concepts (slfcnc08) than students who do not?

(d) Among college-bound students who are always at grade level, do females (gender) have a better self-concept (slfcnc12) than males in twelfth grade?

(e) Among college-bound students who are always at grade level, do females (gender) do better on twelfth grade reading achievement tests (achrdg12) than males?

(f) Among college-bound students who are always at grade level, do those who attended nursery school (nursery) tend to have smaller families (famsiz) than those who did not?

(g) Among college-bound students who are always at grade level, do those who live in the Northeast (region = "Northeast") have mean ses that is higher than that of those who live in the West (region = "West")? To use Levene's test for only two of the regions, use the following command:

levenes.test(NELS\$ses[NELS\$region == "Northeast" | NELS\$region == "West"], NELS\$region[NELS\$region == "Northeast" | NELS\$region == "West"])

Exercise 11.21 relates to the Blood dataset. The creation of a new variable is necessary to perform the independent samples t-test in this example. Note that there is missing data in the Blood dataset; see the instructions for Exercise 11.12 for help getting descriptive statistics on variables with missing values.

11.21 Ten randomly selected African American males are given calcium supplements for 12 weeks, while eleven randomly selected African American males are given a placebo for 12 weeks. At both the beginning and the end of this time period, systolic blood pressure readings of all men were recorded. Create a new variable, reduct; that is, systolc1–systolc2. This variable represents the reduction in blood pressure over the 12 weeks. Conduct an independent samples t-test to determine whether there is a difference in the average blood pressure reduction between the calcium and the placebo groups. Use $\alpha = 0.05$.

Exercise 11.22 involves paired samples t-tests using variables from the Learndis dataset. For inferential purposes, we consider the children in the dataset to be a random sample of all children attending public elementary school in a certain city who have been diagnosed with learning disabilities. Use $\alpha = 0.05$ for all significance tests.

11.22 Answer the following questions about using a paired samples t-test to determine whether public school elementary school children in a certain city diagnosed with learning disabilities perform better in math comprehension (mathcomp) or in reading comprehension (readcomp). Note that there is missing data in the Learndis dataset: some students only have a reading score and some only have a math score. For the paired samples t-test, we need to look at those students who have both scores, so we use the following R code to create read and math variables, which contain scores only for students who have scores for both readcomp and mathcomp.

read = Learndis\$readcomp[complete.cases(Learndis\$readcomp) & complete.cases (Learndis\$mathcomp)]

math = Learndis\$mathcomp[complete.cases(Learndis\$readcomp) & complete.cases (Learndis\$mathcomp)]

  (a) Evaluate the tenability of the normality assumption or indicate why the assumption is not an issue for this analysis, that the results of the test would not be compromised by a failure to meet this assumption.
  (b) Explain why failure to meet the homogeneity of variances assumption for the paired samples t-test would not compromise the results of this test.
  (c) State the null and alternative hypotheses when determining whether public elementary school children in the city diagnosed with learning disabilities perform better in math comprehension or in reading comprehension.
  (d) Use the results of the paired samples hypothesis test to determine whether public elementary school children in the city diagnosed with learning disabilities perform better in math comprehension or in reading comprehension.
  (e) Use the results of the 95 percent confidence interval to determine whether public elementary school children in the city diagnosed with learning disabilities perform better in math comprehension or in reading comprehension.
  (f) Report and interpret Cohen's d as a measure of effect size as a way to measure the practical significance of the test result.

Exercises 11.23–11.24 involve paired samples t-*tests using variables from the Framingham dataset. For inferential purposes, we consider the people in the Framingham dataset to be a random sample of the population of all non-institutionalized adults. Use* α *= 0.05 for all significance tests.*

11.23 Answer the following questions about using a paired samples t-test to determine whether systolic blood pressure (SYSBP1, SYSBP3) increases over time, on average, in non-institutionalized adults. Assume that the normality and equality of variance assumptions are tenable. For the paired samples t-test, we need to look at those individuals who have both scores, so we use the following R code to create bp1 and bp3 variables, which contain scores only for those who have scores for both SYSBP1 and SYSBP3.

bp1 = Framingham\$SYSBP1[complete.cases(Framingham\$SYSBP1) & complete.cases (Framingham\$SYSBP3)]

bp3 = Framingham\$SYSBP3[complete.cases(Framingham\$SYSBP1) & complete.cases (Framingham\$SYSBP3)]

(a) What is the p-value associated with the paired t-test for determining whether among the population of non-institutionalized adults, systolic blood pressure, on average, increases over time?

(b) According to the p-value, does systolic blood pressure increase, on average, over time among non-institutionalized adults?

(c) Report and interpret Cohen's d as a measure of effect size, a measure of the magnitude of practical significance.

11.24 In this exercise, we investigate whether diastolic blood pressure decreases over time (DIABP1, DIABP3). What is the best way to demonstrate that among non-institutionalized adults, the diastolic blood pressure does not does decrease significantly, on average, from time 1 (1956) to time 3 (1968)? Note that there is missing data in the Blood dataset; see the instructions for Exercises 11.22 and 11.23 for help getting descriptive statistics for paired samples with missing values.

Exercises 11.25–11.26 involve paired samples t-tests using variables from the NELS dataset. For inferential purposes, we consider the students in the dataset to be a random sample of the population of all college-bound students who have always been at grade level. Use $\alpha = 0.05$ for all significance tests. Note that there is missing data in the NELS dataset; see the instructions for Exercises 11.22 and 11.23 for help getting descriptive statistics for paired samples with missing values.

11.25 Among the population of college-bound students who have always been at grade level, does the level of science achievement, on average, change from eighth (achsci08) to twelfth grade (achsci12) relative to all students in the grade?

(a) Explain why a paired samples t-test is more appropriate than a one-sample or independent samples test to determine whether the level of science achievement, relative to all students in the grade, changes from eighth to twelfth grade.

(b) Evaluate the tenability of the normality assumption or indicate why the assumption is not an issue for this analysis, that the results of the test would not be compromised by a failure to meet this assumption.

(c) State the null and alternative hypotheses.

(d) Find the p-value associated with the paired samples t-test to determine whether the level of science achievement changes, on average, from eighth to twelfth grade achievement among the population of college-bound students who have always been at grade level.

(e) According to this p-value, does the level of science achievement change from eighth to twelfth grade among this population of college-bound students?

(f) Find the 95 percent confidence interval for the mean difference in science achievement between eighth and twelfth grade.

(g) According to the 95 percent confidence interval, does the level of science achievement change from eighth to twelfth grade for this population?

11.26 Use a paired samples t-test to determine whether among the population of college-bound students who have always been at grade level, the level of self-concept, relative to all students in the grade, increases from eighth (slfcnc08) to twelfth grade (slfcnc12). Be sure to address the underlying assumptions. Interpret the results using either a hypothesis test with $\alpha = 0.05$ or a 95 percent confidence interval. If the result is statistically significant, report and interpret a measure of effect size.

Exercises 11.27– 11.31 involve selection of appropriate tests. Note that there is missing data for some datasets; see the instructions for Exercises 11.12, 11.22, and 11.23 for help getting descriptive statistics when there are missing values.

11.27 A study was undertaken to determine different sources of stress among college students. A sample of 1,000 college students was asked to rate their level of agreement to experiencing stress from different potential sources, such as parents, roommates, partners, and final exams on a 5 point Likert scale. They were also asked to provide demographic information including number of enrolled credits and gender. For each of the following questions relative to this dataset, select an appropriate statistical procedure from the list below for answering this question. Assume for now that the underlying assumptions for these tests have been met.

Procedures:
1. One-tailed, one-sample *t*-test
2. Two-tailed, one-sample *t*-test
3. One-tailed, independent samples *t*-test
4. Two-tailed, independent samples *t*-test
5. One-tailed, paired samples *t*-test
6. Two-tailed, paired samples *t*-test

Questions:
(a) Are undergraduates at large urban universities more stressed by their parents or their roommates?
(b) Are undergraduates at large urban universities more stressed by their parents than their roommates?
(c) Do undergraduates at large urban universities in the Northeast typically take 15 credits per semester?
(d) Are there gender differences in the stress level due to final exams among undergraduates at large urban universities?
(e) Among undergraduates at large urban universities, are males more stressed than females by their partners?

11.28 For each of the following questions based on the NELS dataset, select an appropriate statistical procedure to use to answer it from the list below. Then, use R to conduct the appropriate hypothesis test in cases where the underlying assumptions are tenable. If the result of a hypothesis test is statistically significant, report and interpret an appropriate measure of effect size.

Procedures:
1. One-tailed, one-sample *t*-test
2. Two-tailed, one-sample *t*-test
3. One-tailed, independent samples *t*-test
4. Two-tailed, independent samples *t*-test
5. One-tailed, paired samples *t*-test
6. Two-tailed, paired samples *t*-test

Questions:

(a) Among college-bound students who are always at grade level, do those who attended nursery school (nursery) tend to have higher ses than those who did not?

(b) Among college-bound students who are always at grade level, does self-concept differ in eighth (slfcnc08) and tenth (slfcnc10) grades?

(c) Among college-bound students who are always at grade level, do those who attend public school (schtyp8) perform differently in twelfth grade math achievement (achmat12) from those who attend private school? (Note that to answer this question, the variable schtyp8 will have to be *recoded* to be dichotomous as described in Chapter 4).

(d) Among college-bound students who are always at grade level, do families typically have four members (famsize)?

(e) Among college-bound students who are always at grade level, do students tend to take more years of English (unitengl) than Math (unitmath)?

11.29 In this exercise we demonstrate, by example using the NELS dataset, that the paired samples *t*-test is equivalent to a one-sample *t*-test of the difference scores. For college-bound students who are always at grade level, does relative math achievement change from eighth (achmat08) to twelfth grades (achmat12)? Follow the steps below to use both a paired samples and a one-sample *t*-test to answer the question.

(a) Use a graphical display of your choice to anticipate the answer to the question posed.

(b) Answer the question by using a paired samples *t*-test. Use $\alpha = 0.05$.

(c) Use R to verify that the paired samples *t*-test results are the same as those from a one-sample *t*-test on the difference scores. First use R to create a new variable that represents the difference between eighth and twelfth grade math achievement. You can do this with the command **math_diff = NELS\$achmat12 – NELS\$achmat08**. Then use a one-sample *t*-test on this new variable to answer the question. Use $\alpha = 0.05$.

(d) How do your answers to parts (b) and (c) compare?

(e) Would the results have been the same as the paired *t*-test had we ignored the pairing of scores and conducted an independent samples *t*-test on the eighth and twelfth grade math achievement scores? Explain.

11.30 Explain why a one-sample *t*-test should not be used with the NELS dataset to determine whether the average number of times late for school in twelfth grade (late12) is 4 times (late12 = 4).

11.31 In this exercise, based on the NELS dataset, we contrast a descriptive and inferential approach for determining the relationship, if any, between high school cigarette use and twelfth grade math achievement.

(a) For the students in the NELS dataset, is there a difference in twelfth grade math achievement (achmat12) between those who do and do not smoke cigarettes (cigarett)?

(b) For college-bound students who are always at grade level, is there a difference in twelfth grade math achievement (achmat12) between those who do and do not smoke cigarettes (cigarett)? Use $\alpha = 0.05$.

Exercises 11.32–11.42 include calculations by hand, the use of Table C.2 in Appendix C, and small datasets. Note that there is missing data for some datasets; see the instructions for Exercises 11.12, 11.22, and 11.23 for help getting descriptive statistics when there are missing values.

11.32 Given $t = 2.364$ and $df = 100$ for a one-sample t-test, calculate p or indicate that the result is not statistically significant, under the following conditions:

(a) $H_0: \mu = 30$ vs. $H_1: \mu \neq 30$
(b) $H_0: \mu = 30$ and $H_1: \mu < 30$
(c) $H_0: \mu = 30$ and $H_1: \mu > 30$

11.33 Given $t = 1.283$ and $df = 500$ for an independent samples t-test, calculate p or indicate that the result is not statistically significant, under the following conditions:

(a) $H_0: \mu = 30$ and $H_1: \mu \neq 30$
(b) $H_0: \mu = 30$ and $H_1: \mu < 30$
(c) $H_0: \mu = 30$ and $H_1: \mu > 30$

11.34 Given $t = -1.23$ and $df = 100$ for a paired samples t-test, calculate p or indicate that the result is not statistically significant, under the following conditions:

(a) $H_0: \mu = 30$ and $H_1: \mu \neq 30$
(b) $H_0: \mu = 30$ and $H_1: \mu < 30$
(c) $H_0: \mu = 30$ and $H_1: \mu > 30$

11.35 Given $t = 1.8$ and $df = 800$ for a one-sample t-test, calculate p or indicate that the result is not statistically significant, under the following conditions:

(a) $H_0: \mu = 30$ and $H_1: \mu \neq 30$
(b) $H_0: \mu = 30$ and $H_1: \mu < 30$
(c) $H_0: \mu = 30$ and $H_1: \mu > 30$

11.36 A one-sample t-test, based on the Learndis dataset, was conducted to determine whether the mean intellectual ability score for all children attending public elementary school in the city who have been diagnosed with learning disabilities is 85. Summary statistics for the iq variable are shown in the table below. Use the available information and R or Table C.2 to find the mean difference, t, df, and p. Then, indicate whether the mean intellectual ability score for all children attending public elementary school in the city who have been diagnosed with learning disabilities differs from 85.

Variable	N	Mean	SD	Min.	Max.
iq	105	81.49524	10.94051	51	105

11.37 A one-sample t-test, based on the Learndis dataset, was conducted to determine whether the mean intellectual ability score for all children attending public elementary school in the city who are diagnosed with learning disabilities is 85. Use the table from Exercise 11.36 and R or Table C.2 to find the 95 percent confidence interval for the mean IQ. Then, indicate whether the mean intellectual ability score for all children attending public elementary school in the city who are diagnosed with learning disabilities differs from 85.

11.38 An independent samples t-test, based on the Learndis dataset, was conducted to determine whether there are gender differences in average math comprehension among children attending public elementary school in a certain city who have been diagnosed with learning disabilities. Summary statistics for the mathcomp variable by gender are shown in the table below. Use the available information and R or Table C.2 to obtain the mean difference, t, df, and p, and the 95 percent confidence interval. Then, indicate whether there are gender differences in average math comprehension among children attending public elementary school in a certain city who have been diagnosed with learning disabilities.

Gender	N	Mean	SD	Min.	Max.
female	34	90.20588	14.42174	66	118
male	60	84.05	12.95811	61	121

11.39 A paired samples t-test, based on the Learndis dataset, was conducted to determine whether public school elementary school children in a certain city diagnosed with learning disabilities score differently, on average, in math and reading comprehension. Summary statistics for the readcomp and mathcomp variables are shown in the table below. Use the available information and R or Table C.2 to obtain the mean difference, t, df, p and the 95 percent confidence interval to answer the question posed.

Variable	N	Mean	SD	Min.	Max.
readcomp	76	77.63158	13.07807	22	107
mathcomp	94	86.2766	13.75391	61	121

11.40 From a normally distributed population, the following sample is randomly selected:

25 27 22 20 27 26 24 25 20 30 27 25 29 26 22 25

(a) Use this sample to construct a 95 percent confidence interval for μ. Use your confidence interval to estimate μ and to see whether 27 is one of the plausible values for μ.

(b) Find and interpret the p-value associated with a one-sample t-test on H_0: $\mu = 27$ versus H_1: $\mu \neq 27$ at the significance level $\alpha = 0.05$.

11.41 In order to test whether a new drug for individuals who suffer from high blood pressure affects mental alertness, a random sample of 12 patients suffering from high blood pressure is selected from a large number of such patients who regularly visit an outpatient clinic. Tests of mental alertness are administered to these patients both before and after they receive the drug. Their scores are shown in the following table. Is there evidence of a decrease in mental alertness, on average, after receipt of the drug for the population of all such patients at this outpatient clinic? Assume that the mental alertness scores are normally distributed, both before and after treatment, in the population of all such patients at this outpatient clinic and that the variances are equal in the populations. Use $\alpha = 0.05$.

Before	10	14	5	6	9	15	1	20	10	2	7	10
After	5	9	7	3	10	15	4	16	12	5	3	6

11.42 Eight one-year olds and eight two-year olds took the same test. Scores were compared (on the average, not on an individual paired basis) to determine whether there is an age difference on the skill measured for the populations from which these two samples were randomly selected, at a significance level of $\alpha = 0.05$. Assume that the test scores are normally distributed for both age groups in the population and that the variances are equal in the populations. Complete the analysis using the following data and draw your conclusion:

One-year olds	7	7	0	1	9	3	8	5
Two-year olds	13	13	9	9	13	5	5	5

Exercises 11.43–11.47 are conceptual and do not require the use of R.

11.43 Explain why it is impossible for p to be identically equal to zero for any hypothesis test using the t-distribution.

11.44 As the sample size increases, what happens to the magnitude of t_c in a one-sample t-test?

11.45 As the sample size increases, what happens to the standard error of the mean in a one-sample t-test?

11.46 A researcher conducted a one-tailed, one-sample t-test for which the results were not statistically significant. Should she then conduct a two-tailed test? Explain.

11.47 A researcher conducted a two-tailed independent samples t-test, the results of which were statistically significant. Should she then conduct two one-tailed tests to determine the nature of the mean difference? Explain.

Exercises 11.48–11.51 involve power analyses.

11.48 Suppose you would like to conduct a one-sample t-test with power of approximately 0.80 to detect an effect size of $d = 0.50$ with $\alpha = 0.05$.
   (a) What is the necessary minimum sample size if the test is two-tailed?
   (b) What is the necessary minimum sample size if the test is one-tailed?

11.49 Suppose you would like to detect an effect size of $d = 0.20$ with power 0.80 and $\alpha = 0.05$ in a one-sample t-test with a null hypothesis, $H_0: \mu = 10$.
   (a) What is the necessary minimum sample size if the alternative hypothesis is $H_1: \mu \neq 10$?
   (b) What is the necessary minimum sample size if the alternative hypothesis is $H_1: \mu > 10$?
   (c) Based on your answers to (a) and (b), which test is inherently more powerful, the two-tailed test or the one-tailed test? Explain.

11.50 Suppose you would like to conduct a power analysis to find the necessary minimum sample size to achieve a power of 0.80 in an independent samples t-test to detect an effect size of $d = 0.20$ with $\alpha = 0.05$.
   (a) What is the necessary minimum sample size if the test is two-tailed?
   (b) What is the necessary minimum sample size if the test is one-tailed?

11.51 Suppose you would like to conduct a power analysis to find the minimum sample size necessary to achieve a power of 0.80 in a paired samples t-test to detect an effect size of $d = 0.20$ with $\alpha = 0.05$.
   (a) What is the necessary minimum sample size if the test is two-tailed?
   (b) What is the necessary minimum sample size if the test is one-tailed?

# CHAPTER TWELVE

RESEARCH DESIGN: INTRODUCTION AND OVERVIEW

By this time, you, no doubt, have begun to appreciate the important role analytic methods play in the research process by their ability to enable us to uncover the story contained in our data. The overall research process, however, begins not with the analysis of data, but rather with the posing of questions that interest us. It is the questions we ask that motivate us to conduct research, and it is the nature of these questions, from most simple to most challenging, that gives rise to how we design a research study, how we define and measure relevant variables, and how we collect and analyze our data to answer these questions. In this chapter we will explore many of the different types of questions we may pose, the related types of research designs they engender, and the conclusions they do and do not foster.

QUESTIONS AND THEIR LINK TO DESCRIPTIVE, RELATIONAL, AND CAUSAL RESEARCH STUDIES

We begin by considering a question that is so simple in its nature that, by itself, it hardly constitutes what we think of when we envision a research study: "To what extent do two individuals possess a certain trait?" A more concrete version of this type of question is, "How much do college freshmen John and Mary weigh?"

THE NEED FOR A GOOD MEASURE OF OUR CONSTRUCT: WEIGHT

In thinking through the elements needed to answer this question, we realize that in addition to our two freshmen, Mary and John, we would need a good measure of their respective weights, one that we can rely upon to produce accurate weight values.

In the language of tests and measurement (psychometrics), we would want our measures of weight to have both *validity* and *reliability*[1]. The validity of a measure is the extent to which the measure assesses what it purports to measure (Cohen et al., 2012). The reliability of a measure is the extent to which the measure is free from chance factors (random error) that occur at the time of measurement (e.g., John does not stand in the middle of the scale, the needle on the scale wavers from John's unsteady stance, etc.). If John were weighed more than once on this scale at the same time on each occasion (e.g., at early morning rising), these chance factors would cause John's recorded weight value to vary from one measurement occasion to the next. Because reliable measures are free of this kind of error, they are expected to yield consistent results from one measurement occasion to the next.

---

[1] Covering issues in measurement in greater detail is beyond the scope of this book. The interested reader is referred to Cohen et al. (2012) for further study.

From a more mathematical perspective, in terms of what is known as classical test theory, an observed value X contains both a true weight value component and an error component, expressed by Equation 12.1 as:

$$X = T + E. \tag{12.1}$$

Using Equation 12.1, we may express the reliability of John's observed weight, X, in Equation 12.2 as the variance of John's observed weight ($\mathrm{Var}(X)$) minus the variance of the error component ($\mathrm{Var}(E)$) contained in his observed weight divided by the variance of his observed weight, $\mathrm{Var}(X)$. This expression may, in turn, be expressed as the ratio of the true variance of X ($\mathrm{Var}(T)$) to the observed variance of X ($\mathrm{Var}(X)$), as shown in Equation 12.2:

$$\text{Reliability}(X) = [\mathrm{Var}(X) - \mathrm{Var}(E)]/\mathrm{Var}(X) = \mathrm{Var}(T)/\mathrm{Var}(X). \tag{12.2}$$

As a ratio or proportion, the reliability of a measure will range from 0 to 1. At the extremes, if the measure is error free so that $\mathrm{Var}(E) = 0$, its reliability will equal 1; if the measure is nothing but error so that $\mathrm{Var}(X) = \mathrm{Var}(E)$, its reliability will equal 0.

Measures may have no validity, yet be highly reliable as in a situation in which hair length is used to measure a person's weight from one day to the next. One would be hard-pressed to consider hair length as a measure of weight, yet from one day to the next, one's hair length would remain reasonably consistent or stable (i.e., it would be a reliable, but not a valid, measure of weight). In assessing the reliability of a measure of say, one's mood, one must not confuse the reliability of a measure of mood with the natural day to day variation that occurs in one's mood. The attempt to assess the reliability of a measure of a trait as distinguished from that trait's natural time to time variation makes the assessment of reliability, in general, a challenging task and has given rise to the multiple ways in which reliability is assessed. For traits that do not naturally change from time to time, test–re-test reliability may be used, but for traits that do change naturally from time to time (like mood), assessing the reliability of a measure at a single point in time is more appropriate. One of the most popular approaches to assessing the reliability of a measure at a single point in time is Cronbach's alpha internal consistency reliability coefficient (Cohen et al., 2012). Cronbach's alpha is used when multiple items are used to measure an underlying idea, or *construct*. Like other measures of reliability, Cronbach's alpha ranges from 0 to 1, with higher numbers indicating higher levels of reliability. While the formula for Cronbach's alpha is not reproduced here, we note that the formula is a function of two pieces of information: the number of items in question, and their average correlation.

THE DESCRIPTIVE STUDY

Assuming our measure of weight has both validity and reliability, we may use our two observed weight values to describe or characterize John and Mary's weight, respectively. As such, this type of question leads to what may be called a *descriptive study*. It is descriptive because our aim simply is to describe the *status quo*, or the ways things are, rather than to explain *why* things are the way they are. In a more realistic example of a descriptive study, we may be interested in the question, "How much do male and female college freshmen weigh?" In this case, we are seeking to describe the respective weights of two populations of college freshmen, one male and one female. These two populations may be described as our *target populations* because these are the groups in which we are interested – those about which we would like to draw conclusions (Shadish et al., 2002).

In addition to defining or operationalizing our construct of interest (e.g., weight) and identifying or developing a way to measure that construct well, we also would need to determine the sampling methods[2] by which to select our males and females from their respective populations (assuming it is not possible to obtain information about everyone from both populations), and to determine the statistical methods that would enable us to make an appropriate inference from our respective samples to our respective target populations. Based on our discussion of sampling in Chapter 9, we could obtain a random sample of the male population and another of the female population using, for example, simple random sampling. We could then use the material in Chapter 11 related to estimating a single population mean, μ, to construct two confidence intervals, one based on the unbiased sample mean estimator, $\overline{X}$, of μ for males and the other for females, to estimate their corresponding population means. The respective confidence intervals could then be constructed to contain with high probability the true population mean weight for each of the male and female populations.

FROM DESCRIPTIVE TO RELATIONAL STUDIES

If the aim of the previous question were extended from wanting simply to describe the status quo of male and female college freshmen weight to wanting to explain why things are the way they are, and, perhaps in particular, to determining if there is an association between a college freshman's weight and his/her sex, or even between a college freshman's weight and his/her sex and height, we are in the realm of what may be called a *relational study*. To determine whether there is a relationship between sex and weight considering the population of male and female college freshmen, one could use the independent groups *t*-test discussed in Chapter 11 to test whether such a relationship exists. If the null hypothesis of no difference is not rejected, we would have reason to believe that there is no association between college freshmen weight and sex in the population of college freshmen, and if rejected, we would have reason to believe otherwise. More generally, in relational studies, the use of correlation and regression techniques in the inferential setting are useful in making inferences from sample results to the target populations of interest. Although you already are familiar with correlation and regression techniques in the descriptive setting, these methods will be covered again later in this text in Chapters 15 and 16 within the inferential setting. In Chapter 15, you will see that, in fact, the independent groups *t*-test is equivalent to having computed and tested the correlation in the population between the continuous variable, weight, and the dichotomous variable, sex.

FROM RELATIONAL TO CAUSAL STUDIES

Recalling one of the tenets of correlation analysis covered in Chapter 5, that correlation does not imply causation, one cannot simply use a correlation to answer whether a change in one variable actually causes a change in another variable, called an outcome variable.

---

[2] The method of simple random sampling was discussed in Chapter 9. A more complete discussion of different sampling methods is beyond the scope of this book. The interested reader is referred to Groves et al. (2004).

There are many examples of variables that are correlated but where changing one does not cause the other to change in a predictable way. When we want to determine whether variables are causally related, we conduct a *causal study*. Within the context of our ongoing example about weight, one would need a causal study to address the question, "What is the causal effect of a particular college freshman diet provided by a university on weight gain/loss from September to June?"

If the goal of a study is to make claims that are causal in nature, certain restrictive conditions must hold. In particular, for a study to claim that X causes Y, not only must X be correlated with Y, but X must also precede Y in time, and there must be no alternative plausible explanation for the observed $X-Y$ relationship; that is, the $X-Y$ relationship must not be attributable to any other variable not included in the study (Shadish et al., 2002).

Often a causal claim is made between X and Y, bolstered by the facts that X and Y are correlated and X precedes Y in time, yet alternative plausible explanations exist to offset the validity of the claim. One such example is a study, "Justice at work and reduced risk of coronary heart disease among employees" (Kivimaki et al., 2005), which was reported in the *New York Times* in the article "Environment: Injustices at work may harm men's hearts" (Nagourney, 2005). For the study, approximately 6,500 men between the ages of 35 to 55 completed questionnaires about justice at work, job strain, and effort–reward imbalance during the time period from 1985 to 1990. From 1990 through 1999, the men were tracked for incidence of coronary heart disease (CHD). Given that the authors found that those who perceived a high level of justice at work showed evidence of CHD at 70 percent of the rate of those who did not, can they conclude with authority that "justice at work may protect against CHD," or said differently, that being treated unfairly at work may cause heart problems? Are there variables, other than a perception of being unfairly treated at work, that may be the true cause of the reduction in heart problems? The authors report that men who perceived higher levels of justice were more likely to be older and that "[a]fter adjustment for age, men who perceived higher levels of justice were more likely to be married and have a higher education level, higher employment grade, and lower BMI [Body Mass Index] compared to those with perceived lower levels of justice" (Kivimaki et al., 2005 p. 2247).

Because these factors are clearly potential alternative explanations for the causal claim that a perception of injustice increases the evidence of CHD, the authors controlled for these factors, and still found the relationship to exist. It remains doubtful, however, that the list of variables included in their analysis exhausts all possible variables that may explain the causal relationship noted. In acknowledgement of this situation, Nagourney (2005) extends a note of caution in accepting the causal claim as true by noting that "the results were based on observational data rather than a controlled experiment."

Observational studies are those in which individuals merely are observed and data are collected on an outcome (or outcomes) of interest. In this study, individuals were given a questionnaire to obtain data on their perceptions of job strain and effort–reward imbalance. Other data were then collected over time on indicators of these men's coronary heart problems. There was no attempt made by the investigators to affect the outcome (coronary heart problems) through the administration of a treatment, nor to form treatment and control groups at the outset of the study. Instead, the individuals in this study formed themselves into different comparison groups by their scores on the questionnaire, so that the researcher was working with intact groups. In the context of a two-group design, one may say that, in this case, the "treatment" group was comprised of those who were observed to perceive a high level of justice at work, and the "comparison" or "control" group was comprised of those who were observed to perceive a low or moderate level of justice at work. The problem with studies that are based on intact groups is that they may differ on other important variables in addition to the grouping variable. In this example, the group that perceived higher levels of justice was also more likely to be older, married, and more educated.

In other situations, the investigator decides at the outset who is to be in the treatment group and who is to be in the no-treatment, or control, group. When the investigator assigns individuals to the groups randomly, we have what is called a *randomized control study* or *true experiment*. This is the type of study that Nagourney makes reference to in his word of caution in the Vital Signs column (2005). When, on the other hand, the investigator assigns individuals to treatment and control groups using a method other than random assignment, we have what is called a *non-randomized control study*, which is a type of observational study, also called a *quasi-experimental study*.

THE GOLD STANDARD OF CAUSAL STUDIES: THE TRUE EXPERIMENT AND RANDOM ASSIGNMENT

In short, in order for causal claims to be valid, a true experiment, rather than a non-randomized control study, should be used. The defining feature of a true experiment is that units (e.g., individuals) are *randomly assigned* to treatment and control groups. Those in the treatment group receive the intervention or treatment, while those in the control group do not.

In the study described earlier that a perception of unjust behavior in the workplace causes an increase in the evidence of CHD, the authors acknowledged that men who perceived higher levels of justice were more likely to be older and that "[a]fter adjustment for age, men who perceived higher levels of justice were more likely to be married and have a higher education level, higher employment grade, and lower BMI compared to those with perceived lower levels of justice" (Kivimaki et al., 2005, p. 2247). The two groups being compared differed in ways that could explain the observed difference in the outcome measure and confound the interpretation of results. Accordingly, such variables are called *confounders*. The presence of confounders goes counter to having groups that are *balanced* at the outset of a study.

Although the authors controlled for these confounders, in this study the possibility exists that there still could be other variables on which the two groups differ, and these variables could be the ones that are the real reasons for the observed increase in coronary heart problems by those who perceived the workplace to be unfair. Random assignment to treatment and control groups, however, guarantees that with samples of large enough size, the two groups will be balanced (not different) on all variables. As such, neither the experimental nor the control group will be more endowed on a variable, or set of variables, that might positively affect the outcome, leaving the treatment itself as the only possible cause of the obtained outcome result.

To repeat, groups that are balanced on all variables that might potentially affect the outcome rules out the possibility that some other variable (or variables) lurking in the background (even variables unobserved or unmeasured) is the real reason for having observed the difference on the outcome variable between the two groups. If there is a difference on the outcome variable between the two groups, it must, therefore, be due to the fact that one group was given the treatment and the other group was not, because through randomization with groups of large enough size, the groups are otherwise equivalent at the outset.

It should be noted that with small sample sizes, the two groups could be statistically significantly different at the outset on some variables. Accordingly, although not a perfect or even foolproof way of achieving balanced groups in the case of small samples, random assignment "is nonetheless the only way of doing so, and the essential way" (Cook & Campbell, 1979, p. 15). In this sense, then, a true experiment, defined by random assignment of treatment and control groups, provides the gold standard for reaching causal conclusions.

Of course, random assignment may not always be possible for ethical or practical reasons (Shadish et al., 2002). For example, if one were interested in testing the impact of smoking on the incidence of lung cancer, for ethical reasons, one could not randomly assign individuals to a smoking condition as opposed to a non-smoking condition. Or, if one were studying different approaches to teaching statistics in a college setting, under ordinary circumstances, for practical reasons, the researcher would not be able to randomly assign students to a treatment or control class because college students tend to choose the particular classes they take during a semester based on their own schedules and class availability. Or, in the unjust behavior in the workplace example, intact groups were used as defined by responses to a questionnaire. One could imagine how difficult, for both ethical and practical reasons, it would have been to assign individuals randomly to either "unjust" or "just" supervisors at work. In the next section, we illustrate the extent to which the absence of random assignment to treatment and control groups, for whatever the reason, can result in the wrong causal conclusion regarding the magnitude and even the sign (direction) of the treatment effect.

COMPARING TWO KIDNEY STONE TREATMENTS USING A NON-RANDOMIZED CONTROLLED STUDY

In this study by Charig et al. (1986) the success rates of two treatments, A and B, for kidney stones are compared. Patients with kidney stones were not randomly assigned to one of the two treatments. The table below gives the overall success rates and numbers of cases treated for both treatments, A and B. A comparison of these overall success rates would appear to show quite clearly that overall Treatment B is more effective than Treatment A, since for Treatment B the success rate is 83 percent, while for Treatment A it is only 78 percent.

Success rates (successes/total)	
Treatment A	Treatment B
78% (273/350)	83% (289/350)

However, because individuals were not assigned randomly to Treatments A and B, it may be that those assigned to Treatment A differ from those assigned to Treatment B on variables that could affect the outcome of the study (the success rate of the treatment). One such variable, for example, that is likely to affect the success rate of a treatment, and on which the two groups may differ, is kidney stone size (an indicator of the severity of one's kidney stone problem). As a result, kidney stone size may be a confounding variable lurking in the background of this study, and may be the real reason why Treatment A appears overall to be superior to Treatment B in the analysis above.

As the next table indicates, when kidney stone size is included in the analysis as a control, the same set of treatments suggests a wholly different result. Treatment A now appears to be more effective than Treatment B under both severity scenarios:

Success rates accounting for kidney stone size			
Small stones		Large stones	
Treatment A	Treatment B	Treatment A	Treatment B
Group 1	Group 2	Group 3	Group 4
93% (81/87)	87% (234/270)	73% (192/263)	69% (55/80)

The inequality between the two successes/total ratios is now reversed from what it was before. This reversal (or sign change) in the inequality between the two ratios, which creates what is called *Simpson's paradox*, happens because two effects occur together, or are *confounded* (Julious & Mullee, 1994). In particular, the sizes of the groups which are combined when the lurking variable (kidney stone size) is ignored are very different. Doctors tend to give the severe cases the better treatment (Group 3 in the table above), and the milder cases the inferior treatment (Group 2). Therefore, the overall totals are dominated by these two groups, and not by the much smaller Groups 1 and 4. The lurking variable has a large effect on the ratios, i.e., the success rate is more strongly influenced by the severity of the case than by the choice of treatment. Therefore, Group 3 does worse than Group 2.

This example illustrates a problem that could arise in the computation of a weighted mean (recall that Chapter 3 includes a discussion of the weighted mean) and points to the importance of taking into account variables in an analysis that may confound results, and thereby produce estimates of a treatment effect that are simply wrong (or *biased*) to a great extent. Without including and controlling for the confounder, kidney stone size, Treatment B is deemed to be better than Treatment A, yet with it, the bias is so substantial that the reverse conclusion is reached. In addition to controlling for potentially confounding variables, like kidney stone size, at the analysis stage, one may also control for them in the design itself as the next section describes.

INCLUDING BLOCKING IN A RESEARCH DESIGN

Without including kidney stone size in the analysis, the bias that emerged in estimating the treatment effect was due to the fact that doctors tended to give the severe cases the better treatment and the milder cases the inferior treatment. That is, the severity of the case, as reflected in the size of the kidney stone, was disproportionately represented in the two treatments. If each treatment condition, Treatment A and Treatment B, had an equal probability of being assigned subjects with small and large kidney stones, we would not expect the groups to differ on this important variable that is highly correlated with the outcome of the study, and there would be no bias in the estimate of the treatment effect. If we formed two homogeneous pools of subjects, one with small kidney stones and the other with large kidney stones, and then assigned subjects from each pool randomly to the different treatment conditions, "we would feel quite confident that the groups were nearly equivalent at the outset" (Keppel, 1991, p. 298), not only in terms of the severity of their kidney stone problem, but also in terms of other relevant characteristics as well.

This type of design is called a *blocking design* or a *randomized block design* because the homogeneous pools of subjects are known as *blocks*. If the blocking factor is highly correlated with the outcome (in the kidney stone example, stone size is highly correlated with the outcome, treatment success rate), a blocking design has the additional advantage of having more power than an unblocked design because each of the groups defined by a particular block and treatment condition is more homogeneous relative to the outcome variable. As noted by Keppel, a blocking design is constructed in "two steps: first an initial grouping of subjects into blocks and then the random assignment of subjects within each block to the different conditions" (p. 300). In the next chapter, we will present an analysis, called the one-way analysis of variance, appropriate for analyzing data from a single factor non-blocked design, where individuals are randomly assigned to treatments, and in Chapter 14, we will present an analysis, called a two-way analysis of variance, appropriate for analyzing data from a two-factor (called a *factorial*) design, where one factor may be a treatment factor and the other may be a blocking factor. As will be discussed in Chapter 14, blocking designs can provide greater statistical power, and, as such, may be described as being more statistically valid than non-blocking counterparts.

UNDERSCORING THE IMPORTANCE OF HAVING A TRUE CONTROL GROUP USING RANDOMIZATION

This section is based on Lord (1967) and Holland and Rubin (1982). The randomized block design makes use of randomization to assign individuals within each block to a treatment condition so that the treatment groups to be compared will be equivalent or balanced from the outset. In this section, we take a closer look at estimating a treatment effect when random assignment to treatment and control conditions is difficult or even impossible and return to the question posed in an earlier section of this chapter when the notion of a causal study was first introduced, "What is the causal effect of a particular college freshman diet provided by a university on weight gain/loss from September to June?"

If in the study designed to answer this question, college freshmen were not assigned randomly either to the particular diet under study (the treatment condition) or to a different diet (the control condition), can the researcher ever conclude with certainty that it was the particular diet itself that caused the weight gain/loss, rather than something else, if indeed there was a weight change? If the two groups are not balanced at the outset of the study (in September) on all potential variables that might affect weight gain/loss during freshman year (e.g., the stress of college, the amount of increased exercise from walking greater distances from class to class, the late nights partying), such variables could be the real reasons for any observed average weight gain/loss, rather than the diet itself. In such instances, the average estimate of weight loss caused by the diet itself (called, the *average treatment effect*) would not solely reflect the treatment; it would be biased.

In this particular situation, however, the university has only one diet for its freshmen class. Accordingly, the entire freshman class is assigned this diet, which means that there is no control diet and only a treatment group. We shall designate the treatment group as Group 1. If there were a control group, we would designate that group as Group 0. As one would expect, in order to measure weight gain/loss of its college freshmen from September to June, the university measures the weight of each freshman twice, once in September and then again in June. This type of design is known as a *repeated measures design*, or a *panel design*. The September weight may be viewed as a pretest and the June weight as a posttest, and as such, this particular type of repeated measures design with only two measurement occasions, one before and one after, also is referred to as a *one-group pretest–posttest design* (Shadish et al., 2002). Recall that we analyzed data from this type of design using a paired groups *t*-test in the previous chapter.

Let us depart from this situation for a moment and consider for now a different scenario in which we do not have simply a treatment group, but also a control group, and that, as before, each of these groups is measured twice, once in September and then again in June. Let us also assume that individuals are assigned randomly to one of these two groups; the treatment group is assigned the particular college freshman diet, and the control group is assigned a diet other than the particular college freshman diet. If we let X, in general, represent the students' observed September weights, student i in the treatment group (Group 1) would have their September weight represented by X_{1i}, and student i in the control group (Group 0) would have their September weight represented by X_{0i}. Analogously, if Y represents, in general, the students' observed June weights, then student i in the treatment group would be represented by Y_{1i}, and student i in the control group would have their June weight represented by Y_{0i}.

Because in this situation individuals *are* randomly assigned to treatment and control groups, with large enough sized groups we can expect the two groups to be equal, on average, with respect to their September weights. We also can expect the two groups to be balanced on the host of measured and unmeasured variables that might affect their June weights (e.g., activity level, metabolism, stress level, etc.). Accordingly, in this situation, to obtain an estimate of the average treatment effect of the university diet, we simply would need to compare the average June weight of the college freshmen in the treatment group, denoted $E(Y_1)$, to the average June weight of the college freshmen in the true control group (those randomly not exposed to the university diet), denoted $E(Y_0)$[3]. This comparison may be expressed simply as Equation 12.3, which defines the average treatment effect in equation form:

$$E(Y_1) - E(Y_0). \tag{12.3}$$

But, unfortunately, the situation defined by our university diet problem differs from this one in that *all* college freshmen are assigned the university diet, and as such, they are all in the treatment group. There is no control group to which students have been

---

[3] Through random assignment, we are trying to achieve a situation in which the college freshmen who were not exposed to the university diet (the control group) are basically clones of those who were exposed to the university diet (the treatment group), so that the difference between the average June weights of the two groups is an unbiased estimate of the average treatment effect, due wholly to the treatment itself and to no other lurking variables.

randomly assigned. As a result, we will not have a direct estimate of $E(Y_0)$, namely, the average effect of the diet for a true control group as measured in June.

Without a direct estimate of $E(Y_0)$, it is sensible to ask: How can we solve for Equation 12.3 and obtain the university diet's average treatment effect on weight gain/loss? Said differently, we may ask: How can we assess the university diet's average treatment effect if we do not know *the amount by which the college freshmen's weight would have changed from September to June if they were NOT exposed to the particular diet provided by the university*?

Because, in this example, there is no one in the freshman class who was not exposed to this particular university diet, what we need is information related to a situation that is literally contrary to fact. Such situations are called *counterfactuals* (see Wainer, 2011, pp. 123–126). Some examples of *counterfactuals* are:

- If I had taken three Advil instead of only one, my headache would be gone by now.
- If I were you, I would have applied for the job, eaten more spinach, run the marathon, etc.

The term counterfactual, or potential outcome, is often used as a synonym for control group or comparison. What is the counterfactual? This question just usually means, "To what is the treatment being compared?" When causal claims are made in a research study, it is always sensible to ask, "What is the counterfactual?"

The question before us is: Can we make a causal claim about the effect of the university diet on college freshmen's weight gain/loss without such a counterfactual or true control group?

Without a counterfactual or true control group, we may obtain the average weight change for all college freshmen from September to June by computing each individual student's weight change from September to June as $Y_{1i} - X_{1i}$, and then taking the mean or average of these differences to obtain what is called the *expected value*[4] of these differences, denoted as $E(Y_{1i} - X_{1i})$. Notice in this expression, we use the subscript 1 to convey the fact that everyone is in the treatment group (Group 1), since all are assigned the university diet. There is no one in a control group (Group 0).

If the distribution of weight in September, X_1, is no different from the distribution of weight in June, Y_1, and the mean of the distribution of weight differences calculated between September and June equals zero, we may conclude that the difference in mean weight for college freshmen from September to June is zero, as shown by Equation 12.4:

$$E(Y_{1i} - X_{1i}) = E(Y_1) - E(X_1) = 0. \tag{12.4}$$

The middle part of Equation 12.4 equals the left-hand side because the difference of means equals the mean of differences.

Given the result shown in Equation 12.4, can we conclude also that the diet did not cause a mean change in student weight over the academic year?

Although, at first glance, we might want to agree with this causal claim, on more careful analysis we recall that in order for this causal claim to be valid, according to Equation 12.3, we need to compare $E(Y_1)$, the average weight of college freshmen in June, not to $E(X_1)$,

---

[4] Note: The expected value of X, denoted $E(X)$, is simply the mean of the X distribution.

the average weight of college freshmen in September, but, rather, to $E(i_0)$, the average weight of college freshmen in June assigned to a true control group diet.

If we can assume that $E(X_1) = E(Y_0)$, then we can assume that Equations 12.3 and 12.4 are equivalent, and, if they are equivalent, the causal claim may be deemed to be correct. But, what does it mean to assume that the average weight of college freshmen in September, $E(X_1)$, equals what the average weight of a true control group of college freshmen would have been in June, $E(Y_0)$? It means simply to assume that under some control diet, each student's weight remains constant from September to June, and that the response to that control diet, whatever it might be, is given by the student's weight in September. If this assumption is true, it makes sense to substitute $E(X_1)$ for $E(Y_0)$ in Equation 12.3. On what basis, however, can we decide that this assumption is true?

Without randomization to treatment and control diets, a test of the validity of the assumption that $E(X_1) = E(Y_0)$ would require us to have weight data from September and June on the *same* students exposed to a true control group condition to see if their weights actually did stay the same over this time period. But the same students cannot be exposed to the control diet given they were exposed to the treatment diet, and so our belief in the truth of this assumption must be based only on intuition and/or subject-matter expertise. Unfortunately, this assumption is untestable.

The *fundamental problem of causal inference*[5] is that only either Y_1 or Y_0, but *not* both, can be observed on any one subject. We can never observe both situations (or counterfactuals). And as such, one or more assumptions must be made about what would have happened had that person been in the other group or taken the other path.

In sum, it is *not* the difference $E(Y_1) - E(X_1)$ that measures a treatment effect, but rather the difference $E(Y_1) - E(Y_0)$, and so the extent to which the average difference $E(Y_1) - E(X_1)$ will have causal significance will depend upon the extent to which X_1 can serve as a substitute for the counterfactual Y_0. But, as in the university diet example, assumptions regarding counterfactual outcomes tend to be untestable with the data that are available, and this is what gives causal inference in observational settings an air of uncertainty.

By contrast, as we have discussed in this chapter, random assignment with large enough numbers of individuals allows us to assume that, on average, the experimental and control groups are the same on any number of traits (both observable and unobservable) relevant to the outcome and is what allows us to have confidence in making causal inference in such situations. Without random assignment, one must find a control group that is as close to those in the treatment group as possible so as to reduce bias in the estimate of the treatment effect. Controlling for variables that are known, through literature review and other means, to relate to the outcome variable is important for obtaining an unbiased estimate of the treatment effect. Such control variables, at the individual level, may be socioeconomic status, gender, ability, work status, and include variables at the community or school level (so-called contextual variables), etc., depending upon the outcome to be measured. Because it is not possible to think of all such variables (observed and unobserved) that need to be controlled so as to isolate the treatment effect, important variables may often be omitted in error, as was the case in

---

[5] For a more complete, yet accessible discussion of causal inference, the interested reader is referred to chapter 9 in Gelman and Hill (2007).

analyzing the overall relative effectiveness of the two kidney stone treatments, resulting in a biased estimate of the treatment effects.

ANALYTIC METHODS FOR BOLSTERING CLAIMS OF CAUSALITY FROM OBSERVATIONAL DATA

(This section is optional reading.)

Because of the abundance of observational data, and a general desire to draw causal conclusions based on the analysis of such data, as in the example presented earlier in this chapter on perceived job strain and incidence of coronary heart problems, a number of advanced analytic approaches recently have been developed that seek to bolster a researcher's claim of causality by helping to reduce or even eliminate bias in the estimation of a treatment effect or other variable in which one is interested. Although a full discussion of these cutting edge analytical techniques is beyond the scope of this book, a few of them will be listed here with brief descriptions so as to make the reader aware of what is possible analytically in this emerging field. References for further study for the interested reader are included as well.

Propensity score matching This approach is used in observational studies to attempt to make the treatment and control groups balanced in a way that mimics what would have been the case had there been random assignment to groups. In particular, this approach estimates (usually via logistic regression, an extension of regression modeling to binary outcome variables) the probability (called a propensity score) that an individual (or other unit of analysis) is assigned to the treatment or control groups based on all observed covariates thought to affect the assignment to treatment. Based on the propensity score values, individuals from the treatment group are matched as closely as possible to one or more individuals in the control group using a variety of matching algorithms. The approach is useful in reducing the imbalance between groups to the extent that a substantial overlap in observables can be created between treatment and control groups after matching and that there are no lurking, unobservable, latent variables that have not been accounted for that affect assignment to treatment groups. This approach was introduced by Rosenbaum and Rubin (1983).

Instrumental variables This approach also is used in observational studies to help make the treatment and control groups more balanced so as to reduce bias in estimating the effect of a variable in which one is interested. The use of instrumental variables is used particularly to reduce what is called *endogeneity*, a problem that arises when there is a correlation between the error term in a regression model with one of the independent variables of interest in that regression model. As will be discussed in more detail in Chapter 16 of this book, this type of correlation violates one of the assumptions underlying regression in the inferential context and leads to a biased estimate of the effect of that variable of interest. To reduce or even eliminate this type of correlation, a researcher may attempt to identify new variables, called *instruments*, which correlate directly with the variable of interest and indirectly with the dependent variable through this variable of interest. The following example is based on one used by Card (1995) to illustrate this approach.

Suppose one were interested in estimating the effect of years of schooling on earnings. In this case our variable of interest is years of schooling and our dependent variable is earnings. Assume we do not have information available on an individual's academic ability in the dataset containing the individual's years of schooling and earnings and that therefore our regression model does not include academic ability. Because those with higher academic ability will tend to have more years of schooling and also greater earnings, the error term of the regression model with only years of schooling as a sole regressor will correlate with the unobserved ability. In the instrumental variable approach, one tries to identify a variable that will be an instrument for ability. As an instrument for ability, this variable will not correlate directly with ability, or directly with earnings, yet will correlate directly with years of schooling and will correlate only indirectly with earnings through years of schooling. Such a variable is proximity to a college/university because of the fact that individuals who live far from a college/university will be less likely to attend college/university and, therefore, will tend to have a reduced number of years of schooling compared to those who live near a college/university. It should be noted that instrumental variables are difficult to identify as they must satisfy a number of strong assumptions in order for them to fulfill their role as instruments in reducing bias in the estimation of the effect of a variable of interest, like years of schooling.

Regression discontinuity designs (RDDs) As illustrated in Figure 12.1, regression discontinuity analyses are well suited to situations in which individuals (e.g., children) are placed in a treatment group (e.g., a special program for the gifted and talented) if they score at or just above some cut-off point (e.g., the 90th percentile) on a standardized assessment, and are placed in the control group if they score immediately below that cut-off point, but close enough (87th to 89th percentile, for example) to be cognitively on par with those who did meet the criteria. The treatment and control groups thus created will not only be quite similar on a cognitive dimension related to the outcome of

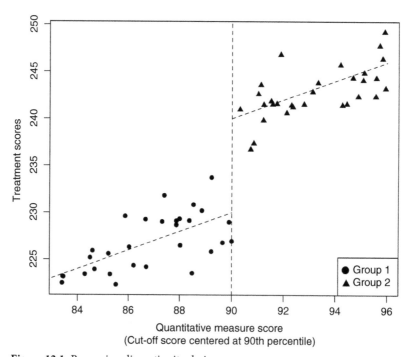

Figure 12.1 Regression discontinuity design

achievement, but also on a motivation-to-achieve dimension because all children in both groups had chosen to take the assessment, deemed a prerequisite for acceptance into the special program. If the assumptions in RDDs hold, the difference between treatment and control groups "close" to the threshold should provide an accurate estimate of the treatment effect (Shadish et al., 2011). Said differently, for this design, the treatment effect is measured as the discontinuity in the regression line at the cut-off. For a more comprehensive review of RDD, the reader is referred to Bloom (2009) and Imbens and Lemieux (2008).

In addition to analytic approaches to help reduce bias in the estimation of a treatment effect, so as to make the causal claims more compelling, one needs to be aware of how elements in the design of a study also can contribute to reducing bias in the estimation of a treatment effect. Accordingly, some of these design elements are considered in the following sections.

QUASI-EXPERIMENTAL DESIGNS

When randomization to treatment and control groups is not possible, yet when one can introduce other aspects of an experimental design into a research study, including the selection of research participants, the use of a control group, the repeated observations before and after the intervention (e.g., a university diet) to gauge the effect of the intervention, and so on, we have what is called a quasi-experimental design (Campbell & Stanley, 1966), as opposed to a true experimental design. What distinguishes a true experimental design from a quasi-experimental design is that a true experimental design includes also the randomization of participants to treatment and control groups.

As discussed earlier in this chapter, we know that without randomization it is likely that the treatment and control groups may not be balanced at the outset, that the two groups may differ systematically on some important variables that might explain the observed effect other than the treatment itself. In carrying out a quasi-experimental design, it is therefore important to consider in a systematic way the alternative plausible explanations for the observed effect other than the intervention itself. As noted by Shadish et al. (2002, p. 14):

In quasi-experiments, the researcher has to enumerate alternative explanations one by one, decide which are plausible, and then use logic, design, and measurement to assess whether each one is operating in a way that might explain any observed effect. The difficulties are that these alternative explanations are never completely enumerable in advance, that some of them are particular to the context being studied, and that the methods needed to eliminate them from contention will vary from alternative to alternative and from study to study.

In the next section, we enumerate some of these factors, referred to by Shadish et al. (2002), that may create bias in the estimation of an average treatment effect. Collectively, these factors are known as threats to the *internal validity* of a quasi-experimental study. In the following section, we describe briefly another type of threat, one that does not potentially compromise the validity of the causal claim itself, but does impact the ability of the researcher to generalize that causal claim to other "populations, settings, treatment variables, and measurement variables"

(Campbell & Stanley, 1966, p. 5). This type of validity is called a study's *external validity*. The interested reader is referred to Shadish et al. (2002) for a full, detailed discussion of these topics, as well as others related to experimental and quasi-experimental design methodology.

THREATS TO THE INTERNAL VALIDITY OF A QUASI-EXPERIMENTAL DESIGN

Threats to the internal validity of a study (Cook & Campbell, 1979; Shadish et al. 2002) are those that provide alternative plausible reasons for the observed result rather than the treatment itself. Accordingly, they can compromise the validity of causal claims made about the treatment's effectiveness by producing a biased (either too low or too high) estimate of the average treatment effect.

History In addition to the treatment, an event external to the study that could produce a differential change in the outcome variable for one of the groups, and, in turn, a biased estimate of a treatment effect.

Maturation Changes in the participants that occur over time within the course of the study that could differentially affect the outcome variable for the groups, such as growing older, more tired, more aware of being in an experiment, etc., and result in a biased estimate of the treatment effect.

Testing Taking the pretest may have a differential practice or other type effect (e. g., sensitization effect) on how one scores on the posttest, resulting in a biased estimate of a treatment effect.

Instrumentation Changing the means by which measures are taken (different tests, different raters or interviewers, etc.) from pretest to posttest may have a differential impact for the two groups on the posttest measure.

Statistical regression The effect produced when one of the groups is selected for being extremely high or low on the pretest measure. On second testing, these extreme scores will regress toward the mean even without an intervention resulting in a biased estimate of the treatment effect. Regression toward the mean is a topic that was covered in Chapter 6 of this book.

Selection bias When there is differential selection of subjects for groups, and subjects in the treatment group compared to the control group have, on average, different endowments on the pretest and other relevant covariates that are known to affect the outcome variable, the estimate of the treatment effect will be biased. This is called *selection bias*, for short. This source of invalidity is probably the most common and is the one that may be a problem in our job strain example. The extent to which this source of invalidity can adversely affect one's estimate of a treatment effect is given by example in the next section.

Experimental mortality When there is differential attrition of subjects from the treatment and control groups, the estimate of the treatment effect might be biased. For example, if a physical fitness course were so demanding in the type of physical exercise imposed on participants in the treatment group that it caused those who were physically weaker to drop out, and yet in the absence of such a demanding protocol of exercise, all participants in the control group continued in their course until the end of the study, the resulting estimate of the treatment effect, the impact of the course on one's physical fitness, would be biased and invalid.

THREATS TO THE EXTERNAL VALIDITY OF A QUASI-EXPERIMENTAL DESIGN

In addition to sources of internal invalidity, which impact the estimate of a treatment effect itself, sources of external invalidity do not impact the estimate of a treatment effect, but do impact the generalizability of a result to other populations, settings, treatment variables, and measurement variables. Although we will not enumerate the possible threats to a study's external validity, these sources typically involve an interaction between some aspect of the design and the treatment group. For example, given a study designed to test whether a film on sexual harassment in the workplace is effective in making individuals more aware of the issues and problems related to such harassment, if, in that study, a pretest were administered before the film was shown to measure an individual's baseline knowledge of sexual harassment issues, the pretest could have the result of sensitizing the individuals in that study to the topic of sexual harassment, in general, and, in turn, amplify the effects of the film for those individuals in the study. This source of external invalidity would be due to what is called a *testing by treatment interaction*, which would limit the generalizability of the amplified effect of the film to pretested populations only, rather than to an intended target population of workers who are not given a pretest before viewing the film.

THREATS TO THE VALIDITY OF A STUDY: SOME CLARIFICATIONS AND CAVEATS

It should be noted that the use of randomization in the design of a study does not guarantee the validity of the resulting causal claim as other factors may intervene after randomization takes place, and experimental and control groups are established, that can compromise the validity of the findings. For example, consider the physical fitness study described earlier under the heading of experimental mortality as a threat to a study's internal validity. In that example, even if the treatment and control groups had been randomly assigned to individuals and balance had been achieved between the two groups at the outset of the study, the fact that the participants with less physical stamina dropped out of the treatment group because it was too physically demanding, while all those in the control group remained until the end of the study, renders questionable the validity of the resulting causal claim regarding the impact of the physical fitness course. Accordingly, even in the context of a true experiment, one should consider the range of alternative plausible factors or threats that could contribute to an invalid causal conclusion. In helping one to consider the role and influence of a threat in a particular study, Shadish et al. (2002) suggest that the following three questions are critical: "(1) How would the threat apply in this case? (2) Is there evidence that the threat is plausible rather than just possible? (3) Does the threat operate in the same direction as the observed effect, so that it could partially or totally explain the observed findings?" (Shadish et al., 2002, p. 40).

The goals of achieving internal and external validity are often at odds with each other. For example, by choosing a more homogeneous set of study participants and randomly assigning them to either the treatment or control group, as one would do in a blocking design, the statistical power is increased as is the internal validity of the design, but with more homogeneous groups, the external validity is compromised. This makes it more difficult to generalize results to other populations. A case in point is the "Justice at work" article referenced earlier in this chapter (Kivimaki et al., 2005). In this article, analyses were carried out on a male sample that was overwhelmingly white. Accordingly, in one of their concluding comments, the authors write, "Finally, as our evidence was based on [an overwhelmingly white sample of] male civil servants, further research is needed to determine whether the effect of justice on heart health is generalizable to women, in other contexts, and across ethnic groups" (Kivimaki et al., 2005, p. 2250).

Given a choice between bolstering the internal versus the external validity of a design, one should give clear priority to bolstering the internal validity and to including elements in the design that do so. After all, and simply stated, only valid causal conclusions are worthy of being generalized.

THREATS TO THE VALIDITY OF A STUDY: SOME EXAMPLES

EXAMPLE 12.1 An approach for teaching early readers how to decode words was developed using a deck of flashcards wherein each flashcard contains a single word. The approach requires the teacher to show each flashcard in turn to students, pronounce each word on a card, and pass through the deck a number of times, repeating the process with each card. To test the efficacy of this approach, students were given a pretest to determine how many words they could decode at baseline and then given a posttest that required each student to read each word off the deck of cards that the teacher had practiced with them. As anticipated by the researchers, students scored higher on the posttest than on the pretest, as they were able to say more words printed on the cards after the treatment than before. The researchers concluded that this approach is highly effective for teaching decoding skills.

Plausible alternative explanation for the causal claim As it turns out, the students had not learned to decode the words; instead, they had memorized extraneous features of the words and cards. For instance, a thumb print, dog-eared corner, or smeared ink enabled them to remember which card contained which word. Rather than the approach to teaching decoding as the cause of the students' impressive performance on the posttest, the students' skills in memorizing the cards' appearances was likely the cause of their success with the task. (From Gough, 1996, pp. 1–20.)

EXAMPLE 12.2 To determine whether the socioeconomic status of undergraduate college students directly impacts their success at obtaining offers for and securing summer internships, an observational study was carried out at a large, private urban university. In particular, after controlling for a number of personal (age and gender) and academic (major, course year, and GPA) characteristics, it was found that summer internships were held predominantly by those students with higher socioeconomic status, and therefore it was concluded that having a higher socioeconomic status caused students to be more successful in gaining offers for and securing a summer internship.

Plausible alternative explanation for the causal claim This study does not consider the extent to which students from higher socioeconomic levels may self-select into the pool of summer internship applicants and therefore receive more internship offers than students of lower socioeconomic levels. Because jobs classified as "internships" typically are unpaid, those from lower socioeconomic backgrounds are less likely to be able to afford, via both actual and opportunity costs, to work in internships and may therefore decide not to apply for internships, but instead to apply for part-time or full-time jobs that come with a salary.

EXAMPLE 12.3 An observational study was conducted to determine if a particular type of therapy for stroke patients improves swallow function to a greater extent for those in the acute phase of recovery (within the first six months post onset) compared to those in the chronic phase of recovery (greater than one year post onset). After controlling for a number of relevant factors, including patient age, gender, socioeconomic status, etiology and severity of the swallowing disorder, and frequency of treatment, it was found that patients in the acute phase of recovery demonstrated greater improvement in swallow function (as evidenced by a decrease in the frequency of overt signs/symptoms of choking/aspiration) following this treatment than patients in the chronic phase of recovery. It was concluded that the treatment was the cause of this difference.

Plausible alternative explanation for the causal claim Because it is well known that brain tissue heals naturally during the first six months following a stroke, causing spontaneous recovery, it may be that rather than the treatment itself, the observed greater improvement in swallow function may be due wholly or in part to this natural healing process that occurs during the first six months and does not extend beyond the first year following a stroke. As such, the natural healing process that occurs during the first six months following a stroke acts as a confounder in this study to bias the estimate of the treatment effect. To correct for this problem, patients within the same time period following a stroke should have been compared.

EXERCISES

In Exercises 12.1–12.7, identify one or more plausible alternative explanations that call into question the validity of the causal claim made.

12.1 To determine if residents of China who have a higher level of education spend more time on the Internet than those with a lower level of education, an observational study was conducted. After controlling for a number of relevant variables, such as gender, race/ethnicity, employment status, occupation, and so on, it was found that those who have a higher level of education did, in fact, spend more time on the Internet than those with a lower level of education. The researchers concluded that having a higher education causes an individual to spend a greater amount of time on the Internet.

12.2 A study at a small Midwestern university was carried out to determine whether a semester-long remedial reading course improves the reading skills of freshmen who, by virtue of their extremely low performance on a test of reading skills, are deemed to be in need of remedial instruction in reading. At the conclusion of the course, the same test that was administered initially to assess these students' reading skills was administered again as a posttest. Based on the average positive gain between the two administrations of this test, the researchers of this study concluded that the remedial reading course caused an improvement in reading skills.

12.3 A study was conducted to determine whether dental students' clinical skills improve more when their lectures are supplemented by instructional videos. Students were randomly assigned to one of two groups. One group was given lectures only and the other group was given both lectures and video instruction. Because the classroom equipped with video equipment was available only in the morning, the group that had both lectures and video instruction met in the morning, whereas the other group met after lunch in the afternoon. Because the group exposed to both lectures and video instruction performed better in the clinical setting than the group with lectures only, it was concluded that video instruction as a supplement to lectures causes an improvement in clinical skills.

12.4 A skateboarding video game was developed to determine whether one's balance could improve after 45 minutes of play. Individuals were invited to participate on a voluntary basis. Using a pretest–posttest design, those who volunteered were administered a balance assessment before and after exposure to the video game. It was found that, on average, the balancing abilities of players were no better after playing the game than before, leading the researchers to conclude that their skateboarding game was not effective in enhancing one's balancing skills.

12.5 To determine if young children of non-working mothers have better communication skills than children of mothers who work full-time, an observational study was carried out. After controlling for a number of relevant variables, including the age, sex, race/ethnicity, and number of siblings of the child, and age of the mother, it was found that the children of non-working mothers did, in fact, have higher communication skills than the children of mothers who work full-time. The researchers concluded that a mother's working outside the home causes a delayed development in a child's communication skills.

12.6 A study was conducted to determine whether a reading intervention could improve the reading ability of the lowest achieving students at a certain school. Those who scored in the bottom 5 percent of all students on the standard reading test at the start of the year were selected for the intervention. At the end of the year, the students' scores on the standard reading test had improved, on average. The researchers concluded that the intervention was effective.

12.7 To determine whether caffeine use increases short-term memory, an experimental study was carried out. Students were randomly assigned to drink either Cocoa Cola, Caffeine-Free Diet Cocoa Cola, or water. They then studied a set of figures in order. After five minutes the figures were taken away, and the students were asked to recreate the sequence. For each student, the number of shapes listed in the correct order was recorded as the measure of short-term memory. It was found that students assigned to drink Cocoa Cola were able to place correctly in order statistically significantly more shapes than students assigned to the other conditions. The researchers concluded that caffeine use does increase short-term memory.

12.8 Read the article "Effects of zinc supplementation in occurrence and duration of common cold in school aged children during cold season: A double blind placebo controlled trial" (Vakili et al., 2009) located in the web resources associated with this text. Answer the following related questions.

(a) What was the purpose of the study?

(b) Is the study observational or experimental?

(c) Why was it important to have a placebo group?

(d) What does it mean for the experiment to be double blind, and why was it important for the experiment to be double blind?

(e) Why was it important to include both males and females in the study?

(f) How many females were in the placebo group?

(g) What was the average number of family members for children in the zinc group?

(h) Why was it important to determine that there were no statistically significant differences in the average number of family members between children in the zinc-supplemented and placebo groups?

(i) Which of the three tests in Chapter 11 could have been conducted to determine that that there were no statistically significant differences in the average number of family members between children in the zinc-supplemented and placebo groups?

(j) What was the statistical support provided for the finding that the occurrence of the common cold differed for the zinc-supplemented and placebo groups?

12.9 Read the following excerpt from the Vital Signs column from the *New York Times* by Roni Caryn Rabin (2011): "Childhood: Obesity and school lunches." Use it to answer the related questions.

Researchers say they have identified another risk factor for childhood obesity: school lunch.

A study of more than 1,000 sixth graders in several schools in southeastern Michigan found that those who regularly had the school lunch were 29 percent more likely to be obese than those who brought lunch from home. Spending two or more hours a day watching television or playing video games also increased the risk of obesity, but by only 19 percent. Of the 142 obese children in the study for whom dietary information was known, almost half were school-lunch regulars, compared with only one-third of the 787 who were not obese.

"Most school lunches rely heavily on high-energy, low-nutrient-value food, because it's cheaper," said Dr. Kim A. Eagle, director of the University of Michigan Cardiovascular Center, and senior author of the paper, published in the December issue of *American Heart Journal*. In some schools where the study was done, lunch programs offered specials like "Tater Tot Day," he said.

(a) Is this study observational or experimental?

(b) Based on the results of this study, if your cousin attended school in southeastern Michigan, would you ask her parents to pack a lunch in order to prevent her from becoming obese?

12.10 In 1999, there was an article published in the journal *Nature* (Quinn et al., 1999; Gee, 1999; available online at https://go.nature.com/37kDloY), whose results indicated that infants who slept in a room with a nightlight were more likely to be nearsighted as adults. Based on the results of this study, should nightlights be removed from infants' rooms?

12.11 Sarah wants to design a study to determine whether students taking statistics who have access to their computers during class do worse than those who do not. She is teaching two sections of statistics and would allow one section to use their computers during class, but would not allow the other to do so. What are three important design considerations?

12.12 Josh wants to design a study to determine whether brushing your teeth in an up-and-down or circular pattern is more effective at eliminating plaque. What are three important design considerations?

12.13 Read the article "Study on parental longevity is short on causation" by Susan Dynarski (2014; available online at https://nyti.ms/2SBMC6J), about the use of natural experiments as an alternative to randomized control experiments.

(a) In the article, Dynarski takes issue with the causal conclusions reached by two sociologists in their study of a child's college attendance and his/her parents' longevity. What is her criticism of that finding?

(b) Propose a question that may be or already has been addressed using a natural experiment.

# CHAPTER THIRTEEN

ONE-WAY ANALYSIS OF VARIANCE

In the previous chapters, we presented statistical models for answering questions about population means when the design involves either one or two groups and when the population standard deviation is not known. In the case of two groups, we distinguished between paired and independent groups designs and presented statistical models tailored to each. In this chapter, we extend the two independent groups model to handle questions about population means of three or more groups.

When there are more than two groups in our design, we will test the null hypothesis that *all* populations have the same mean versus the non-directional alternative that not all populations have the same mean. For example, using the NELS dataset, we may be interested in comparing: (1) the mean number of years of math taken in high school for the populations of students from the Northeast, North Central, South, and West; (2) twelfth grade self-concept by type of high school program (rigorous academic, academic, vocational, and other); or (3) school attendance rate by region.

If there are K populations, we can represent these hypotheses as follows:

$H_0: \mu_1 = \mu_2 = \mu_3 = \cdots = \mu_K$
$H_1:$ not H_0.

The null hypothesis is true only if *all* the population means are equal to one another, and false if any two are not equal to each other.

THE DISADVANTAGE OF MULTIPLE *t*-TESTS

A question that you might be thinking at this point is why must we introduce a new model for testing H_0 against H_1? Why can't we simply use the independent groups t-test introduced in Chapter 11 to test H_0 against H_1 by making all possible pairwise comparisons of means?

For example, if $K = 3$, and the null and alternative hypotheses are:

$H_0: \mu_1 = \mu_2 = \mu_3$
$H_1:$ not H_0,

a set of t-tests, one on each pair of samples, would produce the following three hypothesis tests:

$H_0: \mu_1 = \mu_2$ $H_0: \mu_1 = \mu_3$ $H_0: \mu_2 = \mu_3$
versus   versus   versus
$H_1: \mu_1 \neq \mu_2$ $H_1: \mu_1 \neq \mu_3$ $H_1: \mu_2 \neq \mu_3$

Following this approach, we would reject H_0: $\mu_1 = \mu_2 = \mu_3$ if at least one of the three pairwise tests in the set is statistically significant at $\alpha = 0.05$.

While intuitively appealing, there is a problem that arises in connection with this approach: the probability of making a Type I error and falsely rejecting the null hypothesis (H_0: $\mu_1 = \mu_2 = \mu_3$) will *exceed* the chosen level of significance, 0.05.

Two definitions of Type I error rate are implied here. A Type I error rate attached to each pairwise test (called a *per-comparison error rate* (α)) and a Type I error rate attached to the *complete set* of pairwise tests related to the original null hypothesis (called a *family-wise error rate* (α_{FW})). A "family" of comparisons is a set of comparisons that are logically and conceptually linked.

A family may consist of multiple comparisons conducted on a single dependent variable in a design consisting of more than two groups, or of multiple comparisons conducted on separate dependent variables in a design consisting of two or more groups. A series of three pairwise *t*-tests for testing H_0: $\mu_1 = \mu_2 = \mu_3$ in terms of say, twelfth grade math achievement, is an example of the first type of family. A series of four *t*-tests that compares males and females in terms of twelfth grade math achievement, reading achievement, science achievement, and social studies achievement is an example of the second type of family.

As implied, when several logically linked comparisons are conducted, each at α, the overall family-wise error rate, α_{FW}, will exceed α. The amount by which α_{FW} exceeds α may be obtained from Equation 13.1 that expresses the relationship between these two Type I errors. The probability of making at least one Type I error in conducting a set of K conceptually linked tests is approximated by:

$$\alpha_{FW} = 1 - (1 - \alpha)^K. \tag{13.1}$$

If the number of tests carried out to test H_0: $\mu_1 = \mu_2 = \mu_3$ is $K = 3$, then α_{FW} will equal approximately $1 - (0.95)(0.95)(0.95) = 1 - 0.95^3 = 1 - 0.8574 = 0.1426$.

That is, for every 100 times we tested H_0: $\mu_1 = \mu_2 = \mu_3$ using a set of $K = 3$ mutually independent tests (e.g., a combination of pairwise and more complex comparisons), we would make a Type I error, or reject the H_0 falsely, approximately 14 times on average, instead of 5.

A simpler expression of the relationship between α_{FW} and α is given by Equation 13.2:

$$\alpha_{FW} \leq K\alpha. \tag{13.2}$$

This relationship, proven by Bonferroni, an Italian mathematician, states that the family-wise Type I error rate will always be less than or equal to the per comparison Type I error rate times the number of comparisons conducted.

When $K = 3$ and $\alpha = 0.05$, as in the current illustration, Equation 13.2 suggests that
$$\alpha_{FW} \leq (3)(0.05) = 0.15,$$
which is consistent with our result from Equation 13.1 that $\alpha_{FW} = 0.1426$.

Equations 13.1 and 13.2 make amply clear the fact that as the number of comparisons in a set increases, so does the family-wise error rate relative to α.

To control the family-wise Type I error at the chosen level α, regardless of how many comparisons are conducted, we present two possible approaches: the one-way ANalysis Of VAriance, abbreviated by the acronym ANOVA, and the Bonferroni adjustment.

THE ONE-WAY ANALYSIS OF VARIANCE

One-way ANOVA is a non-directional procedure that tests the equality among two or more population means using independent groups while controlling the family-wise Type I error rate at the chosen level α regardless of the number of groups in the design. When applied to only two groups, the one-way ANOVA is exactly identical to the non-directional t-test for independent groups. Simply stated, one-way ANOVA may be thought of as an extension of the independent two-group t-test to two or more groups.

☞ **Remark.** The name, analysis of variance, given to a procedure to test the equality of population means may seem like a misnomer. Actually, the name comes from the method that is used to test for the equality of means. As we shall see, not unlike the two independent groups t-test, ANOVA tests hypotheses about the equality of means by analyzing variances defined in different ways relative to the groups in the design.

☞ **Remark.** The method of analysis of variance was developed by Ronald Aylmer Fisher, one of the giants in the history of the development of modern statistics, as a way to evaluate the separate effects of various treatments (e.g., fertilizer, soil type, weather, crop variety) on crop production. Hired in 1919 to work at the Rothamsted Agricultural Experimental Station in Harpenden, a rural area north of London, to examine and make sense of the enormous body of data collected in connection with the agricultural experiments that had been conducted to date at that time, Fisher introduced the analysis of variance in an article published in 1923; it was the second in a series of six papers entitled *Studies in Crop Variation* (Salsburg, 2001). As written by Salsburg (2001) "[t]hese papers show a brilliant originality and are filled with fascinating implications that kept theoreticians busy for the rest of the twentieth century, and will probably continue to inspire more work in the years that follow" (p. 43).

A GRAPHICAL ILLUSTRATION OF THE ROLE OF VARIANCE IN TESTS ON MEANS

Suppose the director of a drug rehabilitation center is interested in comparing the effects of three methods of therapeutic treatment on manual dexterity. Accordingly, she selects at random a sample of individuals from the population of applicants to her program and randomly assigns each to one of the three treatments, labeled Treatment 1, Treatment 2, and Treatment 3. After five weeks in the treatment programs, the participants are administered the Stanford Test of Manual Dexterity.

Suppose the three score distributions on this test, for Treatments 1, 2, and 3, are given in Figure 13.1 with means, $\overline{X}_1 = -3, \overline{X}_2 = 0, \overline{X}_3 = 3$, respectively. Based on the differences in these means, can the director conclude that the three treatments differ in their effects on the mean levels of manual dexterity for the population of potential participants from whom the sample was drawn? The answer will depend upon whether the score distributions are separate enough to suggest that each resulted from a different treatment. Because there is no observed overlap among the different group score distributions in Figure 13.1, the groups may be separate enough to suggest that the treatments have an effect on manual dexterity for the population of participants from whom the sample was drawn.

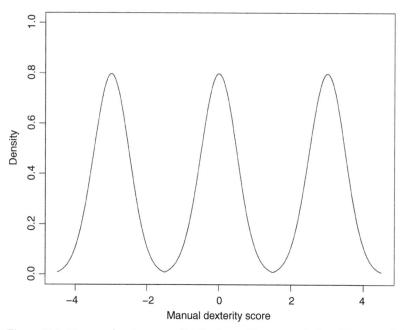

Figure 13.1 Non-overlapping score distributions with means –3, 0, and 3, respectively

Figure 13.2 offers a contrasting scenario to Figure 13.1. While the three means remain the same as in Figure 13.1 ($\overline{X}_1 = -3, \overline{X}_2 = 0, \overline{X}_3 = 3$), in Figure 13.2, considerable overlap exists among the score distributions. Accordingly, in contrast to Figure 13.1, the groups may not be separate enough to suggest that the treatments have a differential effect on manual dexterity for this population. While an individual in Figure 13.1 with a manual dexterity score of 1.00 clearly received Treatment 2, there is a good chance that an individual with the same score in Figure 13.2 received Treatment 2, or to a lesser extent, Treatment 3. There is even a small chance that the individual received Treatment 1.

Clearly, because Figures 13.1 and 13.2 display the same group means, more than mean differences determine the degree of overlap, or separation, between groups. As we shall make more explicit in the next section, we have already measured group separation as more than merely a difference between means in our use of the independent groups t-test.

ANOVA AS AN EXTENSION OF THE INDEPENDENT SAMPLES t-TEST

In the two, independent groups t-test, the t-ratio of the hypotheses $H_0: \mu_1 = \mu_2$ versus H_1: $\mu_1 \neq \mu_2$ is given as:

$$t = \frac{(\overline{X}_1 - \overline{X}_2) - (\mu_1 - \mu_2)}{\sqrt{\dfrac{(N_1 - 1)\hat{\sigma}_1^2 + (N_2 - 1)\hat{\sigma}_2^2}{N_1 + N_2 - 2}\left(\dfrac{1}{N_1} + \dfrac{1}{N_2}\right)}}.$$

We may note that with $H_0: \mu_1 - \mu_2 = 0$, the numerator of this ratio equals the difference between groups as represented by the respective group means $(\overline{X}_1 - \overline{X}_2)$, and the

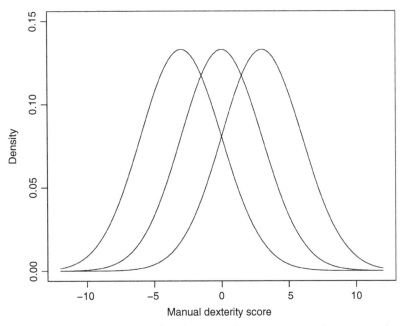

Figure 13.2 Overlapping score distributions with means −3, 0, and 3, respectively

denominator of this ratio equals (a function of) the weighted average of the two variance estimators, $\hat{\sigma}_1^2$ and $\hat{\sigma}_2^2$, computed respectively within each group.

More generally, we may say, that the t-ratio describes the *variability between groups*, expressed as a difference between means, relative to the *variability within groups*, expressed as a weighted average of within group variances. When there are only two groups, the variability between groups may be expressed simply as a difference between means; however, when there are more than two groups, the variability between groups may not be expressed so simply. To express the variability between groups in the case of more than two groups, we compute, instead, the *variance* (or variance estimator) of the group means. That is, we compute a variance on a set of mean values. If the group means are all equal, the variance of the means will be zero. On the other hand, if the group means are quite distinct, the variance of the means will be correspondingly large.

Thus, we may conceptualize the t-test as a test of the relative size of two different variances, a between group variance and a within group variance, for the purpose of judging hypotheses about two independent group means. Like the t-test, the one-way analysis of variance, as discussed in this book, is, by extension, a test of the relative size of a between group variance and a within group variance for the purpose of judging hypotheses about *more than two independent* group means.

☞ **Remark.** A form of analysis of variance, called repeated measures analysis of variance, may be used to test hypotheses about more than two *paired* group means. This procedure is beyond the scope of this book.

DEVELOPING AN INDEX OF SEPARATION FOR THE ANALYSIS OF VARIANCE

To determine whether, in fact, the groups displayed in Figures 13.1 and 13.2 are separate enough to suggest differential treatment effects, we use a single measure of group separation based on the between and within group variances. The *between group variance*, or spread of the means between groups, represents the degree to which the different treatments separate or pull apart individuals (on the test of manual dexterity) by virtue of their exposure to different treatments. The *within group variance*, or spread of scores within each group, represents the naturally occurring variability that exists (in manual dexterity) among individuals who have received the same treatment and may be due to such factors as natural ability, skill, motivation, age, gender, and so on. Such naturally occurring variability among individuals who have received the same treatment is said to be due to *individual differences*. These are differences that are left unexplained by treatment effects and for this reason are referred to not only as within group variance, but also as *residual variance*.

In Figure 13.1 we may note that the between group variance, as measured by the distance of each group mean from another, is quite large relative to the within group variance, as measured by the spread of scores within each group. In Figure 13.2, however, the between group variance is quite small relative to the within group variance. The ratio of these two measures of variance (between to within) may be used to reflect the degree of separation among groups. As in the *t*-test, this ratio will help to determine whether the observed separation among score distributions is sufficiently large to suggest a real difference in the respective population means.

CARRYING OUT THE ANOVA COMPUTATION

Suppose the director of the drug rehabilitation center had selected 30 individuals from the population of applicants to her program and randomly assigned 10 to Treatment 1, 10 to Treatment 2, and 10 to Treatment 3. After five weeks of treatment, a manual dexterity test is administered for which a higher score indicates greater manual dexterity. Suppose the scores on the manual dexterity test are as shown in the table below. These data can be found in the file ManDext.rda. The variable that contains the scores is called ManualDex, and the treatment variable is called Treatment.

Treatment 1	Treatment 2	Treatment 3
6	4	6
10	2	2
8	3	2
6	5	6
9	1	4
8	3	5
7	2	3
5	2	5
6	4	3
5	4	4
$\overline{X}_1 = 7$	$\overline{X}_2 = 3$	$\overline{X}_3 = 4$

Does the variation in treatment group means suggest a real difference in treatment means for the population, using $\alpha = 0.05$? We compute the ratio of between group variance to within group variance to find out.

Because both between and within group variances are variance estimators, we define each as the sum of squared deviations about its respective mean divided by the appropriate degrees of freedom (SS/df). In the context of ANOVA, variance estimators are called *mean squares*, short for mean or average sum of squares, and are denoted by the letters MS. Thus, we say $MS = SS/df$.

To form the ratio of between group variance to within group variance we compute both the mean square between (MS_B) and the mean square within (MS_W). This ratio, (MS_B /MS_W) is our index of separation in the one-way ANOVA.

☞ **Remark.** We may recall that with one group of N values, the degrees of freedom of a variance estimator are $N - 1$. With two groups of N values ($N = N_1 + N_2$), the degrees of freedom are $N_1 + N_2 - 2 = N - 2$ (as in the independent groups t-test). And, therefore, with K groups of N values ($N = N_1 + N_2 + N_3 + \cdots + N_K$), the degrees of freedom are $N - K$. We use this information in presenting the equations for MS_B and MS_W.

The Between Group Variance (MS_B)

The MS_B is computed as a variance on the group means. It is given by Equation 13.3.

$$MS_B = \frac{SS_B}{df} = \frac{\sum_{j=1}^{K} N_j(\overline{X}_j - \overline{\overline{X}})^2}{K - 1}, \tag{13.3}$$

where N_j equals the number of values in group j, $\overline{X}_j$ equals the mean of the values in group j, $\overline{\overline{X}}$ equals the overall or grand mean of all values in all groups (equivalently, the mean of the group means), and K equals the total number of groups in the design.

☞ **Remark.** The between group variance is based on a collection of K mean values. Its degrees of freedom, therefore, are $K - 1$. Because each of the means represents a different group of values, and not all groups are of the same size, we include a weighting factor, N_j, in Equation 13.3. N_j weights each squared deviation from the grand mean by the size of the corresponding group j so that deviations of large-sized groups are weighted more heavily than deviations of small-sized groups.

Using Equation 13.3, we compute the MS_B for the data from our example:

$N_1 = N_2 = N_3 = 10; \overline{X}_1 = 7, \overline{X}_2 = 3, \overline{X}_3 = 4, \overline{\overline{X}} = 4.67; K = 3$
$SS_B = 10(7 - 4.67)^2 + 10(3 - 4.67)^2 + 10(4 - 4.67)^2 = 54.29 + 27.89 + 4.49 = 86.67$
$MS_B = 86.67/(3 - 1) = 86.67/2 = 43.34.$

The Within Group Variance (MS_W)

The MS_W is computed as the sum of the separate sums of squares computed on each group divided by the appropriate degrees of freedom. It is given by Equation 13.4:

$$MS_W = \frac{SS_W}{df} = \frac{\sum_{i,j}(X_{i,j} - \overline{X}_j)^2}{N - K}, \tag{13.4}$$

where $X_{i,j}$ represents the score of individual i in group j (e.g., $X_{1,3}$ represents the score of individual 1 in group 3; $X_{3,1}$ represents the score of individual 3 in group 1).

☞ **Remark.** The within group variance is based on K groups of N values total. Its degrees of freedom are, therefore, $N - K$.

Using Equation 13.4, we compute the MS_W for the data from our example:

$$\begin{aligned}
SS_W &= [(6-7)^2 + (10-7)^2 + (8-7)^2 + (6-7)^2 + (9-7)^2 + (8-7)^2 + (7-7)^2 + (5-7)^2 \\
&\quad + (6-7)^2 + (5-7)^2] + [(4-3)^2 + (2-3)^2 + (3-3)^2 + (5-3)^2 + (1-3)^2 + (3-3)^2 \\
&\quad + (2-3)^2 + (2-3)^2 + (4-3)^2 + (4-4)^2] + [(6-4)^2 + (2-4)^2 + (2-4)^2 + (6-4)^2 \\
&\quad + (4-4)^2 + (5-4)^2 + (3-4)^2 + (5-4)^2 + (3-4)^2 + (4-4)^2] \\
&= 1+9+1+1+4+1+0+4+1+4+1+1+0+4+4+0+1+1+1+0+4+4 \\
&\quad + 4+4+0+1+1+1+1+1+0 \\
&= 60 \\
MS_W &= 60/(30-3) = 60/27 = 2.22.
\end{aligned}$$

The index of separation, MS_B/MS_W, is called the F-ratio. If certain assumptions are satisfied by our K populations, then the distribution of all possible F-ratios, called an F-distribution, will have a particular shape. We use the F-distribution in much the same way we used the t-distribution, to judge whether our observed statistic, in this case, the observed F-ratio, may be attributable to chance.

THE ASSUMPTIONS OF THE ONE-WAY ANOVA

We make the following assumptions in the one-way ANOVA:

1. The null hypothesis is true.
2. The scores are independent of each other.
3. The parent populations are normally distributed for all groups under study.
4. The parent populations have equal variances (this is called homogeneity of variance) for all groups under study.

As with the t-tests introduced in the previous chapters, the reason why a hypothesis test is conducted is to test the first assumption of the one-way ANOVA. If the other assumptions hold, then we may conduct the hypothesis test to assess whether the null hypothesis is true.

Scores are independent if they are randomly selected from their respective parent population so that the selection of scores from one population has no bearing on the selection of scores from any other population. Independence may be achieved if each score is from a separate individual who has been randomly assigned to one of the treatment conditions of the design.

If any of these four conditions is not met, then the statistic obtained may not be distributed as an F-distribution with hypothesized mean difference zero.

In testing the equality of population means, if conditions 2, 3, and 4 are known to be satisfied, and an unusual sample outcome is observed, then the plausibility of the remaining condition, condition 1, becomes questionable and one would decide to reject H_0 as implausible.

Thus, it appears that conditions 2, 3, and 4 need to be satisfied in order to test condition 1 using the F-ratio. For this reason, conditions 2, 3, and 4 are usually referred to as the underlying assumptions of the one-way ANOVA.

In actual research situations, we cannot always be certain whether either or both conditions 3 and 4 hold, and we must expend some effort to investigate the tenability of these assumptions.

Violations of the assumption of normality do not affect, or only minimally affect, the validity of the ANOVA. That is, ANOVA has been shown to produce correct results even when the data are not normally distributed in the population as long as there are at least 30 subjects in each cell. In statistical terms, we say that ANOVA is *robust* to violations of the assumption of normality (see Glass et al., 1972, for a review of studies on the empirical consequences of failing to meet ANOVA assumptions). In the case of a small dataset, however, we recommend checking individual group distributions for outliers and other evidence of non-normality to ensure that a small set of values does not unduly influence the results of the analysis.

Violations of the assumption of homogeneity of variance do not affect, or only minimally affect, the validity of the ANOVA when cell sizes are large and equal. When sample sizes are unequal and small, however, and when populations have heterogeneous variances, the Type I error rate associated with the F-test will actually be greater than what is reported. For example, under such conditions, a reported p-value of 0.05 may actually be 0.10. When samples are larger, yet still unequal in size, and when variances are unequal, there is less distortion in Type I error. That is, reported Type I error levels come closer to actual levels, and the effect of unequal variances is reduced when samples are larger.

In the face of heterogeneity of variance, when sample sizes are neither equal nor large, we recommend that the researcher transform scores nonlinearly to reduce heterogeneity. We recommend also that a more stringent Type I error rate (e.g., 0.01 instead of 0.05) be employed under conditions of heterogeneity to compensate for the tendency of the F-test to report p-values in excess of what they truly are.

TESTING THE EQUALITY OF POPULATION MEANS: THE F-RATIO

If the underlying assumptions are satisfied, then the distribution of all possible ratios MS_B /MS_W that could be observed from these populations will form what is called an *F-distribution with $K - 1$, $N - K$ degrees of freedom*. The $K - 1$ degrees of freedom are associated with MS_B in the numerator, and the $N - K$ degrees of freedom are associated with MS_W in the denominator.

Like the t-distribution, the F-distribution consists of a family of curves. While the t-distribution only uses one parameter for the degrees of freedom, the F-distribution uses two parameters for the degrees of freedom, often called v_1 and v_2, referring to the degrees of freedom of the numerator and denominator, respectively. If a test statistic has an F-distribution with parameters v_1 and v_2, we write $F(v_1, v_2)$. Therefore, in Equation 13.5 produced here, $v_1 = K - 1$, where K is the number of groups, and $v_2 = N - K$, where N is the total sample size of the dataset:

$$F(K-1, \ N-K) = MS_B/MS_W. \tag{13.5}$$

We use Equation 13.5 to determine whether the ratio MS_B/MS_W based on our sample data is likely to be observed when the null hypothesis of equal population means is true. Because we would reject the null hypothesis in favor of the alternative only when MS_B exceeds MS_W (as in Figure 13.1), we are only interested in situations in which MS_B exceeds MS_W and consider areas only in the right tail of the F-distribution. Whenever the observed F-ratio is large enough to be considered unlikely to have occurred by chance (when p is small, say, less than 0.05), we would reject the null hypothesis that all population means are equal in favor of the alternative hypothesis that not all population means are equal.

Figures 13.3(a–d) illustrate four F-distributions each with 27 degrees of freedom in the denominator (as in our example), but with different numbers of degrees of freedom in the numerator: namely, 1, 2, 4, and 16, respectively. The lowest tick on the vertical axis of all four figures represents the probability value of zero.

☞ **Remark.** Notice that as the numerator degrees of freedom increase, the shape of the F-distribution changes considerably and becomes more symmetric. We may note without illustration that the shape of the F-distribution remains relatively constant if we change the denominator degrees of freedom but keep the numerator degrees of freedom the same.

HOW TO READ THE TABLES AND USE R FUNCTIONS FOR THE F- DISTRIBUTION

Table C.3, located in Appendix C and on the website for this textbook, contains an F-distribution summary table that can be used to estimate p-values and F-values that

(a)

Figure 13.3 (a) The $F(1, 27)$ sampling distribution

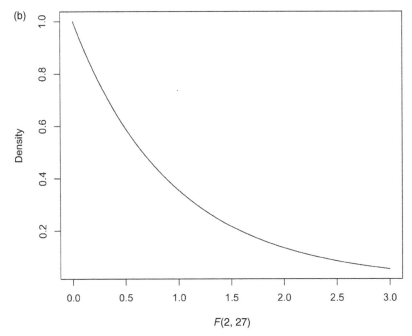

(b) The $F(2, 27)$ sampling distribution

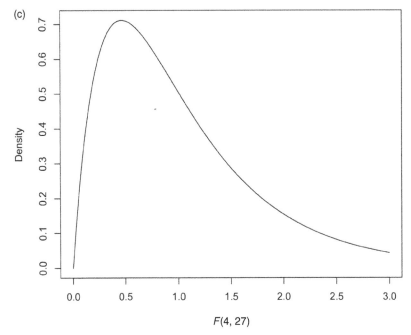

(c) The $F(4, 27)$ sampling distribution

cut off a given area. Two sets of degrees of freedom are associated with the F-statistic, one set for the numerator, or variance due to the effect, and one set for the denominator, or within variance. In the case of one-way ANOVA, the numerator

(d)

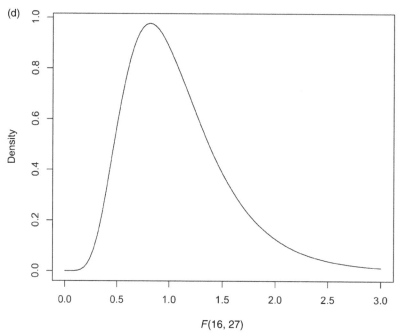

(d) The $F(16, 27)$ sampling distribution

degrees of freedom are given by $K - 1$ and the denominator degrees of freedom are given by $N - K$. In Table C.3, the top row has the numerator degrees of freedom, whereas the leftmost column has the denominator degrees of freedom. For each pair of numerator and denominator degrees of freedom, there are six F-values listed that have area α to their right. For example, we see from the first entry in the table that with 1 degree of freedom in both the numerator and the denominator, $F = 5.83$ has area 0.25 to its right.

So, the F-value associated with 2 degrees of freedom in the numerator and 3 degrees of freedom in the denominator that has area 0.05 to its right is 9.55. We may express the F-value 9.55 associated with 2 degrees of freedom in the numerator and 3 degrees of freedom in the denominator as $F(2, 3) = 9.55$.

EXAMPLE 13.1 Use Table C.3 to estimate the p-value associated with the following F-values.

(a) $F(2, 3) = 8.66$
(b) $F(2, 3) = 1.56$
(c) $F(2, 50) = 3.5$

Solution

(a) The table below contains the F-values and corresponding α's or areas to the right associated with 2 degrees of freedom in the numerator and 3 degrees of freedom in the denominator.

F	α
2.28	0.25
5.46	0.10
9.55	0.05
16.04	0.03
30.82	0.01
148.49	0.001

We find that the F-values that are closest to $F = 8.66$ are $F = 5.46$ and $F = 9.55$. The area to the right of $F = 5.46$ is 0.10 and the area to the right of $F = 9.55$ is 0.05. The p-value, or the area to the right of $F = 8.66$, is less than 0.10 but larger than 0.05. We have the estimate $0.05 < p < 0.10$.

(b) We find that the F-value that is closest to $F = 1.56$ is $F = 2.28$. The area to the right of $F = 2.28$ is 0.25. The p-value, or the area to the right of $F = 1.56$, is greater than 0.25. We have the estimate $p > 0.25$.

(c) Because the table contains no entry for 50 degrees of freedom in the denominator, we take a conservative approach and use the closest value that is smaller than 50, or $df = 40$. We find the estimate $0.03 < p < 0.05$. We may also get a better estimate of these areas by using R. The command **pf(f, df$_1$, df$_2$, lower.tail = F)** returns the area to the right of the value $F = f$. The command **pf(f, df$_1$, df$_2$, lower.tail = T)** returns the area to the left of the value $F = f$.

Returning to the data of our example, $F(2, 27) = MS_B/MS_W = 43.34/2.22 = 19.52$, which, from Figure 13.3(b), appears to fall far into the right tail of the distribution. We will estimate the p-value "by hand" in two ways. First, we will estimate the p-value using Table C.3. Then, we will get a better estimate using R's **pf** command.

To find the proportion of area to the right of 19.52 (that is, the p-value associated with $F(2, 27)$) using Table C.3, we estimate the denominator degrees of freedom as 26 and see that the closest F-value with 2 degrees of freedom in the numerator and 26 degrees of freedom in the denominator is $F = 9.12$, which has area 0.001. Because our observed F-value, 19.52, has less area to its right, we obtain the estimate $p < 0.001$.

MORE R: To find the p-value associated with an F-value with df_1, df_2, type the command,

pf(q, df$_1$, df$_2$, lower.tail = F)

substituting 19.52 for q, 2 for df_1, and 27 for df_2:

pf(19.52, 2, 27, lower.tail = F)

The value that is returned is given in scientific notation and is equivalent to $p = 0.0000057$, which equals the area under the curve to right of 19.52. The p-value suggests that the probability of observing an F-ratio of 19.52 by chance given that the null hypothesis is true (that all population means are equal) is quite small. The α value adopted in this instance is

$\alpha = 0.05$. Accordingly, we reject the null hypothesis in favor of the alternative that not all population means are equal.

Our conclusion is that there are differences in average manual dexterity scores between at least two of the treatments.

For heuristic reasons, we carried out the computations associated with this example by hand. We now show how to use R to provide these same results. We assume these data have been input into a data file with two variables, treatment (Treatment) that signifies the treatment group to which an individual has been assigned and ManualDex that signifies the score on the manual dexterity test.

MORE R: To carry out a one-way ANOVA, type the following syntax into your .R file or into the console based on the ManDext dataset:

results = aov(ManDext$ManualDex ~ ManDext$Treatment)
summary(results)

The first line of the code runs the ANOVA procedure. In this line, the first variable following the command **aov** is the dependent variable, and the second variable is the factor, or group, variable. The second line of the code displays a summary of the results of the ANOVA procedure.

We obtain the following results, including the ANOVA summary table.

	df	Sum sq.	Mean sq.	*F*-value	Pr(>F)
ManDext$Treatment	2	86.67	43.33	19.5	5.75e-06***
Residuals	27	60.00	2.22		

Recall that when we introduced the *F*-ratio, we assumed that all parent populations under study were normally distributed and had equal variances. However, like the independent groups *t*-test, the ANOVA test has been found to be quite insensitive to violations of normality and to violations of the assumption of equal variances as long as relatively large and equal or approximately equal sample sizes are used.

Because these sample sizes are not large, we evaluate the normality assumption by examining skewness for each group. We do so by running the **skew, se.skew,** and **skew. ratio** command from our .R file, or directly into the console window.

MORE R: To obtain the skew, standard error of skewness, and skewness ratio for each treatment group, we run:

skew(ManDext$ManualDex[ManDext$Treatment == 1])
se.skew(ManDext$ManualDex[ManDext$Treatment == 1])
skew.ratio(ManDext$ManualDex[ManDext$Treatment == 1])

skew(ManDext$ManualDex[ManDext$Treatment == 2])
se.skew(ManDext$ManualDex[ManDext$Treatment == 2])
skew.ratio(ManDext$ManualDex[ManDext$Treatment == 2])

```
skew(ManDext$ManualDex[ManDext$Treatment == 3])
se.skew(ManDext$ManualDex[ManDext$Treatment == 3])
skew.ratio(ManDext$ManualDex[ManDext$Treatment == 3])
```

For Treatment = 1: skew = 0.429351; standard error of skewness = 0.68704289; skewness ratio = 0.62492603.
For Treatment = 2: skew = 0; standard error of skewness = 0.68704289; skewness ratio = 0.
For Treatment = 3: skew = 0; standard error of skewness = 0.68704289; skewness ratio = 0.

We see that all of the skewness values are less than 1 (and all skewness ratios less than 2), so the normality assumption is tenable.

To obtain Levene's test for homogeneity of variances, as first described in Chapter 11, in connection with the one-way ANOVA, we use the following R command:

levenes.test

MORE R: To obtain Levene's test for homogeneity of variance, type:

levenes.test(ManDext$ManualDex, ManDext$Treatment)

And we obtain the following output, which provides a p-value. The results of Levene's test indicate that the homogeneity of variance assumption is satisfied, as we fail to reject the null hypothesis.

Levene's test for homogeneity of variance			
	df	F-value	Pr(>F)
group	2	0.675	0.5175
	27		

THE ANOVA SUMMARY TABLE

The ANOVA summary table provides, in a neatly organized way, the results we obtained by hand for the SS_B (between groups, labeled ManDext$Treatment), and for the SS_W (within groups, labeled Residuals). We may also define a new quantity, the total of these sums of squares, denoted SS_T (Total), which has its own meaning. It is simply the total variability contained in the entire set of scores when one ignores group membership. As such, it reflects the distance of each individual score from the overall mean and may be calculated using Equation 13.6.

$$SS_T = \sum (Xi,j - \overline{\overline{X}})^2. \tag{13.6}$$

If there are N scores total in the dataset, then the degrees of freedom associated with SS_T are simply $N - 1$. Using some elementary algebra, it can be shown that the sum of squares total is in fact equal to the sum of the sum of squares between and the sum of squares within:

$$SS_T = SS_B + SS_W. \tag{13.7}$$

Based on our earlier ANOVA summary table result, we may calculate SS_T to be 146.67 = 60 + 86.67.

MEASURING THE EFFECT SIZE

Equation 13.7 offers additional insight into ANOVA. Beginning with a dataset that contains total variability SS_T, Equation 13.7 implies that ANOVA divides or partitions SS_T into two separate components, SS_B and SS_W. SS_B is that part of SS_T that is accounted for, or explained by, group differences; SS_W is that part of SS_T that is left over, or unexplained, after accounting for such group differences.

Figures 13.4 and 13.5 illustrate the partitioning of SS_T into these two components under two scenarios. Figure 13.4 corresponds to the scenario depicted in Figure 13.1 in which between group variance is large relative to within group variance, implying that SS_B accounts for a large proportion of the variability represented by SS_T. Figure 13.5, on the other hand, corresponds to the scenario depicted in Figure 13.2 in which between group variance is small relative to within group variance, implying that SS_B accounts for a small proportion of the variability represented by SS_T. In Figure 13.5 there is much left-over, or *residual*, variability yet to be explained. We shall see in the next chapter that in an attempt to account for or explain this residual variability, one may include another factor (variable) in the design in addition to, say, treatment group and analyze the degree to which it does account for the residual variance.

Because the ratio SS_B/SS_T reflects the magnitude of the effect of the between groups factor (e.g., treatment group), it is useful as a descriptive measure of effect size, expressed as the degree of association between the dependent variable and grouping variable in the sample. Because the measure is independent of sample size and, as a proportion, ranges from 0 to 1, it provides a useful adjunct to the F-test for statistical significance. It should be noted that SS_B/SS_T provides an overestimate of the proportion of dependent variable variance accounted for by the grouping variable in the population.

Applying this ratio to the data from our example, we find that the proportion of manual dexterity variance explained by treatment is $SS_B/SS_T = 86.67/146.67 = 0.59$. This proportion may also be expressed as a percentage: 59 percent of the variance in manual dexterity is explained by treatment.

☞ **Remark.** From here on we shall refer to SS_B/SS_T as R^2 (in the context of ANOVA, R^2 also is referred to as η^2 (read: eta^2)). Following effect size conventions set forth by Cohen (1988), and as noted in Table 10.3, we offer the following scale for evaluating R^2 (relative to $1 - R^2$):

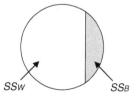

Figure 13.4 SS_B/SS_T is large   **Figure 13.5** SS_B/SS_T is small

$$f = \sqrt{(R^2/(1-R^2))} = 0.10 \text{ represents a ``small'' effect,}$$

$$f = \sqrt{(R^2/(1-R^2))} = 0.25 \text{ represents a ``medium'' effect,}$$

$$f = \sqrt{(R^2/(1-R^2))} = 0.40 \text{ represents a ``large'' effect.}$$

EXAMPLE 13.2 Determine whether there are differences in the mean number of years of mathematics studied in high school (unitmath) among the four regions (region) of the country – Northeast, North Central, South, and West – using the NELS dataset. Let $\alpha = 0.01$.

Solution Because we have *one* grouping variable, or factor, and a dependent variable that is ratio-leveled, we will use a one-way ANOVA to find a solution to this problem. Prior to carrying out the ANOVA, we explore our data using boxplots. Despite the presence of some outliers, these distributions appear to be relatively homogeneous in their variances. Furthermore, given the large number of cases per category, departures from normality, resulting from the outliers, would not pose a problem to the validity of the F-statistic.

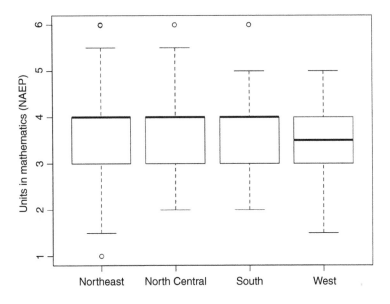

Following the procedure outlined earlier, we run the one-way ANOVA in R by using the following syntax:

results = aov(NELS$unitmath~NELS$region)
summary(results)

We obtain the following results:

	df	**Sum sq.**	**Mean sq.**	*F*-value	**Pr(>F)**
NELS$region	3	11.89	3.962	6.265	0.000352 ***
Residuals	496	313.65	0.632		

According to the ANOVA summary table, we may note that the obtained $F(3, 496) = 6.27$ with $p < 0.0005$, suggesting that it is highly unlikely that the null hypothesis (H$_0$: $\mu_1 = \mu_2 = \mu_3 =$

$\mu_4 = 0$) is true. Our data are more consistent with the alternative hypothesis that a difference exists among means. Hence, we reject the null in favor of the alternative.

We note, however, that $R^2 = SS_B/SS_T = 11.89/325.54 = 3.7$ percent, suggesting that region by itself accounts for a very small proportion of unitmath variance, with a correspondingly small effect size, $f = \sqrt{(R^2/(1 - R^2))} = \sqrt{0.037/0.963} = 0.196$. We may be interested in other factors that need to be considered in addition to region to explain the residual variance in number of years taken in high school (that is, the variance that remains after region has been accounted for).

To assess the homogeneity of variance assumption, we use the R command **levenes.test** and obtain the following results:

Levene's test for homogeneity of variance			
	df	*F*-value	Pr(>F)
group	3	0.8609	0.4613
	496		

The results of Levene's test indicate that the homogeneity of variance assumption is satisfied, as we fail to reject the null hypothesis.

Now that we know that we can reject the null hypothesis that the unitmath means across regions are different in the population, a natural question that arises is which specific region means are different from which others?

Unfortunately, the *F*-test tells us nothing about which means are different, only that not all of them are equal. To find out where specific mean differences exist based on our observation of the data, we use what are called *post-hoc* tests. Post-hoc refers to the fact that we are using the data to decide which comparisons to make, that our decisions are made *after the fact* of obtaining a statistically significant result from the ANOVA and knowing, therefore, that not all population means are equal.

POST-HOC MULTIPLE COMPARISON TESTS

Our goal in conducting post-hoc tests is to extract as much meaningful information from our data as possible while still maintaining the family-wise error rate at a reasonable level. A large number of post-hoc tests exist and recommendations for choosing among them are plentiful. In this book, we present two post-hoc tests that are appropriate when one is interested in making only pairwise comparisons between means. We do so because we believe that most applied research that employs an ANOVA-type design is concerned ultimately with ordering the means of the *K* groups on the dependent variable and a series of pairwise comparisons is useful for this purpose.

Tukey's honestly significant difference (HSD), developed in 1953, directly maintains the family-wise error rate at the chosen level regardless of how many pairwise comparisons are made (Tukey, 1953). The sampling distribution for the HSD is called the *studentized range distribution*. This distribution is based on the expectation that: (1) for random samples drawn from a normal population, the larger the size of the sample, the larger the difference should be between the extreme values in the sample (i.e., the range of the sample); and (2) when K samples are selected from a normal population, the larger K is, the larger the difference should be between the extreme sample means.

Accordingly, when K is greater than two (which it is in an ANOVA-type design), we would expect a larger difference between the two extreme means than if K were only two. The HSD takes this into account by increasing the size of the critical values (or equivalently, by reducing the size of the critical regions, α) associated with statistical significance. In so doing, the HSD makes it more difficult to obtain statistical significance for each comparison and maintains the overall family-wise error rate at the chosen value, say 0.05.

The formula for the Tukey test for comparing the means of treatment groups j and k is given by Equation 13.8 where q, called the *studentized range statistic*, represents a value in the studentized range distribution and the sample sizes for groups j and k are equal:

$$q = \frac{\overline{X}_j - \overline{X}_k}{\sqrt{\dfrac{MS_w}{n}}}, \tag{13.8}$$

where $\overline{X}_j$ and $\overline{X}_k$ are the sample means from treatment groups j and k, respectively, and $\overline{X}_j > \overline{X}_k$. Here, MS_w is the value of the mean square within from the original ANOVA; and n is the common sample size for all treatment groups.

When the treatment groups do not all have a common sample size, an approximate Tukey HSD test statistic can be computed by substituting n' for n, where n' is the harmonic mean of the sample sizes of all the treatment groups. The equation for computing the harmonic mean is:

$$n' = \frac{K}{\left[\dfrac{1}{n_1} + \dfrac{1}{n_2} + \cdots + \dfrac{1}{n_K}\right]}. \tag{13.9}$$

Critical values of the studentized range statistic are provided in Table C.6 of Appendix C. Like the F-test associated with the original ANOVA, the Tukey HSD is a test of a non-directional alternative hypothesis, but uses only the right tail of the sampling distribution for the rejection region. To use Table C.6, one needs both the degrees of freedom associated with the number of treatment groups in the original ANOVA design, K, and the MS_w term from the original ANOVA, df_w.

Another test, Fisher's least significant difference (LSD), known also as the protected t-test, developed in 1935, is not as effective in maintaining the overall family-wise error at the chosen value. The sampling distribution for the LSD is the t-distribution. That is, given a statistically significant F-test associated with the original ANOVA (called the *omnibus F-test*), the LSD follows with a series of t-tests to compare means pairwise. If the original F-test is not statistically significant and the original null hypothesis is not rejected, no further testing would be performed.

The difference between the LSD and a series of t-tests is the requirement of a rejection of the original null hypothesis at the chosen level α. Because the risk of a Type I error in conjunction with the omnibus test is maintained at α, the series of t-tests following a statistically significant ANOVA will be carried out mistakenly (when all population means are truly equal) only 5 times in 100 (if $\alpha = 0.05$). In this way, a statistically significant omnibus ANOVA protects the t-tests carried out subsequently. However, statisticians have pointed out that under certain circumstances, such protection is not enough; the LSD family-wise Type I error may exceed α by some unknown extent that depends, in part, upon the number of pairwise comparisons made.

The choice between the HSD and LSD must depend upon the philosophies and beliefs of the researcher. As we shall demonstrate in our examples, the LSD is generally more powerful than the HSD because for each pairwise comparison, the LSD uses α whereas the HSD uses a reduced α so as to maintain the overall family-wise error rate. Thus, the LSD is able to detect true differences with greater power. On the other hand, the LSD runs a greater risk of committing a Type I error, of declaring a difference between means where there truly is none. Thus, as a researcher, one must consider the number of pairwise comparisons to be made and weigh the risks of both types of error, Type I and Type II, in deciding which procedure makes sense in a particular case.

Alternatively, one could use both procedures and draw conclusions based on the results of both. If results are consistent for the two approaches, then the conclusions to be drawn are clear. If they do not agree, then careful thinking must be done to balance the relative risks of Type I and Type II errors, taking into account the number of comparisons made and other relevant factors particular to the issue being studied. Such thinking should be made public in say, a report of final results, so that a reader or listener can understand the researcher's process in reaching the reported conclusions. With this information, the reader can then decide whether to agree or disagree with these conclusions and to suggest others of his own.

In addition to these two tests, other multiple comparison tests covered in this text are the Scheffe and Bonferroni tests.

EXAMPLE 13.3 Use the Bonferroni, Scheffe, LSD, and Tukey HSD post-hoc tests to determine which methods of therapeutic treatment on manual dexterity for the drug rehabilitation center population are different from which others. Let $\alpha = 0.05$.

Solution We recall that a statistically significant omnibus F-test was obtained in connection with this example, indicating that not all three population means are equal. By calculating summary statistics, we note that the three treatment group means are: $\overline{X}_1 = 7, \overline{X}_2 = 3, \overline{X}_3 = 4$. Accordingly, the mean difference between groups 1 and 2 is 4; between groups 1 and 3 is 3; and between groups 2 and 3 is −1.

To carry out the Tukey HSD test by hand, we compute Equation 13.8 for each pair of treatment means because in this case, $n_1 = n_2 = n_3 = 10$. From the original ANOVA, we note that $MS_w = 2.22$ and $df_w = 27$ and $K = 3$.

1. Comparing μ_1 and μ_2:

$$q = \frac{7 - 3}{\sqrt{\dfrac{2.22}{10}}} = \frac{4}{0.4712} = 8.49.$$

Table C.6 in Appendix C does not list $df_w = 27$ exactly, and so we will use the more conservative values associated with $df_w = 30$. In doing so, we find that 8.49 exceeds 3.49, the critical value associated with $p = 0.05$ when $K = 3$. Hence, we conclude that $\mu_1 \neq \mu_2$ and $p < 0.05$.

2. Comparing μ_1 and μ_3:

$$q = \frac{7-4}{\sqrt{\frac{2.22}{10}}} = \frac{3}{0.47} = 6.38.$$

As in the previous case, 6.38 exceeds 3.49, the critical value associated with $p = 0.05$ when $K = 3$ and $df_w = 30$. Hence, we conclude that $\mu_1 \neq \mu_3$ and $p < 0.05$.

3. Comparing μ_2 and μ_3:

$$q = \frac{4-3}{\sqrt{\frac{2.22}{10}}} = \frac{1}{0.47} = 2.13.$$

The value of 2.13 is less than 3.49, the critical value associated with $p = 0.05$ when $K = 3$ and $df_w = 30$. Hence, we conclude that $\mu_2 = \mu_3$ and $p > 0.05$.Because we already have computed the independent groups t-test by hand, we do not carry out the LSD post-hoc test by hand. Rather, we rely solely on R to carry out this test.

MORE R: To obtain HSD, LSD, Bonferroni, and Scheffe test results, we install (once per computer) and load (once per R session) the DescTools package using the following commands:

install.packages("DescTools")
library(DescTools)

We then run the ANOVA of Manual Dexterity by Treatment and save its output in the variable named **results**:

results = aov(ManDext$ManualDex~ManDext$Treatment)

Next, we use the **PostHocTest** function to calculate the results of the post-hoc tests:

PostHocTest(results, method = "hsd")
PostHocTest(results, method = "lsd")
PostHocTest(results, method = "bonferroni")
PostHocTest(results, method = "scheffe")

The output from the HSD post-hoc comparisons is as follows:

Post-hoc multiple comparisons of means: Tukey HSD 95% family-wise confidence level					
$`ManDext$Treatment`	diff	lwr.ci	upr.ci	pval	
2–1	−4	−5.6529451	−2.347055	6.2e-06	***
3–1	−3	−4.6529451	−1.347055	0.00033	***
3–2	1	−0.6529451	2.652945	0.30679	

The output from the LSD post-hoc comparisons is as follows:

Post-hoc multiple comparisons of means: Fisher LSD 95% family-wise confidence level					
$`ManDext$Treatment`	diff	lwr.ci	upr.ci	pval	
2–1	−4	−5.367887	−2.632113	2.1e−06	***
3–1	−3	−4.367887	−1.632113	0.00012	***
3–2	1	−0.367887	2.367887	0.14522	

The output from the Bonferroni post-hoc comparisons is as follows:

Post-hoc multiple comparisons of means: Bonferroni 95% family-wise confidence level					
$`ManDext$Treatment`	diff	lwr.ci	upr.ci	pval	
2–1	−4	−5.7016392	−2.298361	6.3e-06	***
3–1	−3	−4.7016392	−1.298361	0.00035	***
3–2	1	−0.7016392	2.701639	0.43565	

The output from the Scheffe post-hoc comparisons is as follows:

Post-hoc multiple comparisons of means: Scheffe test 95% family-wise confidence level					
$`ManDext$Treatment`	diff	lwr.ci	upr.ci	pval	
2–1	−4	−5.7266875	−2.273313	1.1e-05	***
3–1	−3	−4.7266875	−1.273313	0.00052	***
3–2	1	−0.7266875	2.726687	0.33940	

Although the specific p-values do not duplicate each other across methods, the results from all methods inform us that the mean difference of −4 between groups 2 and 1 is statistically significant ($p < 0.0005$) as is the mean difference between groups 3 and 1 ($p < 0.0005$). (The p-values are found in the column labeled **pval**.) However, the mean difference between groups 2 and 3 is not statistically significant ($p > 0.140$).

EXAMPLE 13.4 Use the HSD, LSD, Bonferroni, and Scheffe post-hoc tests to determine which specific regions of the country are different from which others in terms of the mean numbers of years of math taken in high school. Let $\alpha = 0.05$.

Solution We recall that a statistically significant omnibus F-test was obtained in connection with this example, indicating that the observed sample mean differences are not attributable to random sampling error. From the table of descriptive statistics, we note that the four treatment group means are: $\overline{X}_{NE} = 3.79, \overline{X}_{NC} = 3.53, \overline{X}_{S} = 3.78, \overline{X}_{W} = 3.41$. The mean differences between groups, along with their respective statistical significance values, are given in the Multiple Comparisons table obtained from R using the procedure detailed above.

The output from the HSD post-hoc comparisons is as follows:

Post-hoc multiple comparisons of means: Tukey HSD 95% family-wise confidence level					
$`NELS$region`	diff	lwr.ci	upr.ci	pval	
North Central–Northeast	−0.25982382	−0.519571701	−7.593135e-05	0.0499	*
South–Northeast	−0.01687547	−0.276980222	2.432293e-01	0.9983	
West–Northeast	−0.38261311	−0.673858453	−9.136776e-02	0.0042	**
South–North Central	0.24294834	0.006641659	4.792550e-01	0.0412	*
West–North Central	−0.12278929	−0.392993325	1.474147e-01	0.6452	
West–South	−0.36573763	−0.636284743	−9.519053e-02	0.0030	**

The output from the LSD post-hoc comparisons is as follows:

Post-hoc multiple comparisons of means: Fisher LSD 95% family-wise confidence level				
$`NELS$region`	diff	lwr.ci	upr.ci	pval
North Central–Northeast	−0.25982382	−0.45780250	−0.06184513	0.01021 *
South–Northeast	−0.01687547	−0.21512616	0.18137522	0.86725
West–Northeast	−0.38261311	−0.60459902	−0.16062719	0.00076 ***
South–North Central	0.24294834	0.06283643	0.42306025	0.00830 **
West–North Central	−0.12278929	0.32873761	0.08315903	0.24199
West–South	−0.36573763	−0.57194744	−0.15952783	0.00054 ***

The output from the Bonferroni post-hoc comparisons is as follows:

Post-hoc multiple comparisons of means : Bonferroni 95% family-wise confidence level					
$`NELS$region`	diff	lwr.ci	upr.ci	pval	
North Central–Northeast	−0.25982382	−0.5267382382	0.007090606	0.0613	
South–Northeast	−0.01687547	−0.2841566060	0.250405663	1.0000	
West–Northeast	−0.38261311	−0.6818940166	−0.083332196	0.0046	**
South–North Central	0.24294834	0.0001218725	0.485774816	0.0498	*
West–North Central	−0.12278929	−0.4004483509	0.154869771	1.0000	
West–South	−0.36573763	−0.6437492350	−0.087726034	0.0032	**

The output from the Scheffe post-hoc comparisons is as follows:

Post-hoc multiple comparisons of means: Scheffe test 95% family-wise confidence level					
$`NELS$region`	diff	lwr.ci	upr.ci	pval	
North Central–Northeast	−0.25982382	−0.54248038	0.02283275	0.0854	
South–Northeast	−0.01687547	−0.29992038	0.26616944	0.9988	
West–Northeast	−0.38261311	−0.69954508	−0.06568113	0.0100	**
South–North Central	0.24294834	−0.01419961	0.50009630	0.0725	
West–North Central	−0.12278929	−0.41682420	0.17124562	0.7122	
West–South	−0.36573763	−0.66014587	−0.07132940	0.0074	**

According to the Bonferroni post-hoc comparison, there are statistically significant differences in the units of math taken between the Northeast and West, between the North Central and South, and between the South and West. The *p*-value for the difference between the Northeast and North Central exceeds 0.05.

The Scheffe post-hoc comparison is the most conservative of all of these, and so the *p*-values are, in general, larger for this procedure than for the others. For the results of this test, only the South and West and the Northeast and West are statistically significantly different in terms of the variable, units of math taken.

By contrast to the Scheffe, the LSD is the most powerful procedure, and results in the smallest *p*-values and the greatest number of significant differences.

The HSD is intermediate in power between the Scheffe and the LSD. For the HSD, the Northeast differs statistically significantly from the North Central and West, and the South differs from the North Central and West.

EXAMPLE 13.5 Does twelfth grade self-concept vary as a function of one of three types of high school program (rigorous academic, academic, and other)? Notice that for this example, the variable hsprog was recoded so that the categories Some Vocational and Other form a single category. The R syntax for doing this recoding is given in the .R file associated with this chapter. Use the NELS dataset and let $\alpha = 0.01$.

Solution Given that type of high school program represents groups or categories and the dependent variable, twelfth grade self-concept, may be considered to be interval-leveled, we use one-way ANOVA to find a solution to the question. To check assumptions and get a sense of what our data look like, we obtain the following boxplots.

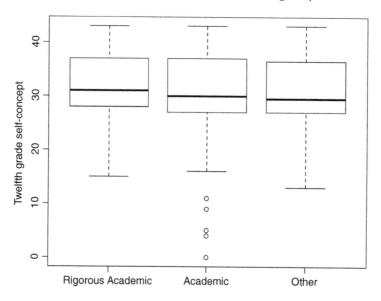

According to the boxplots, aside from the five cases of relatively low self-concept in the academic program category, the distributions appear relatively homogeneous in their variances. Furthermore, given the large number of cases per category, departures from normality resulting, for example, from the five cases of low self-concept in the academic category, would not pose a problem to the validity of the *F*-statistic. We may also note that based on the boxplots alone, twelfth grade self-concept does not appear to vary as a function of high school program type.

We turn to the one-way ANOVA to see whether these sample results are upheld in the population using the following commands (recall that the **levenes.test** command computes Levene's test):

results = aov(NELS\$slfcnc12 ~ NELS\$hsprog2)
summary(results)
levenes.test(NELS\$slfcnc12, NELS\$hsprog2)

The output is as follows:

	df	**Sum sq.**	**Mean sq.**	*F*-**value**	**Pr(>F)**
NELS\$hsprog2	2	56	27.91	0.533	0.587
Residuals	497	26037	52.39		

Levene's test for homogeneity of variance			
	df	*F*-**value**	**Pr(>F)**
group	2	1.3708	0.2549
	497		

Like the boxplot medians, the means are quite homogeneous suggesting that it is unlikely that self-concept varies with type of high school program. We may note that, as expected, Levene's test is non-significant, and the homogeneity of variance assumption is met for these data. The obtained $F = 0.533$ for the one-way ANOVA is non-significant ($p = 0.587$), confirming the impression that the means are not statistically significantly different.

Because there are no differences among self-concept means ($p = 0.587$), no further testing is warranted. Our conclusion is simply that a student's self-concept does not appear to be linked to the type of high school program in which that student is enrolled. While self-concept does vary from individual to individual ($SS_{TOT} = 26037 + 56 = 26093$ units), the amount of that variability due to the type of high school program in which that individual is enrolled is quite low ($SS_B = 56$ units). Other factors need to be considered if we are to understand why there is variability among students in self-concept. Ways to consider these other factors analytically are discussed in the next chapter.

EXAMPLE 13.6 Is there a relationship between school attendance rate and region? Said differently, does school attendance rate depend upon the location of the school, whether it is in the Northeast, North Central, South, or West? Let $\alpha = 0.05$.

Solution Given that there is one grouping variable, region, and that the dependent variable, school attendance rate, is ratio-leveled, a one-way ANOVA is appropriate for answering this question. Following a logical sequence of steps in the analysis, we first examine the data using the boxplot.

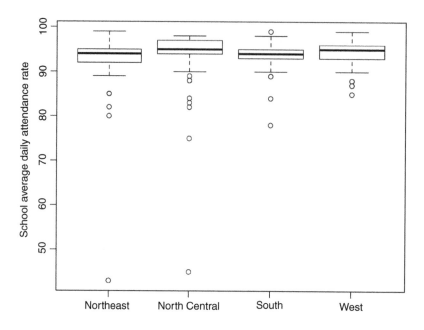

While there are a number of extreme values per region to suggest skewness, there are two cases of particular concern: ID #64 and ID #396. From the NELS dataset itself, we see that the schools that these students attended had average daily attendance rates of 45 and 43, respectively.

We have discussed two ways of handling such outliers. First, if the values are suspicious, it may make sense to eliminate them and report results based on two analyses, one with outliers excluded and another with outliers included. Second, a nonlinear transformation may be applied to reduce the influence of the outliers while using all of the available data in the analysis. Because secondary school attendance rates of 45 percent and 43 percent are suspiciously low, we have chosen here to conduct the analysis without these two cases.

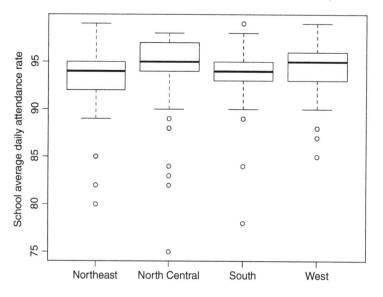

Once these two outliers are eliminated, the variances of the four regions appear to be more reasonably homogeneous. Furthermore, the number of cases per region is sufficiently high for us not to be concerned about violations of the normality assumption. We note that although the vast majority of schools have a daily attendance rate in excess of 90 percent, there does appear to be some waiver in the actual levels of attendance by region. We turn to the ANOVA to determine whether this observed waiver is significant of differences among the respective population means, or whether it may be attributable to random sampling error.

	df	Sum sq.	Mean sq.	F-value	Pr(>F)
NELS$region	3	180	60.01	2.762	0.0418*
Residuals	413	8973	21.73		

And, the results of Levene's test are:

$F = 1.663$, $df(3, 413)$, $Pr > F = 0.174$.

Results based on Levene's test suggest that, as expected, population variances are homogeneous, and there is a statistically significant difference among school mean daily attendance rates $(F(3, 413) = 2.76, p = 0.04)$.

Because the omnibus F-test is statistically significant, we seek to continue our analysis to find which specific means are statistically significantly different from which others. That is, starting with a global analysis of all four means considered simultaneously, we proceed to a local analysis that deals with comparisons between specific means taken pairwise. The results of the HSD, LSD, Bonferroni, and Scheffe post-hoc comparisons are provided below.

The results of the HSD post-hoc comparisons are:

Post-hoc multiple comparisons of means: Tukey HSD 95% family-wise confidence level				
$`NELS$region`	diff	lwr.ci	upr.ci	pval
North Central–Northeast	1.62981850	−0.02436965	3.284007	0.0552
South–Northeast	1.52012740	−0.14198174	3.182237	0.0868
West–Northeast	1.67716411	−0.23605778	3.590386	0.1089
South–North Central	−0.10969110	−1.60979918	1.390417	0.9976
West–North Central	0.04734561	−1.72695297	1.821644	0.9999
West–South	0.15703671	−1.62464896	1.938722	0.9959

The results of the LSD post-hoc comparisons are:

Post-hoc multiple comparisons of means: Fisher LSD 95% family-wise confidence level					
$`NELS$region`	diff	lwr.ci	upr.ci	pval	
North Central–Northeast	1.62981850	0.3692440	2.890393	0.0114	*
South–Northeast	1.52012740	0.2535167	2.786738	0.0188	*
West–Northeast	1.67716411	0.2191929	3.135135	0.0243	*
South–North Central	−0.10969110	−1.2528488	1.033467	0.8505	
West–North Central	0.04734561	−1.3047590	1.399450	0.9452	
West–South	0.15703671	−1.2006973	1.514771	0.8203	

The results of the Bonferroni post-hoc comparisons are:

Post-hoc multiple comparisons of means : Bonferroni 95% family-wise confidence level				
$`NELS$region`	diff	lwr.ci	upr.ci	pval
North Central–Northeast	1.62981850	−0.07022533	3.329862	0.0684
South–Northeast	1.52012740	−0.18805700	3.228312	0.1127
West–Northeast	1.67716411	−0.28909412	3.643422	0.1456
South–North Central	−0.10969110	−1.65138361	1.432001	1.000
West–North Central	0.04734561	−1.77613822	1.870829	1.000
West–South	0.15703671	−1.67403899	1.988112	1.000

The results of the Scheffe post-hoc comparisons are:

Post-hoc multiple comparisons of means: Scheffe test 95% family-wise confidence level				
$`NELS$region`	diff	lwr.ci	upr.ci	pval
North Central–Northeast	1.62981850	0.1702784	3.429915	0.0930
South–Northeast	1.52012740	−0.2885892	3.328844	0.1365
West–Northeast	1.67716411	−0.4048148	3.759143	0.1655
South–North Central	−0.10969110	−1.7421172	1.522735	0.9982
West–North Central	0.04734561	−1.8834562	1.978147	0.9999
West–South	0.15703671	−1.7818037	2.095877	0.9969

Results of the Bonferroni and Scheffe post-hoc tests do not suggest that the daily attendance rate is significantly different across regions. Likewise, the HSD does not suggest that pairwise differences in school mean daily attendance are different from each other.

By contrast, the LSD procedure suggests that the Northeast region is different from all others in terms of school daily attendance rate.

☞ **Remark.** It sometimes happens that although the omnibus F-test is statistically significant, none of the post-hoc pairwise comparisons is statistically significant. Such contradictory results are due to the fact that our inferential estimates are subject to sampling error and that the omnibus F-test is more powerful than the multiple comparison tests that follow. Results based on the F-distribution, the sampling distribution of means for testing the null hypothesis that all K population means are equal, may not agree with results based on an appropriate, yet different, sampling distribution of means based on particular pairwise comparisons. To reduce the probability of such logically contradictory results, we need to reduce the effects of sampling error so that our estimates are more precise and our tests are more powerful. A natural way to do so is through the use of larger samples.

☞ **Remark.** Other logical inconsistencies arise from the presence of random sampling error, which would not arise if we were able to compute the population parameters directly from the entire population, rather than from a random sample of that population. For example, we may observe, based on our sample data, that $\overline{X}_1 \neq \overline{X}_2 \neq \overline{X}_3$. After taking into account sampling error through the inferential process, we may conclude that $\mu_1 = \mu_2$ and that $\mu_2 = \mu_3$, but that $\mu_1 \neq \mu_3$. That is, the observed differences between $\overline{X}_1$ and $\overline{X}_2$, and those between $\overline{X}_2$ and $\overline{X}_3$, are close enough to be attributable to random sampling error, while the observed difference between $\overline{X}_1$ and $\overline{X}_3$ is not. We may note that the inferred pattern of population mean differences appears to contradict the rule of transitivity, that things equal to the same thing are equal to each other. While μ_1 and μ_3 are both equal to μ_2, μ_1 and μ_3 are not equal to each other. The point simply is that in the presence of sampling error, such logical inconsistencies are possible!

THE BONFERRONI ADJUSTMENT: TESTING PLANNED COMPARISONS

In each of the examples presented in this chapter, an analysis of variance was used to test a *global hypothesis* about the equality of means. Following a significant omnibus F-test, and a review of the data obtained, post-hoc multiple comparison tests were then conducted to investigate whether any of the observed mean differences were statistically significant. Sometimes, however, *specific hypotheses* motivate a researcher to plan and conduct a particular study. As we shall discuss in this section, the Bonferroni test may be used for planned comparisons as well.

In our manual dexterity drug rehabilitation example, Treatments 1, 2, and 3 were described merely as different types of treatment that were suspected of having a differential effect on manual dexterity. Accordingly, the purpose of the study was to test a general hypothesis about the equality of population means associated with Treatments 1, 2, and 3. If, on the other hand, however, Treatment 3 had been designed as a control or placebo condition, our interest might naturally have focused on conducting only two specific comparisons – that of Treatments 1 and 2 against the control Treatment 3. In fact, in the initial planning of the design for this study, we might have designated Treatment 3 as the control or placebo so as to draw conclusions about these specific and presumably meaningful comparisons.

Specific comparisons that derive directly from the questions that motivate a researcher to plan a study in the first place are called *planned comparisons*. The use of planned comparisons is an alternative to the analysis of variance that is made without regard to an omnibus F-test. While the method of planned comparisons offers a direct method for testing the specific questions posed, its limitation is that it does not allow for other unanticipated questions to be addressed. For that, one requires the more general approach of the one-way analysis of variance.

To carry out a test of planned comparisons, we must recognize the fact that planned comparisons are another form of multiple comparisons, and as such, give rise to an inflated family-wise Type I error rate. Without adjustment, α_{FW} for these two planned comparisons (Treatment 1 versus Treatment 3 and Treatment 2 versus Treatment 3) approximately equals $1 - (1 - 0.05)^2 = 0.0975$. A similar result is obtained from Equation 13.2, which states that α_{FW} will approximately be equal to, albeit less than, $K\alpha$, where K is the number of planned comparisons. In this example, $K\alpha = 2(0.05) = 0.10$.

Thus, we may use Equation 13.2 to adjust the overall family-wise Type I error to be equal to the desired level, say 0.05, by dividing 0.05 by K. We would then conduct each of the K planned comparisons at the new per-comparison error rate, α_{FW}/K, so as to maintain the overall α_{FW} at 0.05. For a comparison to be called statistically significant, the obtained p-value associated with this comparison must be less than α_{FW}/K. If $K = 3$ and we wish to maintain α_{FW} at 0.05, then each per-comparison α level must be set at $0.05/3 = 0.017$. This adjustment to the per-comparison α level is called the *Bonferroni adjustment* as it is based on the equation developed by Bonferroni.

Clearly, the greater the number of planned comparisons, the smaller each per-comparison α must be to maintain α_{FW} at 0.05. Because the smaller the per-comparison α, the lower the power of each test, Bonferroni adjustments should be reserved for situations in which K is relatively small.

• •

EXAMPLE 13.7 Suppose that a series of recent publications in demography indicated that rural areas have lower socioeconomic status (ses) than either suburban or urban areas. Use planned comparisons to test whether this result is replicated in the NELS dataset (note that the ses variable in NELS is all lowercase). Control the family-wise Type I error rate at 0.05.

Solution To answer this question, we need to draw comparisons: rural ses with suburban ses, and rural ses with urban ses. These comparisons form a family of comparisons, and each comparison may be tested using an independent group one-sided t-test. To control α_{FW} at 0.05, we use the Bonferroni adjustment and divide 0.05 by 2. Each pairwise comparison is conducted at 0.025. The results of the two t-tests are given below.

Rural versus urban
_____

Two sample t-test

data: NELS$ses[NELS$urban == "Rural"]

and NELS$ses[NELS$urban == "Urban"]

$t = -5.4776$ $df = 283$ p-value = 4.763e-08

alternative hypothesis: true difference in means is less than 0

95 percent confidence interval: −Inf   − 3.060953

sample estimates: mean of x   mean of y

                            15.94444   20.32520

Rural versus suburban
_____

Two sample t-test

data: NELS$ses[NELS$urban == "Rural"]

and NELS$ses[NELS$urban == "Suburban"]

$t = -4.7575$ $df = 375$ p-value = 1.401e-06

alternative hypothesis: true difference in means is less than 0

95 percent confidence interval: −Inf   −2.145436

sample estimates: mean of x   mean of y

                            15.94444   19.22791

Because both observed p-values are less than $\dfrac{a}{2} = \dfrac{0.05}{2} = 0.025$, the results reported in the literature are replicated using our NELS dataset.

THE BONFERRONI TESTS ON MULTIPLE MEASURES

Another situation that calls for a Bonferroni adjustment to control the family-wise Type I error rate at a chosen value, say 0.05, arises when groups are compared on multiple measures. The following example illustrates the use of the Bonferroni adjustment in such contexts.

EXAMPLE 13.8 Do males and females differ in twelfth grade achievement in any of the four core areas of math, science, reading, and social studies? Use $\alpha = 0.05$.

Solution Because the intent of this example is to compare males and females on these four core measures considered separately, a series of four independent groups t-tests is appropriate. To avoid an inflated Type I error rate that would result if we were to conduct each of these multiple t-tests at $\alpha = 0.05$, we consider the four tests to be a family of tests and use a Bonferroni adjustment to maintain the family-wise error rate at 0.05. In particular, we conduct each of the four tests at $\alpha = \alpha_{FW}/4 = 0.05/4 = 0.0125$.

To check assumptions and get a sense of what our data look like, we obtain the following boxplots.

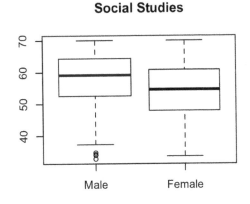

According to the boxplots, there are a few extremely low achievement scores. Given the large number of cases per group, however, such apparent departures from normality cannot be expected to compromise the validity of the t-statistic. The distributions also appear relatively homogeneous in their variances, despite the presence of extreme values in some of the groups. According to these boxplots, in general, males score higher than females. The sample means and results are provided in the following table:

	Math	**Reading**	**Science**	**Social studies**
Male	58.633	55.310	58.420	57.746
Female	55.471	55.844	53.560	53.948
p-value	6.658e-06	0.4572	1.311e-10	6.795e-07

According to results, males perform statistically significantly better than females in math ($t(498) = 4.55$, $p < 0.0005$), science ($t(496) = 6.57$, $p < 0.0005$), and social studies ($t(495) = 5.03$, $p < 0.0005$). Statistically significant gender differences were not detected in reading achievement ($t(498) = -0.744$, $p = 0.46$). Even after the Bonferroni correction to maintain the family-wise error rate, three of the four t-tests are statistically significant.

CONDUCTING POWER ANALYSES FOR ONE-WAY ANOVA

In this section, we will illustrate how to find the sample size for a one-way ANOVA using R's power command, which is available through the **pwr** library. As before, we will set power equal to 0.80, $\alpha = 0.05$, and the effect size, f, equal to a medium effect size, which, as noted in Table 10.3, is 0.25 in the case of ANOVA. We note further that f is defined as $\sqrt{(R^2(1 - R^2))}$. We will consider the situation that the groups are equal in size (called a balanced design).

EXAMPLE 13.9 Use R's **pwr.anova.test** command to determine the sample size required to detect a medium effect size with power = 0.80 and $\alpha = 0.05$ for a balanced design consisting of three groups.

Solution For this example, the R command would be as follows:

pwr.anova.test(k = 3, f = 0.25, power = 0.8, sig.level = 0.05)

Because $\alpha = 0.05$ is the default in this case, we do not need to specify this, but do so for completeness. We obtain the following result:

Balanced one-way analysis of variance power calculation		
k	=	3
n	=	52.3966
f	=	0.25
sig.level	=	0.05
power	=	0.8
Note: n is number in each group		

TABLE 13.1 Flow chart for one-way ANOVA

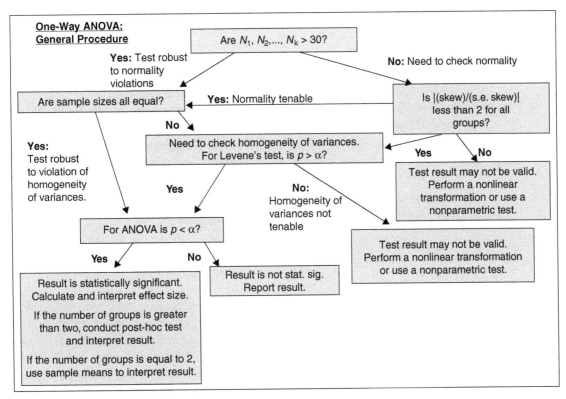

According to these results, we would need 53 cases per group, or 159 cases in total, for the probability of detecting a medium effect size to be 0.80 with $\alpha = 0.05$.

Table 13.1 contains a flow chart for the one-way analysis of variance.

SUMMARY OF R COMMANDS

(See also the .R file for Chapter 13.)

Create	**Command lines**
Calculate the *p*-value associated with an *F*-value of 19.52 and 2 and 27 degrees of freedom	**pf(19.52, 2, 27, lower.tail = F)**
Carry out a one-way ANOVA investigating mean differences in ManualDex by Treatment	**results = aov(ManDext$ManualDex ~ ManDext$Treatment)** **summary(results)**
Find the skew, standard error of skewness, and skewness ratio for Treatment 1	**skew(ManDext$ManualDex[ManDext$Treatment == 1])** **se.skew(ManDext$ManualDex[ManDext$Treatment == 1])** **skew.ratio(ManDext$ManualDex[ManDext$Treatment == 1])**

Create	Command lines
Obtain the results of Levene's test associated with the ANOVA for detecting mean differences in ManualDex by Treatment	levenes.test(ManDext$ManualDex, ManDext$Treatment)
Perform post-hoc testing for the ANOVA for detecting mean differences in ManualDex by Treatment. (Example 13.3)	results = aov(ManDext$Manual Dex~ManDext$Treatment) PostHocTest(results, method = "hsd") PostHocTest(results, method = "lsd") PostHocTest(results, method = "scheffe") PostHocTest(results, method = "bonferroni")
Perform the power analysis for a one-way ANOVA (Example 13.9)	pwr.anova.test(k = 3, f = 0.25, power = 0.8, sig.level = 0.05)

EXERCISES

*Create a .R file for each exercise that requires the use of R. Run code from the .R file by highlighting or having the cursor on the line of code and hitting **control+enter** on a PC computer keyboard or **command+enter** on a Mac computer keyboard. Save each .R file using a name associated with the Exercise for which it was created. It is recommended that you review the .R file for Chapter 13 located on the textbook's website before completing these exercises. To facilitate doing each exercise, it may be helpful to copy and paste relevant code from the .R file for Chapter 13 into your own .R file and modify them as needed.*

Exercises 13.1–13.5 involve one-way ANOVA using variables from the NELS dataset. For inferential purposes, we consider the students in the dataset to be a random sample of the population of all college-bound students who have always been at grade level. Use $\alpha = 0.05$ for all significance tests.

13.1 Does the average math achievement in eighth grade (achmat08) of college-bound students who have always been at grade level vary as a function of whether they are enrolled in a rigorous academic, academic, some vocational, or other high school program (hsprog)? Use the following questions to guide your analysis.

(a) Why is a one-way ANOVA appropriate to use to answer the question posed?

(b) Create a boxplot of achmat08 for each level of hsprog. Based on the boxplots, do the assumptions underlying the one-way ANOVA appear tenable? What do you anticipate the results of the one-way ANOVA to be? Explain.

(c) Evaluate the tenability of the normality assumption or indicate why the assumption is not an issue for this analysis, that the results of the test would not be compromised by a failure to meet this assumption.

(d) Use Levene's test to evaluate the tenability of the homogeneity of variance assumption, or indicate why the assumption is not an issue for this analysis, that the results of the ANOVA would not be compromised by a failure to meet this assumption.

(e) State the null and alternative hypotheses for determining whether or not the average math achievement in eighth grade of college-bound students who always have been at grade level varies as a function of whether they are enrolled in a rigorous academic, academic, or vocational or other high school program.

(f) What is the p-value associated with the one-way ANOVA for testing these null and alternative hypotheses?

(g) Use the p-value to determine whether or not the null hypothesis can be rejected in favor of the alternative.

(h) State the results of the analysis of variance in context. That is, do the ANOVA results suggest that for this population, math achievement in eighth grade varies as a function of high school program type?

(i) Calculate and interpret R^2 as a measure of effect size for the analysis.

(j) Is it necessary to conduct a post-hoc test in this case? If so, report and interpret the results of the Tukey HSD post-hoc tests. If not, explain why. In this exercise, we have included one of the four tests we have learned about in this chapter. Because the method of interpretation is the same, we will rely only on the Tukey HSD test for the rest of the exercises. As you do analyses on your own, you will need to decide, based on a review of your discipline-specific literature and your desired level of conservativeness, the most appropriate test to select.

13.2 Does eighth grade self-concept (slfcnc08) of college-bound students who have always been at grade level vary as a function of whether they live in an urban, suburban, or rural setting (urban)? Use the following questions to guide your analysis.

(a) Address the reason for choosing a one-way ANOVA over an independent samples t-test in this case.

(b) Create a boxplot of slfcnc08 for each level of urban. Based on the boxplots, do the assumptions underlying the one-way ANOVA appear tenable? What do you anticipate the results of the one-way ANOVA to be? Explain.

(c) Evaluate the tenability of the normality and homogeneity of variance assumption or indicate why these assumptions are not an issue for this analysis, that the results of the test would not be compromised by a failure to meet these assumptions.

(d) Conduct the ANOVA and interpret your results in context.

(e) Calculate and interpret R^2 as a measure of effect size for the analysis.

(f) Is it necessary to conduct a post-hoc test in this case? If so, report and interpret the results of the Tukey test. If not, explain why.

(g) Conduct the analysis based on a series of t-tests using the Bonferroni adjustment. Is the result obtained different from the one obtained through post-hoc testing?

13.3 Does the twelfth grade math achievement (achmat12) of college-bound students who have always been at grade level vary as a function of whether or not they ever tried cigarettes (cigarett)? Use the following questions to guide your analysis.

(a) Create boxplots of achmat12 for each level of cigarett. Based on the boxplots, do the assumptions underlying the one-way ANOVA appear tenable? What do you anticipate the results of the one-way ANOVA to be? Explain.

(b) Evaluate the tenability of the underlying assumptions or indicate why these assumptions are not an issue for this analysis, that the results of the test would not be compromised by a failure to meet these assumptions.

(c) Conduct the ANOVA and interpret your results in context.

(d) Calculate and interpret R^2 as a measure of effect size for the analysis.

(e) Is it necessary to conduct a post-hoc test in this case? If so, report and interpret the results of the Tukey HSD test. If not, explain why.

(f) Compare the results of the ANOVA to those of an independent samples t-test. Are they consistent? Is that what you would expect?

(g) Could the one-way ANOVA have been used to determine whether, among college-bound students who are always at grade level, those who never smoked cigarettes perform *better* in twelfth grade math achievement than those who smoked cigarettes at least once? Explain.

13.4 Perform a one-way ANOVA to determine whether the number of units of mathematics taken (unitmath) by college-bound students who have always been at grade level varies as a function of the highest degree the student anticipates earning (edexpect).

(a) Create boxplots of unitmath for each level of edexpect. Based on the boxplots, do the assumptions underlying the one-way ANOVA appear tenable? What do you anticipate the results of the one-way ANOVA to be? Explain.

(b) Evaluate the tenability of the underlying assumptions or indicate why these assumptions are not an issue for this analysis, that the results of the test would not be compromised by a failure to meet these assumptions.

(c) Conduct the ANOVA and interpret your results in context.

(d) Calculate and interpret R^2 as a measure of effect size for the analysis.

(e) Is it necessary to conduct a post-hoc test in this case? If so, report and interpret the results of the Tukey HSD test. If not, explain why.

13.5 Perform a one-way ANOVA to determine whether for college-bound students who have always been at grade level there are differences in the average daily attendance rates (schattrt) of the schools that smokers attended and those that non-smokers attended (cigarett).

(a) Create boxplots of schattrt for each level of cigarett. Based on the boxplots, do the assumptions underlying the one-way ANOVA appear tenable? What do you anticipate the results of the one-way ANOVA to be? Explain.

(b) Evaluate the tenability of the underlying assumptions or indicate why these assumptions are not an issue for this analysis, that the results of the test would not be compromised by a failure to meet these assumptions.

(c) Conduct the ANOVA and interpret your results in context.

(d) Is it necessary to conduct a post-hoc test in this case? If so, report and interpret the results of the Tukey HSD test. If not, explain why.

(e) If a t-test had been carried out instead with a directional alternative hypothesis (that smokers have a lower school attendance rate than non-smokers), would results have been statistically significant?

Exercise 13.6 involves selection of appropriate tests of means.

13.6 For each of the following questions based on the Learndis dataset, select a statistical procedure from the list below that would be appropriate for answering that question. For inferential purposes, we consider the children in the dataset to be a random sample of all children attending public elementary school in an urban area who have been diagnosed with learning disabilities.

1. One-tailed, one-sample t-test
2. Two-tailed, one-sample t-test
3. One-tailed, independent samples t-test
4. Two-tailed, independent samples t-test
5. One-tailed, paired samples t-test
6. Two-tailed, paired samples t-test
7. One-way ANOVA

(a) Do public elementary school females diagnosed with learning disabilities in an urban area perform better in reading comprehension than males drawn from the same population of children with learning disabilities?

(b) Is the average IQ of public-school children with learning disabilities in an urban area equal to 100?

(c) Do public-school children with learning disabilities in an urban area have higher math comprehension scores or reading comprehension scores?

(d) Are there differences in math comprehension by grade?

(e) Do public-school children with learning disabilities in an urban area have higher math comprehension scores than reading comprehension scores?

Exercises 13.7–13.8 may be used to practice calculations by hand.

13.7 A recent study was conducted on levels of tryptophan, a naturally occurring amino acid that is used by the body to produce serotonin, a mood- and appetite-regulating chemical in the brain. The study sought to determine whether bulimics, recovering bulimics, and a control group of people without bulimia differed in their levels of this amino acid. Suppose that 40 individuals from each of the three populations were randomly selected and that the observed group means were 20, 28, and 30, respectively. Complete the ANOVA summary table. Interpret results as best as can be expected with the information available.

ANOVA summary table

	Sum of squares	df	Mean square	F	Sig.
Between groups	2240				
Within groups	26208				
Total					

13.8 In an effort to improve their program for teaching students how to speak French, Western Ohio University language instructors conducted the following experiment. They randomly selected 20 students from all those who registered to take first-term spoken French and randomly divided them into four groups of five students each. Group 1 is taught French the traditional, lecture-recitation way; Group 2 is taught French from a programmed text; Group 3 is taught French from tape-recorded lessons; and Group 4 is taught French from films of people and life in France. At the end of the semester, all 20 students are given the same oral final examination on ability to speak French. The following scores are recorded.

Group 1	Group 2	Group 3	Group 4
75	68	80	87
70	73	65	90
90	70	70	85
80	60	68	75
75	65	72	80

(a) Use these data to perform a test at $\alpha = 0.05$ to determine whether, in general, these four teaching methods have differential mean effects on ability to speak French.

(b) Is it appropriate now to perform a Tukey HSD test to determine specific differences between means? If so, perform the Tukey HSD test and describe the results.

Exercise 13.9 involves power analysis.

13.9 Determine the sample size required to detect a large effect size ($f = 0.40$) with power = 0.80 and $\alpha = 0.05$ for a one-way ANOVA based on a balanced design consisting of three groups.

# CHAPTER FOURTEEN

TWO-WAY ANALYSIS OF VARIANCE

In Chapter 13 we introduced a method for analyzing mean differences on a single dependent variable between two or more independent groups while controlling the risk of making a Type I error at some specified α level. We explained the connection between the method and its name, analysis of variance, and showed how the method was a generalization of the independent groups t-test.

The examples presented were concerned with determining whether the observed variance of the dependent variable (e.g., manual dexterity variance or self-concept variance) was related to a single grouping variable (e.g., gender or type of high school program). The examples were also concerned with determining the proportion of the dependent variable variance that was explained by that grouping variable.

Because, in practice, a single grouping variable is not sufficient to explain all dependent variable variance, we can expect some unexplained portion of dependent variable variance to remain after taking into account the grouping variable. A second grouping variable is often included in a design in an attempt to explain additional residual dependent variable variance and to gain further insight into the nature of the dependent variable.

In this chapter we introduce a method called two-way analysis of variance that is an extension of one-way analysis of variance to designs that contain two grouping or independent variables. The two-way analysis of variance is used to assess mean differences through an analysis of dependent variable variance explained by the two grouping variables. The method also assesses the amount of variance explained by each of the two grouping variables and by the *interaction* between the two grouping variables. The concept of interaction is an important one and will be explained in some detail in this chapter.

THE TWO-FACTOR DESIGN

In the introductory example of Chapter 13, we were interested in comparing the effects of three methods of therapeutic treatment on manual dexterity for a specified population. Thirty individuals were selected randomly from the specified population. Each was then assigned randomly to one of the three treatments resulting in 10 individuals per treatment. After five weeks in the treatment, all 30 were administered the Stanford Test of Manual Dexterity. The scores obtained on this measure are reproduced in Table 14.1 and available in the data file, ManDext.

Under the assumption that all three populations were normally distributed and had equal variances, we used a one-way ANOVA to test the equality of all three population means and obtained $F(2,27) = 19.5$, $p < 0.0005$. Given this result we concluded that not all population means were equal. We also described the effect size for treatment. Treatment

TABLE 14.1 Scores on the Stanford Test of Manual Dexterity by treatment group

Treatment I	Treatment II	Treatment III
6	4	6
10	2	2
8	3	2
6	5	6
9	1	4
8	3	5
7	2	3
5	2	5
6	4	3
5	4	4

	Treatment I	Treatment II	Treatment III
Male			
Female			

Figure 14.1 A schematic of a 2×3 factorial design

accounted for 59 percent of manual dexterity variance. While treatment accounted for an extremely large proportion of manual dexterity variance, it left unexplained 41 percent of this variance.

In this chapter we consider the importance of a second variable, gender, in explaining additional residual manual dexterity variance. Accordingly, we note which of the 30 individuals in our dataset are male and which are female and re-organize the thirty scores into a two-dimensional table (gender by treatment) as shown in Figure 14.1.

Figure 14.1 has two rows and three columns. The row dimension represents the grouping variable, or *factor*, gender, and the column dimension represents the grouping variable, or factor, treatment. Each row represents a category, or *level*, of gender and each column represents a category, or level, of treatment. Each of the six cells in the design represents a unique combination of a level of the gender factor and a level of the treatment factor. For example, the upper left-hand cell represents all subjects in the sample who are male and who received Treatment I.

Because all unique combinations of factor levels are represented in this design (males receive all levels of treatment, I, II, and III as do all females), we call such designs *crossed*. In crossed designs, we may multiply the number of levels of one factor by the number of levels of the second factor to determine the total number of cells in the design. In this example, we multiply 2 by 3 to obtain 6 cells. Because each dimension in the design is defined by a separate factor, such designs also are referred to as *factorial designs*. Taken together, we may say that Figure 14.1 represents a 2×3 (read as "2 by 3") *crossed factorial design*, where 2 refers to the number of levels of the row factor (gender) and 3 refers to the number of levels of the column factor (treatment). We may say also that Figure 14.1 represents a *two-way analysis of variance design*.

We assume for simplicity that each treatment group of 10 individuals contains 5 males and 5 females and that the reorganized raw scores and means are shown in Table 14.2.

☞ **Remark.** We have assumed for simplicity that there are equal numbers of males and females in each treatment. In reality, however, if we were interested in using Sex as a second factor, we would design the study so that equal numbers of males and females would be assigned to each treatment. In particular, we would randomly select equal numbers of males and females from their respective populations and then randomly assign equal numbers of each to each treatment condition. Such designs are called

TABLE 14.2 A 2 x 3 crossed factorial design using the data of Table 14.1

	Treatment I	Treatment II	Treatment III	
Male	10, 9, 8, 8, 7	5, 4, 3, 2, 1	4, 3, 3, 2, 2	Row 1 mean = 4.73
	$\overline{X}_{11} = 8.4$	$\overline{X}_{12} = 3$	$\overline{X}_{13} = 2.8$	
Female	6, 6, 6, 5, 5	4, 4, 3, 2, 2	6, 6, 5, 5, 4	Row 2 mean = 4.60
	$\overline{X}_{21} = 5.6$	$\overline{X}_{22} = 3$	$\overline{X}_{23} = 5.2$	
	Col. 1 mean = 7.0	Col. 2 mean = 3.0	Col. 3 mean = 4.0	Overall mean = 4.67

TABLE 14.3 R representation of the dataset of Table 14.2. For Sex, 1 represents male and 2 represents female

Treatment	Sex	ManualDex
1	1	10
1	1	9
1	1	8
1	1	8
1	1	7
1	2	6
1	2	6
1	2	6
1	2	5
1	2	5
2	1	5
2	1	4
2	1	3
2	1	2
2	1	1
2	2	4
2	2	4
2	2	3
2	2	2
2	2	2
3	1	4
3	1	3
3	1	3
3	1	2
3	1	2
3	2	6
3	2	6
3	2	5
3	2	5
3	2	4

randomized blocks designs. In this case, each category of Sex defines a block. For additional information on such designs, the interested reader is referred to Keppel (1991).

In order to enter the data into R, we require three variables, or columns: one for treatment, one for gender, and one for score. The data as they are displayed by R are given in Table 14.3. We call the treatment variable Treatment. For the variable Sex, 1 represents male and 2 represents female.

MORE R: To calculate individual cell means and standard deviations, type:

aggregate(ManDext$ManualDex ~ ManDext$Sex + ManDext$Treatment, FUN=mean)

aggregate(ManDext$ManualDex ~ ManDext$Sex + ManDext$Treatment, FUN=sd)

Here, **FUN** stands for the function that you would like to calculate. In this case, the first line calculates cell means, and the second calculates cell standard deviations.

To calculate marginal row means and standard deviations, type:

aggregate(ManDext$ManualDex ~ ManDext$Sex, FUN=mean)

aggregate(ManDext$ManualDex ~ ManDext$Sex, FUN=sd)

To calculate marginal column means and standard deviations, type:

aggregate(ManDext$ManualDex ~ ManDext$Treatment, FUN=mean)
aggregate(ManDext$ManualDex ~ ManDext$Treatment, FUN=sd)

To calculate the overall mean and standard deviation, type:

mean(ManDext$ManualDex)
sd(ManDext$ManualDex)

The resulting output is reproduced as Table 14.4.

There are six individual cell means in Table 14.4 (8.4, 3.0, 2.8, 5.6, 3.0, and 5.2). There are also two row means (4.73 and 4.60), three column means (7.0, 3.0, and 4.0), and an overall or *grand mean* (4.67).

Each of the six individual cell means equals the mean on the manual dexterity test of the five subjects in that particular cell. For example, 8.4 equals the manual dexterity mean of the five male subjects who received Treatment I.

Each row mean, also called a *row marginal mean* because it appears in the row margin of the table, equals the mean on the manual dexterity test of those subjects in that parti-

TABLE 14.4 Cell frequencies, means, and standard deviations of manual dexterity of Table 14.2 data

Sex	Treatment			
	I	II	III	Total
Male	5	5	5	15
	8.40	3.00	2.80	4.73
	1.14	1.58	0.84	2.91
Female	5	5	5	15
	5.60	3.00	5.20	4.60
	0.55	1.00	0.84	1.40
Total	10	10	10	30
	7.00	3.00	4.00	4.67
	1.70	1.25	1.49	2.25

cular row. For example, the row marginal mean of 4.73 equals the manual dexterity mean of the 15 male subjects. Alternatively, it equals the mean of the three cell means for males. In computing the row mean, we ignore the treatment the subjects received and consider only the row they are in.

Analogously, each column marginal mean equals the mean on the manual dexterity test of those subjects in that particular column. For example, the column marginal mean of 7.0 equals the manual dexterity mean of the 10 subjects who received Treatment I. In computing the column mean, we ignore the sex of the subject and consider only the column they are in.

Finally, the overall or grand mean equals the mean on the manual dexterity test of all subjects in the study. In this example, it is the manual dexterity mean based on the 30 subjects.

If we ignore row distinctions, and consider only the columns, we have all the information necessary to conduct a one-way ANOVA on manual dexterity to evaluate the effect due to treatment. Analogously, if we ignore column distinctions, and consider only the rows, we have all the information necessary to conduct a one-way ANOVA on Sex to evaluate the effect due to gender. In the context of two-way ANOVA, the effects due to treatment and gender are called *main effects* as each is evaluated "in the main," ignoring the effect of the other factor. Thus, a two-factor design contains all the information necessary to conduct two separate one-way ANOVAs on the two different factors, respectively. It also contains additional information that tells how the two factors interact with each other in terms of the dependent variable.

THE CONCEPT OF INTERACTION

We note that the row marginal mean for males is 4.73 and the row marginal mean for females is 4.60. A comparison of these two values suggests that the mean manual dexterity score for males is similar to the mean manual dexterity score for females; that is, there is no main effect for gender. Because row marginal means represent averaged effects, averaged over all columns in that row, they do not reflect the variation in means contained in that row. By extension, a comparison of row marginal means does not reflect the variation in male–female mean comparisons by treatment. While on average males and females may be quite similar in terms of manual dexterity, it may be that males do better than females under some treatments and worse under others or it may be that their relative performance is constant for all treatments. Only by making such treatment by treatment comparisons between males and females can we gain access to this important information that is carried by the individual cells of the table.

Based on the cell means of Table 14.2, we observe that for Treatment I, males have a substantially higher mean than females (8.4 versus 5.6), for Treatment II, males and females have the same mean (3.0 versus 3.0), and for Treatment III, males have a substantially lower mean than females (2.8 versus 5.2). To show the situation more clearly, we present a line graph of these six means in Figure 14.2. The vertical axis of the graph contains a scale of manual dexterity means, the horizontal axis represents the levels of treatment and each line represents a gender type.

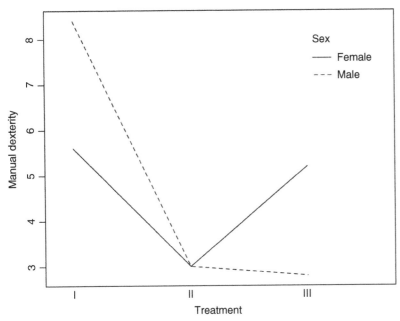

Figure 14.2 Male and female manual dexterity by treatment level: An example of a disordinal interaction

MORE R: To create a line graph of means to illustrate the two-way ANOVA, type:

interaction.plot(ManDext$Treatment, ManDext$Sex, ManDext$ManualDex, xlab = "Treatment", ylab = "Manual Dexterity", trace.label = "Sex")

Note: The **interaction.plot** command requires several arguments. The first two arguments are the factors to be considered, while the third argument is the dependent variable. Afterwards, the next set of arguments label the x-axis, y-axis, and legend. The **trace.label = "Sex"** argument is used so that we know which line represents males and which represents females. The predicted cell values based on the ANOVA are the cell means used for plotting the graph.

From Figure 14.2 it is clear that *treatments do not have a constant effect on manual dexterity performance for males and females.* If an individual were to be assigned to a particular treatment (I, II, or III) for optimal manual dexterity, one would want to know the gender of the individual before making that assignment. Said differently, if one were to ask,

"To which treatment should we assign an individual?" the answer would be "It depends on whether the individual is male or female." If male, the individual would be assigned to Treatment I, if female, the individual would be assigned to Treatment I or, perhaps, Treatment III.

Whenever the relative effects of one factor (e.g., Treatment) change across the levels of the other factor (e.g., males and females), we have what is called an *interaction* between the two factors.

The particular type of interaction illustrated in Figure 14.2 is called a *disordinal interaction* because the lines actually cross in the graph. That is, relative to females, males do better under Treatment I, they do the same under Treatment II, and they do worse under Treatment III. If we computed the difference between the male and female manual dexterity means for each treatment, we would find that these differences change from positive (8.4 − 5.6 = 2.8) to zero (3.0 − 3.0 = 0), to negative (2.8 − 5.2 = −2.4). Mean differences between levels of one factor computed at each level of the second factor will always change sign when interactions are disordinal.

Not all interactions are disordinal, however. Figure 14.3 depicts a different set of sample means using the variable yhat2 in the ManDext2 dataset (ManDext2$yhat2) that illustrates what is called an *ordinal* interaction. In this case, while the relative effects of one factor change across the levels of the other factor, the lines maintain their ordinality; that is, one line remains higher than the other line across all levels of the second factor. The lines do not cross in the graph. As shown in Figure 14.3, males perform better than females under all treatments and their relative superiority on the manual dexterity test increases as treatments change from Treatment I to II to III.

☞ **Remark.** In describing the interactions of Figures 14.2 and 14.3 we may say that there is an *interaction between gender and treatment on manual dexterity*. In so doing, we recognize the role of three variables in defining a two-way interaction, the two independent variables or factors (e.g., gender and treatment) and the dependent variable (e.g., manual dexterity).

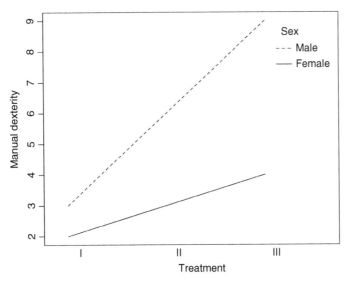

Figure 14.3 Male and female manual dexterity by treatment level: An example of an ordinal interaction

If, on the other hand, the relative effects of one factor are constant across the levels of the other factor, then we say that there is no interaction between the two factors. Figures 14.4(a–d) illustrate four possible scenarios of no interaction in the context of our 2 × 3 factorial design. Assume that these scenarios represent population means, that are, therefore, not subject to sampling error. We may observe that Figures 14.4(a–d) share a common feature: all line segments are equidistant from each other; that is, they are parallel.

Notice that in the absence of an interaction, we would *not* need to take into account gender before assigning an individual to a particular treatment because the pattern of manual dexterity performance remains the same for males and females across all treatments. Figure 14.4(a), based on the variable yhat3 in the ManDext2 dataset (ManDext2 $yhat3), illustrates the situation in which males perform better than females across all treatments. Also, males and females have the same pattern of performance across all levels of treatment. Figures 14.4(b–d) illustrate other possible outcomes. These figures are based respectively on the variables yhat4 through yhat6 in the ManDext2 dataset. The point is that in the absence of an interaction, we do not need to qualify the relative effectiveness of treatments by gender or qualify the relative performance of males and females by the treatment they received. Effects are constant in both directions.

The distances between line segments may be expressed as mean differences in terms of manual dexterity between males and females at Treatment I as $\overline{X}_{11} - \overline{X}_{21}$, at Treatment II as $\overline{X}_{12} - \overline{X}_{22}$, and at Treatment III as $\overline{X}_{13} - \overline{X}_{23}$. When these differences are all equal, all line segments are parallel and there is no interaction. When any two are not equal, all line segments are not parallel and there is an interaction. Thus, a two-way interaction may be observed when the mean differences computed between the levels of one factor for each level of the second factor are not all equal. Alternatively, when there is an interaction between factors, differences between the mean differences are different!

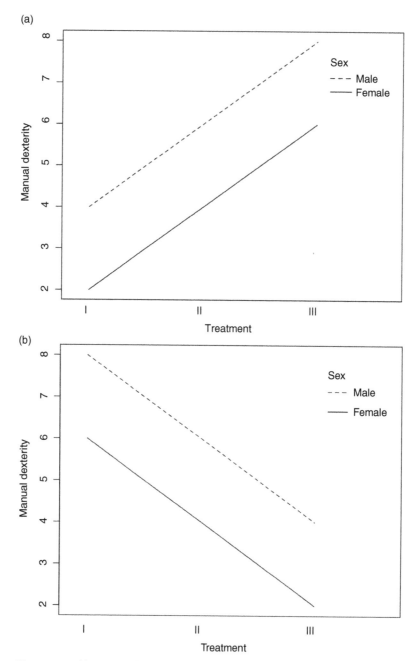

Figure 14.4 (a) Line graph depicting no interaction (b) Line graph depicting no interaction

☞ **Remark.** We have used line graphs to depict interaction effects. While this is standard practice, because the horizontal axis reflects a nominal-leveled variable (i.e., Treatment), one should be cautioned against reading a trend into the result. That is, in Figure 14.4(a), for example, one might be tempted to conclude that manual dexterity increases at a

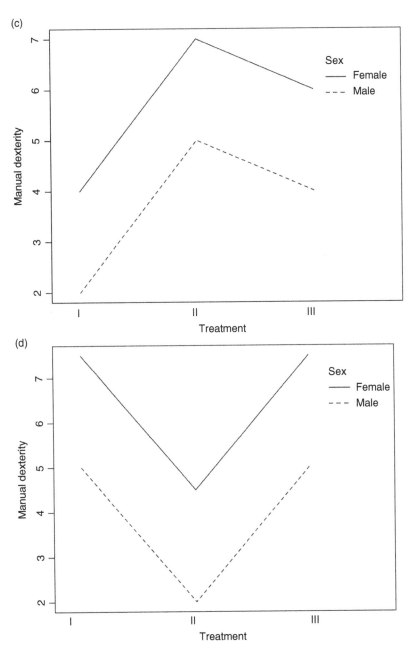

Figure 14.4 (*continued*) (c) Line graph depicting no interaction (d) Line graph depicting no interaction

constant rate across treatments for males and females because of the use of line segments in the graph.

Our discussion thus far has assumed no sampling variability and, in particular, that for example, a difference in sample means implies a difference in population means as well. When sampling variability is present, however, lines do not need to be perfectly parallel to imply no interaction and marginal means do not need to be perfectly equal to imply no main effects. Deviation from parallelism and marginal mean equality due to sampling variability may be present. To determine in practice whether an observed interaction between factors, or an observed difference between marginal means, is large enough to rule out sampling variability and to suggest, therefore, an interaction, or main effect, in the population, we rely on the two-way ANOVA procedure.

THE HYPOTHESES THAT ARE TESTED BY A TWO-WAY ANALYSIS OF VARIANCE

Three separate hypotheses are tested by a two-way ANOVA: a row main effect, a column main effect, and an interaction between the two factors, each at significance level α.

The test of the row main effect is a test of the equality of row marginal means in the population. In our example, it is a test of whether the mean manual dexterity score for males equals that for females in the population. The null and alternative hypotheses for this example are:

$$H_0: {}_R\mu_1 = {}_R\mu_2$$
$$H_1: {}_R\mu_1 \neq {}_R\mu_2.$$

where R represents row and ${}_R\mu_1$ represents the row marginal mean for row 1 (males) and ${}_R\mu_2$ represents the row marginal mean for row 2 (females).

The test of the column main effect is a test of the equality of column marginal means in the population. In our example, it is a test of whether the mean manual dexterity score for Treatment I equals that for Treatment II, which in turn, equals that for Treatment III. The null and alternative hypotheses are:

$$H_0: {}_C\mu_1 = {}_C\mu_2 = {}_C\mu_3$$
$$H_1: \text{not } H_0,$$

where C represents column and ${}_C\mu_1$ represents the column marginal mean for column 1 (Treatment I), and so on.

The null and alternative hypotheses for the test of the 2×3 (Sex $\times$ Treatment) interaction may be expressed simply as:

H_0: There is no interaction in the population between the effects of sex and treatment on manual dexterity.

H_1: There is an interaction in the population between the effects of sex and treatment on manual dexterity.

ASSUMPTIONS OF THE TWO-WAY ANALYSIS OF VARIANCE

As in the one-way ANOVA model of Chapter 13, the two-way ANOVA model in this chapter assumes that the scores are independent. Scores are independent, if, for example, each score is from a separate individual who has been randomly assigned to one of the treatment conditions of the design. In addition, like the one-way ANOVA, the two-way ANOVA model makes distributional assumptions about the scores within each group. In a one-way ANOVA, within-group distributions consist of the sample of scores within each level of the single factor (e.g., scores within Treatment I, scores within Treatment II, and scores within Treatment III). By extension, in a two-way ANOVA, within-group distributions consist of the sample of scores within each combination of factors (i.e., within each cell of the two-way design). The six within-cell distributions in our working example are the distributions of male scores within Treatment I, male scores within Treatment II, male scores within Treatment III, female scores within Treatment I, female scores within Treatment II, and female scores within Treatment III. In the two-way ANOVA, all within-cell samples of scores are assumed to come from populations that are normally distributed with equal variances. Considerations that deal with violations of these assumptions are discussed in Chapter 13 and apply to the two-way ANOVA as well.

Prior to conducting a two-way analysis of variance on the data in Table 14.2, an evaluation of the underlying assumptions of the analysis is performed. The scores are independent because each score is from a separate individual who has been randomly assigned to one of the treatment conditions of the design. Because we have fewer than 30 subjects in each cell, we evaluate the viability of the assumption that the within-cell samples of scores come from populations that are normally distributed.

MORE R: To examine the within-cell normality assumption using R, we examine the skewness, standard error of skewness, and skewness ratio for Manual Dexterity scores by Treatment status and Sex.

As an example, to find the three statistics for Males who received treatment 1, we type:

skew(ManDext$ManualDex[ManDext$Treatment == 1 & ManDext$Sex == "Male"])

se.skew(ManDext$ManualDex[ManDext$Treatment == 1 & ManDext$Sex == "Male"])

skew.ratio(ManDext$ManualDex[ManDext$Treatment == 1 & ManDext$Sex == "Male"])

To find the three statistics for other cells, simply change the arguments to **ManDext$Treatment == 2** (or 3), and **ManDext$Sex == "Female"**.

The skew values are as follows:

Sex	Treatment		
	I	II	III
Male	0.272	0	0.344
Female	−0.408	0	−0.344

Looking at the skewness values for each of the cells, we see that all six are less than 1 in magnitude, indicating that the normality assumption is tenable.

The skew ratio values are as follows:

Sex	Treatment		
	I	II	III
Male	0.297	0	0.376
Female	−0.447	0	−0.376

Looking at the skewness ratios for each of the cells, we see that all six are less than 2 in magnitude, indicating that the normality assumption is tenable.

Because the cell sizes are equal, there are five research participants in each cell, the two-way ANOVA is robust to violations of the homogeneity of variance assumption, so the assumption is not evaluated.

BALANCED VERSUS UNBALANCED FACTORIAL DESIGNS

In the one-way ANOVA, no restriction was placed on the relative sizes of the samples that comprised each level of the factor studied. The model, as described, allowed for either equal or unequal cell sizes. The model presented in this chapter for two-way ANOVA is based on the assumption that the number of subjects in each cell is equal. This is to ensure that the design is *balanced* (or *orthogonal*). An advantage of balanced designs is that they allow us to consider the two main effects as separate entities, which may be tested without regard to each other. For example, the results pertaining to one main effect may be interpreted without regard to the results pertaining to the other main effect. Said differently, the sum of squares due to each main effect in a two-way balanced design equals the sum of squares due to each main effect if each main effect were analyzed separately in a one-way design.

Analytical approaches different from those presented in this chapter are required when applying the two-way ANOVA to non-orthogonal or unbalanced designs. We shall touch on some of the more complicated issues that arise in connection with unbalanced designs in Chapter 16 on multiple regression.

PARTITIONING THE TOTAL SUM OF SQUARES

In Chapter 13, we pointed out that one-way ANOVA partitions the total variability (SS_T) of our dependent variable into two unrelated (orthogonal) components: variability due to the between groups effect (SS_B) and variability that remains unexplained within group after the between groups effect is accounted for (SS_W). Equation 14.1 uses the context of our working example to express the partitioning of the total manual dexterity sum of squares in a one-way design into a sum of squares due to Treatment and a sum of squares due to what remains within group once Treatment is accounted for:

$$SS_{TOT} = SS_{TREAT} + SS_{WITHIN-GROUP}$$
$$146.67 = 86.67 + 60.00$$

(14.1)

In an analogous way, two-way ANOVA also partitions the total sum of squares into unrelated (orthogonal) component parts. In the case of the two-way design of our working example, these components of variability are due to Treatment, Sex, the Sex by Treatment interaction, and what remains unexplained within-cell after all these sources of variation are accounted for. Equation 14.2 expresses this breakdown of variability for the two-way design:

$$SS_{TOT} = SS_{TREAT} + \underbrace{SS_{SEX} + SS_{INTER} + SS_{WITHIN-CELL}}$$

(14.2)

$$146.67 = 86.67 + \qquad\qquad 60.00$$

Notice, that because in both models, the SS_{TOT} is equal to the sum of squares based on the whole set of 30 manual dexterity scores without regard to any grouping variable, the value of SS_{TOT} remains the same in both models (146.67). Analogously, because SS_{TREAT} in the two-way ANOVA continues to equal the sum of squared deviations of the three treatment means about the grand mean without regard to gender, it also has the same value in the two-way ANOVA as in the one-way ANOVA (86.67).

In the two-way design, the addition of the second factor, gender, allows for the opportunity to explain more of the 60 units of residual variability that is left unexplained in the one-way design. According to Equation 14.2, the sum of SS_{SEX}, SS_{INTER} and $SS_{WITHIN-CELL}$ equals 60. If neither Sex nor the interaction between Sex and Treatment accounts for any additional residual variability, then SS_W will remain at 60, and there will be nothing gained by using the two-way design. In general, the degree to which we gain in explanatory power from using the two-way design relates to the amount by which the residual variability left unexplained in the one-way design can be reduced by the additional sources of variation, Sex and Sex by Treatment, in the two-way design.

USING THE *F*-RATIO TO TEST THE EFFECTS IN TWO-WAY ANOVA

To test whether each of the three sources of variation (main effect due to Treatment, main effect due to Sex, and interaction effect due to Sex and Treatment) explains a statistically significant proportion of total variance (that is, a proportion that is not attributable to chance), we carry out a series of three *F*-tests as shown in Table 14.5, each at a specified α level. As in the one-way ANOVA, the denominator of each *F*-test is based on the left-over, residual variance, denoted MS_W, and the numerator of each *F*-test is based on one of the three between group variances defined by its respective source of variation. As before, the degrees of freedom for a main effect equals one less than the number of groups for that main effect (e.g., $R - 1$ for the row main effect). The degrees of freedom for the interaction effect equals the product of $R - 1$ and $C - 1$. The degrees of freedom for the error or within cells effect equals $N - RC$, the total sample size less the total number of cells in the design represented as the product of the number of rows by the number of columns (RC). Finally, the total degrees of freedom equals $N - 1$. We may note that the degrees of freedom for the separate effects in the design sum to the total degrees of freedom for the design (that is, $R - 1 + C - 1 + (R - 1)(C - 1) + N - RC = N - 1$).

Table 14.5 shows how the *F*-ratios are formed to construct the respective *F*-tests beginning with the *SS* terms. In the next section, we describe within a conceptual framework how these *SS* terms are generated and we carry out the two-way ANOVA by hand using our manual dexterity example.

TABLE 14.5 Forming F-ratios in a two-way ANOVA design with a row and a column factor

Source of variation	SS	df	MS	F-ratio
Factor R	SS_R	$R - 1$	$MS_R = SS_R/(R - 1)$	MS_R/MS_W
Factor C	SS_C	$C - 1$	$MS_C = SS_C/(C - 1)$	MS_C/MS_W
$R \times C$ interaction	$SS_{R \times C}$	$(R - 1)(C - 1)$	$MS_{R \times C} = SS_{R \times C}/(R - 1)(C - 1)$	$MS_{R \times C}/MS_W$
Within cells	SS_W	$N - RC$		
Total	SS_T	$N - 1$		

TABLE 14.6 A 2 x 3 crossed factorial design using the data of Table 14.2

	Treatment I	Treatment II	Treatment III	
Male	10, 9, 8, 8, 7	5, 4, 3, 2, 1	4, 3, 3, 2, 2	$_R\overline{X}_1 = 4.73$
	$\overline{X}_{11} = 8.4$	$\overline{X}_{12} = 3$	$\overline{X}_{13} = 2.8$	
Female	6, 6, 6, 5, 5	4, 4, 3, 2, 2	6, 6, 5, 5, 4	$_R\overline{X}_2 = 4.60$
	$\overline{X}_{21} = 5.6$	$\overline{X}_{22} = 3$	$\overline{X}_{23} = 5.2$	
	$_C\overline{X}_1 = 7.0$	$_C\overline{X}_2 = 3.0$	$_C\overline{X}_2 = 4.0$	Overall mean = 4.67

CARRYING OUT THE TWO-WAY ANOVA COMPUTATION BY HAND

The manual dexterity scores of the 30 individuals, organized by the two factors of the two-way design, are given again as Table 14.6.

The sum of squares associated with the row effect, SS_R, is given by Equation 14.3:

$$SS_R = \sum_{i=1}^{r} {}_R N_i ({}_R\overline{X}_i - \overline{\overline{X}})^2, \tag{14.3}$$

where r represents the number of levels of the row factor, $_R N_i$ equals the number of values in row i, $_R\overline{X}_i$ equals the mean of the values in row i, and $\overline{\overline{X}}$ equals the overall or grand mean of all values in the sample.

Using Equation 14.3, we compute SS_R for the manual dexterity example:

$$_R N_1 = {}_R N_2 = 15; \; _R\overline{X}_1 = 4.73, \; _R\overline{X}_2 = 4.60; \overline{\overline{X}} = 4.67; r = 2,$$
$$SS_R = 15(4.6 - 4.67)^2 + 15(4.7 - 4.67)^2 = 0.13.$$

The sum of squares associated with the column effect, SS_C, is given by Equation 14.4:

$$SS_C = \sum_{j=1}^{c} {}_C N_j ({}_C\overline{X}_j - \overline{\overline{X}})^2, \tag{14.4}$$

where c represents the number of levels of the column factor, $_C N_j$ equals the number of values in column j, $_C\overline{X}_j$ equals the mean of the values in column j, and $\overline{\overline{X}}$ equals the overall or grand mean of all values in the sample.

Using Equation 14.4, we compute SS_C for the manual dexterity example:

$$_cN_1 = {}_cN_2 = {}_cN_3 = 10; \; {}_c\overline{X}_1 = 7.0, \; {}_c\overline{X}_2 = 3.0, {}_c\overline{X}_3 = 4.0; \overline{\overline{X}} = 4.67; c = 3,$$
$$SS_C = 10(7 - 4.67)^2 + 10(3 - 4.67)^2 + 10(4 - 4.67)^2 = 86.67.$$

The sum of squares associated with the interaction effect, $SS_{R \times C}$, is given by Equation 14.5.

$$SS_{R \times C} = \sum_{i=1}^{r} \sum_{j=1}^{c} N_{i,j}(\overline{X}_{i,j} - {}_R\overline{X}_i - {}_c\overline{X}_j + \overline{\overline{X}})^2, \tag{14.5}$$

where $N_{i,j}$ equals the number of values in cell i,j, $\overline{X}_{i,j}$ equals the mean of the values in cell i,j, $_R\overline{X}_i$ equals the mean of the values in row i, $_c\overline{X}_j$ equals the mean of the values in column j, and $\overline{\overline{X}}$ equals the overall or grand mean of all values in the sample.

Using Equation 14.5, we compute $SS_{R \times C}$ for the manual dexterity example:

$$N_{11} = N_{12} = N_{13} = N_{21} = N_{22} = N_{23} = 5;$$
$$\overline{X}_{11} = 8.4, \overline{X}_{12} = 3.0, \overline{X}_{13} = 2.8, \overline{X}_{21} = 5.6, \overline{X}_{22} = 3.0, \overline{X}_{23} = 5.2;$$
$$_R\overline{X}_1 = 4.73, \; _R\overline{X}_2 = 4.60; \; _c\overline{X}_1 = 7.0, \; _c\overline{X}_2 = 3.0, \; _c\overline{X}_3 = 4.0; \overline{\overline{X}} = 4.67.$$

$$\begin{aligned} SS_{R \times C} = {} &5(8.4 - 4.73 - 7.0 + 4.67)^2 + 5(3.0 - 4.73 - 3.0 + 4.67)^2 + 5(2.8 - 4.73 - 4.0 \\ &+ 4.67)^2 + 5(5.6 - 4.60 - 7.0 + 4.67)^2 + 5(3.0 - 4.60 - 3.0 + 4.67)^2 + 5(5.2 \\ &- 4.60 - 4.0 + 4.67)^2 = 33.87. \end{aligned}$$

The sum of squares associated with the remaining within-cell variation, SS_W, is given by Equation 14.6:

$$SS_W = \sum_{i,j,k} (X_{i,j,k} - \overline{X}_{i,j})^2, \tag{14.6}$$

where $X_{i,j,k}$ represents the kth score in row i and column j, and $\overline{X}_{i,j}$ represents the mean of the scores in row i and column j.

Using Equation 14.6, we compute SS_W for the manual dexterity example:

$$\begin{aligned} SS_W = {} &(10 - 8.4)^2 + (9 - 8.4)^2 + (8 - 8.4)^2 + (8 - 8.4)^2 + (7 - 8.4)^2 + (5 - 3)^2 + (4 - 3)^2 \\ &+ (3 - 3)^2 + (2 - 3)^2 + (1 - 3)^2 + (4 - 2.8)^2 + (3 - 2.8)^2 + (3 - 2.8)^2 + (2 - 2.8)^2 \\ &+ (2 - 2.8)^2 + (6 - 5.6)^2 + (6 - 5.6)^2 + (6 - 5.6)^2 + (5 - 5.6)^2 + (5 - 5.6)^2 + (4 - 3)^2 \\ &+ (4 - 3)^2 + (3 - 3)^2 + (2 - 3)^2 + (2 - 3)^2 + (6 - 5.2)^2 + (6 - 5.2)^2 + (5 - 5.2)^2 \\ &+ (5 - 5.2)^2 + (4 - 5.2)^2 = 2.56 + 0.36 + 0.16 + 0.16 + 1.96 + 4 + 1 + 0 + 1 + 4 + 1.44 \\ &+ 0.04 + 0.04 + 0.64 + 0.64 + 0.16 + 0.16 + 0.16 + 0.36 + 0.36 + 1 + 1 + 0 + 1 + 1 \\ &+ 0.64 + 0.64 + 0.04 + 0.04 + 1.44 = 26.00. \end{aligned}$$

Finally, the sum of squares associated with the total variability, SS_{TOT}, is given by Equation 14.7:

$$SS_{TOT} = \sum (X_{ijk} - \overline{\overline{X}})^2. \tag{14.7}$$

Using Equation 14.7, we compute SS_{TOT} for the manual dexterity example.

$$\begin{aligned} SS_{TOT} = {} &(10 - 4.67)^2 + (9 - 4.67)^2 + (8 - 4.67)^2 + (8 - 4.67)^2 + (7 - 4.67)^2 + (5 - 4.67)^2 \\ &+ (4 - 4.67)^2 + (3 - 4.67)^2 + (2 - 4.67)^2 + (1 - 4.67)^2 + (4 - 4.67)^2 + (3 - 4.67)^2 \\ &+ (3 - 4.67)^2 + (2 - 4.67)^2 + (2 - 4.67)^2 + (6 - 4.67)^2 + (6 - 4.67)^2 + (6 - 4.67)^2 \end{aligned}$$

$$+ (5 - 4.67)^2 + (5 - 4.67)^2 + (4 - 4.67)^2 + (4 - 4.67)^2 + (3 - 4.67)^2 + (2 - 4.67)^2$$
$$+ (2 - 4.67)^2 + (6 - 4.67)^2 + (6 - 4.67)^2 + (5 - 4.67)^2 + (5 - 4.67)^2 + (4 - 4.67)^2$$
$$= 146.67.$$

Substituting these values for their respective SS, we obtain the second column of Table 14.5.

We then calculate the values of df, MS, and F, following the formulas given in the ANOVA summary in Table 14.5.

We first find these values for the within cells:

$$df_W = N - RC = 30 - 6 = 24, MS_W = SS_W\ df_W = 26/24 = 1.08.$$

For the main effect of gender, we obtain the following values:

$$df_R = R - 1 = 2 - 1 = 1, MS_R = SS_R\ /df_R = 0.13/1 = 0.13.$$
$$F = MS_R\ /MS_W = 0.13/1.08 = 0.12.$$

For the main effect of treatment, we obtain the following values:

$$df_C = C - 1 = 3 - 1 = 2, MS_C = SS_C\ /df_C = 86.76\ /\ 2 = 43.34.$$
$$F = MS_C\ /MS_W = 43.34/1.08 = 40.13.$$

For the interaction effect, we obtain the following values:

$$df_{R \times C} = (R - 1)(C - 1) = 1 \times 2 = 2, MS_{R \times C} = SS_{R \times C}/df_{R \times C} = 33.87/2 = 16.93.$$
$$F = MS_{R \times C}/MS_W = 16.93/1.08 = 15.69.$$

The three p-values are obtained either by using Table C.3 in Appendix C, which may be found online at the Cambridge University Press website for this text (www.cambridge.org/stats-r), or by using the R probability distribution functions. Both approaches are described.

Table C.3 in Appendix C may be used to approximate the associated p-values. To find the p-value for the main effect of gender, we want an estimate of the area to the right of $F = 0.12$ with numerator degrees of freedom 1 and denominator degrees of freedom 24. To do so, we find all of the α values associated with df for numerator = 1 and df for denominator = 24. We see that the F-value 1.39 cuts off area 0.25 to its right, that 2.93 cuts off area 0.10 to its right, etc. Because $F = 0.12$ is less than 1.39, we conclude that the area to the right of $F = 0.12$ is greater than 0.25, that is, that $p > 0.25$.

To find the p-value for the main effect of treatment, we want an estimate of the area to the right of $F = 40.13$ with numerator degrees of freedom 2 and denominator degrees of freedom 24. To do so, we find all of the α values associated with df for numerator = 2 and df for denominator = 24. We find the closest value that is smaller than 40.13. In this case, the F-value 9.34 cuts off area 0.001 to its right. Because $F = 40.13$ is greater than 9.34, it must cut off even less area, so that we conclude that the area to the right of $F = 40.13$ is less than 0.001, that is, that $p < 0.001$.

To find the p-value for the interaction effect, we want an estimate of the area to the right of $F = 15.69$ with numerator degrees of freedom 2 and denominator degrees of freedom 24. As with the main effect of treatment, because $F = 15.69$ is greater than 9.34, $p < 0.001$.

The R F-probability distribution function **pf** may be used to find the associated p-values in the right tail of the F-distribution. In particular, we use:

pf(.12, 1, 24, lower.tail = F) to find the p-value associated with the main effect due to Sex;
pf(40.13, 2, 24, lower.tail = F) to find the p-value associated with the main effect for Treatment; and,
pf(15.69, 2, 24, lower.tail = F) to find the p-value associated with the Sex by Treatment interaction.

MORE R: To carry out a two-way ANOVA with interaction we make use of the * symbol to represent that we are interested in including both main effects and their interaction:

results = aov(ManDext$ManualDex ~ ManDext$Sex*ManDext$Treatment)
summary(results)

The results are summarized in Table 14.7. Note that the values for Pr(>F) are those obtained using R and are rounded to two decimal places.

When interpreting the results of the two-way ANOVA, we compare each of the p-values (found in the Pr(>F) column) to the α level, which in this case is $\alpha = 0.05$. The results of the two-way ANOVA indicate that there is a statistically significant main effect of treatment, $F(2, 24) = 40.13$, $p < 0.005$ and a statistically significant interaction effect $F(2, 24) = 40.13$, $p < 0.005$. Because the presence of a statistically significant interaction indicates that the best treatment depends on the gender, we focus on the interaction instead of the main effect of treatment. In order to understand the nature of the interaction effect, that is, the way in which the best treatment depends on the gender, we conduct post-hoc multiple comparison tests. These are discussed in a later section.

Several comparisons with the one-way ANOVA results are worthwhile. First, we notice that, as expected, the SS_{TOT} and SS_{TREAT} remain the same at 146.67 and 86.67, respectively. Second, we notice that $SS_{SEX} + SS_{INTER} + SS_W = 0.13 + 33.87 + 26.0 = 60$, as we also had expected. Third, we notice that $SS_{TOT} = SS_{TREAT} + SS_{SEX} + SS_{INTER} + SS_W$, suggesting that this two-way ANOVA does partition the total variability of manual dexterity values into these four independent (orthogonal) components.

Finally, we notice that the denominator of the F-ratios, the MS_W term, is smaller in the two-way ANOVA than in the one-way ANOVA, suggesting that we have explained

TABLE 14.7 Summary table of results of the two-way ANOVA on manual dexterity

Source of variation	df	SS	MS	F-ratio	Pr(>F)
Sex	1	0.13	0.13	0.12	0.72
Treatment	2	86.67	43.33	40.13	0.00
Sex × Treatment	2	33.87	16.93	15.69	0.00
Residuals	24	26.00	1.08		
Total	29	146.67			

additional residual variance by the inclusion of Sex and the interaction between Sex and Treatment in the design. Because the denominator of the F-ratio in the two-way design is smaller than in the one-way design, we say that the two-way design is more *precise* than the one-way ANOVA in that it exacts greater control over variation due to individual differences. In the one-way ANOVA, the F-ratio for testing the Treatment effect is only 19.52, while in the two-way design, because of the smaller denominator, the F-ratio for testing the Treatment effect is 40.13. More precise designs give rise to larger F-ratios and, therefore, provide a greater chance of detecting significant differences where they exist. Accordingly, more precise designs are also known as more powerful designs.

Thus, we include additional variables in a design not only because we may be interested in testing the relationships between these variables and the dependent variable, but also because we are interested in enhancing the power of our design by controlling the effects of these other variables. In our example, we have reduced the within-group variance by controlling for individual differences in manual dexterity due to the interaction between Sex and Treatment.

Suppose, instead, we had added a different variable other than Sex, say, preference for ice cream or yogurt, which has nothing to do with manual dexterity, as either a main or interaction effect. In this case, the variable preference would not have helped to control for additional individual differences in manual dexterity and the design would not have been more precise than the one-way design. Accordingly, the power of the two-way ANOVA in testing the Treatment effect would not have improved. In fact, by adding a variable to a design that is not related to the dependent variable, either individually or through interaction, the power of the test will diminish as Example 14.1 illustrates.

EXAMPLE 14.1 Show that the two-way design including Preference for ice cream or yogurt, which is unrelated to the dependent variable of manual dexterity, and Treatment has lower power for testing the Treatment effect than the one-way design with only Treatment.

Solution Because we believe that preference for ice cream or yogurt has nothing (zero) to do with manual dexterity as a main or interaction effect, we set SS_{PREF} and $SS_{PREF \times TREAT}$ to zero in Table 14.5. We leave the degrees of freedom as they are because like Sex, Preference has only two levels: Ice cream and Yogurt. We compute a new, revised SS_W and obtain the following results.

Source of Variation	SS	df	MS	F-ratio
Preference	0	1	0/1 = 0	0/2.5 = 0
Treatment	86.67	2	86.76/2 = 43.34	43.34/2.5 = 17.34
Preference × Treatment	0	2	0/2 = 0	0/2.5 = 0
Within cells	60	24	60/24 = 2.5	
Total	146.67	29		

Notice that the F-ratio for Treatment decreases from a value of 19.52 in the one-way design to a value of 17.34 in the two-way design. Simply stated, adding the variable Preference to our one-way design compromises the power of our test of the Treatment effect. Preference used up one degree of freedom as a main effect and another degree of freedom as an interaction effect without explaining additional residual variance. Variables, such as these, which cannot be expected to "pull their own weight" in a design context are best excluded. Alternatively, variables that are theoretically or otherwise known to relate strongly to the dependent variable as a main or interaction effect ought to be included.

DECOMPOSING SCORE DEVIATIONS ABOUT THE GRAND MEAN

Each of the SS terms used to test for the main and interaction effects in a two-way design derives from a simple mathematical identity that expresses a score's total deviation from the grand mean $(X_{ijk} - \overline{\overline{X}})$ as a sum of its component parts. In particular, we may express this identity as Equation 14.8.

$$X_{ijk} - \overline{\overline{X}} = (_R\overline{X}_i - \overline{\overline{X}}) + (_C\overline{X}_j - \overline{\overline{X}}) + (\overline{X}_{ij} -_R\overline{X}_i -_C\overline{X}_j + \overline{\overline{X}}) + (X_{ijk} - \overline{X}_{ij}). \qquad (14.8)$$

Equation 14.8 makes explicit the notion that each score deviation about the grand mean is represented in two-way ANOVA as a sum of (1) the row deviation about the grand mean, (2) the column deviation about the grand mean, (3) the interaction between the row and column factors, and (4) an individual difference, called error, measured as the difference between an individual's score and the mean of the group for that individual.

☞ **Remark.** What makes Equation 14.8 a mathematical identity is the fact that after simplifying the expression by removing parentheses and rearranging terms, we find, as shown in Equation 14.9, that the value to the left of the equal sign is identical to the value to the right of the equal sign.

$$\begin{aligned} X_{ijk} - \overline{\overline{X}} &= (_R\overline{X}_i - \overline{\overline{X}}) + (_C\overline{X}_j - \overline{\overline{X}}) + (\overline{X}_{ij} -_R\overline{X}_i -_C\overline{X}_j + \overline{\overline{X}}) + (X_{ijk} - \overline{X}_{ij}) \\ &= X_{ijk} +_R\overline{X}_i +_C\overline{X}_j -_R\overline{X}_i -_C\overline{X}_j - \overline{\overline{X}} - \overline{\overline{X}} + \overline{\overline{X}} + \overline{X}_{ij} - \overline{X}_{ij} \\ &= X_{ijk} - \overline{\overline{X}}. \end{aligned} \qquad (14.9)$$

The importance of breaking down $(X_{ijk} - \overline{\overline{X}})$ into its component parts is that it facilitates our understanding of where the SS terms used for testing the main and interaction effects come from. In short, Equation 14.8 makes explicit the connection between the breakdown of the total score deviation into its component parts and the partition of the total SS into its component parts. The total SS associated with the score deviation about the grand mean is also called the *corrected total SS*.

In particular, each score deviation in Equation 14.8 corresponds to a different SS term in Equation 14.2. In particular, the score deviation about the grand mean gives rise to the SS_{TOT}; the row deviation about the grand mean gives rise to the SS_{ROW}; the column deviation about the grand mean gives rise to the SS_{COL}; the interaction term gives rise to the SS_{INTER}; and the error term gives rise to SS_W.

MODELING EACH SCORE AS A SUM OF COMPONENT PARTS

If we add $\overline{\overline{X}}$ to both sides of Equation 14.8, we obtain Equation 14.10 which suggests that each score in ANOVA is comprised of a sum of five parts: (1) the grand mean, (2) the effect due to the row factor, (3) the effect due to the column factor, (4) the effect due to the interaction between row and column factors, and (5) the within-cell deviations that represent the left-over, unexplained individual differences (the error). The grand mean may be thought of as a baseline value to which the value of each effect (row, column, interaction, and error) is added to obtain the score itself.

$$X_{ijk} = \overline{\overline{X}} + (_R\overline{X}_i - \overline{\overline{X}}) + (_C\overline{X}_j - \overline{\overline{X}}) + (\overline{X}_{ij} -_R\overline{X}_i -_C\overline{X}_j + \overline{\overline{X}}) + (X_{ijk} - \overline{X}_{ij}). \quad (14.10)$$

In the context of our working example, Equation 14.10 suggests that two-way ANOVA models the manual dexterity score of each individual as the sum of the grand mean (which may be viewed as a baseline value), plus the effect of the individual's gender, plus the effect of which treatment the individual received, plus the joint effect of the individual's gender and treatment, plus an unexplained amount, called error. The SS associated with the original raw scores are called *raw total SS*.

EXPLAINING THE INTERACTION AS A JOINT (OR MULTIPLICATIVE) EFFECT

We have referred to the interaction between the row and column factors as a joint effect. A joint effect appropriately suggests that the combination of factors produces an effect that is more than the sum of its parts (that is, more than the sum of the effects of the two separate factors). Hays (1973) likened an interaction to what happens when two parts of hydrogen combine with one part of oxygen to produce water. Clearly that combination of hydrogen and oxygen produces an effect that is more than the sum of its parts.

We use a subset of Equation 14.8 to show that, in fact, the interaction effect is more than the sum of its parts. Equation 14.8 describes the total score deviation as a sum of its component parts. These parts may be classified broadly as the between group effects and the within group effect. In this section we consider only between group effects which are based on the difference between each group mean $(\overline{X}_{ij})$ and the grand mean $(\overline{\overline{X}})$. This difference is defined in Equation 14.11 as the sum of the component score deviations representing the two main effects and the interaction:

$$\overline{X}_{ij} - \overline{\overline{X}} = (_R\overline{X}_i - \overline{\overline{X}}) + (_C\overline{X}_j - \overline{\overline{X}}) + (\overline{X}_{ij} -_R\overline{X}_i -_C\overline{X}_j + \overline{\overline{X}}). \quad (14.11)$$

By rearranging the terms we may show that Equation 14.11, like Equation 14.8, is a mathematical identity that simplifies to $\overline{X}_{ij} - \overline{\overline{X}} = \overline{X}_{ij} - \overline{\overline{X}}$. We may isolate the term representing the interaction effect on the right-hand side of the equation by subtracting from the row and column effects from both sides of the equation. In so doing, we obtain Equation 14.12:

$$(\overline{X}_{ij} - \overline{\overline{X}}) - (_R\overline{X}_i - \overline{\overline{X}}) - (_C\overline{X}_j - \overline{\overline{X}}) = (\overline{X}_{ij} -_R\overline{X}_i -_C\overline{X}_j + \overline{\overline{X}}). \quad (14.12)$$

According to Equation 14.12, the interaction is that part of the between groups effect that remains after subtracting out the sum of the separate row and column effects. Said differently, the interaction is what remains after the additive effects of the row and column factors are removed. As such, the interaction effect may be thought of as representing the joint or multiplicative effect of both row and column factors.

MEASURING EFFECT SIZE

In Chapter 13 we measured the size of an effect (e.g., Treatment) as the ratio of the SS due to that effect divided by the SS_{TOT}. As such, this ratio represents the proportion of total variance explained by or accounted for by that effect. We extend this notion to the case of two-way ANOVA where interest is in measuring the magnitude of not one, but rather three effects, the two main effects and the interaction.

By extension, the proportion of total variance explained by the row main effect, denoted as R^2_{ROW} is given by Equation 14.13:

$$R^2_{ROW} = \frac{SS_{ROW}}{SS_{TOT}}. \tag{14.13}$$

The proportion of total variance explained by the column main effect, denoted as R^2_{COL}, is given by Equation 14.14:

$$R^2_{COL} = \frac{SS_{COL}}{SS_{TOT}}. \tag{14.14}$$

The proportion of total variance explained by the interaction effect, denoted as R^2_{INTER}, is given by Equation 14.15:

$$R^2_{INTER} = \frac{SS_{INTER}}{SS_{TOT}}. \tag{14.15}$$

Applying these ratios to the data from our manual dexterity example, we find that the proportion of manual dexterity variance due to Sex is $0.13/146.67 = 0.0009 = 0.09\%$, due to Treatment is $86.67/146.67 = 0.59 = 59\%$, and due to the Sex by Treatment interaction is $33.87/146.67 = 0.23 = 23\%$. Based on the guidelines given in Chapter 10, both the main effect due to Treatment and the Sex by Treatment interaction are very large while the main effect due to Sex is miniscule. The variable Sex contributes to this analysis not as a main effect, but in combination with Treatment as an interaction. Collectively, the three effects account for approximately 82 percent of the total manual dexterity variance, leaving approximately 18 percent unexplained.

An alternative measure of effect size is the ratio of SS due to that effect divided by the sum of the SS due to that effect plus the SS due to unexplained error after controlling for all other effects. As such, this measure of effect size may be thought of as the proportion of variance due to an effect after controlling for all other effects in the design. These measures of effect size are called *partial eta squared* terms because they are based on controlling for or partialling out the other effects in the design. The expressions of partial eta squared, denoted η^2, for the row and column main effects and the interaction effect are given in Equations 14.16 through 14.18, respectively. In general, for any given effect, η^2 will be larger than the corresponding R^2 for that effect:

$$\eta^2_{ROW} = \frac{SS_{ROW}}{SS_{ROW} + SS_W}. \tag{14.16}$$

$$\eta^2_{COL} = \frac{SS_{COL}}{SS_{COL} + SS_W}. \tag{14.17}$$

$$\eta^2_{INTER} = \frac{SS_{INTER}}{SS_{INTER} + SS_W}. \tag{14.18}$$

EXAMPLE 14.2 Use R to conduct a two-way ANOVA on the manual dexterity data. Verify that the answers from R are the same as those we obtained by hand computation.

Solution We open the ManDext dataset, which contains the data we used to conduct the one-way ANOVA consisted of two variables, treatment and Manual Dexterity score. Treatment contains the value of the treatment group (1, 2, or 3) to which an individual has been assigned, and score contains an individual's score on the manual dexterity test. In this analysis, we add another variable, Sex, that represents the sex of an individual.

We obtain the following results:

	df	Sum sq.	Mean sq.	F-value	Pr(>F)	
ManDext$Sex	1	0.13	0.13	0.123	0.729	
ManDext$Treatment	2	86.67	43.33	40.00	2.28e-08	***
ManDext$Sex: ManDext$Treatment	2	33.87	16.93	15.631	4.50e-05	***
Residuals	24	26.00	1.08			
Signif. codes:	0	"***" 0.001	"**" 0.01	"*" 0.05	"." 0.1	" " 1

We notice, as expected, that the model for the two-way design contains a Sex effect, a Treatment effect and an interaction effect denoted by the term **ManDext$Sex:ManDext$Treatment**. The **ManDext$Sex:ManDext$Treatment** term represents the product between the Sex and Treatment variables, and, as such, aligns with the fact that the interaction term represents a joint, multiplicative effect over and above the additive effects of Sex and Treatment.

The values in the two-way ANOVA summary table for each of the effects, including the Residual (aka the within-cell or left-over variability after accounting for main and interaction effects) agree with those we obtained through our hand computation.

The SS for the entire model (120.667) can be obtained by adding the SS values for ManDext$Sex, ManDext$Treatment, and ManDext$Sex:ManDext$Treatment. If we then divide the SS_{MODEL} by SS_{TOTAL} (obtained by adding the SS for the residuals to the SS of the model) we obtain an overall measure of the proportion of total variance explained by the model. As this measure is analogous to the measures presented in Equations 14.13 through 14.15, it too is denoted by R^2. For our working example, we have

$$\begin{aligned} R^2_{MODEL} &= \frac{SS_{MODEL}}{SS_{TOTAL}} \\ &= \frac{120.667}{146.667} \\ &= 0.823, \end{aligned} \tag{14.19}$$

which is the same value we obtained from our hand computation. Because 82.3 percent of the total manual dexterity variance is accounted for by all three model effects taken collectively, we know that approximately 18 percent of this total variance remains unexplained variance.

MORE R: To test for homogeneity of variance using Levene's test you can use the **levenes.test** function, introduced in Chapter 11, as shown with the following code:

levenes.test(ManDext$ManualDex, ManDext$Sex:ManDext$Treatment)

FIXED VERSUS RANDOM FACTORS

In setting up the two-way ANOVA in R, we treated Sex and Treatment as fixed factors. There is also the possibility to consider these variables as random factors.

A *fixed factor* is a factor whose levels have been fixed or specified by the researcher because he or she has interest in those particular levels. Because these are the levels about which the researcher would like to draw conclusions, if a replication were planned, these same levels would be present in the replication as well. Analysis of variance models appropriate for analyzing designs containing only fixed factors are called *fixed-effects models*. In the last analysis we were interested in drawing conclusions specifically about the particular Treatment I, II, and III and about Males and Females.

If, on the other hand, the researcher was not interested in the particular Treatments I, II, and III, but only in these treatments as a random sampling from the whole population of possible drug rehabilitation treatments, we could consider Treatment a *random factor*. A *random factor* is a factor whose levels have been selected randomly from the population of all possible levels. If a replication were planned, the levels used in the first study would not necessarily be present in the replication study because in each study the levels are based on a random selection from the population of all possible levels. Analysis of variance models appropriate for analyzing designs containing only random factors are called *random-effects models*. Analysis of variance models appropriate for analyzing designs containing both fixed and random factors are called *mixed-effects models*.

In this book we restrict our discussion of analysis of variance to fixed-effects models only. For information regarding the other two models, the interested reader is referred to *Designing Experiments and Analyzing Data* by Maxwell and Delaney (2004) and *Design and Analysis: A Researcher's Handbook* by Keppel (1991).

POST-HOC MULTIPLE COMPARISON TESTS

In Chapter 13, following a statistically significant omnibus *F*-test in the one-way ANOVA, we conducted a series of post-hoc tests to determine which specific means differed from which others. We shall do the same in the two-way ANOVA. But, there is a slight difference. In the one-way ANOVA, there is only one omnibus *F*-test. In the two-way ANOVA, there are three, one for the row main effect, another for the column main effect, and a third for the interaction. Hence, in the two-way ANOVA we shall conduct a post-hoc test for each statistically significant effect with one caveat. If an interaction effect is found to be statistically significant, then we shall conduct the post-hoc test associated with the interaction first and then decide whether it is meaningful to conduct the post-hoc tests in connection with any statistically significant main effects.

In the presence of an interaction, we know that the relationship between the two factors and the dependent variable is more complex than is suggested by either of the two main effects alone. Accordingly, in the presence of an interaction effect, we postpone an in-depth analysis of main effects until we understand the more complex nature of the interaction. As we shall see, main effects are often not meaningful in the presence of an interaction effect. In such cases, we carry out post-hoc analyses on the interaction effect only and interpret accordingly.

As we have discussed, a main effect due to a factor is simply the average effect of that factor across all levels of the other factor and is reflected by differences among the population marginal means associated with that factor.

In our working example, there is a statistically significant main effect due to Treatment. This implies that the population means of the manual dexterity scores for Treatments I, II, and III, averaged across males and females, are not all equal. If there were no interaction, we could simply ignore Sex and conduct the post-hoc tests as described in Chapter 13 to determine which treatment means are different from which others. However, there is an interaction, as the non-parallel lines of Figure 14.5, reproduced from Figure 14.2, suggest.

According to the interaction of Figure 14.5, Treatment I appears to be more effective for males, Treatment II appears to be equally as effective for both genders, and Treatment III appears to be more effective for females. Because the main effect estimates the average effect of Treatment across both males and females, it does not convey the complexities that exist in the relationship between treatment, sex, and manual dexterity. To convey these complexities, we must analyze the effect due to Treatment for each gender separately. That is, we analyze the differences in treatment means represented by the solid line segments separately from the differences in treatment means represented by the dashed line segments. In so doing, we are analyzing what are called *simple effects*. If there were no interaction, the Treatment effect would be the same for males and females and there would be no reason to analyze the Treatment effect separately for males and females. In that case, we simply could investigate the Treatment effect averaged over males and females, because, in some sense, we can say, "one size fits all." Such average effects also are called marginal effects.

In more general terms, a *simple effect* is the effect of one factor at a given level of the other factor. There are as many simple effects of one factor as there are levels of the other factor.

In our working example, there are two simple effects due to Treatment because there are two levels of Sex. There is the Treatment effect for males (represented by the dashed line segments) and the Treatment effect for females (represented by the solid line

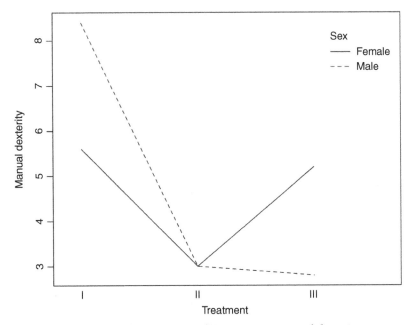

Figure 14.5 Interaction between Sex and Treatment on manual dexterity

segments). Given the interaction between Treatment and Sex, we need to analyze these two distinct simple effects to understand the true nature of the Treatment effect.

In testing for simple effects we increase the number of statistical tests conducted and potentially increase the probability of a family-wise Type I error. To control the family-wise error a popular approach is to use the Bonferroni adjustment for simple effects. To test the simple effects associated with the Row factor (e.g., Sex), use $\alpha = \alpha_{FW}/C$, where C is the number of levels of the column factor. Likewise, to test for simple effects associated with the Column factor (e.g., Treatment), use $\alpha = \alpha_{FW}/R$, where R is the number of levels of the Row factor.

MORE R: To obtain the two tests of simple effects due to Treatment, one for males and one for females, we review the previously created ANOVA object, **results**, within the **interactionMeans** function in the **phia** (post-hoc interaction analysis) package. This code produces a list of (in this case, six) adjusted cell means (also called estimated marginal means) and their standard errors. Before we use the **interactionMeans** function, we must first install the phia package, if it is not already installed, and then load the package into working memory with the library function each time R is reopened.

install.packages("phia")
library(phia)
interactionMeans(results)

The output from the **interactionMeans** function is as follows:

	ManDext $Treatment	ManDext $Sex	adjusted mean	std. error
1	1	Male	8.4	0.4654747
2	2	Male	3.0	0.4654747
3	3	Male	2.8	0.4654747
4	1	Female	5.6	0.4654747
5	2	Female	3.0	0.4654747
6	3	Female	5.2	0.4654747

From these results, we know that the adjusted cell mean for Males in Treatment 1 is 8.4 with standard error 0.465, and so on.

SIMPLE EFFECTS AND PAIRWISE COMPARISONS

To test the simple effects for Treatment at each level of Sex, we can use the **testInteractions** function, also in the phia package. The first argument we will use inside this function will specify our ANOVA model, already created and stored in an object called **results**. This argument is mandatory for the function to work. Remaining available arguments are optional, and for this example we will use the following two: **fixed** to note that we want to fix the values of the variable Sex in the interaction at each of its two values so that we may test the simple effects for Treatment at each of these levels, and **across** to note that we want to compare the means on the outcome variable across the different levels of the variable Treatment in the interaction. The **adjustment** argument is used to specify a p-value adjustment (e.g., Bonferroni). In this example, we will use the default, which is **none**.

The **testInteractions** function as shown below will produce the following output:

testInteractions(results, fixed = "ManDext$Sex", across="ManDext$Treatment", adjustment = "none")

F-test:
P-value adjustment method: none

	ManDext $Treatment1	ManDext $Treatment2	df	Sum of sq.	F	Pr(>F)
Male	5.6	0.2	2	100.93	46.5846	5.455e-09***
Female	0.4	−2.2	2	19.60	9.0462	0.001181**
Residuals			24	26.00		

Because there are three Treatment levels, the *F*-test associated with each simple effect (one for Males and one for Females) has 3 − 1 or 2 degrees of freedom. According to these results, both *F*-tests are statistically significant using the Bonferroni adjustment α level (0.05/2 = 0.025). Thus, we know that there are statistically significant treatment mean differences for both males and females.

☞ **Remark.** Conceptually, we may think of the two tests of simple effects as two one-way analyses of variance. That is, a one-way ANOVA on treatment mean differences based on males only and another one-way ANOVA on treatment mean differences based on females only. While conceptually they are similar, in actuality they are different because the one-way analyses of variance and the tests for simple effects use different error terms. The one-way ANOVA on males, for example, uses an error term based on males only. Likewise, the one-way ANOVA on females, uses an error term based on females only. These error terms are likely to be different as they are based on different groups.

By contrast, the simple effect within males uses the error term from the two-way ANOVA and therefore is based on the data from both males and females combined. Likewise, the simple effect within females also uses the error term from the two-way ANOVA and is based on the data from both males and females combined. Hence, the error terms for both simple effects are equal. Use of this error term based on data from both males and females combined is most appropriate when the homogeneity of variance assumption is met. We should point out as well that when all relevant data are combined to form the estimate of the error term, the statistical power of the test is maximized.

We follow up each simple effect that is statistically significant with a set of Bonferroni-adjusted pairwise comparisons. If, for example, the simple effect for Treatment is statistically significant for males and for females, we would follow up by testing the difference in Treatment group means at each level of Sex, using, once again, the **testInteractions** function. In this case, instead of the **across** argument, we use the **pairwise** argument, specifying the Treatment variable so that each treatment group mean is compared to the mean of the other treatment groups at each level of Sex. We calculate the Bonferroni-adjusted p-values for the individual F-tests conducted on the pairwise comparisons by adding the **adjustment = "bonferroni"** argument to our code and obtain the results below:

testInteractions(results, fixed = "ManDext$Sex", pairwise = "ManDext$Treatment", adjustment = "bonferroni")

F-test:
p-value adjustment method: Bonferroni

		Value	df	Sum of sq.	F	Pr(>F)	
1–2 :	Male	5.4	1	72.9	67.2923	1.211e-07	***
1–3 :	Male	5.6	1	78.4	72.3692	6.274e-08	***
2–3 :	Male	0.2	1	0.1	0.0923	1.00000	
1–2 :	Female	2.6	1	16.9	15.6000	0.00359	**
1–3 :	Female	0.4	1	0.4	0.3692	1.00000	
2–3 :	Female	−2.2	1	12.1	11.1692	0.01631	*
Residuals			24	26.0			
Signif. codes:		0 "***"		0.001"**"	0.01 "*"	0.05 "."	0.1 " " 1

Based on these results, we know that for both males and females, the mean of treatment group 2 is different from the mean of treatment group 1; for males only, the mean of treatment group 3 is different from the mean of treatment group 1, and for females only, the mean of treatment group 2 is different from the mean of treatment group 3.

If, instead, we had not included a Bonferroni adjustment in the **testInteractions()** function, by either omitting the **adjustment** argument or making the argument equal **none**, these are the results we would have obtained:

			Value	df	Sum of sq.	F	Pr(>F)	
1–2	:	Male	5.4	1	72.9	67.2923	2.019e-08	***
1–3	:	Male	5.6	1	78.4	72.3692	1.046e-08	***
2–3	:	Male	0.2	1	0.1	0.0923	0.7638821	
1–2	:	Female	2.6	1	16.9	15.6000	0.0005983	***
1–3	:	Female	0.4	1	0.4	0.3692	0.5491309	
2–3	:	Female	−2.2	1	12.1	11.1692	0.0027178	**
Residuals				24	26.0			

F-test:
p-value adjustment method: none

Signif. codes: 0 "***" 0.001"**" 0.01 "*" 0.05 "." 0.1 " " 1

Given that there are six treatments in this case, three for each level of Sex, the Bonferroni adjustment will compare the obtained p-value to an alpha level divided by 6 or equivalently, multiply the unadjusted p-value by 6. Notice that the unadjusted p-value for the effect 1–2 : Female is $p = 0.0005983$ and the Bonferroni adjusted p-value for this effect is 6 times 0.0005983, or 0.00359, as given in the output above.

To continue the analysis, we now examine the simple effects for Sex at each level of Treatment; i.e., whether males and females have different manual dexterity means at each Treatment level. Because there are only two Sexes, the F-test associated with each simple effect has $2 - 1$ or 1 degree of freedom; i.e., each test is composed of a single contrast. We obtain the following results using the **testInteractions** function with the **fixed** argument for Treatment, the **pairwise** argument for Sex, and the **adjustment** argument for Bonferroni:

testInteractions(results, fixed = "ManDext$Treatment", pairwise = "ManDext$Sex", adjustment = "bonferroni")

			Value	df	Sum of sq.	F	Pr(>F)	
Male–Female	:	1	2.8	1	19.6	18.092	0.0008315	***
Male–Female	:	2	0.0	1	0.0	0.000	1.0000000	
Male–Female	:	3	−2.4	1	14.4	13.292	0.0038473	**
Residuals				24	26.0			

F -test:
p-value adjustment method: Bonferroni

Signif. codes: 0 "***" 0.001"**" 0.01 "*" 0.05 "." 0.1 " " 1

These results suggest that males and females have significantly different Manual Dexterity means using the Bonferroni adjustment for the p-values under Treatments 1 ($p = 0.0008315$) and 3 ($p = 0.0038473$), but not under Treatment 2 ($p = 1.0000000$).

MORE R: We may further explore all pairwise differences between the adjusted cell means using the **CLD** function in the **emmeans** (estimated marginal means) and **multcompView** packages using, in this case, Bonferroni adjusted p-values. This code produces a table of means with a column of codes on the right-hand side that indicate which groups belong together as a homogeneous grouping (they have means that are not significantly different from each other). We first create an **emmeans** object with our ANOVA results object and indicate using ~**Treatment*Sex** that we want the cell mean for each Treatment by Sex combination. We then use the **emmeans** object, **results. emm**, inside the CLD function as the first argument and the Bonferroni adjustment as the second argument:

```
install.packages("emmeans")
install.packages("multcompView")
library(emmeans)
library(multcompView)
results.emm = emmeans(results, ~ Treatment*Sex)
CLD(results.emm, adjust = "bonferroni")
```

The results from this code are as follows:

Treatment	Sex	emmean	SE	df	lower.CL	upper.CL	group
3	Male	2.8	0.4654747	24	1.461716	4.138284	1
2	Female	3.0	0.4654747	24	1.661716	4.338284	1
2	Male	3.0	0.4654747	24	1.661716	4.338284	1
3	Female	5.2	0.4654747	24	3.861716	6.538284	2
1	Female	5.6	0.4654747	24	4.261716	6.938284	2
1	Male	8.4	0.4654747	24	7.061716	9.738284	3

Confidence level used: 0.95
Conf-level adjustment: Bonferroni method for 6 estimates
p-value adjustment: Bonferroni method for 15 tests
significance level used: alpha = 0.05

According to these results, we may note that males in Treatment 1 with a manual dexterity mean of 8.4 are significantly different from all other groups (no other group has the number 3 assigned to it); that females in Treatments 1 and 3 are not different from each other (they both share the number 2), but are different from the other groups, and that females in Treatment 2 and males in Treatments 2 and 3 are not different from each other (they all share the number 1).

SUMMARY OF STEPS TO BE TAKEN IN A TWO-WAY ANOVA PROCEDURE

In summary, we may express the sequence of tests in a two-way analysis of variance as follows.

1. Conduct the two-way ANOVA on the dependent variable (dv) using the **aov** function with the interaction between the two categorical variables x1 and x2 represented as factor variables (i.e., **aov(dv~x1*x2)**) at the given α level.

2. Graph the result using the **interaction.plot** function as demonstrated in the working example.

3. If the interaction term and both main effects are not statistically significant, do not proceed with post-hoc testing.

4. If the interaction term is not statistically significant, but one or both main effects are statistically significant, examine the marginal effects for each main effect that is statistically significant, adjusting the alpha level or p-value using a multiple comparisons adjustment (e.g., Bonferroni or Tukey) as described above.

5. If the interaction term is statistically significant do the following steps as in our working example:

   (a) Test for simple effects of the row factor within the column factor, and if desired, test for simple effects of the column factor within the row factor as well. To control the family-wise Type I error for testing simple effects associated with the Row factor, use $\alpha = \alpha_{FW}/C$ and for testing simple effects associated with the Column factor use $\alpha = \alpha_{FW}/R$.

   (b) Follow all tests of simple effects that are statistically significant with tests of pairwise comparisons on the individual group means within each simple effect adjusting for multiple comparisons using for example, Bonferroni or Tukey adjustments.

   (c) Finally, if meaningful, conduct all pairwise comparisons on the marginal means for each main effect that is statistically significant.

· ·

EXAMPLE 14.3 For this example, we turn to the Wages dataset. Given a sample of 100 males and 100 females randomly selected from the 534 cases that comprised the 1985 Current Population Survey in a way that controls for highest education level attained. The sample of 200 contains 20 males and 20 females with less than a high school diploma, 20 males and 20 females with a high school diploma, 20 males and 20 females with some college training, 20 males and 20 females with a college diploma, and 20 males and 20 females with some graduate school training. As such, the study may be described as a 2 × 5 (gender by education level) factorial design. Use the two-way ANOVA procedure to explore the relationship between gender (male, female), highest education level attained, and hourly wage. Specifically, investigate (a) whether there are differences in hourly wage by gender, and (b) by highest education level attained, and (c) whether there is an interaction between gender and highest education level attained on hourly wage. The data are contained in the Wages dataset.

Solution Using a two-way ANOVA, with the variables sex and education as the independent variables represented as factor variables and hourly wage as the dependent variable, we obtain an omnibus F-test result for the two-way ANOVA. We produce the line graph below with the following code. We use the **as.numeric** function within the **interaction.plot** function to display the numeric values of education levels on the x-axis rather than the factor value labels.

interaction.plot(as.numeric(Wages$ed), Wages$sex, Wages$wage, xlab = "Highest education level", ylab = "Predicted cell means of Wages", trace.label = "Gender")

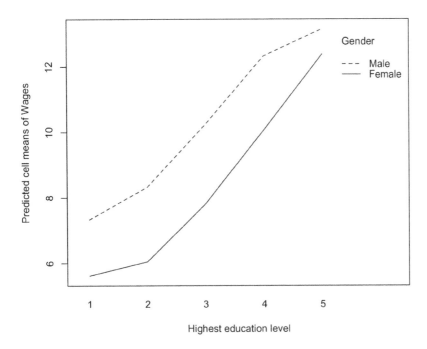

We may note from the plot that males earn more than females (mean hourly wage for males is $10.26 while for females it is $8.38) and that education level varies directly with hourly wage (as education level increases so does hourly wage, from $6.47, to $7.18, to $9.03, to $11.19, and to $12.76). Furthermore, we may note that the relationship between education level and hourly wage appears to be the same for males and females, suggesting that there is no interaction between gender and education level on hourly wage.

In particular, the mean hourly wage for males averaged across education levels is higher than the mean hourly wage for females averaged across education level. Also, the mean hourly wage for each level of education averaged across males and females increases as education level increases. Finally, while not exactly parallel, these two sets of line segments, one for males and one for females, are closely parallel suggesting the absence of an interaction between gender and education level on hourly wage.

Before looking at the results of the two-way ANOVA, we need to evaluate the tenability of the independence, equal cell sizes, normality and homogeneity of variance assumptions. The wages are independent because individuals were randomly selected separately for each cell. Each cell has size $n = 40$ so that the cell sizes are equal. The two-way ANOVA is robust to violations of the normality assumption because each cell contains more than 30 subjects.

In addition, because the sample sizes in each group are equal, however, the validity of the F-test is not compromised and we may proceed with the analysis of variance to determine whether our observed results are significant of differences in the population.

The results of the two-way ANOVA are given below based on the code:

results2 = aov(Wages$wage ~ Wages$ed*Wages$sex) and **summary(results2)**

As expected, these results indicate that while both main effects due to gender and education level are statistically significant, the interaction is not. We use post-hoc comparisons to determine which specific means are different from which others. Because the interaction effect is not statistically significant, we are only interested in comparing the marginal means relative to education level and gender.

The code produces the following results:

	df	Sum sq.	Mean sq.	F-value	Pr(>F)
Wages$sex	1	357	357.5	17.20	0.0000414 ***
Wages$ed	4	2249	562.1	27.04	<0.0000000000000002 ***
Wages$sex: Wages$ed	4	37	9.3	0.45	0.773
Residuals	390	8108	20.8		

Because the interaction is not statistically significant, we only need to conduct pairwise comparisons for each main effect that has more than two levels. Because the sex factor only has two levels, by virtue of the fact that it is statistically significant, we know that males differ from females in terms of wages and from the summary table, know that males' wages exceed those of females. To conduct the pairwise comparisons on education we use the **PostHocTest** function in the DescTools package, introduced in Chapter 13, adjusting the multiple comparisons using the **hsd** adjustment. The following output displays the table of contrasts (pairwise differences in this case) with confidence intervals and p-values obtained from the code **PostHocTest(results2, method = "hsd")$`Wages$ed`**. The code **$`Wages$ed`** tells R to only display the comparisons on education.

We obtain the following results.

	diff	lwr.ci	upr.ci	pval
High school degree–Less than high school degree	0.71225	−1.2634916	2.687992	0.860685706559946
Some college–Less than high school degree	2.55200	0.5762584	4.527742	0.004078444472987
College degree–Less than high school degree	4.71925	2.7435084	6.694992	0.000000001845286
Graduate school–Less than high school degree	6.28975	4.3140084	8.265492	0.000000000000000
Some college–High school degree	1.83975	−0.1359916	3.815492	0.081592228579329
College degree–High school degree	4.00700	2.0312584	5.982742	0.000000503783593
Graduate school–High school degree	5.57750	3.6017584	7.553242	0.000000000000000
College degree–Some college	2.16725	0.1915084	4.142992	0.023440633924968
Graduate school–Some college	3.73775	1.7620084	5.713492	0.000003451538433
Graduate school–College degree	1.57050	−0.4052416	3.546242	0.190042118121591

According to the results of the post-hoc test on education level, the mean hourly wage for those with less than a high school degree is not statistically significantly different from the mean hourly wage for those with a high school degree, but it is statistically significantly lower than all other educational attainments. The mean hourly wage for those with a high school degree is not statistically significantly different from the mean hourly wage for those with some college degree, but it is statistically significantly lower than for those with a college degree or graduate school. All other pairwise differences are statistically significant with the population mean hourly wage for those with a graduate degree the highest, followed by those with a college degree, followed by those with some college.

CONDUCTING POWER ANALYSES FOR TWO-WAY ANOVA

In this section, we will illustrate how to find the sample size for a two-way balanced ANOVA using R's **pwr2** library. In order to use the following functions, you must install and load the **pwr2** library through the commands **install.packages("pwr2")** and **library(pwr2)**. As shown in Table 10.3, we use f as the effect size in this case. We set power equal to 0.80, α = 0.05, and f = 0.25 to represent a medium effect in ANOVA. We will consider three situations, each one corresponding to one of the three model effects tested in this type of design: a main effect due to rows, a main effect due to columns, and an interaction effect.

EXAMPLE 14.4 Use R's **ss.2way** command in the **pwr2** library to determine the sample size required to detect a medium effect size with power = 0.80 and α = 0.05 for each of the hypotheses tested in a 3 × 4 balanced ANOVA design.

Solution The R command to solve this example is provided below. The command requires the following arguments: **a** (the number of rows), **b** (the number of columns), **alpha**, **beta** (1 – power, which is 1 – 0.8 = 0.2 for this example), **f.A** (the effect size we would like to detect for the rows), **f.B** (set equal to 1 as we are not interested in testing the hypothesis pertaining to columns at this point), and **B** (the number of iterations the numerical algorithm should complete, set equal to 100 by default).

To test the *main effect* due to *rows*, for this example, the power command would be:

ss.2way(a = 3, b = 4, alpha = 0.05, beta = 0.2, f.A = 0.25, f.B = 1, B = 100)

We obtain the following results:

Balanced two-way analysis of variance sample size adjustment		
a	=	3
b	=	4
sig.level	=	0.05
power	=	0.8
n	=	14
Note: n is number in each group, total sample = 168		

In similar fashion, we find the sample size for the test of the *main effect* due to *columns* as shown below:

ss.2way(a = 3, b = 4, alpha = 0.05, beta = 0.2, f.A = 1, f.B = 0.25, B = 100)

We obtain the following results:

Balanced two-way analysis of variance sample size adjustment		
a	=	3
b	=	4
sig.level	=	0.05
power	=	0.8
n	=	15
Note: n is number in each group, total sample = 180		

We notice that the n increases as we move from testing a row effect with three rows to a column effect with four columns. The larger n ($n = 180$) should be used as the total sample size for this design. We furthermore note that if it is of interest to be able to detect an interaction effect, a larger sample size may be required. The interested reader is referred to the G*Power (Faul et al., 2007) software for exact sample size calculations in this case.

SUMMARY OF R COMMANDS

Create	**Command lines**
Calculate cell means and standard deviations (Table 14.4)	**aggregate(ManDext$ManualDex ~ ManDext$Sex + ManDext$Treatment, FUN=mean)** **aggregate(ManDext$ManualDex ~ ManDext$Sex + ManDext$Treatment, FUN=sd)**
Calculate marginal row means and standard deviations (Table 14.4)	**aggregate(ManDext$ManualDex ~ ManDext$Sex, FUN=mean)** **aggregate(ManDext$ManualDex ~ ManDext$Sex, FUN=sd)**
Calculate marginal column means and standard deviations (Table 14.4)	**aggregate(ManDext$ManualDex ~ ManDext$Treatment, FUN=mean)** **aggregate(ManDext$ManualDex ~ ManDext$Treatment, FUN=sd)**
Create a line graph of means to illustrate the two-way ANOVA of ManualDex by Sex and Treatment (Figure 14.2)	**interaction.plot(ManDext$Treatment, ManDext$Sex, ManDext$ManualDex, xlab = "Treatment", ylab = "Manual Dexterity", trace.label = "Sex")**
Calculate within-cell skewness, standard error of skewness, and the skewness ratio	**skew(ManDext$ManualDex[ManDext $Treatment == 1 & ManDext$Sex == "Male"])** **se.skew(ManDext$ManualDex[ManDext $Treatment == 1 & ManDext$Sex == "Male"])**

Create	Command lines
	skew.ratio(ManDext$ManualDex [ManDext$Treatment == 1 & ManDext $Sex == "Male"]) To find the three statistics for other cells, simply change the arguments to **ManDext $Treatment == 2** (or 3), and **ManDext $Sex == "Female"**.
Calculate *p*-values for ANOVA	Main effect due to Sex **pf(0.12, 1, 24, lower.tail = F)** Main effect due to Treatment **pf(40.13, 2, 24, lower.tail = F)** Sex by Treatment interaction **pf(15.69, 2, 24, lower.tail = F)**
To obtain the results of Levene's test associated with the two-way ANOVA for detecting mean differences in ManualDex by Treatment and Sex	**levenes.test(ManDext$ManualDex, ManDext$Sex:ManDext$Treatment)**
Perform the two-way ANOVA for detecting mean differences in ManualDex by Treatment and Sex with interaction (Example 14.2)	**results = aov(ManDext$ManualDex ~ ManDext$Sex*ManDext$Treatment)** **summary(results)**
Perform post-hoc testing for mean difference main effects in the ANOVA if there is no interaction.	**install.packages("phia")** **library(phia)** **testInteractions(results, fixed = "ManDext$Sex", across="ManDext $Treatment", adjustment = "none")** **testInteractions(results, fixed = "ManDext $Treatment", across="ManDext$Sex", adjustment = "none")** To compare mean differences: **install.packages("emmeans")** **install.packages("multcompView")** **library(emmeans)** **library(multcompView)** **results.emm = emmeans(results, ~ Treatment*Sex)** **CLD(results.emm, adjust = "bonferroni")**
Perform post-hoc testing for the interaction in the ANOVA for detecting mean differences in ManualDex by Treatment and Sex (Example 14.2)	**testInteractions(results, fixed = "ManDext$Sex", pairwise = "ManDext $Treatment", adjustment = "bonferroni")** **testInteractions(results, fixed = "ManDext $Treatment", pairwise = "ManDext $Sex", adjustment = "bonferroni")**

Create	Command lines
Conduct a two-way ANOVA on the Wages dataset, create a line graph of results, and then conduct pairwise comparisons with an HSD adjustment. Only display comparisons on education (Example 14.3)	**results2 = aov(Wages$wage~Wages$sex*Wages$ed)** **summary(results2)** **interaction.plot(as.numeric(Wages$ed), Wages$sex, Wages$wage, xlab = "Highest education level", ylab = "Predicted cell means of Wages", trace. label = "Gender")** **install.packages("DescTools")** **library(DescTools)** **PostHocTest(results2, method = "hsd") $`Wages$ed`**
Conduct a power analysis to obtain sample size for the main effect due to rows with a power analysis (Example 14.4)	**install.packages("pwr2")** **library(pwr2)** Main effect due to rows **ss.2way(a = 3, b = 4, alpha = 0.05, beta = 0.2, f.A = 0.25, f.B = 1, B = 100)** Main effect due to columns **ss.2way(a = 3, b = 4, alpha = 0.05, beta = 0.2, f.A = 1, f.B = 0.25, B = 100)**

EXERCISES

Create a .R file for each exercise that requires the use of R. Run code from the .R file by highlighting or having the cursor on the line of code and hitting **control+enter** on a PC computer keyboard or **command+enter** on a Mac computer keyboard. Save each .R file using a name associated with the Exercise for which it was created. It is recommended that you review the .R file for Chapter 14 located on the textbook's website before completing these exercises. To facilitate doing each exercise, it may be helpful to copy and paste relevant code from the .R file for Chapter 14 into your own .R file and modify them as needed.

14.1 The following illustrations are of population means and are, therefore, not subject to sampling error. They are based on the results of a fictional study to determine whether there is a relationship between gender, teaching method, and achievement in reading. Assume that each illustration represents a 2 × 3 between-subjects factorial design with equal cell sizes. Use the line graphs to answer the following questions.

For each graph:

(a) Is there a main effect due to gender? What mean values are compared to make this assessment?

(b) Is there a main effect due to teaching method? What mean values are compared to make this assessment?

(c) Is there an interaction effect? What mean values or differences in mean values are compared to make this assessment?

(d) Interpret the relative effectiveness of teaching method for males and females.

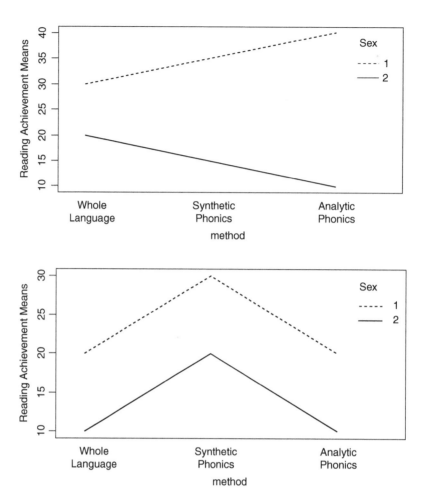

Exercises 14.2–14.3 involve the Framingham dataset. In this series of exercises, we, respectively, investigate whether body mass index and age varied as a function of gender, whether or not the person smoked cigarettes, and the interaction of gender and whether or not the person smoked cigarettes. For inferential purposes, as described in the study itself, we consider the people in the Framingham dataset to be a random sample of the population of all non-institutionalized adults. Use α = 0.05 for all significance tests.

14.2 The Body Mass Index is a tool for indicating weight status in adults. The following questions relate to using a two-way ANOVA to determine whether at the beginning of the Framingham study body mass index (BMI1) varied as a function of gender (SEX), whether the person smoked (CURSMOKE1), and the interaction of gender and smoking status.

(a) State the null and alternative hypotheses for each of the three tests associated with the ANOVA.

(b) Create a multiple line graph of the sample means. Based on this graph, does there appear to be a statistically significant interaction effect? A statistically significant main effect due to gender? A statistically significant main effect due to cigarette use?

(c) Evaluate the tenability of the normality assumption for these data or indicate why the assumption is not an issue for this analysis.

(d) Evaluate the tenability of the homogeneity of variance assumption for these data or indicate why the assumption is not an issue for this analysis.

(e) According to the ANOVA results, is there a statistically significant interaction effect? Is there a statistically significant main effect due to gender? Is there a statistically significant main effect due to cigarette use? Provide statistical support for your answer.

(f) Is post-hoc testing necessary in this case? Why or why not? Interpret results.

(g) Calculate and interpret the effect sizes of the statistically significant effects.

14.3 The following questions relate to using a two-way ANOVA to determine whether at the beginning of the Framingham study that age (AGE1) varied as a function of gender (SEX), whether a person smoked (CURSMOKE1), and the interaction of gender and smoking status. Given the nature of the study design, the ANOVA, in this case, is considered to be robust to both normality and homogeneity of variance assumptions.

(a) Create a multiple line graph of the sample means. Based on this graph, does there appear to be a statistically significant interaction effect? A statistically significant main effect due to gender? A statistically significant main effect due to cigarette use?

(b) According to the ANOVA results, is there a statistically significant interaction effect? A statistically significant main effect due to gender? A statistically significant main effect due to cigarette use? Provide statistical support for your answer.

(c) Given the statistically significant interaction, conduct and interpret simple effects, holding constant, in turn, cigarette use and then gender. If appropriate, conduct additional post-hoc tests as well. Note that in the presence of this statistically significant interaction, main effects are not meaningful and should not be interpreted per se.

(d) Calculate and interpret the effect sizes of the statistically significant effects.

Exercise 14.4 makes use of the Wages dataset. In this exercise we are interested in whether number of years of work experience as of 1985 varies as a function of education level and gender. For inferential purposes, we consider the people in the Wages dataset to be a random sample of the population of all adults living in America in 1985. Use α = 0.05 throughout this example.

14.4 The following questions relate to using a two-way ANOVA to determine whether the number of years of work experience as of 1985 varies as a function of gender (SEX), education level (ED), or the interaction between gender and education level.

(a) Create a multiple line graph of the sample means. Based on this graph, does there appear to be a statistically significant interaction effect? A statistically significant main effect due to gender? A statistically significant main effect due to education level?

(b) Evaluate the tenability of the normality assumption for these data or indicate why the assumption is not an issue for this analysis.

(c) Evaluate the tenability of the homogeneity of variance assumption for these data or indicate why the assumption is not an issue for this analysis.

(d) According to the ANOVA results, is there a statistically significant interaction effect? A statistically significant main effect due to gender? A statistically significant main effect due to education? Provide statistical support for your answer.

(e) Given the statistically significant disordinal interaction, conduct and interpret a test of simple effects, and additional post-hoc tests, if necessary.

(f) Calculate and interpret the effect sizes of the statistically significant effects.

Exercises 14.5 and 14.6 require that you first enter the given data into R. Use $\alpha = 0.05$ for all significance tests.

14.5 Professor Dani teaches an undergraduate introductory statistics course. She teaches students from all four academic years in both morning and afternoon classes. She has reason to believe that either the grade level of the students or the time of the course or both may affect how well undergraduate students at her college do in her course. To test her conjecture, she randomly selects 40 of the students who register for her introductory statistics course the following term, 10 from each academic year, with 20 of those registered for the morning and 20 for the afternoon. At the end of the semester, she gives both classes the same final exam and arranges their final exam scores in a two-way analysis of variance design, as shown in the following table. Use it to answer the following questions.

		Factor B: Academic Year			
		Freshmen	Sophomores	Juniors	Seniors
	Morning	80	85	93	100
		80	80	90	98
Factor A:		75	80	89	95
Time of Course		70	83	87	93
		70	82	87	90
	Afternoon	70	75	85	88
		70	71	84	83
		65	70	80	80
		60	69	73	79
		60	65	72	75

(a) Create a table of cell and marginal means and standard deviations.

(b) Evaluate the tenability of the underlying normality and homogeneity of variance assumptions or indicate why the assumptions are not an issue for this analysis.

(c) Are any of the effects statistically significant? If so, which ones? Provide statistical support for your answer.

(d) What is the proportion of variance explained by each of the statistically significant effects?

(e) Create a line graph of the cell means to illustrate the effects. Explain how the line graph corroborates the results of the significance tests.

(f) Describe the nature of the main effect due to time and explain why a Tukey post-hoc test is not necessary in this case.

(g) Carry out a Tukey HSD post-hoc test on the main effect due to academic year to determine exactly which academic levels are different from which others with respect to final exam performance.

14.6 The data for this exercise are taken from the following website: https://bit.ly/ 2Ssa1IV

Students at Ohio State University conducted an experiment in the fall of 1993 to explore the nature of the relationship between a person's heart rate and the frequency at which that person stepped up and down on steps of various heights. The response variable, heart rate, was measured in beats per minute. For each person, the resting heart rate was measured before a trial (RestHR) and after stepping (HR). There were two different step heights (HEIGHT): 5.75 inches (coded as 0), and 11.5 inches (coded as 1). There were three rates of stepping (FREQUENCY): 14 steps/ min. (coded as 0), 21 steps/min. (coded as 1), and 28 steps/min. (coded as 2). This resulted in six possible height/frequency combinations. Each subject performed the activity for three minutes. Subjects were kept on pace by the beat of an electric metronome. One experimenter counted the subject's heart rate, in beats per minute, for 20 seconds before and after each trial. The subject always rested between trials until her or his heart rate returned to close to the beginning rate. Another experimenter kept track of the time spent stepping. Each subject was always measured and timed by the same pair of experimenters to reduce variability in the experiment.

The data are saved as Stepping, or you may enter them yourself for practice. The following questions relate to using a two-way ANOVA to determine whether final heart rate varies by stepping rate, step height, and the interaction between the two.

Height	Frequency	RestHR	HR
0	0	60	75
0	1	63	84
1	2	69	135
1	0	69	108
0	2	69	93
1	1	96	141
1	0	87	120
0	0	90	99
1	2	93	153
0	2	87	129
1	1	72	99
0	1	69	93
1	0	78	93
0	2	72	99
1	2	78	129
0	0	87	93
1	1	87	111
1	2	81	120
0	2	75	123
0	1	81	96
1	0	84	99
1	0	84	99
1	1	90	129

Height	Frequency	RestHR	HR
0	1	75	90
0	0	78	87
0	0	84	84
0	1	90	108
0	2	78	96
1	1	84	90
1	2	90	147

(a) Evaluate the tenability of the underlying normality and homogeneity of variance assumptions or indicate why the assumptions are not an issue for this analysis.
(b) Is there a statistically significant interaction effect? Provide statistical support for your answer.
(c) Is there a statistically significant main effect due to stepping rate? Provide statistical support for your answer.
(d) Describe the nature of the main effect due to stepping rate.
(e) Is there a statistically significant main effect due to step height? Provide statistical support for your answer.
(f) Describe the nature of the main effect due to step height.

14.7 Three methods of dieting are compared for effectiveness in terms of pounds lost. Because it is believed that a person's gender may influence the relative effectiveness of the three methods, a two-way ANOVA balanced design with equal cell sizes is employed and the summary table is provided.

Tests of between-subjects effort

Dependent variable: weight loss					
Source	Type III sum of squares	df	Mean square	F	Sig
Corrected model	626.400[a]	5	125.280	18.514	0.000
Intercept	4177.200	1	4177.200	6.17.320	0.000
GENDER*TREATMEN	48.133	1	48.133	7.113	0.13
Error	162.400	24	6.767		
Total	4966.000	30			
Corrected Total	788.800	29			

Note: [a]R Squared = 794(Adjusted R Squared = 0.751)

(a) Describe the design by filling in the blanks in the following sentence: The design is a ___ × ___ balanced ANOVA with ___ participants per cell.
(b) Had we performed a one-way ANOVA to look at weight loss by treatment, ignoring gender, how would the results have differed? Complete the following table by filling in the values of the shaded boxes.

Weight Loss by Treatment

	Sum of squares	*df*	Mean square	*F*	Sig.
Between groups					
Within groups					
Total					

(c) Which of the two types of design, the one-way or two-way, is the more powerful test of treatment, in this case? Explain.

14.8 A hypothetical study was conducted to determine whether weight differs by incidence of coronary heart disease (CHD) and cigarette use. One hundred people were randomly selected from among each of the four conditions: no CHD non-smokers, no CHD smokers, CHD non-smokers, and CHD smokers. The following line graph represents the results of the study.

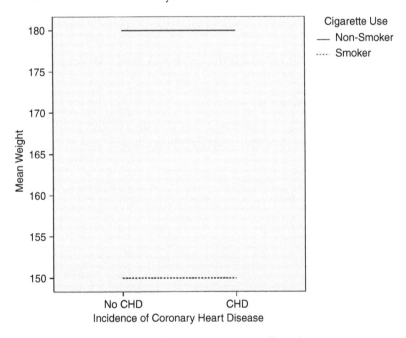

(a) Does the line graph suggest a main effect due to cigarette use? If so, describe the nature of the effect.
(b) Does the line graph suggest a main effect due to incidence of coronary heart disease? If so, describe the nature of the effect.
(c) Does the line graph suggest an interaction effect? If so, describe the nature of the effect.
(d) The factorial ANOVA design in this situation is orthogonal (or balanced) because
  (i) the lines representing the mean weights of the cells are parallel
  (ii) the cell sizes are all equal

(iii) there are two factors represented (cigarette use and incidence of coronary heart disease (CHD)) in a 2 × 2 configuration

(iv) none of the above

(e) Based on the results depicted in the line graph, complete the two-way ANOVA table by filling in the values of the shaded boxes.

Source of variation	SS	df	MS	F-value	p-value
CHD					
Cigarette use					
Interaction					
Error	35,000				
Total	76,000				

14.9 Is the number of sources of variance in a 2 × 3 ANOVA design different from the number of sources of variance in a 3 × 5 ANOVA design? What are these sources of variance?

14.10 Under what conditions, in general, is the two-way ANOVA more powerful than the one-way ANOVA?

Exercise 14.11 involves power analysis.

14.11 Determine the sample size required to detect a medium effect size ($f = 0.25$) with power = 0.80 and $\alpha = 0.05$ for each of the main effect hypotheses tested in a 3 × 5 balanced two-way ANOVA design.

# CHAPTER FIFTEEN

CORRELATION AND SIMPLE REGRESSION AS INFERENTIAL TECHNIQUES

In Chapter 5, we discussed the Pearson product-moment correlation coefficient used to assess the degree of linear relationship between two variables. Recall that in that chapter we assessed the degree of linear relationship between fat grams and calories by type of McDonald's hamburger as one example. In Chapter 6, we discussed how this linear relationship could be used to develop a linear prediction system (a linear regression equation) to predict the value of one variable when the value of the other variable is known. Recall that in that chapter we developed a linear regression equation for predicting the number of calories in a McDonald's hamburger from its fat grams.

In both situations, our discussions were limited to descriptive settings. That is, our measures of linear relationship and accuracy of prediction were confined to the data at hand. In this chapter, we discuss inferential techniques applicable to measures of relationship and linear regression that enable us to generalize our results from a sample to the population from which that sample was randomly selected.

As with other inferential techniques described in this text, the inferential techniques described in this chapter are based also on certain assumptions about the distribution of the parent population. Because the parent population relevant to measuring the linear relationship between two variables is comprised of *pairs of values*, the distribution of this parent population is described as a *joint distribution*, and, in particular, as a *bivariate distribution*. Extending the assumption of population normality in the case of inferential tests based on univariate distributions (e.g., tests of means), the major assumption underlying the inferential test of a linear relationship between two variables is that of *bivariate normality* in the population. That is, the parent population from which the sample of pairs of values has been randomly selected is assumed in this case to have a bivariate normal distribution.

THE BIVARIATE NORMAL DISTRIBUTION

A bivariate distribution is a special case of a joint distribution in which exactly two variables are considered simultaneously, or jointly. If we call one variable X and the other variable Y, we can depict a bivariate distribution graphically by using a scatterplot with the two axes labeled X and Y, respectively. Figure 15.1 shows a bivariate distribution and its corresponding scatterplot.

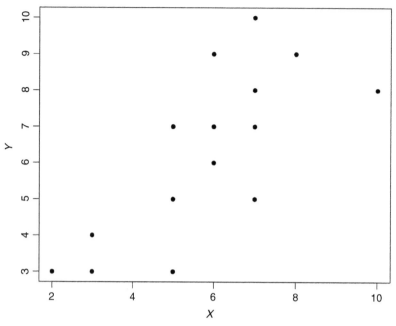

X	Y	f
2	3	1
3	3	1
3	4	1
5	7	1
5	3	1
5	5	1
6	7	1
6	6	1
6	9	1
7	5	1
7	7	1
7	8	1
7	10	1
8	9	1
10	8	1

Figure 15.1 A bivariate distribution and its corresponding scatterplot

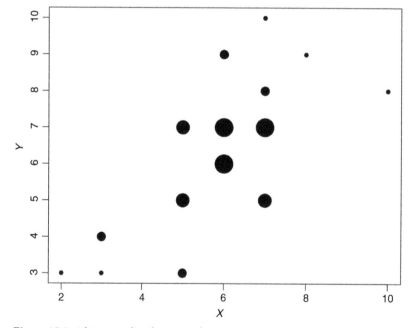

X	Y	f
2	3	1
3	3	1
3	4	2
5	7	3
5	3	2
5	5	3
6	7	4
6	6	4
6	9	2
7	5	3
7	7	4
7	8	2
7	10	1
8	9	1
10	8	1

Figure 15.2 A bivariate distribution and scatterplot with some frequencies greater than 1

While all pairs of values in Figure 15.1 occur with frequency of 1, in other situations, some of the pairs of values, if not all, can occur with frequency greater than 1. Figure 15.2 shows a bivariate distribution with some frequencies of pairs of values greater than 1 along with its scatterplot. In this scatterplot, the different frequencies of the pairs of values are represented by the relative sizes of the points.

If X and Y are both continuous, and they assume all possible values with varied frequencies, we can more effectively represent the frequencies as a third axis perpendicular to the X and Y axes. In this case, the bivariate frequency distribution of X and Y would be represented graphically as a continuous surface (kind of like a tent) sitting on top of the X, Y plane. In this chapter, we are interested in a specific type of bivariate distribution, a *bivariate normal distribution*. Such a distribution has the following seven characteristics.

1. Taken separately, the X and Y variables are both normally distributed.
2. When X is held constant at any value (for example, $X = a$), the distribution of all those Y values corresponding to this value of X (called the conditional distribution of Y given $X = a$) is normally distributed.
3. When Y is held constant at any value (for example, $Y = b$), the distribution of all those X values corresponding to this value of Y (called the conditional distribution of X given $Y = b$) is normally distributed.
4. All the conditional distributions of Y given X have the same standard deviation $\sigma_{Y|X}$.
5. All the conditional distributions of X given Y have the same standard deviation $\sigma_{X|Y}$.
6. The means of all the conditional distributions of Y given X fall along a straight line.
7. The means of all the conditional distributions of X given Y fall along a straight line.

We may cluster the seven characteristics of the bivariate normal distribution into the following three properties:

Normality – Characteristics 1, 2, and 3
Homoscedasticity – Characteristics 4 and 5
Linearity – Characteristics 6 and 7

As we would expect from our experience with univariate normal distributions (normal distributions of one variable), all bivariate normal distributions give rise to frequency or relative frequency curves of a particular shape. This shape is often described as a bell that has been stretched in one direction sitting above the X, Y plane. Figure 15.3 shows a typical bivariate normal distribution curve when there is no stretching in either direction; that is, when the correlation between X and Y is zero. The bivariate normal distribution of Figure 15.3 may be described as a Hershey kiss with its top licked down a bit!

Figure 15.4 shows the same bivariate normal distribution curve composed of a series of cross sections or slices at particular values of X. Each slice is a conditional distribution of Y given X. Notice that all slices satisfy the conditional distribution characteristics of a bivariate normal distribution: they are normally distributed (*normality*) with the same standard deviation $\sigma_{Y|X}$ (*homoscedasticity*), and their means all fall along a straight line (*linearity*).

The assumption of bivariate normality (defined by the characteristics of linearity, homoscedasticity, and normality) in the population is required for the tests of inference introduced in this chapter regarding the Pearson product-moment correlation coefficient. In this chapter we discuss methods to evaluate these assumptions. Correlation is a symmetric index. That is, the value of the correlation indicates the degree to which X relates to Y and the degree to which Y relates to X.

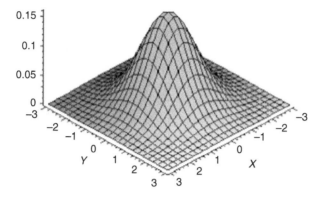

Figure 15.3 A typical bivariate normal distribution

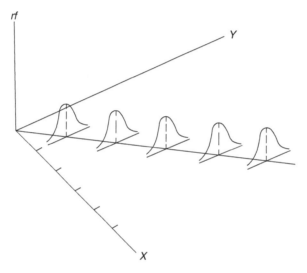

Figure 15.4 Cross sections or slices of a typical bivariate normal distribution curve

☞ **Remark.** Less restrictive assumptions are required for tests of inference regarding (simple) linear regression. The assumptions of linearity, homoscedasticity, and normality are still required but they concern the population conditional Y distributions given X (the slices illustrated in Figure 15.4), and not the conditional X distributions given Y as well. Less restrictive assumptions are appropriate in simple linear regression because it is based on an asymmetric relationship between X and Y. The asymmetric relationship is created by the necessity of designating Y as the outcome variable, and in so doing, emphasizing the importance of Y over X.

TESTING WHETHER THE POPULATION PEARSON PRODUCT-MOMENT CORRELATION EQUALS ZERO

Suppose you are making extra money one summer by selling ice cream on the beach and notice that a positive trend exists between the daily highest temperature and the number of ice cream bars you sell that day. Suppose also that you are an astute businessperson and do not want to have to carry and refrigerate more ice cream than you will be able to sell.

TABLE 15.1 Temperature and ice cream sales for 30 randomly selected summer days

temp	barsold
75	170
70	160
65	155
60	150
72	153
60	142
63	145
68	156
78	170
77	172
75	165
75	167
80	175
82	180
85	180
59	143
86	173
88	176
85	177
90	185
74	163
73	160
71	162
68	148
70	160
73	154
85	169
90	178
70	175
81	164

Accordingly, you check the weather forecast each morning, and the higher the temperature is expected to be, the more ice cream bars you take out with you. In other words, you use the temperature to *predict* your ice cream sales.

But, we can be even more systematic than this in making our predictions. Table 15.1 contains the temperature and ice cream sales for 30 days randomly selected between May 15 and September 6. It is saved as the file IceCream.rda.

Figure 15.5 presents the scatterplot of the bivariate distribution given in Table 15.1. The regression line for predicting sales from temperature is included in the plot as well.

MORE R: To obtain a scatterplot with a regression line superimposed as in Figure 15.5, we use the following command:

plot(IceCream$barsold ~ IceCream$temp, pch = 16, xlab = "Temperature", ylab = "Bars Sold")
abline(lm(IceCream$barsold~IceCream$temp))

The first line creates the two-way scatterplot, and the second line plots the regression fit line over the scatterplot.

According to Figure 15.5, we may surmise that the linear relationship is a strong one as the points hug the regression line rather well. Furthermore, the nature of the relationship is positive – with each unit increase in temperature along the horizontal axis, there is a corresponding increase in sales along the vertical axis.

While this relationship appears to be a strong one, it is based only on 30 randomly selected days. Our question of true interest is whether this relationship based on 30 randomly selected days holds for all summer days during the time period sampled. In this context, we consider the sample correlation (r) as an estimate of the population correlation coefficient (*rho* or ρ) and apply an inferential test to determine whether the correlation between temperature and sales is greater than zero in the population. That is, whether the observed correlation coefficient r based on the sample data is greater enough from zero to infer that the corresponding population parameter ρ based on all summer days during the time period sampled is greater than zero as well.

Because our hypothesis is directional in this case, our null and alternative hypotheses are:

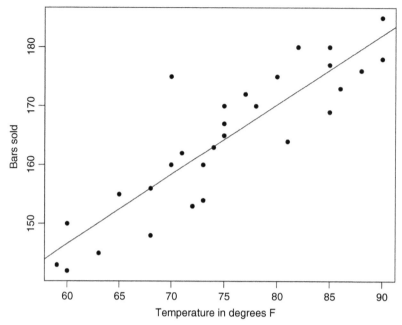

Figure 15.5 Scatterplot of bivariate distribution relating temperature to number of ice creams bars sold

H_0: $\rho = 0$
H_1: $\rho > 0$.

We assume that the parent population from which we have randomly sampled our 30 pairs of values has a bivariate normal distribution (as defined in the previous section). If the null hypothesis, H_0: $\rho = 0$ is true, then it can be shown mathematically that the appropriate sampling distribution is the t-distribution presented earlier in connection with tests on means, and the appropriate t-statistic is:

$$t = \frac{r - 0}{\sqrt{(1 - r^2)/(N - 2)}}$$

(15.1)

$df = N - 2$,

where r represents the sample Pearson product-moment correlation coefficient and $N - 2$ equals the number of degrees of freedom, two less than the number of pairs of values in the sample.

As we have done in Chapter 5, we use R to calculate the Pearson product-moment correlation. Before proceeding, however, we use the scatterplot of this small dataset represented in Figure 15.5 to check informally whether the assumptions of linearity, homoscedasticity, and normality are viable. According to Figure 15.5, violations of these assumptions do not appear to exist. The points conform reasonably well to a linear pattern supporting the assumption of linearity; the spread of ice cream sales for each temperature value (the conditional distributions of ice cream sales given temperature) and the spread of temperature given ice cream sales (the conditional distributions of temperature given ice cream sales) each appear similar, supporting the assumption of homoscedasticity;

overall, there do not appear to be severe outliers either in the univariate or conditional distributions, supporting the assumption of normality.

MORE R: To obtain the Pearson product-moment correlation along with the significance level for this one-tailed test and the one-sided confidence interval, type:

cor.test(IceCream$temp, IceCream$barsold, alternative = "greater")

Note that if the test of interest were a two-sided test, then one would replace **alternative = "greater"** with **alternative = "two.sided"**, or simply omit this argument-because two-sided tests are the default setting of this command.

We obtain the following output:

Pearson's product-moment correlation
data: IceCream$temp
and IceCream$barsold
$t = 10.149$ $df = 28$ p-value = 3.469e-ll
alternative hypothesis: true correlation is greater than 0
95 percent confidence interval: 0.7967975   1.0000000
sample estimates: cor   0.8867125

The correlation between number of ice cream bars sold and temperature in degrees Fahrenheit is 0.887 based on the $N = 30$ pairs of values. The p-value given is 3.469×10^{-11}, indicating significance at the $\alpha = 0.05$ level.

While the significance (p-value) of the correlation that is provided in the output is based on the t-statistic given as Equation 15.1, the t-value itself is also provided. We may confirm this value by calculating it by hand as:

$$t = \frac{r - 0}{\sqrt{(1 - r^2)/(N - 2)}} = \frac{0.887 - 0}{\sqrt{(1 - 0.887^2)/(30 - 2)}} = \frac{0.887}{\sqrt{0.213/28}} = \frac{0.887}{0.087} = 10.20.$$

We may also note that the degrees of freedom for this example are $N - 2 = 30 - 2 = 28$.

If we wish, we may use the obtained t-value and corresponding degrees of freedom to find the p-value using the R function **pt(t, df, lower.tail = F)** or from Table C.2 in Appendix C.

Using R, we find that:

pt(10.20, 28, lower.tail = F) = 3.10e-11 = 0.0000000000310.

Using Table C.2, we obtain the estimate $p < 0.0005$.

☞ **Remark.** Note that the R output from the **cor.test** command includes the confidence interval. We may use this interval to estimate the size of the population correlation coefficient, ρ. Example 15.1 below shows this calculation and how to interpret the confidence interval obtained.

· ·

EXAMPLE 15.1 Use the NELS dataset to determine whether there is a correlation between reading achievement and math achievement in twelfth grade in the population. Estimate the size of the population correlation by constructing a 95 percent confidence interval about ρ.

Solution Using the R **cor.test** command we find that the Pearson product-moment correlation coefficient, r, between achmat12 and achrdg12 equals 0.636 as shown in the following output.

Pearson's product-moment correlation		
data: NELS$achmat12 and NELS$achrdg12		
$t = 18.405$ $df = 498$		p-value $< 2.2e\text{-}16$
alternative hypothesis: true correlation is not equal to 0		
95 percent confidence interval: 0.5809938		0.6857001
sample estimates: cor		0.636268

Because our question is whether the correlation is different from zero, a two-tailed test of significance is appropriate. According to our output, the correlation is statistically significantly different from zero ($p < 0.0005$), and we observe from the sign of the correlation that the relationship is positive. Using our definitions of effect size, we may also note that the relationship is a strong one.

The 95 percent confidence interval given is (0.581, 0.686), suggesting that the population correlation is likely to fall between 0.581 and 0.686. Because zero does not fall within this interval, we know, once again, that the correlation is statistically significantly different from zero. Because the range is in the positive region, we know also that the relationship is positive. Furthermore, because 0.581 is substantially greater than zero, we can be confident that the effect size for this result is large.

REVISITING SIMPLE LINEAR REGRESSION FOR PREDICTION

The discovery of a linear relationship between highest daily temperature and ice cream sales (the higher the temperature, the greater the number of ice cream sales) is an important aspect of the process of setting up a linear regression equation to predict number of ice cream sales from temperature. The linear prediction equation for this example has number of ice cream sales as the outcome variable (otherwise called a *dependent variable*) and highest daily temperature as the predictor variable (otherwise called an *independent variable*).

Because there is only one predictor variable, this type of regression is called *simple linear regression*. When there is more than one predictor variable in the equation (for example, when we use both highest daily temperature *and* humidity to predict ice cream sales) we have what is called *multiple linear regression*. In the following chapter we discuss multiple linear regression and related issues.

Recall that in Chapter 6 we introduced simple linear regression for prediction in a descriptive context. In this chapter we introduce tests of inference in connection with simple linear prediction.

As we recall from Chapter 6, the linear regression (prediction) equation is:

$$\hat{Y} = a + bX \tag{15.2}$$

where

$$b = r\frac{S_Y}{S_X} \tag{15.3}$$

$$a = \overline{Y} - b\overline{X}. \tag{15.4}$$

Equation 15.2 may be represented by a line that has slope b and intercept a. The slope b is also called the *regression coefficient* and is interpreted as the amount of change in Y, on average, for each unit increase in X. The intercept a is interpreted as the predicted Y value associated with $X = 0$. The intercept a is defined to allow the regression line to pass through the center of the bivariate distribution or scatterplot, $(\overline{X}, \overline{Y})$. If your value is at the average of the X variable, you will be predicted to be at the average of the Y variable.

ESTIMATING THE POPULATION STANDARD ERROR OF PREDICTION, $\sigma_{Y|X}$

If the linear regression equation is based on a sample of values randomly selected from a bivariate normal population, then $\hat{Y}$ is an unbiased estimate of the mean of the conditional distribution of Y given X for all values of X within the sampling frame. That is, given that the population has a bivariate normal distribution, as shown in Figure 15.4, the slices of the bivariate distribution for each X value will be normally distributed in the population with mean $\overline{Y} = \hat{Y}$ and standard deviation $\sigma_{Y|X}$. Thus, if Carolyn has a value of $X = X_1$, then the linear regression equation will predict Carolyn's Y value to be equal to the mean of all the Y values for the individuals in the sample who, like Carolyn, have $X = X_1$.

This is a reasonable prediction because among other things, the mean of any normal distribution is that value having the largest frequency. While the prediction is reasonable, the possibility still exists that Carolyn's actual Y score is one of the other Y scores corresponding to $X = X_1$. The accuracy of the prediction will depend upon how closely the Y scores for all individuals who have $X = X_1$ are to one another and to their mean or, in other words, on the spread of the Y distribution for all individuals who have $X = X_1$. The spread of this conditional Y distribution given X_1 is measured by the standard deviation of this conditional Y distribution given X_1, and is denoted as $\sigma_{Y|X_1}$. The less the Y values deviate from their mean for all individuals with $X = X_1$, the smaller the error of prediction can be expected to be. The better the linear model fits the data, the closer $\hat{Y}$ will be to $\overline{Y}$ given $X = X_1$ and the smaller the expected error of prediction for $X = X_1$.

We may generalize from the case of $X = X_1$ to all values of X because of the bivariate normal distribution property of homoscedasticity. This property tells us that *all* the conditional distributions of Y given X have the same standard deviation as the Y distribution corresponding to $X = X_1$. Accordingly, we do not have to link the standard deviation of the conditional Y value given X to any particular X value, like X_1. We may use a more generic measure for the spread of the conditional Y distributions given X for the population at large. This measure is called the *standard error of prediction*, also called the *standard error of estimate*, denoted by $\sigma_{Y|X}$.

We may use the sample data on which the linear regression equation was developed to obtain an estimate of $\sigma_{Y|X}$. This estimate is denoted by $\hat{\sigma}_{Y|X}$ and is given by Equation 15.5:

$$\hat{\sigma}_{Y|X} = \sqrt{\frac{\sum(Y_i - \hat{Y}_i)^2}{N - 2}}, \qquad (15.5)$$

where Y_i = the actual Y score of individual i in the sample, $\hat{Y}_i$ = the predicted Y score of individual i in the sample using the linear regression equation, and N = the number of pairs of values in the sample.

TESTING THE b-WEIGHT FOR STATISTICAL SIGNIFICANCE

The $\hat{Y}$ is an unbiased estimate of the mean of the conditional distribution of Y given X for all values of X. In addition, the slope b of the regression (prediction) line is an unbiased estimate of the slope of the population regression line.

To test whether there is a relationship in the population between Y and the single predictor X, we may test the regression coefficient b for significance. As we shall see, this test is equivalent to the test for the significance of the correlation coefficient r presented earlier in this chapter.

The test of the regression coefficient b is

$$t = \frac{b - 0}{\hat{\sigma}_b} \qquad (15.6)$$

$$df = N - 2,$$

where $\hat{\sigma}_b$ represents the estimated standard error of b, the standard deviation of the sampling distribution of b-weights based on random samples of the same size randomly drawn from the same population. This t-value tests whether the b-coefficient differs from 0 in the population. It has $N - 2$ degrees of freedom, two less than the number of pairs of scores.

As we shall see, the t-value, including the b-coefficient and the standard error of the b-coefficient, along with its two-tailed level of significance are given as part of the R regression output.

For completeness, the equation of the estimated standard error of b is:

$$\hat{\sigma}_b = \sqrt{\frac{\frac{1}{N-2}\sum(Y_i - \hat{Y}_i)^2}{(N-1)\hat{\sigma}_X^2}}. \qquad (15.7)$$

Thus, the estimated standard error of b is a function of the accuracy of the regression equation as measured by $\frac{1}{N-2}\sum(Y - \hat{Y})^2$ relative to (a function of) the variance estimate of X, $\hat{\sigma}_X^2$. In general, then, the estimated standard error of the b-coefficient of X in Equation 15.7 will be smaller when X has a larger variance.

EXAMPLE 15.2 Construct the linear regression equation for predicting number of ice cream bars sold (barsold) from highest daily temperature (temp) for the whole summer. Interpret the equation as well as the various tests of significance reported in the output.

Solution

MORE R: To perform a regression analysis, type:

results = lm(IceCream\$barsold ~ IceCream\$temp)
summary(results)
confint(results)

The third line additionally gives the 95 percent confidence intervals for the intercept and slope of the regression line.

The R output is reproduced below.

Coefficients:

	Estimate	Std. Error	t-value	Pr(> |t|)	
(Intercept)	75.7789	8.7755	8.635	2.21e-09	***
IceCream\$temp	1.1804	0.1163	10.149	6.94e-11	***

Signif. codes: 0 "***" 0.001 "**" 0.01 "*" 0.05 "." 0.1 " " 1
Residual standard error: 5.602 on 28 degrees of freedom

Multiple R-squared: 0.7863   Adjusted R-squared: 0.7786
F-statistic: 103 on 1 and 28 df, p-value: 6.939e-11

From the regression output table, we learn from the column of coefficients that the simple linear regression equation for predicting ice cream sales from highest daily temperature is:

Predicted barsold = 75.78 + 1.18*temp.

The b-coefficient for temp is 1.18, indicating that each additional one degree rise in temperature is associated with 1.18 more ice cream bars sold on average. That is, if we were to compare two months that differed on average by one degree in temperature, the month with the higher temperature would have 1.18 more ice cream bars sold on average. The constant or intercept is 75.78. That is, when temp = 0, the number of ice creams that are predicted to be sold equals 75.78. While in some contexts the constant has a meaningful interpretation, in this one it does not because 0 degrees Fahrenheit is not a plausible or realistic temperature reading for the summer, the time period under study.

Recall that the intercept equals that value that allows the regression line to pass through the center of the scatterplot, $\overline{X}, \overline{Y}$. In this case, the center of the scatterplot is at (74.93, 164.23). When the highest daily temperature is equal to the mean temperature for the days sampled (74.93), the number of bars sold is predicted to be equal to the mean number of bars sold for the days sampled (164.23).

To determine whether the slope (or b-coefficient or b-weight) is statistically significantly different from zero, we refer to the t-test with $N - 2$ degrees of freedom and its corresponding two-tailed significance level, or p-value from the output. In our example, $t(28) = 10.15$, $p < 0.001$, suggesting that, in fact, the regression weight is statistically significantly different from zero. Looking at the sign of b, in this case of simple linear regression, the relationship may be inferred to be positive. That is, the observed positive relationship between ice cream sales and temperature holds for the population of all summer days, not just for the 30 days that comprised our random sample.

We may calculate by hand the estimated standard error of b using Equation 15.7,

$$\hat{\sigma}_b = \sqrt{\frac{\frac{1}{N-2}\sum (Y_i - \hat{Y}_i)^2}{(N-1)\hat{\sigma}_X^2}}.$$ To do so, we first compute $\frac{1}{N-2}\sum (Y_i - \hat{Y}_i)^2$, the mean squared

residual, MS_{RES}. In particular, we obtain the predicted Y values from R using the **predict** command introduced in Example 6.2 of Chapter 6:

$$MS_{RES} = \frac{1}{28}\left((170 - 164.31)^2 + (160 - 158.41)^2 + (155 - 152.51)^2 \right.$$
$$\left. + \ldots + (178 - 182.02)^2 + (175 - 158.41)^2 + (164 - 171.39)^2 \right)$$
$$= 31.385.$$

We may obtain the values for both N (30) and the standard deviation of X, temperature in degrees Fahrenheit, (8.94) by using the **length** and **sd** commands in R. Substituting these values and the value for MS_{RES} into Equation 15.7, we obtain:

$$\hat{\sigma}_b = \sqrt{\frac{31.385}{(30 - 1)(8.94)^2}} = .116,$$ which is the value printed in the output table for the

estimated standard error of b.

We may also verify that the t-value of 10.15 is obtained from Equation 15.6, the ratio of the b-coefficient divided by its estimated standard error, $1.18/0.116 = 10.15$. Finally, we may note that in the case of simple regression, the test of significance for the regression coefficient b is equivalent to the test of significance for the correlation coefficient r.

The t-test of the b-coefficient tells us whether the b-coefficient in the population is statistically significantly different from zero. This is the same test of whether the correlation between bars sold and temperature is statistically significantly different from zero. The 95 percent confidence interval about b gives us an estimate of the likely values of the b-coefficient in the population. We may use the **confint(results)** command to obtain a confidence interval for the b-coefficient and obtain the following output.

	2.5%	97.5%
(Intercept)	57.803140	93.754708
IceCream$temp	0.942186	1.418697

From the printout we may note that reasonable estimates of the b-weight are between 0.942 and 1.419. That the interval does not include zero corroborates the result of the t-test that the b-coefficient is different from zero in the population. That the confidence interval includes only positive values suggests that the b-coefficient in the population is positive, that increases in daily temperature associate with increases in ice cream sales and decreases in daily temperature associate with decreases in ice cream sales.

We turn now to another explanation of simple regression that is based on a decomposition of total sums of squares about the mean. This explanation links simple regression to the analysis of variance framework.

EXPLAINING SIMPLE REGRESSION USING AN ANALYSIS OF VARIANCE FRAMEWORK

Recall that in one-way analysis of variance the total variability (SS_T) of the outcome variable may be decomposed into two unrelated (orthogonal) components: variability due to the between groups effect (SS_B) and variability due to a within effect (SS_W). In the context of regression, SS_B is referred to as SS_{REG}, the sum of squares due to regression and SS_W is referred to as SS_{RES}, the sum of squares due to residual or error. Analogously, we may decompose or partition the total variability of the outcome variable in simple regression. We begin with $Y - \overline{Y}$, which is the error in predicting Y if we were to use $\overline{Y}$ to predict Y. The question is: How much closer can we get to Y by predicting Y from a new variable X using a regression equation?

As shown in Figure 15.6, $Y - \overline{Y}$, the total difference between an actual Y value and its mean, may be expressed as the sum of the two non-overlapping components, $\hat{Y} - \overline{Y}$ and $Y - \hat{Y}$:

$$Y - \overline{Y} = (\hat{Y} - \overline{Y}) + (Y - \hat{Y}) . \tag{15.8}$$

The first component represents that part of the total difference that is explained or accounted for by the relationship of Y with X; the other component represents that part of the total difference that remains after accounting for the relationship of Y with X.

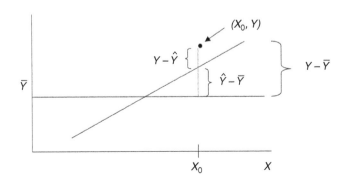

Figure 15.6 Decomposing the difference of the outcome variable from its mean

If both sides of Equation 15.8 are squared, then summed, and simplified using properties of the regression equation, we obtain Equation 15.9:

$$\sum(Y - \overline{Y})^2 = \sum(\hat{Y} - \overline{Y})^2 + \sum(Y - \hat{Y})^2. \tag{15.9}$$

The term on the left-hand side of Equation 15.9 equals the sum of squared deviations of the actual (as opposed to predicted) values of Y about its mean and is what we have called the *total sum of squares* (SS_{TOT}) of Y. The first term on the right-hand side of Equation 15.9 equals the sum of squared deviations of the predicted values of Y, $\hat{Y}$, about the mean of the actual values of Y. Because it represents that part of Y's variability that is due to Y's relation to X (symbolized by $\hat{Y}$), this term is called the *sum of squares due to the regression* (SS_{REG}). The second term on the right-hand side of Equation 15.9 is the sum of the squared deviations between the actual and predicted values of Y. Because it represents that part of Y's variability that is left over after accounting for Y's relation to X (symbolized by $\hat{Y}$), this term is called the sum of squares due to residual (SS_{RES}). We may note that the sum of squares due to residual is related to the standard error of prediction as they are both based on the sum of the squared differences between the actual and predicted Y values.

In diagram form we may illustrate this decomposition as follows:

And we may rewrite Equation 15.9 as:

$$SS_{TOT} = SS_{REG} + SS_{RES}. \tag{15.10}$$

In like manner, the degrees of freedom associated with SS_{TOT} (df_{TOT}) may be decomposed as the sum of df_{REG} and df_{RES} as follows:

$$df_{TOT} = df_{REG} + df_{RES} \tag{15.11}$$

$$N - 1 = P + N - P - 1,$$

where P equals the number of predictors in the regression equation. In the case of simple regression, $P = 1$.

We are now in a position to understand an analysis of variance summary table for regression that is obtained through the command **anova(results)** in R. This summary table provides a test of the statistical significance of the overall fit of the regression model. The table from the temperature/ice cream sales example is given below.

Analysis of variance table						
Response: IceCream$barsold						
	Df	Sum	Sq	Mean Sq F	value	Pr(>F)
IceCream$temp	1	3232.6	3232.6	103	6.939e-ll	***
Residuals	28	878.8	31.4			
Signif. codes:	0 "***"	0.001 "**"	0.01 "*"	0.05 "."	0.1 " "	1

Notice that the sum of SS_{REG} is 3232.6 and SS_{RES} is 878.8. Notice also that the df_{REG} is $P = 1$ and df_{RES} is $N - P - 1 = 30 - 1 - 1 = 28$. As discussed in Chapters 13 and 14 on the analysis of variance, the F-ratio is obtained as MS_{REG}/MS_{RES}.

In the case of simple regression, when $P = 1$, the F-ratio for the regression equals the t-ratio for the b-coefficient squared (i.e., $F = t^2$ when the numerator degrees of freedom for the F-ratio equals 1). In our example, we may note that 103 $= 10.15^2$.

Thus, in summary, in the case of simple regression, the t-test of the significance of r is equivalent to the t-test of the significance of b, and these two t-tests are equivalent to the F-test of the overall regression model. Hence, in the case of simple regression, when r is not statistically significant, b will not be statistically significant, nor will the overall regression equation be statistically significant.

MEASURING THE FIT OF THE OVERALL REGRESSION EQUATION: USING R AND R^2

A measure of the fit of the overall regression equation is given as the statistic R, the correlation between the actual values of the outcome variable and the values of the outcome variable predicted from the linear model, or, in other words, the correlation between Y and $\hat{Y}$. The square of this correlation, R^2, also referred to as the multiple R-squared statistic, is provided by R in the summary output of the regression model. This table is reproduced here as follows:

Residual standard error: 5.602 on 28 degrees of freedom
Multiple R-squared: 0.7863, Adjusted R-squared: 0.7786
F-statistic: 103 on 1 and 28 DF, p-value: 6.939e-ll

The Root MSE (*standard error of estimate*), given in the output as residual standard error, is defined earlier by Equation 15.5. Its value for this example is 5.60 according to the output. We may also find it from the analysis of variance table as the square root of MS_{RES}, the mean square due to residual or error. That is,

$$\sqrt{MS_{RES}} = \sqrt{SS_{RES}/(N-2)} = \sqrt{\sum (Y - \hat{Y})^2/(N-2)} = \hat{\sigma}_{Y|X} = \sqrt{31.385} = 5.60.$$

Recall that in Chapter 6 we defined the effect size for regression in terms of the Pearson product-moment correlation, r, and in terms of the correlation between the actual and predicted values, R. An alternative measure of effect size, or overall fit of the regression equation, is R^2.

We may link the measure of overall fit, R^2, to the analysis of variance framework and, in so doing, explain R^2 as the proportion of Y variance accounted for by X. To do so we divide Equation 15.10 through by SS_{TOT} and obtain Equation 15.12:

$$1 = \frac{SS_{REG}}{SS_{TOT}} + \frac{SS_{RES}}{SS_{TOT}}. \tag{15.12}$$

The total variability of Y, represented by the whole value 1, is decomposed into two non-overlapping components: that proportion due to the regression equation (i.e., that proportion explained by X) and that proportion due to the residual (i.e., that proportion unexplained by X).

For our example,

$$1 = \frac{3232.599}{4111.367} + \frac{878.767}{4111.367}$$

$$= 0.786 + 0.214$$

$$= R^2 + (1 - R^2).$$

This result is true not only for our example, but it is true in general as well. That is,

$$R^2 = \frac{SS_{REG}}{SS_{TOT}} \tag{15.13}$$

$$1 - R^2 = \frac{SS_{RES}}{SS_{TOT}}. \tag{15.14}$$

RELATING R^2 TO $\sigma^2_{Y|X}$

Given the assumption of homoscedasticity, we may express the relationship in the population between R^2, the proportion of Y variance explained by X, and $\sigma^2_{Y|X}$, the common variance of all the conditional Y distributions. In particular, when all conditional Y distributions have the same variance in the population, then it can be shown, from Equation 15.14, that

$$\sigma^2_{Y|X} = \sigma^2_Y(1 - R^2_{POP}) \tag{15.15}$$

where $\sigma^2_{Y|X}$ is the common variance of all conditional Y distributions in the population; σ^2_Y is the variance of the Y values in the population; and R^2_{POP} is the population squared correlation coefficient between X and Y.

We illustrate Equation 15.15 with a concrete situation. For simplicity, assume that X represents gender, a dichotomous variable, and Y represents mathematics achievement. Suppose the scores on the test of mathematical achievement are known to range from 20 to 90 with a variance of 100 in the population. Suppose also that we separate these scores into two distinct groups, male and female, and find that the scores for females range only from 50 to 90 with a variance of 51 and that the scores for males range only from 20 to 60 with a variance of 51. By controlling for gender, we obtain a consequent reduction in the variance of math scores from $\sigma^2_Y = 100$, to $\sigma^2_{Y|X} = 51$, almost half of what it was originally. Said differently, each of the two cross sections of slices of the bivariate distribution, one for males and the other for females, has a variance of 51. Taken together, however, the total variance of math scores is almost doubled.

To find what the correlation between gender and math achievement must be in order to observe such a dramatic reduction in variance we use Equation 15.15:

$$51 = 100(1 - R^2) \rightarrow 51 = 100 - 100R^2 \rightarrow 49 = 100R^2 \rightarrow R^2 = 0.49 \rightarrow R = 0.70.$$

Thus, in order to explain, or account for, 49 percent of the total variance of a variable by another variable, the two variables must correlate 0.70.

In the ice cream example, because $R^2 = 0.786$, we know that highest daily temperature accounts for 78.6 percent of the variance in ice cream sales. This implies that 21.4 percent of ice cream sales variance remains unexplained by highest daily temperature. In the next chapter, we discuss an approach, called multiple regression, which allows us to include other predictor variables into the equation, like humidity, for example. Such other variables may account for some of the variance in Y that remains unexplained and, in so doing, allow us to predict more accurately daily ice cream sales.

TESTING R^2 FOR STATISTICAL SIGNIFICANCE

In the case of simple regression, we have described three different, yet equivalent, ways to test the statistical significance of the regression model: The t-test of the significance of r, the t-test of the significance of b, and the ANOVA F-test of the overall regression model. A fourth, equivalent test is the test of the significance of R^2. Conceptually this makes sense because in the case of simple regression, the magnitude of r, the correlation between the single predictor and Y, equals the magnitude of R, the correlation between the actual and predicted values of Y.

The equation for testing R^2 for statistical significance is:

$$F_{P,N-P-1} = \frac{R^2/P}{(1 - R^2)/(N - P - 1)}, \tag{15.16}$$

where P = the number of predictors in the regression equation (note: in the case of simple regression, $P = 1$; in the next chapter, P will be greater than 1); N = the sample size P; and $N - P - 1$ = the F numerator and denominator degrees of freedom, respectively. In the case of simple regression, these are 1 and $N - 2$, respectively.

For the ice cream sales example, we may note that $F = \dfrac{0.786/1}{0.214/28} = \dfrac{0.786}{0.0076} = 103.00.$

This is the same value that appears in the analysis of variance table and suggests that R^2 is statistically greater than zero in the population, or equivalently, that the fit of the overall regression model to the data is statistically significant.

☞ **Remark.** For the interested reader we provide the algebraic link between the F-test of R^2 as given by Equation 15.16 and the F-test in the analysis of variance table:

$$F = \frac{MS_{REG}}{MS_{RES}} = \frac{SS_{REG}/P}{SS_{RES}/(N-P-1)} = \frac{SS_{REG}/P}{SS_{RES}/(N-P-1)} \times \frac{SS_{TOT}}{SS_{TOT}}$$

$$= \frac{\dfrac{SS_{REG}/SS_{TOT}}{P}}{\dfrac{SS_{RES}/SS_{TOT}}{N-P-1}} = \frac{R^2/P}{(1-R^2)/(N-P-1)},$$

with numerator and denominator degrees of freedom equal to P and $N - P - 1$, respectively.

ESTIMATING THE TRUE POPULATION R^2: THE ADJUSTED R^2

Although the slope b of the regression (prediction) line was described as an unbiased estimate of the slope of the population regression line, the sample R^2 is not an unbiased estimate of the true population R^2, denoted R^2_{POP}. Rather, it is biased upwards; that is, the sample R^2 overestimates the population R^2, R^2_{POP}.

Said differently, when $R^2_{POP} = 0$, then, on average, the sample R^2 will be greater than 0. It will be equal to $P/(N - 1)$. For example, given $R^2_{POP} = 0$, if $P = 1$ and $N = 9$, then, on average, the sample R^2 will equal $1/8 = 0.125$; if $P = 1$ and $N = 5$, then, on average, the sample R^2 will equal $1/4 = 0.25$.

The degree to which the sample R^2 overestimates the population R^2 depends upon both the number of predictors in the equation, P, and the size of the sample, N. The larger P is relative to N, the more the sample R^2 will overestimate the population R^2; the smaller P is relative to N, the less the sample R^2 will overestimate the population R^2.

☞ **Remark.** When $P = N - 1$, the sample R^2 will be equal to one regardless of the size of the population R^2. That is, if you constructed a regression equation with the number of predictors equal to one less than the total sample size (e.g., if $P = 1$ and $N = 2$), the sample R^2 would be one, indicating perfect fit in the population! But certainly, this would not be the case. With $P = 1$ and $N = 2$, the scatterplot consists of only two (X, Y) points, and a line can always be drawn connecting the two, or passing through both. Therefore, your result of $R^2 = 1$ should be taken merely as a reminder of just how upwardly biased the sample R^2 can be when the number of variables is large relative to the sample size.

A more accurate estimate of the population R^2 may be obtained by adjusting the sample R^2 using the following equation:

$$R^2_{ADJ} = 1 - (1 - R^2)\frac{(N-1)}{N-P-1}. \tag{15.17}$$

For the ice cream sales example, we have

$$R^2_{ADJ} = 1 - (1 - R^2)\frac{(N-1)}{N-P-1} = 1 - (1 - 0.786)\frac{30-1}{30-1-1}$$

$$= 1 - 0.214\frac{29}{28} = 1 - 0.221 = 0.779.$$

This is the *adjusted* R^2 value given in the regression output presented earlier, and represents a more accurate estimate of the population R^2 than the original, unadjusted R^2. Because in this case, however, the ratio of predictors to sample size (P:N) is relatively large, 1:30, 0.786 is trivially different from 0.779.

☞ **Remark.** In general, as a rule of thumb, when the ratio of P:N is greater than or equal to 1:30, there will be little difference between the adjusted and unadjusted R^2. When, however, the ratio of P:N is less than or equal to 1:10, the difference between the adjusted and unadjusted R^2 will tend to be large.

☞ **Remark.** The adjusted R^2 is used to provide a more accurate estimate of the population R^2. The original, unadjusted R^2, however, is used in Equation 15.16 for testing R^2 for statistical significance.

EXPLORING THE GOODNESS OF FIT OF THE REGRESSION EQUATION: USING REGRESSION DIAGNOSTICS

Throughout this book we have made the point that summary statistics may be misleading if the data they are purported to characterize are anomalous: if, for example, they contain outliers or do not, in other ways, satisfy the explicit or implicit distributional assumptions upon which these statistics are based. Because the simple regression model serves to characterize, in summary form, the linear relationship between two variables as a line with intercept and slope, it too may be misleading, or in some way, fail to capture the salient features of the data. To be convinced that the resulting intercept and slope are not distorted by outliers and other influential observations contained in the sample, we need to explore ways to validate our linear regression model. To do so, we return to the Anscombe data presented in Chapter 6.

Consider the four panels of Anscombe data reproduced here as Figure 15.7 along with their associated summary statistics. Notice that for all panels, the slope, intercept, correlation, standard error, and t-value are the same. Yet, if we look at the four scatterplots that visually represent these four panels of data, we see to what extent they are different from one another.

Panel I					
Y_1 on X_1:					
Coefficients:					
	Estimate	**Std. Error**	***t*-value**	**Pr(> |t|)**	
(Intercept)	3.0001	1.1247	2.667	0.02573	*
Anscombe\$x1	0.5001	0.1179	4.241	0.00217	**

Panel II					
Y_2 on X_2:					
Coefficients:					
	Estimate	**Std. Error**	***t*-value**	**Pr(> |t|)**	
(Intercept)	3.001	1.125	2.667	0.02576	*
Anscombe\$x2	0.500	0.118	4.239	0.00218	**

Y_3 on X_3:	Panel III				
Coefficients:					
	Estimate	**Std. Error**	**t-value**	**Pr(> |t|)**	
(Intercept)	3.0025	1.1245	2.670	0.02562	*
Anscombe$x3	0.4997	0.1179	4.239	0.00218	**

Y_4 on X_4:	Panel IV				
Coefficients:					
	Estimate	**Std. Error**	**t-value**	**Pr(> |t|)**	
(Intercept)	3.0017	1.1239	2.671	0.02559	*
Anscombe$x4	0.4999	0.1178	4.243	0.00216	**

Notice that in only one case, in Panel I, does the linear model provide a good characterization of the underlying data. In Panel II, the data show a nonlinear relationship, yet the model that is used to characterize these data is not nonlinear; it is linear. In Panel III, the outlier gives rise to a linear regression model that is quite different from the perfectly fitting regression line that would have been created in the absence of the outlier. In Panel IV, the outlier creates a systematic relationship between the dependent and predictor variables and allows a line to be fit to the data that otherwise would not have been able to be fit in the absence of the outlier. That the linear regression models in Panels III and IV are the direct result of a single outlier raises questions about the confidence we may place in these models.

Regression diagnostics are tools with which to explore our data to uncover such anomalies. As we shall see, these tools are useful for determining whether our regression models are in fact meaningful and appropriate characterizations of our data and for suggesting ways to modify our models to improve them if necessary.

RESIDUAL PLOTS: EVALUATING THE ASSUMPTIONS UNDERLYING REGRESSION

From our work on regression, we know that error (also called residual error) is defined for each individual (or more generally, for each case) as the difference between an individual's actual value on the outcome variable, Y, and his or her predicted value, $\hat{Y}$, predicted from the linear regression model. As such, $Y - \hat{Y}$ represents that part of Y that is left over after its linear association with X has been removed.

If the assumptions underlying the linear regression model are met, then the plot of residual values along the vertical axis versus the fitted (or predicted) values of Y along the horizontal axis will be rectangular in shape. A rectangular scatterplot suggests that the relationship between X and Y is a wholly linear one, that after the linear relationship between X and Y is removed, no systematic relationship between X and Y remains. If the relationship between X and Y is not wholly linear, then the scatterplot of the residual values

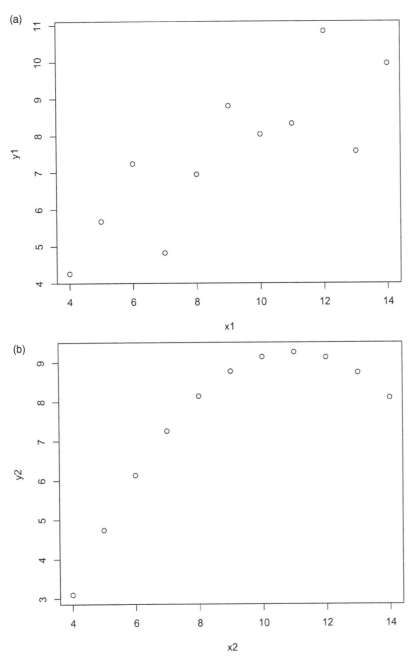

Figure 15.7 Anscombe data revisited (a) Scatterplot of Panel I; (b) Scatterplot of Panel II; (c) Scatterplot of Panel III; (d) Scatterplot of Panel IV

will not be rectangular in shape. An examination of the scatterplot may reveal the presence of a nonlinear relationship between X and Y or the violation of one or more of the other assumptions underlying the linear regression model (normality and homoscedasticity).

Residual plots for the four panels of Anscombe's data, I through IV, that appear in Figure 15.7 are given in Figure 15.8.

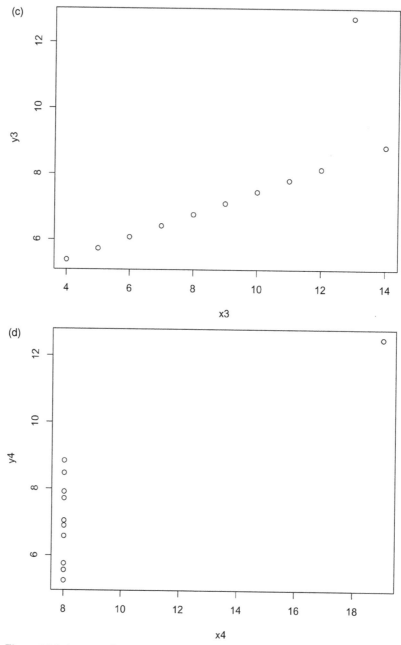

Figure 15.7 (*continued*)

MORE R: To obtain the residual scatterplot of Panel I of Figure 15.8, type:

results1 = lm(Anscombe$y1 ~ Anscombe$x1)
plot(results1, which = 1)

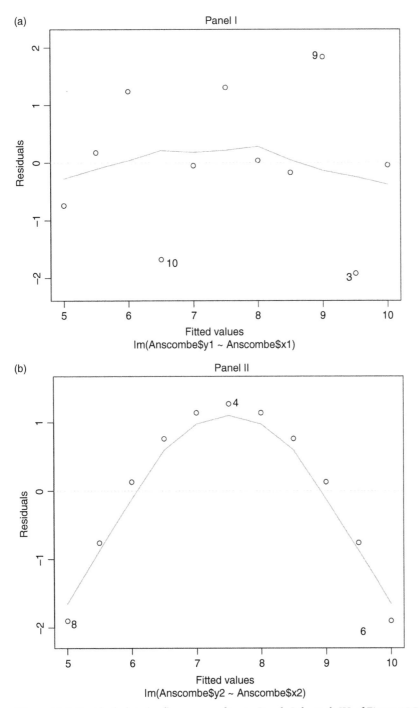

Figure 15.8 Residual plots (a–d) corresponding to Panels I through IV of Figure 15.7

Notice that in Panel I, the points in the scatterplot are rectangular in shape indicating that once the linear relationship between X and Y is removed, there is no other systematic relationship between these two variables.

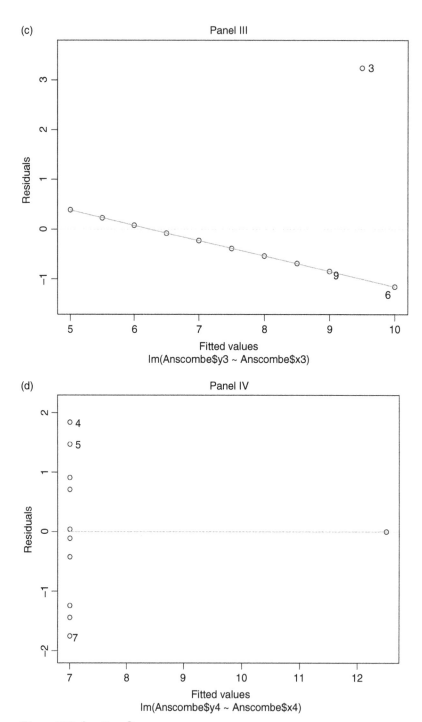

Figure 15.8 (*continued*)

The situation for Panel II is quite different. In this case, after the linear relationship between X and Y is removed, a clearly discernible nonlinear relationship remains between X and Y. The nature of the nonlinear relationship is quadratic. That is, that part of Y that remains after accounting for Y's linear association with X is a function of X^2. What this

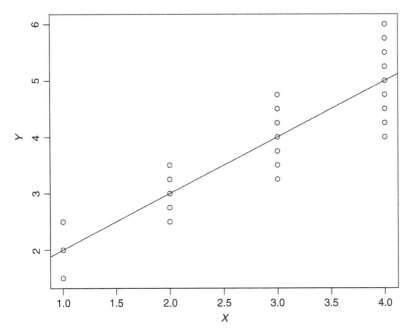

Figure 15.9 Scatterplot with heteroscedasticity

implies is that, in addition to an X term, an X^2 term should be included in the regression model to obtain a more accurate model for predicting Y. We will see how this can be done in the next chapter on multiple regression.

The residual plot of Panel III highlights the existence of the outlier, which, if removed, would make the relationship between X and Y perfect. The residual plot of Panel IV highlights the existence of the outlier which, if removed, would make the concept of a relationship between X and Y meaningless because without the outlier, X would be a constant.

Figure 15.9 contains a scatterplot of X versus Y from a fabricated dataset. Notice that while there is a systematic linear relationship between X and Y ($r_{X,Y} = 0.89$), the variances of the conditional Y distributions given X are not constant as stipulated by the assumption of homoscedasticity, a condition of bivariate normality. In particular, the conditional Y distributions of Figure 15.9 increase with increasing values of X. For example, the variance of the three Y values corresponding to $X = 1$ is smaller than the variance of the five Y values corresponding to $X = 2$, and so on. This funnel shape in the residual plot is indicative of heteroscedasticity.

Figure 15.10 contains the scatterplot of the unstandardized residual plot $Y - \hat{Y}$ versus X corresponding to the data of Figure 15.9. Notice that once that part of X linearly related to Y is removed, no relationship remains ($r = 0$). Thus, while the assumption of linearity appears to be met by these data, the assumption of homoscedasticity is quite clearly violated.

We may transform our data nonlinearly to rectify violations of the assumptions of bivariate normality and to achieve a better fitting model. In this case, the type of transformation we want is one that will produce a constant residual variance. The logarithmic transformation of Y does the trick as shown in Figure 15.11. Not only are the conditional Y distributions of Figure 15.11 homoscedastic, but the linear regression model now provides a slightly better fit to the data ($r_{X,\log(Y)} = 0.90$).

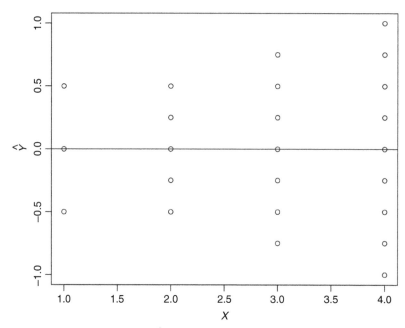

Figure 15.10 Scatterplot of $Y-\hat{Y}$ versus X

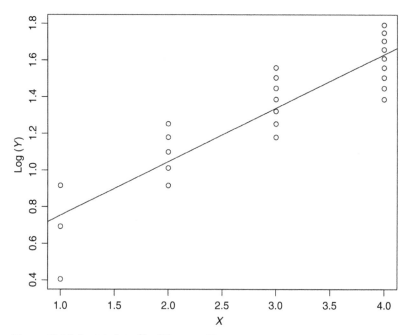

Figure 15.11 Scatterplot of $\log(Y)$ versus X

In addition to residual plots, other diagnostic tools are available for helping to improve the fit of a regression model to data.

DETECTING INFLUENTIAL OBSERVATIONS: DISCREPANCY AND LEVERAGE

In Chapters 2 and 4, we discussed the importance of identifying univariate outliers through the use of boxplots or z-scores. In this section, we expand that discussion to the case of bivariate distributions and introduce ways to identify bivariate outliers in a regression context. For this discussion, a bivariate outlier is a point in the scatterplot that behaves differently from the other points.

Outliers that unduly influence the slope and/or intercept of our regression model are called *influential observations*. Not all outliers are influential observations. Figures 15.12 and 15.13 both contain an outlier, yet in neither case does the outlier unduly influence the parameters of the regression equation.

In Figure 15.12, because the regression outlier is near the mean of $\overline{X}$, it does not affect the slope of the regression line at all, and affects the intercept only slightly. The presence of the outlier raises the regression line to be slightly closer to the points $(1, 3)$, $(2, 4)$, $(4, 6)$, and $(5, 7)$ than it would otherwise. In Figure 15.13, the regression outlier, while far from $\overline{X}$, does not affect the slope or the intercept of the regression line because it falls directly in line with the regression line.

Thus, while the vertical distance of the outlier from the regression line in Figure 15.12 and the horizontal distance of the outlier from $\overline{X}$ in Figure 15.13 characterize both points as outliers, in neither case are these outliers influential observations; in neither case do these points actually influence the slope and/or intercept of the regression model.

The vertical distance of a point from a regression line is called its *residual, discrepancy,* or *deviation*. A function of the horizontal distance of a point from the X mean is called its *leverage*. In general, only when a point has both discrepancy and leverage, as noted in Figure 15.14, does a point influence the slope of a regression equation.

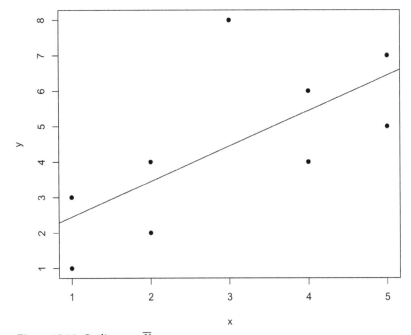

Figure 15.12 Outlier near $\overline{X}$

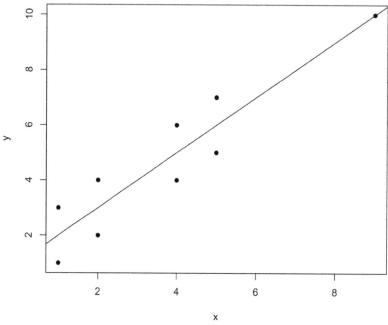

Figure 15.13 Outlier far from $\overline{X}$

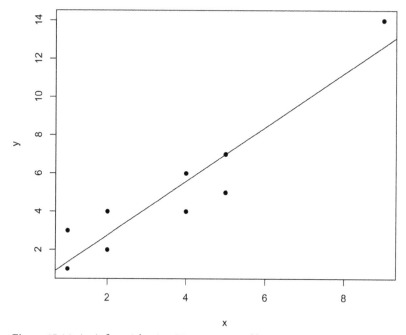

Figure 15.14 An influential point: Discrepancy *and* leverage

We may express the influence of a point on the slope of a regression equation as a function of discrepancy and leverage as shown in Equation 15.18:

$$\text{influence} \approx \text{discrepancy*leverage}. \tag{15.18}$$

TABLE 15.2 Leverage values for the nine points of Figure 15.14

x, y values	Leverage
1, 1	0.2479
1, 3	0.2479
2, 2	0.1645
2, 4	0.1645
4, 4	0.1132
4, 6	0.1132
5, 5	0.1453
5, 7	0.1453
9, 14	0.6581

TABLE 15.3 Studentized residual values for the nine points of Figure 15.12

x, y values	Studentized residual
1, 1	−0.9730
1, 3	0.3514
2, 2	−0.8696
2, 4	0.3178
3, 8	3.2660
4, 4	−0.8696
4, 6	−0.3178
5, 5	−0.9730
5, 7	0.3514

Several diagnostic tools are available in R to measure the degree to which each point in a dataset influences the coefficients of a regression equation.

USING R TO OBTAIN LEVERAGE

The leverage of a point is the distance of a point from $\overline{X}$ in simple regression. Mathematically it is computed as the squared distance of the point from $\overline{X}$ relative to the sum of squared deviations of all points in the dataset from $\overline{X}$.

MORE R: To obtain the leverage of a data point, type:

results = lm(y ~ x)
leverage(results)

Table 15.2 contains the leverage of all nine points of Figure 15.14. Not surprisingly, the leverage of the last point (9, 14) is the highest because this point is farthest from $\overline{X}$ in this dataset.

USING R TO OBTAIN DISCREPANCY

The discrepancy of a point is the vertical distance of the point from the regression line. While discrepancy may be measured as a residual value, for reasons we will not go into here, a better approach is to measure discrepancy as a *studentized residual value*. The studentized residual value of a point is the residual value of the point relative to an estimate of the standard deviation of all residual values for the entire dataset. Studentized residual values follow a *t*-distribution with $N - P - 2$ degrees of freedom.

MORE R: To obtain the studentized residual value for each data point (x, y), type:

results = lm(y ~ x)
rstudent(results)

To exemplify, Table 15.3 contains the studentized residual values of all nine points of Figure 15.12.

As we would expect, the studentized residual value of the point (3, 8) is highest because this point has the greatest vertical distance from the regression line as shown in Figure 15.12.

USING R TO OBTAIN INFLUENCE

The influence of a point is the amount by which the slope of the regression line (the regression coefficient) will change when that point is removed from the dataset and we compute a new slope. The amount of change may be scaled by an index developed by Cook and Weisberg (1983), based loosely on the *F*-statistic, so that we may evaluate which changes are relatively small, moderate, or large.

Many researchers treat cases with Cook's influence scores that are larger than 1 as outliers. We will make particular note of such cases in our analyses.

MORE R: To obtain Cook's influence value for a data point (*x*, *y*), type:

results = lm(y ~ x)
cooks.distance(results)

TABLE 15.4 Cook's influence values for the nine points of Figure 15.14

x, y values	Cook's influence
1, 1	0.0140
1, 3	0.3098
2, 2	0.0354
2, 4	0.0941
4, 4	0.0936
4, 6	0.0066
5, 5	0.2050
5, 7	0.0000
9, 14	2.7360

Table 15.4 contains the Cook's influence values of all nine points of Figure 15.14. As expected, the last value in the dataset (9, 14) has the highest value of Cook's influence (called Cook's distance by R), indicating that this point influences the slope of the regression equation more than any other point in the dataset. It also has a Cook's value that is quite a bit larger than 1.00, so it is classified as an outlier.

Table 15.5 presents the results of the regression analysis based on the total set of nine points in the dataset and on the nine subsets of size eight each with one point removed. Notice that Cook's influence is zero for point (5, 7). Notice also that the regression line based on the sample without this point is identical to the regression line based on the sample that includes this point. Hence, as Cook's influence value suggests, the analysis is not at all influenced by

---

TABLE 15.5 Regression results based on all nine points and on all subsets of eight points, eliminating one point each time

Analysis	Point removed	Sample size	Regression equation
1	1, 1	8	$\hat{Y} = 1.386X - 0.080$
2	1, 3	8	$\hat{Y} = 1.523X - 0.720$
3	2, 2	8	$\hat{Y} = 1.381X + 0.148$
4	2, 4	8	$\hat{Y} = 1.458X - 0.399$
5	4, 4	8	$\hat{Y} = 1.422X - 0.096$
6	4, 6	8	$\hat{Y} = 1.407X - 0.101$
7	5, 5	8	$\hat{Y} = 1.470X - 0.020$
8	5, 7	8	$\hat{Y} = 1.410X - 0.060$
9	9, 14	8	$\hat{Y} = 1.000X - 1.00$
10	none	9	$\hat{Y} = 1.410X - 0.060$

the presence of this point. With or without this point, the results are the same. Notice, however, that as Cook's influence value also suggests, the point with the greatest influence on the equation is point (9, 14). The equation based on the subsample with point (9, 14) removed is quite different from all other equations that are based on samples that include point (9, 14) as one of the points in the sample.

In summary, anomalies in our data may distort the results of our regression analyses. While some anomalies may be corrected easily (e.g., they are the result of data entry mistakes), others may not. Several outliers may be found to cluster together in a dataset, in which case, a separate regression line fit to those points may be warranted. In other cases, transformations of the data may be used to reduce the influence of the outliers. Because the particular course of action taken with regard to outliers will vary with the circumstance of the problem, it is incumbent upon the researcher to provide a clear justification of whatever course of action they choose to use in a particular case.

USING DIAGNOSTICS TO EVALUATE THE ICE CREAM SALES EXAMPLE

We complete the ice cream example with an examination of our data for possible anomalies that may compromise the utility of our regression model. We begin with a scatterplot of Y (barsold) by X (temp) with case ID numbers listed (see Figure 15.15).

MORE R: To create a scatterplot that is labeled by ID numbers, we run the following command:

plot(c(0), type = "n", xlim = range(IceCream$temp), ylim = range(IceCream$barsold), ylab= "", xlab = "")
text(IceCream$barsold ~ IceCream$temp, labels = IceCream$id, pch = 0)

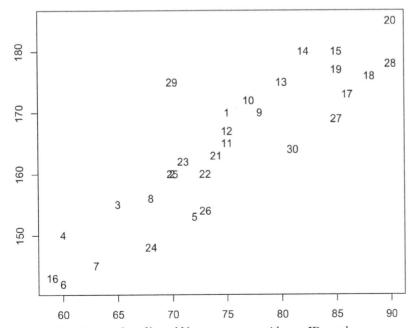

Figure 15.15 Scatterplot of barsold by temperature with case ID numbers

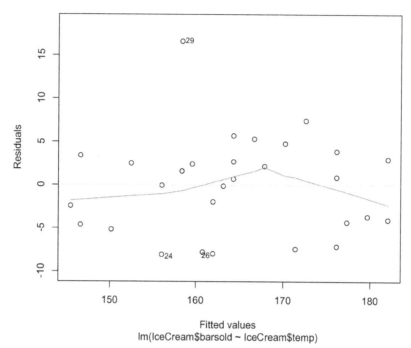

Figure 15.16 Residual plot of $Y - \hat{Y}$ versus X

The first line of code creates an empty plot (**type = "n"**) with axes ranging from the minimum and maximum values of temperature and bars sold, respectively. The second line of code plots the ID value for each point on the scatterplot.

With the exception of case number 29, all points fall fairly close to the regression line and the residual plot, $Y - \hat{Y}$ versus X, given above is fairly rectangular in shape, suggesting that the assumptions of linear regression are met and that transformations of the variables are not needed. Case number 29 warrants further attention (Figure 15.16).

Accordingly, we investigate the vertical discrepancy (as measured by the studentized residuals), the horizontal leverage, and, finally, the influence of all cases in this analysis. Boxplots of these statistics are provided below in Figures 15.17 through 15.19, respectively.

As expected from Figures 15.15 and 15.16, and as illustrated in Figure 15.17, case number 29 has the greatest vertical distance from the regression line as measured by the studentized residual. Because case number 29 is close to the mean temperature value, it does not show up as an outlier with respect to leverage, or horizontal distance from the X mean. Although it does show up as an outlier with respect to influence, the influence value itself is close to 0 (at 0.2) and suggests negligible influence on the regression slope. To confirm this, however, we redo the regression analysis without case number 29 and obtain the following result.

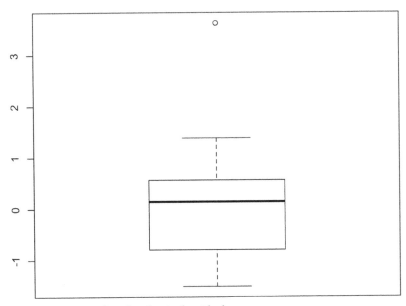

Figure 15.17 Boxplot of studentized residuals

Coefficients:

	Estimate	Std. Error	*t*-value	Pr(> |t|)	
(Intercept)	72.43576	7.38592	9.807	2.15e-10	***
IceCream$temp	1.21734	0.09766	12.465	1.03e-12	***

Signif. codes: 0 "***"   0.001 "**"   0.01 "*" 0.05 "." 0.1 "" 1

Residual standard error: 4.678 on 27 degrees of freedom
Multiple R-squared: 0.852, Adjusted R-squared: 0.8465
F-statistic: 155.4 on 1 and 27 DF, p-value: 1.035e-12

That is, without case number 29, the linear regression equation for predicting barsold from temp is predicted barsold = 72.44 + 1.22(temp), which has a b-weight that is negligibly different from the b-weight of the original equation obtained with case number 29 included: predicted barsold = 75.78 + 1.18(temp).

Notice that the intercept is lower without case number 29 than with case number 29. This is to be expected because of where case number 29 sits relative to the other points in the sample. Case number 29 is near the X mean indicating that it will not affect the b-weight by very much, but it is high above the regression line indicating that it will raise the level of the regression line and increase the Y-intercept as shown.

As one might expect, without case number 29 in the sample, the fit of the regression line to the points is improved (from $R^2 = 0.786$ with case number 29 to $R^2 = 0.852$ without case number 29). However, because there is no compelling reason to eliminate case number 29 from the analysis, we leave it in and acknowledge its influence on our results, albeit small.

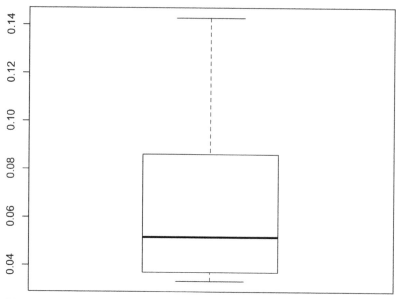

Figure 15.18 Boxplot of leverage values

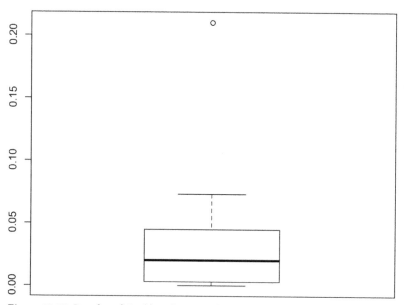

Figure 15.19 Boxplot of Cook's influence values

USING THE PREDICTION MODEL TO PREDICT ICE CREAM SALES

Now that we have shown that our model was appropriately fit to our data using diagnostics and that the result was statistically significant, we can be confident in using our regression equation to predict ice cream sales from temperature. Simply stated, to predict the number of ice cream sales on a particular day with a given forecasted highest daily temperature, we use

predicted barsold = 75.78 + 1.18(temp).

Thus, if the highest daily temperature is forecasted to be 78 °F for a particular day, we would take a predicted barsold = 75.78 + 1.18(78) = 167.82, or 168 bars to the beach.

Given how well our model fits our data (R^2 = 0.786), we can expect our equation to yield reasonably accurate estimates of ice cream sales given particular daily highest temperatures. However, the accuracy of a particular prediction (that we will sell exactly 168 ice cream bars when the daily highest temperature is forecast to reach 78 °F, for example) will depend on several factors. One factor is the distance between the given forecasted daily high (e.g., 78 °F in this case) and the mean daily highest temperature for our sample of data (e.g., 75 °F for these data). Simply stated, the accuracy of our prediction will be better the closer the particular X value is to $\overline{X}$. Thus, in the context of our example, we can expect our prediction of ice cream sales to be more accurate on days when the highest daily temperature is forecast to be around 75 °F than far from 75 °F.

We may also calculate a 95 percent prediction interval around our predicted value. Such an interval would provide a range of values, rather than a single point, for which we would expect the predicted value to be 95 percent of the time.

MORE R: To obtain a 95 percent prediction interval, type:

results = lm(barsold ~ temp, data = IceCream)
predict(results, newdata = data.frame(temp = 78), interval = "predict")

The first line of code runs the regression model of bars sold on temperature. The second line of code provides the 95 percent prediction interval.

The output for the prediction interval we obtain is:

fit	lwr	upr
167.8534	156.1652	179.5415

Therefore, on 95 percent of days where the temperature was 78 °F, we would need to bring between 156.2 and 179.5 ice cream bars to the beach.

SIMPLE REGRESSION WHEN THE PREDICTOR IS DICHOTOMOUS

In Example 11.8 (in Chapter 11), we used the independent samples t-test on the NELS dataset to determine whether gender differences exist in the number of units of mathematics taken in high school among college-bound students from the southern United States. In this problem, gender, a dichotomous variable, may be considered as the predictor variable, and number of units of mathematics taken in high school may be taken as the outcome variable. In this section we compare the result of the independent samples t-test to that of the t-test on the b-weight for predicting units of math taken in high school from gender, and show that they are equivalent.

The R result of the independent samples t-test for this example is reproduced below.

Two sample *t*-test

data: NELS$unitmath[NELS$region == "South" & NELS$gender == "Male"]
and NELS$unitmath[NELS$region == "South" & NELS$gender == "Female"]

$t = 2.1071$ *df* = 148   *p*-value = 0.0368

alternative hypothesis: true difference in means is not equal to 0

95 percent confidence interval: 0.0157010   0.4895371
sample estimates: mean of *x* 3.916667   mean of *y* 3.664048

As discussed in Chapter 11, and as noted in the table above, the mean gender difference in math courses taken of 0.25 is statistically significant, indicating that males in the South take statistically significantly more math than females in the South ($t(148) = 2.11$, $p = 0.04$).

The output from the simple linear regression analysis to predict units of math taken from gender is given below.

Coefficients:

	Estimate	**Std. Error**	**t value**	**Pr(> |t|)**	
(Intercept)	3.91667	0.08972	43.655	<2e-16	***
NELS$gender[NELS$region == "South"] Female	−0.25262	0.11989	−2.107	0.0368	*

Signif. codes: 0   "***"   0.001   "**"   0.01   "*"   0.05   "."   0.1   " "   1

Residual standard error: 0.7289 on 148 degrees of freedom
Multiple *R*-squared: 0.02912, Adjusted *R*-squared: 0.02256
F-statistic: 4.44 on 1 and 148 *df*, *p*-value: 0.0368

Notice that the *t*-test of the *b*-weight is identical (except for the sign) to the *t*-test of the mean difference ($t = -2.11$, $p = 0.04$). The sign change in the *t*-value simply reflects the fact that in one approach, the mean units of math taken by males is subtracted from the mean units of math taken by females, while in the other approach the reverse is the case. Notice that the *b*-weight of −0.253 equals the difference in means between males and females, once again allowing for a sign change due to the way the subtraction is carried out.

Whenever a dichotomous predictor variable is coded 0 for one group (e.g., males) and 1 for the other (e.g., females), the *b*-weight will reflect the difference in means on the outcome variable between the two groups. Furthermore, the constant (3.917 in this case) will equal the mean on the outcome variable of the group coded 0. Hence, we can learn from the regression equation alone that the mean number of math units taken by males is 3.917 and by females is 3.917 − 0.253, or 3.664, which we know to be the case from the descriptive statistics associated with the t-test on means of independent samples. Because X takes only two values, $\hat{Y}$ takes only two, also.

We already have pointed out that the t-test of the b-weight is equivalent to the t-test of the correlation between independent and outcome variables. The output given below corroborates that fact.

Pearson's product-moment correlation

data: NELS\$unitmath[NELS\$region == "South"]
and as.numeric(NELS\$gender[NELS\$region == "South"])

$t = -2.1071$ $df = 148$ p-value = 0.0368

alternative hypothesis: true correlation is not equal to 0

| 95 percent confidence interval: | −0.32211201 | 0.01069122 |
| sample estimates: | cor | −0.1706603 |

Notice that the correlation between gender and units of math taken is $r = -0.17$, which is statistically significant. The t-test on the correlation (note that the t-value is not reported) has a two-tailed p-value of $p = 0.0368$, which is exactly the value given in connection with the t-test on the b-weight and the t-test on the means of the two independent groups.

CONDUCTING POWER ANALYSES FOR CORRELATION AND SIMPLE REGRESSION

In this section, we will use R's **pwr** library to illustrate how to find the sample size for testing the significance of a correlation and the significance of R^2 in simple regression. As shown in Table 10.3, we shall use r as the effect size index for the correlation, and follow Cohen's (1988) guidelines to describe r values of 0.10, 0.30, and 0.50 as small, medium, and large effect sizes, respectively. We, likewise, shall use f^2 as the effect size index for simple regression, and follow Cohen's (1988) guidelines to describe f^2 values of 0.02, 0.15, and 0.35 as small, medium, and large effect sizes, respectively.

We illustrate with power = 0.80, $\alpha = 0.05$, and medium effect sizes in both cases.

EXAMPLE 15.3 Use R's **pwr** library and **pwr.r.test** command to determine the sample size required to detect with power = 0.80 and $\alpha = 0.05$ whether an observed correlation of $r = 0.30$ (a medium effect size) is statistically significantly greater than 0.

Solution R's **power** command for r in this case of a one-tailed test is:

pwr.r.test(r = 0.3, sig.level = 0.05, power = 0.8, alternative = "greater")

where **r** is the value of rho under the alternative hypothesis; **alternative = "greater"** stipulates that the test is one-tailed (default is two-tailed).

We run the **power** command as shown and obtain the following results:

approximate correlation power calculation		
n	=	66.55463
r	=	0.3
sig. level	=	0.05
power	=	0.8
alternative	=	greater

EXAMPLE 15.4 Use R's **power** command to determine the sample size required to detect with power = 0.80 and α = 0.05 whether an observed correlation of r = 0.30 (a medium effect size) is statistically significantly different from 0.

Solution The only difference between this and the previous example is that this example is two-tailed, rather than one-tailed. Accordingly, the **power** command for this example includes the argument **alternative = "two.sided"**. The command is as shown, and the results are as follows:

pwr.r.test(r = 0.3, sig.level = 0.05, power = 0.8, alternative = "two.sided")

approximate correlation power calculation		
n	=	84.07364
r	=	0.3
sig. level	=	0.05
power	=	0.8
alternative	=	two.sided

As pointed out in Chapter 11, all things being equal, two-tailed tests are less powerful than their one-sided counterparts. Accordingly, the sample size required to detect a medium effect size with power equal .80 and alpha equal .05 for this two-tailed test exceeds that of the one-tailed test.

EXAMPLE 15.5 Use R's **pwr.f2.test** command to determine the sample size required to detect with power = 0.80 and α = 0.05 whether an R^2 with a medium effect size ($f^2 = 0.15$, corresponding to Cohen's medium effect size (see Table 10.3)) is statistically significantly different from zero. Recall that because $f^2 = (R^2/(1 - R^2))$, an $f^2 = 0.15$ implies that $R^2 = 0.1304$.

Solution Based on this one-predictor model, the power command to determine with power = 0.80 and alpha = 0.05 the sample size for detecting an $R^2 = 0.1304$ as statistically significantly different from zero is:

pwr.f2.test(u = 1, f2 = 0.15, sig.level = 0.05, power = 0.8)

Note here that the **pwr.f2.test** function requires an input of **u** equal to the number of predictors (not including the intercept) in the regression model. In the case of simple linear regression, as described in this chapter, **u** will always be equal to 1.

The obtained results are as follows:

Multiple regression power calculation		
u	=	1
v	=	52.315
f^2	=	0.15
sig. level	=	0.05
power	=	0.8

The resulting output provides a value for **v**, which represents the degrees of freedom of the F-test. We may calculate the sample size through the formula **n = v + u + 1**. Therefore, for this example, the minimum sample size needed is equal to 52.315 + 1 + 1 = 54.315, or 55.

☞ **Remark.** Had we used the same effect size as in Example 15.4 ($r = 0.30$), transformed to $R^2 = 0.09$, instead of the one we did use, which corresponds to Cohen's medium effect size in the context of simple regression ($R^2 = 0.1304$), the resulting sample size would have been the same.

SUMMARY OF R COMMANDS

Create	Command lines
To obtain a scatterplot with a regression line superimposed (Figure 15.5)	**plot(IceCream$barsold ~ IceCream $temp, pch = 16, xlab = "Temperature", ylab = "Bars Sold")** **abline(lm(IceCream$barsold~IceCream $temp))**
To create a scatterplot that is labeled by ID numbers (Figure 15.15)	**plot(c(0), type = "n", xlim = range(Ice Cream$temp), ylim = range(Ice Cream$barsold), ylab= "", xlab = "")** **text(IceCream$barsold ~ IceCream $temp, labels = IceCream$id, pch = 0)**
To obtain the residual scatterplot (Figure 15.8)	**results1 = lm(Anscombe$y1 ~ Anscombe$x1)** **plot(results1, which = 1)**
Pearson product-moment relation along with the significance level	**cor.test(NELS$achmat12, NELS $achrdg12)**
To perform a regression analysis including summary statistics (Example 15.2)	**results = lm(IceCream$barsold ~ IceCream$temp)** **summary(results)** **confint(results)** **anova(results)**
To obtain the leverage of a data point (Table 15.2)	**results = lm(newY~Figure15_12$xpr)** **leverage(results)**

Create	Command lines
To obtain the studentized residual value for each data point (x, y) (Table 15.3)	results = lm(Figure15_12$y ~ Figure15_12$x) rstudent(results)
To obtain Cook's influence value for a data point (x, y) (Table 15.4)	results = lm(newY~Figure15_12$xpr) cooks.distance(results)
Obtain the sample size required to detect whether an observed correlation of $r = 0.30$ is significantly greater than 0 (Example 15.3)	pwr.r.test(r = 0.3, sig.level = 0.05, power = 0.8, alternative = "greater")
Obtain the sample size required to detect whether an observed correlation of $r = 0.30$ is significantly different from 0 (Example 15.4)	pwr.r.test(r = 0.3, sig.level = 0.05, power = 0.8, alternative = "two.sided")
Obtain the sample size required to detect whether an R^2 with medium effect size is significantly different from 0 (Example 15.5)	pwr.f2.test(u = 1, f2 = 0.15, sig.level = 0.05, power = 0.8)

EXERCISES

Create a .R file for each exercise that requires the use of R. Run code from the .R file by highlighting or having the cursor on the line of code and hitting **control+enter** on a PC computer keyboard or **command+enter** on a Mac computer keyboard. Save each .R file using a name associated with the Exercise for which it was created. It is recommended that you review the .R file for Chapter 15 located on the textbook's website before completing these exercises. To facilitate doing each exercise, it may be helpful to copy and paste relevant code from the .R file for Chapter 15 into your own .R file and modify them as needed.

Exercises 15.1 and 15.2 involve correlation and simple linear regression analyses with interval- or ratio-leveled predictor variables from the Learndis dataset. For inferential purposes, we consider the children in the dataset to be a random sample of all children attending public elementary school in an urban area who have been diagnosed with learning disabilities. Use α = 0.05 for all significance tests.

15.1 Perform correlation analyses to investigate whether grade level (grade), intellectual ability (iq), placement type (placemen, where 1 = Part time resource room and 2 = Full-time self-contained classroom) are statistically significantly associated with reading achievement (readcomp). For now, assume that the underlying assumptions have been verified.

(a) What are the null and alternative hypotheses for testing the linear relationship between reading comprehension and intellectual ability?

(b) Is the linear relationship between reading comprehension and intellectual ability statistically significant? If so, describe its nature and magnitude.

(c) Is the linear relationship between reading comprehension and grade level statis-
     tically significant? If so, describe its nature and magnitude.

(d) Is there a statistically significant difference in reading comprehension scores, on
     average, between the two placement types? If so, describe the nature and magni-
     tude of the difference.

(e) Although data were collected on 105 children attending public school in the urban
     area who had been diagnosed with learning disabilities, reading comprehension
     scores were not available for 29 of the students. By using the R default of list-wise
     deletion of missing data, the scores of only 76 children were included in the
     analyses. Describe how this method of dealing with missing data might impact
     the obtained results. Because a discussion of the many possible ways of handling
     missing data is beyond the scope of this text, all solutions to problems with
     missing data are handled as if the data did not have missing values.

15.2 Perform a correlation and simple linear regression analysis to understand how
mathematics comprehension (mathcomp) may be explained by intellectual ability (iq).

(a) Find the 95 percent confidence interval for ρ.

(b) Find the 95 percent confidence interval for the population b.

(c) Is the coefficient for iq statistically significant? Explain.

(d) Describe, to the extent possible, the nature of the linear relationship between math
     comprehension and intellectual ability.

(e) Describe, to the extent possible, the strength of the linear relationship between
     math comprehension and intellectual ability, using Cohen's scale as a guide.

*Exercises 15.3 and 15.4 involve correlation and simple linear regression analyses with
interval- or ratio-leveled predictor variables from the NELS dataset. For inferential purposes,
we consider the students in the dataset to be a random sample of the population of all college-
bound students who have always been at grade level. Use α = 0.05 for all significance tests.*

15.3 Among college-bound students in an urban setting, what is the relationship between
family size (famsize) and twelfth grade self-concept (slfcnc12)?

(a) Select cases so that the students included in the analysis are from an urban setting
     only. Create a scatterplot between family size (famsize) and twelfth grade self-
     concept (slfcnc12). Use it to comment upon the appropriateness of a correlation
     analysis.

(b) Find the correlation between famsize and slfcnc12 and indicate whether or not it is
     statistically significant.

(c) Find the 95 percent confidence interval for the correlation between famsize and
     slfcnc12. Use it to determine whether or not the correlation between famsize and
     slfcnc12 is statistically significant.

(d) According to Cohen's scale, what is the strength of the linear relationship between
     famsize and slfcnc12 in the population? Which is more useful for making the
     determination: the correlation or the confidence interval?

15.4 Construct a regression model to predict twelfth grade math achievement (achmat12)
from socioeconomic status (ses), reported in eighth grade.

(a) Is the regression model statistically significant? Is the coefficient for ses statistically
     significant?

(b) What is the regression equation for predicting achmat12 (Y) from ses (X)?

(c) What is the interpretation of the slope of the regression equation in the context of this analysis?

(d) Interpret the y-intercept, or constant, within the context of this analysis, or explain why it would not be meaningful to do so.

(e) Report and interpret a measure of effect size for the relationship.

Exercises 15.5 and 15.6 involve simple linear regression analyses with dichotomous predictor variables from the Learndis dataset. For inferential purposes, we consider the children in the dataset to be a random sample of all children attending public elementary school in an urban area who have been diagnosed with learning disabilities. Use $\alpha = 0.05$ for all significance tests.

15.5 Perform a simple linear regression analysis to understand how intellectual ability (iq) may be predicted from gender. Use it to answer the following questions.

(a) Is the b-weight statistically significant? Explain and indicate what part of the output you used to determine the significance of the b-weight.

(b) Explain why, in this case, it is not appropriate to report the regression equation and its components.

15.6 Perform a simple linear regression analysis to determine the proportion of reading comprehension (readcomp) variance explained by type of placement (placemen). For these data, there are two types of placement, part-time resource room, coded 1, and full-time self-contained classroom, coded 2. Use your analysis to answer the following questions.

(a) Is the b-weight statistically significant? Explain and indicate what part of the output you used to determine the significance of the b-weight.

(b) What is the regression equation for predicting reading comprehension scores (Y) from the type of placement (X)?

(c) What is the interpretation of the slope of the regression equation in the context of this analysis?

(d) Interpret the y-intercept, or constant, within the context of this analysis, or explain why it would not be meaningful to do so.

(e) Based on the regression model, what would you predict the reading comprehension score to be for a student within the resource room? Can the predicted score be interpreted as the mean reading comprehension score for all students within the resource room?

(f) Use the regression model to predict the reading comprehension score for a student within the self-contained classroom.

(g) What percentage of the variance in reading comprehension scores is explained by placement type? Explain and indicate what part of the output you used to determine this effect size.

(h) What other inferential test could have been performed to determine how reading comprehension may be predicted from type of placement?

Exercise 15.7 involves simple linear regression analyses with dichotomous predictor variables from the NELS dataset. For inferential purposes, we consider the students in the dataset to be a random sample of the population of all college-bound students who have always been at grade level. Use $\alpha = 0.05$ for all significance tests.

15.7 Develop a regression model to predict twelfth grade math achievement (achmat12) from computer ownership (computer), as reported in eighth grade.

   (a) Is the regression model statistically significant? Is the b-weight statistically significant?

   (b) Report the regression equation for predicting achmat12 (Y) from computer (X).

   (c) What is the interpretation of the slope of the regression equation in the context of this analysis?

   (d) Interpret the y-intercept, or constant, within the context of this analysis, or explain why it is not meaningful.

   (e) Report and interpret two different measures of effect size for the relationship.

Exercise 15.8 involves correlation and simple linear regression analyses with variables from the Brainsz dataset. Recall that the population of students for this study consisted only of those with either extremely high or extremely low intelligence. For inferential purposes, we consider the students in the dataset to be a random sample of all college students with extremely low or high intelligence. Use $\alpha = 0.05$ for all significance tests.

15.8 Perform correlation analyses to investigate whether gender (GENDER) and brain size (MRI) are statistically significantly associated with intelligence as measured by the Full-Scale IQ score of the WAIS-R test (FSIQ). Use these analyses to answer the following questions.

   (a) Is the linear relationship between intelligence and brain size statistically significant? If so, describe its nature and magnitude.

   (b) Is there a statistically significant relationship between intelligence and gender? If so, describe its nature and magnitude.

   (c) Comment upon the effect of the sampling design on the correlation computed in part (a).

   (d) Construct a scatterplot of these two variables with FSIQ on the horizontal axis and brain size as measured by the MRI on the vertical axis.

   (e) Explain why there are two clouds of points in the scatterplot.

   (f) Regress FSIQ on MRI using a single regression model for the entire sample. Comment on the significance and fit of this model.

   (g) Regress FSIQ on MRI using two regression models, one fit to the extremely high FSIQ group and the other fit to the extremely low FSIQ group. Comment on the fit of each model and compare these values to the fit of the model developed on the entire sample and obtained in part (f).

Exercises 15.9 focuses on regression diagnostics using the Learndis dataset. For inferential purposes, we consider the children in the dataset to be a random sample of all children attending public elementary school in an urban area who have been diagnosed with learning disabilities. Use $\alpha = 0.05$ for all significance tests.

15.9 Create a scatterplot that could be used to predict reading comprehension (readcomp) from grade level (grade) for the students in the dataset, labeling the points by the case numbers. Use the scatterplot to answer the following questions.

   (a) Do any of the assumptions (normality, homoscedasticity, and linearity) underlying the correlation analysis between reading comprehension and grade level appear to be violated? Explain.

(b) Which case number has the data point with the largest residual (in magnitude)? Is that residual negative or positive? That is, is that case over- or under-predicted by the model?

(c) Give an example of a case number with relatively large leverage.

Exercises 15.10–15.11 involve regression diagnostics with variables from the NELS dataset. For inferential purposes, we consider the students in the dataset to be a random sample of the population of all college-bound students who have always been at grade level. Use $\alpha = 0.05$ for all significance tests.

15.10 Comment on the appropriateness of using simple linear regression for predicting achmat12 from computer, as we did in Exercise 15.7.

15.11 In Exercise 15.4, we developed a simple regression model to predict achmat12 from ses. In this exercise, we follow up with some regression diagnostics to verify the appropriateness of the model.

(a) Create a scatterplot of the regression for predicting achmat12 from ses. Does the scatterplot suggest a linear relationship between these two variables with no apparent violation of underlying assumptions?

(b) Calculate the studentized residuals and create a residual scatterplot and frequency distribution. What are the lowest and highest values of the studentized residuals? What do these values indicate about the appropriateness of the model?

(c) Calculate the Cook's influence scores and create a boxplot of the distribution. What are the lowest and highest values of the Cook's influence scores? What do these values indicate about the appropriateness of the model?

(d) Using the obtained regression model, what is the value of the predicted twelfth grade math achievement score for the first person in the dataset (with ID = 1)?

(e) Using the obtained regression model, what is the unstandardized residual value of the twelfth grade math achievement score for the first person in the dataset (with ID = 1)?

(f) Which unstandardized residual value has the greatest magnitude? What is its associated ID number?

Exercises 15.12–15.13 involve power analyses for correlation and simple linear regression.

15.12 Determine the sample size required to detect with power = 0.80 and $\alpha = 0.05$ whether an observed correlation of $r = 0.10$ (a small effect size) is

(a) statistically significantly greater than 0

(b) statistically significantly different from 0

15.13 Complete the following to determine the sample size required in simple linear regression to detect with power = 0.80 and $\alpha = 0.05$ whether an R^2 with a small effect size ($f^2 = 0.02$) is statistically significantly different from zero.

(a) What is the value of R^2 that corresponds to $f^2 = 0.02$?

(b) What is the sample size required to detect the effect, in this case?

Exercise 15.14 involves a small dataset.

15.14 Dr. Michelle Knapp, a research pediatrician, is interested in predicting the birth weight of first-born infants (Y) from the amount of weight gained by the mother during her pregnancy (X) for the population of middle-class individuals. She therefore randomly selects 15 middle-class mothers, pregnant for the first time, and follows them through pregnancy. After the mothers give birth, she records their weight gains in pounds and the birth weights of their offspring in pounds. The data are given in the following table. Use them to answer the associated questions.

X Weight gain of mother (pounds)	Y Birth weight of infant (pounds)
14	6.2
23	6.8
28	7.5
27	7.3
12	6.0
19	6.2
25	7.0
24	6.3
34	8.0
21	6.0
30	8.0
32	8.2
26	7.5
27	7.5
23	6.8

(a) Create a scatterplot and, if necessary, a diagnostic analysis, and use them to show that a correlation and simple linear regression analysis is appropriate for these data.

(b) Construct a 95 percent confidence interval for the population correlation, ρ, between the birth weight of the infant and the weight gain of the mother. According to the confidence interval, is the correlation statistically significant? If so, describe its nature and strength.

(c) Construct the linear regression equation for predicting the birth weight of the infant (Y) from the weight gain of the mother (X).

(d) Is the linear regression model statistically significant? Use $\alpha = 0.05$. Explain.

(e) What is the predicted birth weight of a first-born infant whose mother gained 25 pounds during her pregnancy?

Exercises 15.15–15.30 are conceptual in nature and do not require the use of R.

15.15 The b-weight for predicting Y from X is computed in a sample of size 200 drawn randomly from a bivariate population. If this process is repeated 2,000 times, the standard deviation of the 2,000 b-weights is approximately equal to:

(a) the standard deviation of X,

(b) the standard deviation of Y,

(c) the standard error of b for $N = 200$,

    (d) the standard error of b for $N = 2{,}000$,
    (e) none of the above.

15.16 Assume that you are given a simple regression equation for predicting Y from X: $\hat{Y} = bX + a$. When will Var(Y) equal Var(residual)? Hint: The residual is that part of Y that remains after accounting for X, or $Y - \hat{Y}$.
    (a) When the correlation between X and Y is equal to zero?
    (b) When the correlation between X and Y is not equal to zero?
    (c) When the correlation between X and Y is positive, but not when it's negative?
    (d) Always?
    (e) Never?
    (f) None of the above?

15.17 Assume that you are given a simple regression equation for predicting Y from X: $\hat{Y} = bX + a$. When will Var(Y) be less than Var(residual)?
    (a) When the correlation between X and Y is equal to zero?
    (b) When the correlation between X and Y is not equal to zero?
    (c) When the correlation between X and Y is positive, but not when it's negative?
    (d) Always?
    (e) Never?
    (f) None of the above?

Exercises 15.18–15.22 relate to the following scatterplot. The regression line has been added and the points are labeled by their case numbers.

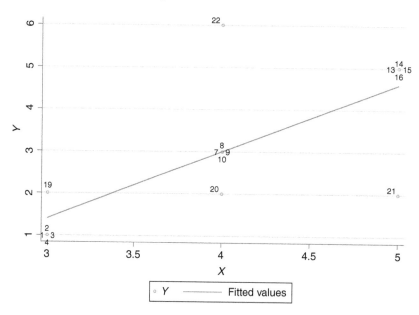

15.18 The value 3 may be described most closely as:
    (a) $\overline{X}$, the mean of X
    (b) $\overline{Y}$, the mean of Y
    (c) both (a) and (b)
    (d) neither (a) nor (b)

15.19 The point with the greatest residual corresponds to case number:
    (a) 19
    (b) 20
    (c) 21
    (d) 22

15.20 The point with the greatest influence corresponds to case number:
    (a) 19
    (b) 20
    (c) 21
    (d) 22

15.21 The slope of the regression equation, in this case is:
    (a) positive
    (b) negative
    (c) zero

15.22 The y-intercept of the regression equation, in this case is:
    (a) positive
    (b) negative
    (c) zero

15.23 Which regression assumption is most likely violated in the following scatterplot?

    (a) linearity
    (b) normality
    (c) homoscedasticity

15.24 Which regression assumption is most likely violated in the following scatterplot?

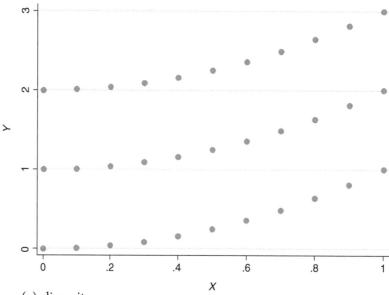

(a) linearity
(b) normality
(c) homoscedasticity

15.25 Which regression assumption is most likely violated in the following scatterplot?

(a) linearity
(b) normality
(c) homoscedasticity

15.26 Which regression assumption is most likely violated in the following scatterplot that depicts the Y scores of 300 males and 300 females?

(a) linearity

(b) normality

(c) homoscedasticity

Exercises 15.27–15.30 come from Becker and Kennedy (1992). Use the following graph to determine the most correct response to the multiple-choice questions.

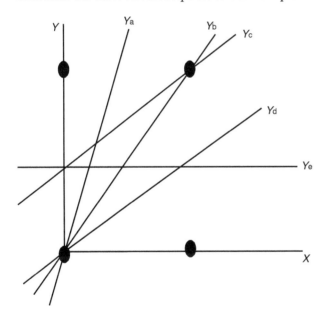

15.27 For the four sample points, which line best represents the average of the Y data? (Note that the point $(0, 0)$ is one of the observations.)

(a) Y_a

(b) Y_b

(c) Y_c

(d) Y_d

(e) Y_e

15.28 For the four sample points, which line best represents the regression line?

(a) Y_a

(b) Y_b

(c) Y_c

(d) Y_d

(e) Y_e

15.29 The value of R^2 for the regression line is:

(a) less than 0

(b) 0

(c) between 0 and 0.5

(d) 0.5

(e) greater than 0.5

15.30 Verify that the mean of the residuals is 0 for any simple linear regression analysis.

# CHAPTER SIXTEEN

AN INTRODUCTION TO MULTIPLE REGRESSION

In Chapter 15, we were concerned with predicting the number of ice cream bars we could expect to sell at the beach from the daily highest temperature. Our goal was to predict that number as accurately as possible so that we would neither take too much ice cream to the beach nor too little. Because of the linear shape depicted in the scatterplot and the strong relationship between number of ice cream sales and daily highest temperature ($r = 0.887$), we were able to construct a reasonably accurate simple linear regression equation for prediction with $R^2 = 0.78$. But, we can try to do even better. That is, we can consider ways to predict ice cream sales even more accurately.

Alternatively, we can shift our focus away from prediction and consider ways to *explain* the observed variability in ice cream sales. That is, rather than use multiple regression for prediction, we may use it to understand and explain phenomena of interest to us and to study the effects that individual predictor variables have on these phenomena. That is, we can use multiple regression to understand the factors that contribute to ice cream sales at the beach rather than to predict the number of ice cream sales we can expect on a particular day at the beach. Clearly, we have already defined temperature as one explanatory factor. We now seek to identify another factor, in addition to temperature, that explains why people buy ice cream at the beach.

Assuming that our beach example takes place in the northeastern part of the United States, another factor might be relative humidity. Like increases in temperature, increases in relative humidity make us feel more uncomfortably hot. Yet, because relative humidity does not correlate highly with temperature when we consider only the summer months in the northeast, relative humidity offers the potential for tapping a set of reasons related to ice cream sales that is different from temperature. Because temperature and humidity are not highly correlated, we say that they are not *redundant* of each other. In general, to optimize the explanatory power of a multiple regression equation, we seek to add new variables to the equation that do not highly correlate with the other predictor variables already in the equation and that do highly correlate with the outcome variable.

While multiple regression, in general, allows for the inclusion of many predictor variables in the equation, we shall restrict our discussion to the case of only two predictor variables. We do so for simplicity and because the principles and concepts that apply in the case of only two predictor variables in the equation generalize easily to the case of more than two predictor variables in the equation. While five or six or more predictor variables are not uncommon in a regression equation, in practice, it is often difficult to identify more than three predictor variables that each contributes new explanatory information over and above the others. Said differently, in general, R^2 will tend not to increase dramatically as the number of predictor variables increases beyond even a few because the new variables will tend to be redundant with those already in the equation.

THE BASIC EQUATION WITH TWO PREDICTORS

When there are two predictor variables (for example, temperature and humidity) and an outcome variable Y (for example, ice cream sales) in a multiple regression equation, the equation has the following form (notice that we have renamed the constant a as b_0):

$$\hat{Y} = b_0 + b_1X_1 + b_2X_2. \tag{16.1}$$

As in the simple linear regression case, the b's are coefficients of the X variables and b_0 is an additive constant (denoted by a in Chapter 15). The right side of Equation 16.1 is called a *linear composite of the X variables*. As Equation 16.1 suggests, the linear composite is obtained by multiplying X_1 by b_1 and X_2 by b_2 and by adding these two products together with the additive constant b_0 to obtain $\hat{Y}$, the predicted value of Y.

The b's of Equation 16.1 are determined to produce the largest possible correlation between the actual value of Y and the linear composite $\hat{Y}$. Once the b's are determined, the constant b_0 is determined so that on average, the predicted value of Y will equal the actual value of Y. That is, so that the mean of $\hat{Y}$ will equal the mean of Y, $\overline{\hat{Y}} = \overline{Y}$. The additive constant b_0 has the following equation:

$$b_0 = \overline{Y} - (b_1\overline{X}_1 + b_2\overline{X}_2). \tag{16.2}$$

The linear composite and additive constant of Equations 16.1 and 16.2 are based on raw or unstandardized scores. When, on the other hand, the predictor variables are standardized to have mean zero and standard deviation one (when they are in z-score form), we may re-express Equation 16.1 as Equation 16.3:

$$\hat{z}_Y = \beta_1z_1 + \beta_2z_2. \tag{16.3}$$

Here, β's (betas) as opposed to b's are used in Equation 16.3 to indicate that the linear composite is based on z-scores as opposed to raw scores. Because this equation is based on z-scores, the additive constant, b_0, is zero.

☞ **Remark.** Because z_Y, z_1, and z_2 are in standardized form, $\overline{z}_Y = \overline{z}_1 = \overline{z}_2 = 0$. If we substitute these means of zero into Equation 16.2 we find that $b_0 = 0$. Regression equations based on z, or standardized, scores all have additive constants equal to zero.

If the independent X variables are converted to z-scores, then the linear composite of the z-scores, $Z_{\hat{Y}}$, may be obtained using Equation 16.3. One simply multiplies β_1 and β_2 by z_1 and z_2, respectively, and computes the sum of these two products.

As in simple linear regression, the correlation between Y and $\hat{Y}$, or between Z_Y and $Z_{\hat{Y}}$, is denoted by R. In the context of multiple regression, however, R is called a *multiple correlation*. R is also denoted as $R_{Y,\hat{Y}}$ or as $R_{Y.12}$. The latter notation explicitly conveys the fact that $\hat{Y}$ is estimated from an equation that contains two predictor variables, X_1 and X_2.

In the next two sections, we give the equations for b, β, and R. In the first of these sections we consider the case when the two predictors are not correlated. In the second, we consider the more general case when the two predictors are correlated.

EQUATIONS FOR b, β, and $R_{Y.12}$ WHEN THE PREDICTORS ARE NOT CORRELATED

When the two predictors in the regression equation are not correlated (i.e., when $r_{X_1,X_2} = 0$), then b_1 and b_2 are expressed simply as Equation 16.4:

$$
\begin{aligned}
b_1 &= r_{Y,X_1} \frac{S_Y}{S_{X_1}} \\
b_2 &= r_{Y,X_2} \frac{S_Y}{S_{X_2}}.
\end{aligned}
\tag{16.4}
$$

Notice that as Equation 16.4 suggests, when the two predictors are uncorrelated, the b-weight for each predictor is simply the b-weight that would be obtained if that predictor were the only one in the equation. That is, the b-weight of a predictor in an equation with two (or more) uncorrelated predictors is obtained simply by ignoring the remaining predictor(s) and calculating the b-weight as though that predictor were the only one in the equation (as in the case of simple linear regression).

The same applies when the two predictors are uncorrelated and all variables are standardized. The equations for β_1 and β_2 are given by Equation 16.5:

$$
\begin{aligned}
\beta_1 &= r_{Y,X_1} \\
\beta_2 &= r_{Y,X_2}.
\end{aligned}
\tag{16.5}
$$

Here again, each beta-weight is determined as if its corresponding predictor were the only one in the equation, as in the case of simple linear regression.

We may find $R_{Y.12}$ by taking the square root of $R^2_{Y.12}$ using Equation 16.6:

$$
R^2_{Y.12} = r^2_{Y,X_1} + r^2_{Y,X_2}.
\tag{16.6}
$$

As Equation 16.6 suggests, when the two predictors are uncorrelated, the squared multiple correlation, $R^2_{Y.12}$, is simply equal to the sum of the squared correlations between each predictor and the outcome variable.

☞ **Remark.** The correlations r_{Y,X_1} and r_{Y,X_1} are called *zero-order correlations* to distinguish them from the other types of correlation we encounter in multiple regression. For notational simplicity, we shall follow common procedure and express r_{Y,X_1} as r_{Y1} and r_{Y,X_2} as r_{Y2}. Likewise, we shall also express the correlation between predictors r_{X_1,X_2} as r_{12} and the standard deviation of X_1, S_{X_1}, as S_1, and so on for S_{X_2}.

In previous work we have noted that R^2 (or r^2) is a measure of overall fit of the regression model to the data, and is interpreted more specifically as the proportion of Y variance explained by the regression. Accordingly, we may use Figure 16.1 to illustrate Equation 16.6.

In Figure 16.1, each circle represents the variance of one of the variables in the equation, Y, X_1, and X_2 and the amount of overlap between two circles represents their squared

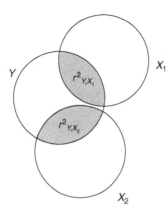

Figure 16.1 The proportion of Y variance explained by the regression when predictors are uncorrelated

correlation. Because X_1 and X_2 are uncorrelated, their circles are non-overlapping. By contrast, X_1 overlaps with Y, and X_2 overlaps with Y, indicating that these two pairs of variables are correlated. The two overlapping areas are shaded and labeled appropriately, r^2_{Y,X_1} and r^2_{Y,X_2}. When X_1 and X_2 are uncorrelated, we may observe quite clearly that the sum of the shaded areas, r^2_{Y,X_1} and r^2_{Y,X_2}, represents the overlap between Y and the two variables taken together, and as such, equals $R^2_{Y.12}$, the proportion of Y variance that is explained by the regression containing X_1 and X_2.

EQUATIONS FOR b, β, and $R_{Y.12}$ When the Predictors Are Correlated

When the predictors are correlated, one cannot ignore the other predictor in the equation when calculating a regression coefficient or the multiple correlation as was the case in the previous section. As a result, the equations for the b-weights and $R_{Y.12}$ are a bit more complex than those given in the previous section. The equation for the b-weights is given in Equation 16.7:

$$b_1 = \frac{r_{Y1} - r_{Y2}r_{12}}{1 - r_{12}^2} \times \frac{S_Y}{S_1}$$
$$b_2 = \frac{r_{Y2} - r_{Y1}r_{12}}{1 - r_{12}^2} \times \frac{S_Y}{S_2}.$$

(16.7)

Equation 16.7 tells us that when the two predictors are correlated, the value of b_1 (both its magnitude and sign) depends upon the correlation between X_1 and Y, denoted r_{Y1}, the correlation between X_2 and Y, denoted r_{Y2}, and the intercorrelation between X_1 and X_2, denoted r_{12}. The same is true for b_2.

☞ **Remark.** When the two predictors are not correlated, when $r_{12} = 0$, Equation 16.7 reduces to Equation 16.4.

Thus, when the predictors of a multiple regression equation are correlated, we do not have the luxury of ignoring the second predictor in the equation when interpreting the importance of the first predictor, and vice versa.

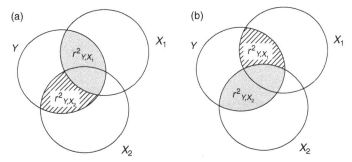

Figure 16.2 (a) The proportion of Y variance explained by X_1 (shaded part) and that part of X_2 unrelated to X_1 (cross-hatched part) (b) The proportion of Y variance explained by X_2 (shaded part) and that part of X_1 unrelated to X_2 (cross-hatched part)

Equation 16.7 reduces to Equation 16.8 when all variables are in standardized form, because the standard deviation of Y, X_1, and X_2 are all equal to 1. Once again, β's are used in place of b's:

$$\beta_1 = \frac{r_{Y1} - r_{Y2}r_{12}}{1 - r_{12}^2}$$
$$\beta_2 = \frac{r_{Y2} - r_{Y1}r_{12}}{1 - r_{12}^2}. \tag{16.8}$$

To help conceptualize the equation for R^2, we present Figures 16.2(a) and (b) which each illustrate the relationships between the correlated predictor variables and the outcome variable. In Figure 16.2(a), the proportion of Y variance explained is expressed as the sum of what is due to X_1 (the shaded part) plus what is due to that part of X_2 unrelated to X_1 (the cross-hatched part). In Figure 16.2(b), the proportion of Y variance explained is expressed as the sum of what is due to X_2 (the shaded part) plus what is due to that part of X_1 unrelated to X_2 (the cross-hatched part).

Equations 16.9(a) and (b) translate what is illustrated, respectively, in Figures 16.2(a) and (b) into an Equation for $R_{Y.12}^2$. Equation 16.9(a) is a direct translation of Figure 16.2(a):

$$R_{Y.12}^2 = r_{Y1}^2 + r_{Y,2(1)}^2, \tag{16.9a}$$

where r_{Y1}^2 equals the proportion of Y variance explained by X_1, $r_{Y,2(1)}^2$ equals the proportion of Y variance explained by X_2 beyond that explained by X_1. And Equation 16.9(b) is a direct translation of Figure 16.2 (b):

$$R_{Y.12}^2 = r_{Y2}^2 + r_{Y,1(2)}^2 \tag{16.9b}$$

where r_{Y2}^2 equals the proportion of Y variance explained by X_2, $r_{Y,1(2)}^2$ equals the proportion of Y variance explained by X_1 beyond that explained by X_2. For both equations, $R_{Y.12}$ is obtained by simply taking the square root.

☞ **Remark.** Both $r_{Y,1(2)}$ and $r_{Y,2(1)}$ are called *semipartial (aka part) correlations*. In particular, $r_{Y,1(2)}^2$ is the semipartial correlation of X_1 squared and may be interpreted as the amount R^2 would drop if X_1 were removed from the equation. Likewise, $r_{Y,2(1)}^2$ is the semipartial correlation of X_2 squared and may be interpreted as the amount R^2 would drop if X_2 were removed from the equation. As we will discuss in more detail later, the semipartial correlation squared is a highly useful measure of the importance of a predictor variable in an equation, and we shall use it as such in our examples in this chapter.

☞ **Remark.** The semipartial correlation of X_1 squared may also be thought of as the *unique contribution* of X_1 to R^2 in the context of the remaining variable in the equation, X_2. An analogous statement may be made for X_2.

SUMMARIZING AND EXPANDING ON SOME IMPORTANT PRINCIPLES OF MULTIPLE REGRESSION

1. R will be high when the predictor variables are each highly correlated with the outcome variable.
2. R will not be less than the highest correlation between any of the predictor variables and the outcome variable.
3. R will be larger when the predictor variables are not redundant of one another, when their intercorrelations are relatively low.
4. R is difficult to estimate from eyeballing the simple, zero-order correlation matrix when the number of predictor variables is large.
5. R based on sample data tends to overestimate the population R. Said differently, the sample R is upwardly biased. The smaller the sample size relative to the number of predictor variables, the more R will be inflated. In situations of prediction, the best way to estimate the extent of inflation is to cross-validate results on a new sample randomly selected from the same population. When there are more than 30 subjects for each predictor variable in the equation, the difference between the sample and cross-validated R's will tend to be small. When, there are fewer than 10 subjects for each predictor variable in the equation, the difference between the sample and cross-validated R will tend to be large.
6. The importance of a predictor variable in an equation is best measured by the amount R^2 would drop if that variable were removed from the equation. This amount may be measured by the squared semipartial (or part) correlation of that variable.
7. The importance of a predictor variable in an equation depends upon what other variables are included in the equation along with that variable. When other variables are included in the equation that correlate strongly with that variable, these other variables will "rob" that variable of some of its unique contribution. As a result, that variable will not appear to be so important in the equation. Of course, if all predictor variables in an equation are highly intercorrelated, none of them will appear to be so important in that equation because they will each "rob" one another of its unique contribution.
8. b_1 measures the *net or marginal effect* of X_1 partialling out or holding constant X_2. Likewise, b_2 measures the net or marginal effect of X_2 partialling out or holding constant X_1. Accordingly, these coefficients are called *partial regression coefficients*. Said differently, the net effect of X_1 equals the *average effect* of X_1 for any given value of X_2; the net effect of X_2 equals the *average effect* of X_2 for any given value of X_1.

9. b_1 and b_2 are calculated on unstandardized values. As a result, the net effects associated with them are measured in terms of the original units of measure for the variables (e.g., in degrees Fahrenheit, in percentage points of relative humidity).

10. β_1 is a standardized partial regression coefficient and measures the net effect of z_1 partialling out or holding constant z_2. Likewise, β_2 is also a standardized partial regression coefficient and measures the net effect of z_2 partialling out or holding constant z_1.

11. β_1 and β_2 coefficients are calculated on standardized values. As a result, the net effects associated with them are measured in standard deviation units rather than in the original units of measure for the variables.

12. In multiple regression, both b's and β's can be greater than 1 or less than −1, even though in the case of simple linear regression, when there is only one predictor variable, β must be between −1 and 1.

Example 16.1 illustrates the points we have made so far in this chapter using our ice cream sales example with humidity included as a predictor variable in addition to temperature.

EXAMPLE 16.1 Given the scenario described in Chapter 15 using the dataset, IceCream, construct a regression equation with both temperature and relative humidity as predictor variables and ice cream sales as the outcome variable. Said differently, construct an equation that regresses ice cream sales on both temperature and relative humidity. The data below contain relative humidity values in addition to daily highest temperature and number of bars sold for each of the thirty days sampled. Interpret the equation as well as the various tests of significance reported in the output.

barsold	temp	relhumid
170	75	70
160	70	72
155	65	73
150	60	72
153	72	70
142	60	72
145	63	60
156	68	70
170	78	73
172	77	85
165	75	70
167	75	70
175	80	89
180	82	95
180	85	98
143	59	75
173	86	82
176	88	88

barsold	temp	relhumid
177	85	93
185	90	97
163	74	70
160	73	75
162	71	73
148	68	68
160	70	78
154	73	72
169	85	72
178	90	95
175	70	88
164	81	65

Solution

MORE R: To perform a multiple regression analysis, we build on the syntax we have used earlier to run a simple linear regression. The general form of the syntax for a multiple regression is:

results = lm(y ~ x1 + x2 + ⋯ + x10)

where y is the outcome variable and the x's are the predictor variables. In the current example, the command would be:

results = lm(IceCream$barsold ~ IceCream$temp + IceCream$relhumid)
summary(results)

To obtain additional correlations related to our regression analysis:

cor.test(IceCream$barsold, IceCream$temp)
cor.test(IceCream$barsold, IceCream$relhumid)
cor.test(IceCream$temp, IceCream$relhumid)

The R output is reproduced and described below

1. From **cor.test(IceCream$barsold, IceCream$temp)**

Pearson's product-moment correlation
data: IceCream$barsold and   IceCream$temp
$t = 10.149$ $df = 28$ p-value = 6.939e-11
alternative hypothesis: true correlation is not equal to 0
95 percent confidence interval: 0.7735616   0.9450732 sample estimates: cor   0.8867125

From **cor.test(IceCream$barsold, IceCream$relhumid)**

Pearson's product-moment correlation
data: IceCream$barsold and   IceCream$relhumid
t = 6.5577   df = 28   p-value = 4.137e-07
alternative hypothesis: true correlation is not equal to 0
95 percent confidence interval: 0.5808154   0.8891983 sample estimates: cor   0.7782383

From **cor.test(IceCream$temp, IceCream$relhumid)**

Pearson's product-moment correlation
data: IceCream$temp and   IceCream$relhumid
$t = 4.5183$ $df = 28$ p-value = 0.0001034
alternative hypothesis: true correlation is not equal to 0
95 percent confidence interval: 0.3773722   0.8182115 sample estimates: cor   0.6493576

We note that the correlations between the outcome variable barsold and the two predictor variables, temp and relhumid, are 0.887 and 0.778, respectively, and that $p < 0.05$ indicating that these relationships are statistically significant. Thus, we may conclude that both predictor variables relate strongly to barsold.

We also may note that temp and relhumid are not uncorrelated as their correlation is 0.649. If we square 0.649, we obtain that approximately 42 percent of the variance of each of these variables is explained by the other.

When we combine the two predictor variables, temp and relhumid, into a regression equation predicting barsold, we can, therefore, expect R to be no smaller than 0.887, the higher of the two correlations with the outcome variable. And, because the two predictor variables are only moderately correlated, we can expect R to exceed 0.887 by a non-negligible amount.

2. From **results = lm(IceCream$barsold ~ IceCream$temp + IceCream$relhumid)**
    summary(results)

Call:
lm(formula = IceCream$barsold ~ IceCream$temp + IceCream$relhumid)
Residuals
Min   IQ   Median   3Q   Max −6.8747   −2.5406   −0.0847   2.6691   10.9952
Coefficients:
Estimate   Std. Error t-value   Pr(> |t|) (Intercept)   67.6216   7.6389   8.852   1.81e-09   ***

Call:

IceCream$temp	0.8778	0.1273	6.894	2.09e-07	***
IceCream$relhumid	0.3970	0.1085	3.659	0.00108	**

Signif. codes: 0 "***"   0.001 "**"   0.01 "*"   0.05 "."   0.1 " " 1

Residual standard error: 4.664 on 27 degrees of freedom
Multiple R-squared:0.8571, Adjusted R-squared:0.8465
F-statistic: 80.99 on 2 and 27 df, p-value: 3.908e-12

According to these regression results, $R^2 = 0.857$ ($R = 0.926$). Thus, temperature and relative humidity *collectively* account for 85.7 percent of ice cream sales variance. While the sample R^2 value is 0.857, we may note that the adjusted R^2 value is 0.847. The small amount of shrinkage from sample to adjusted R^2 is due to the fact that the ratio of subjects to predictor variables exceeds 10:1. For this example, this ratio is 30:2 or 15:1.

We may note as well that R is statistically significant ($F(2, 27) = 80.99$, $p < 0.0005$). The degrees of freedom of 2 and 27 represent, respectively, the number of predictor variables in the equation ($P = 2$) and the sample size minus the number of predictor variables minus 1 ($N - P - 1 = 30 - 2 - 1 = 27$).

Given the coefficients in the output, we note that the multiple regression equation for predicting ice cream sales from both temperature and relative humidity is:

estimated barsold = 67.622 + 0.878*temp + 0.397*relhumid.

We may interpret $b_1 = 0.878$ as follows: For days with a given or specified relative humidity (X_2), each increase in temperature by one degree Fahrenheit is associated with an average increase of 0.878 ice cream bars sold. By this we mean, if we were to compare two groups of days that had the same relative humidity, but differed in temperature by one degree Fahrenheit, then the group with the higher temperature would have 0.878 additional ice cream bars sold, on average. In this sense, b_1 represents the net effect of X_1 (temperature) holding X_2 (relative humidity) constant.

Analogously, we may interpret $b_2 = 0.397$ as follows: For days with a given or specified temperature (X_1), each increase in relative humidity by one percentage point is associated with an average increase of 0.397 ice cream bars sold. By this we mean, if we were to compare two groups of days that had the same temperature, but differed in relative humidity by one percentage point, then the group with the higher relative humidity would have an additional 0.397 ice cream bars sold, on average. In this sense, b_2 represents the net effect of X_2 (relative humidity) holding X_1 (temperature) constant.

A multiple regression equation with one predictor may be represented as a two-dimensional line; with two predictors, it may be represented as a three-dimensional plane as shown in Figure 16.3. As denoted by the plane, which is flat as denoted by the series of parallel lines depicted in it, the slopes of the lines representing the relationship between temp and barsold remain constant at 0.878 across all values of relhumid. Likewise, the slopes of the lines representing the relationship between relhumid and barsold remain constant at 0.397 across all values of temp. For this reason, it makes sense to think of the *b*-weight of temp (0.878) as representing the *average* increase in barsold associated with each unit increase in temp, averaged

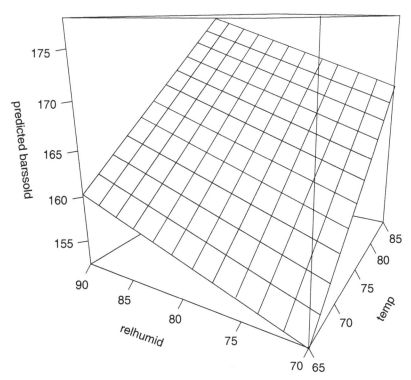

Figure 16.3 A flat plane depicting the regression equation, estimated barsold = 67.622 + 0.878(temp) + 0.397(relhumid)

across the full range of values (levels) of relhumid. Similarly, we may think of the *b*-weight of relhumid (0.397) as representing the *average* increase in barsold associated with each one-unit increase in relhumid, averaged across the full range of values (levels) of temp.

From Equation 16.7, we may note that the relative values of the *b*-coefficients are a function of the relative values of the standard deviations of X_1 and X_2. In particular, the size of a variable's *b*-coefficient varies inversely with that variable's standard deviation; it will be small when its variable's standard deviation is large and large when its variable's standard deviation is small. Accordingly, because a *b*-coefficient is confounded by its variable's standard deviation, *b*-coefficients are not a pure measure of the relative importance of the variables in an equation and cannot be used as such.

To assess the relative importance of variables in an equation, beta coefficients (aka beta weights) are usually more useful because they are based on the standardized values, with each variable having an equal standard deviation of 1.00. To obtain the standardized beta weights of a regression equation, we need to **scale** our variables in the **lm** command as follows (note that the −1 in the command tells R not to estimate an intercept, because intercepts in standardized regression equations are equal to 0):

results = lm(scale(IceCream$barsold) ~ scale(IceCream$temp) + scale(IceCream$relhumid) −1)
summary(results)

Coefficients:					
	Estimate	**Std. Error**	*t*-**value**	**Pr(> |t|)**	
scale(IceCream$temp)	0.65941	0.09393	7.020	0.000000123	***
scale(IceCream$relhumid)	0.35005	0.09393	3.727	0.00087	***

From this coefficients table, we may note that the standardized form of the multiple regression equation is: $z_{\hat{y}} = .659z_1 + .350z_2$. According to this equation, we also may note that temperature is relatively more important than relative humidity in predicting ice cream sales because it receives a higher beta weight.

☞ **Remark.** In general, when there are more than two predictors, the beta weights are not the best measure of relative importance of the variables. The beta weights are not so easily interpreted when the predictor variables are correlated.

☞ **Remark.** Note that for this example the same general conclusion regarding the relative importance of the predictor variables may be obtained from either a comparison of *b*-weights or the beta weights. This is because, in this example, the standard deviation of temperature (11.94) is similar in value to the standard deviation of relative humidity (10.50). That is, the ratio of the two standard deviations is approximately 1:1.

TESTING THE *b*-WEIGHTS FOR STATISTICAL SIGNIFICANCE

Following the same procedures described in Chapter 15, we may test each of the partial regression coefficients for statistical significance by way of the *t*-ratio:

$$t = \frac{b}{\hat{\sigma}_b},$$
(16.10)

where $\hat{\sigma}_b$ equals the standard error of b, the standard deviation of the sampling distribution of b-weights based on random samples of the same size randomly drawn from the same population. This *t*-ratio tests whether the b-coefficient differs from 0 in the population. With P predictor variables in the equation, the *t*-test has $N - P - 1$ degrees of freedom. (In Chapter 15, we considered the case of only one predictor variable in the equation. Thus, P equaled 1 and the degrees of freedom for the *t*-test of the b-weight were noted as being $N - 2$.) If a b-coefficient differs significantly from 0, the variable associated with that b contributes significantly to the prediction over and above the contribution of the other variables.

We may obtain the *t*-ratios for b_1 and b_2 from the output in Example 16.1. The *t*-ratio for b_1 is 6.894 (derived from the *t*-ratio 0.878/0.127) is statistically significant ($p < 0.0005$) and suggests that b_1 is different from zero in the population. We conclude that the temperature is a statistically significant predictor of the number of ice cream bars sold over what is predicted by relative humidity. Likewise, the *t*-ratio for b_2 is 3.659 (derived from the *t*-ratio 0.397/0.108) is statistically significant ($p = 0.001$) and suggests that b_2 is different from zero in the population. We conclude that the relative humidity is a statistically significant predictor of the number of ice cream bars sold over what is predicted by temperature.

We further noted that the overall regression equation containing both temperature and relative humidity is statistically significant and that, therefore, temperature and relative humidity *collectively* predict ice cream sales. From the *t*-test results, we now know that *individually* temperature and relative humidity each contributes uniquely to the prediction of ice cream sales beyond the contribution of the other variable in the model.

To estimate the respective values of the *b*-coefficients in the population we may use confidence intervals as described in Chapter 15. The two-tailed 95 percent confidence intervals for b_1 and b_2 in Example 16.1 may be obtained from the table of coefficients associated with the **conf.int** command. We may note from the following output that reasonable estimates of b_1 in the population are between 0.617 and 1.139, while reasonable estimates of b_2 in the population are between 0.174 and 0.620. While there is some overlap between the two estimates, b_1 is likely to be the larger of the two weights in the population.

	2.5%	97.5%
(Intercept)	51.9479453	83.2952947
IceCream$temp	0.6165560	1.1391212
IceCream$relhumid	0.1743992	0.6195666

ASSESSING THE RELATIVE IMPORTANCE OF THE PREDICTOR VARIABLES IN THE EQUATION

As noted earlier, while the beta weights are often useful in assessing the relative importance of the predictor variables in an equation, a preferred approach is to use the amount R^2 will drop when that variable is removed from the equation, or equivalently, the amount R^2 will increase when that variable is added to the equation last.

The amount R^2 will drop when X_2, for example, is removed from an equation that contains both X_1 and X_2 equals the cross-hatched area of Figure 16.2(a). Likewise, the amount R^2 will drop when X_1 is removed from the equation that contains both X_1 and X_2 equals the cross-hatched area of Figure 16.2(b).

Without X_2, R^2 would only be equal to r_{Y1}^2 as it would no longer include the cross-hatched area of Figure 16.2(a). Without X_1, R^2 would only be equal to r_{Y2}^2 as it would no longer include the cross-hatched area of Figure 16.2(b).

From Equation 16.9(a), we know that the cross-hatched area of Figure 16.2(a) may be expressed directly as $r_{Y,2(1)}^2$, defined earlier as the square of the semipartial (or part) correlation of X_2. From Equation 16.9(b), we know that the cross-hatched area of Figure 16.2(b) may be expressed directly as $r_{Y,1(2)}^2$, defined earlier as the square of the semipartial (or part) correlation of X_1.

☞ **Remark.** As the cross-hatched area of Figure 16.2(a) suggests, the square of the semipartial (aka part) correlation of X_2 may be defined more explicitly as the square of the correlation between Y and that part of X_2 uncorrelated with (or orthogonal to) X_1. The part of X_2 uncorrelated with (or orthogonal to) X_1 is that part of X_2 that remains after removing the linear relationship of X_2 with X_1, likewise for the semipartial correlation of X_1.

Thus, to assess the relative importance of temperature and relative humidity in Example 16.1, we may use the values of their semipartial correlations, which may be obtained using the **ppcor** library in R. To access the functions within this package, it must first be installed through the **install.packages("ppcor")** command, and then loaded each time R is reopened using the **library(ppcor)** command.

spcor.test(IceCream$barsold, IceCream$temp, IceCream$relhumid) provides the semipartial correlation for temp, with output shown below:

estimate	p.value	statistic	n	gp	Method
0.5014674	0.005582367	3.011756	30	1	pearson

spcor.test(IceCream$barsold, IceCream$relhumid, IceCream$temp) provides the semipartial correlation for relhumid, with output shown below:

estimate	p.value	statistic	n	gp	Method
0.2662055	0.1627632	1.435025	30	1	pearson

From these results, we note that the semipartial correlations of temperature (X_1) and relative humidity (X_2), are respectively 0.501 and 0.266, and semipartial correlations squared may be calculated to be 0.251 and 0.071, respectively. Therefore, the amount that the overall R^2 of 0.857 would drop if temperature were removed from the equation is 0.251, and the amount that the overall R^2 of 0.857 would drop if relative humidity were removed from the equation is 0.071. From these statistics, it is clear that temperature is the more important variable of the two.

MEASURING THE DROP IN R^2 DIRECTLY: AN ALTERNATIVE TO THE SQUARED SEMIPARTIAL CORRELATION

If we so choose, we may carry out a series of regression analyses to obtain the amount that R^2 will drop when a variable is removed from the equation. In particular, to find the amount that R^2 will drop when temperature is removed from the equation with both temperature and humidity, we construct one regression equation with both temperature and humidity to obtain $R^2_{Y.12}$. We then construct another equation without temperature to obtain $R^2_{Y.2}$. The difference, $R^2_{Y.12} - R^2_{Y.2}$ is the amount by which $R^2_{Y.12}$ will drop when temperature is removed from the equation.

For our example, we find that $R^2_{Y.12} = 0.857$ and $R^2_{Y.2} = 0.605$, and that therefore, $R^2_{Y.12} - R^2_{Y.2} = 0.252$, which is the amount R^2 drops when temperature is removed from the equation. Notice that, within rounding error, this amount equals $(0.501)^2$, the square of the part correlation for temperature.

We may use an analogous procedure to find $R^2_{Y.12} - R^2_{Y.1}$, the drop in R^2 when humidity is removed from the equation. As before, this amount equals the part correlation of humidity squared.

EVALUATING THE STATISTICAL SIGNIFICANCE OF THE CHANGE IN R^2

Intuitively, it should make sense that whenever the b-weight of a predictor variable is statistically significant, the increase in R^2 obtained when that variable is added last to the equation will also be statistically significant. It can be shown that the t-test of the statistical significance of the b-weight of a predictor variable is equivalent to the corresponding F-test associated with the increase in R^2 when that variable is added last to the equation.

Consider the following two equations, the first with only X_1 and the second with both X_1 and X_2:

$$\begin{aligned} \hat{Y} &= b_0 + b_1 X_1 \\ \hat{Y} &= b_0 + b_1 X_1 + b_2 X_2 \end{aligned}. \tag{16.11}$$

Because the two models represented in Equation 16.11 are different, in general, we would expect the b_1 and b_0 values to be different in the two equations as well.

The squared multiple correlations of the first and second equations are designated $R^2_{Y.1}$ and $R^2_{Y.12}$, respectively. As discussed earlier, a test of whether the effect of X_2 (relative humidity), controlling for X_1 (temperature), is statistically significant is given by the t-test of b_2 that appears in the output ($t(27) = 3.659, p = 0.001$) associated with the **lm** command. Alternatively, it is given by the following associated F-test of the increment in R^2 due to X_2:

$$F_{(1, N-2-1)} = \frac{(R^2_{Y.12} - R^2_{Y.1})/1}{(1 - R^2_{Y.12})/(N-2-1)}. \tag{16.12}$$

For our ice cream example, we have $R^2_{Y.12} = 0.857, R^2_{Y.1} = 0.787$, and $N = 30$. Substituting these values into Equation 16.12 and simplifying we find that $F_{(1,27)} = \dfrac{0.07}{0.143/27} = \dfrac{0.07}{0.00529} = 13.22$, which equals within rounding error $t^2 = 3.659^2 = 13.39$.

Likewise, the t-test on the b-weight of temperature, b_1 in our equation is equivalent to the F-test associated with the increase in R^2 when temperature is added last to the equation (when it is added to the equation that already includes relative humidity).

MORE R: To test the statistical significance of the change in R^2 of two nested equations.

Because the first Equation 16.11 includes only X_1 and the second equation includes both X_1 and X_2, the first equation is said to be *nested* within the second equation. Accordingly, to evaluate the statistical significance of the change in R^2 for these two nested equations, we may use the **anova** command:

results1 = lm(IceCream$barsold ~ IceCream$temp)
results2 = lm(IceCream$barsold ~ IceCream$temp + IceCream$relhumid)
anova(results1, results2)

Note: This set of commands will run two separate regressions, saving the first as **results1** and the second as **results2**. The first will regress barsold on temp. The second will regress barsold on both temp and relhumid. The use of the **anova** command will test whether the change in R^2 between the first and second models is statistically significant.

The relevant output follows:

Analysis of variance table
Model 1:   IceCream\$barsold ~ IceCream\$temp
Model 2:   IceCream\$barsold ~ IceCream\$temp + IceCream\$relhumid

	Res. Df	RSS	df	Sum of sq.	F	Pr(>F)	
1	20	878.77					
2	27	587.41	1	291.35	13.392	0.001081	**

Looking at the last row of the output, we have $F(1, 27) = 13.39$ with $p = 0.001$. We conclude that relative humidity explains a statistically significant proportion of variance in ice cream sales over and above what was explained by temperature.

THE *b*-WEIGHT AS A PARTIAL SLOPE IN MULTIPLE REGRESSION

Recall that in the case of simple regression, the single *b*-weight or regression coefficient is interpreted as a slope that signifies the expected average change in the outcome variable, Y, for each unit increase in the predictor variable, X. Just as b is the slope of the line that relates Y to X, we can also describe b_1 and b_2 as slopes, or more precisely, as *partial slopes*. In particular, b_1 can be described as the slope of the line that relates Y to X_1 after X_2 *is partialled from X_1*. Likewise, b_2 can be described as the slope of the line that relates Y to X_2 after X_1 *is partialled from X_2*. X_1 with X_2 partialled from it may be represented graphically as the shaded area of Figure 16.4(a). Likewise, X_2 with X_1 partialled from it may be represented graphically as the shaded area of Figure 16.4(b). As Figures 16.4(a) and (b) indicate, what remains of X_1 after X_2 is partialled from it is that part of X_1 unrelated (or orthogonal) to X_2, and what remains of X_2 after X_1 is partialled from it is that part of X_2 unrelated (or orthogonal) to X_1.

If we wanted to create a new variable that represents the shaded part of Figure 16.4(a), for example, we may do so by setting up a simple regression equation to predict X_1 from X_2 as shown in Equation 16.13:

$$\hat{X}_1 = b_0 + bX_2 \qquad\qquad (16.13)$$

and then compute $X_1 - \hat{X}_1$. Recall that $X_1 - \hat{X}_1$ is also called the residual of X_1 after accounting for X_2 and may be denoted as $X_{1.2}$. It is that part of X_1 (temp) orthogonal to X_2 (relhumid). Analogously, to find $X_{2.1}$ we compute $X_2 - \hat{X}_2$, where $\hat{X}_2$ is obtained from Equation 16.14:

$$\hat{X}_2 = b_0 + bX_1. \qquad\qquad (16.14)$$

Figure 16.4 (a) That part of X_1 unrelated (orthogonal) to X_2. (b) That part of X_2 unrelated (orthogonal) to X_1

Relating this discussion to our ice cream example, X_1 represents temperature and X_2 represents relative humidity. We may create the new variables $X_{1.2}$ and $X_{2.1}$ by constructing the respective simple regression Equations 16.13 and 16.14, and obtaining the two respective residuals $X_1 - \hat{X}_1$ and $X_2 - \hat{X}_2$. In so doing we will be creating that part of temperature unrelated to humidity ($X_{1.2}$) and that part of humidity unrelated to temperature ($X_{2.1}$). Note that the correlation between ($X_{1.2}$) and ($X_{2.1}$) is 0.

We use R to create the new variable $X_{1.2}$ and show that b_1, which equals 0.878, is simply the slope of the regression line that predicts Y from $X_{1.2}$. In Exercise 16.10 you will show that b_2, which equals 0.397, is simply the slope of the regression line that predicts Y from $X_{2.1}$.

MORE R: To create the variable $X_{1.2}$ that depicts that part of X_1 orthogonal to X_2, we use the **lm** command to regress one predictor variable X_1 (temp) on X_2 (relhumid). We then generate the set of unstandardized residuals, representing that part of X_1 (temp) that is orthogonal to X_2 (relhumid):

results3 = lm(IceCream\$temp ~ IceCream\$relhumid)
results3\$resid

Table 16.1 contains the results of the R analysis that we use to show that b_1, which is 0.878, equals the *b*-weight in the simple regression equation that predicts ice cream sales (Y) from that part of temperature unrelated or orthogonal to humidity ($X_{1.2}$). In so doing, we can begin to appreciate why b_1 is described as a *partial slope*.

EXAMPLE 16.2 Use the data of Table 16.1 to predict ice cream sales (Y) from that part of temperature unrelated to humidity ($X_{1.2}$) and show that the *b*-weight of $X_{1.2}$ is equal to b_1, the *b*-weight associated with temperature in the regression equation containing both temperature and humidity. For this to be the case, the simple *b*-weight from this analysis should equal 0.878.

Solution To find the slope, *b*, of the simple regression equation that predicts number of ice cream sales from that part of temperature unrelated to humidity, we use the linear regression procedure with ice cream sales as the outcome variable and $X_{1.2}$, the unstandardized residual, as the predictor variable. The following output is obtained as part of our results:

Coefficients:

	Estimate	Std Error	*t*-value	Pr(> |t|)	
(Intercept)	164.2333	1.9141	85.803	<0.0000000000000002	***
results3\$resid	0.8778	0.2862	3.067	0.00476	**

Notice that, as expected, $b = 0.878$.

TABLE 16.1 Data to illustrate that b_1 is a partial slope

Ice cream bars sold (Y)	Temperature (X_1)	That part of temperature unrelated to humidity ($\mathbf{X}_{1.2}=X_1-\hat{X}_1$)
170	75	4.30772
160	70	−1.79864
155	65	−7.35182
150	60	−11.79864
153	72	1.30772
142	60	−11.79864
145	63	−2.16048
156	68	−2.69228
170	78	5.64818
172	77	−1.98999
165	75	4.30772
167	75	4.30772
175	80	−1.20271
180	82	−2.52179
180	85	−1.18133
143	59	−14.45819
173	86	8.66955
176	88	7.35047
177	85	1.58457
185	90	4.37185
163	74	3.30772
160	73	−.45819
162	71	−1.35182
148	68	−1.58592
160	70	−5.11773
154	73	1.20136
169	85	13.20136
178	90	5.47821
175	70	−10.64953
164	81	13.07362

MULTIPLE REGRESSION WHEN ONE OF THE TWO PREDICTOR VARIABLES IS DICHOTOMOUS

In the examples presented thus far in this chapter, the predictor variables, temperature and relative humidity, were at least interval-leveled. We consider in Example 16.3 the situation in which one of the two predictor variables is dichotomous.

EXAMPLE 16.3 Using the NELS dataset, regress twelfth grade self-concept (slfcnc12) on both eighth grade self-concept (slfcnc08) and gender. In doing so, determine the extent to which twelfth grade self-concept variance is explained collectively by eighth grade self-concept and gender. In addition, determine whether eighth grade self-concept is associated with twelfth grade self-concept after gender is controlled for and whether gender is associated with twelfth grade self-concept after eighth grade self-concept is controlled for.

Solution Using the same commands as for Example 16.1, we obtain the following results. The following output shows a statistically significant moderate positive correlation between twelfth grade and eighth grade self-concept ($r = 0.444$, $p < 0.001$).

Pearson's product-moment correlation
data: NELS$slfcnc12
and NELS$slfcnc08
$t = 11.045$ $df = 498$ p-value < 2.2e-16
alternative hypothesis: true correlation is not equal to 0
95 percent confidence interval: 0.3702860   0.5113731
sample estimates: cor   0.4435735

Furthermore, there is a statistically significant yet low correlation between twelfth grade self-concept and gender ($r = -0.161$, $p < 0.001$).

Pearson's product-moment correlation
data: NELS$slfcnc12
and as.numeric(NELS$gender)
$t = -3.634$ df = 498   p-value = 0.000308
alternative hypothesis: true correlation is not equal to 0
95 percent confidence interval: −0.24496482   −0.07408034
sample estimates: cor   −0.1607268

The first correlation indicates that students who had relatively low self-concept in eighth grade tended also to have relatively low self-concept in twelfth grade and that students who had relatively high self-concept in eighth grade tended also to have relatively high self-concept in twelfth grade. Given the coding for gender (1 for male, 2 for female), the negative correlation implies that on average males have higher self-concept scores than females in twelfth grade.

Pearson's product-moment correlation
data: NELS$slfcnc08
and as.numeric(NELS$gender)
$t = -4.3471$ df = 498   p-value = 1.674e-05
alternative hypothesis: true correlation is not equal to 0
95 percent confidence interval: −0.2742946   −0.1052776
sample estimates: cor   −0.191203

The above output shows that the statistically significant intercorrelation between the two predictor variables is also low ($r = -0.191$) and implies, as before, that on average males have higher scores than females in eighth grade as well.

```
Coefficients:
                    Estimate   Std error   t-value   Pr(> |t|)
(Intercept)         21.17430   1.18328     17.895    <2e-16     ***
NELS$slfcnc08        0.51894   0.04942     10.501    <2e-16     ***
NELS$genderFemale   −1.14327   0.59205     −1.931    0.054

Signif. codes:   0 "***"  0.001 "**"  0.01 "*" 0.05 "." 0.1 " " 1

Residual standard error: 6.47 on 497 degrees of freedom
Multiple R-squared: 0.2027, Adjusted R-squared: 0.1995
F-statistic: 63.19 on 2 and 497 df, p-value: < 2.2e-16
```

Given that R^2 equals 0.2027, we know that $R = 0.450$; namely, that a linear composite of gender and eighth grade self-concept maximally correlates $R = 0.450$ with twelfth grade self-concept. Because 0.450 is only marginally greater than 0.444, the simple, zero-order correlation between twelfth grade and eighth grade self-concept, we can infer that gender is likely to be contributing little, if anything at all, to the equation over and above eighth grade self-concept. Said differently, gender does not appear to relate to twelfth grade self-concept after eighth grade self-concept is accounted for.

We may determine the proportion of variance accounted for by gender over and above eighth grade self-concept by examining the R^2 values. We know that the overall R^2 with both eighth grade self-concept and gender in the equation is 0.203. Thus, collectively, eighth grade self-concept and gender account for 20.3 percent of twelfth grade self-concept variation. From the correlation output, we know that eighth grade self-concept, by itself, accounts for $r^2 = 0.444^2 = 0.197$ of twelfth grade self-concept variance. The difference between 0.203 and 0.197 is the proportion of twelfth grade self-concept variance due to gender after eighth grade self-concept is accounted for. This difference, at 0.006, is certainly negligible, suggesting again that gender does not have much explanatory power over and above eighth grade self-concept.

To assess the statistical significance of the individual, unique contribution of each variable and to obtain the regression equation itself, we consult the above output of coefficients.

The unstandardized regression equation is:

estimated slfcnc12 = 21.174 + (.519)(slfcnc08) − (1.143)(gender).

According to the significance values associated with the t-tests on the regression coefficients, we may note that while eighth grade self-concept is statistically significant, gender is not. This result is consistent with what our earlier analysis based on the correlations showed.

Because the b-weight associated with eighth grade self-concept is statistically significant, we may say that controlling for gender, every one-point increase in eighth grade self-concept associates with a 0.519-point increase in twelfth grade self-concept on average. Because the b-weight associated with gender is not statistically significant, we know that after controlling for eighth grade self-concept, the magnitude of the difference in twelfth grade self-concept between males and females is not likely to be different from zero. That is, the gender difference in twelfth grade self-concept represented by the statistically significant zero-order correlation coefficient between gender and twelfth grade self-concept appears to be explained by the difference in self-concept in eighth grade. Said differently, gender differences in twelfth grade self-concept do not exist after partialling out or controlling for eighth grade self-concept.

☞ **Remark.** Notice that if we subtract the male mean from the female mean we obtain −1.143, the value of the *b*-weight associated with gender. Hence, as noted earlier, the *b*-weight associated with the dichotomous variable equals the difference between the outcome variable means for the two groups represented by the dichotomy. In our example, it equals the difference between the twelfth grade self-concept means for males and females (30.961 − 32.104 = −1.143). Because the *b*-weight associated with gender is not statistically significant, we know that after controlling for eighth grade self-concept, the populations of males and females are not different, on average, in terms of twelfth grade self-concept.

EXAMPLE 16.4 The Basketball file contains data regarding the top 20 scoring professional basketball players in the United States for the 2014–2015 season. The commands used to obtain the results for this problem are in the solution to this example. They also may be found in the .R file associated with this chapter.

1. Obtain summary statistics for average number of points scored per game (points) and weight in pounds (weightlb) as well as the correlation between these two variables. Obtain the regression equation for predicting points from weightlb.
2. Interpret the regression equation.
3. If you were a scout for a professional basketball team, this result would imply that you should recommend hiring as team members heavier players over lighter ones. Does this conclusion make sense?
4. Construct a scatterplot with points on the vertical axis and weightlb on the horizontal axis. Superimpose the fitted regression line on this scatterplot. Verify that the regression line passes through the point (21.95, 202.70), the respective means of the variables, points and weightlb.
5. Redo the scatterplot, coloring each observation by gender to generate (a) a scatterplot of all points labelled by gender, (b) a regression line fitted to the female points, and (c) a regression line fitted to the male points.
6. Describe the slope of each of the regression lines. Do they convey the same positive relationship that the total regression line did?
7. Obtain the regression equation for predicting points from both weightlb and gender. Is the coefficient for weightlb still positive and statistically significant?
8. What is the moral of this example?

Solution
1. We use the following commands to answer part 1:

   mean(Basketball$points)
   sd(Basketball$points)
   mean(Basketball$weightlb)
   sd(Basketball$weightlb)
   cor.test(Basketball$points, Basketball$weightlb)
   results = lm(Basketball$points ~ Basketball$weightlb)
   summary(results)

The mean and standard deviation of the variables points and weightlb respectively are: mean = 21.95, sd = 4.47 and mean = 202.70, sd = 38.28. The correlation between the two variables is 0.709.

The regression equation is:

predicted points = 5.153 + 0.083(weightlb)

The *t*-value associated with the coefficient for weightlb is $t = 4.266$, $p < 0.0005$, suggesting that the relationship between weight in pounds and points scored per game is statistically significant.

2. According to the *b*-coefficient, each pound increase in a player's weight is associated with an average of 0.083 additional points scored per game.

3. Something seems awry with this result, as such a conclusion does not make sense. Perhaps an important variable has been omitted from the regression model that results in a biased estimate of the coefficient for weightlb.

4. We use the commands below to create the following graph:

plot(Basketball$points~Basketball$weightlb, xlab = "Weight", ylab = "Points", pch = 16)
abline(lm(Basketball$points ~ Basketball$weightlb))

Yes, from the graphic, we note that the regression line does pass through (21.95, 202.70), the respective means of points and weightlb.

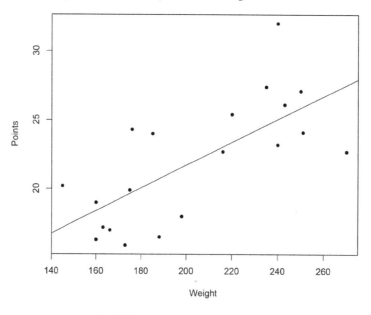

5. To generate the following graph, we use the commands below.

plot(Basketball$points~Basketball$weightlb, xlab = "Weight", ylab = "Points", pch = 16, col = Basketball$gender)
abline(lm(Basketball$points[Basketball$gender == "Male"] ~ Basketball$weightlb [Basketball$gender == "Male"]))
abline(lm(Basketball$points[Basketball$gender == "Female"] ~ Basketball$weightlb [Basketball$gender == "Female"]), col = "red")
legend("topleft", c("Male", "Female"), pch = 16, col = c(1,2))

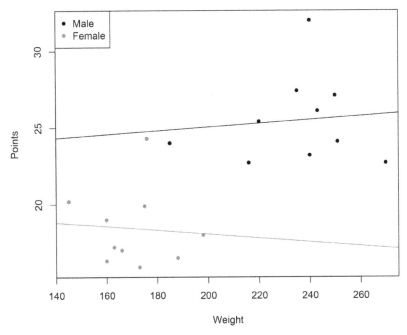

6. The slope of the regression line for males is positive, although close to zero, and the slope of the regression line for females is negative, although also close to zero, suggesting that when gender is held constant, the magnitude of the relationship between points and weight is near zero. The partial relationship between points and weightlb controlling for gender makes more sense than the earlier result based on the total set of points, without controlling for gender. As suggested by the scatterplot of part 5, the earlier positive coefficient for weightlb based on the total set of scores is a result of having combined the two genders into a single analysis, and the fact that one gender, females, has both lower weight and lower average points scored than the male gender.

7. We use the command: **lm(Basketball\$points ~ Basketball\$weightlb + Basketball\$gender)** to obtain the regression equation with both regressors in the equation:

predicted points = 24.358 + 0.005(weightlb) – 6.734(gender)

The t-value associated with the coefficient for weightlb is $t = 0.142$, $p = 0.889$, suggesting that the (partial) relationship between weight in pounds and points scored per game after controlling for gender is no longer statistically significant.

8. By omitting from a regression equation a variable that correlates with the outcome variable as well as with a regressor in the equation in whose coefficient we are interested in estimating, we obtain a biased estimate of that coefficient; that is, the coefficient will be either too big or too small. In this example, omitting gender from the regression equation resulted in an estimate of the coefficient of weightlb that was too big. We have seen another instance of "the omitted variable problem" in our kidney stone example in Chapter 12. In that example, the severity of the kidney stone was the omitted variable, which we called a confounder.

CONTROLLING VARIABLES STATISTICALLY: A CLOSER LOOK

As Example 16.4, Exercise 16.16, and the kidney stone example of Chapter 12 make amply clear, when we omit even one critical variable from an analysis, our results and our conclusions based on those results are often in error. Said differently, when critical variables are statistically controlled for (held constant, accounted for, or partialled out), our conclusions can be radically different.

One well-known example of this is the Berkeley sex-bias case in the 1970s. The University of California-Berkeley was sued for bias against women applying to graduate school. The admission figures showed that men applying were more likely than women to be admitted, and the difference was so large that it was unlikely to be due to chance (Bickel et al., 1975). When examining the individual departments (i.e., controlling for departments), however, it was found that no department was significantly biased against women. In fact, most departments had a small bias against men. The incorrectness of the initial interpretation came about because of what is called *self-selection*: women tended to apply to departments with low rates of admission; men tended to apply to departments with high rates of admission. As a result, in order to obtain a correctly specified model, one that would not produce self-selection bias, it was critical, in this case, to control for the variable for department in the model. The question of which variables to control for in a particular model falls under the general heading of what is called *model specificity*.

Although this term may be unfamiliar, as readers of the popular press, there is little doubt that you all have been concerned about model specificity on at least one occasion. You encounter headlines that shout, for example: those who are first-born children have higher IQs than those who are later-born; daily soft drinks, diet and regular, can lead to diabetes and heart problems; and red wine is effective in preventing heart attacks. On reading these headlines, we often ask, "but did the researcher control for … ?" We do so to be assured that the results reported provide information that is meaningful.

Given a list of relevant variables that are important to control for in a study, as described in Chapter 12, one may do so, for example, by using an experimental design that utilizes random assignment of cases to treatment and control groups, if one were particularly interested in drawing causal conclusions from the results. Another way is by using regression analysis.

For example, in a study on the gender gap in faculty salaries at a university, in order to obtain a meaningful result, among the relevant variables that would need to be controlled for are a faculty member's tenure status, year of PhD, academic rank (assistant, associate, or full professor), discipline of study, age, administrative positions held, etc. In this analysis, salary would be the outcome variable, the above-mentioned list would be the set of control variables, and gender would be the single research variable to be tested for statistical significance. If after controlling for the set of control variables, gender is statistically significant, we would conclude that there is a gender gap in faculty salaries, otherwise not.

A HYPOTHETICAL EXAMPLE

Consider the following very simple (simulated) dataset that consists of the number of hours eight individuals spend at the gym on a weekly basis along with measures of their upper body strength. The dataset is labeled UpperBodyStrength. The graphic representing the values in this dataset is given by Figure 16.5.

Figure 16.5 Upper body strength by weekly hours at gym

A simple regression analysis on the eight cases yields the following results:

Coefficients:

	Estimate	**Std. Error**	**t-value**	**Pr(> |t|)**	
(Intercept)	8.9634	1.7746	5.051	0.00233	**
UpperBodyStrength$gym	−0.6098	0.2449	−2.490	0.04718	*

Signif. codes: 0 "***" 0.001 "**" 0.01 "*" 0.05 "." 0.1 " " 1

Residual standard error: 2.218 on 6 degrees of freedom
Multiple *R*-squared: 0.5081, Adjusted *R*-squared: 0.4262
F-statistic: 6.198 on 1 and 6 *df*, *p*-value: 0.04718

Based on these results, we have the following model:

$$\hat{Y} = 8.96 - 0.61X,$$

where $\hat{Y}$ = strength and X = gym. This suggests, unfortunately, that longer sessions at the gym associates with *lower* upper body strength! We know that cannot be right.

So, we begin to think in terms of what variable(s) we might have omitted from this model, that if added, would give us a more meaningful result. Given men are known to have greater upper body strength than women, there is likely to be a correlation between gender and upper body strength, which could mean that the relationship reported between hours at the gym and upper body strength does not reflect the unique relationship between upper body strength and hours at the gym, but rather one that incorporates the explanatory power of gender. To obtain a more accurate assessment of the unique relationship between upper body strength and hours at the gym that is not shared with gender, we fit a regression line separately to males and females using the two commands:

results_male = lm(UpperBodyStrength$strength[UpperBodyStrength$gender == "male"]~UpperBodyStrength$gym[UpperBodyStrength$gender == "male"])
results_female = lm(UpperBodyStrength$strength[UpperBodyStrength$gender == "female"]~UpperBodyStrength$gym[UpperBodyStrength$gender == "female"])

We obtain the following two regression lines, where $\hat{Y}$ = strength and X = gym, for:

$$\text{males: } \hat{Y} = 4 + X,$$
$$\text{females: } \hat{Y} = 7 + X$$

From these results, we are relieved to see that the relationship for each group is now positive. The regression coefficient for females is +1 and likewise for males, indicating that each additional hour of time spent at the gym is associated with an increase in one unit of upper body strength on average.

Rather than fitting a separate regression line for males and females, we may obtain these same results by using a more parsimonious approach by adding a dichotomous group membership variable, which we call Z, to the regression equation. That equation would have the following general form:

$$\hat{Y} = b_0 + b_1X + b_2Z,$$

where X represents time spent at the gym, and Z is coded 0 for males and 1 for females. We fit this new model to the entire sample and obtain the following result:

$$\hat{Y} = 4 + X - 11Z.$$

We may verify that this single regression equation yields the same result as the two separate regression equations by substituting the values of 0 and 1 for Z as follows:

$$\text{for females: } \hat{Y} = 4 + X - 11(1) = -7 + X;$$
$$\text{for males: } \hat{Y} = 4 + X - 11(0) = 4 + X.$$

By adding the variable Z to the model to represent gender, we have, in effect, fit two separate regression equations for predicting upper body strength, one for females and one for males. Said differently, the Z-variable serves to control for gender in the model; it allows the model to be *conditioned* on gender in addition to weekly hours at the gym. Using this model, we are now able to answer the question: "What can we expect one's upper body strength to be, given a particular number of hours at the gym (e.g., $X = 3$) and a particular gender (e.g. $Z = 0$)?"

This is what is meant by statistical control – what can we expect the response, Y, to be conditioned on, or holding constant (fixed at a particular value), all other predictor/regressor variables?

With each new relevant variable we add to the regression equation, we produce a more tailored fit of the model to our data seeking to explain more accurately the variance of our outcome of interest.

CONDUCTING POWER ANALYSES FOR MULTIPLE REGRESSION

In this section, we will use R's **pwr** library and **pwr.f2.test** command to illustrate how to find the sample size for testing the significance of R^2 in multiple regression based on all the predictors in the model to be tested for significance, which would be two in this case. As shown in Table 10.3, we shall use f^2 as the effect size index for regression, and follow

Cohen's (1988) guidelines to describe f^2 values of 0.02, 0.15, and 0.35 as small, medium, and large effect sizes, respectively.

As in previous applications of the power command, we illustrate with power = 0.80, α = 0.05, and a medium effect size.

•••

EXAMPLE 16.5 Use R's **pwr.f2.test** command to determine the sample size required to detect with power = 0.80 and α = 0.05 whether a medium effect size (f^2 = 0.15, corresponding to Cohen's medium effect size (see Table 10.3)) is statistically significantly different from zero based on a total model that contains two predictors to be tested for significance.

Solution The power command and obtained results for this example are:

pwr.f2.test(u = 2, f2 = 0.15, sig.level = 0.05, power = 0.8)

Here, **u** is the number of predictors in the model, equal to 2 for our example. We get the following output:

Multiple regression power calculation		
u	=	2
v	=	64.31932
f2	=	0.15
sig.level	=	0.05
power	=	0.8

The resulting output provides a value for **v**, which represents the degrees of freedom of the F test. We may calculate the sample size through the formula **n = v + u + 1**. Therefore, for this example, the minimum sample size needed is equal to 64.319 + 2 + 1 = 67.319, or 68.

SUMMARY OF R COMMANDS

Create	Command lines
Perform a multiple regression of barsold on temp and relhumid (Example 16.1)	**results = lm(IceCream$barsold ~ IceCream $temp + IceCream$relhumid)** **summary(results)**
Perform a multiple regression of barsold on temp and relhumid with standardized beta coefficients	**results = lm(scale(IceCream$barsold) ~ scale(IceCream$temp) + scale(IceCream $relhumid) -1)** **summary(results)**
Calculate the semipartial correlations for each of two predictor variables (temp and relhumid) with the outcome variable barsold	**spcor.test(IceCream$barsold, IceCream $temp, IceCream$relhumid)** **spcor.test(IceCream$barsold, IceCream $relhumid, IceCream$temp)**
Test the statistical significance of the change in R^2 of two nested equations	**results1 = lm(IceCream$barsold ~ IceCream$temp)**

Create	Command lines
where the first equation includes only X_1 and the second equation includes both X_1 and X_2 Regress one predictor variable, X_1 (temp), on another, X_2 (relhumid). Then generate the set of unstandardized residuals, representing that part of X_1 (temp) that is orthogonal to X_2 (relhumid) (Example 16.2)	results2 = lm(IceCream$barsold ~ IceCream$temp + IceCream$relhumid) anova(results1, results2) results3 = lm(IceCream$temp ~ IceCream$relhumid) results3$resid
Obtain pairwise correlations and run a multiple regression analysis with one interval-leveled predictor variable and one dichotomous predictor variable (Example 16.3)	cor.test(NELS$slfcnc12, NELS$slfcnc08) cor.test(NELS$slfcnc12, as.numeric (NELS$gender)) cor.test(NELS$slfcnc08, as.numeric (NELS$gender)) results = lm(NELS$slfcnc12 ~ NELS $slfcnc08 + NELS$gender summary(results)
Construct a scatterplot with points on the vertical axis and weightlb on the horizontal axis. Superimpose the fitted regression line on this scatterplot (Example 16.4(d))	plot(Basketball$points~Basketball $weightlb, xlab = "Weight", ylab = "Points", pch = 16) abline(lm(Basketball$points ~ Basketball $weightlb))
Construct a scatterplot with points on the vertical axis and weightlb on the horizontal axis, coloring each observation by gender to generate (1) a scatterplot of all points labeled by gender, (2) a regression line fitted to the female points, and (3) a regression line fitted to the male points (Example 16.4(e))	plot(Basketball$points~Basketball $weightlb, xlab = "Weight", ylab = "Points", pch = 16, col = Basketball $gender) abline(lm(Basketball$points[Basketball $gender == "Male"] ~ Basketball $weightlb[Basketball$gender == "Male"])) abline(lm(Basketball$points[Basketball $gender == "Female"] ~ Basketball $weightlb[Basketball$gender == "Female"]), col = "red") legend("topleft", c("Male", "Female"), pch = 16, col = c(1,2))
Run a power analysis for a regression model with two predictors, a medium effect size of 0.15, an alpha of 0.05, and power of 0.8 (Example 16.5)	pwr.f2.test(u = 2, f2 = 0.15, sig.level = 0.05, power = 0.8)

EXERCISES

Create a .R file for each exercise that requires the use of R. Run code from the .R file by highlighting or having the cursor on the line of code and hitting **control+enter** on a PC computer keyboard or **command+enter** on a Mac computer keyboard. Save each .R file using a name associated with the Exercise for which it was created. It is recommended that you review the .R file for Chapter 16 located on the textbook's website before completing these exercises. To facilitate doing each exercise, it may be helpful to copy and paste relevant code from the .R file for Chapter 16 into your own .R file and modify them as needed.

Exercises 16.1–16.3 make use of the NELS dataset. For inferential purposes, we consider the students in the dataset to be a random sample of the population of all college-bound students who have always been at grade level. Use $\alpha = 0.05$ for all significance tests.

16.1 In this exercise, we will use multiple regression to determine whether there is a gender (gender) difference in twelfth grade math achievement (achmat12) after controlling for amount of math taken (unitmath) and to investigate related questions. Exercise 16.6 utilizes regression diagnostics to determine aspects of the model fit and whether underlying assumptions appear to be met.

   (a) Conduct initial univariate and bivariate analyses of the variables involved in the multiple regression model.
   (b) Is the regression model for predicting achmat12 from gender and unitmath statistically significant? Provide statistical support for your answer.
   (c) Report and interpret the value of R^2.
   (d) Write down the regression equation for predicting achmat12 from gender and unitmath.
   (e) Use the regression equation to predict the twelfth grade math achievement score of a male who took 4 units of math in high school. Note that even though the gender variable is coded as 1 = "Male" and 2 = "Female," when run in a regression equation, only one of these categories appears in the output (in this case, NELS $genderFemale). To use the regression equation properly, assign 1 to gender if the student belongs to this category and 0 if they do not.
   (f) Which of the two predictor variables makes a greater unique contribution to the regression model? Explain and provide statistical support for your answer.
   (g) Interpret the value of the *y*-intercept or indicate why it would not be appropriate to do so.
   (h) Interpret the value of the coefficient (slope) of unitmath in the regression equation.
   (i) Interpret the value of the coefficient (slope) of gender in the regression equation.
   (j) After controlling for number of years of math taken, is there a gender difference in twelfth grade math achievement among college-bound students who are always at grade level? If so, what is the nature of the gender difference? Explain and provide statistical support for your answer.

16.2 In this exercise, we will see that predictor variables each by themselves may be statistically significantly correlated to the outcome variable in the bivariate sense, but when examined together in the same regression equation, both may not be statistically significant. Perform a multiple regression analysis to determine whether twelfth grade self-concept (slfcnc12) is related to mathematics achievement as measured by both twelfth grade math achievement (achmat12) and the number of units of mathematics taken in high school (unitmath). Exercise 16.7 utilizes regression diagnostics to determine aspects of model fit and whether underlying assumptions appear to be met.

(a) Conduct initial univariate and bivariate analyses of the variables involved in the multiple regression model.

(b) Perform a multiple regression analysis with slfcnc12 as the outcome variable and achmat12 and unitmath as predictor variables. Is the regression model statistically significant? Provide statistical support for your answer.

(c) What proportion of variance in slfcnc12 is explained by both predictor variables?

(d) Which, if any, of the predictor variables make a statistically significant unique contribution to the regression model? Provide statistical support for your response.

(e) Interpret the value of the y-intercept or indicate why it would not be appropriate to do so.

(f) Interpret the value of the statistically significant b-weight coefficient (slope) of achmat12 in the regression equation.

16.3 In this exercise, we look at the individual and unique contributions of math achievement (achmat12) and socioeconomic status (ses) in explaining reading achievement (achrdg12) variance.

(a) What proportion of the variance in reading achievement scores can be explained by socioeconomic status? Is this proportion statistically significant? Explain and provide statistical support for your response.

(b) What proportion of the variance in reading achievement scores can be explained by math achievement? Is this proportion statistically significant? Explain and provide statistical support for your response.

(c) What is the intercorrelation between ses and achmat12? Is it statistically significant?

(d) What proportion of the variance in reading achievement scores can be explained by math achievement after controlling for socioeconomic status? Said differently, what proportion of reading achievement variance can be explained uniquely by math achievement? Is this proportion statistically significant? Explain and provide statistical support for your response.

(e) What proportion of the variance in reading achievement scores can be explained by socioeconomic status after controlling for math achievement? Said differently, what proportion of reading achievement variance can be explained uniquely by socioeconomic status? Is this proportion statistically significant? Explain and provide statistical support for your response.

(f) What is another way to determine whether the proportion of variance in reading achievement scores that can be explained by socioeconomic status controlling for math achievement is statistically significant?

(g) Why is it that the proportion of variance in reading achievement that can be explained by socioeconomic status is larger than the proportion of variance in reading achievement that can be explained by socioeconomic status after *controlling for math achievement*?

(h) Explain why R^2 for the model with both predictor variables is less than $r^2_{achrdg12,\ ses} + r^2_{achrdg12,\ achmat12}$.

Exercise 16.4 makes use of the Learndis dataset. For inferential purposes, we consider the children in the dataset to be a random sample of all children attending public school in the urban area who have been diagnosed with learning disabilities. Many students in the dataset have missing values for either math or reading comprehension, or both. Such omissions can lead to problems when generalizing results. There are statistical remedies for missing data that are beyond the scope of this text. For these exercises, we will assume that there is no pattern to the missing values, and that our sample is representative of the population. Use α = 0.05 for all significance tests.

16.4 Recall that students diagnosed with learning disabilities in this urban area are placed in one of two classroom situations: resource room for part of the day (coded as 1) or in a full-time self-contained classroom (coded as 2). Use multiple regression analysis to determine whether reading comprehension (readcomp) variance can be explained by math comprehension (mathcomp) and type of placement (placemen).

(a) Conduct initial univariate and bivariate analyses of the variables involved in the multiple regression model.

(b) Is the regression model for predicting readcomp from mathcomp and placement statistically significant? Are the predictor variables statistically significant in the equation? Provide statistical support for your response.

(c) Report and interpret the value of $R^2_{adjusted}$.

(d) Compare the values of R^2 and $R^2_{adjusted}$. Explain why they are similar or different.

(e) What is the regression equation for predicting readcomp from mathcomp and placement?

(f) Interpret value of the y-intercept or indicate why it would not be meaningful to do so.

(g) Controlling for type of placement, are higher math comprehension scores associated with higher or lower reading comprehension scores? Provide statistical support for your response.

(h) Interpret the value of the slope of mathcomp.

(i) Controlling for math comprehension, does reading comprehension statistically significantly differ for children attending public school in the urban area who have been diagnosed with learning disabilities depending on placement type? Provide statistical support for your response. If there is a difference, describe its nature.

(j) Interpret the value of the slope of placemen.

(k) Use your regression equation to predict the reading comprehension score of a student in a resource room placement who has a mathcomp score of 84.

(l) Explain why you should not use the regression equation to predict the reading comprehension score of a student in a resource room placement who has a mathcomp score of 40.

Exercise 16.5 makes use of the Framingham dataset. For inferential purposes, we consider the people in the Framingham dataset to be a random sample of the population of all non-institutionalized adults. Use α = 0.05 for all significance tests.

16.5 In this exercise we use regression to model total serum cholesterol at time 3 (TOTCHOL3) using initial systolic blood pressure at time 1 (SYSBP1) and diastolic blood pressure at time 1 (DIABP1).

(a) Conduct initial univariate and bivariate analyses of the variables involved in the multiple regression model.

(b) Is the regression model for predicting TOTCHOL3 from SYSBP1 and DIABP1 statistically significant? Is the individual contribution of any of the variables statistically significant?

(c) Why do you suppose the model is statistically significant, but none of the predictor variables are?

(d) What is an appropriate model for predicting TOTCHOL3?

(e) Compare the proportion of variance in TOTCHOL3 explained by DIABP1 alone to that explained by the combination of DIABP1 and SYSBP1.

Exercises 16.6–16.8 involve regression diagnostics and nonlinear transformations using the NELS dataset. For inferential purposes, we consider the students in the dataset to be a random sample of the population of all college-bound students who have always been at grade level. Use $\alpha = 0.05$ for all significance tests.

16.6 In Exercise 16.1, we created a model to predict twelfth grade math achievement (achmat12) from gender and the number of units of math taken in high school (unitmath). In this exercise, we will conduct a series of residual analyses to examine more closely the fit of the model to these data.

(a) Run the multiple regression model from Exercise 16.1 and save the studentized residuals to the dataset as a variable called rstu. Then create a scatterplot between the studentized residual scores and the continuous regressor with a horizontal line at 0. Examine this plot for evidence of nonlinearity. *Hint:* To add a horizontal line at 0, use the **abline** command with the sole argument **h = 0**.

(b) Name two cases that have relatively high positive residuals and two cases that have relatively low negative residuals. What do the residuals say about these four cases? Hint: Subset the id variable to cases with rstu values greater than 2 and then to cases with rstu values less than −2.

(c) Create boxplots of Cook's distance and leverage values. What do they tell you about the appropriateness of the regression model?

(d) Based on these diagnostic analyses, comment on the appropriateness of this regression equation.

16.7 In Exercise 16.2, we created a model to predict twelfth grade self-concept (slfcnc12) from twelfth grade math achievement (achmat12) and units of math taken in high school (unitmath). In this exercise, we will perform regression diagnostics on the model to determine whether it can be improved.

(a) Run the multiple regression model from Exercise 16.2 and save the studentized residuals to the dataset as a variable called rstu. Then create scatterplots between the studentized residual scores and each of the two continuous regressors, adding a horizontal line at 0 on each plot. Examine these plots for evidence of nonlinearity.

(b) Determine whether there are any bivariate outliers in the model – that is, points whose standardized residual is greater than 2 in magnitude. Indicate the number of such points and give their case numbers.

(c) Create boxplots of Cook's distance and leverage values. What do they tell you about the appropriateness of the regression model?

(d) Based on these diagnostic analyses, comment on the appropriateness of this regression equation.

16.8 In this exercise, we will create a multiple regression model to determine how expected income at age 30 (expinc30) can be explained by gender and socioeconomic status (ses).

(a) Conduct initial univariate and bivariate analyses of the variables involved in the multiple regression model.

(b) Because of its severe positive skew, transform expinc30 using both the square root and log transformations to try to reduce that skew. Which of the two transformations is more effective in symmetrizing expinc30?

(c) Conduct bivariate analyses using the square root of expected income at age 30.

(d) Conduct the multiple regression analysis with the square root of expinc30 as the outcome variable and ses and gender as the predictor variables. Is the model statistically significant? Provide statistical support for your response.

(e) Compare the proportion of variance explained with the untransformed and the transformed expinc30.

(f) Write down the regression for predicting the transformed expinc30 from ses and gender.

(g) Use your model to predict the transformed expected income at age 30 of a male with ses 15. Then undo the transformation to find the expected income.

16.9 This exercise makes use of the Exercise dataset and is adapted from Darlington (1990). In this exercise, we illustrate the importance of controlling for confounding variables in a regression equation to achieve b-weight estimates that are less clearly biased and more credible. The variable FoodIntake is defined as the average daily number of calories consumed in one particular week that is more than a baseline of 1,000 calories as measured in increments of 100 calories. That is, for example, a person who has a score of 2 on the FoodIntake variable has consumed a daily average of 1,200 calories: namely, 200 more than the baseline number of 1,000 calories for that week. The WeightLoss variable is defined as the number of pounds lost in that week. The variable Exercise is defined as the average daily number of hours exercised in that week.

(a) Using R, obtain and write out the regression equation for predicting WeightLoss from FoodIntake. Additionally, obtain and report the correlation between WeightLoss and FoodIntake and the means of these two variables.

(b) Interpret the coefficients from the regression equation obtained in part (a). Is the value of the b-weight consistent with what you would have expected? Might the problem be an omitted variable that, in its absence, causes the b-weight to be biased?

(c) Construct a scatterplot with WeightLoss on the vertical axis and FoodIntake on the horizontal axis. Add the regression line fit on the total dataset to the plot and verify that the regression line passes through the point $(\overline{X}, \overline{Y})$.

(d) Redo the scatterplot coloring points by the Exercise variable to indicate the number of hours each person exercised (0, 2, or 4). Then superimpose three regression lines on the scatterplot, one for each exercise group. Remember to include a legend for the exercise groups. Hint: Usually we color points by a categorical variable with group names coded by R as 1, 2, 3, etc. However, Exercise is a numeric variable, so R will try to color the plot using the numbers 0, 2, and 4, leading to the "0" group not being plotted. To correct this, refer to the Exercise variable as **factor(Exercise$Exercise)** within the plotting command.

(e) Do these three regression lines of WeightLoss on FoodIntake controlling for Exercise have positive or negative slopes? Said differently, is the (partial) relationship between FoodIntake and WeightLoss, controlling for Exercise, positive or negative? Is this result consistent with what you would have expected?

(f) What is the F-test associated with the regression equation containing both FoodIntake and Exercise? Is it statistically significant? Hint: Check the F-test associated with the ANOVA summary table provided in the R multiple regression output.

(g) Obtain the regression equation for predicting WeightLoss from both FoodIntake and Exercise. Is the partial regression coefficient (b-weight) for FoodIntake (controlling for Exercise) positive or negative? Is it consistent with what you would have expected?

(h) Is the contribution of FoodIntake over and above Exercise statistically significant? Test this in two ways: by the t-test associated with the b-weight for FoodIntake and by the F-test associated with the change in R^2 resulting from adding FoodIntake to the equation. These two tests will produce identical results in this situation.

Exercise 16.10 relates to an example from the chapter.

16.10 In the section entitled, "The b-weight as a partial slope in multiple regression," we used R to create the new variable $X_{1.2}$ and showed that b_1, which equals 0.878, is simply the slope of the regression line that predicts Y from $X_{1.2}$. For this exercise, show that b_2, which equals 0.397, is simply the slope of the regression line that predicts Y from $X_{2.1}$.

The following exercises are conceptual and are not based on a specific dataset.

16.11 Given the regression equation, $\hat{Y} = 10 + 1.2X_1 + 0.6X_2$.
(a) X_1 is more important than X_2
(b) X_1 is less important than X_2
(c) X_1 is equally as important as X_2
(d) One cannot tell the relative importance of X_1 and X_2 from the information given.

16.12 In general, higher R^2 values will arise when the correlation between each regressor and Y is _____ and the intercorrelation between the regressors is _____.
(a) high, high
(b) high, low
(c) low, high
(d) low, low

16.13 Given a regression equation with two regressors: $\hat{Y} = b_0 + b_1X_1 + b_2X_2$. If b_1 is *not* statistically significant, then _____ will also *not* be statistically significant.

(a) R
(b) r_{Y1}
(c) $r_{Y1(2)}$
(d) none of the above

16.14 Given a regression equation with two regressors: $\hat{Y} = b_0 + b_1X_1 + b_2X_2$. The largest discrepancy between R^2 and $R^2_{adjusted}$ will occur when
(a) N = 100
(b) N = 10
(c) N = 5
(d) cannot tell from the information given

16.15 Given Y and two different X variables, X_1 and X_2, with the following two different scatterplots, A and B. Assume the Y sum of squares equals 100 ($SS_Y = 100$) in both situations.

(A)

(B)

If we construct two regression equations, one for predicting Y from X_1 and another for predicting Y from X_2, which is most descriptive of situations A and B?

(a) For (A), $SS_{REG} = 90$ and $SS_{ERROR} = 10$; For (B), $SS_{REG} = 60$ and $SS_{ERROR} = 40$
(b) For (A), $SS_{REG} = 60$ and $SS_{ERROR} = 40$; For (B), $SS_{REG} = 90$ and $SS_{ERROR} = 10$
(c) For (A), $SS_{REG} = 50$ and $SS_{ERROR} = 50$; For (B), $SS_{REG} = 50$ and $SS_{ERROR} = 50$
(d) For (A), $SS_{REG} = 90$ and $SS_{ERROR} = 60$; For (B), $SS_{REG} = 10$ and $SS_{ERROR} = 40$

16.16 Under what circumstances would the weights for variables X_1 and X_2 not change when a third variable X_3 is added to the multiple regression equation?

# CHAPTER SEVENTEEN

TWO-WAY INTERACTIONS IN MULTIPLE REGRESSION

The regression model for the examples we have considered in Chapter 16 have had the following form:

$$\hat{Y} = b_0 + b_1 X_1 + b_2 X_2. \tag{17.1}$$

In this model, because the estimate of Y, $\hat{Y}$, equals the sum of two variables, X_1 and X_2, each weighted by its respective regression coefficient, b_1 and b_2 plus a constant, b_0, it is called an *additive model*. From Chapter 16, we may recall that the regression coefficients (b-weights) are obtained by minimizing the sum of squared errors, $(Y - \hat{Y})^2$, across all cases. This model was used in Chapter 16 to estimate ice cream sales as the sum of the two variables, temperature and relative humidity, each weighted by its respective regression coefficient, plus a constant. With b-weights rounded to the nearest hundredth, the model that was obtained is:

$$\hat{Y} = 67.62 + 0.88 \text{temp} + 0.40 \text{relhumid}. \tag{17.2}$$

According to Equation 17.2, and as discussed in Chapter 16, holding relative humidity constant at a fixed value, each one-degree Fahrenheit increase in temperature is associated with an estimated 0.88 more ice cream bars sold on average. This is true regardless of the value at which relative humidity is held constant. Likewise, holding temperature constant at a fixed value, each one-percentage increase in relative humidity is associated with an estimated 0.40 more ice cream bars sold on average regardless of the value at which temperature is held constant. If we define the value of 67 percent as low relative humidity and 88 percent as high relative humidity, and fix the values of relative humidity at these values, then plot the relationship between temperature and ice cream sales for each of these values of relative humidity, we obtain the graph shown in Figure 17.1.

A noticeable feature of the graph in Figure 17.1 is that the lines are parallel, depicting the fact that whether the relative humidity is low or high, the relationship between temperature and ice cream sales remains the same. Had we had selected to fix the values of relative humidity to be different from 67 percent (low) and 88 percent (high), the lines representing the relationship between ice cream sales and temperature would still be parallel. In short, when models are additive, as in Equation 17.1, the relationship between Y and X_1 will not change as a function of value of X_2.

Suppose, however, we believed that the relationship between temperature and ice cream sales might not the same under conditions of low and high relative humidity. More specifically, based on our own experiences with ice cream, we believed that with low relative humidity (67 percent), the number of ice cream bars sold would increase more

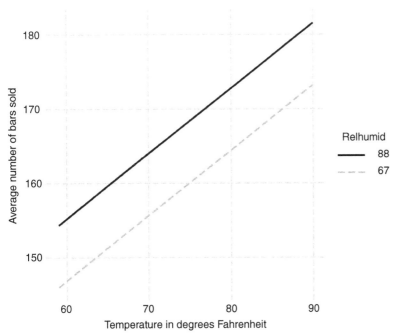

Figure 17.1 The relationship between ice cream sales and temperature remains constant whether relative humidity equals 67 percent or 88 percent: No interaction

dramatically with an increase in temperature than when relative humidity is high (88 percent). If this were the case, we would say there exists a *joint* (or *multiplicative*) effect of temperature and relative humidity on ice cream sales over and above the additive effects of these two predictors. This situation is depicted in Figure 17.2.

As Figure 17.2 shows, under conditions of low relative humidity, the relationship between temperature and ice cream sales is stronger than under conditions of high relative humidity. Said differently, we would say that the relationship between temperature and ice cream sales varies as a function of relative humidity. Based on our discussion of interaction in Chapter 14 in connection with two-way ANOVA, we may note that Figure 17.2 depicts a *two-way interaction* between temperature and humidity on ice cream sales, that humidity *moderates* the relationship between temperature and ice cream sales. When a variable, like humidity, moderates the relationship between two other variables, that variable is said to be a *moderator*. The moderator variable and the variable whose relationship it moderates with the outcome variable also are called *interacting* variables.

If, more generally, the two interacting variables are X_1 and X_2, then the product, $X_1 \cdot X_2$, will represent their multiplicative or joint effect. If we add this product term to the additive model given by Equation 17.1, we obtain Equation 17.3. Equation 17.3 is called an *interaction model* (as opposed to an additive model). We may test whether the interaction of X_1 and X_2 on Y is statistically significant by testing the significance of the *b*-weight, b_3, associated with this product term in Equation 17.3:

$$\hat{Y} = b_0 + b_1 X_1 + b_2 X_2 + b_3 X_1 X_2. \tag{17.3}$$

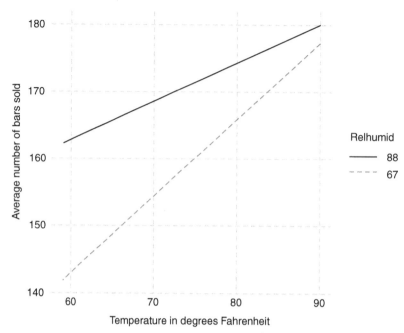

Figure 17.2 The relationship between ice cream sales and temperature changes as the value of relative humidity changes: relhumid moderates the relationship between barsold and temp

By rearranging the terms in Equation 17.3, we can show more clearly how the slope of X_1 in Equation 17.3, which depicts the relationship of X_1 with Y, varies with the value of X_2.

$$\hat{Y} = b_0 + b_1X_1 + b_2X_2 + b_3X_1X_2$$
$$= b_0 + (b_1 + b_3X_2)X_1 + b_2X_2. \tag{17.4}$$

From Equation 17.4, we note that the slope of the line relating X_1 (temperature) to Y (ice cream sales) is not simply b_1, but rather $(b_1 + b_3X_2)$ and the constant is not simply b_0, but rather $(b_2X_2 + b_0)$. As a result, Equation 17.4 may be viewed as a family of equations with slope $b_1 + b_3X_2$ and intercept $b_2X_2 + b_0$ where each equation in the family has a slope and an intercept influenced by the value of X_2. Said differently, we may say that the relationship between X_1 and Y is conditional on X_2.

In terms of the ice cream example, if X_1 represents temperature and X_2 represents relative humidity, Equation 17.4 shows that if relative humidity is low ($X_2 = 67$ percent) we would obtain one slope for X_1 and a different slope if relative humidity is high ($X_2 = 88$ percent). The two differently-sloped lines would not be parallel, as shown in Figure 17.2, and would suggest a two-way interaction between X_1 and X_2 on Y.

Because the family of equations represented by Equation 17.4 exists only if there is a two-way interaction between X_1 and X_2 (if the product $X_1 \cdot X_2$ belongs in the model), we note that a two-way interaction exists in the population if and only if $b_3 \neq 0$ in the population. We may test whether $b_3 \neq 0$ in the population by using the t-test given in Equation 16.10 in Chapter 16.

☞ **Remark.** We may interpret b_1 and b_2 in Equation 17.3 as follows: b_1 represents the slope of the line that describes the relationship between Y and X_1 when X_2 is zero; b_2

represents the slope of the line that describes the relationship between Y and X_2 when X_1 is zero. *If an interaction term is in the equation, b_1 and b_2 are easily interpreted as long as the value of zero is a meaningful one for X_1 and X_2.* If an interaction term is *not* in the equation, b_1 represents the average effect of X_1 averaged across the full range of values of X_2 and b_2 represents the average effect of X_2 averaged across the full range of values of X_1.

☞ **Remark.** As illustrated more clearly in Equation 17.4, we may interpret b_3 in Equation 17.3 as follows: For every unit change in X_2, the slope of the line that describes the relationship between Y and X_1 changes by b_3 units. Because interaction is a symmetric notion, we may say, as well, that for every unit change in X_2 the slope of the line that describes the relationship between Y and X_1 changes by b_3 units.

TESTING THE STATISTICAL SIGNIFICANCE OF AN INTERACTION USING R

EXAMPLE 17.1 Test whether there is an interaction between temperature and humidity on ice cream sales. If there is an interaction, what proportion of ice cream sales variance does it explain?

Solution Compute the product of temperature and relative humidity as a new variable in the Ice Cream dataset and give that new variable the name, product (note that any other variable name would do equally as well):

IceCream$product = IceCream$temp*IceCream$relhumid

The new variable carries the interaction between temperature and relative humidity and we now include it as a predictor in the **lm** command that regresses barsold on temp (x_1) and relhumid (x_2). Alternatively, we can include **temp*relhumid** as the only predictor term in the **lm** command, and R will provide coefficient estimates for both the main effects and the interaction term. The R commands for this analysis (which includes summary statistics and bivariate correlations) are:

```
summary(IceCream[, c("temp", "barsold", "relhumid", "product")])
cor(IceCream[, c("temp", "barsold", "relhumid", "product")])
results3 = lm(barsold ~ temp + relhumid + product, data = IceCream)
summary(results3)
```

or

```
results4 = lm(barsold ~ temp*relhumid, data = IceCream)
summary(results4)
```

temp		barsold		relhumid		product	
Min.	59.00	Min.	142.0	Min.	60.00	Min.	3780
1st Qu.	70.00	1st Qu.	155.2	1st Qu.	70.00	1st Qu.	5040
Median	74.50	Median	164.5	Median	73.00	Median	5260
Mean	74.93	Mean	164.2	Mean	77.67	Mean	5879
3rd Qu.	81.75	3rd Qu.	174.5	3rd Qu.	87.25	3rd Qu.	6925
Max.	90.00	Max.	185.0	Max.	98.00	Max.	8730

☞ **Remark.** It should come as no surprise that the mean of the variable product is very large since that variable is formed by multiplying the values of temp and relhumid.

	temp	barsold	relhumid	product
temp	1.0000000	0.8867125	0.6493576	0.8860942
barsold	0.8867125	1.0000000	0.7782383	0.8990884
relhumid	0.6493576	0.7782383	1.0000000	0.9255073
product	0.8860942	0.8990884	0.9255073	1.0000000

☞ **Remark.** We may note that the correlations between the product term and its component parts are both very high. The correlation between product and temp is $r = 0.886$; the correlation between product and relhumid is $r = 0.926$. The reason for these high correlations is that the variable, product, carries within it some of the main (or *first-order*) effects of its component parts (temperature and relative humidity). In order for the product term to truly represent an interaction, it must represent the multiplicative effects of temp and relhumid after the additive effects of temp and relhumid are controlled for or partialled out. As such, authors have referred to the interaction as a *partialled product*. In the case of two predictor variables, the partialled product is simply obtained by entering the product term into an equation that already contains its two component, first-order effects. The test of the b-weight associated with the product term is then a test of the unique contribution of the product term after controlling for the two first-order effects that are already in the equation. In the context of this problem, a test of the b-weight associated with the product term is a test of the interaction between temperature and relative humidity on ice cream sales *as long as both first-order component terms are already in the equation.*

	Estimate	Std. Error	t-value	Pr(> |t|)	
(Intercept)	−98.67536	64.67668	−1.526	0.1392	
temp	2.96785	0.81640	3.635	0.0012	**
relhumid	2.58340	0.85116	3.035	0.0054	**
temp:relhumid	−0.02724	0.01053	−2.586	0.0157	*

Signif. codes: 0 "***" 0.001 "**" 0.01 "*" 0.05 "." 0.1 " " 1

Residual standard error: 4.239 on 26 degrees of freedom
Multiple R-squared: 0.8864, Adjusted R-squared: 0.8732
F-statistic: 67.6 on 3 and 26 DF, p-value: 2.087e-12

The unstandardized regression equation for estimating ice cream sales (Y) from temperature (temp), relative humidity (relhumid), and their interaction (product = temp*relhumid) is:

$$\hat{Y} = 2.968(\text{temp}) + 2.583(\text{relhumid}) - 0.0272(\text{product}) - 98.675.$$

The b-weight associated with the product term is statistically significant ($p = 0.016$), suggesting that there is an interaction between temperature and relative humidity on ice cream sales; that the relationship between temperature and ice cream sales varies as a function of relative humidity, or likewise, that the relationship between relative humidity and ice cream sales varies as a function of temperature.

Analysis of variance table					
Response: barsold					
	df	Sum sq.	Mean sq.	*F*-value	Pr(>F)
Temp	1	3232.6	3232.6	179.8863	3.427e-13 ***
Relhumid	1	291.4	291.4	16.2131	0.0004362 ***
temp:relhumid	1	120.2	120.2	6.6882	0.0156599 *
Residuals	26	467.2	18.0		

Signif. codes: 0 "***" 0.001 "**" 0.01 "*" 0.05 "." 0.1 " " 1

To assess the overall goodness of fit of the model that contains the two main effects and the interaction term we may create and consult an analysis of variance (ANOVA) table of model summary statistics with the R command **anova(lm(barsold ~ temp*relhumid, data = IceCream))**. By dividing SS_{MODEL} by SS_{TOTAL} (3232.6 + 291.4 + 120.2)/(3232.6 + 291.4 + 120.2 + 467.2) or reading the R-squared value directly from the regression output, we find that approximately 89 percent of the ice cream sales variance is accounted for by temperature, relative humidity, and their interaction.

We also may use the *hierarchical* multiple regression approach to test the statistical significance of the interaction term by evaluating the statistical significance of the change in R^2 when the interaction term is introduced to the model. In this approach, the main effects of temp and relhumid are entered simultaneously in the first block and then the interaction term product is entered in the second block. Analyses that are carried out using blocks are called *hierarchical analyses* because they rely on a hierarchy or order of entry of terms into the equation. In this example, that order was main effects entered as the first block, followed by the interaction or product term entered as the second block.

MORE R: Create two regression objects and compare the R-squared of each model using the **anova** function to test the significance of the interaction term:

```
model1 = lm(barsold ~ temp + relhumid, data = IceCream)
summary(model1)
model2 = lm(barsold ~ temp + relhumid + product, data = IceCream)
summary(model2)
anova(model1, model2)
```

Note: Model 1 contains the predictors temp and relhumid; Model 2 contains all three predictors with the product term having been added to Model 1. Accordingly, Model 1 is nested within Model 2. The **anova** function tests the significance in the change in R^2 when the product term is added to Model 1.

We obtain the following results:

Analysis of variance table

Model 1: barsold ~ temp + relhumid
Model 2: barsold ~ temp + relhumid + product

	Res.Df	RSS	df	Sum of sq.	F-value	Pr(>F)
1	27	587.41				
2	26	467.23	1	120.19	6.6882	0.01566 *

Signif. codes:　0 "***" 0.001 "**" 0.01 "*" 0.05 "." 0.1 " " 1

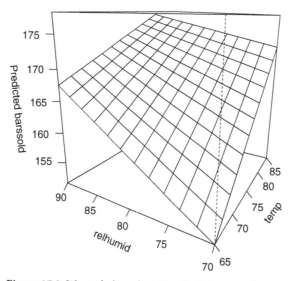

Figure 17.3 Warped plane depicting the interaction between relhumid and temp

The change in R^2 associated with introducing the interaction term into the equation is statistically significant ($F(1, 26) = 6.69$, $p = 0.016$). Thus, as we noted before from the t-test value associated with the product term, there is an interaction between temperature and relative humidity on ice cream sales. We emphasize the fact that the F-test on R^2_{Change} is identical to the t-test of the b-weight associated with the product term. Note that both have p-values equal to 0.016 and by squaring the t-value of −2.586 we obtain the F-value of 6.688. Recall that with 1 degree of freedom in the numerator, $F = t^2$. Finally, we note once again that the overall R^2 equals 0.886, suggesting that approximately 89 percent of the ice cream sales variance is accounted for by all three terms in the equation, temperature, relative humidity, and their interaction. Figure 17.3 illustrates the regression equation, including the interaction, as a three-dimensional plane. As we noted earlier, with one predictor, we may plot the regression equation as a two-dimensional line, but with two predictors, we need one more dimension to plot the equation.

By contrast to the flat plane of Figure 16.3, the plane of Figure 17.3 is warped. Consistent with the flat plane of Figure 16.3, the slopes of the lines relating temp to barsold are equal across all values (levels) of relhumid, and the lines themselves are parallel. In the warped plane of Figure 17.3, however, these slopes are not equal across values of relhumid, and the lines are not parallel. Rather, when relhumid is low (e.g., at 70 and vicinity) the slopes are more steep and when relhumid is high (e.g., at 90 and vicinity) they are less steep. In particular, with each unit increase in relhumid, the *b*-weight for temp changes by the value of the *b*-weight for the interaction (product) term (−0.0272). Likewise, with each unit increase in temp, the *b*-weight for relhumid changes by −0.0272 as well. Because in the presence of an interaction, the slope of the line relating temp to barsold is different for each value of relhumid, one cannot say that the *b*-weight for temp represents the average effect of temp on barsold, averaged across all values (levels) of relhumid. Rather, we say that the *b*-weight for temp is *conditional on* the value of relhumid and must be interpreted with respect to specific values of relhumid.

COMPARING THE *Y*-HAT VALUES FROM THE ADDITIVE AND INTERACTION MODELS

The **anova** results reported in the previous section provide the equations for Models 1 and 2, rounded to the nearest hundredth.

Model 1 (the additive model) with only temperature and humidity, is:

$\hat{Y} = 0.88\text{temp} + 0.40\text{relhumid} + 67.62.$

Model 2 (the interaction model) with temperature, humidity, and their interaction, is:

$\hat{Y} = 2.97\text{temp} + 2.58\text{relhumid} - 0.027\text{product} - 98.68.$

In order to understand more fully the differences between the additive and interaction models, in this section, we produce a table of the predicted number of ice cream bars sold for both models based on three values of temperature and two values of relative humidity. We choose these six values to reflect prototypical values for each variable. In the case of temperature, we choose the values that are 1 standard deviation below the mean (−1 *SD*), at the mean (0 *SD*), and 1 standard deviation above the mean (+1 *SD*). These three values typically are used to capture the range within which the majority of values in a predictor's distribution falls. Because the mean and standard deviation of temperature are, respectively, 75 and 9, rounded to the whole number, these three prototypical values are, respectively, 66, 75, and 84. In the case of relative humidity, we choose the values 67 percent and 88 percent that have been representing, respectively, low and high relative humidity in this example.

Substituting these values into the respective equations, we obtain the following Table 17.1 of predicted ice cream sales for our six prototypical values, rounded to the nearest whole number, for both Models 1 and 2:

TABLE 17.1 Predicted ice cream sales for six prototypical values of temp and relhumid

	Temp = 66 (−1 *SD*)	Temp = 75 (0 *SD*)	Temp = 84 (+1 *SD*)
Model 1			
Low humidity (67%)	152	160	168
High humidity (88%)	*160*	168	*176*
Model 2			
Low humidity (67%)	151	161	172
High humidity (88%)	*168*	173	*178*

Differences between the models are most noticeable in the cells in italics and bold font. The interaction term adjusts the number of ice cream bars sold downward under conditions of high humidity as the temperature increases, and does the reverse under conditions of low humidity. This is consistent with the notion that we effectively are fitting a separate slope and intercept under conditions of low and high humidity.

We may infer from this table that under high humidity conditions, one can expect ice cream sales to increase relatively less dramatically with increasing temperature as compared to under low humidity conditions.

We may interpret this result directly from the equation of Model 2, the interaction model, if we explicitly express the product in terms of its two component variables and rearrange terms as follows:

estimated ice cream bar sales = 2.97temp + 2.58relhumid − 0.027temp*relhumid − 98.68 = (2.97 − 0.027relhumid)temp + (2.58relhumid − 98.68).

Note that as relhumid increases by one percentage point, the slope of temp decreases by 0.027 units. Accordingly, as relative humidity increases 11 percentage points, from low to high, the slope of temperature decreases 0.297 percentage points (11 × 0.027). This situation is depicted in Figure 17.2 where we can observe the temperature slope under conditions of high humidity to be less steep than under conditions of low humidity.

CENTERING FIRST-ORDER EFFECTS IF THE EQUATION HAS AN INTERACTION

As indicated in an earlier remark in this chapter, if an equation contains a product term (representing the interaction between two variables already in the equation), the interpretation of the b-weights associated with the first-order effect variables is a bit more complicated than if the equation does not contain that product term. In our example, the b-weight associated with temperature represents the slope of the line that describes the relationship between ice cream sales and temperature when relative humidity is 0; the b-weight associated with relative humidity represents the slope of the line that describes the relationship between ice cream sales and relative humidity when temperature is 0. Because both zero temperature and zero relative humidity are not meaningful in the context of this problem set in the northeast during the summer months, the interpretation of these b-weights also is not meaningful.

To impart meaning to the b-weights of first-order effect variables in an equation that contains an interaction term, we may rescale each of the first-order effect variables so as to make the value of zero in each variable correspond to something meaningful. A reasonable choice is to set the mean of each rescaled variable at zero by subtracting the mean from each variable value. Such rescaling is called *centering* and the newly rescaled variables are called *centered variables*. Another advantage to centering is that it allows us to test the interaction term with greater power than if we had not centered the variables (Cohen et al., 2003). In general, a product term that is based on centered first-order effect variables will correlate less strongly with each of the centered first-order variables already in the equation than a product term that is not based on centered first-order variables will correlate with each of the uncentered first-order effect variables already in the equation. As a result, the product term will have a greater unique contribution to make over and above the first-order effect variables, and we will be able to test the interaction with greater power. To find the centered temperature variable, we subtract the mean temperature (74.93) from each temperature value in the distribution; to find the centered relative humidity variable, we subtract the mean relative humidity (77.67) from each relative humidity value in the distribution. The product term would then be the product of each centered variable. The analysis of the interaction from Example 17.1 using the centered temperature and relative humidity variables is left for the reader to complete as Exercise 17.7.

PROBING THE NATURE OF A TWO-WAY INTERACTION

A statistically significant two-way interaction informs us that the effect of X_1 (temperature) is not the same across all levels of X_2 (relative humidity) and likewise the effect of X_2 is not the same across all levels of X_1. To examine more closely how the relationship between the outcome variable and each predictor varies as a function of the other predictor we could plot a graphic of the interaction to visualize it. Figure 17.2 illustrates such a graphic. It depicts the nature of the relationship between temperature and ice cream sales at the two fixed values of relative humidity, 67 and 88. Although we could have fixed humidity at values other than 67 and 88, these particular values were chosen because they represent meaningful humidity values; namely, low and high humidity, respectively. The graphic allows us to observe that the slope of the line for high humidity is flatter than that of low humidity, which is useful in helping us to describe the nature of the relationship between ice cream sales and temperature and humidity. The slope of each line at each of these two humidity values is called a *simple slope*. In ANOVA, the comparable term is called a simple effect.

From the *t*-test of the *b*-weight associated with the product term, we know that the simple slopes representing these relationships are different from each other, but we do not know whether each simple slope is significantly different from zero. In this section, we describe more fully how to produce plots of an interaction, and to test whether a simple slope is statistically significantly different from zero. Having this additional information allows us to describe our results more completely.

To plot the interaction and obtain a plot such as the one in Figure 17.2, we use the **interact_plot** function in the **interactions** package.

MORE R: To produce the graphic of Figure 17.2, we use the following R code, which also is given in the .R file for Chapter 17 and can be found online at www.cambridge.org /stats-r:

```
results2 = lm(barsold ~ temp*relhumid, data = IceCream)
interact_plot(results2, pred="temp", modx = "relhumid", modx.values = c(67,88),
x.label = "Temperature in Degrees Fahrenheit",
y.label = "Average Number of Bars Sold",
main.title = "Relating Ice Cream Sales to Temp and Relhumid \n
Relhumid Moderates the Relationship between Barsold and Temp",
legend.main = "Relhumid")
```

Note: **modx** defines which of the variables is to be designated as the moderator variable in the graphic (in this case it is relhumid); **modx.values** defines the moderator variable values that are to be plotted.

We reproduce Figure 17.2 as Figure 17.4.

To obtain the predicted values of barssold, rather than estimating from the graphic, we may use the **make_predictions** command, which also is in the interactions package. This function uses the model from the regression analysis to estimate predicted values of the outcome variable and the associated values of the predictor variable at −1, 0, and +1 *SD* of the moderator variable, stored in a new dataset called **predicted**.

MORE R: To make predictions from the model used in the regression analysis and estimate predicted values of the outcome variable and to list them, we use the following commands:

predictions = make_predictions(results2, pred = "temp", modx = "relhumid")
predictions

Another function in the interactions package, **sim_slopes**, is highly useful because it calculates and reports the values of the simple slopes and their standard errors at particular (fixed) values of the other variables in the equation, and tests whether each of these simple slopes is significantly different from zero. For the ice cream example, we could, for

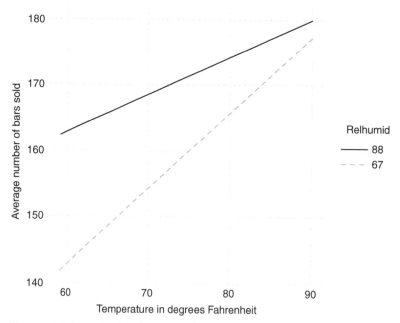

Figure 17.4 A graph of the interaction between temperature and humidity on ice cream sales: relhumid moderates the relationship between barsold and temp

example, test the significance from zero of each of the two simple slopes for temperature, one at low humidity and the other at high humidity, using the following command:

MORE R: To calculate and report the values of the simple slopes and their standard errors at particular (fixed) values of the other variables in the equation, we use the following command:

sim_slopes(results2, pred = "temp", modx = "relhumid", modx.values = c(67,88))

The output from executing this command is the following:

Simple slopes analysis			
Slope of temp when relhumid = 88.00:			
Est.	S.E.	*t*-val.	*p*
0.60	0.16	3.78	0.00
Slope of temp when relhumid = 67.00:			
Est.	S.E.	*t*-val.	*p*
1.17	0.16	7.23	0.00

Accordingly, we know that when relative humidity is low, the slope of the line relating ice cream sales to temperature is 1.17, and when relative humidity is high, it is 0.60, and we know that each is statistically significantly different from zero. Therefore, when relative humidity is low, each degree increase in temperature associates with an additional 1.17 ice cream bars sold on average, but when relative humidity is high, each degree increase in temperature associates with only an additional 0.60 bars of ice cream sold on average.

In summary, the results of our analysis of ice cream sales suggest that both temperature and humidity are related to summer ice cream sales at the beach in the northeast and that relative humidity moderates the relationship between temperature and ice cream sales. We know from the overall test of the interaction that the slopes of the lines relating temperature to ice cream sales vary as a function of relative humidity. From the **sim_slopes** test we know additionally that the simple slopes relating temperature to ice cream sales at low and high relative humidity are each significantly different from zero.

In completing this analysis, we should also have paid attention to the diagnostics we discussed in the previous chapter to verify that our model was not influenced unduly by outliers and that the assumptions underlying the procedure are met. Often, to determine to what extent outliers influence the results of a regression analysis, the analysis is carried out both with and without outliers and changes in results are noted and evaluated. Such analyses are called "sensitivity analyses" because they are measuring the sensitivity of the results to what appear to be critical changes in the dataset. We ask you to complete this aspect of the analysis in Exercise 17.8.

INTERACTION WHEN ONE OF THE PREDICTOR VARIABLES IS DICHOTOMOUS AND THE OTHER IS CONTINUOUS

In this example, we examine the extent to which eighth grade self-concept and gender explain twelfth grade self-concept. Specifically, we examine whether there is an interaction between eighth grade self-concept and gender on twelfth grade self-concept. That is, whether the relationship between eighth grade self-concept and twelfth grade self-concept varies as a function of gender.

● ●

EXAMPLE 17.2 Determine whether there is an interaction between eighth grade self-concept and gender on twelfth grade self-concept. Construct a plot to facilitate the interpretation of the interaction, if one exists.

Solution In the solution to this example we shall center the eighth grade self-concept variable to have a mean of zero to illustrate how to carry out an analysis of interactions using centered variables for variables that are continuous. By centering, the value of zero on the self-concept scale will be a meaningful quantity for interpretation purposes. In addition, because the values for the categorical variable gender are 2 for females and 1 for males, we subtract 1 from each value so as to make 0 a meaningful quantity for the interpretation of gender. In particular, after the subtraction, a 0 value simply connotes males.

Prior to conducting the regression analysis, we center the variables and form the product term to represent the interaction. To center eighth grade self-concept, we generate a new variable, called ctrslf08, by subtracting the mean of slfcnc08 from every score of slfcnc08. The syntax for doing this follows:

MORE R: Center the variables, form the product term that carries the interaction, and conduct the regression analysis:

***Center the variables:

```
NELS$ctrslf08 = NELS$slfcnc08 – mean(NELS$slfcnc08, na.rm = TRUE)
NELS$gendernew = as.numeric(NELS$gender) – 1
```

***Form the product term:

```
NELS$product = NELS$gendernew*NELS$ctrslf08
```

***Run the regression analysis:

```
summary(NELS[, c("slfcnc12", "ctrslf08", "gendernew", "product")])
cor(NELS[, c("slfcnc12", "ctrslf08", "gendernew", "product")]
results5 = lm(slfcnc12 ~ ctrslf08 + gendernew + product, data = NELS)
anova(results5)
summary(results5)
```

The results of the regression analysis are reproduced and analyzed below.

slfcnc12		ctrslf08		gendernew		product	
Min. :	0.00	Min. :	−21.062	Min. :	0.000	Min. :	−21.0620
1st Qu.:	27.00	1st Qu.:	−4.062	1st Qu.:	0.000	1st Qu.:	−2.0620
Median :	31.00	Median :	−0.062	Median :	1.000	Median :	0.0000
Mean :	31.48	Mean :	0.000	Mean :	0.546	Mean :	−0.5679
3rd Qu.:	37.00	3rd Qu.:	4.938	3rd Qu.:	1.000	3rd Qu.:	0.0000
Max. :	43.00	Max. :	10.938	Max. :	1.000	Max. :	10.9380

	slfcnc12	ctrslf08	gendernew	product
slfcnc12	1.0000000	0.4435735	−0.1607268	0.4010131
ctrslf08	0.4435735	1.0000000	−0.1912030	0.8072183
gendernew	−0.1607268	−0.1912030	1.0000000	−0.1090761
product	0.4010131	0.8072183	−0.1090761	1.0000000

Notice, that as expected, the mean of the centered eighth grade self-concept variables is zero. The mean of gendernew is 0.546. Because the new values of gender are 0 and 1 (where 1 is now the code for females and 0 for males), 0.546 indicates that 54.6 percent of the sample is female. The mean of the twelfth grade self-concept variable is the same as it was earlier because the variable was not changed.

Because centering is a translation, a form of linear transformation that does not involve reflection, the correlations between the first-order effect variables remain the same. The correlations of product with its component parts are non-zero, suggesting once again that the product term, by itself, is not the interaction. Rather, the interaction is the *partialled product*, the product with its component parts removed or partialled out.

Analysis of variance table
Response: slfcnc12

	df	Sum sq.	Mean sq.	F-value	Pr(>F)	
ctrslf08	1	5134.0	5134.0	123.3758	< 2e-16	***
gendernew	1	156.1	156.1	3.7508	0.05335	
product	1	163.1	163.1	3.9187	0.04830	*
Residuals	496	20639.7	41.6			

Signif. codes:　0 "***" 0.001 "**" 0.01 "*" 0.05 "." 　0.1 " " 1

Model summary statistics inform us that the overall model, consisting of the product, gender, and centered eighth grade self-concept variables, is statistically significant ($p < 0.0005$). Both the ratio SS_{MODEL}/SS_{TOTAL} and the R-squared value inform us that 20.9 percent of twelfth grade self-concept variance is explained by this model.

Coefficients:

	Estimate	Std. Error	t-value	Pr(> |t|)	
(Intercept)	32.27032	0.44063	73.237	< 2e-16	***
ctrslf08	0.38615	0.08323	4.639	4.48e-06	***
gendernew	−1.23485	0.59213	−2.085	0.0375	*
product	0.20443	0.10327	1.980	0.0483	*

Signif. codes: 0 "***" 0.001 "**" 0.01 "*" 0.05 "." 0.1 " " 1

Residual standard error: 6.451 on 496 degrees of freedom
Multiple R-squared: 0.209, Adjusted R-squared: 0.2042
F-statistic: 43.68 on 3 and 496 df, p-value: < 2.2e-16

Given that the overall model is statistically significant, we construct the regression equation using the unstandardized weights and to determine whether the interaction is statistically significant. The unstandardized regression equation for $\hat{Y}$ = predicted twelfth grade self-concept (slfcnc12) is:

$$\hat{Y} = 0.386(\text{ctrslf08}) - 1.235(\text{gendernew}) + 0.204(\text{product}) + 32.27$$

or equivalently

$$\hat{Y} = 0.386(\text{ctrslf08}) - 1.235(\text{gendernew}) + 0.204(\text{ctrslf08*gendernew}) + 32.27.$$

Because the b-weight associated with the product term is statistically significant (p = 0.048), the interaction is statistically significant. Therefore, the relationship between eighth grade and twelfth grade self-concept is not constant for males and females; rather, it varies as a function of gender. Because the relationship between eighth grade self-concept and twelfth grade self-concept is different for males and females in the population, we can create two separate regression equations, one for each gender.

To find the regression equation for males, we substitute gendernew = 0 into:

$$\hat{Y} = 0.386(\text{ctrslf08}) - 1.235(\text{gendernew}) + 0.204(\text{ctrslf08*gendernew}) + 32.27$$
$$\hat{Y} = 0.386(\text{ctrslf08}) - 1.235(0) + 0.204(\text{ctrslf08*0}) + 32.27$$
$$\hat{Y} = 0.386(\text{ctrslf08}) + 32.27.$$

To find the regression equation for females, we substitute gendernew = 1 into:

$$\hat{Y} = 0.386(\text{ctrslf08}) - 1.235(\text{gendernew}) + 0.204(\text{ctrslf08*gendernew}) + 32.27$$
$$\hat{Y} = 0.386(\text{ctrslf08}) - 1.235(1) + 0.204(\text{ctrslf08*1}) + 32.27$$
$$\hat{Y} = 0.386(\text{ctrslf08}) - 1.235 + 0.204(\text{ctrslf08}) + 32.27$$
$$\hat{Y} = 0.590(\text{ctrslf08}) + 31.035.$$

Looking at the two slopes, we see that for males, every one-point increase in eighth grade self-concept is associated with a 0.39 point increase in twelfth grade self-concept on average, whereas for females, every one-point increase in eighth grade self-concept is associated with a 0.59 point increase in twelfth grade self-concept on average. The statistical significance of the interaction term tells us that these two slopes are significantly different from each other. That the slope for females, 0.59, is greater than the slope for males, 0.39, suggests that females exhibit greater growth in self-concept than males between grades 8 and 12. To test whether each (simple) slope is significantly different from zero, we use the **sim_slopes** function in the interactions package. In order to do so, however, we need to re-do the regression using **ctrslf08*gendernew** as the only covariate term:

results6 = lm(slfcnc12 ~ ctrslf08*gendernew, data = NELS)
sim_slopes(results6, pred = "ctrslf08", modx = "gendernew")

The obtained results from the **sim_slopes** command are given below. Notice that the simple slopes for males and females are calculated to be 0.39 and 0.59, respectively, and are identical to the values we obtained earlier by computing these simple slopes by hand. In addition to calculating the simple slopes, the **sim_slopes** command estimates the standard errors of these slopes, allowing it to test the significance of the simple slopes from zero.

Simple slopes analysis			
Slope of ctrslf08 when gendernew = 1.00 (1):			
Est.	S.E.	*t*-val.	p
0.59	0.06	9.66	0.00
Slope of ctrslf08 when gendernew = 0.00 (0):			
Est.	S.E.	*t*-val.	p
0.39	0.08	4.64	0.00

We plot the interaction in Figure 17.5 using the **interact_plot** function in the interactions package,which includes 95 percent confidence interval bands when including the **interval=TRUE** argument so you can see at which values males and females differ from each other in terms of slfcnc12.

The following **interact_plot** command plots predicted values with ctrslf08 as the *x*-axis and gender as the moderator:

interact_plot(results6, pred="ctrslf08", modx = "gendernew",
x.label = "ctrslf08", y.label = "12th Grade Self-Concept", interval = TRUE,
main.title = "12th Grade Self-Concept Related to Gender & 8th Grade Self-Concept",
legend.main = "Gender", modx.labels = c("Male", "Female"))

MORE R: An alternative way to achieve a graph similar to Figure 17.5, but with the points of the scatterplot included is adding the argument **plot.points=TRUE** to the **interact_plot** command:

interact_plot(results6, pred="ctrslf08", modx = "gendernew", plot.points = TRUE,
x.label = "ctrslf08", y.label = "12th Grade Self-Concept", interval = TRUE, main.
  title = "12th Grade Self-Concept Related to Gender & 8th Grade Self-Concept",
  legend.main = "Gender", modx.labels = c("Male","Female"))

The resulting graph is provided as Figure 17.6.

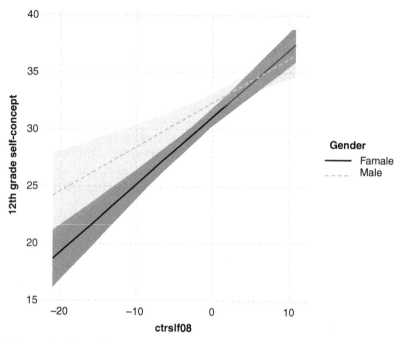

Figure 17.5 Plot of the interaction between eighth grade self-concept and gender on twelfth grade self-concept with gender as moderator

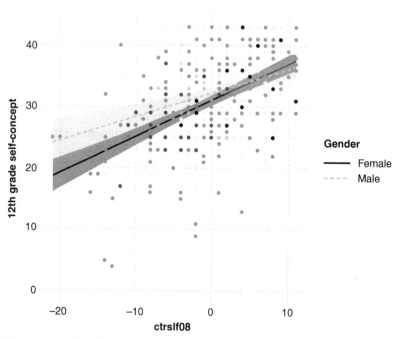

Figure 17.6 Plot of the interaction between eighth grade self-concept and gender on twelfth grade self-concept with gender as moderator and plotted points

We also may find it helpful to depict the interaction with gender on the *x*-axis and eighth grade self-concept as the moderator. The following **interact_plot** command provides that plot by having **gendernew** as the predictor and **ctrslf08** as the moderator and specifying the values of the moderator you want to see using the **modx.values** argument (see Figure 17.7).

interact_plot(results6, pred="gendernew", modx = "ctrslf08", modx.values = c(−20, −10,0,10,20),x.label = "Gender", y.label = "12th Grade Self-Concept", interval = TRUE,pred.labels = c("Male","Female"),
main.title = "12th Grade Self-Concept Related to Gender & 8th Grade Self-Concept",
legend.main = "8th Grade Self-Concept", modx.labels = c("−20", "−10", "0", "10", "20"))

The results of these analyses suggest that females who have average or lower than average self-concept in eighth grade continue to have lower self-concept than males, on average, in twelfth grade, but females who have higher than average self-concept in eighth grade appear to be no different from males in twelfth grade. Had there been no interaction, the difference between males and females in twelfth grade self-concept would have remained the same across the different values of eighth grade self-concept. Without the interaction, we could have said in terms of the two lines depicting changes in self-concept from eighth to twelfth grade that "one size fits all."

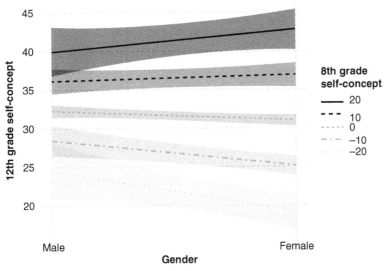

Figure 17.7 Plot of the interaction between eighth grade self-concept and gender on twelfth grade self-concept with eighth grade self-concept as moderator

METHODS USEFUL FOR MODEL SELECTION

With the possibility of creating any number of seemingly appropriate models to explain or predict an outcome variable, the question naturally arises as to which model should one choose; i.e., which model is most appropriate.

One method to help with model selection is the R^2 based on the calibration sample. Because this R^2 will increase, however minimally, when new variables are added to the equation, it is not a very good method by which to select the most appropriate model. A better method would be to use the *adjusted* R^2 (discussed in Chapter 15, see Equation 15.17) and Equation 17.5 below:

$$R^2_{ADJ} = 1 - (1 - R^2)\frac{N-1}{N-P-1},\qquad(17.5)$$

where N = sample size and P = number of predictors in the regression model.

Unlike R^2, the adjusted R^2 will not continuously increase with the addition of predictors into the equation. In fact, it will decrease when predictors are added that are superfluous to the model. For example, if newly added predictors are redundant with predictors already in the model, R^2 will increase only negligibly, and $(1 - R^2)$ in the above equation will therefore stay basically the same. However, because P, the number of predictors in the equation, has increased, the overall amount subtracted from 1 in the above equation will increase, resulting in a reduction in the adjusted R^2.

Other approaches exist for use with model selection based on what is called the *information criterion* (*ic*), and are denoted as AIC (Akaike, 1974) and BIC (Bayesian or Schwarz information criterion; Schwarz, 1978).

Both AIC and BIC are defined when maximum likelihood rather than ordinary least squares (OLS) estimation is used to fit the regression models. However, when errors are normally distributed, maximum likelihood and least squares are the same. As a result, although R uses OLS to estimate the linear regression parameters, it reports the measure of fit used by maximum likelihood estimation (the maximized log-likelihood, *lnL*) and provides AIC and BIC values in the regression output as defined in Equations 17.6.

$$\begin{aligned}\text{AIC} &= -2\ lnL + P\\ \text{BIC} &= -2\ lnL + P\ lnN.\end{aligned}\qquad(17.6)$$

where *lnL* is the maximized log-likelihood of the model, P is the number of parameters estimated.

In general, given two models, the one with the smaller AIC fits the data better than the one with the larger AIC, and likewise for BIC. In general, BIC places a heavier penalty on models with many variables, and so by using the BIC statistic one would select a more parsimonious model (i.e., a model with fewer variables). Both AIC and BIC are useful for comparing models that are not necessarily nested, one within the other.

EXAMPLE 17.3 In Example 17.1, we used the Ice Cream dataset to predict barsold from temp, relhumid and their interaction. Calculate and comment upon the values of adjusted R^2, AIC and BIC as they relate to model selection.

Solution. We run the following code to generate these statistics for three models. Model 1 predicts barsold from temp. Model 2 predicts barsold from temp and relhumid. Model 3 predicts barsold from temp, relhumid, and their interaction.

MORE R: To obtain the AIC, BIC, and adjusted R^2 from a regression model that predicts barsold from temp, we may type the following commands (see Table 17.2):

```
results = lm(barsold ~ temp, data = IceCream)
AIC(results)
BIC(results)
summary(results)$adj.r.squared
```

TABLE 17.2 Adjusted R^2, AIC, and BIC values for the three models

Model	AIC	BIC	Adjusted R^2
1	192.46	196.65	0.7786
2	182.37	187.97	0.8465
3	177.50	184.51	0.8732

The decreasing AIC and BIC values and the increasing adjusted R^2 values across models suggest that Model 3 is the model of choice for this example.

☞ **Remark.** Hirotugu Akaike (1927–2009) was born in Fujinomiya City, Shizuoka Prefecture, Japan. He was the son of a silkworm farmer. He gained BA and DSc degrees from the University of Tokyo. Akaike's career from 1952 at the Institute of Statistical Mathematics in Japan culminated in service as Director General; after 1994, he was Professor Emeritus (Stata Manual).

☞ **Remark.** Gideon E. Schwarz (1933–2007) was a Professor of Statistics at the Hebrew University, Jerusalem. He was born in Salzburg, Austria, and obtained an MSc in 1956 from the Hebrew University and a PhD in 1961 from Columbia University. His interests included stochastic processes, sequential analysis, probability, and geometry (Stata Manual).

Still another approach for helping to decide whether a model is most appropriate from a number of alternatives is to estimate how well a model developed in a calibration sample performs in a *cross-validation* sample. One way to carry out the cross-validation is to:

1. Randomly divide the whole sample into two equal halves, a Sample A and Sample B.
2. Fit a regression model to the data in Sample A and obtain R^2_A.
3. Use the regression model developed in Sample A to obtain the $\hat{Y}$ values from the data in Sample B.
4. Calculate the squared correlation between the actual Y values in Sample B and the $\hat{Y}$ values obtained in step (3) to obtain R^2_B.

☞ **Remark.** R^2_B may be thought of as the *shrunken* R^2 and the difference between R^2_A and R^2_B is referred to as the amount of shrinkage in R^2. Models with large shrinkage should not be selected as they may not generalize to other samples from the same population of interest.

☞ **Remark.** The end-of-chapter exercises will offer an opportunity to practice the first three of these statistics useful for model selection: adjusted R^2, AIC, and BIC.

SUMMARY OF R COMMANDS

Create	Command lines
Compute the product of temperature and relative humidity and give that new variable the name product (Example 17.1)	IceCream$product = IceCream$temp*IceCream$relhumid
Perform a multiple regression of barsold on temp and relhumid with the interaction term (Example 17.1)	summary(IceCream[, c("temp", "barsold", "relhumid", "product")]) cor(IceCream[, c("temp", "barsold", "relhumid", "product")]) results3 = lm(barsold ~ temp + relhumid + product, data = IceCream) summary(results3)
Use a nested regression to test the statistical significance of the interaction term (Example 17.1)	model1 = lm(barsold ~ temp + relhumid, data = IceCream) summary(model1) model2 = lm(barsold ~ temp + relhumid + product, data = IceCream) summary(model2) anova(model1, model2)
Create the graph of the interaction between two scale variables (Figure 17.2)	results2 = lm(barsold ~ temp*relhumid, data = IceCream) interact_plot(results2, pred="temp", modx = "relhumid", modx.values = c (67,88), x.label = "Temperature in Degrees Fahrenheit", y.label = "Average Number of Bars Sold", main.title = "Relating Ice Cream Sales to Temp and Relhumid \n Relhumid Moderates the Relationship between Barsold and Temp", legend.main = "Relhumid", colors = "Greys")
Test the significance from zero of each of the two simple slopes for temperature, one at low humidity and the other at high humidity	sim_slopes(results2, pred = "temp", modx = "relhumid", modx.values = c(67,88))
To center the variables, form the product term that carries the interaction, and conduct the regression analysis (Example 17.2)	NELS$ctrslf08 = NELS$slfcnc08 − mean (NELS$slfcnc08, na.rm = TRUE) NELS$gendernew = as.numeric(NELS$gender) − 1 NELS$product = NELS$gendernew*NELS$ctrslf08

Create	Command lines
	summary(NELS[, c("slfcnc12", "ctrslf08", "gendernew", "product")]) cor(NELS[, c("slfcnc12", "ctrslf08", "gendernew", "product")]) results5 = lm(slfcnc12 ~ ctrslf08 + gendernew + product, data = NELS) anova(results5) summary(results5)
Test whether each (simple) slope is significantly different from zero. (Example 17.2)	results6 = lm(slfcnc12 ~ ctrslf08*gendernew, data = NELS) sim_slopes(results6, pred = "ctrslf08", modx = "gendernew", colors = "Greys")
To create the plot depicting the interaction between a scale and a dichotomous variable (Figure 17.5)	interact_plot(results6, pred="ctrslf08", modx = "gendernew", x.label = "ctrslf08", y.label = "12th Grade Self-Concept", interval = TRUE, main.title = "12th Grade Self-Concept Related to Gender & 8th Grade Self-Concept", legend.main = "Gender", modx.labels =c("Male","Female"), colors = "Greys")
Adapt the plot by adding scatterplot points (Figure 17.6)	interact_plot(results6, pred="ctrslf08", modx = "gendernew", plot.points = TRUE, x.label = "ctrslf08", y.label = "12th Grade Self-Concept", interval = TRUE, main.title = "12th Grade Self-Concept Related to Gender & 8th Grade Self-Concept", legend.main = "Gender", modx.labels = c("Male","Female"), colors = "Greys")
Depict the interaction in Figure 17.5 and Figure 17.6 but with gender on the *x*-axis and 8th grade self-concept as the moderator (Figure 17.7)	interact_plot(results6, pred="gendernew", modx = "ctrslf08", modx.values = c(−20,−10,0,10,20), x.label = "Gender", y.label = "12th Grade Self-Concept", interval = TRUE, pred.labels = c("Male", "Female"), main.title = "12th Grade Self-Concept Related to Gender & 8th Grade Self-Concept", legend.main = "8th Grade Self-Concept", modx.labels = c("−20", "−10", "0", "10", "20"), colors = "Greys")

Create	Command lines
Calculate adjusted R^2 and AIC and BIC indicators for different models predicting barsold (Example 17.3)	model1 = lm(barsold ~ temp, data = IceCream) AIC(model1) BIC(model1) summary(model1)\$adj.r.squared model2 = lm(barsold ~ temp + relhumid, data = IceCream) AIC(model2) BIC(model2) summary(model2)\$adj.r.squared model3 = lm(barsold ~ temp*relhumid, data = IceCream) AIC(model3) BIC(model3) summary(model3)\$adj.r.squared

EXERCISES

Create a .R file for each exercise that requires the use of R. Run the commands from the .R file by highlighting them and hitting **control+enter** on a PC computer keyboard or **command+enter** on a Mac computer keyboard. Save each .R file using a name associated with the Exercise for which it was created. It is recommended that you review the .R file for Chapter 17 located on the textbook's website before completing these exercises. To facilitate doing each exercise, it may be helpful to copy and paste relevant commands from the .R file for Chapter 17 into your own .R file and modify them as needed.

Exercises 17.1–17.5 involve interactions in the NELS dataset. For inferential purposes, we consider the students in the dataset to be a random sample of the population of all college-bound students who have always been at grade level. Use $\alpha = 0.05$ for all significance tests.

17.1 Predict twelfth grade math achievement (achmat12) from whether or not the student attended public school (schtypdi), whether or not the student took advanced math in eighth grade (advmath8), and the interaction of the two.
  (a) Create schtypdi, a variable with 0 = public and 1 = private (both religious and non-religious) from the variable schtyp8. How many students attended private school?
  (b) Create a multiple line graph depicting the predicted twelfth grade math achievement by school type and whether or not advanced math was taken in eighth grade and use it to anticipate the results.
  (c) Create the product term of the two predictor variables. Report the mean of the product term to verify that you did it correctly.
  (d) Is the model that predicts achmat12 from schtypdi, advmat8, and their interaction statistically significant?

(e) Is the interaction statistically significant?

(f) What percentage of the variance in twelfth grade math achievement can be explained by the two main effects and the interaction effect? What percentage can be explained by the interaction alone?

(g) Calculate adjusted R^2 and AIC and BIC indicators for the model that includes both main effects and the model that includes both main effects and the interaction. Comment upon the relative benefits of the two models.

(h) What is the regression equation?

(i) Describe the nature of the interaction by writing down and interpreting separate regression equations for predicting twelfth grade math achievement from school type for those who did not take advanced math in eighth grade and for those who did.

(j) Interpret the slopes of these two equations.

(k) What is contained in your .R file for this analysis?

17.2 In this exercise, we expand on Exercise 16.1 by investigating whether there is an interaction between gender and unitmath on achmat12.

(a) Center the variable unitmath by computing a new variable, unitmatc (unitmatc = unitmath − 3.637, where 3.637 is the mean of unitmath for those values included in the analysis). Verify that the mean of the centered variable is 0.

(b) Create the interaction term, product, as unitmatc*gender. What is the mean of this product term?

(c) To determine if there is an interaction, conduct a hierarchical multiple regression analysis with achmat12 as the outcome variable, unitmatc and gender in the first block, and product in the second block. Is there a statistically significant interaction between gender and number of years of math taken on achievement in math? Explain.

(d) What can you conclude from the results of the test of significance of the interaction?

17.3 In Exercise 16.8, we constructed a regression model to predict the square root of expected income at age 30 plus one (sqrt(expinc30 + 1) from gender and socioeconomic status (ses). In this exercise, we will investigate whether it is appropriate to include an interaction term in the model.

(a) Create a scatterplot that summarizes the analysis. Superimpose two fit lines, one for males and the other for females. Based on the scatterplot, do you anticipate that there is a statistically significant interaction between the two predictor variables on the outcome variable? Explain.

(b) Is the interaction statistically significant? Provide statistical support for your answer using both the relevant b-weight and the F-change statistic.

17.4 In this exercise, we will use multiple regression to determine if expected income at age 30 (expinc30) can be explained by eighth grade self-concept (slfcnc08), socioeconomic status (ses) and their interaction.

(a) Conduct initial univariate and bivariate analyses of the variables involved in the multiple regression model.

(b) Center the variables slfcnc08 and ses to create slfc8c and sesc. Conduct a hierarchical multiple regression analysis with expinc30 as the outcome variable, slfc8c and sesc in the first block, and the product of slfc8c and sesc in the second block. Calculate the significance of F-change. Is the interaction represented by product statistically significant? Provide statistical support for your response.

(c) What is the regression equation for the full model, including the interaction?

(d) Clarify the nature of the interaction by using the regression equation to estimate the expected income at age 30 at one standard deviation above and one standard deviation below 0 (0 is the mean because the variables have been centered) for both slfc8c and sesc.

(e) Create a line graph like that of Figure 17.4, which is a summary of the interaction, using the −1 SD and +1 SD estimates of the moderator sesc.

(f) Describe the nature of the interaction.

17.5 Perform a multiple regression analysis to determine whether ses can be explained by the NAEP units of mathematics taken in high school (unitmath), nursery school attendance (nursery) and their interaction.

(a) Conduct initial univariate and bivariate analyses of the variables involved in the multiple regression model.

(b) Center unitmath and create the product term of the centered unitmath variable with nursery and conduct a simultaneous regression analysis with the three predictor variables. Is the full regression model including the interaction term statistically significant? Is the interaction term statistically significant? Provide statistical support for your answer.

(c) What is the regression equation for the full model, including the interaction?

(d) For those who attended nursery school, what is the regression equation for predicting ses from unitmath?

(e) For those who did not attend nursery school, what is the regression equation for predicting ses from unitmath?

(f) Are the regression equations given in parts (c) and (d) statistically significantly different? How can you tell?

(g) Test the significance from 0 of each of the two simple slopes for units of mathematics taken, one for students who attended nursery school and one for those who didn't.

(h) Create a graph that depicts the interaction.

(i) Describe the nature of the interaction.

(j) What does it mean that the interaction term is statistically significant, but that the b-weights units of math taken in high school is not statistically significant?

Exercise 17.6 involves interactions in the Learndis dataset. In this chapter, we consider the children in the dataset to be a random sample of all children attending public school in the urban area who have been diagnosed with learning disabilities. Use $\alpha = 0.05$ for all significance tests.

17.6 Perform a multiple regression analysis to determine whether reading comprehension (readcomp) can be explained by a combination of math comprehension (mathcomp), grade level (grade), and their interaction. Prior to the analysis, center the variables math comprehension and grade level.

(a) What is the average reading comprehension score for public school students diagnosed with learning disabilities in this urban area?

(b) Is the standard deviation of the centered math comprehension variable (13.75) different from the standard deviation of the original non-centered math comprehension variable? Explain.

(c) Look at the three-dimensional picture of the regression equation. Does there appear to be an interaction? How can you tell?

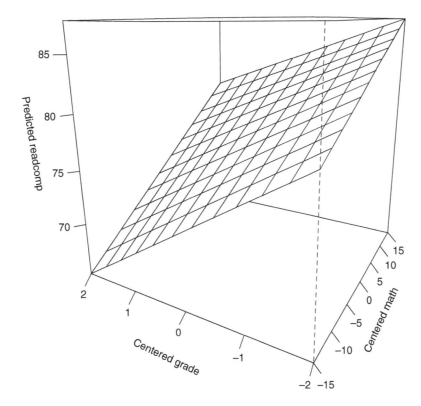

(d) Is the interaction effect statistically significant? Explain.

(e) What is the regression equation with main effects only? Are these main effects statistically significant? Why is the regression equation that includes only main effects a better model for these data?

(f) Using the equation with main effects only, interpret b_1, the b-weight for centered math comprehension, within the context of the problem.

(g) Using the equation with main effects only, interpret b_2, the b-weight for centered grade, within the context of the problem.

(h) What is the proportion of outcome variable variance explained by these two variables?

Exercises 17.7–17.8 relate to examples from the chapter.

17.7 In Example 17.1, we analyzed the relationship between ice cream sales, temperature, humidity, and the interaction between temperature and relative humidity. We did not center the variables before conducting our analysis. For this exercise, re-run the analysis using the centered variables and compare these results to those obtained in the chapter based on the non-centered variables.

(a) Open the Ice Cream dataset in R. Center temp. Center relhumid. Using the centered variables, test whether there is an interaction between temperature and relative humidity on ice cream sales. What proportion of variance in ice cream sales is explained by the model including the interaction term? How do your results compare to those obtained in Example 17.1 based on non-centered variables?

(b) Interpret the coefficient of centered temperature in the regression equation.

(c) Interpret the coefficient of centered relative humidity in the regression equation.

(d) Explain why the plot of the interaction between temperature and relative humidity, given in Figure 17.2, is the same for the two analyses.

17.8 In completing the analysis of the relationship between ice cream sales, temperature, relative humidity, and the interaction between temperature and relative humidity, we should also have paid attention to the diagnostics we discussed in the previous chapter to verify that our model was not influenced unduly by outliers and that the assumptions underlying the procedure are met. We ask you to complete this aspect of the analysis in this exercise. Use the centered variables that you created in Exercise 17.7.

(a) As part of the regression analysis, save the standardized residuals and the Cook's distances. Are any of the standardized residuals less than −2 or greater than 2? Are any of the values for Cook's distance greater than 1?

(b) Conduct a sensitivity analysis by re-running the regression without the values with studentized residuals greater than 2 in magnitude.

(c) Construct two scatterplots, one with centered temp vs. the standardized residuals and one with centered relhumid vs. the standardized residuals. Place the residuals on the vertical axis. Do any of the assumptions (normality, homoscedasticity, and linearity) underlying the multiple regression analysis appear to be violated? Explain.

# CHAPTER EIGHTEEN

NONPARAMETRIC METHODS

In the situations of statistical inference that we have discussed regarding the mean and the variance, the outcome variable Y was tacitly assumed to be at the interval level of measurement. In addition, the statistical tests (e.g., t and F) required the assumptions of normality and, sometimes, homogeneity of variance of the parent population distributions. In the situations of statistical inference regarding correlation and regression, the Y variable was tacitly assumed to be at the interval level of measurement, and the statistical tests required the assumption of homogeneous variances and bivariate normality of the parent population distribution. When one or more of these assumptions regarding the population distributions and parameters are not reasonable, alternative methods of statistical inference must be employed. The focus of this chapter is on the development and use of such alternative methods.

PARAMETRIC VERSUS NONPARAMETRIC METHODS

Because the validity of the inferential tests we have discussed so far in this book relies on explicit assumptions about population distributions and parameters, these tests are called "parametric" or "distribution-tied" methods. There are occasions, however, when the use of parametric methods is not warranted. One such instance occurs when the outcome variable is not at the interval level of measurement, but rather at the nominal or ordinal levels of measurement, as in the case of categorical or ranked data. Another instance occurs when one or more of the required assumptions regarding the parent population distributions are not reasonable, as in the case of studying the mean of a non-normal population using a small sample of data.

In situations where the use of parametric or distribution-tied methods is inappropriate, alternative methods called "nonparametric" or "distribution-free" may be employed. In this chapter, we first present nonparametric techniques that can be used for nominal-leveled variables, and then we present techniques that can be used for ordinal-leveled variables.

Although nonparametric methods have the advantage of being relatively free from assumptions about population distributions and parameters, they have the disadvantage of having lower power generally than comparable parametric methods when these parametric methods do apply. It should also be pointed out that the hypotheses tested using nonparametric methods are not exactly the same as the hypotheses tested using parametric methods. For example, although the parametric two-group t-test specifically tests a hypothesis about the equality of two population means, the comparable nonparametric alternative (to be discussed later in this chapter) tests a hypothesis about the equality of two population distributions, providing information about the equality of the two medians as a by-product.

NONPARAMETRIC METHODS WHEN THE OUTCOME VARIABLE IS AT THE NOMINAL LEVEL

In this section, we present two commonly used nonparametric techniques of statistical inference based on the chi-square distribution, which are applicable when the outcome variable is at the nominal level of measurement. The first method, the chi-square goodness-of-fit test, can be used to analyze the distribution of subjects among the categories of a nominal-leveled variable. For example, it can be used to answer questions such as "Is the distribution of car sales in the eastern United States in the current year for Nissans, Mazdas, Toyotas, and Hondas the same as the known distribution of the previous year?" and "Are college-bound students who are always at grade level equally divided among the four regions of the United States?" The second method, the chi-square test of independence, can be used to determine whether a maximum of two ordinal-leveled variables are related. For example, it can be used to answer questions such as "Is there a relationship between gender and political party affiliation in the United States?," "Among college-bound students in the South who are always at grade level, is there a relationship between nursery school attendance and gender?," and "Among college-bound students who are always at grade level, does computer ownership differ by region of residence?"

THE CHI-SQUARE DISTRIBUTION (χ^2)

Given a *normal* distribution with mean μ and variance σ^2, we select at random a value X from this population. We then form the corresponding z-score and square it to obtain z^2, as follows:

$$z^2 = \left(\frac{X - \mu}{\sigma}\right)^2 = \frac{(X - \mu)^2}{\sigma^2}.$$

The distribution of all z^2 values that could be obtained in this way is shown in Figure 18.1. This distribution is called a chi-square distribution with one degree of freedom (*df*), and it is denoted by the symbol $\chi^2_{(1)}$, where the (1) represents the degrees of freedom of the chi-square distribution.

If instead of drawing a single value at random from the population, we select two values at random from the population and for each value compute the corresponding z^2, we obtain:

$$z_1^2 = \frac{(X_1 - \mu)^2}{\sigma^2} \text{ and } z_2^2 = \frac{(X_2 - \mu)^2}{\sigma^2}$$

If we now add these two z^2 values together and plot the distribution of all such sums that could be obtained in this way (from the given population), we have what is called a chi-square distribution with two degrees of freedom, which is denoted by the symbol $\chi^2_{(2)}$.

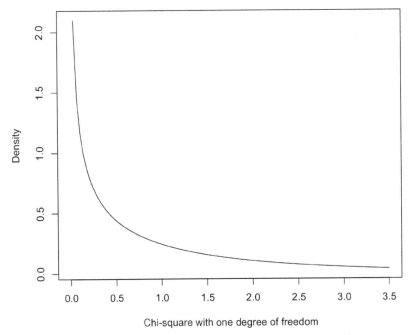

Figure 18.1 The chi-square distribution with one degree of freedom (df)

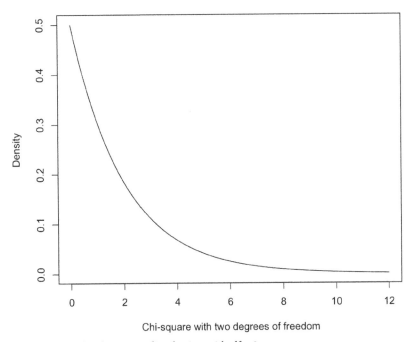

Figure 18.2 The chi-square distribution with $df = 2$

This distribution is shown in Figure 18.2. Note that, as before, all $\chi^2_{(2)}$ values are nonnegative because the $\chi^2_{(2)}$ values are sums of z^2 values, and all squared values are nonnegative.

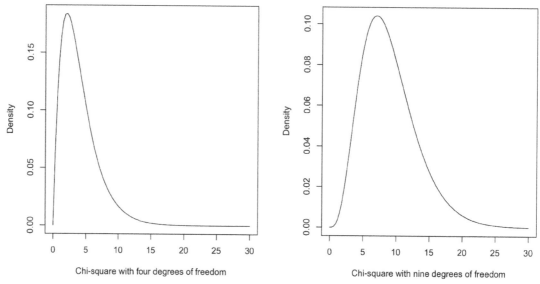

Figure 18.3 Two chi-square distributions

In general, the values of a chi-square distribution with N degrees of freedom are of the form

$$\chi^2_{(N)} = \sum_{i=1}^{N} z_i^2 = \sum_{i=1}^{N} \frac{(X_i - \mu)^2}{\sigma^2},$$

where $X_1, X_2, X_3, \ldots, X_N$ is a random sample of size N drawn from a given normally distributed population with mean μ and variance σ^2.

Figure 18.3 illustrates two chi-square distributions with 4 and 9 degrees of freedom, respectively.

In terms of summary statistics, the mean, mode, and standard deviation of the chi-square distribution are all functions of its degrees of freedom (df). The chi-square distribution has mean equal to df, mode equal to $df - 2$ (as long as $df > 2$), and standard deviation $= \sqrt{2(df)}$.

At this point, we turn to the question of how to use this chi-square distribution (really a family of distributions, just like the t-distributions) to find p-values. To do so, we may use either the R function, which gives the right-tail probability of a chi-square distribution for the value x, or Table C.5 in Appendix C, which also gives the chi-square distribution for right-tailed areas.

EXAMPLE 18.1 Estimate the p-value associated with $\chi^2_3 = 23.18$, first using R syntax and then using Table C.5 in Appendix C.

Solution Executing **pchisq(23.18, 3, lower.tail = F)** leads to the estimate $p = 0.00003686$, which may be rounded to 0.00004.

Turning to Table C.5 in Appendix C, we see that the degrees of freedom are listed down the leftmost column and that they range from 1 to 100 inclusive. Listed across the top row of Table C.5 are selected probability values corresponding to the right tails of the curve. That is, these probability values refer to the amount of area located under the chi-square distribution curve that falls to the right of the chi-square value listed in the table. In our example, we look at the row with $df = 3$. To find the p-value associated with $\chi^2_3 = 23.18$, we find that the closest χ^2 value to 23.18 is 16.27 and we conclude that $p < 0.001$. Note that the two methods, using R and the table, lead to consistent decisions, but that the value obtained from R is a more precise estimate.

If the number of degrees of freedom is not listed in the table, the conservative approach is to take the chi-square value closest to, but lower than, the desired degrees of freedom value. Alternately, the R function **pchisq()** may be used.

THE CHI-SQUARE GOODNESS-OF-FIT TEST

Consider the problem of determining whether the distribution of car sales in the eastern United States in the current year for Nissans, Mazdas, Toyotas, and Hondas is the same as the known distribution of the previous year, which is given hypothetically in Table 18.1.

Setting this question up as a hypothesis test, we have as our null and alternative hypotheses:

H_0: The current year's sales distribution is the same as that of the previous year (Nissan: 18 percent, Mazda: 10 percent, Toyota: 35 percent, Honda: 37 percent).
H_1: The current year's sales distribution is not the same as that of the previous year.

From Motor Vehicle Bureau records, we select a random sample of 1,000 families residing in the eastern United States who have purchased one of these four types of foreign cars in the current year, and we note which type of car was purchased. From this information, we arrive at the sample distribution given in Table 18.2.

If H_0 is true, we would *expect* approximately 18 percent of this sample to have bought Nissans (18 percent of 1,000 = $0.18 \times 1000 = 180$); approximately 10 percent to have bought Mazdas (10 percent of 1,000 = $0.10 \times 1,000 = 100$); approximately 35 percent to have bought Toyotas (35 percent of 1,000 = $0.35 \times 1,000 = 350$); and approximately 37 percent to have bought Hondas (37 percent of 1,000 = $0.37 \times 1,000 = 370$). We create Table 18.3 to compare the sales frequencies *observed* in this sample of 1,000 (as given in Table 18.2) to the sales frequencies *expected* if the hypothesis is true.

Making use of a procedure developed by Karl Pearson in 1900 (Pearson, 1900), we may now determine how unlikely it is for the observed values (O_i) to differ as much as they do from the expected values (E_i), given that the null hypothesis is true. If we compare the observed and expected frequencies shown in Table 18.3 according to the equation

TABLE 18.1 Previous year's sales distribution of selected foreign cars in the eastern United States

Type of car	Percentage
Nissan	18%
Mazda	10%
Toyota	35%
Honda	37%

TABLE 18.2 Current sales distribution of selected foreign cars in the eastern United States (sample size = 1,000)

Type of car	Frequency
Nissan	150
Mazda	65
Toyota	385
Honda	400

$$\chi^2_{K-1} = \sum_{i=1}^{K} \frac{(O_i - E_i)^2}{E_i}, \tag{18.1}$$

the obtained value will be distributed as a chi-square with $df = K - 1$ degrees of freedom, where K is the number of cells (or categories). We can then use the chi-square distribution to calculate the associated p-value to decide whether to retain the null hypothesis that the current year's sales distribution is the same as that of the previous year. The test is always a one-tailed (and in particular a right-tailed) test, because only large, positive values of χ^2 indicate a significant discrepancy between observed and expected values. If we observe a significant discrepancy between the observed and expected values, then this would lead us to reject the null hypothesis in favor of the alternative.

TABLE 18.3 Comparison of observed and expected car sales in our sample of 1,000

Type of car	Observed frequency (O_i)	Expected frequency (E_i)
Nissan	150	180
Mazda	65	100
Toyota	385	350
Honda	400	370

Using the data given in Table 18.3 and Equation 18.1, we test our hypothesis that the current year's distribution of foreign car sales is the same as the previous year's distribution of foreign car sales at significance level $\alpha = 0.05$.

We calculate the observed chi-square as

$$\chi^2_3 = \sum_{i=1}^{4} \frac{(O_i - E_i)^2}{E_i} = \frac{(O_1 - E_1)^2}{E_1} + \frac{(O_2 - E_2)^2}{E_2} + \frac{(O_3 - E_3)^2}{E_3} + \frac{(O_4 - E_4)^2}{E_4}$$

$$= \frac{(150 - 180)^2}{180} + \frac{(65 - 100)^2}{100} + \frac{(385 - 350)^2}{350} + \frac{(400 - 370)^2}{370}$$

$$= \frac{(-30)^2}{180} + \frac{(-35)^2}{100} + \frac{(35)^2}{350} + \frac{(30)^2}{370} = \frac{900}{180} + \frac{1225}{100} + \frac{1225}{350} + \frac{900}{370}$$

$$= 5.00 + 12.25 + 3.50 + 2.43 = 23.18.$$

To find the associated p-value, we may use Table C.5 in Appendix C as illustrated in Example 18.1 or R as described below.

MORE R: To find the p-value associated with a chi-square goodness-of-fit test, we use the R function below:

pchisq(23.19, 3, lower.tail = F)

The obtained result is $p = 0.00004$. That is, if the distribution of sales is the same as in the previous year, the probability of obtaining the observed sample distribution, or one more extreme, is approximately 0.00004. Thus, our decision is to reject H_0 and switch to H_1. We conclude that the current year's distribution of foreign car sales for these selected types is not the same as that of the previous year.

We carried out the hypothesis test by hand for heuristic reasons. We now use R. Given the values in Table 18.2, we may enter the data in tabulated form to create our dataset.

MORE R: To enter in the tabulated data, we type:

type = c("Nissan", "Mazda", "Toyota", "Honda")
freq = c(150, 65, 385, 400)
prob = c(.18, .10, .35, .37)

Note that we enter in the names of the cars first, followed by the observed frequencies, followed by the expected probabilities (rather than the expected counts). (See Table 18.4.)

MORE R: To perform the chi-square goodness-of-fit test on tabulated data, we type:

chisq.test(freq, p = prob)

We obtain the following output:

Chi-square test for given probabilities
data: freq
χ-squared = 23.182,   *df* = 3,   *p*-value = 3.7e-05

The results report the observed χ^2 value, its associated degrees of freedom, and the *p*-value: chisq(3) is 23.18 and p = 3.7e-0.5, or 0.000037.

These values agree with those obtained by hand, and we conclude, as before, that the current year's distribution of foreign car sales for these selected types is not the same as that of the previous year.

Note that we rejected the null hypothesis in favor of the alternative because the fit between the observed and the expected cell values was not good enough. For this reason, this type of chi-square test is known as the *chi-square goodness-of-fit test*.

As discussed previously, because the chi-square goodness-of-fit test is a nonparametric method, its validity does not rely on assumptions about the population from which the sample is selected. The validity of the test, however, does rely on several assumptions about the

TABLE 18.4 The tabulated dataset associated with the data of Table 18.2

car_type	freq
1	150
2	65
3	385
4	400

sample and the treatment of the sample data. First, the cells must be mutually exclusive and exhaustive; that is, each observed piece of information must fit into one and only one of the cells. Therefore, the probabilities associated with each of the categories must sum to 1. Second, the observations must be independent of each other; that is, the result of any one observation must tell us nothing about the result of any other observation. Third, the *expected* frequency in each cell must be at least 5. Fourth and last, the sum of the expected frequencies must equal the sum of the observed frequencies. To justify the use of $K - 1$ degrees of freedom rather than K, the number of cells, we note that the sum of the observed cell frequencies must be equal to the sample size, so that once the first $K - 1$ observed frequencies are known, the Kth is completely determined.

In the special case where the number of degrees of freedom is 1 (when there are two cells), the distribution of values obtained from Equation 18.1 departs markedly from a chi-square distribution. A correction called Yates' correction is used when $df = 1$ to enhance the validity of the test (Yates, 1943). When $df = 1$, the equation for the observed chi-square value is

$$\chi^2_{(1)} = \frac{(|O_1 - E_1| - 0.5)^2}{E_1} + \frac{(|O_2 - E_2| - 0.5)^2}{E_2}.$$ (18.2)

Note that the absolute value of the difference $O_i - E_i$ is taken *before* subtracting 0.5 and squaring.

☞ **Remark.** In R, the argument **correct = T** within the **chisq.test()** command runs the test with Yates' correction, while **correct = F** runs the test without this correction. The default setting for the **chisq.test()** function changes depending on the number of observations in each cell.

• •

EXAMPLE 18.2 Are college-bound high school students who have always been at grade level in the United States equally divided among the four census regions? That is, do the students in the NELS dataset come from a population in which 25 percent of the students are in each region? Use $\alpha = 0.05$.

Solution

In this case, we solve using R only.

The null and alternative hypotheses in this problem are

H_0: The distribution by region is uniform (25 percent in each region).
H_1: The distribution by region is not uniform.

MORE R: To perform the chi-square goodness-of-fit test on raw data, we once again use the **chisq.test** function:

chisq.test(table(NELS$region), p = c(0.25, 0.25, 0.25, 0.25))

In this example, each of the four regions has an expected percentage of 25 percent (or 0.25). If we were to complete this test by hand, we would need to find the expected frequency for each region. To do this, we would multiply 0.25 by the sample size 500 to obtain $0.25 \times 500 = 125$.

The output from R gives the results of the chi-square goodness-of-fit test. Note that because there are four regions, the degrees of freedom equal 4 − 1 or 3.

Chi-square test for given probabilities

data: table(NELS$region)

χ-squared = 21.488, $df = 3$, p-value = 8.336e-05

We see that in this case, our obtained chi-square value is $\chi_3^2 = 21.49$, which has $p < 0.0005$. Because $p < \alpha$, we conclude that such students in the USA are not uniformly distributed among the four regions.

THE CHI-SQUARE TEST OF INDEPENDENCE

In this section, we present another application of the Pearson chi-square distribution, one that enables us to determine whether two categorical variables are related. For example, suppose we were interested in determining whether the gender (Male, Female) and ppa (Political Party Affiliation [Democrat, Republican, Neither]) are related (dependent). If they are related, then knowing the gender of an individual would predict the individual's political party affiliation, and otherwise would not.

Suppose that a random sample of 200 individuals drawn from a population of interest produces the following observed frequencies, organized in Table 18.5 as what is called a bivariate contingency table or cross-tabulation.

TABLE 18.5 Political party affiliation by gender

	Democrat	Republican	Neither
Male	40	10	50
Female	60	20	20

If we can determine the expected frequency in each cell given that the two variables are mutually independent, then, as in the chi-square goodness-of-fit test, we can compare observed with expected cell frequencies. We do so by using Equation 18.3,

$$\chi_{(C-1)(R-1)}^2 = \sum_{i,j} \frac{(O_{ij} - E_{ij})^2}{E_{ij}}, \tag{18.3}$$

which gives values that are distributed as a chi-square with $(C-1)(R-1)$ degrees of freedom, where C is the number of columns and R is the number of rows in the contingency table. In Table 18.5, there are three columns and two rows, so the number of degrees of freedom is $df = (C-1)(R-1) = (3-1)(2-1) = (2 \times 1) = 2$. We compute p based on this chi-square value to determine how unlikely it is for the observed frequencies (O_{ij}) to differ as much as they do from the expected frequencies (E_{ij}), given that the null hypothesis is true that the two variables are mutually independent.

The p-value is the area to the right of the observed chi-square value. If the fit between observed and expected values is poor, then the observed chi-square value will be large, and we will reject the hypothesis of independence. We show how to determine the expected cell frequencies for all cells using the data (observed cell frequencies) of Table 18.5.

We first sum all the frequencies in each row to find the row marginal frequencies. We also sum all the frequencies in each column to find the column marginal frequencies. The marginal frequencies are given in Table 18.6. The marginal frequency for the first row (Males) is 40 + 10 + 50 = 100; the marginal frequency for the second row (Females) is 60 + 20 + 20 = 100; the marginal frequency for the first column (Democrat) is 40 + 60 = 100; the marginal frequency of the second column (Republican) is 10 + 20 = 30; and, the marginal frequency of the third column (Neither) is 50 + 20 = 70. The marginal frequencies tell us that there are 100 males and 100 females in the entire sample of 200 individuals and that there are 100 Democrats, 30 Republicans, and 70 of neither party in the same sample of 200 individuals.

If the two variables gender and political party affiliation truly are independent of each other, because we have the same number of males and females in the sample, we would expect the number of male Democrats to equal the number of female Democrats, the number of male Republicans to equal the number of female Republicans, and the number of males of neither party to equal the number of females of neither party. That is, because there are a total of 100 Democrats, we would expect 50 of them to be male and 50 of them to be female. Because there are a total of 30 Republicans, we would expect 15 of them to be male and 15 of them to be female. And because there are a total of 70 of neither party, we would expect 35 of them to be male and 35 of them to be female.

These expected frequencies, along with the observed frequencies, are given in Table 18.7.

A more formal method for finding the expected frequency of a given cell is simply to multiply the marginal frequency of the row the cell is in by the marginal frequency of the column the cell is in, and divide by the total sample size N.

TABLE 18.6 Cross-tabulation of political party affiliation by gender with marginal frequencies

gender	Democrat	ppa Republican	Neither	Total
Male	40	10	50	100
Female	60	20	20	100
Total	100	30	70	

TABLE 18.7 Observed and expected frequencies for political party affiliation by gender

	Democrat	Republican	Neither
Male	$O = 40$	$O = 10$	$O = 50$
	$E = 50$	$E = 15$	$E = 35$
Female	$O = 60$	$O = 20$	$O = 20$
	$E = 50$	$E = 15$	$E = 35$

For example, to find the expected frequency for "Male Democrats," the cell in row 1 and column 1 of Table 18.6, we multiply the marginal frequency of row 1 (100) by the marginal frequency of column 1 (100) to obtain $100 \times 100 = 10,000$. We then divide this product by the total sample size $N = 200$ to obtain an expected frequency of $10,000/200 = 50$, the value we obtained earlier in Table 18.7. Similarly, to find the expected frequency for "Male Republicans," the cell in row 1 and column 2 in Table 18.6, we multiply the marginal frequency of row 1 (100) by the marginal frequency of column 2 (30) to obtain $100 \times 30 = 3,000$. We then divide this product by the total sample size $N = 200$ to obtain an expected frequency of $3,000/200 = 15$, the value we obtained earlier in Table 18.7.

Given these expected frequencies, we now test the null and alternative hypotheses.

H_0: Gender and political party affiliation are independent.
H_1: Gender and political party affiliation are dependent.

Because there are two rows and three columns in this example, the number of degrees of freedom is $df = (C - 1)(R - 1) = (3 - 1)(2 - 1) = (2 \times 1) = 2$.

Using Equation 18.3, we obtain the following observed chi-square value:

$$\chi_2^{(2)} = \sum_{i,j} \frac{(O_{ij} - E_{ij})^2}{E_{ij}}$$

$$= \frac{(40 - 50)^2}{50} + \frac{(10 - 15)^2}{15} + \frac{(50 - 35)^2}{35} + \frac{(60 - 50)^2}{50} + \frac{(20 - 15)^2}{15} + \frac{(20 - 35)^2}{35}$$

$$= \frac{100}{50} + \frac{25}{15} + \frac{225}{35} + \frac{100}{50} + \frac{25}{15} + \frac{225}{35} = \frac{200}{50} + \frac{50}{15} + \frac{450}{35} = 4 + 3.33 + 12.86$$

$$= 20.19.$$

To find the associated p-value, we use R or the chi-square table in Appendix C. In this case, the R syntax **pchisq(20.19, 2, lower.tail = F)** gives $p = 0.00004$. Alternatively, the estimated p-value using Table C.5 in Appendix C is $p < 0.001$.

Thus, if there were no relationship between political party affiliation and gender, the probability of obtaining the observed sample data is approximately 0.00004. Accordingly, we reject H_0 in favor of H_1, that gender and political party affiliation are related, for the population under study. Said differently, the distribution of political party affiliation for males is different from that for females. The data of Table 18.5 indicate that while females tend to be Democrats, males are more evenly split between Democrats and neither political party.

We now illustrate how to perform the chi-square test of independence using R.

MORE R: To perform the chi-square test of independence, we type:

chisq.test(table(Politics\$Gender, Politics\$Party))

The output gives the results of the chi-square test of independence.

Pearson's chi-square test

data: table(Politics$Gender, Politics$Party)

χ-squared = 20.19 $df = 2$ p-value = 4.128e-05

The Pearson chi-square results from R are consistent with those obtained by hand in that $\chi^2_{(2)} = 20.19$ with $p < 0.0005$. As before, we conclude that the distribution of political party affiliation for males is different from that for females.

Assumptions of the Chi-Square Test of Independence

The basic assumptions underlying the use of the chi-square test of independence are as follows:

1. The individual observations are independent of each other (no observation has any effect on any other observation).
2. The expected cell frequencies are not too small (the minimum expected cell frequency required in a particular problem depends on the significance level α and how similar in size the expected cell frequencies are to each other). In general, however, a good minimum expected cell frequency is 5; that is, each cell should have an expected frequency of 5 or more.

For the analysis of the relationship between gender and political party affiliation, we see that the first assumption was met by the sampling design. The second assumption can be assessed by looking at Table 18.5, and seeing that the minimum cell frequency is 10.

• •

EXAMPLE 18.3 Using the NELS dataset, is there a relationship between nursery school attendance and gender among college-bound high school students who are always at grade level?

Solution Note that in Example 5.6(1), we asked whether there is a relationship between nursery school attendance and gender among students in the NELS dataset. To answer this descriptively, we used both the correlation (phi coefficient, in this case) and the contingency table. We now answer this question inferentially and draw conclusions to the larger population from which the students in the NELS dataset have been selected.

The null and alternative hypotheses are:

H_0: There is no relationship between nursery school attendance and gender in the population (they are independent).

H_1: There is a relationship between nursery school attendance and gender in the population (they are dependent).

MORE R: To perform the chi-square test of independence with raw (non-tabulated) data, we type:

chisq.test(table (NELS$gender, NELS$nursery), correct = F)

The output gives the *p*-value associated with the chi-square test of independence:

Pearson's chi-square test
data: table(NELS$Gender, NELS$nursery)
χ-squared = 0.35504 *df* = 1   *p*-value = 0.5513

In this case, $\chi^2_{(1)} = 0.36$ and $p = 0.55$, indicating that we should fail to reject the null hypothesis. We conclude that there is no relationship between gender and nursery school attendance among college-bound high school students who are always at grade level.

In a situation such as this one that has two dichotomous variables, there is an alternative approach to determine whether there is a relationship between nursery school attendance and gender among college-bound high school students who are always at grade level. That approach is via the use of the Pearson correlation coefficient.

MORE R: To obtain the correlation between nursery school attendance and gender, we type:

cor.test(as.numeric(NELS$nursery), as.numeric(NELS$gender))

We obtain the following output:

Pearson's product-moment correlation
data: as.numeric(NELS$nursery) and as.numeric(NELS$gender)
$t = -0.59468$ *df* = 418   *p*-value = 0.5524
alternative hypothesis: true correlation is not equal to 0
95 percent confidence interval: −0.12441469   0.06679743
sample estimates: cor   −0.02907461

We see that $r = -0.029$ with $p > 0.05$, corroborating the results of the chi-square test of independence.

. . . .

EXAMPLE 18.4 Do families of eighth graders who are college bound and always at grade level differ on computer ownership according to the region of the country in which they reside?

Solution

Note that we answered this question descriptively in Example 5.9, confining our conclusions to the 500 individuals in our NELS dataset. We now answer this question inferentially and draw inferences to the larger population from which the students in the NELS dataset have been selected.

The null and alternative hypotheses are

H_0: There is no relationship between region and computer ownership in the population (they are independent).
H_1: There is a relationship between region and computer ownership in the population (they are dependent).

MORE R: To perform the chi-square test of independence using raw data, type:

chisq.test(table(NELS\$region, NELS\$computer))

The output gives the results of the Pearson chi-square test of independence.

Pearson's chi-square test
data: table(NELS\$region, NELS\$computer)
χ-squared = 9.4481 df = 3 p-value = 0.02389

In this case, chisq(3) = 9.45 and p = 0.02, indicating that we should reject the null hypothesis as implausible in favor of the alternative. We conclude that there is a relationship between region and computer ownership among college-bound high school students who are always at grade level.

FISHER'S EXACT TEST

The p-values obtained through the chi-square test of independence are only approximations to the true or exact p-values. In the case of a 2×2 contingency table, an approach that does provide exact p-values is the Fisher's exact test. The approximate p-values of the chi-square test of independence depart from the true or exact p-values especially when sample sizes are small, and in such cases, the Fisher's exact test result should be used as it provides the more accurate result.

The Fisher's exact test was first proposed in 1934 by R. A. Fisher (Fisher, 1934) and makes use of a probability distribution called the hypergeometric probability distribution for obtaining the exact probability values associated with the observed outcome or an outcome that is more extreme than the observed outcome, given that the null hypothesis is true.

By contrast to the Pearson chi-square test, the calculation of exact probabilities using the hypergeometric probability distribution is quite laborious even when sample sizes are small. We illustrate this fact with an example that makes use of the same variables found in Example 18.3, but with a far smaller sample size. In practice, however, we simply may rely on the computer to obtain these Fisher's exact probability values using R.

EXAMPLE 18.5 Is there a relationship between nursery school attendance and gender given a sample of size $N = 12$, randomly selected without replacement from a relatively small population of college-bound high school students from one particular area in the South?

In Example 18.3, notice that the ratio of those who attended nursery school to those who did not is approximately 2:1. Likewise, the ratio of males to females is approximately 1:1. For comparability, these same ratios will be used in the current example. That is, for this example, we assume that of the 12 students randomly selected, 8 have attended nursery school and 4 have not; and that 6 are male and 6 are female. Accordingly, the marginal values of our 2×2 contingency table are as follows:

	Male	Female	Total
Nursery School – No			8
Nursery School – Yes			4
Total	6	6	12

Given these marginal values, the Fisher's exact test provides the exact probability of whether the observed, or even more extreme, distribution of the proportion of males and females who attend nursery school is consistent with the null hypothesis that there is no difference between the proportion of males and females who attend nursery school.

Assume that we have observed the following number of males and females to have attended nursery school or not:

MORE R: To perform the Fisher's exact test, we first create a matrix object with our data:

data = matrix(c(2,6,4,0), nrow = 2, byrow = T)

A matrix is a two-dimensional data structure consisting of rows and columns. In this case, we enter 2 and 6 into the first row, and 4 and 0 into the second row, as displayed in Table 18.8. The argument **byrow = T** indicates that it is True that we are entering the data row by row.

The following line runs Fisher's exact test:

fisher.test(data)

Using this procedure, we obtain the following results:

> Fisher's exact test for count data
>
> data: data
>
> p-value = 0.06061
>
> alternative hypothesis: true odds ratio is not equal to 1
>
> 95 percent confidence interval: 0.000000   1.099161
> sample estimates: odds ratio   0

For this example, the Fisher's exact test 2-sided probability is $p = 0.061$, resulting in the conclusion not to reject the null hypothesis.

Calculating the Fisher's Exact Test by Hand Using the Hypergeometric Distribution

For those interested, in this section we provide the general form of the Fisher's exact test for the 2×2 case using the hypergeometric distribution.

Given N subjects categorized into a 2×2 contingency table as follows:

	A_1	A_2	
B_1	a	b	$a + b$
B_2	c	d	$c + d$
	$a + c$	$b + d$	N

If the marginal values are considered fixed, and sampling is without replacement from a relatively small population, the 1-sided exact probability of observing the relative frequencies a, b, c, and d in the 2×2 table is given by the hypergeometric distribution as follows:

$$\frac{\binom{a+c}{a}\binom{b+d}{b}}{\binom{N}{a+b}} = \frac{(a+b)!(c+d)!(a+c)!(b+d)!}{N!a!b!c!d!}. \tag{18.4}$$

Given the observed nursery school/gender results provided by Table 18.8, using Equation 18.4, we find that the one-sided exact probability of obtaining this particular set of frequencies, with the marginal values considered fixed, is:

$$\frac{8!4!6!6!}{12!2!6!4!0!} = \frac{1}{33} = 0.0303.$$

Doubling this value, we obtain the two-sided exact probability to be 0.0606, or 0.061 as given by R in its rounded form.

This is the exact probability of obtaining by chance the observed outcome or an outcome more extreme, given the null hypothesis is true. Accordingly, since 0.0606 exceeds the 0.05 significance level, we cannot reject the null hypothesis in favor of the alternative. We conclude that there appears to be no relationship between nursery school attendance and sex based on this example.

☞ **Remark.** Because the observed result given in Table 18.8 is as extreme as possible in one direction (we know this to be the case because of the presence of the 0 in one of the cells), we needed only to compute the hypergeometric probability for this one case. Given that a test of the null hypothesis addresses the generic question "What is the probability, given the null hypothesis is true, of obtaining the result observed or results even less consistent with the null hypothesis (i.e., more extreme)?", the calculation of the exact probability in question must consider not only the result observed, but also all possible results that are more extreme (or more disproportionate) than the result observed (if the result is not already the most extreme, as it was in our example). Simply stated, the calculation of the exact probability in question must be based not only on the result observed, but also on all possible results that may be observed that are increasingly more extreme (increasingly less consistent with the null hypothesis of no relationship) than the result observed, until the smallest cell frequency is 0; the exact probability equals the sum of the hypergeometric probabilities of all such possible increasingly more extreme results, beginning with the result observed. We illustrate by assuming that the observed result is given in Table 18.9, rather than in Table 18.8.

Given the marginal values of 8 and 4, and 6 and 6, respectively, we may note that the cell frequencies of Table 18.9 are more consistent with the null hypothesis of no relationship between nursery school attendance and sex (and therefore less extreme) than those of Table 18.8.

TABLE 18.8 Observed frequencies for nursery school attendance by gender

	Male	Female	Total
Nursery School – No	2	6	8
Nursery School – Yes	4	0	4
Total	6	6	12

TABLE 18.9 New observed frequencies for nursery school attendance by gender

	Male	Female	Total
Nursery School – No	3	5	8
Nursery School – Yes	3	1	4
Total	6	6	12

Using Equation 18.4, we find that the one-sided exact probability of obtaining the particular set of cell frequencies given in Table 18.9, with the marginal values considered fixed, to be:

$$\frac{8!4!6!6!}{12!3!5!3!1!} = \frac{8}{33} = 0.2424.$$

Adding this probability value to the probability value associated with the more extreme result given in Table 18.8, yields the following one-sided exact probability value $p = 0.2424 + 0.0303 = 0.2727$. Doubling this value we find the two-sided exact probability value to be $p = 0.5454$, which is the value given by the following R output, obtained using the previously used R input and **fisher.test** commands (see the .R file associated with this chapter for the specific commands):

Fisher's exact test for count data

data: data

p-value = 0.5455

alternative hypothesis: true odds ratio is not equal to 1

95 percent confidence interval: 0.00319446   4.50042353

sample estimates: odds ratio   0.2303567

Because the exact probability ($p = 0.545$) of obtaining by chance the observed outcome of Table 18.9 or an outcome more extreme, given the null hypothesis is true, exceeds the 0.05 significance level, we cannot reject the null hypothesis in favor of the alternative in this case. We conclude, therefore, that there appears to be no relationship between nursery school attendance and sex based on the observed result given in this example.

☞ **Remark.** Although it is too advanced for inclusion in this book, we should mention the existence of a general technique called log-linear analysis that can be used to estimate and test complex models involving outcome variables measured at the nominal level. The model for log-linear analysis is similar to the model for analysis of variance in that it allows for the estimation and testing of both main and interaction effects. The interested reader should consult a more advanced book that covers this topic in detail (Marascuilo & Busk, 1987; Marascuilo & Serlin, 1988).

NONPARAMETRIC METHODS WHEN THE OUTCOME VARIABLE IS ORDINAL-LEVELED

In this section, we present a few commonly used nonparametric techniques that are applicable when the outcome variable is at the ordinal level of measurement. In particular, we present: the Wilcoxon sign test for matched pairs, the nonparametric analog to the t-test on means for dependent groups; the Mann–Whitney U-test, the nonparametric analog to the t-test on means for independent groups; and the Kruskal–Wallis "Analysis of Variance," the nonparametric analog of the one-way ANOVA. These tests were first introduced in the mid to late 1940s.

☞ **Remark.** Frank Wilcoxon, then a chemist at American Cyanimid, published a revolutionary paper, "Individual comparisons by ranking methods," in 1945 (Wilcoxon, 1945) that introduced the notion that statistical hypothesis tests do not necessarily need to be based on estimates of distribution parameters (e.g., the mean, variance, or correlation), but rather could be based more simply on assigning ranks to the observed data and comparing those ranks to ranks that would be expected randomly, or by chance. As noted earlier, because such tests do not require the estimation of a parameter, they are called *nonparametric* tests. Working independently, and in the same vein, Henry B. Mann, an economist, and D. Ransom Whitney, a graduate student in statistics at Ohio State University, published a paper two years later that served to continue a focus on nonparametric tests

(Mann & Whitney, 1947). As noted by Salsburg (2001, p. 164), "[t]he work of Wilcoxon and Mann and Whitney had opened a new window of mathematical investigation by directing attention to the underlying nature of ordered ranks." One such later example is the paper by Kruskal and Wallis (1952).

A nonparametric measure of association between two variables, each in rank order form, is the Spearman rank correlation coefficient. Recall that this measure of association was discussed and illustrated in Chapter 5 as a special case of the Pearson correlation coefficient. Consequently, although the Spearman rank correlation coefficient is a nonparametric technique, it will not be presented in this chapter.

WILCOXON SIGN TEST

Perhaps the simplest nonparametric procedure is the sign test for matched pairs. The sign test tests the null hypothesis that two population distributions are identical. It is used with pairwise matched (or related) samples to determine whether or not two conditions (or treatments) have identical population distributions for the outcome variable. The proportion in the population is denoted π.

The null hypothesis of the sign test assumes that there is no difference between conditions, and consequently that chance alone determines whether the difference between scores on the outcome variable for each sample pair is positive or negative. If the signs of the pairwise differences are due to chance alone, then the probability that any particular pairwise difference is positive (or negative) is 0.50, and the probabilities of all possible outcomes of the experiment (i.e., the number of positive pairwise differences, Pos) may be represented by a binomial model with $p = 0.50$ and N equal to the number of matched pairs. In the event of ties (i.e., pairwise differences of 0), the procedure is to drop the tied pairs from the sample and to reduce the sample size accordingly. The null hypothesis of equal treatment effects in the population (H_0: $\pi = 0.50$) is tested using the binomial distribution. We carry out the sign test procedure by hand and then using R in Example 18.6.

● ●

EXAMPLE 18.6 In a study to determine if weights recorded on packaged snack food items (muffins, cookies, cakes, candy bars, potato chips, and pretzels) are accurate, two of each item type was randomly selected, removed from its packaging, and weighed on a high precision scale. Recorded package weights and obtained (actual) weights in ounces are given pairwise below.

Sample 1 (recorded weights): 11.5, 10.0, 17.0, 16.0, 12.5, 9.0, 8.75, 6.0, 8.0, 20.5, 5.75, 16.0.
Sample 2 (actual weights): 11.8, 10.0, 16.5, 16.0, 13.0, 9.5, 9.00, 6.0, 8.2, 19.5, 6.20, 16.2.

The paired samples t-test could be appropriate, in this case. We assume, for the purposes of this example, that at least one of the assumptions underlying the paired samples t-test is not tenable (namely, that either the two parent populations are not normally distributed or that they do not have equal variances). Accordingly, we employ instead its nonparametric analog, the sign test. We use a 0.05 level of significance. Because a direction of difference is not specified, the test is two-tailed.

Solution The data are reproduced and the signs of the differences between the recorded and actual weights are noted as well.

Sample 1 (recorded weights): 11.5, 10.0, 17.0, 16.0, 12.5, 9.0, 8.75, 6.0, 8.0, 20.5, 5.75, 16.0
Sample 2 (actual weights): 11.8, 10.0, 16.5, 16.0, 13.0, 9.5, 9.0, 6.0, 8.2, 19.5, 6.2, 16.2
Sign of difference (recorded−actual): − 0 + 0 − − − 0 − +− −.

Because there are three tied pairs (sign of difference = 0), we eliminate these pairs and reduce the sample size from $N = 12$ to $N = 9$. Using Table C.2 of the binomial probability distribution with $N = 9$ and $p = 0.50$, we find the two-tailed rejection region to be 0, 1, 8, or 9 positive differences. Note that we must include the two lowest and two highest differences in our rejection region because the test of interest is a two-sided test. We observe that the number of positive pairwise differences as $Pos = 2$. Because 2 is not in the rejection region, we cannot reject the null hypothesis of equal weights and we conclude that weights recorded on such packaged snack food items are accurate; they are not statistically significantly different from actual weights.

We may note also from the binomial distribution table with $N = 9$ and $p = 0.50$ that the probability of obtaining 2 or more extreme (in both directions because the test is two-sided) positive differences is:

Prob(0 or 1 or 2 or 7 or 8 or 9)

= Prob(0) + Prob(1) + Prob(2) + Prob(7) + Prob(8) + Prob(9)

= 0.002 + 0.0176 + 0.0703 + 0.0703 + 0.0176 + 0.002 = 0.1798 or 0.18.

Because 0.18 exceeds 0.05, our conclusion, once again, is not to reject the null hypothesis in favor of the alternative.

MORE R: To carry out the sign test, first we enter our data using the following commands:

recordwt = c(11.5, 10.0, 17.0, 16.0, 12.5, 9.0, 8.75, 6.0, 8.0, 20.5, 5.75, 16.0)
actualwt = c(11.8, 10.0, 16.5, 16.0, 13.0, 9.5, 9.0, 6.0, 8.2, 19.5, 6.2, 16.2)

Next, we must install (only once per computer) and load (once per R session) the BSDA package with the following commands:

install.packages("BSDA")
library(BSDA)

Once the data are entered as 12 records of two variables each (recordwt and actualwt), and the package is loaded, we use the following command:

SIGN.test(recordwt, actualwt)

The results corroborate with those obtained above.

Dependent-samples sign-test

data: recordwt
and actualwt
$S = 2$ p-value = 0.1797

alternative hypothesis: true median difference is not equal
to 0

95 percent confidence interval   0.4340455   0.0000000
sample estimates: median of x−y   −0.2

As mentioned earlier, the *t*-test on related samples is the parametric alternative to the sign test. When the parametric assumptions underlying the *t*-test are true, the power of the *t*-test will be greater than that of the corresponding nonparametric sign test. Consequently, if the underlying assumptions of the parametric test are satisfied, we should use the more powerful parametric procedure, the *t*-test on related groups, in this case. If one or more of the assumptions are not satisfied, however, then the nonparametric procedure, the sign test for matched pairs, in this case, is the best available alternative.

☞ **Remark.** As noted in Chapter 8, when Np and Nq both exceed 5, the binomial distribution is well approximated by the normal. Because $p = 0.50$ for the sign test, N must exceed 10 to use the normal as an approximation of the binomial. In this case, the normal distribution has mean and standard deviation given by Equation 18.5:

$$\text{mean} = \mu_{Pos} = Np = N(0.5) = \frac{N}{2},$$

$$\text{standard deviation} = \sigma_{Pos} = \sqrt{Npq} = \sqrt{N(0.5)(0.5)} = \sqrt{N}(0.5) = \frac{\sqrt{N}}{2}. \tag{18.5}$$

We may determine the significance of an observed value of *Pos* by transforming it to a *z*-value using Equation 18.6:

$$z = \frac{2Pos - N + C}{\sqrt{N}}, \tag{18.6}$$

where

$C = +1$ if $(2Pos - N) < 0$
$C = -1$ if $(2Pos - N) > 0$.

The *z*-value obtained in Equation 18.5 may be compared to an appropriate critical *z*-value to determine its statistical significance. The letter C in this equation is a correction for continuity factor, which is included to enhance the fit between the binomial model (which is discrete) and the normal model (which is continuous).

THE MANN–WHITNEY U-TEST OR WILCOXON RANK-SUM TEST

Like the sign test, the Mann–Whitney U-test tests the null hypothesis that two population distributions are identical. Unlike the sign test, however, the Mann–Whitney U-test is designed for use with unrelated or independent samples, and uses the ranks of the sample scores rather than the scores themselves. The Mann–Whitney U-test is equivalent to a test known as Wilcoxon's rank-sum test.

The Mann–Whitney U-test assumes that there is no difference between populations, and consequently, if both populations were combined into one large group, there would be a complete intermingling of scores. If we select a random sample from each population, and combine both samples into one large group, we would expect a complete intermingling of sample scores similar to that of the population scores, but with some separation due to sampling error. The question is whether the observed separation between samples is significant of a true separation in the population, or can be accounted for by chance factors alone.

What we need is a measure of the extent to which the two groups are not completely intermingled; that is, the extent to which the scores of one group are generally smaller than, equal to, or larger than the scores of the other group. What is also needed is a sampling distribution against which to compare this measure to determine if the difference between the two groups is statistically significant. Such a measure is provided by the U-statistic, which is defined as the number of times a score from one group is smaller than a score from the other group. For simplicity, we shall assume that all scores are unique and that there are no ties. For situations in which there are tie scores, the interested reader is referred to Siegel & Castellan (1988), a more advanced book on this topic. We illustrate with an example.

EXAMPLE 18.7 Use the Mann–Whitney U-test to determine whether a random sample of four boys and a random sample of five girls who participate in varsity college soccer come from identical populations when one considers the number of injuries sustained in a season of play. Use a 0.05 level of significance. The data are given below.

Boys:	14	17	18	25	
Girls:	7	13	15	16	12

Solution We will compute U as the number of times a value in the sample of boys is smaller than a value in the sample of girls. Looking at the data, we see that 14 is smaller than 2 values in the sample of girls; 17 is smaller than none of the 5 values in the sample of girls; 18 is smaller than none of the 5 values, and likewise for 25. Consequently, $U = 2 + 0 + 0 + 0 = 2$.

☞ **Remark.** It may be noted that the value of U will always be between 0 and $(N_1)(N_2)$. A value of U near 0 indicates that the values in the first group are generally larger than the values in the second group. A value of U near the middle of the range, $(N_1)(N_2)/2$, indicates that the values in the first group are generally intermingled with the values in the second group. A value of U near $(N_1)(N_2)$ indicates that the values in the first group are generally smaller than the values in the second group.

In this example, U can range between 0 and $(N_1)(N_2) = (4)(5) = 20$, so the obtained U value of 2 suggests that the number of injuries sustained by the sample of boys is generally larger than the number of injuries sustained by the sample of girls.

To determine whether the sample data are consistent with the null hypothesis that the two population distributions are identical, we compare the obtained value of U to an appropriate sampling distribution of U values. We reject the null hypothesis of identical population distributions if the obtained value of U is in the rejection region, otherwise we do not.

A table of critical U values, organized by rows and columns, is given in Table C.7 of Appendix C. The rows are indexed by N_1, the size of Sample 1, and the columns are indexed by N_2, the size of Sample 2.

In this example, $N_1 = 4$ and $N_2 = 5$. Therefore, the critical values, contained in the column labeled $N_1 = 4$ and the row labeled $N_2 = 5$, for $\alpha = 0.05$, two-tailed, are 1 and 19 and the rejection region for U is 0, 1, 19, 20. Because the obtained U value of 2 is not in the rejection region, we retain belief in the null hypothesis that the two population distributions are identical.

An alternative method for obtaining the U statistic that is based on the ranks of the scores is given in Equation 18.7:

$$U = N_1 N_2 + \frac{N_1(N_1 + 1)}{2} - R_1, \tag{18.7}$$

where N_1 is the size of Sample 1, N_2 is the size of Sample 2, and R_1 is the sum of the ranks of Sample 1 when all scores from both samples are combined and rank-ordered from smallest (assigned a rank of 1) to largest (assigned a rank of $N_1 + N_2$).

We illustrate the use of Equation 18.7 using the data of Example 18.7.

The nine scores rank ordered from smallest to largest are:

Raw Score:	7	12	13	14	15	16	17	18	25
Rank:	1	2	3	4	5	6	7	8	9

The sum of Sample 1 ranks is: $R_1 = 4 + 7 + 8 + 9 = 28$. Substituting the relevant values into Equation 18.7, we obtain:

$$U = (4)(5) + \frac{(4)(4 + 1)}{2} - 28 = 2,$$

the same value obtained in connection with the approach presented previously.

Our conclusion, once again, is not to reject the null hypothesis in favor of the alternative.

MORE R: To carry out the Mann–Whitney U- (or Wilcoxon's rank-sum) test.

We first enter our data as two vectors, labeled "girls" and "boys":

girls = c(7, 13, 15, 16, 12)
boys = c(14, 17, 18, 25)
wilcox.test(girls, boys)

Using R, we obtain the following results:

> Wilcoxon rank sum test
>
> data: girls and boys
>
> W = 2 p-value = 0.06349
>
> alternative hypothesis: true location shift is not equal to 0

Because the p-value obtained above (0.063) is greater than 0.05, we fail to reject the null hypothesis, which corroborates the results obtained above.

EXAMPLE 18.8 In a small study to determine whether boys have a more positive attitude than girls toward organized baseball at a co-ed summer camp, eight boys and five girls of the same age were randomly selected from a particular summer camp and given an attitude questionnaire on this topic. The following data were obtained. Higher scores indicate more positive attitudes.

Boys	25	32	16	11	29	31	22	15
Girls	9	10	12	26	24			

Use a Mann–Whitney U-test with the stated hypothesis at = 0.05.

Solution The null hypothesis is that the distributions of boys' attitude scores and girls' attitude scores are identical in the population. Because the alternative hypothesis is directional, we use a one-tailed test. Arbitrarily, we let the boys be Sample 1 and the girls Sample 2. Because the value of U measures the degree to which the scores in Sample 1 are smaller than the scores in Sample 2 (that is, higher values of U suggest that boys score lower than girls, in this case), the one-tailed test for this example is left-tailed.

A combined ranking for all 13 participants is:

Score	9	10	11	12	15	16	22	24	25	26	29	31	32
Rank	1	2	3	4	5	6	7	8	9	10	11	12	13

$$R_1 = 3 + 5 + 6 + 7 + 9 + 11 + 12 + 13 = 66.$$

Substituting the relevant values into Equation 18.7 we obtain:

$$U = (8)(5) + \frac{(8)(9)}{2} - 66 = 40 + 36 - 66 = 10.$$

Because the range of possible values of U in this example is from 0 to (8)(5) = 40, with midpoint 20, the obtained U- value of 10 indicates that, in general, for these data boys' attitude scores are higher than girls' attitude scores, or, equivalently, that the girls' attitude scores are lower than the boys' attitude scores. We consult Table C.7 in Appendix C to determine whether the obtained U value is statistically significant at the chosen level of alpha.

From column $N_1 = 8$ and $N_2 = 5$, we find the left critical value for $\alpha = .005$ to be 6 and the rejection region is $U \le 6$. Hence, our obtained value of U, $U = 10$, does not fall in the rejection region and our conclusion is not to reject the null hypothesis that the boys' and girls' attitude distributions in the population are identical.

Using R, we may obtain the following one-tailed p-value of 0.08547 as shown below.

Wilcoxon rank sum test

data: girls and boys

W = 10 p-value = 0.08547

alternative hypothesis: true location shift is not equal to 0

☞ **Remark.** Had we arbitrarily designated the boys as Sample 2 and the girls as Sample 1, the test would be right-tailed because a larger value of U in this case would suggest, as hypothesized, that girls score lower than boys. In this case, $R_1 = 25$ and U, from Equation 18.7, equals:

$$U = (5)(8) + \frac{(5)(6)}{2} - 25 = 40 + 15 - 25 = 30.$$

The right tail critical value from Table C.7 in Appendix C for $N_1 = 5$ and $N_2 = 8$ is $U = 34$, and the rejection region is therefore $U \geq 34$. Notice that the sum of the left and right tail critical U values equals the product of N_1 and N_2, or $(5)(8) = 40$, in this case. Because $U = 30$ is not in the rejection region, we reach the same conclusion as before.

THE KRUSKAL–WALLIS ANALYSIS OF VARIANCE

The Kruskal–Wallis analysis of variance may be considered an extension of the Mann–Whitney U-test to three or more populations using unrelated samples. It tests the null hypothesis that all population distributions are identical, against the non-directional alternative that at least one of the population distributions is different from at least one of the others.

As with the Mann–Whitney U-test, the Kruskal–Wallis test is carried out using the ranks of the scores when they are all combined into a single group. To determine whether the differences among the samples are due to more than chance factors, we compare the obtained measure of separation, in this case referred to as H, against an appropriate sampling distribution. As long as the size of each group is at least five, the chi-square distribution with $K - 1$ degrees of freedom is a good approximation to the appropriate sampling distribution, where K is the number of groups or samples. Because H is a measure of separation, H is compared to a right-tail rejection region. Like the Mann–Whitney, H relies on the sum of the ranks in each of the K groups. H is given by Equation 18.8:

$$H = \frac{12}{N(N+1)} \sum_{j=1}^{K} \frac{R_j^2}{N_j} - 3(N+1), \tag{18.8}$$

where K = number of groups, N_j = size of Sample j, N = total number of scores from all samples, and R_j = sum of ranks for the scores in Sample j.

For simplicity, we shall assume that all scores are unique and that there are no ties. For situations in which there are tie scores, the interested reader is referred to a more advanced book on this topic (e.g., Siegel & Castellan, 1988). We illustrate with an example.

EXAMPLE 18.9 In a study to determine whether there is a relationship between age and time spent on the Internet, 8 college students, 10 adults between the ages of 35 and 45, and 7 adults between the ages of 60 and 70 were randomly selected from their respective populations of known Internet users. Participants were asked to indicate on a survey the average number of minutes they spent each day on the Internet. The data are given below. Use the Kruskal–Wallis test to test the null hypothesis that the three population distributions of time are identical. Set $\alpha = 0.05$.

College students	Adults aged 35 to 45	Adults aged 60 to 70
48	28	15
42	33	19
40	26	20
46	34	25
35	29	18
39	36	27
32	31	16
41	22	
	21	
	17	

Solution Grouping all 25 times together and rank-ordering them from lowest to highest, we obtain:

15	16	17	18	19	20	21	22	25	26	27	28	29	31	32	33	34	35	36	39	40	41	42	46	48	Times
1	2	3	4	5	6	7	8	9	10	11	12	13	14	15	16	17	18	19	20	21	22	23	24	25	Ranking
3	3	2	3	3	3	2	2	3	2	3	2	2	2	1	2	2	1	2	1	1	1	1	1	1	Group

$$N_1 = 8 \qquad N_2 = 10 \qquad N_3 = 7 \qquad N = 5$$
$$R_1 = 168 \qquad R_2 = 119 \qquad R_3 = 38 \qquad K = 3$$

Substituting these values into Equation 18.8, we obtain:

$$H = \frac{12}{(25)(26)}\left[\frac{168^2}{8} + \frac{119^2}{10} + \frac{38^2}{7}\right] - 3(26) = (0.01846)(5150.3857) = 95.08 - 78$$

$$= 17.08.$$

From Table C.5 in Appendix C, we note that a chi-square value closest, but less than, 17.08 with $K - 1 = 2$ degrees of freedom is 13.82. This value marks off area 0.001 to its right, suggesting that the probability of observing 13.82 or higher is less than 0.001. Since 0.001 is less than 0.05, our conclusion is to reject the null hypothesis in favor of the alternative that the populations from which these samples were drawn do not have identical distributions in terms of average daily time spent on the internet.

MORE R: To carry out the Kruskal–Wallis test, we first enter our data:

time = c(48, 42, 40, 46, 35, 39, 32, 41, 28, 33, 26, 34, 29, 36, 31, 22, 21, 17, 15, 19, 20, 25, 18, 27, 16)
group = c(rep(1, 8), rep(2, 10), rep(3, 7))

We then run:

kruskal.test(time~group)

We obtain the following results, which corroborate those obtained above:

> Kruskal–Wallis rank-sum test
>
> data: time by group
>
> Kruskal–Wallis chi-squared = 17.084 $df = 2$ p-value = 0.0001951

SUMMARY OF R COMMANDS

Create	Command lines
Estimate the p-value associated with $\chi_3^2 = 23.18$ (Example 18.1)	**pchisq(23.19, 3, lower.tail = F)**
Perform the chi-square goodness-of-fit test for tabulated or summary data	**type = c("Nissan", "Mazda", "Toyota", "Honda")** **freq = c(150, 65, 385, 400)** **prob = c(.18, .10, .35, .37)** **chisq.test(freq, p = prob)**
Perform the chi-square goodness-of-fit test for raw data (Example 18.2)	**chisq.test(table(NELS\$region), p = c (0.25, 0.25, 0.25, 0.25))**
Perform the chi-square goodness-of-fit test for tabulated or summary data	**chisq.test(table(Politics\$Gender, Politics\$Party))**

Create	Command lines
Perform the chi-square goodness-of-fit test for raw data (Example 18.3)	**chisq.test(table(NELS$gender, NELS$nursery), correct = F)**
Perform the Fisher's exact test (Example 18.5)	**data = matrix(c(2,6,4,0), nrow = 2, byrow = T)** **fisher.test(data)**
Carry out the sign test (Example 18.6)	**SIGN.test(recordwt, actualwt)**
To carry out the Mann–Whitney *U*-test (Example 18.7)	**wilcox.test(girls, boys)**
To carry out the Kruskal–Wallis test (Example 18.9)	**kruskal.test(time~group)**

EXERCISES

Create a .R file for each exercise that requires the use of R. Run code from the .R file by highlighting or having the cursor on the line of code and hitting **control+enter** on a PC computer keyboard or **command+enter** on a Mac computer keyboard. Save each .R file using a name associated with the Exercise for which it was created. It is recommended that you review the .R file for Chapter 18 located on the textbook's website before completing these exercises. To facilitate doing each exercise, it may be helpful to copy and paste relevant code from the .R file for Chapter 18 into your own .R file and modify them as needed.

Exercises 18.1–18.5 relate to the Learndis dataset. For inferential purposes, we consider the children in the dataset to be a random sample of all children attending public school in the urban area who have been diagnosed with learning disabilities. Use α = 0.05 for all significance tests.

18.1 There are two different types of placement for these students diagnosed with learning disabilities: resource room for part of the day and full-time self-contained classroom (placemen). Perform a chi-square goodness-of-fit test to determine whether children attending public school in this urban area who have been diagnosed with learning disabilities are equally likely to be in either type of placement or whether one of the two placements is statistically significantly more prevalent than the other. Explain the results.

18.2   Are there gender differences in the type of placement assigned to public school children in this urban area who have been diagnosed with learning disabilities? Perform a chi-square test of independence to make the determination.

   (a) According to the chi-square test of independence, are there gender differences in the type of placement assigned to public school children in this urban area who have been diagnosed with learning disabilities?

   (b) What other statistical significance test could we have performed to determine whether there are gender differences in the type of placement assigned to public school children in this urban area who have been diagnosed with learning disabilities?

18.3   In Exercise 11.22, we used a paired samples *t*-test to determine whether elementary school children in the city diagnosed with learning disabilities perform better in math comprehension or in reading comprehension. According to the descriptive statistics, the skewness ratio for math comprehension is 2.28 and the skewness ratio for reading comprehension is −3.46, indicating that both variables are statistically significantly skewed. Because the sample size was adequate, $N = 74$, we determined that the paired samples t-test was robust to the violation of the normality assumption. In this exercise, use an alternative approach, the sign test to answer the same question.

(a) According to the results of the sign test, do elementary school children in the city diagnosed with learning disabilities perform better in math comprehension or in reading comprehension? Explain.

(b) Do these results corroborate those obtained in Exercise 11.22?

18.4 Is there a statistically significant difference in reading achievement depending on type of placement?

(a) Why might someone question the appropriateness of the independent samples t-test, in this case?

(b) Conduct the Mann–Whitney U-test. Is there a statistically significant difference in reading achievement depending on type of placement?

18.5 Are there statistically significant differences in reading achievement by grade? Calculate relevant descriptive statistics and conduct the Kruskal–Wallis analysis of variance. Use your results to answer the following questions.

(a) Why might one question the use of a one-way ANOVA to determine whether there is a statistically significant difference in reading achievement by grade?

(b) Using the results of the Kruskal–Wallis test, is there a statistically significant difference in reading achievement by grade? Explain.

18.6 Data were gathered on a random sample of 200 people visiting the Museum of Natural History in New York City in order to understand the background of visitors to the museum. The variable descriptions of the various measures taken are contained in the following table.

Variable name	What the variable measures	How the variable measures it
EDLEVEL	Highest educational level achieved	1 = Less than H.S.
		2 = H.S Graduate
		3 = B.A. or more
MUSEUMS	Annual charitable contributions to museums	1 = $0
		2 = $0.01–$100
		3 = $100.01–$500
		4 > $500
WILDLIFE	Annual charitable contributions to wildlife conservation	1 = $0
		2 = $0.01–$100
		3 = $100.01–$500
		4 > $500
LOCATION		1 = Resident of NYC
		2 = Tourist
MEMBER	Whether the person is a member of the Museum of Natural History	0 = No
		1 = Yes

For each of the following questions based on this dataset, select an appropriate statistical procedure from the list below to answer each of the following questions based on this dataset. A nonparametric analysis is to be used. In some instances, more than one procedure may be appropriate. Also, procedures may be selected more than once. Note that you do not have to perform any analyses to complete this exercise, just specify the analyses that should be performed.

Procedures
1. Chi-square goodness-of-fit test
2. Chi-square test of independence
3. Sign test
4. Mann–Whitney U-test
5. Kruskal–Wallis analysis of variance

Questions
(a) Which is typically higher, charitable contributions to museums, or charitable contributions to wildlife preservation?
(b) Is there a difference in charitable contributions to museums according to the highest educational level achieved?
(c) Is the distribution of charitable contributions to museums between tourists and residents different from the distribution of charitable contributions to wildlife preservation between tourists and residents?
(d) Is the amount of charitable contributions to museums higher among tourists or among residents?
(e) Are visitors to the museum evenly divided between tourists and residents?
(f) Is there a difference in the highest educational level attained between tourists and residents?
(g) Is there a relationship between highest educational level attained and membership in the museum?

Exercises 18.7–18.11 relate to the NELS dataset. For inferential purposes, we consider the students in the dataset to be a random sample of the population of all college-bound students who have always been at grade level. Use $\alpha = 0.05$ for all significance tests.

18.7 Using cross-tabulation introduced in Chapter 5, we may determine descriptively that there is a relationship between region and urban.
   (a) What nonparametric test is appropriate to determine whether this relationship is statistically significant?
   (b) Use this test to determine whether this relationship is statistically significant.

18.8 Is there a statistically significant difference in the frequency of cut classes by seniors (cuts12) and the frequency of missed school by seniors (absent12)? If so, which occurs more often?
   (a) What nonparametric test is appropriate to determine whether this difference is statistically significant?
   (b) Why is the test specified in your answer to part (a) more appropriate than a paired-samples t-test, in this case?
   (c) Is the nonparametric test statistically significant?

18.9 Is there a statistically significant difference in perceived teacher interest (tcherint) between those students taking a challenging curriculum and those taking a less challenging curriculum (advmath8)?
   (a) What two nonparametric tests are appropriate to determine whether this difference is statistically significant?
   (b) Are these tests statistically significant?

18.10 In the *Marijuan* dataset, we see that in 1992, 32.6 percent of high school seniors in the United States reported smoking marijuana at least once. The same information was measured for the college-bound students in the NELS dataset, when they were seniors in 1992. For those students, 92 reported that they had tried marijuana, while 408 reported that they never had. Do college-bound students report the same incidence of marijuana use as that of the population of all high school seniors?
   (a) What nonparametric test is appropriate to determine whether college-bound students report the same incidence of marijuana use as that of the population of all high school seniors?
   (b) Conduct the test specified in your answer to part (a). Use $\alpha = 0.05$.

18.11 Does time spent on homework outside school by high school seniors (hwkout12) vary by urbanicity (urban)?
   (a) Explain why a nonparametric test is appropriate, in this case.
   (b) Which nonparametric test would you use?
   (c) Conduct the test specified in your answer to part (b). Use $\alpha = 0.05$.

18.12 According to an article in the *New York Times* on June 1, 2000, the New York State health commissioner suspended the licenses of two doctors who were accused of falsifying mammogram test results for poor women. These radiologists, who screened approximately 10,000 women in the Bronx for breast cancer over the course of five years, were accused of providing faulty tests and billing for tests that they did not perform. The problem was detected by looking at the rate at which the two doctors reported abnormal mammogram results and comparing it to the average rate for all doctors in New York State. Of the 10,000 women evaluated by these doctors, only 13 screened positive for breast cancer, while the rate for the rest of the state is 52 positive screens per 10,000 patients. Conduct a hypothesis test at $\alpha = 0.05$ to determine whether the difference in rates is statistically significant.

18.13 According to data from the Department of Health and Human Services, there is an association between estrogen use and cardiovascular death rates. To corroborate these results, 1,500 people were randomly selected from the population of female Americans over 50; 750 took estrogen supplements and 750 did not. The results are summarized in the following table. Use them to conduct a nonparametric hypothesis test of the association between estrogen use and cardiovascular death rates. Use $\alpha = 0.05$.

		Status	
		Alive	Dead
Takes estrogen supplements?	Yes	746	4
	No	740	10

18.14 A researcher is studying whether the education level of first-born sons in a small rural community in the Midwest is higher than the education level of their fathers. Accordingly, the researcher randomly selects 15 adult males from this community who are first-born sons and asks them to indicate on a questionnaire the highest level of education attained by themselves and by their fathers. To measure the variable, highest level of education attained, the following scale is used:

1 = graduated from elementary school
2 = graduated from middle school
3 = graduated from high school
4 = graduated from two-year college
5 = graduated from four-year college
6 = at least some graduate training

The data are as follows:

Highest level of education attained

Sons	3	3	3	5	6	4	3	5	2	4	4	1	4	3	6
Fathers	1	2	1	3	3	2	3	4	3	3	2	1	2	2	4

Run an appropriate nonparametric analysis on these data at $\alpha = 0.05$. Interpret your results within the context of the problem.

18.15 A researcher is interested in determining the degree of overall competitiveness between high-school-aged siblings from two-child families. In particular, she is interested in determining whether siblings of the same sex are more competitive overall than siblings of the opposite sex. Accordingly, she selects at random 10 high-school-aged students with younger siblings of the same sex in high school and 10 high-school-aged students with younger siblings of the opposite sex in high school. Each student selected is asked to respond to a questionnaire in which degree of perceived competitiveness with younger siblings is sought in each of four areas (academic, athletic, personal appearance, and social). Each area is to be rated on a scale from 0 (no competition) to 10 (extreme competition). A total score of perceived overall competitiveness is obtained by summing the individual responses in each of the four areas. Assume that this competitiveness score is measured on an ordinal scale.

Same sex siblings	15	23	38	35	29	22	31	26	39	36
Opposite sex siblings	24	25	16	10	13	18	9	37	27	33

Perform an appropriate nonparametric analysis at $\alpha = 0.05$. Interpret your results within the context of the problem.

18.16 In a study to interpret the effects of music on mood, 12 adults are asked to spend 30 minutes in a room into which one of three different types of music is piped (slow classical, soft rock, or hard rock). At the end of the 30 minutes, participants are asked to complete a questionnaire designed to measure mood. Low scores on this test suggest a relaxed mood, whereas high scores suggest a relatively tense mood. Assume that these mood scores are measured at the ordinal level. The 12 participants are randomly assigned to one of the three music conditions. The data are as follows:

Slow Classical	1	3	4	2
Soft Rock	5	8	6	7
Hard Rock	9	12	11	10

Perform an appropriate nonparametric analysis at $\alpha = 0.05$ to determine whether mood differed depending on music type. Interpret your results within the context of the problem.

DATASET DESCRIPTIONS

ANSCOMBE

This dataset is used to illustrate the importance of statistical display as an adjunct to summary statistics. Anscombe (1973) fabricated four different bivariate datasets such that, for all datasets, the respective X and Y means, X and Y standard deviations, and correlations, slopes, intercepts, and standard errors of estimate are equal. Accordingly, without a visual representation of these four panels, one might assume that the data values for all four datasets are the same. Scatterplots illustrate, however, the extent to which these datasets are different from one another.

BASKETBALL

The dataset consists of the heights and weights of the 24 scoring leaders, 12 each from the US Women's and Men's National Basketball Association, for the 2012–2015 season. These data are adapted from the ESPN website at espn.com.

Variable name	Variable definition	Additional description
player	Player name	
gender	Gender	1 = Male; 2 = Female
heightin	Height in inches	
weightlb	Weight in pounds	
games	Games played	
points	Average total points scored per game	

BLOOD

The data were collected to determine whether an increase in calcium intake reduces blood pressure among African American adult males. The data are based on a sample of 21 African American adult males selected randomly from the population of African American adult males. Ten of the 21 men were randomly assigned to a treatment condition that required them to take a calcium supplement for 12 weeks. The remaining 11 men received a placebo for the 12 weeks. At both the beginning and the end of this time period, systolic blood pressure readings of all men were recorded. These data are adapted from the Data and Story Library (DASL) website.

Variable name	Variable definition	Additional description
id	Case number	
treatmen	Treatment condition	1 = Placebo; 2 = Calcium
systolc1	Initial blood pressure	
systolc2	Final blood pressure	

BRAINSZ

The data are based on a study by Willerman et al. (1991) of the relationships between brain size, gender, and intelligence. The research participants consisted of 40 right-handed introductory psychology students with no history of alcoholism, unconsciousness, brain damage, epilepsy, or heart disease who were selected from a larger pool of introductory psychology students with total Scholastic Aptitude Test Scores higher than 1350 or lower than 940. The students in the study took four subtests (Vocabulary, Similarities, Block Design, and Picture Completion) of the Wechsler (1981) Adult Intelligence Scale-Revised (WAIS-R). Among the students with Wechsler full-scale IQs of at most 103, 10 males and 10 females were randomly selected. Similarly, among the students with Wechsler full-scale IQs of at least 130, 10 males and 10 females were randomly selected, yielding a randomized blocks design. MRI scans were performed at the same facility for all 40 research participants to measure brain size. The scans consisted of 18 horizontal MRI images. The computer counted all pixels with non-zero gray scale in each of the 18 images, and the total count served as an index for brain size. The dataset and description are adapted from the Data and Story Library (DASL) website.

Variable name	Variable definition	Additional description
ID	Case number	
GENDER	Gender	1 = Male; 2 = Female
FSIQ	Full-scale IQ score based on WAIS-R	
VIQ	Verbal IQ score based on WAIS-R	
PIQ	Performance IQ score based on WAIS-R	
MRI	Pixel count from 18 MRI scans	
IQDI	Group membership based on FSIQ score	1 = Lower IQ; 2 = Higher IQ

CURRENCY

This dataset contains, for the smaller bill denominations, the value of the bill and the total value in circulation. The source for these data is *The World Almanac and Book of Facts 2014.*

Variable name	Variable definition
BillValue	Denomination
TotalCirculation	Total currency in circulation in US dollars
NumberCirculation	Total number of bills in circulation

EXERCISE

A simulated dataset constructed by Darlington (1990) to demonstrate the importance of including all relevant variables in an analysis. This dataset contains information about exercise, food intake, and weight loss for a fictional set of dieters.

Variable name	Variable definition
ID	Case number
Exercise	The average daily number of hours exercised in that week
FoodIntake	The average daily number of calories consumed in one particular week that is more than a baseline of 1,000 calories, as measured in increments of 100 calories
WeightLoss	The number of pounds lost in that week

FRAMINGHAM

The Framingham Heart Study is a long-term prospective study of the etiology of cardio-vascular disease among a population of non-institutionalized people in the community of Framingham, Massachusetts. The Framingham Heart Study was a landmark study in epidemiology in that it was the first prospective study of cardiovascular disease and identified the concept of risk factors and their joint effects. The study began in 1956 and 5,209 subjects were initially enrolled in the study. In our dataset, we included variables from the first examination in 1956 and the third examination, in 1968. Clinic examination data has included cardiovascular disease risk factors and markers of disease such as blood pressure, blood chemistry, lung function, smoking history, health behaviors, ECG tracings, echocardiography, and medication use. Through regular surveillance of area hospitals, participant contact, and death certificates, the Framingham Heart Study reviews and adjudicates events for the occurrence of any of the following types of coronary heart disease (CHD): angina pectoris, myocardial infarction, heart failure, and cerebrovascular disease.

The associated dataset is a subset of the data collected as part of the Framingham study and includes laboratory, clinic, questionnaire, and adjudicated event data on 400 participants. These participants for the dataset have been chosen so that among all male participants, 100 smokers and 100 non-smokers were selected at random. A similar procedure resulted in 100 female smokers and 100 female non-smokers. This procedure resulted in an over-sampling of smokers. The data for each participant is on one row. People who had any type of CHD in the initial examination period are not included in the dataset.

Variable name	Variable definition	Additional description
ID	Case number	
SEX	Sex	1 = Men; 2 = Women
TOTCHOL1	Serum cholesterol (mg/dL) at initial examination	
AGE1	Age (years) at initial examination	
SYSBP1	Systolic blood pressure (mmHg) at initial examination	
DIABP1	Diastolic blood pressure (mmHg) at initial examination	
CURSMOKE1	Indicator that participant currently is a cigarette smoker at initial examination	1 = No; 2 = Yes
CIGPDAY1	Cigarettes smoked per day at initial examination	Coded as factor (categorical) variable
BMI1	Body Mass Index (kg/(M*M)) at initial examination	
DIABETES1	Indicator that participant is diabetic at initial examination	1 = Not a diabetic; 2 = Diabetic
BPMEDS1	Use of anti-hypertensive medication at initial examination	1 = Not currently used; 2 = currently used
HEARTRTE1	Ventricular rate (beats/min) at initial examination	
GLUCOSE1	Casual glucose (mg/dL) at initial examination	
PREVCHD1	Prevalent CHD (angina pectoris, myocardial infarction, or coronary insufficiency) at initial examination	1 = Free of CHD; 2 = Prevalence of CHD
TIME1	Days since initial examination	
TIMECHD1	Days from initial examination to any CHD event	
TOTCHOL3	Serum cholesterol (mg/dL) at third examination	
AGE3	Age (years) at third examination	
SYSBP3	Systolic blood pressure (mmHg) at third examination	
DIABP3	Diastolic blood pressure (mmHg) at third examination	
CURSMOKE3	Indicator that participant currently is a cigarette smoker at third examination	1 = No; 2 = Yes
CIGPDAY3	Cigarettes smoked per day at third examination	Coded as numeric variable

Variable name	Variable definition	Additional description
BMI3	Body Mass Index (kg/(M*M)) at third examination	
DIABETES3	Indicator that participant is diabetic at third examination	1 = Not a diabetic; 2 = Diabetic
BPMEDS3	Use of anti-hypertensive medication at third examination	1 = Not currently used; 2 = currently used
HEARTRTE3	Ventricular rate (beats/min) at third examination	
GLUCOSE3	Casual glucose (mg/dL) at third examination	
PREVCHD3	Prevalent CHD (angina pectoris, myocardial infarction, or coronary insufficiency) at third examination	1 = Free of CHD; 2 = Prevalence of CHD
TIME3	Days since initial examination at third examination	
HDLC3	HDL cholesterol (mg/dL) at third examination	
LDLC3	LDL cholesterol (mg/dL) at third examination	
TIMECHD3	Days from initial examination to any CHD event at third examination	
ANYCHD4	Indicator of event of hospitalized myocardial infarction, angina pectoris, coronary insufficiency, or fatal CHD by the end of the study	1 = CHD Event did not occur; 2 = CHD Event did occur

HAMBURGER

This dataset contains the fat grams and calories associated with the different types of hamburger sold by McDonald's. The data are from McDonald's Nutrition Information Center.

Variable name	Variable definition	Additional description
name	Type of burger	
fat	Grams of fat	
calories	Total calories	
cheese	Cheese added	1 = No; 2 = Yes

ICE CREAM

This dataset contains fabricated data for the temperature, relative humidity, and ice cream sales for 30 days randomly selected between May 15 and September 6.

Variable name	Variable definition	Additional description
id	Case number	
temp	Temperature in degrees Fahrenheit	
barsold	Number of ice cream bars sold	
relhumid	Relative humidity	

IMPEACH

On February 12, 1999, for only the second time in the nation's history, the US Senate voted on whether to remove a president, based on impeachment articles passed by the US House. Professor Alan Reifman of Texas Tech University created the dataset consisting of descriptions of each senator that can be used to understand some of the reasons that the senators voted the way they did. The data are taken from the *Journal of Statistics Education* (available online at http://jse.amstat.org).

Variable name	Variable definition	Additional description
name	Senator's name	
state	State the senator represents	
region	Geographic region of the U.S.	1 = Northeast; 2 = Midwest; 3 = South; 4 = West
vote1	Vote on perjury	1 = Not Guilty; 2 = Guilty
vote2	Vote on obstruction of justice	1 = Not Guilty; 2 = Guilty
guilty	Total number of guilty votes	
party	Political party of senator	1 = Democrat; 2 = Republican
conserva	Conservatism score, defined as the senator's degree of ideological conservatism, based on 1997 voting records as judged by the American Conservative Union, where the scores ranged from 0 to 100 and 100 is most conservative	
supportc	State voter support for Clinton, defined as the percent of the vote Clinton received in the 1996 presidential election in the senator's state	
reelect	Year the senator's seat is up for reelection	2000, 2002, or 2004
newbie	Indicator for whether the senator is in their first term	1 = No; 2 = Yes

LEARNDIS

This dataset is a subset of data from a study by Susan Tomasi and Sharon L. Weinberg (1999), which profiled learning disabled students in an urban setting. According to Public Law 94.142, enacted in 1976, a team may determine that a child has a learning disability (LD) if a severe discrepancy exists between a child's actual achievement in, for example, math or reading, and his or her intellectual ability. The dataset consists of six variables, described below, on 105 elementary school children from an urban area who were classified as LD and who, as a result, had been receiving special education services for at least three years. Of the 105 children, 42 are female and 63 are male. There are two main types of placements for these students: part-time resource room placements, in which the students get additional instruction to supplement regular classroom instruction, and self-contained classroom placements, in which students are segregated full time. In this dataset, 66 students are in resource room placements while 39 are in self-contained classroom placements. For inferential purposes, we consider the children in the dataset to be a random sample of all children attending public elementary school in a certain city who have been diagnosed with learning disabilities. Many students in the dataset have missing values for either math or reading comprehension, or both. Such omissions can lead to problems when generalizing results. There are statistical remedies for missing data that are beyond the scope of this text. In this case, we will assume that there is no pattern to the missing values, so that our sample is representative of the population.

Variable name	Variable definition	Additional description
grade	Student's grade level	1, 2, 3, 4, or 5
gender	Student's gender	1 = Male; 2 = Female
placemen	Type of placement: "RR" for part time in resource room or "MIS" for full time in self-contained classroom	1 = RR; 2 = MIS
readcomp	Reading comprehension score, with possible range of 0 to 200	Higher scores ↔ greater reading comprehension
mathcomp	Math comprehension score, with possible range of 0 to 200	Higher scores ↔ greater math comprehension
iq	Student's intellectual ability, as measured by IQ score with possible range of 0 to 200	Higher scores ↔ greater IQ

LIKERT

This dataset contains fabricated data for a single survey item measured on a Likert scale. It is given that a survey was administered to 30 individuals and included an item measuring assertiveness by having the individual indicate agreement with the statement: "I have the ability to stand up for my own rights without denying the rights of others." The response options were: 1 = "strongly agree"; 2 = "agree"; 3 = "neutral"; 4 = "disagree"; 5 = "strongly disagree." Notice that on this scale, high scores are associated with low levels of assertiveness.

Variable name	Variable definition	Additional description
Assertiveness	Five-point Likert-scale score of assertiveness, with high scores associated with low levels of assertiveness	This variable is given as a numeric, not factor (categorical), object See dataset description for response option associated with each number

MANDEXT

This fictional dataset contains the treatment group number and the manual dexterity scores for 30 individuals selected by the director of a drug rehabilitation center. There are three treatments, and the individuals are randomly assigned ten to a treatment. After five weeks of treatment, a manual dexterity test is administered for which a higher score indicates greater manual dexterity.

Variable name	Variable definition
ManualDex	Manual dexterity score
Sex	Individual's sex
Treatment	Treatment group assignment

MARIJUANA

The dataset contains the year and percentage of twelfth graders who have ever used marijuana for several recent years. The source for these data is *The World Almanac and Book of Facts 2014*.

Variable name	Variable definition
Year	Year for which data was collected
MarijuanaUse	Percentage of twelfth graders who reported that they have ever used marijuana

NELS

In response to pressure from federal and state agencies to monitor school effectiveness in the United States, the National Center for Education Statistics (NCES) of the US Department of Education conducted a survey in the spring of 1988, the National Education Longitudinal Study (NELS). The participants consisted of a nationally representative sample of approximately 25,000 eighth graders to measure achievement outcomes in four core subject areas (English, history, mathematics, and science), in addition to personal, familial, social, institutional, and cultural factors that might relate to these outcomes. Details on the design and initial analysis of this survey may be referenced in Horn, Hafner, and Owings (1992). A follow-up of these students was conducted during tenth grade in the spring of 1990; a second follow-up was conducted during the twelfth grade in the spring of 1992; and, finally, a third follow-up was conducted in the spring of 1994.

For this dataset, we have selected a sub-sample of 500 cases and 48 variables. The cases were sampled randomly from the approximately 5,000 students who responded to all four administrations of the survey, who were always at grade level (neither repeated nor skipped a grade), and who pursued some form of post-secondary education. The particular variables were selected to explore the relationships between student and home background variables, self-concept, educational and income aspirations, academic motivation, risk-taking behavior, and academic achievement.

Variable name	Variable definition	Additional description
absent12	Number of times student missed school in twelfth grade	1 = Never; 2 = 1–2 Times; 3 = 3–6 Times; 4 = 7–9 Times; 5 = 10–15 Times; 6 = Over 15 Times
achmat08	Math achievement in eighth grade	Similar to achrdg08
achmat10	Math achievement in tenth grade	Similar to achrdg08
achmat12	Math achievement in twelfth grade	Similar to achrdg08
achrdg08	Reading achievement in eighth grade	Gives a score for the student's performance in eighth grade on a standardized test of reading achievement. Actual values range from 36.61 to 77.2, from low to high achievement.
achrdg10	Reading achievement in tenth grade	Similar to achrdg08
achrdg12	Reading achievement in twelfth grade	Similar to achrdg08
achsci08	Science achievement in eighth grade	Similar to achrdg08
achsci10	Science achievement in tenth grade	Similar to achrdg08
achsci12	Science achievement in twelfth grade	Similar to achrdg08
achsls08	Social studies achievement in eighth grade	Similar to achrdg08
achsls10	Social studies achievement in tenth grade	Similar to achrdg08
achsls12	Social studies achievement in twelfth grade	Similar to achrdg08
advmath8	Indicator for whether advanced math taken in eighth grade	1 = No; 2 = Yes
alcbinge	Indicator for whether ever binged on alcohol	1 = Never; 2 = Yes
algebra8	Indicator for whether algebra taken in eighth grade	1 = No; 2 = Yes
apoffer	Number of advanced placement courses offered by school	

Variable name	Variable definition	Additional description
approg	Indicator for whether advanced placement program taken	1 = No; 2 = Yes
cigarett	Indicator for whether smoked cigarettes ever	1 = Never; 2 = Yes
computer	Indicator for whether computer owned by family in eighth grade	1 = No; 2 = Yes
cuts12	Number of times skipped/cut classes in twelfth grade	1 = Never; 2 = 1–2 Times; 3 = 3–6 Times; 4 = 7–9 Times; 5 = 10–15 Times; 6 = Over 15 Times
edexpect	Highest level of education expected	1 = Less than College Degree; 2 = Bachelor's Degree; 3 = Master's Degree; 4 = PhD., MD, JD, etc.
excurr12	Time spent weekly on extracurricular activities in twelfth grade, in hours	1 = None; 2 = Less than 1 Hour; 3 = 1–4 Hours; 4 = 5–9 Hours; 5 = 10–14 Hours; 6 = 15 – 19 Hours; 7 = 20–24 Hours; 8 = 25 or More Hours
expinc30	Expected income at age 30, in dollars	
famsize	Student's family size	
gender	Student's gender	1 = Male; 2 = Female
homelang	Home language background	1 = Non-English Only; 2= Non-English Dominant; 3 = English Dominant; 4 = English Only
hsprog	Type of high school program	1= Rigorous Academic; 2 = Academic; 3 = Some Vocational; 4 = Other
hwkin12	Time spent on homework weekly in school per week in twelfth grade	1 = None; 2 = Less than 1 Hour; 3 = 1–3 Hours; 4 = 4–6 Hours; 5 = 7–9 Hours; 6 = 10–12 Hours; 7 = 13–15 Hours; 8 = 16–20 Hours; 9 = Over 20 Hours
hwkout12	Time spent on homework out of school per week in twelfth grade	1 = None; 2 = Less than 1 Hour; 3 = 1–3 Hours; 4 = 4–6 Hours; 5 = 7–9 Hours; 6 = 10–12 Hours; 7 = 13–15 Hours; 8 = 16–20 Hours; 9 = Over 20 Hours
id	Case number	
late12	Number of times late for school in twelfth grade	

Variable name	Variable definition	Additional description
		1 = Never; 2 = 1–2 Times; 3 = 3–6 Times; 4 = 7–9 Times; 5 = 10–15 Times; 6 = Over 15 Times
marijuan	Indicator for whether smoked marijuana ever	1 = Never; 2 = Yes
numinst	Number of post-secondary institutions attended	
nursery	Indicator for whether nursery school attended	1 = No; 2 = Yes
parmarl8	Parents' marital status in eighth grade	1 = Divorced; 2 = Widowed; 3 = Separated; 4= Never Married; 5 = Marriage-Like Relationship; 6 = Married
region	Geographic region of school	1= Northeast; 2 = North Central; 3 = South; 4 = West
schattrt	School average daily attendance rate	Gives the average daily attendance rate for the secondary school the student attends.
schtyp8	School type in eighth grade	Classifies the type of school each student attended in eighth grade, where 1 = Public; 2 = Private, Religious; 3 = Private, Non-Religious.
ses	Socioeconomic status score, ranging from 0 to 35, and given as a composite of father's education level, mother's education level, father's occupation, mother's occupation, and family income	Gives a score representing the socioeconomic status (ses) of the student, a composite of father's education level, mother's education level, father's occupation, mother's occupation, and family income. Values range from 0 to 35, from low to high ses.
slfcnc08	Self-concept in eighth grade	Similar to slfcnc12
slfcnc10	Self-concept in tenth grade	Similar to slfcnc12
slfcnc12	Self-concept in twelfth grade	Gives a score for student self-concept in twelfth grade. Values range from 0 to 43. Self-concept is defined as a person's self-perceptions, or how a person feels about himself or herself. Four items comprise the self-concept scale in the NELS

Variable name	Variable definition	Additional description
		questionnaire: I feel good about myself; I feel I am a person of worth, the equal of other people; I am able to do things as well as most other people; and, on the whole, I am satisfied with myself. A self-concept score, based on the sum of scores on each of these items, is used to measure self-concept in the NELS study. Higher scores associate with higher self-concept and lower scores associate with lower self-concept.
tcherint	Likert-scale variable classifying student agreement with the statement, "My teachers are interested in students"	1 = Strongly Agree; 2 = Agree; 3 = Disagree; 4 = Strongly Disagree
unitcalc	Units in calculus (NAEP), or number of years of calculus taken in high school	
unitengl	Units in English (NAEP), or number of years of English taken in high school	
unitmath	Units in mathematics (NAEP), or number of years of math taken in high school	
urban	Urbanicity	Classifies the type of environment in which each student lives where 1 = Urban, 2 = Suburban, and 3 = Rural.

POLITICS

This dataset contains data on a fabricated random sample of 200 individuals, 100 females and 100 males, drawn from a population of interest. There are only two variables, both of which are categorical: gender and political party affiliation.

Variable name	Variable definition	Additional description
Gender	Individual's gender	1 = Female; 2 = Male
Party	Individual's political party affiliation	1 = Democrat; 2 = Neither; 3 = Republican

STATES

This dataset includes different educational measures of the 50 states and Washington, DC. These data are from *The World Almanac and Book of Facts 2014*.

Variable name	Variable definition	Additional description
state	Name of state	
region	Region of the country in which the state is located	1 = Northeast; 2 = Midwest; 3 = South; 4 = West
enrollmt	Total public school enrollment 2011–2012	
stuteach	Average number of pupils per teacher 2011–2012	
teachpay	Average annual salary for public school teachers 2011–2012	
eduexpe	Average expenditure per pupil 2011–2012	
satcr	Average SAT Critical Reading score 2013	
satm	Average SAT Math score 2013	
satw	Average SAT Writing score 2013	
pertak	Percentage of eligible students taking the SAT 2012	

STATISTICIANS

This dataset includes data on 12 statisticians who each have contributed significantly to the field of modern statistics.

Variable name	Variable definition	Additional description
Statistician	Name of statistician	
Gender	Gender of statistician	1 = "Female"; 2 = "Male" This variable is given as a numeric, not factor (categorical), object
Birth	Year of birth	
Death	Year of death	
AmStat	Number of references in *The American Statistician*, 1995–2005	

STEPPING

Students at Ohio State University conducted an experiment in the fall of 1993 to explore the nature of the relationship between a person's heart rate and the frequency at which that person stepped up and down on steps of various heights. The response variable, heart rate, was measured in beats per minute. For each person, the resting heart rate was measured before a trial (HRInit) and after stepping (HRFinal). There were two different step heights (Height): 5.75 inches (coded as 1 = Low), and 11.5 inches (coded as 2 = High). There were three rates of stepping (Freq): 14 steps/min. (coded as 1 = Slow), 21 steps/min. (coded as 2 = Medium), and 28 steps/min. (coded as 3 = Fast). This resulted in six possible height/frequency combinations. Each subject performed the activity for three minutes. Subjects were kept on pace by the beat of an electric metronome. One experimenter counted the subject's heart rate, in beats per minute, for 20 seconds before and after each trial. The subject always rested between trials until her or his heart rate returned to close to the beginning rate. Another experimenter kept track of the time spent stepping. Each subject was always measured and timed by the same pair of experimenters to reduce variability in the experiment. The dataset and description are adapted from the Data and Story Library (DASL) website.

Variable name	Variable definition	Additional description
Order	Overall performance order of the trial	
Block	Subject and experimenters' block number	
Height	Step height	1 = Low; 2 = High
Freq	Rate of stepping	1 = Slow; 2 = Medium; 3 = Fast
HRInit	Resting heart rate of the subject before a trial, in beats per minute	
HRFinal	Final heart rate of the subject after a trial, in beats per minute	

TEMP

This dataset gives the average monthly temperatures (in degrees Fahrenheit) for Springfield, MO and San Francisco, CA. These data are from Burrill et al. (1993).

Variable name	Variable definition	Additional description
City	City where temperature was measured	1 = Springfield, MO; 2 = San Francisco, CA
Temperature	Average monthly temperature, in degrees Fahrenheit	

UPPERBODYSTRENGTH

This simulated dataset consists of the number of hours eight individuals spend at the gym on a weekly basis along with measures of their upper body strength.

Variable name	Variable definition	Additional description
gym	Number of hours spent at the gym weekly	
strength	Upper body strength score	
gender	Individual's gender	1 = male; 2 = female

WAGES

This is a sub-sample of 100 males and 100 females randomly selected from the 534 cases that comprised the 1985 Current Population Survey in a way that controls for highest education level attained. The sample of 200 contains 20 males and 20 females with less than a high school diploma, 20 males and 20 females with a high school diploma, 20 males and 20 females with some college training, 20 males and 20 females with a college diploma, and 20 males and 20 females with some graduate school training. The data include information about gender, highest education level attained, and hourly wage.

Variable name	Variable definition	Additional description
id	Case number	
educ	Number of years of education	
south	Indicator for whether individual lives in the South	1 = does not live in South; 2 = lives in South
sex	Individual's sex	1 = Male; 2 = Female
exper	Number of years of work experience	
wage	Wage (dollars per hour)	
occup	Occupation category	1 = Management; 2 = Sales; 3 = Clerical; 4 = Service; 5 = Professional; 6 = Other
marr	Marital status	1 = Not married; 2 = Married
ed	Highest education level	1 = Less than a high school degree; 2 = High school degree; 3 = Some college; 4 = College degree; 5 = Graduate school

.R FILES AND DATASETS IN R FORMAT

This appendix details how to access several resources that accompany this textbook.

CAMBRIDGE UNIVERSITY PRESS WEBSITE

The website associated with this book, which can be accessed at www.cambridge.org /stats-r, contains the following resources available for download:

- .R script files that reproduce the tables and figures found in each chapter.
- Datasets in R format.
- Solutions to end-of-chapter exercises.
- PowerPoint slides summarizing the methods discussed in each chapter.

R PACKAGE

All datasets and some functions used in this textbook are contained within a package especially designed for this textbook, which we have called "sur." This package can be accessed only after the R package is installed and loaded. Once the R package is installed and loaded, you may download sur directly from the CRAN server by opening R or RStudio and then typing install.packages("sur"). This needs to be done only once for each computer you will be using in connection with this textbook. Each time you reopen R or RStudio, however, you will need to type library(sur) to have access to the sur package during that session.

R TUTORIAL

Accompanying this textbook is an interactive tutorial that teaches basic concepts relating to data frame management in R. We encourage you to make use of it, especially if you are new to R.

To run the tutorial, open RStudio, and type the following lines of code:

library(sur)
learnr::run_tutorial("R_Basics", package = "sur")

This will open the tutorial as an HTML file in your default Internet browser. To exit the tutorial, you must close the tab in the browser, and also press the Escape key in the RStudio console window. Note that when you close the tutorial, your progress will be saved for the next time you re-open it. If you decide to clear your progress, before closing the tutorial, click the Start Over button at the bottom of the browser screen.

STATISTICAL TABLES

TABLE C.1 Areas under the standard normal curve (to the right of the z-score)
For example, the area to the right of $z = 1.96$ is found by decomposing 1.96 as $1.9 + 0.06$ and referencing the entry in the row labeled 1.9 and the column labeled 0.06. This right-tailed area is 0.0250. To obtain the area to the left, calculate $1 - 0.0250$. The left-tailed area equals 0.9750. Because the normal curve is symmetric about its mean, the area to the left of $z = -1.96$ is equal to the area to the right of $z = 1.96$.

	0	0.01	0.02	0.03	0.04	0.05	0.06	0.07	0.08	0.09
0.0	.5000	.4960	.4920	.4880	.4840	.4801	.4761	.4721	.4681	.4641
0.1	.4602	.4562	.4522	.4483	.4443	.4404	.4364	.4325	.4286	.4247
0.2	.4207	.4168	.4129	.4090	.4052	.4013	.3974	.3936	.3897	.3859
0.3	.3821	.3783	.3745	.3707	.3669	.3632	.3594	.3557	.3520	.3483
0.4	.3446	.3409	.3372	.3336	.3300	.3264	.3228	.3192	.3156	.3121
0.5	.3085	.3050	.3015	.2981	.2946	.2912	.2877	.2843	.2810	.2776
0.6	.2743	.2709	.2676	.2643	.2611	.2578	.2546	.2514	.2483	.2451
0.7	.2420	.2389	.2358	.2327	.2296	.2266	.2236	.2206	.2177	.2148
0.8	.2119	.2090	.2061	.2033	.2005	.1977	.1949	.1922	.1894	.1867
0.9	.1841	.1814	.1788	.1762	.1736	.1711	.1685	.1660	.1635	.1611
1.0	.1587	.1562	.1539	.1515	.1492	.1469	.1446	.1423	.1401	.1379
1.1	.1357	.1335	.1314	.1292	.1271	.1251	.1230	.1210	.1190	.1170
1.2	.1151	.1131	.1112	.1093	.1075	.1056	.1038	.1020	.1003	.0985
1.3	.0968	.0951	.0934	.0918	.0901	.0885	.0869	.0853	.0838	.0823
1.4	.0808	.0793	.0778	.0764	.0749	.0735	.0721	.0708	.0694	.0681
1.5	.0668	.0655	.0643	.0630	.0618	.0606	.0594	.0582	.0571	.0559
1.6	.0548	.0537	.0526	.0516	.0505	.0495	.0485	.0475	.0465	.0455
1.7	.0446	.0436	.0427	.0418	.0409	.0401	.0392	.0384	.0375	.0367
1.8	.0359	.0351	.0344	.0336	.0329	.0322	.0314	.0307	.0301	.0294
1.9	.0287	.0281	.0274	.0268	.0262	.0256	.0250	.0244	.0239	.0233
2.0	.0228	.0222	.0217	.0212	.0207	.0202	.0197	.0192	.0188	.0183
2.1	.0179	.0174	.0170	.0166	.0162	.0158	.0154	.0150	.0146	.0143
2.2	.0139	.0136	.0132	.0129	.0125	.0122	.0119	.0116	.0113	.0110
2.3	.0107	.0104	.0102	.0099	.0096	.0094	.0091	.0089	.0087	.0084
2.4	.0082	.0080	.0078	.0075	.0073	.0071	.0069	.0068	.0066	.0064
2.5	.0062	.0060	.0059	.0057	.0055	.0054	.0052	.0051	.0049	.0048
2.6	.0047	.0045	.0044	.0043	.0041	.0040	.0039	.0038	.0037	.0036
2.7	.0035	.0034	.0033	.0032	.0031	.0030	.0029	.0028	.0027	.0026
2.8	.0026	.0025	.0024	.0023	.0023	.0022	.0021	.0021	.0020	.0019
2.9	.0019	.0018	.0018	.0017	.0016	.0016	.0015	.0015	.0014	.0014
3.0	.0013	.0013	.0013	.0012	.0012	.0011	.0011	.0011	.0010	.0010
3.1	.0010	.0009	.0009	.0009	.0008	.0008	.0008	.0008	.0007	.0007
3.2	.0007	.0007	.0006	.0006	.0006	.0006	.0006	.0005	.0005	.0005
3.3	.0005	.0005	.0005	.0004	.0004	.0004	.0004	.0004	.0004	.0003
3.4	.0003	.0003	.0003	.0003	.0003	.0003	.0003	.0003	.0003	.0002
3.5	.0002	.0002	.0002	.0002	.0002	.0002	.0002	.0002	.0002	.0002

TABLE C.2 *t*-distribution values for right-tail areas

[For example, the *t*-value with 22 degrees of freedom that has to its right an area of 0.05 is found at the intersection of the row labeled df = 22 and column labeled 0.05. The *t*-value is 1.717. Because the *t*-curve is symmetric about its mean, the *t*-value with 22 degrees of freedom that has to its left an area of 0.05 is −1.717. The table also may be used to find approximate *p*-values corresponding to given *t*-values. For example, to estimate the *p*-value associated with a *t*-value of 8.42 with 83 degrees of freedom, we look at the line corresponding to the df value that is closest to and smaller than or equal to 83. In this case, we estimate the answer using 80 degrees of freedom. On the line corresponding to 80 degrees of freedom, we find the *t*-value that is closest to, but smaller than 8.42. In this case, the value is 3.416. We conclude that $p < 0.0005$. If the *t*-value had been 0.5, with 83 degrees of freedom, we would see that there are no values smaller than or equal to 0.5 on the line and we would conclude that $p > 0.25$.]

df	0.25	0.20	0.15	0.10	0.05	0.025	0.02	0.01	0.005	0.001	0.0005
1	1.000	1.376	1.963	3.078	6.314	12.706	15.894	31.821	63.656	318.289	636.578
2	0.816	1.061	1.386	1.886	2.920	4.303	4.849	6.965	9.925	22.328	31.600
3	0.765	0.978	1.250	1.638	2.353	3.182	3.482	4.541	5.841	10.214	12.924
4	0.741	0.941	1.190	1.533	2.132	2.776	2.999	3.747	4.604	7.173	8.610
5	0.727	0.920	1.156	1.476	2.015	2.571	2.757	3.365	4.032	5.894	6.869
6	0.718	0.906	1.134	1.440	1.943	2.447	2.612	3.143	3.707	5.208	5.959
7	0.711	0.896	1.119	1.415	1.895	2.365	2.517	2.998	3.499	4.785	5.408
8	0.706	0.889	1.108	1.397	1.860	2.306	2.449	2.896	3.355	4.501	5.041
9	0.703	0.883	1.100	1.383	1.833	2.262	2.398	2.821	3.250	4.297	4.781
10	0.700	0.879	1.093	1.372	1.812	2.228	2.359	2.764	3.169	4.144	4.587
11	0.697	0.876	1.088	1.363	1.796	2.201	2.328	2.718	3.106	4.025	4.437
12	0.695	0.873	1.083	1.356	1.782	2.179	2.303	2.681	3.055	3.930	4.318
13	0.694	0.870	1.079	1.350	1.771	2.160	2.282	2.650	3.012	3.852	4.221
14	0.692	0.868	1.076	1.345	1.761	2.145	2.264	2.624	2.977	3.787	4.140
15	0.691	0.866	1.074	1.341	1.753	2.131	2.249	2.602	2.947	3.733	4.073
16	0.690	0.865	1.071	1.337	1.746	2.120	2.235	2.583	2.921	3.686	4.015
17	0.689	0.863	1.069	1.333	1.740	2.110	2.224	2.567	2.898	3.646	3.965
18	0.688	0.862	1.067	1.330	1.734	2.101	2.214	2.552	2.878	3.610	3.922
19	0.688	0.861	1.066	1.328	1.729	2.093	2.205	2.539	2.861	3.579	3.883
20	0.687	0.860	1.064	1.325	1.725	2.086	2.197	2.528	2.845	3.552	3.850
21	0.686	0.859	1.063	1.323	1.721	2.080	2.189	2.518	2.831	3.527	3.819
22	0.686	0.858	1.061	1.321	1.717	2.074	2.183	2.508	2.819	3.505	3.792
23	0.685	0.858	1.060	1.319	1.714	2.069	2.177	2.500	2.807	3.485	3.768
24	0.685	0.857	1.059	1.318	1.711	2.064	2.172	2.492	2.797	3.467	3.745
25	0.684	0.856	1.058	1.316	1.708	2.060	2.167	2.485	2.787	3.450	3.725
26	0.684	0.856	1.058	1.315	1.706	2.056	2.162	2.479	2.779	3.435	3.707
27	0.684	0.855	1.057	1.314	1.703	2.052	2.158	2.473	2.771	3.421	3.689
28	0.683	0.855	1.056	1.313	1.701	2.048	2.154	2.467	2.763	3.408	3.674
29	0.683	0.854	1.055	1.311	1.699	2.045	2.150	2.462	2.756	3.396	3.660
30	0.683	0.854	1.055	1.310	1.697	2.042	2.147	2.457	2.750	3.385	3.646
35	0.682	0.852	1.052	1.306	1.690	2.030	2.133	2.438	2.724	3.340	3.591
40	0.681	0.851	1.050	1.303	1.684	2.021	2.123	2.423	2.704	3.307	3.551
50	0.679	0.849	1.047	1.299	1.676	2.009	2.109	2.403	2.678	3.261	3.496
60	0.679	0.848	1.045	1.296	1.671	2.000	2.099	2.390	2.660	3.232	3.460
70	0.678	0.847	1.044	1.294	1.667	1.994	2.093	2.381	2.648	3.211	3.435
80	0.678	0.846	1.043	1.292	1.664	1.990	2.088	2.374	2.639	3.195	3.416
90	0.677	0.846	1.042	1.291	1.662	1.987	2.084	2.368	2.632	3.183	3.402
100	0.677	0.845	1.042	1.290	1.660	1.984	2.081	2.364	2.626	3.174	3.390
500	0.675	0.842	1.038	1.283	1.648	1.965	2.059	2.334	2.586	3.107	3.310
1000	0.675	0.842	1.037	1.282	1.646	1.962	2.056	2.330	2.581	3.098	3.300
∞	0.674	0.841	1.036	1.282	1.645	1.960	2.054	2.326	2.576	3.091	3.291

TABLE C.3 *F*-distribution values for right-tail areas

[For example, the *F*-value with numerator degrees of freedom 2 and denominator degrees of freedom 3 that has to its right an area of 0.05 is found at the intersection of the row with *df* FOR DENOM = 3 and α = 0.05 and column with *df* FOR NUMERATOR = 2. The *F*-value is 9.55. The table may also be used to find approximate *p*-values corresponding to given *F*-values. For example, to find the *p*-value associated with *F* = 8.66 with numerator degrees of freedom = 2 and denominator degrees of freedom = 3, we find all of the values associated with *df* FOR DENOM = 3 and *df* FOR NUMERATOR = 2. We find that the *F*-values that are closest to *F* = 8.66 are *F* = 5.46 and *F* = 9.55. The area to the right of *F* = 5.46 is 0.10 and the area to the right of *F* = 9.55 is 0.05. The *p*-value, or the area to the right of *F* = 8.66 is less than 0.10 but larger than 0.05. We have the estimate $0.05 < p < 0.10$. If, however, given the same degrees of freedom, we wished to find the *p*-value associated with *F* = 1.56, we find that the *F*-value that is closest to *F* = 1.56 is *F* = 2.28. The area to the right of *F* = 2.28 is 0.25. The *p*-value, or the area to the right of *F* = 1.56 is greater than 0.25. We have the estimate $p > 0.25$.

					df FOR NUMERATOR				
df FOR DENOM	α	1	2	3	4	5	6	7	8
1	0.25	5.83	7.50	8.20	8.58	8.82	8.98	9.10	9.19
1	0.10	39.86	49.50	53.59	55.83	57.24	58.20	58.91	59.44
1	0.05	161.45	199.50	215.71	224.58	230.16	233.99	236.77	238.88
1	0.03	647.79	799.48	864.15	899.60	921.83	937.11	948.20	956.64
1	0.01	4.E+03	5.E+03	5.E+03	6.E+03	6.E+03	6.E+03	6.E+03	6.E+03
1	0.001	4.E+05	5.E+05	5.E+05	6.E+05	6.E+05	6.E+05	6.E+05	6.E+05
2	0.25	2.57	3.00	3.15	3.23	3.28	3.31	3.34	3.35
2	0.10	8.53	9.00	9.16	9.24	9.29	9.33	9.35	9.37
2	0.05	18.51	19.00	19.16	19.25	19.30	19.33	19.35	19.37
2	0.03	38.51	39.00	39.17	39.25	39.30	39.33	39.36	39.37
2	0.01	98.50	99.00	99.16	99.25	99.30	99.33	99.36	99.38
2	0.001	998.38	998.84	999.31	999.31	999.31	999.31	999.31	999.31
3	0.25	2.02	2.28	2.36	2.39	2.41	2.42	2.43	2.44
3	0.10	5.54	5.46	5.39	5.34	5.31	5.28	5.27	5.25
3	0.05	10.13	9.55	9.28	9.12	9.01	8.94	8.89	8.85
3	0.03	17.44	16.04	15.44	15.10	14.88	14.73	14.62	14.54
3	0.01	34.12	30.82	29.46	28.71	28.24	27.91	27.67	27.49
3	0.001	167.06	148.49	141.10	137.08	134.58	132.83	131.61	130.62

(*continued*)

9	10	12	15	20	24	30	40	60	120	10000
9.26	9.32	9.41	9.49	9.58	9.63	9.67	9.71	9.76	9.80	9.85
59.86	60.19	60.71	61.22	61.74	62.00	62.26	62.53	62.79	63.06	63.32
240.54	241.88	243.90	245.95	248.02	249.05	250.10	251.14	252.20	253.25	254.30
963.28	968.63	976.72	984.87	993.08	997.27	1.0E+03	1.0E+03	1.0E+03	1.0E+03	1.0E+03
6.E+03	6.E+03	6.E+03	6.E+03	6.E+03	6.E+03	6.E+03	6.E+03	6.E+03	6.E+03	6.E+03
6.E+05	6.E+05	6.E+05	6.E+05	6.E+05	6.E+05	6.E+05	6.E+05	6.E+05	6.E+05	6.E+05
3.37	3.38	3.39	3.41	3.43	3.43	3.44	3.45	3.46	3.47	3.48
9.38	9.39	9.41	9.42	9.44	9.45	9.46	9.47	9.47	9.48	9.49
19.38	19.40	19.41	19.43	19.45	19.45	19.46	19.47	19.48	19.49	19.50
39.39	39.40	39.41	39.43	39.45	39.46	39.46	39.47	39.48	39.49	39.50
99.39	99.40	99.42	99.43	99.45	99.46	99.47	99.48	99.48	99.49	99.50
999.31	999.31	999.31	999.31	999.31	999.31	999.31	999.31	999.31	999.31	999.31
2.44	2.44	2.45	2.46	2.46	2.46	2.47	2.47	2.47	2.47	2.47
5.24	5.23	5.22	5.20	5.18	5.18	5.17	5.16	5.15	5.14	5.13
8.81	8.79	8.74	8.70	8.66	8.64	8.62	8.59	8.57	8.55	8.53
14.47	14.42	14.34	14.25	14.17	14.12	14.08	14.04	13.99	13.95	13.90
27.34	27.23	27.05	26.87	26.69	26.60	26.50	26.41	26.32	26.22	26.13
129.86	129.22	128.32	127.36	126.43	125.93	125.44	124.97	124.45	123.98	123.46

df FOR DENOM	α	1	2	3	4	5	6	7	8	9	10	12	15	20	24	30	40	60	120	10000
4	0.25	1.81	2.00	2.05	2.06	2.07	2.08	2.08	2.08	2.08	2.08	2.08	2.08	2.08	2.08	2.08	2.08	2.08	2.08	2.08
4	0.10	4.54	4.32	4.19	4.11	4.05	4.01	3.98	3.95	3.94	3.92	3.90	3.87	3.84	3.83	3.82	3.80	3.79	3.78	3.76
4	0.05	7.71	6.94	6.59	6.39	6.26	6.16	6.09	6.04	6.00	5.96	5.91	5.86	5.80	5.77	5.75	5.72	5.69	5.66	5.63
4	0.03	12.22	10.65	9.98	9.60	9.36	9.20	9.07	8.98	8.90	8.84	8.75	8.66	8.56	8.51	8.46	8.41	8.36	8.31	8.26
4	0.01	21.20	18.00	16.69	15.98	15.52	15.21	14.98	14.80	14.66	14.55	14.37	14.20	14.02	13.93	13.84	13.75	13.65	13.56	13.46
4	0.001	74.13	61.25	56.17	53.43	51.72	50.52	49.65	49.00	48.47	48.05	47.41	46.76	46.10	45.77	45.43	45.08	44.75	44.40	44.05
5	0.25	1.69	1.85	1.88	1.89	1.89	1.89	1.89	1.89	1.89	1.89	1.89	1.89	1.88	1.88	1.88	1.88	1.87	1.87	1.87
5	0.10	4.06	3.78	3.62	3.52	3.45	3.40	3.37	3.34	3.32	3.30	3.27	3.24	3.21	3.19	3.17	3.16	3.14	3.12	3.11
5	0.05	6.61	5.79	5.41	5.19	5.05	4.95	4.88	4.82	4.77	4.74	4.68	4.62	4.56	4.53	4.50	4.46	4.43	4.40	4.37
5	0.03	10.01	8.43	7.76	7.39	7.15	6.98	6.85	6.76	6.68	6.62	6.52	6.43	6.33	6.28	6.23	6.18	6.12	6.07	6.02
5	0.01	16.26	13.27	12.06	11.39	10.97	10.67	10.46	10.29	10.16	10.05	9.89	9.72	9.55	9.47	9.38	9.29	9.20	9.11	9.02
5	0.001	47.18	37.12	33.20	31.08	29.75	28.83	28.17	27.65	27.24	26.91	26.42	25.91	25.39	25.13	24.87	24.60	24.33	24.06	23.79
6	0.25	1.62	1.76	1.78	1.79	1.79	1.78	1.78	1.78	1.77	1.77	1.77	1.76	1.76	1.75	1.75	1.75	1.74	1.74	1.74
6	0.10	3.78	3.46	3.29	3.18	3.11	3.05	3.01	2.98	2.96	2.94	2.90	2.87	2.84	2.82	2.80	2.78	2.76	2.74	2.72
6	0.05	5.99	5.14	4.76	4.53	4.39	4.28	4.21	4.15	4.10	4.06	4.00	3.94	3.87	3.84	3.81	3.77	3.74	3.70	3.67
6	0.03	8.81	7.26	6.60	6.23	5.99	5.82	5.70	5.60	5.52	5.46	5.37	5.27	5.17	5.12	5.07	5.01	4.96	4.90	4.85
6	0.01	13.75	10.92	9.78	9.15	8.75	8.47	8.26	8.10	7.98	7.87	7.72	7.56	7.40	7.31	7.23	7.14	7.06	6.97	6.88
6	0.001	35.51	27.00	23.71	21.92	20.80	20.03	19.46	19.03	18.69	18.41	17.99	17.56	17.12	16.90	16.67	16.44	16.21	15.98	15.75
7	0.25	1.57	1.70	1.72	1.72	1.71	1.71	1.70	1.70	1.69	1.69	1.68	1.68	1.67	1.67	1.66	1.66	1.65	1.65	1.65
7	0.10	3.59	3.26	3.07	2.96	2.88	2.83	2.78	2.75	2.72	2.70	2.67	2.63	2.59	2.58	2.56	2.54	2.51	2.49	2.47
7	0.05	5.59	4.74	4.35	4.12	3.97	3.87	3.79	3.73	3.68	3.64	3.57	3.51	3.44	3.41	3.38	3.34	3.30	3.27	3.23
7	0.03	8.07	6.54	5.89	5.52	5.29	5.12	4.99	4.90	4.82	4.76	4.67	4.57	4.47	4.41	4.36	4.31	4.25	4.20	4.14
7	0.01	12.25	9.55	8.45	7.85	7.46	7.19	6.99	6.84	6.72	6.62	6.47	6.31	6.16	6.07	5.99	5.91	5.82	5.74	5.65
7	0.001	29.25	21.69	18.77	17.20	16.21	15.52	15.02	14.63	14.33	14.08	13.71	13.32	12.93	12.73	12.53	12.33	12.12	11.91	11.70

8	0.25	1.54	1.66	1.67	1.66	1.66	1.65	1.64	1.64	1.63	1.63	1.62	1.62	1.61	1.60	1.60	1.59	1.59	1.58	1.58
8	0.10	3.46	3.11	2.92	2.81	2.73	2.67	2.62	2.59	2.56	2.54	2.50	2.46	2.42	2.40	2.38	2.36	2.34	2.32	2.29
8	0.05	5.32	4.46	4.07	3.84	3.69	3.58	3.50	3.44	3.39	3.35	3.28	3.22	3.15	3.12	3.08	3.04	3.01	2.97	2.93
8	0.03	7.57	6.06	5.42	5.05	4.82	4.65	4.53	4.43	4.36	4.30	4.20	4.10	4.00	3.95	3.89	3.84	3.78	3.73	3.67
8	0.01	11.26	8.65	7.59	7.01	6.63	6.37	6.18	6.03	5.91	5.81	5.67	5.52	5.36	5.28	5.20	5.12	5.03	4.95	4.86
8	0.001	25.41	18.49	15.83	14.39	13.48	12.86	12.40	12.05	11.77	11.54	11.19	10.84	10.48	10.30	10.11	9.92	9.73	9.53	9.34
9	0.25	1.51	1.62	1.63	1.63	1.62	1.61	1.60	1.60	1.59	1.59	1.58	1.57	1.56	1.56	1.55	1.54	1.54	1.53	1.53
9	0.10	3.36	3.01	2.81	2.69	2.61	2.55	2.51	2.47	2.44	2.42	2.38	2.34	2.30	2.28	2.25	2.23	2.21	2.18	2.16
9	0.05	5.12	4.26	3.86	3.63	3.48	3.37	3.29	3.23	3.18	3.14	3.07	3.01	2.94	2.90	2.86	2.83	2.79	2.75	2.71
9	0.03	7.21	5.71	5.08	4.72	4.48	4.32	4.20	4.10	4.03	3.96	3.87	3.77	3.67	3.61	3.56	3.51	3.45	3.39	3.33
9	0.01	10.56	8.02	6.99	6.42	6.06	5.80	5.61	5.47	5.35	5.26	5.11	4.96	4.81	4.73	4.65	4.57	4.48	4.40	4.31
9	0.001	22.86	16.39	13.90	12.56	11.71	11.13	10.70	10.37	10.11	9.89	9.57	9.24	8.90	8.72	8.55	8.37	8.19	8.00	7.82
10	0.25	1.49	1.60	1.60	1.59	1.59	1.58	1.57	1.56	1.56	1.55	1.54	1.53	1.52	1.52	1.51	1.51	1.50	1.49	1.48
10	0.10	3.29	2.92	2.73	2.61	2.52	2.46	2.41	2.38	2.35	2.32	2.28	2.24	2.20	2.18	2.16	2.13	2.11	2.08	2.06
10	0.05	4.96	4.10	3.71	3.48	3.33	3.22	3.14	3.07	3.02	2.98	2.91	2.85	2.77	2.74	2.70	2.66	2.62	2.58	2.54
10	0.03	6.94	5.46	4.83	4.47	4.24	4.07	3.95	3.85	3.78	3.72	3.62	3.52	3.42	3.37	3.31	3.26	3.20	3.14	3.08
10	0.01	10.04	7.56	6.55	5.99	5.64	5.39	5.20	5.06	4.94	4.85	4.71	4.56	4.41	4.33	4.25	4.17	4.08	4.00	3.91
10	0.001	21.04	14.90	12.55	11.28	10.48	9.93	9.52	9.20	8.96	8.75	8.45	8.13	7.80	7.64	7.47	7.30	7.12	6.94	6.76
11	0.25	1.47	1.58	1.58	1.57	1.56	1.55	1.54	1.53	1.53	1.52	1.51	1.50	1.49	1.49	1.48	1.47	1.47	1.46	1.45
11	0.10	3.23	2.86	2.66	2.54	2.45	2.39	2.34	2.30	2.27	2.25	2.21	2.17	2.12	2.10	2.08	2.05	2.03	2.00	1.97
11	0.05	4.84	3.98	3.59	3.36	3.20	3.09	3.01	2.95	2.90	2.85	2.79	2.72	2.65	2.61	2.57	2.53	2.49	2.45	2.41
11	0.03	6.72	5.26	4.63	4.28	4.04	3.88	3.76	3.66	3.59	3.53	3.43	3.33	3.23	3.17	3.12	3.06	3.00	2.94	2.88
11	0.01	9.65	7.21	6.22	5.67	5.32	5.07	4.89	4.74	4.63	4.54	4.40	4.25	4.10	4.02	3.94	3.86	3.78	3.69	3.60
11	0.001	19.69	13.81	11.56	10.35	9.58	9.05	8.65	8.35	8.12	7.92	7.63	7.32	7.01	6.85	6.68	6.52	6.35	6.18	6.00

(continued)

df FOR NUMERATOR

df FOR DENOM	α	1	2	3	4	5	6	7	8	9	10	12	15	20	24	30	40	60	120	10000
12	0.25	1.46	1.56	1.56	1.55	1.54	1.53	1.52	1.51	1.51	1.50	1.49	1.48	1.47	1.46	1.45	1.45	1.44	1.43	1.42
12	0.10	3.18	2.81	2.61	2.48	2.39	2.33	2.28	2.24	2.21	2.19	2.15	2.10	2.06	2.04	2.01	1.99	1.96	1.93	1.90
12	0.05	4.75	3.89	3.49	3.26	3.11	3.00	2.91	2.85	2.80	2.75	2.69	2.62	2.54	2.51	2.47	2.43	2.38	2.34	2.30
12	0.03	6.55	5.10	4.47	4.12	3.89	3.73	3.61	3.51	3.44	3.37	3.28	3.18	3.07	3.02	2.96	2.91	2.85	2.79	2.73
12	0.01	9.33	6.93	5.95	5.41	5.06	4.82	4.64	4.50	4.39	4.30	4.16	4.01	3.86	3.78	3.70	3.62	3.54	3.45	3.36
12	0.001	18.64	12.97	10.80	9.63	8.89	8.38	8.00	7.71	7.48	7.29	7.00	6.71	6.40	6.25	6.09	5.93	5.76	5.59	5.42
13	0.25	1.45	1.55	1.55	1.53	1.52	1.51	1.50	1.49	1.49	1.48	1.47	1.46	1.45	1.44	1.43	1.42	1.42	1.41	1.40
13	0.10	3.14	2.76	2.56	2.43	2.35	2.28	2.23	2.20	2.16	2.14	2.10	2.05	2.01	1.98	1.96	1.93	1.90	1.88	1.85
13	0.05	4.67	3.81	3.41	3.18	3.03	2.92	2.83	2.77	2.71	2.67	2.60	2.53	2.46	2.42	2.38	2.34	2.30	2.25	2.21
13	0.03	6.41	4.97	4.35	4.00	3.77	3.60	3.48	3.39	3.31	3.25	3.15	3.05	2.95	2.89	2.84	2.78	2.72	2.66	2.60
13	0.01	9.07	6.70	5.74	5.21	4.86	4.62	4.44	4.30	4.19	4.10	3.96	3.82	3.66	3.59	3.51	3.43	3.34	3.25	3.17
13	0.001	17.82	12.31	10.21	9.07	8.35	7.86	7.49	7.21	6.98	6.80	6.52	6.23	5.93	5.78	5.63	5.47	5.30	5.14	4.97
14	0.25	1.44	1.53	1.53	1.52	1.51	1.50	1.49	1.48	1.47	1.46	1.45	1.44	1.43	1.42	1.41	1.41	1.40	1.39	1.38
14	0.10	3.10	2.73	2.52	2.39	2.31	2.24	2.19	2.15	2.12	2.10	2.05	2.01	1.96	1.94	1.91	1.89	1.86	1.83	1.80
14	0.05	4.60	3.74	3.34	3.11	2.96	2.85	2.76	2.70	2.65	2.60	2.53	2.46	2.39	2.35	2.31	2.27	2.22	2.18	2.13
14	0.03	6.30	4.86	4.24	3.89	3.66	3.50	3.38	3.29	3.21	3.15	3.05	2.95	2.84	2.79	2.73	2.67	2.61	2.55	2.49
14	0.01	8.86	6.51	5.56	5.04	4.69	4.46	4.28	4.14	4.03	3.94	3.80	3.66	3.51	3.43	3.35	3.27	3.18	3.09	3.01
14	0.001	17.14	11.78	9.73	8.62	7.92	7.44	7.08	6.80	6.58	6.40	6.13	5.85	5.56	5.41	5.25	5.10	4.94	4.77	4.61
15	0.25	1.43	1.52	1.52	1.51	1.49	1.48	1.47	1.46	1.46	1.45	1.44	1.43	1.41	1.41	1.40	1.39	1.38	1.37	1.36
15	0.10	3.07	2.70	2.49	2.36	2.27	2.21	2.16	2.12	2.09	2.06	2.02	1.97	1.92	1.90	1.87	1.85	1.82	1.79	1.76
15	0.05	4.54	3.68	3.29	3.06	2.90	2.79	2.71	2.64	2.59	2.54	2.48	2.40	2.33	2.29	2.25	2.20	2.16	2.11	2.07
15	0.03	6.20	4.77	4.15	3.80	3.58	3.41	3.29	3.20	3.12	3.06	2.96	2.86	2.76	2.70	2.64	2.59	2.52	2.46	2.40
15	0.01	8.68	6.36	5.42	4.89	4.56	4.32	4.14	4.00	3.89	3.80	3.67	3.52	3.37	3.29	3.21	3.13	3.05	2.96	2.87
15	0.001	16.59	11.34	9.34	8.25	7.57	7.09	6.74	6.47	6.26	6.08	5.81	5.54	5.25	5.10	4.95	4.80	4.64	4.48	4.31

16	0.25	1.42	1.51	1.51	1.50	1.48	1.47	1.46	1.45	1.44	1.44	1.43	1.41	1.40	1.39	1.38	1.37	1.36	1.35	1.34
16	0.10	3.05	2.67	2.46	2.33	2.24	2.18	2.13	2.09	2.06	2.03	1.99	1.94	1.89	1.87	1.84	1.81	1.78	1.75	1.72
16	0.05	4.49	3.63	3.24	3.01	2.85	2.74	2.66	2.59	2.54	2.49	2.42	2.35	2.28	2.24	2.19	2.15	2.11	2.06	2.01
16	0.03	6.12	4.69	4.08	3.73	3.50	3.34	3.22	3.12	3.05	2.99	2.89	2.79	2.68	2.63	2.57	2.51	2.45	2.38	2.32
16	0.01	8.53	6.23	5.29	4.77	4.44	4.20	4.03	3.89	3.78	3.69	3.55	3.41	3.26	3.18	3.10	3.02	2.93	2.84	2.75
16	0.001	16.12	10.97	9.01	7.94	7.27	6.80	6.46	6.20	5.98	5.81	5.55	5.27	4.99	4.85	4.70	4.54	4.39	4.23	4.06
17	0.25	1.42	1.51	1.50	1.49	1.47	1.46	1.45	1.44	1.43	1.43	1.41	1.40	1.39	1.38	1.37	1.36	1.35	1.34	1.33
17	0.10	3.03	2.64	2.44	2.31	2.22	2.15	2.10	2.06	2.03	2.00	1.96	1.91	1.86	1.84	1.81	1.78	1.75	1.72	1.69
17	0.05	4.45	3.59	3.20	2.96	2.81	2.70	2.61	2.55	2.49	2.45	2.38	2.31	2.23	2.19	2.15	2.10	2.06	2.01	1.96
17	0.03	6.04	4.62	4.01	3.66	3.44	3.28	3.16	3.06	2.98	2.92	2.82	2.72	2.62	2.56	2.50	2.44	2.38	2.32	2.25
17	0.01	8.40	6.11	5.19	4.67	4.34	4.10	3.93	3.79	3.68	3.59	3.46	3.31	3.16	3.08	3.00	2.92	2.83	2.75	2.65
17	0.001	15.72	10.66	8.73	7.68	7.02	6.56	6.22	5.96	5.75	5.58	5.32	5.05	4.78	4.63	4.48	4.33	4.18	4.02	3.85
18	0.25	1.41	1.50	1.49	1.48	1.46	1.45	1.44	1.43	1.42	1.42	1.40	1.39	1.38	1.37	1.36	1.35	1.34	1.33	1.32
18	0.10	3.01	2.62	2.42	2.29	2.20	2.13	2.08	2.04	2.00	1.98	1.93	1.89	1.84	1.81	1.78	1.75	1.72	1.69	1.66
18	0.05	4.41	3.55	3.16	2.93	2.77	2.66	2.58	2.51	2.46	2.41	2.34	2.27	2.19	2.15	2.11	2.06	2.02	1.97	1.92
18	0.03	5.98	4.56	3.95	3.61	3.38	3.22	3.10	3.01	2.93	2.87	2.77	2.67	2.56	2.50	2.44	2.38	2.32	2.26	2.19
18	0.01	8.29	6.01	5.09	4.58	4.25	4.01	3.84	3.71	3.60	3.51	3.37	3.23	3.08	3.00	2.92	2.84	2.75	2.66	2.57
18	0.001	15.38	10.39	8.49	7.46	6.81	6.35	6.02	5.76	5.56	5.39	5.13	4.87	4.59	4.45	4.30	4.15	4.00	3.84	3.67
19	0.25	1.41	1.49	1.49	1.47	1.46	1.44	1.43	1.42	1.41	1.41	1.40	1.38	1.37	1.36	1.35	1.34	1.33	1.32	1.30
19	0.10	2.99	2.61	2.40	2.27	2.18	2.11	2.06	2.02	1.98	1.96	1.91	1.86	1.81	1.79	1.76	1.73	1.70	1.67	1.63
19	0.05	4.38	3.52	3.13	2.90	2.74	2.63	2.54	2.48	2.42	2.38	2.31	2.23	2.16	2.11	2.07	2.03	1.98	1.93	1.88
19	0.03	5.92	4.51	3.90	3.56	3.33	3.17	3.05	2.96	2.88	2.82	2.72	2.62	2.51	2.45	2.39	2.33	2.27	2.20	2.13
19	0.01	8.18	5.93	5.01	4.50	4.17	3.94	3.77	3.63	3.52	3.43	3.30	3.15	3.00	2.92	2.84	2.76	2.67	2.58	2.49
19	0.001	15.08	10.16	8.28	7.27	6.62	6.18	5.85	5.59	5.39	5.22	4.97	4.70	4.43	4.29	4.14	3.99	3.84	3.68	3.52

(continued)

df FOR DENOM	α	1	2	3	4	5	6	7	8	9	10	12	15	20	24	30	40	60	120	10000
20	0.25	1.40	1.49	1.48	1.47	1.45	1.44	1.43	1.42	1.41	1.40	1.39	1.37	1.36	1.35	1.34	1.33	1.32	1.31	1.29
20	0.10	2.97	2.59	2.38	2.25	2.16	2.09	2.04	2.00	1.96	1.94	1.89	1.84	1.79	1.77	1.74	1.71	1.68	1.64	1.61
20	0.05	4.35	3.49	3.10	2.87	2.71	2.60	2.51	2.45	2.39	2.35	2.28	2.20	2.12	2.08	2.04	1.99	1.95	1.90	1.84
20	0.03	5.87	4.46	3.86	3.51	3.29	3.13	3.01	2.91	2.84	2.77	2.68	2.57	2.46	2.41	2.35	2.29	2.22	2.16	2.09
20	0.01	8.10	5.85	4.94	4.43	4.10	3.87	3.70	3.56	3.46	3.37	3.23	3.09	2.94	2.86	2.78	2.69	2.61	2.52	2.42
20	0.001	14.82	9.95	8.10	7.10	6.46	6.02	5.69	5.44	5.24	5.08	4.82	4.56	4.29	4.15	4.00	3.86	3.70	3.54	3.38
22	0.25	1.40	1.48	1.47	1.45	1.44	1.42	1.41	1.40	1.39	1.39	1.37	1.36	1.34	1.33	1.32	1.31	1.30	1.29	1.28
22	0.10	2.95	2.56	2.35	2.22	2.13	2.06	2.01	1.97	1.93	1.90	1.86	1.81	1.76	1.73	1.70	1.67	1.64	1.60	1.57
22	0.05	4.30	3.44	3.05	2.82	2.66	2.55	2.46	2.40	2.34	2.30	2.23	2.15	2.07	2.03	1.98	1.94	1.89	1.84	1.78
22	0.03	5.79	4.38	3.78	3.44	3.22	3.05	2.93	2.84	2.76	2.70	2.60	2.50	2.39	2.33	2.27	2.21	2.14	2.08	2.00
22	0.01	7.95	5.72	4.82	4.31	3.99	3.76	3.59	3.45	3.35	3.26	3.12	2.98	2.83	2.75	2.67	2.58	2.50	2.40	2.31
22	0.001	14.38	9.61	7.80	6.81	6.19	5.76	5.44	5.19	4.99	4.83	4.58	4.33	4.06	3.92	3.78	3.63	3.48	3.32	3.15
24	0.25	1.39	1.47	1.46	1.44	1.43	1.41	1.40	1.39	1.38	1.38	1.36	1.35	1.33	1.32	1.31	1.30	1.29	1.28	1.26
24	0.10	2.93	2.54	2.33	2.19	2.10	2.04	1.98	1.94	1.91	1.88	1.83	1.78	1.73	1.70	1.67	1.64	1.61	1.57	1.53
24	0.05	4.26	3.40	3.01	2.78	2.62	2.51	2.42	2.36	2.30	2.25	2.18	2.11	2.03	1.98	1.94	1.89	1.84	1.79	1.73
24	0.03	5.72	4.32	3.72	3.38	3.15	2.99	2.87	2.78	2.70	2.64	2.54	2.44	2.33	2.27	2.21	2.15	2.08	2.01	1.94
24	0.01	7.82	5.61	4.72	4.22	3.90	3.67	3.50	3.36	3.26	3.17	3.03	2.89	2.74	2.66	2.58	2.49	2.40	2.31	2.21
24	0.001	14.03	9.34	7.55	6.59	5.98	5.55	5.24	4.99	4.80	4.64	4.39	4.14	3.87	3.74	3.59	3.45	3.29	3.14	2.97
26	0.25	1.38	1.46	1.45	1.44	1.42	1.41	1.39	1.38	1.37	1.37	1.35	1.34	1.32	1.31	1.30	1.29	1.28	1.26	1.25
26	0.10	2.91	2.52	2.31	2.17	2.08	2.01	1.96	1.92	1.88	1.86	1.81	1.76	1.71	1.68	1.65	1.61	1.58	1.54	1.50
26	0.05	4.23	3.37	2.98	2.74	2.59	2.47	2.39	2.32	2.27	2.22	2.15	2.07	1.99	1.95	1.90	1.85	1.80	1.75	1.69
26	0.03	5.66	4.27	3.67	3.33	3.10	2.94	2.82	2.73	2.65	2.59	2.49	2.39	2.28	2.22	2.16	2.09	2.03	1.95	1.88
26	0.01	7.72	5.53	4.64	4.14	3.82	3.59	3.42	3.29	3.18	3.09	2.96	2.81	2.66	2.58	2.50	2.42	2.33	2.23	2.13
26	0.001	13.74	9.12	7.36	6.41	5.80	5.38	5.07	4.83	4.64	4.48	4.24	3.99	3.72	3.59	3.44	3.30	3.15	2.99	2.82

ν_2	α																			
28	0.25	1.24	1.25	1.27	1.28	1.29	1.30	1.31	1.33	1.34	1.36	1.37	1.38	1.39	1.40	1.41	1.43	1.45	1.46	1.38
28	0.10	1.48	1.52	1.56	1.59	1.63	1.66	1.69	1.74	1.79	1.84	1.87	1.90	1.94	2.00	2.06	2.16	2.29	2.50	2.89
28	0.05	1.65	1.71	1.77	1.82	1.87	1.91	1.96	2.04	2.12	2.19	2.24	2.29	2.36	2.45	2.56	2.71	2.95	3.34	4.20
28	0.03	1.83	1.91	1.98	2.05	2.11	2.17	2.23	2.34	2.45	2.55	2.61	2.69	2.78	2.90	3.06	3.29	3.63	4.22	5.61
28	0.01	2.07	2.17	2.26	2.35	2.44	2.52	2.60	2.75	2.90	3.03	3.12	3.23	3.36	3.53	3.75	4.07	4.57	5.45	7.64
28	0.001	2.70	2.86	3.02	3.18	3.32	3.46	3.60	3.86	4.11	4.35	4.50	4.69	4.93	5.24	5.66	6.25	7.19	8.93	13.50
30	0.25	1.23	1.24	1.26	1.27	1.28	1.29	1.30	1.32	1.34	1.35	1.36	1.37	1.38	1.39	1.41	1.42	1.44	1.45	1.38
30	0.10	1.46	1.50	1.54	1.57	1.61	1.64	1.67	1.72	1.77	1.82	1.85	1.88	1.93	1.98	2.05	2.14	2.28	2.49	2.88
30	0.05	1.62	1.68	1.74	1.79	1.84	1.89	1.93	2.01	2.09	2.16	2.21	2.27	2.33	2.42	2.53	2.69	2.92	3.32	4.17
30	0.03	1.79	1.87	1.94	2.01	2.07	2.14	2.20	2.31	2.41	2.51	2.57	2.65	2.75	2.87	3.03	3.25	3.59	4.18	5.57
30	0.01	2.01	2.11	2.21	2.30	2.39	2.47	2.55	2.70	2.84	2.98	3.07	3.17	3.30	3.47	3.70	4.02	4.51	5.39	7.56
30	0.001	2.59	2.76	2.92	3.07	3.22	3.36	3.49	3.75	4.00	4.24	4.39	4.58	4.82	5.12	5.53	6.12	7.05	8.77	13.29
40	0.25	1.19	1.21	1.22	1.24	1.25	1.26	1.28	1.30	1.31	1.33	1.34	1.35	1.36	1.37	1.39	1.40	1.42	1.44	1.36
40	0.10	1.38	1.42	1.47	1.51	1.54	1.57	1.61	1.66	1.71	1.76	1.79	1.83	1.87	1.93	2.00	2.09	2.23	2.44	2.84
40	0.05	1.51	1.58	1.64	1.69	1.74	1.79	1.84	1.92	2.00	2.08	2.12	2.18	2.25	2.34	2.45	2.61	2.84	3.23	4.08
40	0.03	1.64	1.72	1.80	1.88	1.94	2.01	2.07	2.18	2.29	2.39	2.45	2.53	2.62	2.74	2.90	3.13	3.46	4.05	5.42
40	0.01	1.81	1.92	2.02	2.11	2.20	2.29	2.37	2.52	2.66	2.80	2.89	2.99	3.12	3.29	3.51	3.83	4.31	5.18	7.31
40	0.001	2.23	2.41	2.57	2.73	2.87	3.01	3.15	3.40	3.64	3.87	4.02	4.21	4.44	4.73	5.13	5.70	6.59	8.25	12.61
60	0.25	1.15	1.17	1.19	1.21	1.22	1.24	1.25	1.27	1.29	1.30	1.31	1.32	1.33	1.35	1.37	1.38	1.41	1.42	1.35
60	0.10	1.29	1.35	1.40	1.44	1.48	1.51	1.54	1.60	1.66	1.71	1.74	1.77	1.82	1.87	1.95	2.04	2.18	2.39	2.79
60	0.05	1.39	1.47	1.53	1.59	1.65	1.70	1.75	1.84	1.92	1.99	2.04	2.10	2.17	2.25	2.37	2.53	2.76	3.15	4.00
60	0.03	1.48	1.58	1.67	1.74	1.82	1.88	1.94	2.06	2.17	2.27	2.33	2.41	2.51	2.63	2.79	3.01	3.34	3.93	5.29
60	0.01	1.60	1.73	1.84	1.94	2.03	2.12	2.20	2.35	2.50	2.63	2.72	2.82	2.95	3.12	3.34	3.65	4.13	4.98	7.08
60	0.001	1.89	2.08	2.25	2.41	2.55	2.69	2.83	3.08	3.32	3.54	3.69	3.86	4.09	4.37	4.76	5.31	6.17	7.77	11.97

(continued)

df FOR NUMERATOR

df FOR DENOM	α	1	2	3	4	5	6	7	8	9	10	12	15	20	24	30	40	60	120	10000
120	0.25	1.34	1.40	1.39	1.37	1.35	1.33	1.31	1.30	1.29	1.28	1.26	1.24	1.22	1.21	1.19	1.18	1.16	1.13	1.10
120	0.10	2.75	2.35	2.13	1.99	1.90	1.82	1.77	1.72	1.68	1.65	1.60	1.55	1.48	1.45	1.41	1.37	1.32	1.26	1.19
120	0.05	3.92	3.07	2.68	2.45	2.29	2.18	2.09	2.02	1.96	1.91	1.83	1.75	1.66	1.61	1.55	1.50	1.43	1.35	1.26
120	0.03	5.15	3.80	3.23	2.89	2.67	2.52	2.39	2.30	2.22	2.16	2.05	1.94	1.82	1.76	1.69	1.61	1.53	1.43	1.31
120	0.01	6.85	4.79	3.95	3.48	3.17	2.96	2.79	2.66	2.56	2.47	2.34	2.19	2.03	1.95	1.86	1.76	1.66	1.53	1.38
120	0.001	11.38	7.32	5.78	4.95	4.42	4.04	3.77	3.55	3.38	3.24	3.02	2.78	2.53	2.40	2.26	2.11	1.95	1.77	1.55
10000	0.25	1.32	1.39	1.37	1.35	1.33	1.31	1.29	1.28	1.27	1.26	1.24	1.22	1.19	1.18	1.16	1.14	1.12	1.08	1.01
10000	0.10	2.71	2.30	2.08	1.95	1.85	1.77	1.72	1.67	1.63	1.60	1.55	1.49	1.42	1.38	1.34	1.30	1.24	1.17	1.03
10000	0.05	3.84	3.00	2.61	2.37	2.21	2.10	2.01	1.94	1.88	1.83	1.75	1.67	1.57	1.52	1.46	1.40	1.32	1.22	1.03
10000	0.03	5.03	3.69	3.12	2.79	2.57	2.41	2.29	2.19	2.11	2.05	1.95	1.83	1.71	1.64	1.57	1.49	1.39	1.27	1.04
10000	0.01	6.64	4.61	3.78	3.32	3.02	2.80	2.64	2.51	2.41	2.32	2.19	2.04	1.88	1.79	1.70	1.59	1.48	1.33	1.05
10000	0.001	10.83	6.91	5.43	4.62	4.11	3.75	3.48	3.27	3.10	2.96	2.75	2.52	2.27	2.14	1.99	1.84	1.66	1.45	1.06

TABLE C.4 Binomial distribution table

The entries in the table below give the probability of K successes in N trials where p is the probability of success on a single trial. For example, to find the probability of obtaining 2 heads in 3 coin tosses, we have $N = 3$, $K = 2$, and $p = 0.5$. The probability of obtaining 2 heads in 3 coin tosses is 0.375.

N	K						P				
		0.05	**0.10**	**0.15**	**0.20**	**0.25**	**0.30**	**0.35**	**0.40**	**0.45**	**0.50**
2	0	0.9025	0.8100	0.7225	0.6400	0.5625	0.4900	0.4225	0.3600	0.3025	0.2500
	1	0.0950	0.1800	0.2550	0.3200	0.3750	0.4200	0.4550	0.4800	0.4950	0.5000
	2	0.0025	0.0100	0.0225	0.0400	0.0625	0.0900	0.1225	0.1600	0.2025	0.2500
3	0	0.8574	0.7290	0.6141	0.5120	0.4219	0.3430	0.2746	0.2160	0.1664	0.1250
	1	0.1354	0.2430	0.3251	0.3840	0.4219	0.4410	0.4436	0.4320	0.4084	0.3750
	2	0.0071	0.0270	0.0574	0.0960	0.1406	0.1890	0.2389	0.2880	0.3341	0.3750
	3	0.0001	0.0010	0.0034	0.0080	0.0156	0.0270	0.0429	0.0640	0.0911	0.1250
4	0	0.8145	0.6561	0.5220	0.4096	0.3164	0.2401	0.1785	0.1296	0.0915	0.0625
	1	0.1715	0.2916	0.3685	0.4096	0.4219	0.4116	0.3845	0.3456	0.2995	0.2500
	2	0.0135	0.0486	0.0975	0.1536	0.2109	0.2646	0.3105	0.3456	0.3675	0.3750
	3	0.0005	0.0036	0.0115	0.0256	0.0469	0.0756	0.1115	0.1536	0.2005	0.2500
	4	0.0000	0.0001	0.0005	0.0016	0.0039	0.0081	0.0150	0.0256	0.0410	0.0625
5	0	0.7738	0.5905	0.4437	0.3277	0.2373	0.1681	0.1160	0.0778	0.0503	0.0313
	1	0.2036	0.3281	0.3915	0.4096	0.3955	0.3602	0.3124	0.2592	0.2059	0.1563
	2	0.0214	0.0729	0.1382	0.2048	0.2637	0.3087	0.3364	0.3456	0.3369	0.3125
	3	0.0011	0.0081	0.0244	0.0512	0.0879	0.1323	0.1811	0.2304	0.2757	0.3125
	4	0.0000	0.0005	0.0022	0.0064	0.0146	0.0284	0.0488	0.0768	0.1128	0.1563
	5	0.0000	0.0000	0.0001	0.0003	0.0010	0.0024	0.0053	0.0102	0.0185	0.0313
6	0	0.7351	0.5314	0.3771	0.2621	0.1780	0.1176	0.0754	0.0467	0.0277	0.0156
	1	0.2321	0.3543	0.3993	0.3932	0.3560	0.3025	0.2437	0.1866	0.1359	0.0938
	2	0.0305	0.0984	0.1762	0.2458	0.2966	0.3241	0.3280	0.3110	0.2780	0.2344
	3	0.0021	0.0146	0.0415	0.0819	0.1318	0.1852	0.2355	0.2765	0.3032	0.3125
	4	0.0001	0.0012	0.0055	0.0154	0.0330	0.0595	0.0951	0.1382	0.1861	0.2344
	5	0.0000	0.0001	0.0004	0.0015	0.0044	0.0102	0.0205	0.0369	0.0609	0.0938
	6	0.0000	0.0000	0.0000	0.0001	0.0002	0.0007	0.0018	0.0041	0.0083	0.0156
7	0	0.6983	0.4783	0.3206	0.2097	0.1335	0.0824	0.0490	0.0280	0.0152	0.0078
	1	0.2573	0.3720	0.3960	0.3670	0.3115	0.2471	0.1848	0.1306	0.0872	0.0547
	2	0.0406	0.1240	0.2097	0.2753	0.3115	0.3177	0.2985	0.2613	0.2140	0.1641
	3	0.0036	0.0230	0.0617	0.1147	0.1730	0.2269	0.2679	0.2903	0.2918	0.2734
	4	0.0002	0.0026	0.0109	0.0287	0.0577	0.0972	0.1442	0.1935	0.2388	0.2734
	5	0.0000	0.0002	0.0012	0.0043	0.0115	0.0250	0.0466	0.0774	0.1172	0.1641
	6	0.0000	0.0000	0.0001	0.0004	0.0013	0.0036	0.0084	0.0172	0.0320	0.0547
	7	0.0000	0.0000	0.0000	0.0000	0.0001	0.0002	0.0006	0.0016	0.0037	0.0078
8	0	0.6634	0.4305	0.2725	0.1678	0.1001	0.0576	0.0319	0.0168	0.0084	0.0039
	1	0.2793	0.3826	0.3847	0.3355	0.2670	0.1977	0.1373	0.0896	0.0548	0.0313
	2	0.0515	0.1488	0.2376	0.2936	0.3115	0.2965	0.2587	0.2090	0.1569	0.1094
	3	0.0054	0.0331	0.0839	0.1468	0.2076	0.2541	0.2786	0.2787	0.2568	0.2188
	4	0.0004	0.0046	0.0185	0.0459	0.0865	0.1361	0.1875	0.2322	0.2627	0.2734
	5	0.0000	0.0004	0.0026	0.0092	0.0231	0.0467	0.0808	0.1239	0.1719	0.2188
	6	0.0000	0.0000	0.0002	0.0011	0.0038	0.0100	0.0217	0.0413	0.0703	0.1094
	7	0.0000	0.0000	0.0000	0.0001	0.0004	0.0012	0.0033	0.0079	0.0164	0.0313
	8	0.0000	0.0000	0.0000	0.0000	0.0000	0.0001	0.0002	0.0007	0.0017	0.0039

(continued)

N	K	P									
		0.05	0.10	0.15	0.20	0.25	0.30	0.35	0.40	0.45	0.50
9	0	0.6302	0.3874	0.2316	0.1342	0.0751	0.0404	0.0207	0.0101	0.0046	0.0020
	1	0.2985	0.3874	0.3679	0.3020	0.2253	0.1556	0.1004	0.0605	0.0339	0.0176
	2	0.0629	0.1722	0.2597	0.3020	0.3003	0.2668	0.2162	0.1612	0.1110	0.0703
	3	0.0077	0.0446	0.1069	0.1762	0.2336	0.2668	0.2716	0.2508	0.2119	0.1641
	4	0.0006	0.0074	0.0283	0.0661	0.1168	0.1715	0.2194	0.2508	0.2600	0.2461
	5	0.0000	0.0008	0.0050	0.0165	0.0389	0.0735	0.1181	0.1672	0.2128	0.2461
	6	0.0000	0.0001	0.0006	0.0028	0.0087	0.0210	0.0424	0.0743	0.1160	0.1641
	7	0.0000	0.0000	0.0000	0.0003	0.0012	0.0039	0.0098	0.0212	0.0407	0.0703
	8	0.0000	0.0000	0.0000	0.0000	0.0001	0.0004	0.0013	0.0035	0.0083	0.0176
	9	0.0000	0.0000	0.0000	0.0000	0.0000	0.0000	0.0001	0.0003	0.0008	0.0020
10	0	0.5987	0.3487	0.1969	0.1074	0.0563	0.0282	0.0135	0.0060	0.0025	0.0010
	1	0.3151	0.3874	0.3474	0.2684	0.1877	0.1211	0.0725	0.0403	0.0207	0.0098
	2	0.0746	0.1937	0.2759	0.3020	0.2816	0.2335	0.1757	0.1209	0.0763	0.0439
	3	0.0105	0.0574	0.1298	0.2013	0.2503	0.2668	0.2522	0.2150	0.1665	0.1172
	4	0.0010	0.0112	0.0401	0.0881	0.1460	0.2001	0.2377	0.2508	0.2384	0.2051
	5	0.0001	0.0015	0.0085	0.0264	0.0584	0.1029	0.1536	0.2007	0.2340	0.2461
	6	0.0000	0.0001	0.0012	0.0055	0.0162	0.0368	0.0689	0.1115	0.1596	0.2051
	7	0.0000	0.0000	0.0001	0.0008	0.0031	0.0090	0.0212	0.0425	0.0746	0.1172
	8	0.0000	0.0000	0.0000	0.0001	0.0004	0.0014	0.0043	0.0106	0.0229	0.0439
	9	0.0000	0.0000	0.0000	0.0000	0.0000	0.0001	0.0005	0.0016	0.0042	0.0098
	10	0.0000	0.0000	0.0000	0.0000	0.0000	0.0000	0.0000	0.0001	0.0003	0.0010
11	0	0.5688	0.3138	0.1673	0.0859	0.0422	0.0198	0.0088	0.0036	0.0014	0.0005
	1	0.3293	0.3835	0.3248	0.2362	0.1549	0.0932	0.0518	0.0266	0.0125	0.0054
	2	0.0867	0.2131	0.2866	0.2953	0.2581	0.1998	0.1395	0.0887	0.0513	0.0269
	3	0.0137	0.0710	0.1517	0.2215	0.2581	0.2568	0.2254	0.1774	0.1259	0.0806
	4	0.0014	0.0158	0.0536	0.1107	0.1721	0.2201	0.2428	0.2365	0.2060	0.1611
	5	0.0001	0.0025	0.0132	0.0388	0.0803	0.1321	0.1830	0.2207	0.2360	0.2256
	6	0.0000	0.0003	0.0023	0.0097	0.0268	0.0566	0.0985	0.1471	0.1931	0.2256
	7	0.0000	0.0000	0.0003	0.0017	0.0064	0.0173	0.0379	0.0701	0.1128	0.1611
	8	0.0000	0.0000	0.0000	0.0002	0.0011	0.0037	0.0102	0.0234	0.0462	0.0806
	9	0.0000	0.0000	0.0000	0.0000	0.0001	0.0005	0.0018	0.0052	0.0126	0.0269
	10	0.0000	0.0000	0.0000	0.0000	0.0000	0.0000	0.0002	0.0007	0.0021	0.0054
	11	0.0000	0.0000	0.0000	0.0000	0.0000	0.0000	0.0000	0.0000	0.0002	0.0005
12	0	0.5404	0.2824	0.1422	0.0687	0.0317	0.0138	0.0057	0.0022	0.0008	0.0002
	1	0.3413	0.3766	0.3012	0.2062	0.1267	0.0712	0.0368	0.0174	0.0075	0.0029
	2	0.0988	0.2301	0.2924	0.2835	0.2323	0.1678	0.1088	0.0639	0.0339	0.0161
	3	0.0173	0.0852	0.1720	0.2362	0.2581	0.2397	0.1954	0.1419	0.0923	0.0537
	4	0.0021	0.0213	0.0683	0.1329	0.1936	0.2311	0.2367	0.2128	0.1700	0.1208
	5	0.0002	0.0038	0.0193	0.0532	0.1032	0.1585	0.2039	0.2270	0.2225	0.1934
	6	0.0000	0.0005	0.0040	0.0155	0.0401	0.0792	0.1281	0.1766	0.2124	0.2256
	7	0.0000	0.0000	0.0006	0.0033	0.0115	0.0291	0.0591	0.1009	0.1489	0.1934
	8	0.0000	0.0000	0.0001	0.0005	0.0024	0.0078	0.0199	0.0420	0.0762	0.1208
	9	0.0000	0.0000	0.0000	0.0001	0.0004	0.0015	0.0048	0.0125	0.0277	0.0537
	10	0.0000	0.0000	0.0000	0.0000	0.0000	0.0002	0.0008	0.0025	0.0068	0.0161
	11	0.0000	0.0000	0.0000	0.0000	0.0000	0.0000	0.0001	0.0003	0.0010	0.0029
	12	0.0000	0.0000	0.0000	0.0000	0.0000	0.0000	0.0000	0.0000	0.0001	0.0002

N	K	P									
		0.05	0.10	0.15	0.20	0.25	0.30	0.35	0.40	0.45	0.50
13	0	0.5133	0.2542	0.1209	0.0550	0.0238	0.0097	0.0037	0.0013	0.0004	0.0001
	1	0.3512	0.3672	0.2774	0.1787	0.1029	0.0540	0.0259	0.0113	0.0045	0.0016
	2	0.1109	0.2448	0.2937	0.2680	0.2059	0.1388	0.0836	0.0453	0.0220	0.0095
	3	0.0214	0.0997	0.1900	0.2457	0.2517	0.2181	0.1651	0.1107	0.0660	0.0349
	4	0.0028	0.0277	0.0838	0.1535	0.2097	0.2337	0.2222	0.1845	0.1350	0.0873
	5	0.0003	0.0055	0.0266	0.0691	0.1258	0.1803	0.2154	0.2214	0.1989	0.1571
	6	0.0000	0.0008	0.0063	0.0230	0.0559	0.1030	0.1546	0.1968	0.2169	0.2095
	7	0.0000	0.0001	0.0011	0.0058	0.0186	0.0442	0.0833	0.1312	0.1775	0.2095
	8	0.0000	0.0000	0.0001	0.0011	0.0047	0.0142	0.0336	0.0656	0.1089	0.1571
	9	0.0000	0.0000	0.0000	0.0001	0.0009	0.0034	0.0101	0.0243	0.0495	0.0873
	10	0.0000	0.0000	0.0000	0.0000	0.0001	0.0006	0.0022	0.0065	0.0162	0.0349
	11	0.0000	0.0000	0.0000	0.0000	0.0000	0.0001	0.0003	0.0012	0.0036	0.0095
	12	0.0000	0.0000	0.0000	0.0000	0.0000	0.0000	0.0000	0.0001	0.0005	0.0016
	13	0.0000	0.0000	0.0000	0.0000	0.0000	0.0000	0.0000	0.0000	0.0000	0.0001
14	0	0.4877	0.2288	0.1028	0.0440	0.0178	0.0068	0.0024	0.0008	0.0002	0.0001
	1	0.3593	0.3559	0.2539	0.1539	0.0832	0.0407	0.0181	0.0073	0.0027	0.0009
	2	0.1229	0.2570	0.2912	0.2501	0.1802	0.1134	0.0634	0.0317	0.0141	0.0056
	3	0.0259	0.1142	0.2056	0.2501	0.2402	0.1943	0.1366	0.0845	0.0462	0.0222
	4	0.0037	0.0349	0.0998	0.1720	0.2202	0.2290	0.2022	0.1549	0.1040	0.0611
	5	0.0004	0.0078	0.0352	0.0860	0.1468	0.1963	0.2178	0.2066	0.1701	0.1222
	6	0.0000	0.0013	0.0093	0.0322	0.0734	0.1262	0.1759	0.2066	0.2088	0.1833
	7	0.0000	0.0002	0.0019	0.0092	0.0280	0.0618	0.1082	0.1574	0.1952	0.2095
	8	0.0000	0.0000	0.0003	0.0020	0.0082	0.0232	0.0510	0.0918	0.1398	0.1833
	9	0.0000	0.0000	0.0000	0.0003	0.0018	0.0066	0.0183	0.0408	0.0762	0.1222
	10	0.0000	0.0000	0.0000	0.0000	0.0003	0.0014	0.0049	0.0136	0.0312	0.0611
	11	0.0000	0.0000	0.0000	0.0000	0.0000	0.0002	0.0010	0.0033	0.0093	0.0222
	12	0.0000	0.0000	0.0000	0.0000	0.0000	0.0000	0.0001	0.0005	0.0019	0.0056
	13	0.0000	0.0000	0.0000	0.0000	0.0000	0.0000	0.0000	0.0001	0.0002	0.0009
	14	0.0000	0.0000	0.0000	0.0000	0.0000	0.0000	0.0000	0.0000	0.0000	0.0001
15	0	0.4633	0.2059	0.0874	0.0352	0.0134	0.0047	0.0016	0.0005	0.0001	0.0000
	1	0.3658	0.3432	0.2312	0.1319	0.0668	0.0305	0.0126	0.0047	0.0016	0.0005
	2	0.1348	0.2669	0.2856	0.2309	0.1559	0.0916	0.0476	0.0219	0.0090	0.0032
	3	0.0307	0.1285	0.2184	0.2501	0.2252	0.1700	0.1110	0.0634	0.0318	0.0139
	4	0.0049	0.0428	0.1156	0.1876	0.2252	0.2186	0.1792	0.1268	0.0780	0.0417
	5	0.0006	0.0105	0.0449	0.1032	0.1651	0.2061	0.2123	0.1859	0.1404	0.0916
	6	0.0000	0.0019	0.0132	0.0430	0.0917	0.1472	0.1906	0.2066	0.1914	0.1527
	7	0.0000	0.0003	0.0030	0.0138	0.0393	0.0811	0.1319	0.1771	0.2013	0.1964
	8	0.0000	0.0000	0.0005	0.0035	0.0131	0.0348	0.0710	0.1181	0.1647	0.1964
	9	0.0000	0.0000	0.0001	0.0007	0.0034	0.0116	0.0298	0.0612	0.1048	0.1527
	10	0.0000	0.0000	0.0000	0.0001	0.0007	0.0030	0.0096	0.0245	0.0515	0.0916
	11	0.0000	0.0000	0.0000	0.0000	0.0001	0.0006	0.0024	0.0074	0.0191	0.0417
	12	0.0000	0.0000	0.0000	0.0000	0.0000	0.0001	0.0004	0.0016	0.0052	0.0139
	13	0.0000	0.0000	0.0000	0.0000	0.0000	0.0000	0.0001	0.0003	0.0010	0.0032
	14	0.0000	0.0000	0.0000	0.0000	0.0000	0.0000	0.0000	0.0000	0.0001	0.0005
	15	0.0000	0.0000	0.0000	0.0000	0.0000	0.0000	0.0000	0.0000	0.0000	0.0000

(*continued*)

N	K					P					
		0.05	0.10	0.15	0.20	0.25	0.30	0.35	0.40	0.45	0.50
16	0	0.4401	0.1853	0.0743	0.0281	0.0100	0.0033	0.0010	0.0003	0.0001	0.0000
	1	0.3706	0.3294	0.2097	0.1126	0.0535	0.0228	0.0087	0.0030	0.0009	0.0002
	2	0.1463	0.2745	0.2775	0.2111	0.1336	0.0732	0.0353	0.0150	0.0056	0.0018
	3	0.0359	0.1423	0.2285	0.2463	0.2079	0.1465	0.0888	0.0468	0.0215	0.0085
	4	0.0061	0.0514	0.1311	0.2001	0.2252	0.2040	0.1553	0.1014	0.0572	0.0278
	5	0.0008	0.0137	0.0555	0.1201	0.1802	0.2099	0.2008	0.1623	0.1123	0.0667
	6	0.0001	0.0028	0.0180	0.0550	0.1101	0.1649	0.1982	0.1983	0.1684	0.1222
	7	0.0000	0.0004	0.0045	0.0197	0.0524	0.1010	0.1524	0.1889	0.1969	0.1746
	8	0.0000	0.0001	0.0009	0.0055	0.0197	0.0487	0.0923	0.1417	0.1812	0.1964
	9	0.0000	0.0000	0.0001	0.0012	0.0058	0.0185	0.0442	0.0840	0.1318	0.1746
	10	0.0000	0.0000	0.0000	0.0002	0.0014	0.0056	0.0167	0.0392	0.0755	0.1222
	11	0.0000	0.0000	0.0000	0.0000	0.0002	0.0013	0.0049	0.0142	0.0337	0.0667
	12	0.0000	0.0000	0.0000	0.0000	0.0000	0.0002	0.0011	0.0040	0.0115	0.0278
	13	0.0000	0.0000	0.0000	0.0000	0.0000	0.0000	0.0002	0.0008	0.0029	0.0085
	14	0.0000	0.0000	0.0000	0.0000	0.0000	0.0000	0.0000	0.0001	0.0005	0.0018
	15	0.0000	0.0000	0.0000	0.0000	0.0000	0.0000	0.0000	0.0000	0.0001	0.0002
	16	0.0000	0.0000	0.0000	0.0000	0.0000	0.0000	0.0000	0.0000	0.0000	0.0000
17	0	0.4181	0.1668	0.0631	0.0225	0.0075	0.0023	0.0007	0.0002	0.0000	0.0000
	1	0.3741	0.3150	0.1893	0.0957	0.0426	0.0169	0.0060	0.0019	0.0005	0.0001
	2	0.1575	0.2800	0.2673	0.1914	0.1136	0.0581	0.0260	0.0102	0.0035	0.0010
	3	0.0415	0.1556	0.2359	0.2393	0.1893	0.1245	0.0701	0.0341	0.0144	0.0052
	4	0.0076	0.0605	0.1457	0.2093	0.2209	0.1868	0.1320	0.0796	0.0411	0.0182
	5	0.0010	0.0175	0.0668	0.1361	0.1914	0.2081	0.1849	0.1379	0.0875	0.0472
	6	0.0001	0.0039	0.0236	0.0680	0.1276	0.1784	0.1991	0.1839	0.1432	0.0944
	7	0.0000	0.0007	0.0065	0.0267	0.0668	0.1201	0.1685	0.1927	0.1841	0.1484
	8	0.0000	0.0001	0.0014	0.0084	0.0279	0.0644	0.1134	0.1606	0.1883	0.1855
	9	0.0000	0.0000	0.0003	0.0021	0.0093	0.0276	0.0611	0.1070	0.1540	0.1855
	10	0.0000	0.0000	0.0000	0.0004	0.0025	0.0095	0.0263	0.0571	0.1008	0.1484
	11	0.0000	0.0000	0.0000	0.0001	0.0005	0.0026	0.0090	0.0242	0.0525	0.0944
	12	0.0000	0.0000	0.0000	0.0000	0.0001	0.0006	0.0024	0.0081	0.0215	0.0472
	13	0.0000	0.0000	0.0000	0.0000	0.0000	0.0001	0.0005	0.0021	0.0068	0.0182
	14	0.0000	0.0000	0.0000	0.0000	0.0000	0.0000	0.0001	0.0004	0.0016	0.0052
	15	0.0000	0.0000	0.0000	0.0000	0.0000	0.0000	0.0000	0.0001	0.0003	0.0010
	16	0.0000	0.0000	0.0000	0.0000	0.0000	0.0000	0.0000	0.0000	0.0000	0.0001
	17	0.0000	0.0000	0.0000	0.0000	0.0000	0.0000	0.0000	0.0000	0.0000	0.0000
18	0	0.3972	0.1501	0.0536	0.0180	0.0056	0.0016	0.0004	0.0001	0.0000	0.0000
	1	0.3763	0.3002	0.1704	0.0811	0.0338	0.0126	0.0042	0.0012	0.0003	0.0001
	2	0.1683	0.2835	0.2556	0.1723	0.0958	0.0458	0.0190	0.0069	0.0022	0.0006
	3	0.0473	0.1680	0.2406	0.2297	0.1704	0.1046	0.0547	0.0246	0.0095	0.0031
	4	0.0093	0.0700	0.1592	0.2153	0.2130	0.1681	0.1104	0.0614	0.0291	0.0117
	5	0.0014	0.0218	0.0787	0.1507	0.1988	0.2017	0.1664	0.1146	0.0666	0.0327
	6	0.0002	0.0052	0.0301	0.0816	0.1436	0.1873	0.1941	0.1655	0.1181	0.0708
	7	0.0000	0.0010	0.0091	0.0350	0.0820	0.1376	0.1792	0.1892	0.1657	0.1214
	8	0.0000	0.0002	0.0022	0.0120	0.0376	0.0811	0.1327	0.1734	0.1864	0.1669
	9	0.0000	0.0000	0.0004	0.0033	0.0139	0.0386	0.0794	0.1284	0.1694	0.1855
	10	0.0000	0.0000	0.0001	0.0008	0.0042	0.0149	0.0385	0.0771	0.1248	0.1669
	11	0.0000	0.0000	0.0000	0.0001	0.0010	0.0046	0.0151	0.0374	0.0742	0.1214
	12	0.0000	0.0000	0.0000	0.0000	0.0002	0.0012	0.0047	0.0145	0.0354	0.0708
	13	0.0000	0.0000	0.0000	0.0000	0.0000	0.0002	0.0012	0.0045	0.0134	0.0327
	14	0.0000	0.0000	0.0000	0.0000	0.0000	0.0000	0.0002	0.0011	0.0039	0.0117

N	K					P					
		0.05	0.10	0.15	0.20	0.25	0.30	0.35	0.40	0.45	0.50
	15	0.0000	0.0000	0.0000	0.0000	0.0000	0.0000	0.0000	0.0002	0.0009	0.0031
	16	0.0000	0.0000	0.0000	0.0000	0.0000	0.0000	0.0000	0.0000	0.0001	0.0006
	17	0.0000	0.0000	0.0000	0.0000	0.0000	0.0000	0.0000	0.0000	0.0000	0.0001
	18	0.0000	0.0000	0.0000	0.0000	0.0000	0.0000	0.0000	0.0000	0.0000	0.0000
19	0	0.3774	0.1351	0.0456	0.0144	0.0042	0.0011	0.0003	0.0001	0.0000	0.0000
	1	0.3774	0.2852	0.1529	0.0685	0.0268	0.0093	0.0029	0.0008	0.0002	0.0000
	2	0.1787	0.2852	0.2428	0.1540	0.0803	0.0358	0.0138	0.0046	0.0013	0.0003
	3	0.0533	0.1796	0.2428	0.2182	0.1517	0.0869	0.0422	0.0175	0.0062	0.0018
	4	0.0112	0.0798	0.1714	0.2182	0.2023	0.1491	0.0909	0.0467	0.0203	0.0074
	5	0.0018	0.0266	0.0907	0.1636	0.2023	0.1916	0.1468	0.0933	0.0497	0.0222
	6	0.0002	0.0069	0.0374	0.0955	0.1574	0.1916	0.1844	0.1451	0.0949	0.0518
	7	0.0000	0.0014	0.0122	0.0443	0.0974	0.1525	0.1844	0.1797	0.1443	0.0961
	8	0.0000	0.0002	0.0032	0.0166	0.0487	0.0981	0.1489	0.1797	0.1771	0.1442
	9	0.0000	0.0000	0.0007	0.0051	0.0198	0.0514	0.0980	0.1464	0.1771	0.1762
	10	0.0000	0.0000	0.0001	0.0013	0.0066	0.0220	0.0528	0.0976	0.1449	0.1762
	11	0.0000	0.0000	0.0000	0.0003	0.0018	0.0077	0.0233	0.0532	0.0970	0.1442
	12	0.0000	0.0000	0.0000	0.0000	0.0004	0.0022	0.0083	0.0237	0.0529	0.0961
	13	0.0000	0.0000	0.0000	0.0000	0.0001	0.0005	0.0024	0.0085	0.0233	0.0518
	14	0.0000	0.0000	0.0000	0.0000	0.0000	0.0001	0.0006	0.0024	0.0082	0.0222
	15	0.0000	0.0000	0.0000	0.0000	0.0000	0.0000	0.0001	0.0005	0.0022	0.0074
	16	0.0000	0.0000	0.0000	0.0000	0.0000	0.0000	0.0000	0.0001	0.0005	0.0018
	17	0.0000	0.0000	0.0000	0.0000	0.0000	0.0000	0.0000	0.0000	0.0001	0.0003
	18	0.0000	0.0000	0.0000	0.0000	0.0000	0.0000	0.0000	0.0000	0.0000	0.0000
	19	0.0000	0.0000	0.0000	0.0000	0.0000	0.0000	0.0000	0.0000	0.0000	0.0000
20	0	0.3585	0.1216	0.0388	0.0115	0.0032	0.0008	0.0002	0.0000	0.0000	0.0000
	1	0.3774	0.2702	0.1368	0.0576	0.0211	0.0068	0.0020	0.0005	0.0001	0.0000
	2	0.1887	0.2852	0.2293	0.1369	0.0669	0.0278	0.0100	0.0031	0.0008	0.0002
	3	0.0596	0.1901	0.2428	0.2054	0.1339	0.0716	0.0323	0.0123	0.0040	0.0011
	4	0.0133	0.0898	0.1821	0.2182	0.1897	0.1304	0.0738	0.0350	0.0139	0.0046
	5	0.0022	0.0319	0.1028	0.1746	0.2023	0.1789	0.1272	0.0746	0.0365	0.0148
	6	0.0003	0.0089	0.0454	0.1091	0.1686	0.1916	0.1712	0.1244	0.0746	0.0370
	7	0.0000	0.0020	0.0160	0.0545	0.1124	0.1643	0.1844	0.1659	0.1221	0.0739
	8	0.0000	0.0004	0.0046	0.0222	0.0609	0.1144	0.1614	0.1797	0.1623	0.1201
	9	0.0000	0.0001	0.0011	0.0074	0.0271	0.0654	0.1158	0.1597	0.1771	0.1602
	10	0.0000	0.0000	0.0002	0.0020	0.0099	0.0308	0.0686	0.1171	0.1593	0.1762
	11	0.0000	0.0000	0.0000	0.0005	0.0030	0.0120	0.0336	0.0710	0.1185	0.1602
	12	0.0000	0.0000	0.0000	0.0001	0.0008	0.0039	0.0136	0.0355	0.0727	0.1201
	13	0.0000	0.0000	0.0000	0.0000	0.0002	0.0010	0.0045	0.0146	0.0366	0.0739
	14	0.0000	0.0000	0.0000	0.0000	0.0000	0.0002	0.0012	0.0049	0.0150	0.0370
	15	0.0000	0.0000	0.0000	0.0000	0.0000	0.0000	0.0003	0.0013	0.0049	0.0148
	16	0.0000	0.0000	0.0000	0.0000	0.0000	0.0000	0.0000	0.0003	0.0013	0.0046
	17	0.0000	0.0000	0.0000	0.0000	0.0000	0.0000	0.0000	0.0000	0.0002	0.0011
	18	0.0000	0.0000	0.0000	0.0000	0.0000	0.0000	0.0000	0.0000	0.0002	0.0011
	19	0.0000	0.0000	0.0000	0.0000	0.0000	0.0000	0.0000	0.0000	0.0000	0.0000
	20	0.0000	0.0000	0.0000	0.0000	0.0000	0.0000	0.0000	0.0000	0.0000	0.0000

TABLE C.5 Chi-square distribution values for right-tailed areas
[For example, the area to the right of $\chi^2 = 3.841$ with $df = 1$ is 0.05.]

df	0.10	0.05	0.025	0.01	0.001
1	2.706	3.841	5.024	6.635	10.83
2	4.605	5.991	7.378	9.210	13.82
3	6.251	7.815	9.348	11.34	16.27
4	7.779	9.488	11.14	13.28	18.47
5	9.236	11.07	12.83	15.09	20.51
6	10.64	12.59	14.45	16.81	22.46
7	12.02	14.07	16.01	18.48	24.32
8	13.36	15.51	17.53	20.09	26.12
9	14.68	16.92	19.02	21.67	27.88
10	15.99	18.31	20.48	23.21	29.59
11	17.28	19.68	21.92	24.73	31.26
12	18.55	21.03	23.34	26.22	32.91
13	19.81	22.36	24.74	27.69	34.53
14	21.06	23.68	26.12	29.14	36.12
15	22.31	25.00	27.49	30.58	37.70
16	23.54	26.30	28.85	32.00	39.25
17	24.77	27.59	30.19	33.41	40.79
18	25.99	28.87	31.53	34.81	42.31
19	27.20	30.14	32.85	36.19	43.82
20	28.41	31.41	34.17	37.57	45.31
21	29.62	32.67	35.48	38.93	46.80
22	30.81	33.92	36.78	40.29	48.27
23	32.01	35.17	38.08	41.64	49.73
24	33.20	36.42	39.36	42.98	51.18
25	34.38	37.65	40.65	44.31	52.62
26	35.56	38.89	41.92	45.64	54.05
27	36.74	40.11	43.19	46.96	55.48
28	37.92	41.34	44.46	48.28	56.89
29	39.09	42.56	45.72	49.59	58.30
30	40.26	43.77	46.98	50.89	59.70
32	42.58	46.19	49.48	53.49	62.49
34	44.90	48.60	51.97	56.06	65.25
36	47.21	51.00	54.44	58.62	67.98
38	49.51	53.38	56.90	61.16	70.70
40	51.81	55.76	59.34	63.69	73.40
50	63.17	67.50	71.42	76.15	86.66
60	74.40	79.08	83.30	88.38	99.61
70	85.53	90.53	95.02	100.4	112.3
80	96.58	101.9	106.6	112.3	124.8
90	107.6	113.1	118.1	124.1	137.2
100	118.5	124.3	129.6	135.8	149.4

TABLE C.6 The critical q-values

		K (number of groups)									
df_w	α	2	3	4	5	6	7	8	9	10	11
5	.05	3.64	4.60	5.22	5.67	6.03	6.33	6.58	6.80	6.99	7.17
	.01	5.70	6.98	7.80	8.42	8.91	9.32	9.67	9.97	10.24	10.48
6	.05	3.46	4.34	4.90	5.30	5.63	5.90	6.12	6.32	6.49	6.65
	.01	5.24	6.33	7.03	7.56	7.97	8.32	8.61	8.87	9.10	9.30
7	.05	3.34	4.16	4.68	5.06	5.36	5.61	5.82	6.00	6.16	6.30
	.01	4.95	5.92	6.54	7.01	7.37	7.68	7.94	8.17	8.37	8.55
8	.05	3.26	4.04	4.53	4.89	5.17	5.40	5.60	5.77	5.92	6.05
	.01	4.75	5.64	6.20	6.62	6.96	7.24	7.47	7.68	7.86	8.03
9	.05	3.20	3.95	4.41	4.76	5.02	5.24	5.43	5.59	5.74	5.87
	.01	4.60	5.43	5.96	6.35	6.66	6.91	7.13	7.33	7.49	7.65
10	.05	3.15	3.88	4.33	4.65	4.91	5.12	5.30	5.46	5.60	5.72
	.01	4.48	5.27	5.77	6.14	6.43	6.67	6.87	7.05	7.21	7.36
11	.05	3.11	3.82	4.26	4.57	4.82	5.03	5.20	5.35	5.49	5.61
	.01	4.39	5.15	5.62	5.97	6.25	6.48	6.67	6.84	6.99	7.13
12	.05	3.08	3.77	4.20	4.51	4.75	4.95	5.12	5.27	5.39	5.51
	.01	4.32	5.05	5.50	5.84	6.10	6.32	6.51	6.67	6.81	6.94
13	.05	3.06	3.73	4.15	4.45	4.69	4.88	5.05	5.19	5.32	5.43
	.01	4.26	4.96	5.40	5.73	5.98	6.19	6.37	6.53	6.67	6.79
14	.05	3.03	3.70	4.11	4.41	4.64	4.83	4.99	5.13	5.25	5.36
	.01	4.21	4.89	5.32	5.63	5.88	6.08	6.26	6.41	6.54	6.66
15	.05	3.01	3.67	4.08	4.37	4.59	4.78	4.94	5.08	5.20	5.31
	.01	4.17	4.84	5.25	5.56	5.80	5.99	6.16	6.31	6.44	6.55
16	.05	3.00	3.65	4.05	4.33	4.56	4.74	4.90	5.03	5.15	5.26
	.01	4.13	4.79	5.19	5.49	5.72	5.92	6.08	6.22	6.35	6.46
17	.05	2.98	3.63	4.02	4.30	4.52	4.70	4.86	4.99	5.11	5.21
	.01	4.10	4.74	5.14	5.43	5.66	5.85	6.01	6.15	6.27	6.38
18	.05	2.97	3.61	4.00	4.28	4.49	4.67	4.82	4.96	5.07	5.17
	.01	4.07	4.70	5.09	5.38	5.60	5.79	5.94	6.08	6.20	6.31
19	.05	2.96	3.59	3.98	4.25	4.47	4.65	4.79	4.92	5.04	5.14
	.01	4.05	4.67	5.05	5.33	5.55	5.73	5.89	6.02	6.14	6.25
20	.05	2.95	3.58	3.96	4.23	4.45	4.62	4.77	4.90	5.01	5.11
	.01	4.02	4.64	5.02	5.29	5.51	5.69	5.84	5.97	6.09	6.19
24	.05	2.92	3.53	3.90	4.17	4.37	4.54	4.68	4.81	4.92	5.01
	.01	3.96	4.55	4.91	5.17	5.37	5.54	5.69	5.81	5.92	6.02
30	.05	2.89	3.49	3.85	4.10	4.30	4.46	4.60	4.72	4.82	4.92
	.01	3.89	4.45	4.80	5.05	5.24	5.40	5.54	5.65	5.76	5.85
40	.05	2.86	3.44	3.79	4.04	4.23	4.39	4.52	4.63	4.73	4.82
	.01	3.82	4.37	4.70	4.93	5.11	5.26	5.39	5.50	5.60	5.69
60	.05	2.83	3.40	3.74	3.98	4.16	4.31	4.44	4.55	4.65	4.73
	.01	3.76	4.28	4.59	4.82	4.99	5.13	5.25	5.36	5.45	5.53
120	.05	2.80	3.36	3.68	3.92	4.10	4.24	4.36	4.47	4.56	4.64
	.01	3.70	4.20	4.50	4.71	4.87	5.01	5.12	5.21	5.30	5.37
∞	.05	2.77	3.31	3.63	3.86	4.03	4.17	4.29	4.39	4.47	4.55
	.01	3.64	4.12	4.40	4.60	4.76	4.88	4.99	5.08	5.16	5.23

Note: Adapted from E. S. Pearson and H. O. Hartley (eds.) (1966). *Biometrika Tables for Statisticians.* New York: Cambridge University Press, vol. 1, table 29. Used by permission.

TABLE C.7 The critical U values
Critical values of the U distribution (0.01 level, two-tailed)[a]

N_1	1	2	3	4	5	6	7	8	9	10	11	12	13	14	15	16	17	18	19	20
	–	–	–	–	–	–	–	–	–	–	–	–	–	–	–	–	–	–	–	–
2	–	–	–	–	–	–	–	–	–	–	–	–	–	–	–	–	–	–	0	0
																			38	40
3	–	–	–	–	–	–	–	–	0	0	0	1	1	1	2	2	2	2	3	3
									27	30	33	35	38	41	43	46	49	52	54	57
4	–	–	–	–	–	0	0	1	1	2	2	3	3	4	5	5	6	6	7	8
						24	28	31	35	38	42	45	49	52	55	59	62	66	69	72
5	–	–	–	–	0	1	1	2	3	4	5	6	7	7	8	9	10	11	12	13
					25	29	34	38	42	46	50	54	58	63	67	71	75	79	83	87
6	–	–	–	0	1	2	3	4	5	6	7	9	10	11	12	13	15	16	17	18
				24	29	34	39	44	49	54	59	63	68	73	78	83	87	92	97	102
7	–	–	–	0	1	3	4	6	7	9	10	12	13	15	16	18	19	21	22	24
				28	34	39	45	50	56	61	67	72	78	83	89	94	100	105	111	116
8	–	–	–	1	2	4	6	7	9	11	13	15	17	18	20	22	24	26	28	30
				31	38	44	so	57	63	69	75	81	87	94	100	106	112	118	124	130
9	–	–	0	1	3	5	7	9	11	13	16	18	20	22	24	27	29	31	33	36
			27	35	42	49	56	63	70	77	83	90	97	104	111	117	124	131	138	144
10	–	–	0	2	4	6	9	11	13	16	18	21	24	26	29	31	34	37	39	42
			30	38	46	54	61	69	77	84	92	99	106	114	121	129	136	143	151	158
11	–	–	0	2	5	7	10	13	16	18	21	24	27	30	33	36	39	42	45	48
			33	42	so	59	67	75	83	92	100	108	116	124	132	140	148	156	164	172
12	–	–	1	3	6	9	12	15	18	21	24	27	31	34	37	41	44	47	51	54
			35	45	54	63	72	81	90	99	108	117	125	134	143	151	160	169	177	186
13	–	–	1	3	7	10	13	17	20	24	27	31	34	38	42	45	49	53	56	60
			38	49	58	68	78	87	97	106	116	125	125	144	153	163	172	181	191	200
14	–	–	1	4	7	11	15	18	22	26	30	34	38	42	46	50	54	58	63	67
			41	52	63	73	83	94	104	114	124	134	144	154	164	174	184	194	203	213
15	–	–	2	5	8	12	16	20	24	29	33	37	42	46	51	55	60	64	69	73
			43	55	67	78	89	100	111	121	132	143	153	164	174	185	195	206	216	227
16	–	–	2	5	9	13	18	22	27	31	36	41	45	50	55	60	65	70	74	79
			46	59	71	83	94	106	117	129	140	!51	163	174	185	196	207	218	230	241
17	–	–	2	6	10	15	19	24	29	34	39	44	49	54	60	65	70	75	81	86
			49	62	75	87	100	112	124	136	148	160	172	184	195	207	219	231	242	254
18	–	–	2	6	11	16	21	26	31	37	42	47	53	58	64	70	75	81	87	92
			52	66	79	92	105	118	131	143	156	169	181	194	206	218	231	243	255	268
19	–	0	3	7	12	17	22	28	33	39	45	51	56	63	69	74	81	87	93	99
		38	54	69	83	97	111	124	138	151	164	177	191	203	216	230	242	255	268	281
20	–	0	3	8	13	18	24	30	36	42	48	54	60	67	73	79	86	92	99	105
		40	57	72	87	102	116	130	144	158	172	186	200	213	227	241	254	268	281	295

[a]Adapted from D. V. Lindley and W. F. Scott, *New Cambridge Elementary Statistical Tables.* London: Cambridge University Press, 1984, Table 21. Used by permission.

Note: The rows are indexed by N_1, the size of Sample 1, and the columns are indexed by N_2, the size of Sample 2.

Critical values of the U distribution (0.01 level, one-tailed) (*continued*)

1	2	3	4	5	6	7	8	9	10	11	12	13	14	15	16	17	18	19	20
—	—	—	—	—	—	—	—	—	—	—	—	—	—	—	—	—	—	—	—
—	—	—	—	—	—	—	—	—	—	—	—	0	0	0	0	0	0	1	1
												26	28	30	32	34	36	37	39
—	—	—	—	—	—	0	0	1	1	1	2	2	2	3	3	4	4	4	5
						21	24	26	29	32	34	37	40	42	45	47	50	52	55
—	—	—	—	0	1	1	2	3	3	4	5	5	6	7	7	8	9	9	10
				20	23	27	30	33	37	40	43	47	50	53	57	60	63	67	70
—	—	—	0	1	2	3	4	5	6	7	8	9	10	11	12	13	14	15	16
			20	24	28	32	36	40	44	48	52	56	60	64	68	72	76	80	84
—	—	—	1	2	3	4	6	7	8	9	11	12	13	15	16	18	19	20	22
			23	28	33	38	42	47	52	57	61	66	71	75	80	84	89	94	98
—	—	0	1	3	4	6	7	9	11	12	14	16	17	19	21	23	24	26	28
		21	27	32	38	43	49	54	59	65	70	75	81	86	91	96	102	107	112
—	—	0	2	4	6	7	9	11	13	15	17	20	22	24	26	28	30	32	34
		24	30	36	42	49	55	61	67	73	79	84	90	96	102	108	114	120	126
—	—	1	3	5	7	9	11	14	16	18	21	23	26	28	31	33	36	38	40
		26	33	40	47	54	61	67	74	81	87	94	100	107	113	120	126	133	140
—	—	1	3	6	8	11	13	16	19	22	24	27	30	33	36	38	41	44	47
		29	37	44	52	59	67	74	81	88	96	103	110	117	124	132	139	146	153
—	—	1	4	7	9	12	15	18	22	25	28	31	34	37	41	44	47	50	53
		32	40	48	57	65	73	81	88	96	104	112	120	128	135	143	151	159	167
—	—	2	5	8	11	14	17	21	24	28	31	35	38	42	46	49	53	56	60
		34	43	52	61	70	79	87	96	104	113	121	130	138	146	155	163	172	180
—	0	2	5	9	12	16	20	23	27	31	35	39	43	47	51	55	59	63	67
	26	37	47	56	66	75	84	94	103	112	121	130	139	148	157	166	175	184	193
—	0	2	6	10	13	17	22	26	30	34	38	43	47	51	56	60	65	69	73
	28	40	50	60	71	81	90	100	110	120	130	139	149	159	168	178	187	197	207
—	0	3	7	11	15	19	24	28	33	37	42	47	51	56	61	66	70	75	80
	30	42	53	64	75	86	96	107	117	128	138	148	159	169	179	189	200	210	220
—	0	3	7	12	16	21	26	31	36	41	46	51	56	61	66	71	76	82	87
	32	45	57	68	80	91	102	113	124	135	146	157	168	179	190	201	212	222	233
—	0	4	8	13	18	23	28	33	38	44	49	55	60	66	71	77	82	88	93
	34	47	60	72	84	96	108	120	132	143	155	166	178	189	201	212	224	234	247
—	0	4	9	14	19	24	30	36	41	47	53	59	65	70	76	82	88	94	100
	36	50	63	76	89	102	114	126	139	151	163	175	187	200	212	224	236	248	260
—	1	4	9	15	20	26	32	38	44	50	56	63	69	75	82	88	94	101	107
	37	53	67	80	94	107	120	133	146	159	172	184	197	210	222	235	248	260	273
—	1	5	10	16	22	28	34	40	47	53	60	67	73	80	87	93	100	107	114
	39	55	70	84	98	112	126	140	153	167	180	193	207	220	233	247	260	273	286

(*continued*)

Critical values of the U distribution (0.05 level, two-tailed) (*continued*)

	1	2	3	4	5	6	7	8	9	10	11	12	13	14	15	16	17	18	19	20
	–	–	–	–	–	–	–	–	–	–	–	–	–	–	–	–	–	–	–	–
2	–	–	–	–	–	–	–	0	0	0	0	1	1	1	1	1	2	2	2	2
								16	18	20	22	23	25	27	29	31	32	34	36	38
3	–	–	–	–	0	1	1	2	2	3	3	4	4	5	5	6	6	7	7	8
					15	17	20	22	25	27	30	32	35	37	40	42	45	47	50	52
4	–	–	–	0	1	2	3	4	4	5	6	7	8	9	10	11	11	12	13	13
				16	19	22	25	28	32	35	38	41	44	47	50	53	57	60	63	67
5	–	–	0	1	2	3	5	6	7	8	9	11	12	13	14	15	17	18	19	20
			15	19	23	27	30	34	38	42	46	49	53	57	61	65	68	72	76	80
6	–	–	1	2	3	5	6	8	10	11	13	14	16	17	19	21	22	24	25	27
			17	22	27	31	36	40	44	49	53	58	62	67	71	75	80	84	89	93
7	–	–	1	3	5	6	8	10	12	14	16	18	20	22	24	26	28	30	32	34
			20	25	30	36	41	46	51	56	61	66	71	76	81	86	91	96	101	106
8	–	0	2	4	6	8	10	13	15	17	19	22	24	26	29	31	34	36	38	41
		16	22	28	34	40	46	51	57	63	69	74	80	86	91	97	102	108	111	119
9	–	0	2	4	7	10	12	15	17	20	23	26	28	31	34	37	39	42	45	48
		18	25	32	38	44	51	57	64	70	76	82	89	95	101	107	114	120	126	132
10	–	0	3	5	8	11	14	17	20	23	26	29	33	36	39	42	45	48	52	55
		20	27	35	42	49	56	63	70	77	84	91	97	104	111	118	125	132	138	145
11	–	0	3	6	9	13	16	19	23	26	30	33	37	40	44	47	51	55	58	62
		22	30	38	46	53	61	69	76	84	91	99	106	114	121	129	136	143	151	158
12	–	1	4	7	11	14	18	22	26	29	33	37	41	45	49	53	57	61	65	69
		23	32	41	49	58	66	74	82	91	99	107	115	123	131	139	147	155	163	171
13	–	1	4	8	12	16	20	24	28	33	37	41	45	50	54	59	63	67	72	76
		25	35	44	53	62	71	80	89	97	106	115	124	132	141	149	158	167	175	184
14	–	1	5	9	13	17	22	26	31	36	40	45	50	55	59	64	67	74	78	83
		27	37	47	57	67	76	86	95	104	114	123	132	141	151	160	171	178	188	197
15	–	1	5	10	14	19	24	29	34	39	44	49	54	59	64	70	75	80	85	90
		29	40	50	61	71	81	91	101	111	121	131	141	151	161	170	180	190	200	210
16	–	1	6	11	15	21	26	31	37	42	47	53	59	64	70	75	81	86	92	98
		31	42	53	65	75	86	97	107	118	129	139	149	160	170	181	191	202	212	222
17	–	2	6	11	17	22	28	34	39	45	51	57	63	67	75	81	87	93	99	105
		32	45	57	68	80	91	102	114	125	136	147	158	171	180	191	202	213	224	235
18	–	2	7	12	18	24	30	36	42	48	55	61	67	74	80	86	93	99	106	112
		34	47	60	72	84	96	108	120	132	143	155	167	178	190	202	213	225	236	248
19	–	2	7	13	19	25	32	38	45	52	58	65	72	78	85	92	99	106	113	119
		36	50	63	76	89	101	114	126	138	151	163	175	188	200	212	224	236	248	261
20	–	2	8	13	20	27	34	41	48	55	62	69	76	83	90	98	105	112	119	127
		38	52	67	80	93	106	119	132	145	158	171	184	197	210	222	235	248	261	273

Critical values of the U distribution (0.05 level, one-tailed) (*continued*)

	1	2	3	4	5	6	7	8	9	10	11	12	13	14	15	16	17	18	19	20
1	–	–	–	–	–	–	–	–	–	–	–	–	–	–	–	–	–	–	0	0
																			19	20
2	–	–	–	–	0	0	0	1	1	1	1	2	2	2	3	3	3	4	4	4
					10	12	14	15	17	19	21	22	24	26	27	29	31	32	34	36
3	–	–	0	0	1	2	2	3	3	4	5	5	6	7	7	8	9	9	10	11
			9	12	14	16	19	21	24	26	28	31	33	35	38	40	42	45	47	49
4	–	–	0	1	2	3	4	5	6	7	8	9	10	11	12	14	15	16	17	18
			12	15	18	21	24	27	30	33	36	39	42	45	48	50	53	56	59	62
5	–	0	1	2	4	5	6	8	9	11	12	13	15	16	18	19	20	22	23	25
		10	14	18	21	25	29	32	36	39	43	47	50	54	57	61	65	68	72	75
6	–	0	2	3	5	7	8	10	12	14	16	17	19	21	23	25	26	28	30	32
		12	16	21	25	29	34	38	42	46	50	55	59	63	67	71	76	80	84	88
7	–	0	2	4	6	8	11	13	15	17	19	21	24	26	28	30	33	35	37	39
		14	19	24	29	34	38	43	48	53	58	63	67	72	77	82	86	91	96	101
8	–	1	3	5	8	10	13	15	18	20	23	26	28	31	33	36	39	41	44	47
		15	21	27	32	38	43	49	54	60	65	70	76	81	87	92	97	103	108	113
9	–	1	3	6	9	12	15	18	21	24	27	30	33	36	39	42	45	48	51	54
		17	24	30	36	42	48	54	60	66	72	78	84	90	96	102	108	114	120	126
10	–	1	4	7	11	14	17	20	24	27	31	34	37	41	44	48	51	55	58	62
		19	26	33	39	46	53	60	66	73	79	86	93	99	106	112	119	125	132	138
11	–	1	5	8	12	16	19	23	27	31	34	38	42	46	50	54	57	61	65	69
		21	28	36	43	50	58	65	72	79	87	94	101	108	115	122	130	137	144	151
12	–	2	5	9	13	17	21	26	30	34	38	42	47	51	55	60	64	68	72	77
		22	31	39	47	55	63	70	78	86	94	102	109	117	125	132	140	148	156	163
13	–	2	6	10	15	19	24	28	33	37	42	47	51	56	61	65	70	75	80	84
		24	33	42	50	59	67	76	84	93	101	109	118	126	134	143	151	159	167	176
14	–	2	7	11	16	21	26	31	36	41	46	51	56	61	66	71	77	82	87	92
		26	35	45	54	63	72	81	90	99	108	117	126	135	144	153	161	170	179	188
15	–	3	7	12	18	23	28	33	39	44	50	55	61	66	72	77	83	88	94	100
		27	38	48	57	67	77	87	96	106	115	125	134	144	153	163	172	182	191	200
16	–	3	8	14	19	25	30	36	42	48	54	60	65	71	77	83	89	95	101	107
		29	40	50	61	71	82	92	102	112	122	132	143	153	163	173	183	193	203	213
17	–	3	9	15	20	26	33	39	45	51	57	64	70	77	83	89	96	102	109	115
		31	42	53	65	76	86	97	108	119	130	140	151	161	172	183	193	204	214	225
18	–	4	9	16	22	28	35	41	48	55	61	68	75	82	88	95	102	109	116	123
		32	45	56	68	80	91	103	114	123	137	148	159	170	182	193	204	215	226	237
19	0	4	10	17	23	30	37	44	51	58	65	72	80	87	94	101	109	116	123	130
	19	34	47	59	72	84	96	108	120	132	144	156	167	179	191	203	214	226	238	250
20	0	4	11	18	25	32	39	47	54	62	69	77	84	92	100	107	115	123	130	138
	20	36	49	62	75	88	101	113	126	138	151	163	176	188	200	213	225	237	250	262

References

Akaike, H. (1974). A new look at the statistical model identification. *IEEE Transactions on Automatic Control* 19(6), 716–723. DOI:10.1109/TAC.1974.1100705.

Anscombe, F. J. (1973). Graphs in statistical analysis. *American Statistician*, 27(1), 17–21. DOI:10.1080/00031305.1973.10478966.

Bakan, D. (1966). The test of significance in psychological research. *Psychological Bulletin*, 66 (6), 423–437.

Becker, W. and Kennedy, P. (1992). A lesson in least squares and R squared. *The American Statistician*, 46(4), 282–283.

Bem, S. L. (1977). *Bem Sex-Role Inventory Professional Manual.* Palo Alto, CA: Consulting Psychologists Press, Inc.

Bickel, P.J., Hammel, E.A., and J.W. O'Connell (1975). Sex bias in graduate admissions: data from Berkeley. *Science*, 187: 398–404.

Bloom, H. (2009). Modern Regression Discontinuity Analysis. MDRC Working Papers on Research Methodology. An MDRC publication. Available online at www.mdrc.org/sites/default/files/full_446.pdf.

Burrill, G., Hopfensperger, P., Demana, F. D., and Waits, B. K. (1993). *Exploring Statistics with the T1-81.* Reading, MA: Addison-Wesley.

Campbell, D. T. and Stanley, J. C. (1966). *Experimental and quasi-experimental designs for research.* Chicago: Rand McNally.

Card, D. (1995). Using geographic variation in college proximity to estimate the return to schooling. In L. Christofides, E. Kenneth Grant and R. Swindinsky (eds.) *Aspects of Labour Economics: Essays in Honour of John Vanderkamp.* Toronto: University of Toronto Press.

Carver, R. P. (1978). The case against statistical significance testing. *Harvard Educational Review*, 48(3), 378–398.

Charig, C. R., Webb, D. R., Payne, S. R., and Wickham, J. E. (1986). Comparison of treatment of renal calculi by open surgery, percutaneous nephrolithotomy, and extracorporeal shockwave lithotripsy. *British Medical Journal (Clin Res Ed)*, 292(6524), 879–882.

Cohen, J. (1988). *Statistical Power Analysis for the Behavioral Sciences* (2nd edition). Hillsdale, NJ: Lawrence Erlbaum Associates.

Cohen, J. (1990). Things I have learned (so far). *American Psychologist*, 45, 1304–1312.

Cohen, J. (1994). The earth is round ($p < .05$). *American Psychologist*, 49(12), 997–1003.

Cohen, J., Cohen, P., West, S.G., and Aiken, L. S. (2003). *Applied Multiple Regression/Correlation Analysis for the Behavioral Sciences* (3rd edition). Mahwah, NJ: Lawrence Erlbaum Associates.

Cohen, R. J. and Swerdlik, M. (2005). *Psychological Testing and Assessment: An Introduction to Tests and Measurement* (6th edition). Boston, MA: McGraw Hill.

Cohen, R. J., Swerdlik, M., and Sturman, E. (2012). *Psychological Testing and Assessment: An Introduction to Tests and Measurement.* New York: McGraw-Hill Education.

Cook, R. D. and Weisberg, S. (1983). Diagnostics for heteroscedasticity in regression.

Biometrika 70(1), 1–10. DOI:https://doi.or g/10.1093/biomet/70.1.1.

Cook, T. D. and Campbell, D. T. (1979). *Quasi-Experimentation: Design and Analysis Issues for Field Settings*. Boston, MA: Houghton-Mifflin.

Darlington, R. B. (1990). *Regression and Linear Models*. New York: McGraw Hill.

de Moivre, A. (1756). *The Doctrine of Chances* (3rd edition). London: Millar.

Dynarski, S. (2014). Study on parental longevity is short on causation. *The New York Times*, August 6.

Elmore, J. Barton, M. B., Moceri, V. M., et al. (1998). Ten-year risk of false positive screening mammograms and clinical breast examinations. *The New England Journal of Medicine*, 338(16), 1089–1096.

Falk, R. and Greenbaum, C. W. (1995). Significance tests die hard. The amazing persistence of a probabilistic misconception. *Theory and Psychology*, 5(1), 75–98.

Faul, F., Erdfelder, E., Lang, A.-G., and Buchner, A. (2007). G*Power 3: A flexible statistical power analysis program for the social, behavioral, and biomedical sciences. *Behavior Research Methods*, 39, 175–191.

Fisher, R. A. (1934). *Statistical Methods for Research Workers*. Edinburgh, UK: Oliver and Boyd.

Fisher, R. A. (1959). *Statistical Methods and Scientific Inference* (2nd edition). Edinburgh, UK: Oliver and Boyd.

Galton, F. (1886). Regression towards mediocrity in hereditary stature. *The Journal of the Anthropological Institute of Great Britain and Ireland*, 15, 246–263.

Gee, H. (1999) Keep your babies in the dark, Nature News Archive available online at https://go.nature.com/3c2GEEK.

Gelman, A. and Hill, J. (2007). *Data Analysis Using Regression and Multilevel/Hierarchical Models*. Cambridge, UK: Cambridge University Press.

Glass, G.V., Peckham, P.D., and Sanders, J. R. (1972). Consequences of failure to meet assumptions underlying the fixed effects analyses of variance and covariance, *Review of Educational Research*, 42 (3), 237–288.

Gough, P. (1996). How children learn to read and why they fail. *Annals of Dyslexia*, 46(1), 1–20.

Groves, R. M., Fowler, Jr. F. J., Couper, M. P., et al. (2004). *Survey Methodology*. Hoboken, NJ: John Wiley and Sons.

Hagen, R. L. (1997). In praise of the null hypothesis statistical test. *American Psychologist*, 52, 15–24.

Harlow, L. L., Mulaik, S. A., and Steiger, J. H. (eds.) (1997). *What If There Were No Significance Tests?* Mahwah, NJ: Lawrence Erlbaum Associates.

Hays, W. L. (1973). *Statistics for the Social Sciences* (2nd edition). New York: Holt, Rinehart, and Winston.

Holland, P. W. and Rubin, D. B. (1982). On Lord's Paradox. Program Statistical Research, Technical Report No. ETS RR-82–36, Princeton, NJ: Educational Testing Service.

Horn, L., Hafner, A., and Owings, J. (1992). A profile of American eighth-grade mathematics and science instruction. National Education Longitudinal Study of 1988. Statistical Analysis Report. ERIC Document (ERIC Document Reproduction Service No. ED337094). US Department of Education.

Imbens, G. W. and Lemieux, T. (2008). Regression discontinuity designs: A guide to practice. *Journal of Economics*, 142, 615–635.

Julious, S. A. and Mullee, M.A. (1994). Confounding and Simpson's paradox. *British Medical Journal*, 309(6967), 1480–1481.

Kaplan, A. (1964). *The Conduct of Inquiry: Methodology for Behavioral Science*. San Francisco, CA: Chandler Publishing Company.

Keppel, G. (1991). *Design and Analysis: A Researcher's Handbook*. Englewood, NJ: Prentice Hall.

Kirk, R. E. (1996). Practical significance: A concept whose time has come. *Educational and Psychological Measurement*, 56(5), 746–759.

Kivimaki, M., Ferrie, J. E., Brunner, E., et al. (2005). Justice at work and reduced risk of coronary heart disease among employees. *Archives of Internal Medicine*, 165(19), 2245–2251.

Kruskal, W. H. and Wallis, W. A. (1952). Use of ranks in one-criterion variance analysis. *Journal of the American Statistical Association*, 47(260), 583–621.

Lord, F. M. (1967) A paradox in the interpretation of group comparisons. *Psychological Bulletin*, 68, 304–305.

Lykken, D. T. (1968). Statistical significance in psychological research. *Psychological Bulletin*, 70, 151–159.

Mann, H. B. and Whitney, D. R. (1947). On a test of whether one of two random variables is stochastically larger than the other. *The Annals of Mathematical Statistics*, 18, 50–60.

Marascuilo, L. A. and Busk, P. L. (1987). Loglinear models: a way to study main effects and interactions for multidimensional contingency tables with categorical data. *Journal of Counseling Psychology*, 34(4), 443–455.

Marascuilo, L. A. and Serlin, R. C. (1988). *Statistical Methods for the Behavioral Sciences*. New York: W. H. Freeman.

Maxwell, S. E. and Delaney, H. D. (2004). *Designing Experiments and Analyzing Data: A Model Comparison Perspective* (2nd edition). Mahwah, NJ.: Lawrence Erlbaum Associates.

Meehl, P. E. (1967). Theory testing in psychology and physics: A methodological paradox. *Philosophy of Science*, 34, 103–115.

Nagourney, E. (2005). Environment: Injustices at work may harm men's hearts. Vital Signs Column, *The New York Times*. November 1.

Pearson, K. (1900). On the criterion that a given system of deviations from the probable in the case of a correlated system of variables is such that it can be reasonably supposed to have arisen from random sampling. *Philosophical Magazine,* series 5, 50, 157–175. Reprinted in Pearson, K. (1956), *Early Statistical Papers.*

Cambridge, UK: Cambridge University Press, pp. 339–357.

Quinn, G. E., Shin, C. H., Maguire, M. G., and Stone, R. A. (1999). Myopia and ambient lighting at night. *Nature*, 399, 113–114.

Rosenbaum, P. R. and Rubin, D. B. (1983). The central role of the propensity score in observational studies for causal effects. *Biometrika* 70(1), 41–55.

Rosnow, R. L. and Rosenthal, R. (1989). Statistical procedures and the justification of knowledge in psychological science. *American Psychologist*, 44, 1276–1284.

Rozeboom, W. W. (1960). The fallacy of the null hypothesis significance test. *Psychological Bulletin*, 57, 416–428.

Salsburg, David. (2001). *The Lady Tasting Tea: How Statistics Revolutionized Science in the Twentieth Century*. New York: Henry Holt/A.W.H. Freeman/Owl Book Edition.

Satterthwaite, F. W. (1946). An approximate distribution of estimates of variance components. *Biometrics Bulletin*, 2, 100–144.

Schau, C., Stevens, J., Dauphinee, T. et al. (1995). The development and validation of the Survey of Attitudes toward Statistics. *Educational & Psychological Measurement*, 55(5), 868–876.

Schwarz, G. E. (1978). Estimating the dimension of a model. *Annals of Statistics* 6(2), 461–464. DOI:10.1214/aos/1176344136.

Shadish, W. R., Cook, T.D., and Campbell, D. T. (2002). *Experimental and Quasi- Experimental Designs for Generalized Causal Inference*. Boston MA: Houghton Mifflin.

Shadish, W. R., Galindo, R., Wong, V.C., et al. (2011). A randomized experiment comparing random and cutoff-based assignment. *Psychological Methods*, 16(2), 179–191.

Siegel, S. and Castellan, Jr., N. J. (1988). *Nonparametric Statistics for the Behavioral Sciences*. New York: McGraw-Hill.

Stanton, J. (2001). Galton, Pearson, and the peas: A brief history of linear regression for statistics instructors. *Journal of Statistics Education*, 9(3), 1–13.

Stevens, S. S. (1946). On the theory of scales of measurement. *Science*, 103(2684), 677–680.

Stevens, S. S. (1951). Mathematics, measurement, and psychophysics. In S. S. Stevens (ed.), *Handbook of Experimental Psychology*. New York: John Wiley and Sons.

Stigler, S. M. (1986). *The History of Statistics: The Measurement of Uncertainty Before 1900*. Cambridge, MA: Harvard University Press.

Stigler, S. M. (1997). Regression toward the mean, historically considered. *Statistical Methods in Medical Research*, 6(2), 103–114.

Thompson, B. (1994). The concept of statistical significance testing. ERIC/AE Digest. ERIC Document (ERIC Document Reproduction Service No. ED366654).

Thompson, B. (1996). AERA editorial policies regarding statistical significance testing: Three suggested reforms. *Educational Researcher*, 25, 26–30.

Thorndike, R. L. and Hagen, E. P. (1969). *Measurement and Evaluation in Psychology and Education*. New York: John Wiley & Sons.

Tomasi, S. and Weinberg, S. L. (1999). Classifying children as learning disabled: An analysis of current practice in an urban setting. *Learning Disability Quarterly*, 22, 31–42.

Tukey, J. W. (1953). The problem of multiple comparisons. In *The Collected Works of John W. Tukey VIII. Multiple Comparisons: 1948-1983*. New York: Chapman and Hall, pp. 1–300.

Tukey, J. (1977). *Exploratory Data Analysis*. Reading, MA: Addison-Wesley.

Vakili, R., Vahedian, M., Khodaei, G. et al. (2009). Effects of zinc supplementation in occurrence and duration of common cold in school aged children during cold season: A double-blind placebo-controlled trial. *Iranian Journal of Pediatrics*, 19(4), 376–380.

Wainer, H. (2011). *Uneducated Guesses: Using Evidence to Uncover Misguided Education Policies*. Princeton, NJ: Princeton University Press.

Wechsler, D. (1981). *Manual for the Wechsler Adult Intelligence Scale-Revised*. New York: Psychological Corporation.

Wilcoxon, F. (1945). Individual comparisons by ranking methods. *Biometrics Bulletin*, 1, 80–83.

Willerman, L., Schultz, R., Rutledge, J. N., and Bigler, E. (1991). In vivo brain size and intelligence. *Intelligence* 15, 223–228.

World Almanac and Book of Facts 2006. (2006). New Jersey: World Almanac Books.

World Almanac and Book of Facts 2014. (2014). New Jersey: World Almanac Books.

Yates, F. (1943). Contingency tests involving small numbers and the χ^2 test. *Journal of the Royal Statistical Society Supplement*, 1, 217–235.

Index

Lightning Source UK Ltd.
Milton Keynes UK
UKHW030631060222
398252UK00013B/186